Readings in Microeconomics

Tim Jenkinson

OXFORD UNIVERSITY PRESS

2000

OXFORD
University Press, Great Clarendon Street, Oxford OX2 6DP

Oxford University Press is a department of the University of Oxford.
It furthers the University's objective of excellence in research, scholarship,
and education by publishing worldwide in

Oxford New York

Athens Auckland Bangkok Bogotá Buenos Aires Calcutta
Cape Town Chennai Dar es Salaam Delhi Florence Hong Kong Istanbul
Karachi Kuala Lumpur Madrid Melbourne Mexico City Mumbai
Nairobi Paris São Paulo Shanghai Singapore Taipei Tokyo Toronto Warsaw
with associated companies in Berlin Ibadan

Published in the United States
by Oxford University Press Inc., New York

British Library Cataloguing in Publication Data
Data available

Library of Congress Cataloging in Publication Data
Data available
ISBN 0–19–8776306

Typeset
by Oxford Review of Economic Policy
Printed in Great Britain by
Bath Press Ltd., Bath, Avon

Readings in Microeconomics

For Rebecca, Thomas, and Henry

Preface

Demand often results in supply. The idea of producing a book collecting together many of the important and widely cited papers published in the *Oxford Review of Economic Policy* initially came from my students. They complained to me about the difficulty of finding copies of the *Review* in libraries when everyone taking a course was after the same issue. They told me how good it would be to have a selection of the most useful papers readily available. They even told me they might buy such a collection. And so the idea to produce this reader on microeconomics, along with the companion volume on macroeconomics, was born.

The first editions of these volumes were published in 1996, and, thankfully, confirmed a healthy demand. The second editions contain many of the articles that were included in the first edition, some of which have been updated and revised, along with some new papers that have been published more recently.

The first volume of the *Oxford Review of Economic Policy* was published in 1985. Two features have continued to distinguish the *Review* from other economics journals: the thematic approach, whereby each issue is focused on a particular subject, with leading authorities commissioned to contribute, and an insistence that articles should be written in a non-technical style. From the start the editors have stressed that articles should be accessible to students, policymakers, journalists—in fact, anyone with an interest in economic issues. There has also been an insistence that policy implications should be discussed fully, rather than relegated to an occasional footnote. As much of economics has become more technical, specialized, and mathematically sophisticated, the role played by the *Review* in cutting through the algebra and stating ideas in words has become increasingly valuable. As a result, the *Review* has established a strong and growing readership amongst students, academics, journalists, teachers, and economists in the private and public sectors, as well as an impressive list of contributing authors.

These volumes of collected papers draw together some of the most important and widely cited articles published in the first fourteen volumes of the *Oxford Review of Economic Policy*. I hope that the books will fulfil a number of aims. First, they will ensure that the original articles remain easily accessible. Second, they will provide a resource to those teaching core micro- and macroeconomics courses, and may be used as a ready-made 'reading pack' by lecturers (hence avoiding the trouble and cost of obtaining copyright clearance on individual articles). Third, they will enable students and others interested in economic policy to acquire a selection of the most useful papers at a low cost and reduce the need to spend hours slaving over the photocopier.

The production of these volumes also presented a useful opportunity to up-date or revise the original articles in the light of developments since they were first published. Many of the authors have taken advantage of this opportunity and have updated and revised their papers to take into account recent advances in the literature, policy developments, and more recent data. This periodic spring-cleaning should ensure that even the papers published in early volumes of the *Review* stay relevant and useful. Some papers, especially those published relatively recently, have not been changed.

By far the most difficult task in putting together these volumes was to decide which papers to include. A large number of high quality and widely-cited papers have been published in the *Review*—many more than could be included in two books of a reasonable length. In making the selection I was concerned to cover all the main areas of macro- and microeconomics, which inevitably meant that some of the less 'mainstream' areas were neglected altogether. This is not to deny the significance and importance of these areas. A slightly different problem was that some issues contained many important articles, but only one or two could be included. There are thus many interesting and important papers not included in this selection.

An important criterion used in selecting papers was that the volume should contain a balance between those papers that surveyed a particular theoretical literature and those that were more focused on applied policy issues. It was also decided to go for depth of coverage rather than breadth. Consequently, the volume contains two or three articles on each of the six selected areas:

- Industrial Organization
- R&D
- Competition and Regulatory Policy
- Externalities and the Environment
- International Trade
- Education and Training

While this has resulted in the exclusion of several other areas—such as the microeconomics of the labour market and corporate finance—all the selected subject areas have been the focus of extensive academic research and policy debate in recent years, and would be covered by intermediate or advanced courses on microeconomics.

Finally, I should like to thank Alison Gomm who has managed the production of these volumes—including dealing with revisions, liaising with authors, and much more—with her characteristic effectiveness. Over the years that I have been managing editor of the *Oxford Review of Economic Policy* I have accumulated a tremendous debt of gratitude to Alison, whose contribution has been far greater than that of a conventional production editor.

Last and certainly not least, the success of the *Oxford Review of Economic Policy* owes much to the efforts and vision of the current set of editors—Chris Allsopp, Andrea Boltho, Andrew Glyn, Dieter Helm, Colin Mayer, Ken Mayhew, and David Vines—along with past editors Derek Morris and Gerry Holtham. We have all been greatly assisted by an active and supportive editorial board. Their editorial input was critical in the commissioning and production of the original papers.

Tim Jenkinson
July 2000

Contents

List of Figures

List of Tables

PART I

INDUSTRIAL ORGANIZATION

Strategic competition among the few—some recent developments in the economics of industry

JOHN VICKERS

All Souls College, Oxford

I. Introduction

The title of this article is intended as a signal of two things. First, we are concerned with industries where several—but not many—firms are actually or potentially in competition with each other. Thus our topic is competition among the few,[1] or oligopoly, rather than the polar extremes of textbook perfect competition and pure monopoly. Secondly, we are interested in the *strategic* nature of competition between firms, where the meaning of 'strategic' can be explained as follows:

If the essence of a game of strategy is the dependence of each person's proper choice of action on what he expects the other to do, it may be useful to define a 'strategic move' as follows: A strategic move is one that influences the other person's choice, in a manner favourable to one's self, by affecting the other person's expectations of how one's self will behave. Schelling (1960, p. 150)

The definition is taken from Thomas Schelling's classic book *The Strategy of Conflict*, which has inspired much recent work on strategic moves such as threats, promises and commitments in the economics of industry. This work is sometimes described as 'The New Industrial Economics', but we shall steer clear of the controversial business of applying that label.

The recent work on strategic competition among the few can be compared with the older traditions in

industrial economics associated with Harvard and Chicago. The structure–conduct–performance paradigm pioneered by Edward Mason at Harvard in the 1930s was developed by Joe Bain and others in the 1950s and 1960s. This approach regards market *structure* (the number and sizes of firms in the industry, entry barriers, etc.) as determining the *conduct* of firms (their policies regarding price, advertising, capacity, innovation, etc.), which in turn determines the performance of the industry (its allocative efficiency and technological progress, for example). Of course proponents of this view would not claim that causality flows in one direction only—from structure to conduct to performance—but they do emphasize relationships involving that causal flow (see Scherer (1980) pp. 4–5). The recent work on strategic competition has explored many of the aspects of industry structure and conduct that were recognized as being important by economists in the Harvard tradition. A prime example is the theory of entry barriers and entry deterrence, which will be described below. But there are important differences between the approaches that should be noted. The apparently general applicability of the structure–conduct–performance paradigm caused attention to be focused on features shared by different industries, rather than upon the idiosyncracies of particular industries. More recently, however, there has been some tendency to study industries on a case by case basis (see Schmalensee (1982) and Spence (1981)). A second difference is that much recent work has been concerned with the determinants of market structure, rather than with the dependence of conduct and performance upon structure. One concern has

First published in *Oxford Review of Economic Policy*, vol. 1, no. 3 (1985).
[1] This phrase is borrowed (i.e. stolen) from the title of Fellner's (1949) book on oligopoly. For an excellent recent survey of the economics of industry, see Waterson (1984).

been to show how the fundamentals of consumer preferences and technological relationships, together with the behaviour of firms, determine market structure endogenously.

The 'Chicago tradition' has been to view industrial economics 'through the lens of price theory'.[2] This approach places much greater faith in the operation of market forces than does the Harvard approach, and is correspondingly less convinced of the need or desirability of government intervention to do something about apparent 'market power'. To the contrary, government policy is seen as being one of the main causes of restrictions upon free competition—for example legal barriers to entry into certain markets. These views are closely linked with the emphasis of the 'Austrian School' upon dynamic competition by innovation and the threat of new entry. Such topics as these have also been addressed in the recent work that is reported below, but the conclusions reached—especially regarding government policy—have often differed markedly from those of the Chicago school.

The lens of *game theory* has been used to study the economics of strategic competition. Game theory provides a framework for analysing situations in which there is interdependence between agents in the sense that the decisions of one agent affect the other agents. It is not necessary to use game theory to study pure monopoly (where there is only one decision-maker) or perfect competition (where each individual is too small to have any appreciable effect upon others), but game theory is most appropriate to the study of competition among the few. The next section contains a very brief outline of some basic notions in game theory, and introduces some illustrative examples that are developed in the subsequent discussion.

Section III discusses strategic competition between existing firms, and section IV is concerned with strategic competition between existing firms and potential rivals. These two issues are closely related, but it is helpful as a first step to address them separately. Section III has three main themes: the dynamic nature of strategic competition between firms, the dependence of market structure on the fundamental conditions of consumer preferences and technology, and the role of strategic commitment. The first theme is illustrated in part 1 of the section, which is about collusion between firms. Using the perspective of repeated games, it is shown how firms may be able effectively to collude noncooperatively, i.e. in the absence of explicit cartel arrangements. This demonstrates that it would

be fallacious to argue that such collusion would inevitably be undermined by each firm's incentive to undercut its rivals. The theme of the endogeneity of market structure is developed in parts 2 and 3, which are concerned with R & D competition and product differentiation, respectively. The final part discusses strategic commitment of R & D as an illustration of how the decisions of a firm are made partly with a view to influencing the behaviour of its rivals in the industry. Each firm attempts to gain a position of strategic advantage over its rivals, and to avoid being put at a disadvantage by its rivals' efforts. It is hoped that these examples convey some of the flavour of main theories of strategic competition between existing firms. They do not constitute an exhaustive survey.

Section IV is concerned with the effect of potential competition upon firms already in a market. The seminal work of Bain (1956) on barriers to new competition has recently been subject to intensive reappraisal. Baumol (1982) and others have proposed a controversial theory of 'contestable markets', in which there are no barriers to new competition. Other authors, more in the spirit of Bain, have shown in a rigorous fashion how an existing firm in a market might be able to deter entry into the market by strategic investment in capacity, R & D advertising, brand proliferation, or predatory pricing, for example. These developments are reviewed below.

Section V draws some broad implications for policy. The other articles in this volume provide more detailed discussions of antitrust and industrial policy. The first broad implication is that market structure and conduct are determined jointly by the fundamental conditions of consumer preferences and technological relationships. This contrasts with the view that market structure is somehow given, and that it determines conduct in the industry. Rather, industry structure may be as much a symptom of underlying factors as a root cause of undesirable conduct and performance. A related implication is the importance of potential competition. The threat of new entry can be a potent influence upon the behaviour of existing firms; on the other hand that threat may be thwarted by strategic moves by existing firms. A third broad implication is that competition among the few does not necessarily produce socially desirable results—a point well illustrated by R & D competition. It follows that there is an important role for public policy to influence the outcome of strategic competition among the few. As a final point, recent work in industrial economics should not be seen as delivering generally applicable policy prescriptions. On the contrary, it has served to highlight the heterogeneous nature of industries while pro-

---

[2] This phrase is due to Aaron Director—see Williamson (1979, p. 919).

viding useful tools and valuable perspectives for the study of particular cases.

II. Interdependent decision-making

When there are only a few firms in an industry, they are *interdependent* in the following sense. The behaviour of any one firm has an appreciable effect upon the other firms, and the best plan of action for one firm to adopt depends upon the plans of action chosen by the other firms. Each firm is trying to second-guess the others—the behaviour of one firm depends upon what it expects the other firms to do, and they in turn are making their decisions on the basis of their expectations of what their rivals (including the first firm) will do. The situation is rather like that found in games like poker, bridge, or the children's game involving scissors, paper and rocks. Indeed, the framework for studying situations of interdependent decision is called the *theory of games*. This theory was developed by von Neumann and Morgenstern and has been refined and employed in numerous applications.

This section has two purposes. The first is informally to describe some basic notions of game theory, which will be useful for the economic analysis to follow. The second is to introduce two illustrations of games—concerning cooperation between firms and predatory pricing—which will be developed in the subsequent sections.

1. Some elements of game theory

A situation of interdependent decision-making, as described in the paragraphs above, is called a *game*. The participants in the game are the *players*. In our case the firms in the industry are the players. Each player pursues some objective: each player is intent upon maximizing his *payoff*. The payoff that a player receives measures how well he achieves his objective. We shall suppose for the most part that the payoff of a firm is its profit (or, in dynamic contexts, the discounted value of its profit stream). Thus we are assuming that firms are intent upon maximizing their profits. The payoffs of the players depend upon the decisions that they make. In general, the payoff of player 1 depends not only on his decision, but also upon the decisions made by the other players. This is precisely the element of interdependence that game theory attempts to study.

Each player chooses a *strategy*. A strategy is a plan of action, or a complete contingency plan,

which specifies what the player will do in any of the circumstances in which he might find himself. A strategy is therefore quite different from a *move*. A move is the action that a player makes on a particular occasion, whereas his strategy specifies for the whole range of possible circumstances what move he would make in each particular circumstance. The distinction is rather like the difference in chess between Karpov's game plan (his strategy) and his move pawn-to-king-four.

To summarize so far: the description of a game includes:

(i) the set of *players*;
(ii) the set of *strategies* available to each player from which each player chooses one; and
(iii) each player's *payoff*, which depends on the strategies chosen by the various players.

It is sometimes necessary to describe a game in more detail. A fuller description would include:

(iv) the *move order* in the game—i.e. who moves when; and
(v) the *information* conditions in the game.

By (v) is meant the knowledge that each player has at every stage concerning (a) the prior moves made by the various players, and (b) the motivations of, and strategies available to, the other players in the game.

One way to categorize games is according to the degree of harmony or disharmony between the interests of the players. At one extreme is the pure *coordination* game, in which all players have the same objective. At the other extreme is the game of pure *conflict*, in which there are two players with completely opposed interests—what is good for one is bad for the other. Usually, however, there is a mixture of conflict and co-ordination of interests. Such *mixed motive* games will be our main concern.

It was stated above that in most games the best strategy for one player to choose depends upon what the other players choose. Hence the importance of expectations about the others' choices. But sometimes a player has a strategy that is best irrespective of what the others do. This is called a *dominant* strategy, and the other, inferior strategies are called *dominated* strategies. The first example in the next subsection is one in which each player has a dominant strategy.

It is easy to deduce what will happen in games with dominant strategies—each player simply chooses his dominant strategy. But in general it is hard to work out what will happen, because the best strategy for each player depends upon what the others do. A situation in which each player is choosing the best strategy available to him, given the strategies chosen by the other players, is called a *Nash equilibrium*. Nash equilibrium corresponds to the idea of self-fulfilled expectations. If each player expected the others to play their part in the equilibrium, then it would be rational for him to do likewise. If the same is true for all players, then all have their expectations fulfilled at equilibrium. Similarly, Nash equilibrium corresponds to the idea of a tacit, self-supporting agreement. If the players were somehow to agree to a plan of Nash equilibrium behaviour, then none would have an incentive to depart from the agreement. No external mechanism would be required to enforce the agreement. However, any agreement that is not a Nash equilibrium would require a means of enforcement.

The concept is named after John Nash, an economist who made some fundamental advances in game theory in the 1950s. The concept is in fact a development of that introduced in the 1830s by Cournot, a French mathematician, who examined the output decisions of the two firms in a duopoly. He defined equilibrium as a position in which each firm is producing his optimal output level, given the output level chosen by the other firm.

2. Two illustrations

Following the rather general outline of game theory above, we now consider two illustrative examples. They are concerned with

(i) the problems of collusion; and
(ii) predatory pricing.

Both examples will be developed in later sections of this paper.

(i) The problem of collusion

Figure 1.1 represents a very simple game[3] in which the players are two firms, A and B. Each firm has a choice between two alternatives—a high output strategy or a low output strategy. The numbers in the boxes give the payoffs of the players, which can be thought of as the firms' profits. The convention is that firm A's payoff is written in the bottom left-hand corner of a box, and B's payoff appears in the top right-hand corner.

In the example, the best thing that can happen for a firm is for it to produce high output while its rival produces low output. The low output level of its rival means that price is not driven down too much, and so

Figure 1.1. The Prisoners' Dilemma

a good profit margin is earned. The worst thing that can happen is to produce low output while the rival produces high output. Then price is fairly low—due to the rival's high output—and revenues are barely sufficient to cover total costs. If both firms produce high output, then price is low but profits are positive. It is better for both to restrain output, and thereby to raise price. We shall refer to this as the collusive outcome.

What will happen in this game? In fact it is a dominant strategy for each firm to choose a high output level. This is the best strategy for firm A whether firm B produces a high level of output or a low one. Similarly for firm B. Thus the 'noncooperative' outcome is for each firm to get a payoff of 1. However, if the firms had somehow been able to attain the collusive outcome (i.e. both produce low levels of output), then both would have received a superior payoff of 2. The problem of collusion is for the firms to achieve this superior outcome notwithstanding the seemingly compelling argument that high output levels will be chosen. In section 3 it will be seen how this problem can be resolved when a game such as that depicted in figure 1.1 is repeated. After all, in reality firms are in competition on a long-term basis; they are not engaged in a 'one-shot' game like the one just considered. When account is taken of this fact, collusion can be sustained by threats of retaliation against non-cooperative behaviour.

(ii) Predatory pricing

Figure 1.2 represents a simple game[4] in which predatory pricing is possible. Note that the method of representation differs from that in figure 1.1. Here we have made the order of moves explicit. The players are two firms—a potential entrant is contemplating entry into a market currently dominated by an incumbent firm.

---

[3] The game is a version of the well-known Prisoners' Dilemma Game.

[4] Dixit's excellent (1982) survey contains an account of this game.

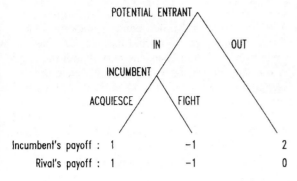

Figure 1.2. An entry game

The potential entrant chooses between going IN to the market, or remaining OUT of it.

If entry occurs, the incumbent can either FIGHT entry, which is costly to both firms, or he can ACQUI-ESCE so as to arrive at some peaceful coexistence, which is more profitable. The best thing for the incumbent is for entry not to take place. In that event, the potential entrant does better than if its entry were fought, but not as well as if its entry were met with acquiescence.

What will happen in the game? In fact there are two Nash equilibria:

(a) Potential entrant chooses IN, and incumbent chooses to ACQUIESCE in the event of entry, and
(b) Potential entrant chooses OUT, and incumbent chooses to FIGHT in the event of entry.

In each case, each player gets his maximum payoff given the strategy chosen by the other player. But equilibrium (b) is implausible, because it is clear that, faced with the fact of entry, the incumbent would find it profitable to ACQUIESCE, rather than to FIGHT entry. Relying on this fact, the potential entrant would choose IN, and we would get equilibrium (a). In other words, the incumbent's threat to FIGHT is not *credible*—it is an empty threat that would not be believed. The concept of Nash equilibrium has been refined to rule out these peculiar equilibria involving incredible threats. The concept of *perfect equilibrium*, developed by Selten (1965; 1975), requires that the strategies chosen by the players be a Nash equilibrium, not only in the game as a whole, but also in every subgame of the game. In figure 1.2 there is a subgame beginning at the node alongside the word 'incumbent'. Perfect equilibrium rules out the undesirable equilibrium (b), leaving only the intuitively reasonable equilibrium (a): entry occurs and is met with acquiescence.

The game in figure 1.2 is sufficiently simple for it to be possible to work out what will happen without bothering with the jargon above. But in more sophisticated—and realistic—examples this is not so. The two examples above were intended to illustrate how game theory is used to analyse strategic competition among the few, and to prepare some of the ground for the discussion to follow.

III. Strategic competition between existing firms

The aim of this section is to describe some recent developments in the analysis of strategic competition between existing firms. The next section considers competition between existing firms and potential rivals. Neither section is intended to be anything like a survey. Rather, the intention is to try to convey the flavour of some recent developments, by way of illustrative examples.

The present section has four parts. The first continues the discussion of collusion from the previous section. It is shown that, using the perspective of repeated games, it may be possible for firms effectively to collude in the absence of explicit agreement to do so, even though each is exclusively concerned to maximize its own profits. The second and third parts of this section both develop the theme of the 'endogeneity' of market structure by showing the importance of the fundamentals of consumer preferences and technological relationships. The model of R & D competition by Dasgupta and Stiglitz (1980) is the main subject of part 2, and part 3 discusses recent work on product differentiation, notably that of Shaked and Sutton (1983). Strategic commitment is the topic in the final part of this section, which contains an account of Brander and Spencer's (1983) model in which firms choose their levels of R & D activity partly with a view to influencing their rivals' behaviour.

1. Non-cooperative collusion

The paradoxical title of this subsection indicates that we are asking whether collusive outcomes can be sustained by non-cooperative behaviour, i.e. in the absence of explicit, enforceable agreements between firms. In the simple illustration of figure 1.1 above this was not possible, but that illustration had evident short-comings. In particular, it represented a 'one-shot' game, whereas in reality firms are commonly in competition with their rivals on a longer-term basis.

That is to say, they are in a *repeated* game. Is non-co-operative collusion possible in a repeated game?

The answer to this question depends upon at least four things:

(i) whether the game is repeated indefinitely, or only a finite number of times;
(ii) whether the players in the game are fully informed as to the objectives of, and opportunities available to, their rivals;
(iii) whether the players know the prior moves made by their rivals—so that 'cheating' can be detected; and
(iv) how much weight the players attach to the future in their calculations.

The particular circumstances of an industry determine what it is appropriate to assume in relation to (i)–(iv). Rather than look at particular industries, our approach here will be to explore the consequences of the various assumptions that could be made.

Initially, we shall do this by developing the illustrative example shown in figure 1.1.

Suppose for the moment that the game is repeated a finite number of times, and that there is complete and perfect information. Firms are assumed to maximize the (possibly discounted) sum of their profits in the game as a whole. Unfortunately (for the firms) the collusive low output outcome cannot be sustained. Suppose that the game is repeated 137 times. At the last round, it is clear from previous argument that it is a dominant strategy for both firms to produce high output. This fact implies that neither firm has any incentive to cooperate by producing low output at the 136th repetition, since it is clear to all what will happen at the last round. And the same is true at the 135th repetition. The argument proceeds, by backwards induction, to the conclusion that there is never any collusion—both firms produce high output at every stage of the game. Since there is nothing special about the number 137, the same conclusion holds for any finite number of repetitions of the game.

As well as being unhappy (for the firms), this result is rather unsatisfactory. First, our intuition suggests that some collusion would occur, at least early on in the game, despite the fact that the number of repetitions is finite. Secondly, the experimental evidence (see Axelrod (1984)) accords with this intuition. How can this intuition, supported by experimental evidence, be squared with apparently compelling game theoretical logic?

Before answering this question, let us consider the *infinitely* repeated version of the game depicted in figure 1.1. Suppose that firms discount the future at rate w, where w is a number between zero and one. That is, firms attach weight w to what happens next period, weight w^2 to what happens the period after that, and so on. The closer w is to zero, the less weight they attach to the future relative to the present, i.e. the more short-sighted they are.

Provided that w is not too small, it is now possible for non-cooperative collusion to occur. Suppose that firm B plays the *trigger strategy*, which is to choose low output in period 1 and in any subsequent period provided that firm A has never produced high output, but to produce high output forever more once firm A ever produces high output.[5] The idea is that firm B cooperates with A unless and until A 'defects', in which case B is triggered into perpetual non-cooperation. What is A's best response to this trigger strategy by B? If A were also to adopt the trigger strategy, then there would always be collusion—each firm would always choose low output and receive 2 in each period. The discounted value of this profit flow is

$$2 + 2w + 2w^2 + \ldots = 2/(1-w).$$

In fact A gets this payoff with any strategy in which he is not the first to defect. If, however, A chooses a strategy in which he defects at any stage, then he gets a payoff of 3 in the first period of defection (because B chooses low output), and a payoff of no more than 1 in every subsequent period (because B has been triggered into perpetual non-cooperation). So his payoff is at most

$$3 + w + w^2 + w^3 + \ldots = 3 + w/(1-w).$$

Comparing the two payoffs, we see that it is better not to defect so long as

$$w \geq 1/2$$

This precise answer depends of course upon the particular numbers chosen for the illustration. But the general point is clear. Provided that the firms give enough weight to the future, then non-cooperative collusion can be sustained, for example by trigger strategies. The collusion is non-cooperative in the sense that the firms are not acting in concert; each is independently doing the best it can given the strategy adopted by the other firm. In other words, the trigger strategies constitute a Nash equilibrium, or a self-enforcing agreement. Trigger strategies are not the only way to sustain the collusive outcome non-cooperatively. Another leading strategy is tit-for-tat, accord-

---

[5] See Friedman (1971).

ing to which a player chooses in the current period what the other player chose in the previous period.

Now let us return to the question of how collusion might occur non-cooperatively, even in the finitely repeated game. Recall that we found a tension between intuition and experimental evidence on one hand, and game theoretic logic on the other. Intuition said that collusion could happen—at least in the earlier rounds—but game theory apparently said that it could not. An important and elegant resolution of this paradox has been provided by Kreps et al. (1982). They relax the assumption of complete information, and suppose instead that one player has a small amount of doubt in his mind as to the motivation of the other player. Suppose, for example, that A is not absolutely certain that B's payoffs are as described above (i.e. the discounted sum of the payoffs in figure 1.1). Suppose that A attaches some tiny probability p to B preferring —or being committed—to playing the trigger strategy.[6] It turns out that even if p is very small indeed, the players will effectively collude until some point towards the end of the game. This occurs because it is not worth A defecting in view of the risk that the non-collusive outcome will obtain for the rest of the game, and because B wishes to maintain his *reputation* for possibly preferring, or being committed to, the trigger strategy. Thus the analysis also yields a satisfying account of how reputation can operate to maintain effective collusion, at least for a substantial part of the time. What is remarkable about the result is that a small degree of doubt about the motivation of one of the players can yield much effective collusion. Once the strict assumption of complete information is slightly relaxed, the outcome of the game changes radically.[7]

So far in the discussion of collusion we have focused on the simple example in figure 1.1, in which two firms have a choice between a high or a low output level. But there may be several firms in an industry, and in fact firms have a much broader choice. If output is their decision variable, they can choose from a wide range of possible output levels. Or it may be that their decision variable is price, not to mention other aspects of company behaviour such as investment, advertising and R & D. Be that as it may, more or less the same analysis can be applied straightforwardly in the more complex settings. In those settings new possibilities arise. For example, Abreu (1984) has investigated the most effective credible strategies for 'punishing' de-

viations from collusive behaviour. The more effective the punishment, the greater is the deterrent effect, and the greater is the degree of collusion than can be sustained. In an infinitely repeated game where firms choose output levels, the most effective credible punishment strategy consists of a stick and a carrot—the carrot is the attraction of collusion, and the stick is a swift episode of high output levels and a correspondingly low price level. If any firm deviates from collusive behaviour, there would immediately occur one unpleasant period of punishment (the stick), followed by a return to collusion (the carrot). This punishment strategy is credible because it would be entirely rational for the other firms to punish the defector in the way described. In the model no firm actually chooses to defect, because the credible threat of punishment acts as a sufficient deterrent.

We have not yet faced up to the problem of detecting defection from a collusive arrangement. Implicitly we have been supposing that firms can observe one another's behaviour, but this assumption of perfect information may be unjustified. It is perhaps more reasonable to suppose that the firms in a collusive arrangement can observe the price prevailing in their market, but not the output levels chosen by the individual firms that are party to the arrangement. If the demand curve facing the industry is not known for certain, then one firm cannot infer exactly what the others have done. Suppose that a low price is observed in some period. That might be because demand for the product of the industry is low; or it might be because some firm has defected from the collusive arrangement by producing a high level of output. There is the problem of inferring which is the true cause.

This question has been examined by Green and Porter (1984). They consider equilibrium strategies in which firms collude so long as price remains above some critical level P, but they revert to an episode of more aggressive, non-cooperative behaviour if price ever falls below P, before restoring collusive behaviour T periods after the initial price drop.[8] The (credible) threat of the episode of non-cooperative behaviour is sufficient to deter defection from the collusive outcome, but occasionally there is an episode of non-cooperation when demand is especially low. This theory offers an interesting interpretation of the pattern of prices in an industry characterized by occasional, temporary falls in price. One view is to regard the falls in price as *collapses* in cartel discipline, but the

[6] In fact Kreps et al. (1982) suppose that the small probability is attached to B playing the tit-for-tat strategy, which had emerged as a successful strategy in experiments—see Axelrod (1984).
[7] The same point emerges in the work on predatory pricing by Kreps et al. (1982).
[8] Abreu et al. (1984) have shown that in Green and Porter's (1984) model, the most effective way to police the cartel is to have a severe reversionary episode lasting one period. The parallel with Abreu (1984) is clear.

account given by Green and Porter suggests the alternative view that they *help ensure* cartel discipline.

There are numerous other devices that might be used by firms to facilitate non-cooperative collusion by ologopolists. Salop (1985) has explored *facilitating practices* such as most-favoured-nation (MFN) clauses and meeting-competition-clauses (MCCs) that are commonly observed in sales contracts. An MFN clause is one that promises the buyer that the seller will not supply another buyer at a lower price. (If the commodity in question is an input for the buyer's business, then the buyer would not face the risk that another buyer would gain a competitive advantage over him by obtaining the input more cheaply). Several common pricing conventions—for example posting list prices—have effects similar to an MFN clause. An MCC says that the seller will match the price of any seller supplying at a lower price. The effect of practices of this sort is to alter the incentives of the firms in the oligopoly in such a way that price reductions are less attractive. In addition, they tend to make it easier for one firm to monitor the behaviour of others. Thus they facilitate oligopolistic collusion. In similar vein Klemperer (1984) has shown how switching costs can promote collusive behaviour.[9] Switching costs are present when it is costly for a consumer to switch from his current supplier to a different supplier (even though ex ante suppliers are on a par). Examples are accountants, and airlines that offer frequent flyer discounts. Sometimes switching costs occur naturally (as with accountants), but sometimes they occur because of the deliberate actions of firms (as with airline discounts), although the motivation for those actions is not necessarily to facilitate collusion.

We conclude this discussion of non-cooperative collusion by mentioning some problems for public policy that will be developed in section V. We have seen that effective collusion does not necessarily require explicit agreements between firms. Antitrust policy generally declares explicit agreements to be unlawful, but it is not clear how it can or should be directed against tacit, non-cooperative collusion. One difficulty is to identify the actions of firms that are unlawful. After all, if each firm is independently pursuing its legitimate business interests. Nevertheless we saw that in some contexts the process of collusion might be facilitated by certain practices—for example price clauses in sales contracts. The question arises of whether these facilitating practices are a suitable target for antitrust policy.

2. Market structure and cost reducing innovation

One of the themes emphasized in the introduction was the endogeneity of market structure. Rather than take market structure as given, we wish to understand how the basic conditions of consumer preferences, technology, and so on determine market structure and the conduct of firms. To make the point very crudely, we wish to see how the basic conditions jointly determine structure, conduct and performance, whereas the traditional S–C–P paradigm is more concerned with the causal flow from structure to conduct to performance.

Below we set out the model of market structure and cost-reducing innovation due to Dasgupta and Stiglitz (1980).[10] It is very much a 'bare bones', stylized model, and deliberately so. It shows with great clarity that relationships and correlations—such as those between market structure and R & D efforts—do not necessarily imply causality, and that other explanations are available. This affects how we interpret empirical correlations between market structure and innovation.

The model brings out another, quite separate point. The message of much economic theory concerning the production decisions of firms is that the free market generates results that are broadly desirable from the social point of view, especially if the market is competitive. It is well-known, however, that this happy conclusion breaks down in a wide range of circumstances. Technological competition is a leading case in point. After presenting the Dasgupta-Stiglitz model, we shall discuss why this is so.

The model

The unit costs of a firm are assumed to depend on its R & D efforts. Let $c(x)$ be the unit production costs of a firm that spends x on R & D. As x increases, c falls. There are n identical firms in the industry producing the same product. We will see shortly how n is determined. If total industry output is Q, price is $P(Q)$, where P falls as Q rises. The profits of a firm with output q and R & D expenditure x can be written

$$\pi = [P(Q) - c(x)]q - x$$

The term in square brackets is the profit margin. When multiplied by q this gives gross profit, from which R & D expenditure x is deducted. If all firms produce the same level of output q then total industry output Q is equal to nq.

---

[9] By contrast, von Weizsäcker (1984) has constructed a model in which higher switching costs cause there to be more competition. See Klemperer (1984) for a discussion.

[10] See also Dasgupta (1985) for a review of the theory of technological competition.

Each firm chooses its output q and its R & D expenditure x to maximize its profits π. Each firm assumes that its own decisions about x and q do not affect the decisions of other firms about their output and R & D. In other words, we are interested in the Nash equilibrium of the game.

As to the determination of n, the number of firms, there are two leading possibilities. One is that n is given exogenously—there happen to be n firms and that's that. But this assumption seems to be rather arbitrary. At least it calls for some justification. Another possibility is that n is determined endogenously, by *free entry* into the industry. If there is free entry, then firms will continue to come into the industry until it would be unprofitable for the next firm to do so. As an approximation, we may say that entry occurs up to the point where profits are zero. The free entry condition is not the only way that n could be determined endogenously. Alternatively one could suppose that barriers to entry do exist, and these could be modelled explicitly. However, we shall assume free entry in this illustration, because it suffices to make the points at hand.

Let us remind ourselves of the variables of interest. Our index of market *structure* is n, the number of firms. As n falls, the industry becomes more concentrated. The *conduct* of firms includes their decisions on output q and R & D expenditure x. The *performance* of the industry is measured by such things as profits π, the price-cost margin (P − c)/P, and innovative advance (i.e. the rate of cost reduction).

It remains to say more about consumer *preferences* and *technological* relationships. Consumer preferences determine demand conditions for the output of the industry, i.e. the relationship between P and Q. To be specific, let the (inverse) demand curve have the form

$$P(Q) = \sigma Q^{-\varepsilon} \qquad ; \qquad \sigma, \varepsilon > 0.$$

This specification turns out to be particularly convenient. The size of the market is measured by σ and the sensitivity of price to output is measured by ε. The price elasticity of demand is 1/ε. As to technological conditions, the relationship between unit costs and R & D expenditure is given the form

$$c(x) = \beta x^{-\alpha} \qquad ; \qquad \alpha, \beta > 0.$$

Here β measures the level of costs, and α measures the sensitivity of unit costs to R & D expenditure. When α is large, unit costs fall more rapidly with R & D efforts. Thus, 'innovative opportunities' are greater.

The four parameters, α, β, ε and σ are the basic conditions of demand and technology. Together they determine the structure, conduct and performance variables in the model. It turns out that α and ε (the elasticities of cost reduction and of demand) are especially important. A number of interesting results hold at the (free entry) equilibrium in the model.

The number of firms is given by

$$n = \varepsilon (1 + \alpha)/\alpha.$$

Thus an industry is more concentrated (n is smaller) when innovation opportunities (α) are greater. Industries with less elastic demand (that is, lower 1/ε, or higher ε) are less concentrated. The size of the market (σ) does not affect n. If the market is larger, the level of R & D per firm is greater, and unit costs are correspondingly lower.

The price-cost margin at equilibrium is

$$\frac{P-c}{P} = \frac{\varepsilon}{n}$$

Thus the price-cost margin is negatively related to the elasticity of demand (1/ε) and positively related to the level of concentration (1/n). However, care is necessary in interpreting this familiar relationship, because n is determined endogenously, within the model, rather than being fixed. Indeed, by combining the last two equations we obtain

$$\frac{P-c}{P} = \frac{\alpha}{1+\alpha}$$

The price-cost margin is seen to depend on the basic parameter α. This margin is greater in industries where innovative opportunities are greater. This is because firms' R & D expenditures—which have to be covered by the price-cost margin—are higher in these industries. In fact research intensity, as measured by the ratio of R & D expenditure to sales revenue is

$$\frac{nx}{PQ} = \frac{\alpha}{1+\alpha}$$

which is the same price-cost margin. Recall that industries with greater innovative opportunities also tend to be more concentrated. *Thus there tends to be a positive relationship between concentration, the price-cost margin, and research intensity, but there is no causal relationship between these variables*: they are all determined by the underlying parameters of technology and demand.

The equilibrium outcome described above can be compared with the socially optimal research and production plan. In the Dasgupta-Stiglitz (1980) model, costs are not reduced as much as is socially optimal, and price is too high. At the same time, total R & D expenditure is likely to be too great, because there is excessive duplication between the research efforts of different firms.

Spence (1984) examines cost reducing innovation in a richer model. He focuses on the classic appropriability problem in R & D. The problem has two parts: (i) the incentive of a firm to do R & D depends on the degree to which it appropriates the benefits of its R & D; if there are 'spillovers', so that one firm benefits from the R & D of another, then incentives are reduced; (ii) on the other hand, knowledge is optimally diffused among firms if it is priced at the marginal cost of its dissemination (which is often close to zero). The problem, then, is that incentives for innovation require inefficient diffusion of knowledge. Spence shows that the market may perform poorly irrespective of concentration and the extent of spillovers, but potential performance improves when spillovers are high. R & D *subsidies* improve market performance substantially. They drive a wedge between the price received by a supplier of R & D output and the price paid by its buyers. A possible solution to the problem of excessive duplication of R & D efforts is to encourage cooperative R & D. However, there is the danger that this facilitates anti-competitive behaviour, such as collusion in product markets or entry deterrence. For a discussion of policy towards R & D intensive sectors, see Ordover and Willig (1985).

This subsection has described only a tiny fraction of the work that has been done on the relationships between market structure and innovation. It has concentrated on cost-reducing innovation, where the costs of a firm depend smoothly upon its (and possibly its rivals') R & D efforts. Product innovation has not been discussed, and nor have R & D contests such as patent races. On these important matters see the extensive surveys by Kamien and Schwartz (1982), and Stoneman (1983).

3. Product differentiation and market structure

The study of product differentiation has been central to industrial economics ever since its inception. The 'spatial' representation of product differentiation, first used in Hotelling's 1929 *Economic Journal* article, has been the basic framework for much work on the topic. In Hotelling's representation, sellers are positioned at points along a line, along which consumers are distributed. One can think of the line as, for example, a stretch of beach (with the sellers being ice-cream vendors) or as a representation of the sweetness/dryness of cider (with very sweet cider at one end and very dry cider at the other). Consumers prefer to patronize sellers positioned close to them (because they save on 'travel costs'), and are therefore prepared to pay some price premium to obtain their favoured variety. The framework can be extended in many directions—to several dimensions, circles rather than lines, and so on. Several interesting questions can be posed within this framework. For example, will there be a tendency for sellers to differentiate their products as much as possible, or will they tend to agglomerate at a point? How does the nature of price competition between firms depend on their locations? Can an incumbent monopolist deter entry into his market by introducing a proliferation of brands at different locations? And so on.

Rather than discuss any of these questions in the Hotelling tradition, I shall focus instead upon recent work on *vertical* product differentiation, and its bearing on the issue of the determination of market structure. Products are said to be 'vertically differentiated' when they differ in respect of *quality*. If two vertically differentiated products were offered to consumers at the same price, one of the two products would be preferred by all—i.e. the one with higher quality. (This is of course *not* the case in Hotelling's framework, where there is 'horizontal' product differentiation. In that case, if two goods were offered at the same price, some consumers would prefer one of them, and other consumers would prefer the other—a consumer would prefer the product closer to him in product space). Since quality differences are manifest features of many markets, it is clearly important to study vertical product differentiation.

Shaked and Sutton (1983) have examined the determination of market structure in markets with vertically differentiated products (see also Shaked and Sutton (1982)). Their major result concerning market structure is that there may be an upper limit to the number of firms than can coexist at equilibrium irrespective of the size of the market. In that case, a certain degree of market concentration is inevitable. (By 'equilibrium' is meant Nash equilibrium in prices given quality levels).

A market in which this property holds is called a *natural oligopoly*. This result contrasts with the property of horizontally differentiated markets that there is no limit to the number of firms that can coexist at equilibrium if the market is large enough.

Whether or not a market is a natural oligopoly depends in a subtle way upon the interaction between consumer preferences and the technology of product improvement. Let c(u) be the unit variable cost of supplying a product with quality level u. We would expect c to increase with u, but what matters is how rapidly c increases with u. If unit variable costs rise 'sufficiently slowly' as quality increases, then the market is a natural oligopoly—there is a limit to the number of firms that can coexist at equilibrium, no matter how big the market is. More generally, this result holds if it is the case that all consumers would have the same ranking of products if all products were offered at their respective unit variable costs. If this property does not hold, it is possible for a new firm to attract custom by entering with a quality level intermediate between two existing quality levels and selling at a price close to unit variable cost. It follows that there is no limit to the number of firms that can exist as the market grows. However, when the property does hold, a firm adopting such a policy would not necessarily gain any custom, because consumers would be prepared to pay the extra for the higher quality product already on the market, for example.

The details of Shaked and Sutton's analysis are complex and subtle; the account above does not do justice to them. The central point to emerge is that market structure depends critically upon the technology of product improvement and upon consumers' preferences—in particular their willingness to pay for quality improvements.

Shaked and Sutton observe that the condition that the cost of quality improvement does not rise rapidly in relation to consumers' willingness to pay for it, is most likely to be met in industries where product quality depends more on fixed costs (e.g. R & D) than on unit variable costs. Expenditure on quality improvement and the number and sizes of firms in the market therefore jointly depend upon consumer preferences and upon technological relationships. Thus we have seen in this section—as in the last—that market structure is not the exogenously given determinant of firms' conduct. Rather, conduct and structure are jointly determined by the fundamentals of preferences and technology.

4. Strategic commitment with R & D

Strategic moves are an important feature of competition between existing firms. Recall that a strategic move is one designed to induce another player to make a choice more favourable to the strategic mover than would otherwise have happened. The purpose of this subsection is to examine strategic commitment in the particular contexts of R & D competition, following Brander and Spencer (1983).

Consider an industry containing two firms, each of which is to decide on its level of cost-reducing R & D expenditure. Whereas in subsection (2) it was assumed that firms chose their R & D and output levels simultaneously, we shall now suppose that R & D decisions are made *before* output decisions are made. This is realistic inasmuch as R & D expenditures are irreversible and long-term in nature, whereas output decisions are more readily changed. Since the firms' output decisions now depend partly upon their R & D decisions, a *strategic motive* is added to the efficiency motive for research expenditures. In particular, firm 1 would like to curb the output of firm 2, because market price is then higher. By reducing its own costs through research expenditure, firm 1 credibly threatens to produce greater output. This has the desired effect of discouraging firm 2 from producing such high output. High R & D expenditure is thus a strategic move that works by influencing the output decision of the other firm. Owing to the attractiveness of this move, firms tend to overinvest in R & D, in the sense that the output that they eventually supply is produced inefficiently: too much R & D, and too little of the other factors of production, are employed. This strategic source of inefficiency is quite separate from those mentioned earlier in this section.

In more precise terms, the problem is analysed as a two-stage game. Levels of R & D are chosen at stage one, and output levels are chosen at stage two. Being interested only in threats that are credible, we characterize the perfect equilibrium of the game. The easiest way to do this is first to calculate the equilibrium outputs at stage two as a function of the R & D levels chosen at stage one. Having found the dependency of outputs upon R & D, it is then possible to find equilibrium in the choice of R & D levels at stage one. In fact the analysis does not depend on the strategic variable being R & D. Exactly the same applies to any fixed factor of production that reduces costs—such as capital. However, the analysis is sensitive to the assumptions that are made about stage two of the game. We assumed that the firms achieved equilibrium in output levels, in which case there is excessive R & D. But if equilibrium is in prices, the opposite result can hold: each firm underinvests in R & D to induce the other to charge a higher price. The intuitive explanation is that by investing less in R & D, a firm causes its equilibrium price to be slightly higher. This in turn causes the rival's equilibrium price to be slightly higher, which is beneficial to the first firm. This sort of sensitivity of results to assumptions that appear equally plausible bedevils theorists of market structure.

Strategic commitment with R & D is but one illustration of the strategic nature of competition between existing firms. Other instruments of commitment include advertising, the introduction of new brands, and patenting. These themes are taken up again when strategic commitment to deter new entry is examined.

IV. Potential competition and strategic entry deterrence

The threat to existing firms posed by potential competitors has long been recognized as an important influence upon market structure and conduct. The force of this threat depends on the extent to which there are *barriers to entry* into the market. In his classic analysis, Bain (1956, p. 3) defines barriers to entry as

the advantages of established sellers in an industry over potential entrant sellers, those advantages being reflected in the extent to which established sellers can persistently raise their prices above a competitive level without attracting new firms to enter the industry.

He identified three sources of barriers to new competition:

  (i) Product Differentiation: customer loyalty to existing products puts new entrants at a disadvantage.
 (ii) Absolute Cost Advantages: incumbent firms might enjoy absolute cost advantages, due perhaps to exclusive access to superior technologies, or to accumulated experience.
(iii) Economies of Scale: if the minimum efficient scale of production for a firm is large in relation to total demand in the market, then a new entrant faces a dilemma—entry at small scale involves high production costs, but entry at efficient scale would expand industry supply so that price would fall.

Bain's analysis has been subject to recent critical scrutiny (see for example von Weizsäcker (1980)) and at the same time attempts have been made to develop his insights in a rigorous, detailed fashion. As to the causes of barriers to entry, an important distinction, due to Salop (1979), is between *innocent* and *strategic* barriers to entry. An innocent barrier to entry is the incidental result of the short-run profit-maximizing behaviour of existing firms. A strategic barrier to entry is constructed by design, with the intent of

deterring new entrants into the market. The erection of a strategic barrier to entry involves the sacrifice of short-run profits with a view to the longer-run gains of deterring entry. Strategic entry deterrence is the subject of section IV.2. The next section, however, is about the controversial theory of contestable markets, in which there are no barriers to new competition and the threat of entry is at its most potent.

1. The theory of contestable markets

The idea that potential competition affects the conduct of existing firms is by no means novel, but it has recently been examined in its purest form in the theory of contestable markets, developed by Baumol, Panzar and Willig (1982) and their colleagues. Much of their work concerns the economics of multi-product industries, but here we shall concentrate on their analysis of *new entry* into markets. (Although there are important relationships between the topics of entry and multi-product firms, most of the main ideas concerning the former can be discussed with reference to single-product industries). Important claims have been made on behalf of contestability theory. Baumol (1982, p. 1) in his Presidential address to the American Economic Association claims that the theory

enables us to look at industry structure and behaviour in a way that is novel in some respects, that it provides a unifying analytical structure to the subject area, and that it offers useful insights for empirical work and for the formulation of policy.

A contestable market is one into which there is ultra-free entry (to use Shepherd's (1984) phrase). All firms —actual and potential—have access to the same technology and hence they enjoy the same cost function. Furthermore, and most importantly, exit from a contestable market is absolutely costless, in the sense that an entrant incurs no *sunk costs* (i.e. irrecoverable expenditures). Thus a contestable market is vulnerable to *hit-and-run entry*:

Even a very transient profit opportunity need not be neglected by a potential entrant, for he can go in, and, before prices change, collect his gains and then depart without cost, should the climate grow hostile. (Baumol (1982, p. 4)).

Contestability is not inconsistent with the existence of economies of scale. Even if there are fixed costs of production, a market can be contestable provided that there are no sunk costs.

The following conditions hold at equilibrium in a contestable market.

(i) Profits are zero. If they were positive, then new firms would be attracted to enter. If they were negative, then some existing firms would exit from the market.

(ii) Production is efficient. Otherwise a new firm would enter the market, attracted by the prospect of producing efficiently, undercutting the existing inefficient firms, and making a profit.

(iii) Price P is at least as great as marginal cost MC. Otherwise a new firm would be able to make more profits than some existing firm by entering on a slightly smaller scale.

(iv) When there are two or more firms in the market, P cannot exceed MC. Together with (iii), this implies that P = MC. This condition is desirable from the point of view of welfare (ignoring 'second best problems'), because it implies that production occurs up to the point where the marginal cost of output equals its marginal benefit as measured by price. (When just one firm is in the market, this condition might not hold: see Baumol (1982, p. 5)).

(v) There is no cross-subsidization between products. Otherwise there would again be a profit opportunity for a new firm. This follows from (iii).

(vi) The number and configuration of firms is always such as to produce the industry's output at minimum total cost.

Properties (i) to (vi) are highly desirable, according to the canons of traditional welfare economics.[11] The final property is of particular interest. It is another instance of the idea that market structure is endogenously determined by the basic conditions of demand and technology, rather than being given exogenously.

The theory has been subject to critical review—see, for example, Shepherd (1984). It is most implausible that real-world markets (or at any rate a significant number of them) fit the assumptions of the theory of contestable markets, even approximately. In particular, the theory depends on the twin assumptions:

(a) that there are no sunk costs; and

(b) that an entrant can come into a market, and set up on full scale, before the existing firm(s) respond by changing price.

Both these assumptions are dubious in respect of real-world markets. Assumption (b) is the *opposite* of the natural assumption to make, since price can be generally altered more rapidly than a new firm can establish itself in a market.

Against these criticisms, it might be said that, although real-world markets do not exactly fit the assumptions of the theory, a significant number of them approximately do so, or could be made to do so by appropriate policy measures. It is unclear how this response could meet the objection to assumption (b), and in any event there is a further difficulty. It is that if the assumptions of contestability theory are changed slightly (for example by supposing that sunk costs are positive but small), the predictions of the theory can alter radically. For instance, even tiny sunk costs can substantially reduce—or even eliminate—the force of the threat of entry upon existing firms. This *lack of robustness* is a major reason to doubt the applicability of the theory to practical problems.

That being said, the theory of contestable markets is a timely reminder that the threat of new entry can be a potent force that shapes market structure and the conduct of existing firms. It underlines the importance of measures to liberalize markets by reducing barriers to entry and exit, where it is possible to do so.[12] However, the theory is not built on sufficiently strong foundations to justify the confidence that is sometimes placed in the 'invisible hand' results derived from it. For example, it would be a grave error to suppose that there is no need to regulate private natural monopolists, on the grounds that the threat of entry compels them to behave benignly.

2. Strategic entry deterrence

In a contestable market, the only way to deter the entry of new firms is to meet the needs of consumers with maximum efficiency. This is far from being true in other, perhaps more plausible, contexts. The purpose of this subsection is to describe some of the devices that existing firms might use to deter entry in a strategic fashion. That is to say, we are interested in strategic moves designed to benefit existing firms by inducing potential rivals to choose not to enter their markets. Salop (1979) gives an account of early work on this topic. See also Salop (1981).

For the sake of simplicity, we shall focus on the case where one incumbent firm is seeking to deter the entry of one potential rival.[13] The entry decision of the

---

[11] Another property is that in multiproduct natural monopoly industries, 'Ramsey prices' obtain at equilibrium for the product set of the industry in question: see Baumol *et al.* (1982). Ramsey prices maximize social welfare subject to the constraint that the firms earn a given profit level.

[12] Most economists would agree with the proposition that on the whole it is desirable for entry to be as free as possible. This statement is qualified because in some circumstances it is possible that free entry would damage welfare: see e.g. von Weizsäcker (1980).

[13] The case where several incumbents seek non-cooperatively to deter entry has been studied by Gilbert & Vives (1985).

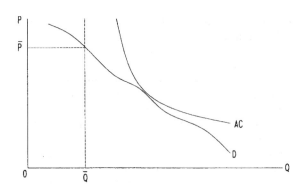

Figure 1.3. Limit pricing

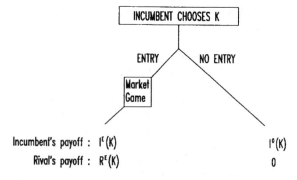

Figure 1.4. Commitment and entry deterrence

rival depends upon his beliefs as to the likely profit-ability of being in the market. Entry will occur if and only if the expected profits exceed the expected costs of entry. How can the incumbent influence those be-liefs in such a way as to deter entry?

We shall address this question in two steps. First, we shall suppose that each firm is fully informed about the behaviour, opportunities and motivation of the other. In that case, the game between firms is one of complete and perfect information. Secondly, we shall relax these assumptions about the information avail-able to the firms, and examine the roles of signalling and reputation in entry deterrence.

An instructive place to start is with the Bain-Sylos model of entry deterrence.[14] According to the Bain-Sylos postulate, the rival assumes that the output of the incumbent after entry would be the same as his output before entry. Given this postulate, it follows that the incumbent can influence the rival's assessment of post-entry profitability by varying his own pre-en-try output. Figure 1.3 shows the 'limit output', and cor-responding 'limit price' sufficient to deter entry. The demand curve for the industry is D, which is drawn relative to the vertical axis at 0. The AC curve is the average cost curve of the rival. It is drawn relative to the vertical axis given by the dashed line at output level $\overline{Q}$ because the D curve relative to that axis is the re-sidual demand faced by the rival.

The limit output and limit price are $\overline{Q}$ and $\overline{P}$, re-spectively. If output is less than $\overline{Q}$, the AC curve is shifted left, and a portion of it would lie below the de-mand curve, in which case the rival could enter profit-ably. An output level greater than or equal to $\overline{Q}$ suffices to deter entry. The incumbent may choose to deter or to accommodate entry, depending on the profitabil-ity to him of each course of action.

The above analysis is instructive, but not altogether convincing. The difficulty lies with the postulate that the rival expects the incumbent not to change his out-put level in the event of entry. Dixit (1980, p. 97) ques-tions the postulate on two counts:

First, faced with an irrevocable fact of entry, the established firm will usually find it best to make an accommodating out-put reduction. On the other hand, it would like to threaten to respond to entry with a predatory increase in output. The problem is to make the latter threat credible given the pro-spective entrant's knowledge of the former fact.

Similarly, Friedman (1979) has observed that in a game of complete and perfect information, and with no intertemporal interdependencies of cost or demand conditions, the incumbent's output level before the entry decision ought to make no difference to the rival's assessment of the profitability of entry. Once entry occurs, a new game begins, and the parameters of that game are independent of previous behaviour.

This suggests that flexible instruments such as price or quantity are less likely to be the means of entry deterrence than instruments that have a more lasting effect upon cost or demand conditions. The key is for the incumbent to *commit* himself to a course of con-duct that would be detrimental to an entrant. A large literature, from which but a few items will be men-tioned,[15] has explored this theme. Figure 1.4 above sketches a simple schema.

First, the incumbent chooses the level of some stra-tegic variable K. Numerous interpretations can be given to K, but for the moment regard it as the incum-bent's capacity level. If the rival chooses not to enter, he gets zero, and the incumbent gets $I^O(K)$, as shown at the foot of the right-hand branch. Note that the in-cumbent's payoff depends on K even if entry does not

---

[14]   See Bain (1956) and Sylos-Labini (1964).

[15]   A fuller survey, and an extensive bibliography, are provided by Geroski and Jacquemin (1984).

occur. If entry does take place, a duopoly exists. Without examining the details of the duopolists' interactions, let us assume that the upshot of the 'market game' between them is that the incumbent gets $I^E(K)$ and the rival gets $R^E(K)$ in the event of entry. The schema is broad enough to allow for the rival also to choose some strategic variable, after the incumbent's choice of K. This would be included in the black box of the market game.

The incumbent's choice of K deters entry if $R^E(K)$ < 0. It may be that entry is deterred even by the level of K that would have been chosen by a pure monopolist facing no threat of entry. Then entry is said to be blockaded. Or it may be that the incumbent does better to permit entry than to deter it. But here our concern is with the remaining case, in which strategic entry deterrence is optimal for the incumbent.

What are the likely instruments of entry deterrence? It is useful to distinguish between those that affect costs (the incumbent's and/or the rival's) and those that affect demand. As to the former, Dixit (1980) showed how the incumbent's choice of *capacity* could deter entry, but in Dixit's model, excess (in the sense of idle) capacity is not observed.[16] More generally, K can be interpreted as the incumbent's level of *capital input*. Strategic entry deterrence commonly implies overcapitalization, in the sense that the output eventually produced by the incumbent could have been produced more efficiently with a lower level of capital, and a correspondingly higher level of variable factors of production (see Spence 1977). The same holds when K is interpreted as the incumbent's cost-reducing R & D expenditure. (Note the parallel with section III.4 above). In all these examples, the incumbent's commitment of high K promises that he will supply a high output level, or charge a low price, in the market game. The choice of K is therefore unattractive to the rival, not because of its direct effects, but because of its indirect influence upon the outcome of the market game.

In criticism of the Bain-Sylos analysis, it was stated above that the incumbent's pre-entry output would not affect the rival's entry decision if there were no inter-temporal interdependences of cost or demand. But such interdependences do hold if the *experience curve* effect operates—i.e. if a firm's cost level is a declining function of its cumulative output. In that case it is possible for the incumbent's choice of output to deter entry strategically: see Spence (1981) and Fudenberg and Tirole (1983).

As well as the incumbent lowering his own costs, there may be ways for him to *raise the rival's cost*: see

Salop and Scheffman (1983). For example, by setting high wage rates in the industry, the incumbent increases his own costs and those of an entrant. The direct effect of this upon the incumbent is unfavourable, but if the indirect effect is to deter the rival's entry, then the ploy may well be beneficial to him in overall terms.

Another way in which entry might be deterred is for the incumbent to deny the rival access to technology that would allow him to compete. Gilbert and Newbery (1982) examine *pre-emptive patenting*—the acquisition of a patent by an incumbent firm with the purpose of denying the patent, and hence an entry opportunity, to a potential rival. An important factor here is that the incumbent's incentive to win the patent is likely to exceed the rival's incentive, even if the patent is for a technology inferior to that already enjoyed by the incumbent. This is because the incumbent's monopoly persists if he denies entry to the rival, whereas competition, which is less profitable than monopoly, occurs in the event of entry. This result has an important bearing on the question of the persistence of monopoly, for the advantage of the incumbent arises from his *strategic position*; intrinsically the incumbent may be no different from the rival. The result also offers an explanation of the phenomenon of sleeping (i.e. unused) patents, because the pre-emption result does not depend upon the patent being for a technology that is superior to the incumbent's existing technology.

Turning from the cost side to the demand side, there are further ways in which an incumbent firm can make the prospect of entry unattractive for a rival firm. In some circumstances, strategic *advertising* deters entry, although in Schmalensee's (1983) exploration of advertising and entry deterrence, it emerged that low advertising was the way to deter entry. The reason was that high advertising would cause the incumbent to have a higher price in the market game. For the rival, the favourable latter effect outweighed the disadvantage of high advertising, and made entry more attractive. *Brand proliferation*—the introduction of numerous new products—can also serve to deter entry (see Schmalensee (1978)). To use the locational analogy common in the analysis of product differentiation, brand proliferation fills up product space in such a way that there are no remaining slots or niches for profitable entry.

Product differentiation was one of Bain's three sources of barriers to entry. Although advertising is often regarded as a measure of product differentiation, Bain did not see it as the heart of the problem. Schmalensee (1982) shows how buyers' uncertainty

---

[16] Bulow *et al.* (1985a) show that idle capacity is possible when Dixit's assumptions on demand are relaxed.

about the quality of new brands can give established (or pioneering) brands an advantage in a differentiated market. The new brand would have to be priced substantially below the existing brand to induce consumers to experiment with it; part of the cost of the experiment is the loss of surplus currently being enjoyed on the existing brand. This is again an example where the incumbent has strategic advantage solely because of already being in the market.

To summarize so far, there are numerous ways in which an incumbent firm can influence cost and/or demand conditions by strategic investments in such a way as to discourage entry into his market. Bulow *et al.* (1985b) and Fudenberg and Tirole (1984) have examined in general terms various types of entry deterrence. Returning to the schema of figure 1.4 above, we can ask whether over-or-under-investment in the strategic variable K deters entry. The answer depends of course upon the specification of the market game. In some instances (such as excess capacity deterring entry), the incumbent deters entry by being 'large'. Fudenberg and Tirole call this the Top Dog Effect. In other instances, the incumbent deters entry by being 'small', and thereby promises an aggressive response in the event of entry. This is the Lean and Hungry Look. It may be better for the incumbent to accommodate, rather than deter entry. Then he will act strategically to influence the nature of entry, either by being 'large' (a Top Dog) or 'small' (the Puppy Dog Ploy). The aim of all these strategic moves is to cause the rival to choose to act more favourably for the incumbent than he would otherwise do.

So far we have supposed that firms are fully informed about each other's opportunities and motivation, but we now turn to the second step in the analysis of strategic entry deterrence by relaxing this assumption. Milgrom and Roberts (1982b) have shown how limit pricing may be used to deter entry when the potential entrant is uncertain as to the cost level of the incumbent firm. The rival's expectations concerning that cost level—and hence his entry decision—are influenced by the price charged by the incumbent before the entry decision is made. Therefore the pre-entry price can act as a *signal* of the incumbent's efficiency. An incumbent with low costs would like to signal that fact, because the potential rival would then be more reluctant to enter his market. By the same token, an inefficient incumbent would like to masquerade as a low-cost firm in order to make entry less likely. This incentive to signal in an uncertain environment means that the incumbent's pricing may be used as an instrument of entry deterrence. Note that consumers benefit from this kind of limit pricing insofar as it lowers

price. Other interesting issues arise when there is uncertainty about demand as well as the incumbent's cost level. Then a low pre-entry price might signal either low demand or low costs: see Matthews and Mirman (1983).

Milgrom and Roberts (1982a) and Kreps and Wilson (1982) have explored another context in which uncertainty about the incumbent plays a role in entry deterrence, namely in connection with *predatory pricing*. They examine a game due to Selten (1978) in which an incumbent firm—a chain store—is threatened by entry in each of a number of towns. More precisely, they look at a game in which the predatory pricing game in figure 1.2 is repeated a finite number of times. Intuitively, one would expect that the incumbent would fight entry if challenged in town early in the sequence, in order to deter later entrants. However, this is not so if the entrants have complete information about the opportunities and motivation of the incumbent, because in that case he would never fight entry. This is because it is common knowledge that he would not fight in the last town; and so he would not fight in the last but one; and so on. But if the assumption of complete information is very slightly relaxed—so that there is a possibility that the incumbent is somehow committed to fighting—then even an uncommitted incumbent would (rationally) fight entry in early towns to keep up the *reputation* of possibly being a committed fighter. This reputation effect is very powerful, in the sense that a very small amount of imperfect information can make it rational to fight in a large number of towns. There is an exact parallel between this and the work of Kreps *et al.* (1982) on the repeated Prisoners' Dilemma described in section III.1.

3. Potential competition: concluding remarks

To summarize, potential competition affects the behaviour of existing firms insofar as it impels them to behave in such a way that entry is an unattractive prospect. In a contestable market, where entry is ultrafree, entry is unattractive only when existing firms, singly and in combination, meet consumers' demands with maximum efficiency. In other, perhaps more realistic circumstances, this need not be so. Incumbent firms may choose to act strategically to deter entry. Since the key to strategic commitment is some degree of irreversibility, price is perhaps less likely to be the instrument of strategic entry deterrence than non-price instruments such as capacity, R & D or brand proliferation (although price was regarded as the instrument in conventional theory of entry deterrence). However, when firms are uncertain about each other and their environment, richer possibilities exist, and firms' behaviour may be chosen partly with a view to the signals conveyed to rivals. The theory of industrial organization has made important advances in understanding these matters.

V. Conclusions and policy implications

The purpose of this paper has been to explain some recent developments in industrial economics so as to give a background for the consideration of policy. In this concluding section, some of the main themes of the foregoing discussion are highlighted, and it is suggested how they bear on policy questions.

A major theme is the *endogeneity of market structure* (see e.g. sections III.2 and III.3 above). Recent theory has examined the dependence of market structure and conduct upon the basic parameters of technology and demand, whereas previously much emphasis was placed upon the causal flow from structure to conduct and performance. If structure is regarded as a symptom of underlying forces, rather than as the root cause of (say) undesirable forms of conduct, then the perspective on policy alters.

A related theme is the role of *potential competition*. If conditions of entry into an industry are free and easy, then, even though there may be only a few firms actually in the industry, they may be compelled to perform well, in terms of productive, dynamic and allocative efficiency, due to the threat of entry. It is for this reason that policies designed to liberalize entry are on the whole desirable. The results of the liberalization of the US airline markets, and of the market for terminal equipment in telecommunications, are examples in point. As a theoretical proposition it is not always the case that liberalization is desirable, but there must be a strong—though rebuttable—presumption in favour of that claim.

There are numerous ways in which incumbent firms can seek to thwart the threat of entry—for example by predatory practices. Unless these practices are somehow checked, the danger is that other measures of liberalization will not be effective. If threats of predatory behaviour deter entry, then liberalization has not properly taken place.[17] In any event, it would be a serious

mistake to suppose that measures of liberalization are always sufficient to ensure good industry performance. In a contestable market (see section IV.1 above) that is indeed the case, but the assumptions of the theory of contestable markets are both strict and sensitive to small variations. The implications of that theory for policy are therefore doubtful, save insofar as the theory underlines the point that entry conditions are important. In some industries (including natural monopolies) no amount of liberalization will ensure good industry performance. There is then a case for regulation—either in the form of control of public enterprise, or as regulation of private enterprise.[18]

Another broad theme is that strategic competition among the few can produce results that are not socially desirable. For example, it was shown in section III.1 that effective collusion between firms can occur even when there is no opportunity for them to make enforceable agreements. In section III.4 it was shown how a firm might over-invest in R & D or capital equipment (and therefore produce its output inefficiently) in an attempt to gain strategic advantage relative to its competitors. Section IV.2 on strategic entry deterrence contained numerous examples of entry deterring devices that are costly to society both directly and because they thwart competition.

The classic example of market failure is perhaps that of R & D competition (see section III.2), which has been a major topic in recent industrial economics. The free market allocates resources inefficiently to R & D for several reasons, including appropriability problems (the innovator requires reward, but static efficiency requires free access to his results) and duplication of research. These considerations are the justification for government policies such as patent protection, subsidies for R & D, and measures to promote collaborative R & D (e.g. joint ventures). By its industrial policies, government can influence conditions in the game between firms—their payoffs, strategies, and so on—and thereby influence its outcome. Moreover, one government may be engaged in a game with others, in which each is choosing industrial and commercial policies to further its objectives. Many of the tools and concepts recently employed in industrial economics—such as commitments, threats and collusion—are being applied to the study of government policy using this game perspective.

Recent developments in the theory of industrial organization have added considerably to our understanding of the workings of competition between the

---

[17] For a brief account of the economics of predatory practices, see Vickers (1985) and the references therein.

[18] The natural monopoly problem in general, and electricity and telecommunications in particular, are discussed in Vickers and Yarrow (1985).

few. Although the perspective gained should and will influence the making and the implementation of competition policy and industrial policy, the new theory has not delivered generally applicable policy guidelines, and it is unlikely that it will do so in future. It would be wrong to blame theory for this shortcoming, for the reason is that industries are intrinsically different from one another, and the prospect of generally applicable guidelines is therefore unlikely. However, recent developments in industrial economics are providing most illuminating perspectives on the nature of industrial conflict.

Appreciation of the strategic nature of competition among the few underlines this point. The successful strategist (say a threatener or a promiser) is he who arranges things in such a way that the other parties think it sufficiently likely that the threat or promise will be carried out. Whether and how this can be done depends on the particular circumstances at hand, and is largely a matter of tactics and opportunism. The economists recently studying strategic competition among the few have been investigating phenomena well-known to others: an eminent businessman, who had just been told of recent developments in the economics of industry exclaimed: 'I feel like the character in Molière who learns that all the while he has been speaking prose'.

References

Abreu, D. (1984), 'Infinitely repeated games with discounting: a general theory', unpublished paper, Princeton University.

Abreu, D., D. Pearce and E. Stacchetti (1984), 'Optimal cartel equilibrium with imperfect monitoring', Harvard Institute of Economic Research Discussion Paper 1090.

Axelrod, R. (1984), *The Evolution of Cooperation*, (Basic Books, New York).

Bain, J. (1956), *Barriers to new competition* (Harvard University Press, Cambridge, MA).

Baumol, W., J. Panzar and R. Willig (1982), *Contestable markets and the theory of industry structure*, (Harcourt Brace Jovanovich, San Diego, CA).

Baumol, W. (1982), 'Contestable Markets: an uprising in the theory of industry structure', *American Economic Review*, **72**, 1–15.

Brander, J., and B. Spencer (1983), 'Strategic commitment with R & D: the symmetric case', *Bell Journal of Economics*, **14**, 225–35.

Bulow, J., J. Geanakopolos and P. Klemperer (1985a), 'Holding idle capacity to deter entry', *Economic Journal*, **95**, 178–82.

Bulow, J., J. Geanakopolos and P. Klemperer (1985b), 'Multi-market oligopoly', *Journal of Political Economy*, **93**, 488–511.

Dasgupta, P. (1985), 'The theory of technological competition' in F. Mathewson and J. Stiglitz (eds.) *New developments in the analysis of market structure*, (MIT Press, Boston, MA).

Dasgupta, P., and J. Stiglitz (1980), 'Industrial structure and the nature of innovative activity', *Economic Journal*, **90**, 266–293.

Dixit, A. (1980), 'The role of investment in entry deterrence', *Economic Journal*, **90**, 95–106.

Dixit, A. (1982), 'Recent developments in oligopoly theory', *American Economic Review Papers and Proceedings*, **72**, 12–17.

Fellner, W. (1949), *Competition among the few*, (Knopf, New York).

Friedman, J. (1971), 'A non-cooperative equilibrium for supergames', *Review of Economic Studies*, **28**, 1–12.

Friedman, J. (1977), *Oligopoly and the theory of games*, (North-Holland, Amsterdam).

Friedman, J. (1979), 'On entry preventing behaviour and limit price models of entry', in Brams *et al.* (eds.) *Applied Game Theory* (Physica-Verlag, Vienna).

Fudenberg, D., and J. Tirole (1983), 'Learning by doing and market performance', *Bell Journal of Economics*, **14**, 522–30.

Fudenberg, D., and J. Tirole (1984), 'The fat-cat effect, the puppy-dog ploy, and the lean and hungry look', *American Economic Review Papers and Proceedings*, **74**, 361–6.

Geroski, P. and A. Jacquemin (1984), 'Dominant firms and their alleged decline', *International Journal of Industrial Organisation*, **2**, 1–27.

Gilbert, R., and D. Newbery (1982), 'Pre-emptive patenting and the persistence of monopoly', *American Economic Review*, **72**, 514–526.

Gilbert, R., and X. Vives (1985), 'Non-cooperative Entry deterrence and the free rider problem', mimeo, University of Pennsylvania.

Green, E., and R. Porter (1984), 'Non-cooperative collusion under imperfect price information', *Econometrica*, **52**, 87–100.

Kamien, M., and N. Schwartz (1982), *Market structure and innovation* (Cambridge University Press, Cambridge).

Klemperer, P. (1984), 'Collusion via switching costs', Stanford University Graduate School of Business Discussion Paper no. 786.

Kreps, D., P. Milgrom, J. Roberts and R. Wilson (1982), 'Rational cooperation in a finitely repeated prisoners' dilemma game', *Journal of Economic Theory*, **27**, 245–252.

Kreps, D., and R. Wilson (1982), 'Reputation and imperfect information', *Journal of Economic Theory*, **27**, 253–279.

Matthews, S., and L. Mirman (1983), 'Equilibrium limit pricing: the effects of private information and stochastic demand', *Econometrica*, **51**, 981–996.

Milgrom, P., and J. Roberts (1982a), 'Predation, reputation and entry deterrence', *Journal of Economic Theory*, **27**, 280–312.

Milgrom, P., and J. Roberts (1982b), 'Limit pricing and entry under incomplete information: An equilibrium analysis', *Econometrica*, **50**, 443–459.

Ordover, J., and R. Willig (1985), 'Antitrust for high-technology industries: assessing research joint ventures and mergers', Woodrow Wilson School Discussion Paper no. 87.

Salop, S. (1979), 'Strategic entry deterrence', *American Economic Review Papers and Proceedings*, **69**, 335–8.

Salop, S. (ed.) (1981), *Strategy, predation and antitrust analysis*, (F. T. C., Washington, DC).

Salop, S. (1985), 'Practices that facilitate Oligopoly Coordination', in F. Mathewson and J. Stiglitz (eds.), *New developments in the analysis of market structure* (MIT Press, Boston, MA).

Salop, S., and D. Scheffman (1983), 'Raising rivals' costs', *American Economic Review Papers and Proceedings*, **73**, 267–71.

Schelling, T. (1960), *The strategy of conflict*, (Harvard University Press, Cambridge, MA).

Scherer, F. (1980), *Industrial Market Structure and Economic Performance*, (2nd ed., Rand-McNally, Chicago).

Schmalensee, R. (1978), 'Entry deterrence in the ready to eat breakfast cereal industry', *Bell Journal of Economics*, **9**, 305–327.

Schmalensee, R. (1982), 'Product Differentiation Advantages of Pioneering Brands', *American Economic Review*, **82**, 349–365.

Schmalensee, R. (1983), 'Advertising and Entry Deterrence: an Exploratory Model', *Journal of Political Economy*, **90**, 636–53.

Selten, R. (1965), 'Spieltheoretische Behandlung eines Oligopolmodells mit Nachfrageträgheit', *Zeitschrift für die gesamte Staatswissenschaft*, **121**, 301–324 and 667–89.

Selten, R. (1975), 'Re-examination of the Perfectness Concept for Equilibrium Points in Extensive Games', *International Journal of Game Theory*, **4**, 25–55.

Selten, R. (1978), 'The Chain Store Paradox', *Theory and Decision*, **9**, 127–159.

Shaked, A., and J. Sutton (1982), 'Relaxing Price Competition through Product Differentiation', *Review of Economic Studies*, **49**, 3–14.

Shaked, A., and J. Sutton (1983), 'Natural Oligopolies', *Econometrica*, **51**, 1469–84.

Shepherd, W. (1984), '"Contestability" vs. Competition', *American Economic Review*, **74**, 572–587.

Spence, M. (1977), 'Entry, capacity, investment and oligopolistic pricing', *Bell Journal of Economics*, **8**, 534–44.

Spence, M. (1981), 'The learning curve and competition', *Bell Journal of Economics*, **12**, 49–70.

Spence, M. (1984), 'Cost Reduction, Competition, and Industry Performance', *Econometrica*, **52**, 101–21.

Stoneman, P. (1983), *The Economic Analysis of Technological Change* (Oxford University Press, Oxford).

Sylos-Labini, P. (1962), *Oligopoly and Technical Progress*, Cambridge, Mass.: Harvard University Press.

Vickers, J. (1985), 'The Economics of Predatory Practices', *Fiscal Studies*, **6**(3), 24–36.

Vickers, J., and G. Yarrow (1985), *Privatization and the Natural Monopolies*, London: Public Policy Centre.

von Weizsäcker, C. (1980), 'A Welfare Analysis of Barriers to Entry', *Bell Journal of Economics*, **11**, 399–420.

von Weizsäcker, C. (1984), 'The costs of substitution', *Econometrica*, 52, 1085–116.

Waterson, M. (1984), *Economic Theory of the Industry*, Cambridge: Cambridge University Press.

Williamson, O. (1979), 'Symposium on Antitrust Law and Economics: Symposium Introduction', University of Pennsylvania Law Review, **127**, 918–24.

Tacit collusion

RAY REES

University of Munich[1]

I. Introduction

The word collusion describes a type of conduct or form of behaviour whereby decision-takers agree to co-ordinate their actions. This in general would seem to involve two elements: a process of communication, discussion, and exchange of information with the aim of reaching an agreement; and, where there are gains to reneging on the agreement given that the others comply, some kind of mechanism for punishing such violations and so enforcing the agreement. In the economics of oligopolistic markets the distinction between 'explicit' and 'tacit' collusion turns on the first of these elements. It is possible that firms could agree to co-ordinate their actions in some way without explicit communication and discussion. For example, it may become tacitly accepted practice in a market exactly to match the price changes of the largest firm. All firms are aware of this 'tacit agreement' or 'conscious parallelism', and no process for reaching agreement is strictly necessary. However, the second element must always be present: typically there are at least short-run gains from reneging on an agreement and so tacit collusion requires the perception that to do so would in the end turn out to be unprofitable because of punitive reactions by the other firms.

Indeed, at the extreme, it could be argued that whether or not there is explicit communication is irrelevant: what matters is whether a collusive agreement, however arrived at, can be sustained by the self-interest of the parties involved. If this is not the case,

then explicit communication is simply 'cheap talk'. This is most easily seen in the context of a market which takes place only once. For example, suppose that a government wishes to sell off, once and for all, the mineral rights on a tract of land and invites sealed bids which will specify required acreage and a price per acre. There are just two firms which will bid, though the minerals extracted will subsequently be sold on a competitive world market. Each firm knows that the value of the land is £100 per acre, and knows the other knows this and that the government does not. The government places a reservation value of £10 an acre on the land. If the firms bid competitively, they will each bid £100 an acre for the entire acreage. It would clearly be in their interests for them to agree to bid £10 an acre for one-half the acreage each. Such an agreement would not, of course, be legally enforceable. Moreover, it is not sustainable by the self-interest of the firms. If one firm believed that the other would bid according to the agreement, it is in its interest to bid slightly more than £10 an acre for the entire acreage. But then it would realize that the other firm would have also worked that out, and it should raise its bid. But the other firm will also have worked this out . . . and so on. Whatever the firms may have discussed and agreed, this is merely cheap talk if the agreement cannot be enforced: under the conditions of this example, the firms will end up making competitive bids.

The enforceability of collusive agreements by some means can, therefore, be taken as a necessary condition for their existence. We shall consider at some length below circumstances under which this condition is met even when enforcement through the courts is not available. If the distinction between tacit and explicit collusion is to mean anything, it must also be shown that the ability to communicate in some way affects the likely existence and stability of collusion. Is collusion indeed *ever really* 'tacit', or is it the case that

First published in *Oxford Review of Economic Policy*, vol. 9, no. 2 (1993). This version has been updated and revised to incorporate recent developments.

[1] I am grateful to Asha Sadanand and to participants at the conference run by *Oxford Review of Economic Policy* and the Centre for Business Strategy at the London Business School in January 1993, in particular to Donald Hay, for helpful comments on an earlier draft of this paper.

what may appear to be tacit collusion is actually explicit collusion in which the process of agreement is simply concealed? The statement by Adam Smith that businessmen's meetings, even for 'merriment and diversion', usually end up in connivance to restrict competition, is often quoted, but the sentence which follows it is equally perceptive: 'It is impossible indeed to prevent such meetings, by any law which either could be executed, or would be consistent with liberty and justice.' Moreover, short of methods of surveillance which are also not 'consistent with liberty and justice' it may be impossible to obtain evidence on what transpired at such meetings.

Turning now to antitrust policy, a major difference among advanced industrial countries in respect of their policy towards collusion lies in whether collusion is in most instances *per se* illegal, as in the US, or whether attention is directed at appraising the results of collusive behaviour, as for example in the UK. In the former case there is understandably much more emphasis on deciding whether or not collusion has in fact taken place. The problem here is that, quite apart from the possibility that collusion might be concealed, the observation that firms communicated and appeared to reach agreement need not imply that the collusive outcome was actually achieved (as in the above bidding example), while if collusion is tacit there will be no evidence of communication and negotiation. The observation of communication is neither necessary nor sufficient for existence of collusion.

II. Equilibrium concepts

Until relatively recently, oligopoly theory was typically presented as a collection of models each based on a particular *ad hoc* set of assumptions about firms' perceptions of their rivals' reactions to their own choices of prices or outputs. The leading models in the literature are:

The Cournot model: in the traditional story firms independently choose outputs on the assumption that their rivals make no response to their choices—even though this assumption may be continually falsified—and market equilibrium is achieved through a sequence of alternating output choices which converges over time.

The Stackelberg model: a leader makes a choice of output, the other firms act as followers and make their profit-maximizing response to this output. The leader takes account of these responses in choosing its output and is able to do better than it would under Cournot

reactions—there is a 'first mover' or precommitment advantage.

The 'kinked demand curve' model: each firm believes that an increase in its output (reduction in its price) will be matched by its rivals, while a reduction in output (increase in price) will not be followed. This creates a kink in the firm's perceived demand curve at its current price–output pair (the levels of which are, however, unexplained) which then tends to remain the same despite changes in marginal cost, because of a discontinuity in the firm's marginal revenue at the kink.

The Bertrand model: again in the traditional story firms independently choose prices, on the assumption that their rivals make no response to their choices. Where firms produce identical outputs and have identical constant marginal costs equilibrium price ends up equal to this common cost. If the constant marginal costs differ, then only the firm with the lowest marginal cost is left in the market and it sets a price just below the marginal cost of the next-to-lowest cost firm. If marginal costs are non-constant then no equilibrium price exists unless outputs are non-homogeneous, i.e. there is product differentiation.

The Edgeworth model: firms choose prices as in the Bertrand model, with identical constant marginal costs, but with fixed output capacities. There is a range of possible types of outcome, including those of the Cournot and Bertrand models, but the novel possibility is that of 'price cycles'. There is a range of prices the upper and lower limits of which are determined by demand, cost, and capacity parameters. As firms set prices alternately over consecutive periods, price falls by small steps from the upper limit of the interval until it reaches the lower limit and then jumps back to the upper limit and the cycle begins again.

Recent developments in game theory have had an important impact on the way we interpret these models. Game theory forces us to be precise about three sets of assumptions on which a model rests:

(i) the possibility of binding commitments. If it is possible for firms to make binding commitments, for example legally enforceable contracts, to carry out certain agreed actions, then this raises a fundamentally different set of issues than if no such commitments are possible. In the former case the firms are involved in a *co-operative game*, the problem is to reach agreement on division of the gains from co-operation. In the latter case, whether or not explicit communication takes place, each firm has to decide on the choice of action which is in its own best interest in the light of the fact that the others are behaving in the same way: we have a *non-co-operative game*. All the oligopoly models just discussed are examples of non-co-operative games, and in the light of the antitrust laws in most advanced industrial countries this would seem to be appropriate.

(ii)   The frequency of market interaction. This is something that is often somewhat ambiguously specified in the traditional economic models. The models are usually formulated as 'one-shot games': firms are making their choices relative to market and cost conditions at a given point in time as if there were no past and no future. Nevertheless, time enters through the back door in the discussion of reaction patterns. The very concept of 'action' and 'reaction' must presuppose at least two points in time, but the discussions underlying the Cournot and Bertrand models implicitly require much more, possibly an infinity of time periods as the processes of convergence to an equilibrium work themselves out. Likewise the price cycles in the Edgeworth model take place through real time. If market interaction takes place repeatedly, however, why is it that firms are assumed to ignore this and treat each decision as if it were a move in a 'one-shot' game? Surely if the market is held repeatedly firms would realize this and formulate strategies that determine their actions over time. But then, as we shall see, it may become possible to rationalize the kind of collusive behaviour which is simply not contemplated in the standard models.

(iii)   The way in which firms form their expectations of their rivals' choices. A rational player in a game cannot be thought of as simply taking his rivals' actions as given by some *ad hoc* assumption. The analysis of a game is concerned precisely with the question of the expectations of the behaviour of his rivals it is rational for any one player to form. The general answer game theory gives to this question is contained in the concept of Nash Equilibrium (NE). The choices made by players in a game must be mutually consistent in the sense that each player's choice is the best for him given the choices made by the others. The NE choices have the property that if each player knows the others will make their NE choices, he has no reason to deviate from making his own NE choice. The argument to suggest that a non-NE set of choices cannot be an equilibrium outcome of the game proceeds as follows. Suppose player 1 assumes that player 2 will choose action A, and that 1's best (most profitable) response to this is action B. Suppose, further, that 2's best response to B is *not* A. Should 1 continue to assume that 2 will choose A? If 2 *had* been going to choose A, she would work out that 1 would plan to choose B, in which case she would change her planned action to whatever is the best response to B, so falsifying the initial assumption that she would choose A. Thus 1 cannot persist in believing

2 will choose A if he knows that she is as rational and well-informed as he is. Only the NE choices are immune to this kind of contradiction.

The classic oligopoly models can then be thought of as one-shot, non-co-operative games to which the NE concept can be applied to find a solution. They differ not in respect of reaction patterns but in the economic characteristics of the market concerned, and it is a matter of fact, not logic, to decide which model is appropriate for any particular market under study. An interesting point is that in the three leading models, those of Cournot, Bertrand, and Stackelberg, the NE outcomes are identical to those traditionally derived; only the reasoning underlying the derivation of those equilibria changes. Since the games are played just once, with the firms making output or price choices simultaneously, the equilibria cannot be rationalized by appeal to a process of action and reaction through time. The explanation of the equilibrium outcomes is that they *are* the NE outcomes in these games.

It is useful to consider the antitrust implications of the outcomes in these three market games. First, firms are behaving non-co-operatively and, it seems safe to say, non-collusively. Communication between firms is unnecessary to achieve the market equilibrium, since this is done by the firms independently thinking through the logic of the situation.[2] In the absence of the ability to make binding agreements any such communication would in any case be cheap talk—the only outcomes that are sustainable by the self-interest of the firms are the NE outcomes, and any agreement to choose non-NE outcomes would be reneged upon, as in our earlier example (which can be thought of as a model of Bertrand competition). Thus a charge of collusion could not be made to stick.[3] At the same time, in two of the three models the equilibrium outcomes could be quite bad from the welfare point of view. In the Bertrand case with constant identical marginal costs we have, in fact, the perfectly competitive market outcome, with price equal to marginal cost and no excess profit, but in the Cournot and Stackelberg cases prices exceed marginal costs and the firms make excess profit. Moreover, in these models, if the firms have different and non-constant marginal costs, a further source of inefficiency is that total market output will be produced at more than minimum total cost—the marginal costs of firms are not equalized at the equilibrium. It is

---

[2]   Note, however, that the firms are assumed to have full knowledge of each other's profit functions, which, at the least, requires knowledge of each other's cost functions. There is clearly a role for exchange of information to achieve this, as we discuss more fully below.

[3]   This is, in fact, recognized in US antitrust law, as we discuss more fully in section III.

certainly true that the Cournot and Stackelberg equilibria in general involve smaller welfare losses, and lower levels of excess profit, than would be the case if the firms acted as a joint profit-maximizing monopoly or cartel but, none the less, contingent on market parameters, allocative inefficiency could still be quite large.

It seems clear then that an antitrust policy based on the behaviour of firms, in particular on whether or not this is collusive, could come to different conclusions to one which was based upon appraisal of the inefficiency and extent of excess profits associated with the market outcome. Except in the special Bertrand case, even if the self-interest of the firms does not lead them to collude, it would not lead them to behave as perfectly competitive firms either.

The assumption that the market takes place just once is, of course, patently unrealistic: repeated market interaction among firms would appear to be the rule. Some care has to be taken, however, in specifying the time horizon in a model of a multi-period market. To simplify the dynamics of the model, it is usual to assume that the market situation in each period is the same: the same population of firms faces the same market demand with the same cost conditions in each period. The key distinction is that between the case in which there is a known, finite number of periods in which firms will choose prices or outputs, and those in which either the number of periods, though finite, is not known with certainty, or the time horizon can be regarded as infinite. When there is a known, finite number of periods, an argument based on backward induction can be constructed, to the effect that the equilibrium strategies for the multi-period game consist simply of repetitions of the single-period NE, for example the one-period Cournot equilibrium outputs in a market in which firms make output choices.[4] Nothing of substance, therefore, is added by analysing the market in a multi-period setting. On the other hand, if there is no known, certain last period from which this

backward induction argument can begin, it makes sense to discuss the conditions under which *collusive* behaviour can be sustained as a *non-co-operative* equilibrium of the repeated game.

The intuitive argument is straightforward. If firms agree to set outputs or prices which give them higher profits than those they would earn in a one-shot NE, and one of them reneges on this agreement, then in the following period(s) punitive actions can be undertaken, for example a price war, to wipe out the gains from the deviation. The threat of this *ex ante* can then be used to ensure adherence to the agreement. The existence of a future in which to apply punishment allows current collusion to be sustained by the self-interest of the firms.

There are two respects in which this intuition must be taken more rigorously. First, it must be established that sufficiently large future losses can be threatened so that, when discounted to a present value, they offset the gain from reneging in the current period. Second, the threat to inflict these losses must be credible. We consider each of these points in turn.

The fact that future losses from punishment have to be set against current gains to defection implies that the rate at which a firm discounts the future will be important. This rate will in general reflect a firm's (marginal) cost of capital. In an imperfect capital market it need not be the same for all firms, and in an economy subject to cyclical fluctuations in economic activity it need not be the same over time. In general, the more heavily firms discount the future (i.e. the higher their cost of capital) the smaller will be the present value of future losses of profit caused by punishment, relative to the immediate gains from cheating on an agreement. In a particular market, given its underlying cost and demand parameters, it will usually be possible to define a range of discount rates over which agreement on some collusive set of outputs or prices can be sustained by some threatened punishment strategy. In general this range will vary with the set of outputs or prices to be sustained, the punishment strategy and the characteristics of the individual firm. We shall explore how these factors interact more fully below. It suffices to note here that the more heavily firms discount the future the less likely is it that collusion among them can be sustained.

The gain to a firm from reneging on the collusive agreement will depend partly on cost, demand, and capacity parameters and partly on the length of time for which a higher profit than that realized under the agreement can be earned before retaliation by the other firms takes place. For example, if technology is such that production is subject to a fixed maximum rate of

[4] Even in finite horizon games, there are cases in which collusive behaviour may constitute a non-co-operative equilibrium. If there are multiple Nash equilibria of the constituent game, over which players have strict preferences, then collusion can be sustained by threats to play less-preferred Nash equilibrium strategies. If the end-period of the finite horizon game is not known with certainty, then at each period there is a probability there will be a next period in which punishment can take place, and by factoring this probability into the discount rate the model becomes similar to the infinite horizon case. Finally, if each player believes that there is a non-zero probability that the other will play co-operatively, because she is 'crazy' or not individually rational, than as Kreps *et al.* (1982) show, even in a finite horizon game, if the horizon is long enough, firms may play co-operatively. In the interests of simplicity, and since similar issues arise, we subsume all these cases under the 'infinite horizon' case.

capacity output, and for each firm its output under the collusive agreement is just about at capacity, then there would be virtually no short-run gain to reneging on the agreement. On the other hand, if there is significant excess capacity at the agreed output, and the agreed price is well above marginal cost, then a significant output expansion would be both feasible and profitable and so reneging on the agreement could appear attractive. The longer the other firms take to detect a deviation and implement a punitive response, the greater will be the duration of the flow of profit from reneging and the further into the future the losses from punishment will be delayed, thus reducing their present value.

The extent of losses from punishment of course depends on the form of punishment adopted (we consider the question of the *credibility* of this punishment below, here we examine only its extent). In the literature[5] three main types of punishment strategy have been analysed.

(i) *Nash reversion.*   It is generally expected that the profits firms receive as a result of collusion exceed those they would earn in the one-shot NE, otherwise they might as well not collude. In that case, one way of inflicting a loss of profit in retaliation for reneging on the agreement would be to revert to the NE of the one-shot game, either permanently or for a number of periods sufficient to wipe out the gains from reneging, if that is possible. One limitation of this as a punishment is that it may not be very severe—it may imply a moderate loss of profit relative to the collusive agreement—and so may support collusion only for a small set of discount rates. A second limitation, at least if the joint profit-maximizing (cartel) allocation is thought to be a likely objective of the collusion, is that this allocation may not be sustainable by threats of reversion to a Cournot–Nash equilibrium. It is not difficult to construct cases in which firms have unequal marginal costs and some firms earn higher profits at the Nash equilibrium than at the joint profit-maximizing allocation.

(ii) *Minimax punishment.*   For each firm in the market, it is possible to define its profit maximizing action (an output or price) or *best response* given the actions of all other firms. We can then find the values of the latter which make the firm's best-response profit as small as possible. This is the firm's minimax profit, and it is also often referred to as its 'security level', since the firm cannot be forced to take a lower profit than that. Clearly the most drastic punishment for a firm

[5]   For expository surveys, at varying levels of difficulty, see Friedman (1986), Gravelle and Rees (1992), Martin (1992), Tirole (1988), Fudenberg and Tirole (1989), and Shapiro (1989).

that has reneged on the collusive agreement would be for the other firms to force it to its security level, either forever or for some specified number of time periods. It is straightforward to show that the threat of minimax punishment forever is always capable of enforcing a collusive agreement which gives a firm a higher profit than its security level for *some* set of interest rates. Thus denote the firm's security level profit by π^s, the profit level under the agreement by $\pi^* > \pi^s$, and the maximum profit the firm can earn when it reneges on the agreement in a single period by $\pi^R > \pi^*$. Then in contemplating reneging the firm must weigh up the one-off gain $\pi^R - \pi^*$, against the present value of the infinite future stream of profit it loses as a result of punishment, $(\pi^* - \pi^s)/r$, where r is the per-period interest rate. The firm will not renege if

$$\pi^R - \pi^* < (\pi^* - \pi^s)/r$$

or

$$r < (\pi^* - \pi^s)/(\pi^R - \pi^*)$$

and since the right-hand side is always positive there must be some set of interest rates for which this will hold. This proposition goes under the name of the Folk Theorem in the theory of repeated games. In a given market, the set of profits which can be sustained by minimax punishments could be very large indeed.

(iii) *Simple Penal Codes:*   Abreu's theory of simple penal codes involves a 'stick and carrot' form of punishment. For each firm that is party to the agreement, a 'punishment path' is formulated, which specifies outputs (or prices) for each firm to be adopted if the firm in question deviates from the agreement. This punishment path involves two phases: a phase of expanded outputs (lower prices) which inflicts loss of profit on the deviant; then the remainder of the path consists of a return to the original collusive outputs. Thus the path could be thought of as a period of price warfare followed by reversion to collusion. The loss of profit in the punishment phase must be enough to wipe out the gain from reneging. If the deviant reneges again in the punishment phase, this is met with a reimposition of the punishment phase *from its beginning*, thus postponing the date of reversion to the more profitable collusive phase. This reversion to collusion is the carrot to induce the deviant to accept whatever is meted out to it in the punishment phase. If one of the non-deviant firms fails to carry out its role in punishing the cheat by producing its punishment output, it in turn is treated as having reneged and the firms adopt the punishment path for this firm. It can be shown that again a large set of collusive allocations can be supported by threats of punishment of this kind provided firms do not discount the future 'too heavily'.

These three types of punishment strategy will sustain different sets of collusive allocations, but the main point of interest in comparing them is that of the credibility of the strategies. Clearly, if a threat of punishment is to be effective in sustaining collusion the firms must believe that the punishment would actually be carried out if the need arose. This not only requires the firm reneging on the agreement to 'accept its punishment'. Since in general inflicting punishment may be costly to the non-reneging firms, it must be credible that they would in fact do so. In the case of the first two of the above punishment strategies, Nash reversion and minimax, the acceptance of punishment by the deviant is not an issue. In each case the punishment profit corresponds to its best response to the actions of the other firms. In the case of a simple penal code, acceptance of its punishment is the best action by the deviant given that the alternative is reimposition of the punishment path: punishment outputs are so chosen that it is better not to postpone the date of reversion to collusion than to make a short-term gain from deviating from the punishment path. We shall, therefore, focus on the question of the credibility of the threat that the non-deviating firms will actually carry out the punishment.

Study of the general question of credibility of threats in dynamic games has led to the formulation of the 'refinement' of the Nash equilibrium concept termed 'subgame perfect equilibrium'. We can illustrate with the case of minimax punishment and, for simplicity, assume that there are just two firms. If each firm believes the other's threat to minimax forever following a defection, its best response is not to defect. Now, consider what would be the situation at the beginning of the period immediately following a defection. In the game beginning at that time, which is a proper subgame of the original game, it is not in the best interest of the non-deviating firm actually to minimax the other. For suppose this firm believes that the deviant believes that it will be minimaxed, and so will produce the corresponding output. Then the punishing firm's best response to this is *not* to carry out the punishment but to produce its corresponding profit maximizing output. There is nothing to make it in the firm's best interests actually to follow through with the punishment in the *period following* a deviation, given the game that then presents itself. This will then be perceived in the previous period, and so the threat of minimax punishment will not be credible. To be credible, it must be in a firm's best interest to carry out the threat at the time it is called

upon to do so. This criterion of credibility is more formally embodied in Selten's equilibrium concept of *subgame perfection*. According to this, a subgame perfect equilibrium strategy for a game is one which gives a Nash equilibrium strategy for *every subgame* of the game. The above example of a minimax punishment strategy was not subgame perfect because, in the subgame beginning in the period just after a defection, the minimax choices did not constitute a Nash equilibrium.

Both Nash reversion and Abreu's simple penal codes are subgame perfect equilibrium strategies and so satisfy this criterion of credibility. The former does so because a strategy of playing Nash equilibrium in every constituent game is also a Nash equilibrium of an entire repeated game. In the case of the simple penal code, the essential reason it is in the interest of a firm in this case to carry out the threat of punishment is that it believes that if it does not it itself will be punished. This in turn is credible because if any other firm does not join in this punishment it will be punished, and so on. Thus belief in the credibility of punishment is sustained by the expectation that each firm will prefer to be the punisher than the punished. This can be put in its least intuitively reasonable light if we assume just two firms. If firm 1 reneges, firm 2 in the next period must punish it. If firm 2 reneges on punishment, then in the following period firm 1 must punish firm 2 for not having punished it in the previous period, and so on.

This reliance on 'self-lacerating' punishment strategies has led a number of authors to propose an alternative criterion of credibility, known as 'renegotiation proofness'. Here we shall discuss that formulation due to Farrell and Maskin (1989). They begin by asking the question: in the period immediately following a defection, what would stop the firms getting together and, instead of actually carrying out the punishment, agreeing to reinstitute the collusive agreement? The game from that period looks just as it did when the original agreement was concluded—because of the infinite horizon assumption every subgame is identical to the original game—and so if it was in the firms' interests to negotiate that agreement initially it will be in their interests now to renegotiate that agreement. But if firms perceive that a deviation will be followed by renegotiation rather than punishment this means that punishment would never be carried out, and so agreement to collude could not be reached in the first place. Abreu's strategies appear to assume away such renegotiation possibilities—an agreement is made once and for all and can never be reopened.

This argument leads to the *renegotiation proofness* criterion of credibility of threats. Punishment strategies are credible only if they are not only subgame perfect but also not capable of being pre-empted by renegotiation of the agreement if the occasion arises that they must be implemented. Informally put, in the case of an oligopolistic market this can be achieved by an agreement which specifies that the punishing firms choose outputs or prices which yield them higher profit than at the collusive allocation, so that they would actually gain in the punishment phase. This ensures that they would not be prepared to renegotiate back to the original agreement.

These theories suggest that collusion may or may not be successful in a particular market: that depends on the values taken by a set of market or firm-specific parameters. The assumption that the same constituent game is repeated period after period also implies that collusion, if achieved, is perfectly stable and never breaks down. Although the non-co-operative collusive equilibrium is sustained by threats, those threats never have to be implemented because they are successful. Thus we would never observe price wars. Given that price wars *are* observed, the question arises of how to explain them within this type of approach. A great insight of George J. Stigler provides one basis for an answer, which has been further developed by Green and Porter (1984), Rotemberg and Saloner (1986), and Rees (1985), among others.[6] Here we focus on the first of these.

Stigler's insight was that randomness in demand provides scope for cheating on a collusive agreement, and creates a problem of statistical inference in enforcing that agreement. In Green and Porter's model it is assumed that a firm's choice of output cannot be observed by another firm, and the sum of all outputs determines market price according to a demand function which is subject to unobservable random shocks. Then, when price is low firms do not know for sure whether it was because someone cheated (produced a larger than agreed output), or because demand was low. The strategy for maintaining collusion consists of choosing a critical level of price such that, if market price falls below that level, firms infer cheating and enter a punishment phase, a price war. It is always possible (for some set of discount rates) to find a critical price level that will fully enforce adherence to the agreement—no one cheats. There is now, however, a non-zero probability that in any time period a price war will break out, and in an infinitely repeated market it is virtually certain that one will be observed. The

interesting, though not necessarily plausible, feature of this result is that firms know that when the price falls below the critical level this is due to a random shock, because they know it pays no one to cheat, but nevertheless they must still go into the punishment phase to enforce the collusive agreement. This is clearly very much open to the critique based upon renegotiation-proofness, even more so than in the case without uncertainty. From the point of view of this paper, an important aspect of the model is that it shows the costs that can be imposed (in the form of probable price wars) when firms' outputs are unknown to each other and demand is stochastic. We return to this point when we consider the subject of information agreements later.

This concludes our brief survey of equilibrium concepts and the models of oligopoly in which they are embedded. We now consider what they imply for the analysis of tacit collusion.

III. Facilitating tacit collusion

Many theorists see the models surveyed in the previous section as giving analytical precision to the idea of tacit collusion. For example, Fudenberg and Tirole (1989) take a simple example of homogeneous output-setting duopoly with identical (non-decreasing) costs, and note that:

patient, identical Cournot duopolists can implicitly collude by each producing one-half the monopoly output, with any deviation triggering a switch to the Cournot outcome. This would be 'collusive' in yielding the monopoly price. The collusion is 'implicit' (or 'tacit') in that the firms would not need to enter into binding contracts to enforce their co-operation. (p. 280)

In this quotation, however, both the words 'collusion' and 'tacit' are being interpreted in a different sense to that adopted in this paper. 'Collusion' should, certainly for antitrust purposes, refer to a form of conduct, not the value of an outcome: collusive behaviour might well result in less than monopoly profits. It is tacit not simply because of the absence of a binding (legally enforceable) agreement, but because of the absence of any explicit agreement whatsoever. Explicit collusion would involve the firms in talking to each other, explicitly agreeing to produce half the monopoly output each, and, quite possibly, agreeing also that deviation by one would be punished by a price war. The fact that the agreement is sustained by threats of market sanctions rather than a binding contract makes it no less

---

[6] Abreu *et al.* (1986) in particular show how the Green and Porter model can be extended by replacing Nash reversion punishments with Abreu's simple penal code.

explicit,[7] at least in the eyes of antitrust law. Tacit collusion, on the other hand, would involve no explicit agreement but simply the unspoken acceptance by the two firms that it was in their best interests each to produce half the monopoly output on the understanding that failure to do so would provoke a price war.

As with non-co-operative playing of the one-shot game, the tacitly collusive equilibrium still requires information. In the simple model above each firm must know that the other's costs are identical to its own, and must know that they have the same beliefs about the market demand function as well as in the credibility of the punishment that would result from a deviation. It is easy to see that these information requirements expand considerably with the number of firms, product heterogeneity, spatial dispersion of markets, uncertainty about future demands and costs, rate of technological change, and the extent of threats from entry of new firms. If firms are to collude tacitly, they must somehow choose prices and outputs which are sustainable by a credible punishment strategy that also has to be tacitly agreed upon. We have seen that there may be many punishment strategies, and relative to any one of them there may be a very large set of sustainable price–output configurations. The firms must somehow define the set of feasible agreements, reach a point within it, preserve stability of the agreement, and make the threat of punishment as effective and credible as possible.

It is, therefore, natural that in real-world markets many so-called 'facilitating devices' would have been developed. These are arrangements or practices which can be construed as helping firms in at least one of the four steps to stable, successful tacit collusion: defining the possible agreements; focusing upon one; preserving it; and providing for credible effective punishment. It should also be noted that in many cases they would also facilitate explicit collusion, and so their use does not rule out the (possibly concealed) existence of this. We shall consider them in order of increasing specificity.

Information exchange: a flow of information among firms is clearly essential for all four aspects of successful collusion. Firms may enter into formal information agreements, under which they undertake to exchange information on costs, outputs, prices, and discounts. Exchange of cost information is clearly important in defining the set of possible agreements and arriving at one. Exchange of price and output data is important in detecting deviation: the shorter the lag between cheating and detection, the smaller the incentive to cheat. Such exchange of information is, of course, possible in the absence of a formal information agreement.

Trade associations: many industries have a central organization which may function fairly innocuously, handling public relations at the industry-wide level and organizing conventions, trade fairs, etc. However, they may also act as facilitating devices, collecting and disseminating information on costs, outputs, and prices, suggesting price lists (for example, the professional associations for lawyers, doctors, and architects publish 'recommended fee scales') and policing the (tacit) agreement. For example, the trade association in the UK nut and bolt industry actually employed individuals who posed as buyers and tried to obtain discounts on prices from sellers suspected of cheating. Trade associations may also carry out services such as demand forecasting and capacity planning for the market as a whole. This can be important both in achieving agreement on prices in the short run, and in preventing the development of excess capacity, which can pose a serious threat to collusion in the long run. At the very least, trade associations often provide the opportunities for the 'meetings of merriment and diversion' mentioned in Adam Smith's famous remark.

Price leadership: it is usual to distinguish between 'dominant firm' and 'barometric' price leadership. In the former, the largest firm first announces price changes and the other firms then follow within a short space of time; in the latter, some non-dominant firm, which presumably is considered the best at judging the market conditions, plays this role. In many markets, however, the identity of the firm initiating a price change may vary over time, possibly to avoid the impression that there *is* a price leader, or to spread more equitably the unpopularity of being the first firm to raise prices. Clearly, the practice of price leadership is a way of solving the problem of choosing one price agreement in the set of possible agreements. If the leader is good at finding mutually acceptable prices, or has the market power to punish deviants from its prices sufficiently, agreement can be entirely tacit. For many writers the 'conscious parallelism' in prices associated with price leadership is the very essence of tacit collusion.[8]

Collaborative research and cross-licensing of patents: for sound reasons—high fixed costs, economies of scale, and risk-sharing—firms may pool research and development (R & D) resources and set up a common R & D agency. This obviously limits competition in

---

[7] One may speak of a 'legal' or 'formal' cartel to cover this latter case.

[8] At the same time, price leadership may also be a way of implementing an agreement arrived at by explicit, though secret, negotiations. Colluding firms may well choose to announce price increases in a non-simultaneous way.

product design and innovation and facilitates uniform pricing of the resulting products. In the case of cross-licensing on the other hand, firms license use of the results of their own research out to their competitors. It is legal under the terms of these licenses to specify selling prices and to place other restrictions on sale, for example geographical area. Thus what may at first sight appear to be something that facilitates competition can actually be a form of legal collusion.

MFN and MC clauses in buyer–seller contracts: Salop (1986) pointed out that 'most favoured nation' (MFN) and 'meeting competition' (MC) clauses in contracts between buyers and sellers can act to facilitate collusion among sellers. A MFN clause guarantees to a buyer that if, when the contract is concluded or within some specified time period later, the seller makes a sale to another buyer at a lower price, then the buyer in question will also receive that lower price. A MC clause guarantees that if the buyer can find another seller offering a lower price, then the seller in question will match that price upon presentation of appropriate evidence. Salop argues convincingly that both these types of clauses help sustain collusion. Note first that since they form part of a contract between buyer and seller they are legally enforceable and that in itself is an important advantage because it reduces the cost of enforcing collusion. Moreover, the buyer has an incentive to detect and report deviations from the price agreement, either by the seller in question (under MFN) or by other sellers (under MC). A MFN clause sustains collusion because it makes it costly for a seller to reduce price in a discriminatory way, which is how secret cheating on a price agreement often takes place. If price cuts have to be paid to all buyers this reduces their profitability as well as increasing their detectability. A MC clause obviously sustains collusion by creating an incentive for a buyer to report to a seller keeping to the agreement the prices of a seller who may be cheating on the agreement, at the same time nullifying the effect of the latter.

Resale price maintenance: this is a system under which manufacturers contractually control the minimum level of prices charged by retailers. This obviously stops collusion at the manufacturing stage being undone by price competition at the point of sale to the ultimate buyer.

Basing point pricing: this is a pricing system often encountered in industries, such as steel and cement, where transport costs are high relative to production costs and buyers and sellers are spatially dispersed. In one variant, manufacturing plants of each seller are designated as bases, and a 'base price' is set at each of them. There is also a standard table of transport charges.

Then, a buyer at any given location will be quoted a price by each seller, equal to the base price at the nearest base plus the standard charge for transporting the product from the base to the buyer's location. The result is then that *delivered* prices to any buyer are always uniform across sellers, and there is no price competition. Clearly sellers must exchange information—the list of bases and base prices, the standard transport charges—but no *explicit* agreement to collude on prices need be made.

Common costing books: in some industries where there may be variation in the form of the finished product because of variation in the buyer's specifications (for example, industrial engines, building services) a book may be circulated by a trade association which shows how the overall cost of the specific product variant can be calculated. This encourages price uniformity among sellers and makes it less easy to label price-cutting a computational mistake.

This list covers the most generally encountered facilitating devices. Particular markets may provide examples of practices specific to them. For example, if airlines share a computerized reservation system this makes it easy to monitor and collude on prices. Insurance companies may collaborate in working out loss probabilities and this leads to uniformity in premium rates.[9] It should also be noted that there are many opportunities for company representatives to make their views known to each other on the state of the market and the direction prices should take, for example, in after-dinner speeches, newspaper interviews, articles in trade publications as well as while doing lunch.

IV. Policy implications

We now turn to the relation between tacit collusion and antitrust policy in the US, UK, and the EC. In all three jurisdictions explicit collusion is clearly dealt with.[10] In respect of tacit collusion there is far less clarity. In the US explicit collusion is, with a few exceptions,[11] *per se* illegal, and so it is simply necessary in a given case to establish whether or not collusion has existed. In the UK the Restrictive Trade Practices Court and the Monopolies and Mergers Commission (MMC) exist to investigate whether collusive agreements exist or

---

[9] See, for example, the discussion of the *Concordato Incendio* case in the paper by Sapir *et al.* (1993).
[10] For much fuller discussion of policy in these three jurisdictions, see the papers by Sapir *et al.* (1993), Williams (1993), and White (1993), and the references given there.
[11] For discussion of these see White (1993).

collusive conduct has taken place and, if so, whether they have operated against the public interest. For the EC, Article 85 of the Treaty of Rome prohibits agreements designed to prevent, restrict, or distort competition within the common market, though specific agreements may be exempted by the European Commission if they are found to have overall net benefits. In a 1989 White Paper and 1992 Green Paper (DTI, 1989, 1992) the UK government declared an intention to revise UK law in the direction of consistency with Articles 85 and 86 of the Treaty of Rome.[12]

In relation to tacit collusion the US legislation is, to use White's term, 'sloppy'.[13] Price leadership is not illegal, and 'conscious parallelism' does not amount to collusion. Thus, to quote Scherer:[14]

Oligopolists refraining from price competition merely because they recognize the likelihood of rival retaliation do not violate the law as long as their decisions are taken independently. And by avoiding any suggestion of encouraging or compelling rivals to co-operate, they may also facilitate uniform and non-aggressive pricing through such devices as price leadership and open price-reporting systems.

At the same time, there have been cases[15] in which 'the inference of illegal conspiracy' has been drawn from 'detailed similarity of behaviour'. From the economic point of view, the problem is that in most cases the US antitrust process is concerned with deciding whether *conduct* has been illegal, rather than with the appraisal of the economic consequences of whatever conduct may have taken place. In this respect the UK system, though it also has substantial defects, is superior, as I shall now try to establish.

In theoretical language, we could state the core of the problem as being that tacit collusion is a form of non-co-operative equilibrium, just as is Nash equilibrium in a one-shot oligopoly game (which, as we argued earlier, would never be regarded as collusive). The equilibrium results from rational pursuit of individual self-interest in a situation of perceived mutual interdependence. The behaviour of firms need not be conspiratorial in the legal sense. Therefore a conduct-based approach such as that underlying US antitrust law inevitably encounters difficulties.

To bring out the contrast with UK policy, we can consider a specific case, that of the MMC inquiry into the White Salt Market.[16] Two firms supplied virtually the entire UK salt market and, over the 13-year period

taken by the MMC, their prices had been identical and had changed identically within a few weeks of each other. The identity of the price leader had changed from time to time with no obvious pattern. One firm would inform the other of its proposed price increases by letter, usually a month before they came into effect, and the other would usually respond within that period. The firms argued that this was because they bought quantities of salt from each other (usually small), and it was usual to notify important buyers in advance of price changes. They also pointed out that in a competitive market for a homogeneous product it was to be expected that prices would be identical and follow each other closely. The firms denied collusion. It is also clear that they understood the logic of tacit collusion, put very clearly by one firm:[17]

if [we] raised prices to a lesser amount than [our competitor] and [it] failed to lower its own prices to the same level, there would be an immediate transfer of business [to us] . . . This would lead to a long-term retaliation by [our competitor].

I would contend that it is a major strength of the British legislation that the MMC *did not have to decide* whether the firms had 'really colluded'. By examining the costs, prices, and profits of the two firms they were able to conclude that the outcome of the conduct of the firms, however that conduct may be described, was against the public interest or, in economic terms, highly distortive of economic efficiency. It is hard to disagree with that decision.

Under a prohibition system such as that of the EEC, it *would* have to be established that the firms had colluded. In the absence of any concrete evidence of an agreement it is unlikely that this could have been done. In fact, the 1992 Green Paper explicitly recognizes (p. 27) that under a prohibition system in the case of price leadership or parallel pricing it is 'unlikely that breach of the prohibition would be established in the absence of anti-competitive behaviour'. I take this to mean that price leadership or parallel pricing are not in themselves regarded as anti-competitive: the firms would have to have followed some specifically anti-competitive course of conduct, for example exclusive dealing or discriminatory discounting, to fall foul of the law.

It would appear, then, that since many of the facilitating devices listed in the previous section are not subject to prohibition (information agreements are the only type of device that are, although Resale Price Maintenance is also usually excluded by law), a move to a purely prohibition system would make the British system as helpless in the face of tacit collusion as the

---

[12] Williams (1993) gives a very thorough discussion of these proposals.
[13] See also Scherer (1980), chs. 19 and 20.
[14] Scherer (1980), p. 525.
[15] For discussion of these see Scherer (1980).
[16] For a more extensive treatment of this fascinating case, see Rees (1993).

[17] MMC (1986), para 28.11.

American.[18] Given that there are advantages in other aspects to be derived from introducing a prohibition system (especially with the attendant threats of fines and private action for damages and injunctive relief), this argues for adopting the Green Paper's proposal for a dual system (option 3). Under this, prohibition replaces the Competition Act 1980 provisions on anti-competitive practices, but the provisions of the Fair Trading Act 1973 remain in force, thus allowing tacit collusion to be dealt with by the MMC.

V. Conclusions

In this concluding section I shall try to pull together the preceding discussions of the theory, practice, and policy relating to tacit collusion. The theoretical models reflect the strengths and weaknesses of modern game theory: they provide a rigorous characterization of what 'credible punishment' might mean, and a formal analysis of the way in which discount rates and demand, capacity, and cost parameters interact to determine the sustainability of tacit collusion. At the same time nothing is said about the way in which firms will converge on one of the large set of possible equilibrium agreements (given that collusion is sustainable). Firms are assumed to have unbounded capacity for working out strategies and payoffs, and for working through the abstract chains of reasoning which lead them to non-co-operative equilibrium strategies. Do firms 'really do' all that?

In practice it is very probable that they do not. Firms clearly do share the intuition underlying the idea of collusion sustained by punishment threats (recall the quotation given above from the White Salt report) and it seems very obvious to them. Moreover, numerical examples, experimental games, and such empirical case studies as have been carried out (see, for example, Rees, 1993) seem to suggest that typically punishments far outweigh the gains to short-run deviation for empirically reasonable discount rates and so it is really not hard to explain collusion. Not only may firms be unable, for reasons of bounded rationality, to work through the complex mathematics of these models, they may not have to because the answer is to them so obvious. It has been shown in the experimental literature on the prisoners' dilemma game that the strategy of 'tit for tat' is a very effective and frequently chosen way of sustaining co-operation even though it is far simpler than Abreu's strategies (and neither subgame

perfect nor renegotiation-proof). Moreover, as we have seen, firms have developed facilitating devices such as information agreements, trade associations, and price leadership to help them solve the problem of achieving and maintaining agreements. These can be seen as practical methods of resolving the kinds of problems identified by the theory.[19]

Turning now to policy, it seems clear that a prohibitions-based or *per se* illegality form of legislation cannot effectively deal with tacit collusion. This is because that kind of approach is aimed at conduct which is explicitly conspiratorial. Tacit collusion is a form of non-co-operative equilibrium: it results from the rational, independent pursuit of self-interest, which courts tend to find not nearly as reprehensible, to say the least, as conspiratorial conduct. Further complications are created by the fact that secret explicit collusion may be observationally equivalent to tacit collusion given surveillance methods constrained by considerations of 'liberty and justice'. There will always be the problem of trying to infer whether apparently tacit collusion really was well-concealed explicit collusion.

These problems are avoided by an effects-based approach such as that underlying the UK legislation. Whether firms 'really' colluded is not a central issue. What matters is the appraisal of the outcomes of their behaviour from the point of view of economic efficiency. To eliminate the possibility of this would seem to be a retrograde step. Indeed, there is every argument for strengthening it by introducing penalties and allowing MMC findings on the outcomes of firms' behaviour to form the basis for private actions for damages. This is all the more necessary because, although some facilitating devices such as information agreements may be made the subject of prohibitions, the majority of them appear to escape these.

References

Abreu, D., Pearce, D., and Stacchetti, E. (1986), 'Optimal Cartel Equilibria with Imperfect Monitoring', *Journal of Economic Theory*, **39**, 251–69.

DTI (1989), 'Opening Markets: New Policy on Restrictive Trade Practices', Cm 727, London, HMSO.

---

[18] This seems, in fact, to be fully recognized in paras 3.14 and 3.15 of the Green Paper.

[19] In this author's opinion, the major contribution of the models surveyed in section II has been to liberate the literature of oligopoly theory from almost exclusive concern with one-shot models, in which collusion cannot be rationalized, and to extend rigorous analysis to a wide and important set of economic phenomena. It has re-focused theoretical attention on the right questions even if all of them have not yet been answered.

—— (1992), 'Abuse of Market Power', Cm 2100, London, HMSO.

Farrell, J., and Maskin, E. (1989), 'Renegotiation in Repeated Games', *Games and Economic Behaviour*, **1**, 327–60.

Friedman, J. (1986), *Game Theory with Applications to Economics*, Oxford, Oxford University Press.

Fudenberg, D., and Tirole, J. (1989), 'Noncooperative Game Theory for Industrial Organisation: An Introduction and Overview', ch. 5 in R. Schmalensee and R. Willig (eds.), *Handbook of Industrial Organisation*, Vol. 1, Amsterdam, North-Holland.

Gravelle, H. S. E., and Rees, R. (1992), *Microeconomics*, London, Longman.

Green, E., and Porter, R. (1984), 'Noncooperative Collusion under Imperfect Price Information', *Econometrica*, **52**, 87–100.

Kreps, D., Milgrom, P., Roberts, J., and Wilson, R. (1982), 'Rational Cooperation in the Finitely Repeated Prisoners' Dilemma', *Journal of Economic Theory*, **27**, 245–52.

Martin, S. (1992), *Advanced Industrial Economics*, Oxford, Blackwell.

MMC (1986), 'White Salt: A Report on the Supply of White Salt in the United Kingdom by Producers of Such Salt', London, HMSO.

Rees, R. (1985), 'Cheating in a Duopoly Supergame', *Journal of Industrial Economics*.

—— (1993), 'Collusive Equilibrium in the Great Salt Duopoly', *The Economic Journal*, **103**, 883–48.

Rotemberg, J., and Saloner, G. (1986), 'A Supergame-theoretic Model of Business Cycles and Price Wars during Booms', *American Economic Review*, **76**, 390–407.

Salop, S. C. (1986), 'Practices that (Credibly) Facilitate Oligopoly Coordination', ch. 9 in J. E. Stiglitz and G. F. Matthewson (eds.), *New Developments in the Analysis of Market Structure*, London, MacMillan Press.

Sapir, A., Buigues, P., and Jacquemin, A. (1993), 'European Competition Policy in Manufacturing and Services: A Two-speed Approach?', *Oxford Review of Economic Policy*, **9**(2), 113–32.

Scherer, F. M. (1980), *Industrial Market Structure and Economic Performance* (2nd edn.), Chicago, Rand McNally.

Shapiro, C. (1989), 'Theories of Oligopoly Behavior', ch. 6 of R. Schmalensee and R. Willig (eds.), *Handbook of Industrial Organization*, Vol. 1, Amsterdam, North-Holland.

Tirole, J. (1988) *The Theory of Industrial Organization*, Cambridge MA, MIT Press.

White, L. J. (1993), 'Competition Policy in the United States: An Overview', *Oxford Review of Economic Policy*, **9**(2), 133–53.

Williams, M. E. (1993), 'The Effectiveness of Competition Policy in the United Kingdom', *Oxford Review of Economic Policy*, **9**(2), 94–112.

3

Vertical integration and vertical restraints

MICHAEL WATERSON

University of Warwick

I. Introduction

'Cut out middleman's profits—buy direct from the manufacturer' is a phrase often seen in newspaper advertisements, implying that the retailing and whole-saling functions are otiose, or at least inefficient. On the other hand, certain of our major retailers (e.g. Tesco) are commonly thought of as models of efficiency, and their 'own brands' command widespread respect—the typical consumer does not think twice about which factory or by whom they are made. Manufacturers of complex products such as cars seldom make a feature of the source of their inputs—whose brake system, whose gearbox (perhaps a competitor's), or whatever ('Intel inside' computers is a striking exception here). There is also a certain amount of secrecy, or lack of communication, about vertical arrangements more generally. Is Specsavers a chain of opticians or not? Is MacDonalds a vertically integrated firm? Why do tyre retailers not say they are (in large part) owned by tyre manufacturers, and why then do they sell competitors' products? Why will aluminium producers agree to pay for electricity even if they do not use it? How 'free' is a free public house?

Clearly, vertical arrangements take a variety of forms, and they are an important feature of industrial society, indeed have been so since the Industrial Revolution. Two quite directly opposing views on their policy significance prevail. One views unusual vertical arrangements with suspicion, presuming that they are made so as to prevent others entering the industry, to raise margins and thereby increase profits at the

expense of consumers. The alternative benign view is that all contracts are made, broadly speaking, to ease the flow of product. Thus, according to Bork (1978, p. 245) 'in the absence of a most unlikely proved predatory power and purpose, anti-trust should never object to the verticality of any merger' and, much more straightforward, 'every vertical restraint should be completely lawful' (p. 288).

As we shall see, the hostile view is linked to some extent with strategic theories about the existence of vertical links, whereas the benign view relates to a contractarian approach. Unusually, explanations from more than one school of thought constitute the mainstream view here. However, the match between theoretical school and policy implication is by no means exact. In later sections, the major theoretical contributions aimed at understanding vertical linkages will be outlined, and subsequently policy implications will be drawn from them. Before that, the legal position in the UK will be outlined in brief, and issues raised by recent investigations will be considered.

Definitions: For simplicity, throughout the theoretical and policy section the world will be taken to have only two vertical stages below final consumers—called manufacturers and retailers—rather than many. Vertical integration will be taken to mean the complete interlinkage of a manufacturer and a retailer under one owner or organizer. Conceptually at least, this is reasonably straightforward.

Vertical restraints come under a number of guises. There is retail price maintenance by the manufacturer, both maximum price and minimum price. Or a manufacturer could specify minimum quantity (quantity forcing), or details of service and demonstration facilities, or quality criteria (e.g. no hamburger to be sold more than two minutes after being cooked). The

First published in *Oxford Review of Economic Policy*, vol. 9, no. 2 (1993). This version has been updated and revised to incorporate recent developments, in particular legislative changes.

manufacturer could impose full-line forcing, obliging the retailer to take a whole range of its products if it takes one, or tie-in sales, no X sold without Y. It could impose exclusive purchasing (no products of a certain description to be bought from anywhere but itself), and may offer selective and exclusive distribution agreements (suppliers have to meet certain criteria in order to be selected to distribute a product, and may be offered an exclusive territory or even absolute territorial protection). It may package a number of these restraints as a business format franchise, and charge a fee or a royalty, or some combination. Retailers with power will, perhaps less commonly, use it to invoke restraints such as slotting allowances for the right of a manufacturer's product to be on the shelves of a supermarket.

II. The policy framework

1. The law

This short section does not purport to be a complete statement of the legal position regarding vertical activity. It is at best an outline of the main points in a rather complex field. For a more authoritative view, a book such as Whish (1993) is helpful.

Vertical mergers are treated little differently from horizontal mergers by the law. They are still covered by the Fair Trading Act 1973 (FTA), under which mergers involving the takeover of assets worth (currently) £70m or more may be referred to the Monopolies and Mergers Commission (MMC). However, it is widely known that only a small proportion of such qualifying mergers are referred, and further that vertical mergers are a small proportion of the total. Moreover, the current rules or guidelines focus on the impact on competition as the ground for referral by the Secretary of State. Hence few vertical mergers are investigated. Vertical mergers having a Community dimension can be investigated under the EC Merger Regulation.

The legal position on vertical restraints is currently (1999) subject to significant changes, with a new Competition Act 1998 coming into force in March 2000 in the UK and many of the details of the Community treatment of vertical restraints being currently under discussion. Therefore it is difficult to give an appreciation of how policy will be operating. Instead, the focus here is on broad principles, an outline of the current structure, and indications of how the new structure will look.

European policy on vertical restraints is governed by what were Articles 85 and 86 of EC law, now renumbered 81 and 82. Article 82 concerns 'abuse of a dominant position', Article 81 tackles agreements between traders. A vertical restraint may take on one of two forms: one is unilateral imposition of substantive conditions for supply, for example a manufacturer saying 'you may not take my product X unless you also take my product Y'. If the player is dominant (has significant monopoly power) enforcing such a position may fall foul of Article 83. The second is mutual agreement that substantive conditions of supply will hold, for example 'in exchange for you granting me an exclusive territory, I promise to sell only your products in that territory'. Most mutual agreements of this type would be caught by Article 81(1), but may benefit from a block Exemption or an individual exemption under 81(3).

Over the period of operation, there have been created a significant number of Block Exemptions for particular vertical agreements, all time-limited. The current proposal is to replace all but one of these with a single widely drawn Block Exemption covering most vertical restraints apart from those viewed as 'hardcore'. Below a threshold level of market share, the presumption is that vertical restraints outside the hardcore have no negative impact. Above a (possibly higher) threshold, a vertical restraint may be investigated and either cleared or prohibited. The hardcore will contain resale price maintenance (RPM). Though significant details are not yet clear, this structure may simplify the situation by moving away from block exemptions concerned with the form which an agreement takes, rather than its effect.

The law can have real bite. Recently, the Commission imposed a fine of over 100m ECU against Volkswagen for engaging in vertical restraints designed to force its dealers in Italy to refuse to sell cars to foreign buyers, thereby infringing Article 85(1).

UK law in the area is moving significantly towards the EU structure, with some notable differences. The Competition Act 1998 has a Chapter I prohibition on agreements which parallels Article 81. However, an Order will be introduced with the effect that this prohibition will not apply to vertical agreements in the main; again RPM is an exception. This new structure has the potential to reduce significantly the wasteful registering and examining of restrictive practices of little or no significant economic effect, which now happens under the Restrictive Trade Practices Act 1976 (which is replaced by the new Act).

Chapter II of the Competition Act prohibits abuse of a dominant position. Thus vertical restraints which have the effect of market foreclosure, raising rivals' costs or competition dampening when imposed by a dominant firm, may be investigated for abuse. Examples would include exclusive purchasing obligations or full-line forcing imposed by a dominant manufacturer, making entry by new manufacturers difficult. In addition, the 'complex monopoly' provisions of the Fair Trading Act (FTA) will be retained. Hence, where a group of companies all have similar practices (say, again, exclusive purchasing obligations) the Director General of Fair Trading and subsequently the Competition Commission may investigate.

The biggest change to the culture of UK policy comes from the fact that finding of an abuse (or, where relevant, an agreement) will lead to financial penalties being imposed, as in the case of cross-border activities covered by Community law. Previously, the Monopolies and Mergers Commission (MMC; the predecessor to the Competition Commission) investigated vertical practices and could recommend changes. But it could not fine. One thing that remains to be seen is whether the Director General will decide to 'claw back' the special (favourable) treatment accorded non-price vertical agreements practised by groups of firms, thereby making them subject to the Competition Act rather than the FTA. The significance lies in the fact that penalties may then be applied, which may in turn have a deterrent effect. Another interesting question is whether affected third parties (e.g. a retailer adversely affected by refusal to supply) will find it easier to take action under the new regime.

Lastly, it should not be forgotten that the common law, through the restraint of trade doctrine, has a potential role to play. Some vertical agreements, such as exclusive distribution and exclusive purchasing, have been examined under this framework.

2. Some important cases

In a remarkable series of investigations, the MMC examined the practices in beer, petroleum, and motor vehicle supply. These are the three main areas in which the relationship between manufacturer and final consumer is affected by vertical restraints, covering perhaps 30 per cent of UK retail trade by value. Thus together they amount to a concerted attempt to investigate whether or not any form of vertical behaviour is to be allowed. Because of the high profile of the industries, the reports have aroused considerable interest.

The Supply of Beer (MMC, 1989), the first of these reports, is in some ways also the most noteworthy. It set the tone for the others by being massive—500 pages

in A4 format. Included are appendices containing a certain amount of relatively sophisticated economic analysis—diagrams and algebra. The Commission found that the various vertical practices, including brewers' imposition of exclusive-purchase obligations for a range of products including beer (the 'tied house'), and connected with this, the use of loans at preferential rates of interest, 'prevent, restrict and distort competition from the point of view of both suppliers and consumers' (p. 250, para 11.21). As a result of these and other factors, a number of detriments to the public interest resulted, including (a) real increases in beer prices of 15 per cent in the six years ending December 1986; (b) raised margins on lager above cost compared with beer; (c) a restricted choice of beers and other drinks; (d) limited independence of tenants, and (e) a restricted role for independent wholesalers.

Unusually the MMC (or rather a majority of its serving members) proposed a structural remedy. Only on a few occasions have they gone this far; where they suggest changes they will often be limited to 'undertakings' or promises. (This was the case for example with the report (MMC, 1986) into the vertical merger of BT with Mitel, an equipment maker.) The major recommendation was that brewers be prevented from owning or leasing, or having an interest in, or an exclusive relationship with any more than 2,000 on-licensed outlets in the UK. This implied structural changes for all the big brewers. In addition there were behavioural remedies proposed in order to reduce the extent of the product tie. Following the report, although the then Secretary of State at first indicated he would implement its recommendations in full, they were subsequently modified to make them less swingeing. The national brewers' various structural responses, which have included vertical disintegration as well as sales of tied estate, have been replaced in part by exclusive dealing relationships (on which, see below) and the growth of 'pub chains'.

Another feature of interest in this report concerns the relationship between UK and EC law. The Brewers' Society contended that arrangements with their outlets fell within the block exemption of exclusive purchasing agreements 1984/83, and therefore that the UK would be in breach of its obligations under the Treaty of Rome if it prohibited such arrangements. The MMC pointed out that the block exemption only applied if there were no effective competition, no refusal to supply, or if it were not true that less favourable conditions were imposed on those with an exclusive purchasing obligation. They argued that these conditions were not satisfied and, therefore, that there was no legal difficulty in remedying adverse effects in the UK.

The Supply of Petrol (MMC, 1990) came to quite different conclusions regarding the superficially similar vertical arrangements in that industry. The MMC found no grounds to suggest that the pattern of ownership, 'solus' ties or pricing arrangements in the industry, operated against the public interest. They therefore recommended no structural or behavioural changes, though they did feel that continued monitoring of the industry by the OFT was necessary.

New Motor Cars (MMC, 1992a) is the longest of all, and almost certainly the longest MMC report ever, at nearly 850 pages including appendices. Again, there are complex vertical linkages in the industry and, again, there is a block exemption which covers distribution arrangements within the industry, provided they remain within certain parameters (which the European Community's DG IV believe they do not in some respects). The MMC found that restrictions in the selective and exclusive distribution agreements prevent efficient dealers from growing strong, promoting outside their territory, obtaining competing franchises and gaining bargaining power, thereby bargaining for better terms and obtaining more customers by passing some of these benefits on to final consumers. Therefore these features operate against the public interest. The MMC proposed a behavioural remedy, that in their agreements with manufacturers, franchised dealers be allowed to advertise outside their designated territories and to acquire dealerships outside that territory, and not be limited as to the number of cars they may sell. They also proposed that dealers may hold competing dealerships in an area and provide other ser-vices outside their territories. No major changes resulted from this report, and, at the time of writing, the industry was again under investigation by the Competition Commission with a report due in December 1999.

Accompanying this investigation was a related, less extensive inquiry into motor car parts (MMC, 1992b), in which industry there are also substantial vertical interlinkages. However, the MMC, although finding areas of potential concern, did not propose any remedies.

There are cases in quite different spheres which suggest a perceived considerable importance in vertical arrangements. Prime amongst these is the electricity industry in England and Wales. In 1990 the industry, which was both vertically and horizontally integrated, became separated into different units (for fuller details, see e.g. Vickers and Yarrow, 1991). Generation was initially in the hands of two main concerns, National Power and PowerGen, together with input from Nuclear Electric, imports from Scotland and France,

but, in due course, competition from independent producers has developed. The generators have to bid for the right to supply electricity to the National Grid, the central player in the system. It operates on behalf of suppliers such as the regional electricity companies (RECs) in buying and transmitting power to them. They then distribute (and supply) electricity to final consumers, except the largest ones. The RECs can generate electricity on their own account but are strictly limited in the extent to which they can do so.

One major concern in creating this structure seems to have been the recognition that competition in generation was feasible and capable in principle of producing cost reductions, but that the structure of the interrelationship between generation and distribution had to be carefully designed. Electricity is essentially non-storable, so total generated supply has to equal total demand at every point in time. Hence there is a regulated market system organized by the Grid interposed between the two, determining prices and supply for each half-hour period. (Previously there had been a shadow market, based upon operating-cost information.) The system as a whole is overseen by the Director General of Gas and Electricity Markets, who has a duty to promote competition in generation and supply. The extent of vertical integration in gas supply has also been reduced, with the aim of aiding the development of competition.

Finally, in devising structures for essentially new but potentially problematic industries (problematic as a result of natural monopoly issues) such as cable TV and mobile telephone communication, the government has experimented with a variety of vertical systems and restraints. Clearly, vertical arrangements are not matters which can be left to chance in all circumstances.

III. Theoretical analyses of vertical linkages

1. Technological economies

The first set of factors leading to close vertical linkages is fairly straightforward-technological interdepend-ence. The classic example concerns various stages of the steelmaking process, where unnecessary cooling and reheating is avoided by siting these activities in close proximity to each other, usually under common ownership. However, there are certainly other industries where it is normal to group activities in this way.

A rather different example is newspapers, where typesetting, printing, and publishing are all commonly carried out on the same premises by one company. This is quite different from the case with books where the activities are very often carried out in different locations. But with newspapers, speed is essential for economic production, hence the proximity to minimize delay. The example also illustrates the influence of technology—now that data is easily transferred electronically, typesetting and printing of newspapers is often carried out in different places, with printing taking place at several locations.

Nor need the activities necessarily be performed by the same firm. Electricity generation is quite often carried out at coal-mine mouths, but (as Joskow, 1985, has documented) under a variety of contractual relationships. Vertical linkages can be used rather than vertical integration. The same is true of relationships between aluminium smelters and electricity suppliers. Contractual arrangements between the parties can lead to disputes, but it is not clear that these are the concern of competition policy authorities.

2. The transactions cost approach

From one point of view, the theory of vertical integration and vertical restraints is but a special case of the theory of the firm. The employment relation or contract, which characterizes all firms larger than sole proprietorships and certain partnerships, is a form of vertical integration. Thus a second approach is to look at vertical linkages as a way of minimizing transaction costs, or reducing them below market transaction levels.

The approach originates from the insights of Coase (1937) but has largely been developed by Williamson (e.g. 1971, 1975, and 1985). For reasons which will become apparent, I will not provide more than a brief overview of this approach.

A major element in this analysis is the concept of asset specificity. Assets are specific to a transaction to the extent to which their costs are sunk. If I, a plastics factory owner, decide to make a rear-lamp cluster for a particular car, either I or the car assembler will have to invest in the specific mould to produce it. The subsequent bargaining position between me and the assembler will depend a great deal on the nature of the ownership structure regarding this asset, and may be subject to dispute, especially if I acquire some knowledge as a result of using it.

This first element interacts with the second, uncertainty. If we knew what the future would bring, our contract regarding the specific asset (and other matters) could be well and completely thought out. But

what if demand is lower than expected—must I keep to my quoted price? If demand is higher than expected, can I object if the manufacturer asks another producer also to make the same product? If there was no asset specificity, then there would be no commitment on either side, and hence no problem.

Frequency of exchange is also important. Suppose the same sort of bargain will have to be concluded quite often, then it may make sense to devise a framework, or 'governance structure' or protocol, to facilitate it.

Thus market exchange has its weaknesses, as well as its strengths (competition, anonymity, flexibility). It is noteworthy that General Motors and Toyota developed quite different responses to the problem exemplified, the former specializing in vertical integration, the latter in vertical linkages well short of that, but both some distance from anonymous market exchange.

3. A contractual rights approach

A more recent outgrowth of the transactions cost approach stems from the work of Grossman, Hart, and Moore (GHM) (Grossman and Hart, 1986; Hart and Moore, e.g. 1990). This accepts that integration provides benefits identified by Coase, Williamson, and others, but is critical of their analysis of the costs. In caricatures of the Coase–Williamson view, one might expect the firm to grow without limit, in the absence of the costs of overburdening bureaucracy. But what, more precisely, are these costs?

To answer this question, GHM define ownership as control over the (residual rights in the) firm's assets, the firm itself being viewed as a collection of assets. Naturally, the firm has employees but, in the absence of slavery, the workers have inalienable rights. A manager can order an employee to carry out a specific task. If the employee refuses then, in an extreme case, he or she will be fired. The manager is no better off, seemingly, than if the employee were a sub-contractor, whose contract could be rescinded for poor performance. Thus control over employees, and the incentives of employees, come indirectly through management's ownership of assets, which in turn defines the status quo, within this framework.

An example from Hart (1989) will illustrate the costs as well as benefits of ownership of two successive stages of production. The example involves a car assembler and a car-body manufacturer. Suppose the two are separate. Then if the assembler wants to make changes to the contract, the body-maker is in a strong position because it can threaten to keep both employees and assets working to the original contracts. However, if the two are integrated, those running the body-making division are in a weaker position if asked to make changes, since they have no independent control rights over the assets they manage. This is a benefit of integration. On the other hand, those running the body-making division of an integrated firm would have a dulled incentive to come up with cost-saving or quality-enhancing innovations for producing bodies than would an independent body-maker. Management in the latter would appropriate a surplus created by the innovation to a far greater extent than in the integrated firm, assuming that the innovation is asset-specific. This dulled incentive to enhance productivity is a cost of integration that must be borne in mind when amalgamation is contemplated. Integration does not yield the outcome which would arise under complete contracts. The example sketched out above concerns those relatively high up in the hierarchy, but it can be extended to cover other employees of the body-maker.

These ideas can be developed into a theory of the boundaries of the firm. The first result is that complementary assets should be owned by a single firm. If a product may only be realized by the use of two sets of assets, and each set has no alternative use, then when both sets are under common control, fewer parties can hold up any non-contracted changes to the production process. On the other hand, when assets are economically independent, integration would bring in outside control which would dilute incentives in the division being controlled. Hence the second result, that independent assets should be separately owned. Less polar cases will depend upon a balance of forces. Thus there are, in principle, limits to the scope of a firm based upon the technology and transactions involved in its production and output processes.

This theory builds upon transactions cost theory but, its proponents would argue, provides clearer predictions. In both frameworks, firms are in a second-best world; first-best contractual arrangements are not available *ex ante* (and the Coase theorem, therefore, does not apply). Firms have an incentive to opt for particular levels or types of integration. Whether in practice they act in this way has not been established convincingly.

The main gap in the theoretical analysis in both cases is any consideration of whether or when there is likely to be a divergence between the private and socially desirable directions of vertical integration for contractual reasons. The fact that firms find it in their mutual interests to combine, or to develop lasting links, does not mean that such links are socially desirable in the wider sense (as Williamson, for example, would agree). Thus whilst transactions cost and contractual rights

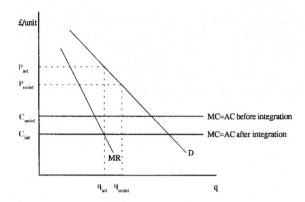

Figure 3.1. Cost and price changes on vertical integration

approaches are capable of considerable insights, and have strong links with delegation and strategic issues which will be discussed later, they do not yet lend themselves very readily to propositions in welfare economics. This is the reason for comparative neglect in the material that follows.

4. Monopolistic motives for integration

The third main set of arguments will be the most extensively covered, under a number of sub-headings. First, there are a number of standard arguments regarding integration which, although widely available in texts, should be briefly reviewed.

Following Vernon and Graham (1971), if variable proportions may be used in production, but one input is monopolized and priced above marginal cost whereas the other is not, then merger between the upstream monopolized input supplier and the final producer(s) can remove the inefficiency caused by the factor distortion in production. However, it simultaneously increases the monopolist's market, since possibilities of substitution away from the monopolized input are eliminated. Hence final price may rise (particularly if the downstream stage was competitive) and social welfare could fall—see Schmalensee (1973). The possibility is illustrated in Figure 3.1.

If (with Greenhut and Ohta, 1976) the upstream and downstream stages were connected by fixed proportions, with upstream being a monopoly and downstream an oligopoly, then integration would remove successive mark-ups at different stages in favour of a single mark-up. Monopoly power would not increase, but price would fall and a welfare gain would ensue.

Clearly these two effects can be combined (Waterson, 1982). Thus, if the elasticity of substitution is fairly low (high), and numbers at the downstream stage prior to integration are low (high), social welfare is likely to rise (fall) on integration. This modelling framework can also be extended to include oligopoly at each level and firm by firm integration, at the cost of some complexity.

Two comments on this analysis are in order. First, it assumes there are no contractual means to eliminate the problems of successive mark-ups/input pricing distortions in the absence of complete integration despite potential benefits to the parties involved. Second, it is sometimes said that the pure vertical effects of integration are always positive in a welfare sense—they only become negative because of associated horizontal effects, for example as a result of a reduction in the number of downstream firms. But this is of little comfort, since the two are commonly inextricably intertwined.

From the point of view of policy, there is a substantial difference between horizontal mergers and vertical mergers, based upon this analysis. In the absence of scale economy benefits, horizontal mergers are likely to be socially undesirable. The presumption with a vertical merger is that unless a substantial horizontal impact is involved, it will be socially beneficial on balance. Of course some parties will be adversely affected, but the overall effect takes this into account.

One particular element of concern here is what is known as the foreclosure issue. If one of the few upstream firms integrates with a downstream firm, then its previous customers may find their supply of input dries up, or is subject to onerous terms. This was a factor in the merger between BMC and Pressed Steel Fisher some years ago (Monopolies Commission, 1966). In this particular case, there seems to have been no question of halting supply, but undertakings were sought that, in times of high demand, outside customers (Rootes, etc.) would receive fair attention to their orders.

More recently, the question has been raised analytically by Salinger (1988). He argues that in the absence of diminishing returns to production of the intermediate or final good, or some element of product differentiation at intermediate or final levels, or the need for a firm's intermediate product division to be held to being competitive, then vertically integrated firms will not participate in the intermediate good market. Thus, under certain circumstances intermediate good prices in the unintegrated sector can rise as a result of integration, and vertical merger can thereby cause a rise in final good prices. However, it will be noted that the list of qualifications under which participation in the intermediate market will not take place is extensive. As a matter of fact, such participa-

tion often takes place. And some recent work (Abiru et al., 1998) questions this analysis in any case. Therefore the importance of the foreclosure issue as regards overall welfare is rather unclear.

A further element may enter here to complicate the picture. Suppose upstream scale economies are extensive. A downstream firm may wish to integrate backwards, despite the scale economies, in order to value (shadow price) additional units of input at marginal cost. But this will have adverse effects on remaining upstream firms, who will be faced with a thinner market over which to cover their costs, and may harm overall welfare. Again this assumes there is no contractual means, for example a two-part tariff, by which to enable the intending integrator to obtain additional units at or near marginal cost.

Finally, suppose that the upstream firm's product has two uses with very different elasticities of demand. In order to sustain price discrimination between the two sets of purchasers, it may decide to integrate into the area of relatively elastic demand and charge a high price to the other. Of course we must remember that the welfare implications of price discrimination are not clear-cut.

5. Vertical restraints and the 'externality problem'

At first sight, it might be thought that a manufacturer would be keen on retailing being as competitive as possible. This argument goes as follows: There is a demand by consumers for the product of manufacturer *X*. But the manufacturer faces a derived demand from dealers/retailers in the product. If the retail sector is competitive, the derived demand curve will be the same shape as the final demand curve, and below it by a distance representing the marginal cost of retailing. If the retail sector were imperfectly competitive, the derived demand curve would be steeper in slope, and if it were inefficient the derived demand curve would be a greater distance below. Neither possibility would be in the manufacturer's interest. All other things being equal, the smaller the retailing mark-up, the greater the profit share for the manufacturer. So what is wrong with this argument?

In essence, the complication is that retailers provide 'much more than mere warehousing' (Marvel and McCafferty, 1984, p. 348). They provide both specific and general services to customers and potential customers—demonstration facilities, information, stocks, and so on. But these do not come free. Retailers incur fixed costs, many of which contain a sunk element, for example fixtures and fittings. Manufacturers gain through having their product demonstrated, or even through having it present in a store (or else they would be unwilling to pay 'slotting allowances' to supermarkets), so that demand is not exogenous to retailing. The fact that there are fixed costs means perfect competition is an unattainable ideal framework for retailing. Moreover, for many goods, competition is localized due to the spatial nature of retailing. When modelling vertical restraints, it becomes important to incorporate these features (see e.g. Dixit, 1983; Mathewson and Winter, 1984).

Once a model incorporating a manufacturer with some monopoly power and (say) a monopolistically competitive retail sector has been set up, it becomes apparent that manufacturer and retailer interests diverge; the retailers may want more or less margin than the manufacturer would like to impose. For example, Gallini and Winter (1983) show that a typical retailer would want a margin [(price – input cost)/price] of $1/\varepsilon_r$, whereas the manufacturer would want the retail margin to be $\varepsilon_n/\varepsilon_R$, ε_r being the elasticity of demand when one retailer changes price, ε_R the elasticity when all retailers do likewise and ε_n, the elasticity of demand with respect to changes in the number of retailers. Moreover, the numbers entering retailing may be suboptimal from the manufacturer's point of view. This divergence of views can be seen (following Mathewson and Winter, 1984) as arising out of a set of externalities.

(i)   Retailers do not gain all the benefits of action taken to improve sales; some goes to manufacturers. For every extra unit a retailer sells by modifying pricing or advertising strategies, the manufacturer gains an amount given by the difference between the wholesale price and marginal production costs. Thus, there is a positive externality bestowed on the manufacturer by such retailers' actions, which in turn means that retailers will tend to set prices too high and advertising too low from the manufacturer's point of view (i.e. high prices are a negative vertical externality).

(ii)   On the other hand, retailers when raising price confer benefits on neighbouring retailers, by increasing demand for their products. This is a positive horizontal externality created by one retailer on others; in attempting to gain a greater margin for itself, it drives some custom away. It will tend to mean retailers will keep prices lower than they would be in the absence of rivals.

Clearly, these two opposing effects imply that it is unlikely there will be a dominant direction to the outcome over all modelling variants.

(iii)   Each retailer confers a positive externality on other retailers and on the manufacturer by engaging in advertising of the product, unless the advertising is very specifically targeted. There is a similar effect regarding other services—demonstration facilities and so on. Because the horizontal and vertical externalities here operate in the same direction, the clear prediction is that, in the absence of any agreements, too little promotional and demonstration activity will take place. Some retailers will attempt to 'free ride' on others, perhaps offering low prices and a warehouse-type ambiance, once customers have had a product demonstrated elsewhere.

(iv)   Retailers left to themselves would be likely to set location sufficiently distant from rivals to permit supernormal returns to their location but not sufficient to make entry worthwhile. This assumes an element of sunkness about location (which Mathewson and Winter did not), so that potential entrants believe they are unlikely to be able to push established firms out of current locations. In this case, the retailers' locational choices confer a negative externality on the manufacturer leading to a suboptimal density of suppliers from the manufacturer's point of view.

Vertical restraints imposed by the manufacturer can in principle control all these problems or deal with the externalities involved. Resale price maintenance, quantity forcing, specification of demonstration service and promotional facilities, franchise fees, allocation of territories, and so on, can all be used to this end, assuming the manufacturer has sufficient information regarding the underlying cost and demand parameters, and assuming all are legal.

To call something an externality is potentially emotive. In welfare economics we are taught that to internalize externalities by appropriate contracts is socially desirable. But that should not lead us to assume that the same holds for the externalities identified here. Internalization will be in the manufacturer's interest, but the manufacturer and society do not have the same set of preferences. The manufacturer's interest in a high price, for example, may be in opposition to the social desirability of a low price.

The positive analysis of vertical restraints within this framework can be taken a little further, with implications for normative issues. Still assuming a deterministic setting, and given sufficient mathematical regularity in the underlying functions, the number of instruments needed might be expected to equal the number of variables to be controlled. (Uncertainty will be introduced later.) Thus in the absence of the fourth externality discussed above, it is price and advertising levels (and thereby quantity, as well) set by retailers which the manufacturer wishes to control. Two instruments are sufficient. Depending on the framework, it can be shown that alternative pairs of instruments can be used.

Moving to policy issues, if two alternative pairs with the same properties exist, then if one set is deemed socially (un)desirable, so should the other set be. Mathewson and Winter note an asymmetry between the treatment of RPM and various territorial and franchise restrictions in the law of the US (and the same is true of the UK). Pricing restraints are treated much more harshly than non-price restraints. If it is true that they are simply used as substitutes, the law is making an economically illegitimate distinction.

In fact, I have argued (Waterson, 1988) that things are not as straightforward as this. Cases are documented where what are seen in Mathewson and Winter as potential substitutes (territory distribution and RPM) were used together. There are, I believe, two reasons, first that closed territory distribution (sales outside an area being prohibited) is normally infeasible and second that the fourth externality may be of importance. Hence to ban one but not the other may not be as ridiculous as a simple interpretation of their model would suggest. Moreover, there are circumstances under which simple vertical restraints do not perform as Mathewson and Winter suggest (see Bolton and Bonanno, 1988; O'Brien and Shaffer, 1992). There is also the question of the relationship between maximum and minimum RPM (see Perry and Besanko, 1991).

But there is one important general point which holds regardless of these specific criticisms. For economists, a focus on the effects of a set of practices is what matters. Whether they take one particular legal form or another, whether they involve particular instruments or another set, is not of first importance. Thus the idea that instruments are substitutes at all is rather damning for a restrictive practices policy which, like that currently (1999) in operation in the UK, is based upon form rather than effect.

Finally, one general feature of the framework of this subsection is worthy of note, in order to facilitate comparisons between models. The manufacturer's ideal would be complete vertical control—vertical integration. The restraints are imposed in an attempt to mimic this. But then there is no rationale within the model for restraints *per se*. Perhaps restraints are imposed because the history of the industry precludes vertical integration. Perhaps the manufacturer lacks sufficient capital to build the network. It cannot be a lack of expertise, given the framework. Other models soon to

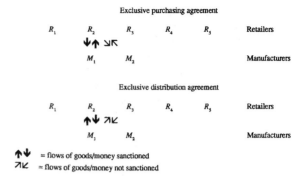

Figure 3.2. Exclusive purchasing and exclusive distribution

be discussed have more fundamental reasons for vertical restraints, as opposed to vertical integration.

6. Interbrand v. intrabrand competition

In almost every purchase one makes, from a butter substitute to a bathroom suite, there are two forms of competition. Do I want Flora or St Ivel Gold, is one form; do I buy from Tesco or Sainsbury is the other. (With some products, like the bathroom suite, there is a further question—within the Armitage Shanks range, do I want the Sandringham-Envoy with Silverspa taps, or some higher specification? I will not consider this issue any further in the present context.) The models of the previous section, by assuming a monopoly manufacturer, neglected interbrand competition and the role of exclusive purchasing agreements.

An exclusive purchasing agreement obliges a retailer to purchase its supply of a particular good or set of goods solely from one manufacturer. In Figure 3.2, R_2 must buy from M_1 not M_2, but M_1 is unconstrained. This gives the manufacturer some immunity from interbrand competition and, as a first-order effect, increases the manufacturer's margin, which is privately but not socially desirable.

In practice (as, for example, in car retailing, and commonly in franchising) it is often coupled with an exclusive distribution agreement. Again in Figure 3.2, M_1 says it will sell to R_2 but not to R_3, a neighbour of R_2. R_2 will often be given a 'territory', although this will not normally mean that R_2 makes all sales of M_1's product inside the territory. However, other retailers of the product will normally be under some obligation not to seek customers actively in R_2's industry. Thus it gives the retailer some immunity from intrabrand competition, as discussed above, and as a first-order effect increases the retailer's margin.

There will be additional effects as a result of these marketing agreements. For example, the exclusive purchasing agreement by itself raises the manufacturer's margin, but may lower the retail margin. If retailers are spread around the country, in some places it will transpire that there is room for only one seller of both manufacturer M_1's and manufacturer M_2's product. If exclusive purchasing is then instituted, there may be enough custom for one retailer of each product. This increases competition at the retail level, all other things being equal, compared with the no-restraint position, and so reduces retail margins (see Waterson, 1990). Therefore the effects of exclusive purchasing agreements on social welfare are not clear; sometimes restrictions will be desirable, sometimes not, dependent upon particular parameters of the model. However, it appears that the higher the cross-elasticity of demand between rival goods or brands, the more likely are exclusive purchasing agreements to be socially desirable, and vice versa (see Besanko and Perry, 1994; Dobson and Waterson, 1994). Also, there is a greater private than social incentive for manufacturers to impose exclusive purchasing. There are similar considerations related to exclusive distribution, as the preamble to the legislation on the block exemption suggests (see also Rey and Stiglitz, 1995).

7. Strategic effects and vertical separation

So far, much of the analysis has implied that firms are likely to want vertical integration and that, though in many cases it would be socially desirable, in some it may not be. A rather different type of argument suggests there may be strategic advantages in manufacturers remaining separate from retailers, whilst having distinct linkages.

Suppose two manufacturers produce goods which are partial substitutes, and (for whatever reason) competition in the market is through price. Suppose they are each integrated with their retailing operation. If the goods are close substitutes, competition between them will drive price down near to marginal cost. Now let the retailing operations be separate. In order to avoid successive mark-up problems, the manufacturers may each decide to charge input at marginal cost, but gain benefits by imposing a positive franchise fee. However, if the products are very close, the price mark-up retailers can charge above marginal cost will be low, so the level at which the franchise fee can be set will not prove very rewarding to the manufacturers.

Therefore, let us consider an alternative scenario, in which one manufacturer decides to raise its input

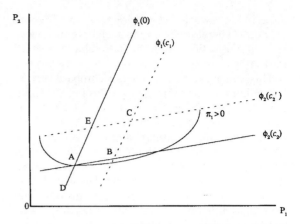

Figure 3.3. Best-reply functions with vertical integration

price (possibly at the same time reducing the franchise fee). This will raise its retailer's costs, so causing an increase in price and reduction in output. Provided the manufacturer can claw back the benefits, this will increase its profitability. In fact, Bonanno and Vickers (1988, p. 260) show the following proposition: 'if franchise fees can be used to extract the retailers' profits, it is in the individual interest of each manufacturer to choose vertical separation and charge his retailer a wholesale price in excess of unit production cost' whether the other is integrated or separated.

The point may be illustrated in a best-reply function diagram. Because the products' prices are strategic complements (in the Bulow et al., 1985 sense) their best-reply functions will be upward sloping—see Figure 3.3. The line $\phi_1(0)$ is the best-reply function of manufac-turer 1 whilst $\phi_2(c_2)$ is the best-reply function of the retailer of 2's product when charged an input price $c_2 > 0$ (costs are assumed here to equal zero). When charged an input price of 0, $\phi_1(0)$ is also the best-reply function of the retailer of good 1. The franchise fee will determine the point D, below which the retailer would make losses. When the manufacturer charges a unit price c_1 somewhat above zero, the retailer sets a higher price for any given price of retailer 2, leading to the best-reply function $\phi_1(c_1)$ and equilibrium at B rather than A. The same argument can be made for manufacturer 2. Hence the eventual position will be at a point like C.

Intuitively, what is happening here is that the force which argues for an increase in output (fall in prices) from the double marginalization position in monopoly is being outweighed by a force which argues for a decrease in output (increase in price) from the duopoly position. This increases manufacturer profits, as long as the surplus can be captured. But notice that position A is socially preferred to B or C, involving as it does lower prices and greater output for both products. Therefore, from the social point of view, vertical integration would be preferable to vertical separation.

This model can be extended to compare vertical separation with the complete absence of vertical linkages, through an adaptation of the model of Ordover *et al.* (1990); see also Rey and Stiglitz (1988, 1995). Here there are two manufacturers and two retailers. The manufacturers produce identical products (say, for simplicity). Therefore price competition between them for the right to sell to the retailers would drive price to marginal cost. The retailers' products are somewhat differentiated, so that price competition would still leave a mark-up above costs.

Suppose now that manufacturer 1 signs a selective and exclusive distribution agreement with retailer 1, promising not to supply retailer 2. Manufacturer 2 can then raise its price to retailer 2 above cost, because there is no alternative source of supply. Hence, by signing the agreement, retailer 1 has raised rival's costs in the manner suggested by Salop and Scheffman (1987). In terms of the figure, $\phi_2(c_2)$ shifts up to $\phi_2(c_2')$, so that if the original outcome was point A it now moves to E (or if the original outcome were B, it moves to C). Thus manufacturer 1 and retailer 1 have some surplus to share. Once manufacturer 1 and retailer 1 have signed their agreement, it may pay manufacturer 2 and retailer 2 to sign a similar agreement.

Again it appears that vertical separation (here vertical restraints, of the exclusive distribution kind) are socially less desirable than the alternative, in this case complete absence of vertical links. Obviously the result is dependent on there being not too much differentiation at the upstream stage, or the double mar-ginalization effect of no linkage would dominate. Also important is the limited availability of alternative sources for retailer 2 once the first agreement is signed. This harks back to the foreclosure issue. But the general point is that vertical restraints should not be thought of, in social welfare terms, as intermediate between no linkage and complete integration.

8. Risk, uncertainty, and agency

Discussion of the benefits to the manufacturer of vertical separation and of imposing restraints on downstream firms reminds us that one way the whole issue can be thought of is as a principal–agent problem of delegation. The manufacturer delegates to the agent the task of setting final price (usually), output, presale ser-vices, and so on, but is rather careful about the con-

struction of the award schedule. Still in this vein, one element not so far introduced is risk and uncertainty and its impact on the modelling of frameworks and outcomes. It is once these are introduced that traditional agency factors come into play.

Rey and Tirole (1986) have a model in which a manufacturer supplies a number of retailers, but cannot observe a retailer's profit or quantity sold. There is the possibility of demand uncertainty and cost uncertainty in the retail markets. Also retailers may be risk-averse. They show that in general RPM and exclusive territories are not equivalent (they would be in their model without uncertainty). The manufacturer is likely to prefer one or the other depending upon the nature of uncertainty and the risk preferences of retailers. Gal Or (1991*b*) in a development of this model, finds some relative strengths of RPM. Social and private preferences may also diverge.

Moreover, agency considerations may conflict with strategic considerations. The following example developed from Slade (1998) will illustrate the point. Suppose some retailers are more risk-averse than others. Traditional agency theory then suggests that the more risk-averse be given contracts which force them to bear less of the risk involved in the venture. The outcome will be influenced by their effort, but they need to be heavily compensated for bearing risks. This may be tackled for example by paying them a relatively higher fixed salary with less dependent upon the outcome. In other words, they are more vertically integrated. Thereby, they work hard. In the context of a petrol station, the risk-averse are offered a salary plus a small performance bonus for running the station, whereas the less risk-averse are offered petrol at wholesale price and are free to decide how to behave.

Suppose also that there are two groups of petrol stations. Those which offer petrol alone have relatively higher cross elasticities of demand between them than those which have additional facilities (carwash, repairs, retailing, and so on). In other words, in the former price and profits are more likely to be affected by price wars. Thus it is in the former that the manufacturer has the greater strategic motive for vertical separation, setting wholesale prices and charging franchise fees.

However, if the typical person running the latter group of stations (those with additional facilities) is also less risk-averse than the typical person running the former, then there is a conflict. Strategic motives would imply vertical separation for the petrol-only stations; agency motives would imply the opposite (see also Gal Or, 1991*a*). Clearly, whether this is an important issue or conflict can only be answered empirically. In her paper, Slade finds that strategic motives are important in determining contract choice. This is comforting for applications to policy questions of previously discussed results of the vertical separation literature.

IV. Policy implications

A nihilistic view about the policy implications of recent theoretical work in the area of vertical restraints would be that, since almost anything can happen, nothing can be said about policy. In fact, although there is an element of truth to this position, the previous the-oretical analysis is arguably of substantial assistance in commenting upon the current framework of the law. A number of points may be made (see also Dobson and Waterson (1996) for further discussion).

(i)   The element of truth certainly resides in the point that there is no direct link between competition and social welfare in the area of vertical relationships. One arrangement (e.g. vertical integration) may involve less competition in some sense but may be socially more desirable than another. This is rather unlike horizontal competition. But this point is already clearly recognized in the legal framework through such elements as the block exemptions. Thus the general lessons are that a concentrated vertical market structure is not necessarily undesirable, and that freely negotiated contractual relationships are not necessarily benign. The theory gives little support to Bork's (1978) position. Moreover, combinations of factors can conspire to turn vertical effects into horizontal effects, for example the combination of vertical linkages and the necessity for licences at the retail stage (as in the supply of beer) or the general use of exclusive territories to facilitate collusion.

(ii)   Moving on to more specific issues, theory gives comparatively little support to the legal position that resale price maintenance should be treated differently from other vertical restraints. There is some justification, in that RPM may be the most direct method of maintaining high prices. But combinations of other controls which are viewed benignly may very easily lead to similar effects, given market power somewhere in the system. Indeed, some people would argue they are worse, if anything. What is, unfortunately, not clear as a general proposition is whether the controls on RPM should be relaxed, or whether exclusive dealing and so on should be viewed with greater suspicion.

(iii)   There is another factor which arises in this connection. If one set of instruments can substitute for another, policy is in any case badly served by a legal framework which focuses on form rather than ef-

fect, as the UK restrictive practice legislation does. (Kay, 1990, extends this argument to say that effect should be valued over intent as well.) Two sets of words may amount to the same thing, but one set may be caught by the Act and another set not. Those formulating agreements are obviously better advised to avoid the particular frameworks captured by the Act. But then the Act loses its utility. This lesson appears to have been accepted in the new structure of the Competition Act 1999, as well as in Community law.

(iv)   The case for block exemption of franchising does not appear clear in economic theory. It is perhaps implicitly assumed that each franchise chain has little market power. Otherwise the fact that RPM is disallowed but that franchisors can 'recommend' selling prices to franchisees would be quite remarkable. Alternatively, it is perhaps assumed that without franchises there would be a vertically integrated chain, which would be less socially desirable. But neither is this necessarily the case. This leads to a more general point.

(v)   The law appears so far to have almost entirely failed to rise to the challenge of the vertical separation literature. Vertical integration is not strongly controlled, but vertical (non-price) restraints are commonly exempted from control. Clearly this is likely to encourage development of the latter, including franchising. But we have seen that vertical separation with restraints may well be more socially undesirable than vertical integration. This is not a curiosum: the types of arrangements in the beer and petrol industries in which tied retailers face a higher unit price and possibly subsidised fixed costs (i.e. a negative franchise fee) seem to accord quite closely with the predictions of some theoretical models. Admittedly in the beer industry the MMC took the position that, although there were block exemptions, they could be negated under certain circumstances if the agreements were detrimental. But the point was not very forcefully made, and vertical restraints did in some cases replace vertical integration.

References

Abiru, M., Nahata, B., Raychaudhuri, S., and Waterson, M. (1998), 'On the Profitability of Vertical Integration', *Journal of Economic Behavior and Organization*, **37**, 463–80.
Besanko, D., and Perry, M. K. (1994), 'Exclusive Dealing in a Spatial Model of Retail Competition', *International Journal of Industrial Organization*, **12**, 299–329.
Bolton, P., and Bonanno, G. (1988), 'Vertical Restraints in a Model of Vertical Differentiation', *Quarterly Journal of Economics*, **103**, 555–70.
Bonanno, G., and Vickers, J. (1988), 'Vertical Separation', *Journal of Industrial Economics*, **36**, 257–65.

Bork, R. H. (1978), *The Antitrust Paradox*, New York, Basic Books.

Bulow, J., Geanakoplos, J., and Klemperer, P. (1985), 'Multi-market Oligopoly: Strategic Substitutes and Complements', *Journal of Political Economy*, **93**, 488–511.

Coase, R. M. (1937), 'The Nature of the Firm', *Economica*, NS4, 386–405.

Dixit, A. K. (1983), 'Vertical Integration in a Monopolistically Competitive Industry', *International Journal of Industrial Organization*, **1**, 63–78.

Dobson, P. W., and Waterson, M. (1994), 'The Effects of Exclusive Purchasing on Interbrand and Intrabrand Rivalry', Warwick Economics Working Paper no. 94–15, University of Warwick.

—— and —— (1996), *Vertical Restraints in Competition Policy*, Office of Fair Trading, Research Paper No. 12, London.

Gallini, N. T., and Winter, R. A. (1983), 'On Vertical Control in Monopolistic Competition', *International Journal of Industrial Organisation*, **1**, 275–86.

Gal Or, E. (1991*a*), 'Optimal Franchising in Oligopolistic Markets with Uncertain Demand', *International Journal of Industrial Organisation*, **9**, 343–64.

—— (1991*b*), 'Vertical Restraints with Incomplete Information', *Journal of Industrial Economics*, **39**, 503–16.

Greenhut, M., and Ohta, H. (1976), 'Related Market Conditions and Interindustrial Margins', *American Economic Review*, **66**, 267–77.

Grossman, S. J., and Hart, O. D. (1986), 'The Costs and Benefits of Ownership: A Theory of Vertical and Lateral Integration', *Journal of Political Economy*, **94**, 691–719.

Hart, O. D. (1989), 'An Economist's Perspective on the Theory of the Firm', *Columbia Law Review*, **89**, 1757–74.

—— Moore, J. (1990), 'Property Rights and the Nature of the Firm', *Journal of Political Economy*, **98**, 1119–58.

Joskow, P. (1985), 'Vertical Integration and Long-Term Contracts: The Case of Coal-burning Electric Utilities', *Journal of Law, Economics and Organisation*, **1**, 33–80.

Kay, J. (1990), 'Vertical Restraints in European Competition Policy', *European Economic Review*, **34**, 551–61.

Marvel, H. R., and McCafferty, S. (1984), 'Resale Price Maintenance and Quality Certification', *Rand Journal of Economics*, **15**, 346–59.

Mathewson, G. F., and Winter, R. A. (1984), 'An Economic Theory of Vertical Restraints', *Rand Journal of Economics*, **15**, 27–38.

Monopolies Commission (1966), *The British Motor Corporation Ltd. and the Pressed Steel Company Ltd: A Report on the Merger*, HCP 46, London, HMSO.

Monopolies and Mergers Commission (1986), *British Telecommunications plc/Mitel Corporation*, Cmnd 9715, London, HMSO.

—— (1989), *The Supply of Beer*, Cm 651, London, HMSO.

—— (1990), *The Supply of Petrol*, Cm 972, London, HMSO.

Monopolies and Mergers Commission (1992*a*), *New Motor Cars*, Cm 1808, London, HMSO.

—— (1992*b*), *Motor Car Parts*, Cm 1818, London, HMSO.

O'Brien, D. P., and Shaffer, G. (1992), 'Vertical Control with Bilateral Contracts', *Rand Journal of Economics*, **23**, 299–308.

Ordover, J. A., Saloner, G., and Salop, S. C. (1990), 'Equilibrium Vertical Foreclosure', *American Economic Review*, **86**, 137–41.

Perry, M. K., and Besanko, D. (1991), 'Resale Price Maintenance and Manufacturer Competition for Exclusive Dealerships', *Journal of Industrial Economics*, **39**, 517–44.

Rey, P., and Stiglitz, J. (1988), 'Vertical Restraints and Producers' Competition', *European Economic Review*, **32**, 561–8.

——, and —— (1995), 'The Role of Exclusive Territories in Producers' Competition', *Rand Journal of Economics*, **26**, 431–51.

—— Tirole, J. (1986), 'The Logic of Vertical Restraints', *American Economic Review*, **76**, 921–39.

Salinger, M. A. (1988), 'Vertical Merger and Market Foreclosure', *Quarterly Journal of Economics*, **103**, 345–56.

Salop, S. C., and Scheffman, D. (1987), 'Cost-raising Strategies', *Journal of Industrial Economics*, **36**, 19–34.

Schmalensee, R. (1973), 'A Note on the Theory of Vertical Integration', *Journal of Political Economy*, **81**, 442–9.

Slade, M. (1998), 'Strategic Motives for Vertical Separation: Evidence from Retail Gasoline', *Journal of Law, Economics and Organization*, **14**, 84–113.

Utton, M. (1994), 'Anti-competitive Practices and the UK Competition Act 1980', *Antitrust Bulletin*, **39**, 485–539.

Vernon, J., and Graham, D. (1971), 'Profitability of Monopolisation by Vertical Integration', *Journal of Political Economy*, **79**, 924–5.

Vickers, J., and Yarrow, G. (1991), 'The British Electricity Experiment', *Economic Policy*, **12**, 187–232.

Waterson, M. (1982), 'Vertical Integration, Variable Proportions and Oligopoly', *Economic Journal*, **92**, 129–44.

—— (1988), 'On Vertical Restraints and the Law: A Note', *Rand Journal of Economics*, **19**, 293–7.

—— (1990), 'Some Economics of Exclusive Purchasing Obligations', University of Reading Discussion Papers in Industrial Economics No. 22.

Whish, R. (1993), *Competition Law*, (3rd edn.), London, Butterworths.

Williamson, O. E. (1971), 'The Vertical Integration of Production: Market Failure Considerations', *American Economic Review*, **61**, 112–23.

—— (1975), *Markets and Hierarchies: Analysis and Antitrust Implications*, New York, Free Press.

—— (1985), *The Economic Institutions of Capitalism*, New York, Free Press.

PART II

RESEARCH AND DEVELOPMENT

The economics of technology policy

PAUL STONEMAN

University of Warwick

JOHN VICKERS[1]

All Souls College, Oxford

The Government has ... a general responsibility to support science and technology because this is fundamental to the social and economic well-being of the country.

House of Lords Select Committee on Science and Technology (1986)

Firms themselves are best able to assess their own markets and to balance the commercial risks and rewards of financing R & D and innovation. The Government should not take on responsibilities which are principally those of industry.

Department of Trade and Industry (1988)

The long-run performance of any economy depends upon its success in innovating new products and processes. Few would doubt that the spectacular post-war economic record of Japan, as compared to that of the US or the UK, has had much to do with its superior achievements in developing and applying new technologies. However, it is much harder to agree on what factors, let alone which government policies, promote good technological performance. In this paper we do not claim to have reached definitive conclusions on these major questions. Rather, the aim is to clarify and examine—both theoretically and empirically—a number of economic issues in technology policy, in the hope of contributing to recent debates. In the final section of the paper, however, we attempt to illustrate how the lessons learnt from the discussion can illuminate the arguments, as illustrated in the two contradictory quotes above, over an appropriate technology policy for the UK.

It is useful to begin with some basic definitions. First we define technological change, following Schumpeter, as changes in products, processes of production, raw materials, and management methods. A classic trilogy that has informed and conditioned many of the debates on technology and technology policy, again attributed to Schumpeter, is that which characterizes three stages in the process of technological change: *invention*—the generation of new ideas; *innovation*—the transformation of those ideas into, for example, new marketable products and processes; and *diffusion*—the spread of use and ownership of new technology. Implicit in this trilogy is the knowledge base which underlies technological change and which is itself continually changing and evolving. The trilogy should not be taken to be unidirectional or lacking in feedback, but it is a useful organizing framework. It should also be realized that a country's technology does not always have to be produced at home: new technology can be and is often imported from overseas. Moreover, technology does not necessarily come from a formal Research and Development effort: phenomena such as learning-by-doing can be important sources of technology. It is also worth noting that it is only at the diffusion stage that the economy obtains benefit from and is affected by new technology. Nevertheless much of the literature and technology policy debate tends to focus upon R & D spending although this is in fact more related to invention and innovation than diffusion.

A distinction often made is that between Science and Technology. At a general level it is common to associate science with the knowledge base and technology with invention, innovation, and diffusion. However, Dasgupta and David (1986) argue persuasively that the

First published in *Oxford Review of Economic Policy*, vol. 4, no. 4 (1988).
[1] We are grateful to Chris Allsopp, Tim Jenkinson, and Colin Mayer for their comments on an earlier version of this paper.

difference between the two lies in the respective goals of the scientific and technological communities. For the former, knowledge is a public good, and scientists compete to be first to publish new ideas. For technologists, however, the value of being first to innovate lies not in public esteem but in private return. The distinction is not hard and fast, and it would be a serious mistake to think that science policy and technology policy can be considered in isolation from one another. Scientists and technologists have different incentive systems—for reasons that will become more apparent below—but they are intimately connected in the process of technological change. For example, science is the main source of technological labour.

What then exactly does 'technology policy' mean? In the present context technology policy is defined as a set of policies involving government intervention in the economy with the *intent* of affecting the process of technological change. However, even with this definition the economics of technology policy is a complex subject. Some of the reasons for this are that, first, the incentives that firms have to invest in new technology are influenced by such diverse factors as the nature of product market competition (including international competition), the degree of 'spillover' from one firm's technological change to the technological capability of another, the availability of skilled personnel, the extent of public subsidy (direct or via procurement policy), and the availability of finance for technological change. Some of those factors, for example market structure, are in turn influenced by the outcome of technological competition, and hence the reciprocal interactions become yet more complicated.

Second, technological change and thus technology policy proceed in an environment of uncertainty and often very incomplete information. This not only complicates analysis but makes the design of policy subject to such problems as informational poverty, adverse selection, and moral hazard. Moreover, attitudes to risk and uncertainty greatly influence the funding of technological activity and thus bring issues of finance to the fore of technology policy discussions.

Third, as will already be apparent, several government policy instruments have interacting effects on incentives to advance technology. As well as direct instruments of technology policy, enforcement of property rights over information, subsidies, public R & D, etc., it is essential to consider the impact of other microeconomic policies, notably competition policy (see Baumol and Ordover (1988)), trade policy (see Hausman and Mackie-Mason (1988)), and education and training policies.

Fourth, there are severe difficulties of measurement.

Neither input measures (e.g. R & D expenditure) nor output measures (e.g. patents filed) are perfect indicators of innovative activity. Nevertheless, measurements have to be made, and data problems overcome, for empirical analysis to proceed (see Pavitt and Patel (1988)).

Fifth, there are problems of evaluation. It is hard enough for firms themselves to make sensible assessments of the private return to technological activity, and it is harder still to assess social returns. Quite apart from difficulties in gauging the (probabilities of) future returns, there is the question of what discount rate to apply to them, and in particular how to take risk into account.

Sixth, assessment of the national return from technology policy is complicated by international rivalry. For example there may be dangers of countries attempting to 'free-ride' on each others' R & D efforts, or, on the other hand, governments might compete in a zero sum game to support their 'national champions' in the hope of gaining them strategic advantages in international markets.

Easy answers, therefore, are not to be had. However, that is no excuse for agnosticism and inaction, because one fact is clear: unassisted market forces cannot be relied upon to secure an efficient allocation of resources to technological activity—market failure is pervasive (see the paper by Dasgupta in this volume). The 'invisible hand' may be tolerably good at achieving static efficiency in many circumstances, though with notable exceptions and probably with undesirable distributional consequences, but dynamic efficiency is quite another matter. A *laissez-faire* technology policy would therefore be a dangerous thing, but, on the other hand, the problems facing policy design in practice are quite daunting.

The purpose of this paper is to give an overview of the economics of technology policy (see Stoneman, 1987, for a fuller account). Our focus will be on microeconomic analysis, notwithstanding the importance of technology policy for macroeconomic performance, and we shall discuss UK technology policy in particular. We begin, in section 1, with a discussion of various types of technological activity in the UK and an outline of the current pattern of R & D expenditure by government and industry, including international comparisons. Some broad 'stylized facts' will be derived from the data. Section 2 examines why unassisted market forces are unlikely to produce socially desirable rates and directions of innovative activity, and establishes the general case for government intervention. The pros and cons of various policy instruments are considered in section 3. Section 4 discusses recent debates and government policy statements on technology policy in the UK. Section 5 contains conclusions.

I. Technological activity in the UK

We have discussed above the problems associated with measuring technological activity. Of the several imperfect measures available we have most data on R & D expenditure, and this section mainly concentrates on R & D data (Pavitt and Patel (1988) consider others) although we shall make one or two comments on diffusion as well. R & D is an aggregate measure and can be disaggregated in several ways. One division is between basic, strategic, and applied research, and development, which were defined by the House of Lords Select Committee (1986, p. 13) as

'basic (pure or fundamental) research—research undertaken primarily to acquire new knowledge and with no specific applications in mind;

strategic research—research undertaken with eventual practical applications in mind even though these cannot be clearly specified;

applied research—research directed primarily towards specific practical aims or objectives;

development—systematic work drawing on existing knowledge to produce new products, processes, etc.'

R & D activity can also be characterized according to who pays for it and who carries it out. The bulk of publicly funded R & D is conducted either intramurally (within government institutions), or by universities and research councils, or by public and private industry. Most industry R & D is performed intramurally and may be funded by industry itself, by government, or from overseas. The nature of the explicit or implicit 'research contracts' associated with these relationships create particular difficulties where R & D is concerned, partly because inputs and outputs are hard to measure. That is one reason why reward is often accorded to priority of discovery, both in the scientific and technological communities—priority is easier to observe than effort. Dasgupta's paper in this volume provides a fuller discussion of these issues.

In Tables 4.1 to 4.6 below we present some data on R & D spending in the major OECD economies. Table 4.1 illustrates that UK R & D as a percentage of GDP is broadly in line with, although generally somewhat lower than, the spending of its main international competitors. More striking, however, is the decline of the UK from a position of international preeminence in 1965 to a much lower status in 1985. Moreover, given

Table 4.1. R & D as percentage of GDP 1963–1985

Country	R & D/GDP %	
	1963	1985
UK	2.2	2.3
Japan	1.4	2.6
Sweden	1.2	2.8
W. Germany	1.5	2.7
Italy	n.a.	1.1
France	n.a.	2.3
USA	3.1	2.8

Source: OECD (1984) and Cabinet Office (1988), Table 4.10.

Table 4.2. Government finance of R & D

Country	Government finance as percentage of gross expenditure on R & D 1985
Italy	51.7
France	52.9
W. Germany	36.7
Japan	19.1
Sweden	34.0
USA	50.3
UK	43.1

Source: Cabinet Office (1988), Table 4.10.

Table 4.3. Government funding of R & D 1986

Country	Defence R & D (£m)	Civil R & D (£m)	Total R&D (£m)	Defence as % of Total
Italy	229	2,465	2,695	8.5
France	1,775	3,667	5,421	32.7
W. Germany	596	4,324	4,920	12.1
Sweden	199	566	764	26.0
USA	21,159	9,320	30,479	69.4
UK	2,259	2,330	4,589	49.2

Source: Cabinet Office (1988), Table 4.8.

Table 4.4. UK government spending on R & D 1987/8 by type (percentage of totals)

	Civil	Defence	Total
Basic	36.7	—	18.2
Strategic	27.6	1.7	14.5
Applied	24.8	14.9	19.8
Development	10.9	83.5	47.5
Total	100.0	100.0	100.0

Source: Cabinet Office (1988), Table 1.23.

Table 4.5. Industrial R & D in the UK (£m)

Year	R & D at current prices	R & D at 1975 prices
1986	5,673	1,883
1985	5,146	1,752
1983	4,163	1,564
1981	3,792	1,661
1978	2,324	1,566
1975	1,340	1,340
1972	830	1,418
1969	680	1,513
1968	639	1,506
1967	604	1,514
1966	580	1,504
1964	489	1,400

Source: Survey of Industrial R & D, British Business, various dates.

Table 4.6. UK industrial R & D by sector (percentage of total industrial R & D)

Industry	1975	1981	1986
Chemicals	16.9	16.3	18.3
Mech. Engineering	7.3	6.9	4.7
Electronic Engineering	21.2	32.6	34.1
Other Electrical	5.4	3.2	2.9
Motor Vehicles	6.6	4.8	6.9
Aerospace	21.7	20.1	16.9
Other Manufactures	15.8	8.8	7.7
Non Manufactures	4.8	7.4	8.4
Total	100.0	100.0	100.0

Source: as Table 4.5.

the relatively poor GDP growth performance in the UK in international terms over these last twenty years, total R & D expenditure in the UK is now below that of many other nations and this may be a more relevant statistic.

The proportion of total R & D financed from public sources is lower in the UK than in the USA, France, and Italy but is higher than in Germany and much higher than in Japan (Table 4.2). As can be seen from the data in Table 4.3, the proportion of government funded R & D that is defence related is high in the UK. This pattern is repeated in the USA and France, but in Germany and Japan only a limited amount of government funded R & D is defence related. The overall result of this pattern and level of government funding is that in the UK a high proportion of total R & D is defence related. As a proportion of total R & D approximately 22 per cent is devoted to defence in the UK, this is far greater than in Germany (4.4 per cent), France (16.5 per cent), Italy (5.1 per cent), and Japan (no accurate

figures) but less than in the USA (34 per cent). The obvious corollary of this when combined with the data on R & D spent as a proportion of GDP is that the UK devotes proportionately less of its GDP to civil R & D than do its major international competitors.

In Table 4.4 we show the composition of government spending—civil and defence—as between basic, strategic and applied research, and development. It should be noted that defence R & D is never classed as basic in the UK. These and other data illustrate that the UK Government allocates a relatively high proportion of its R & D expenditure to development, but this spending is predominantly defence related. Civil spending is directed away from development and towards basic, applied, and strategic research. Current government policy is to increase the emphasis in civil spending away from the 'near market' end.

R & D performed in UK industry recovered in the 1980s (with a hiccup in 1983) after a prolonged decline between the mid-sixties and the mid- to late seventies (see Table 4.5). The sectoral breakdown of industrial R & D in the UK (see Table 4.6) illustrates, however, that it is concentrated, with the exception of chemicals, in defence-related sectors. Further data in Cabinet Office (1988), not presented here, also illustrates certain patterns in the finance of industrial R & D. One trend is the increasing proportion of funding for UK industrial R & D that comes from overseas. This has risen secularly from 4 per cent in 1967 to 13 per cent in 1986. This finance is concentrated in the chemicals and electronics sectors. Government finance of industrial R & D rose from 29 per cent of the total spent in 1967 to peak at 33 per cent in 1972, but fell back to 23 per cent in 1985 and 1986. In particular this proportion fell from 30 per cent in 1983 to 23 per cent in 1985. The share of finance for industrial R & D in the UK provided by industry itself (i.e. 1 minus the government share) is relatively low in international terms (OECD figures not strictly comparable to those above put the UK share at 48 per cent in 1985 compared with the USA at 65 per cent, Germany 80 per cent, and Japan 100 per cent). To some degree the high contribution of government in the UK could be attributed to the high level of defence contracts placed with UK industry. However, the support for *civil* R & D in industry by the UK Government may well be quite low, although accurate data on this are not available.

The overall picture as described above can thus be summarized as a decline in the UK's share of GDP devoted to R & D relative to that in other countries and an excessive emphasis on defence. Recently there has been a rise in industrial R & D expenditure, but this expenditure has been biased towards defence. There has been an increasing reliance on overseas funds to finance industrial R & D in the UK and a decline in the government's contribution to industrial R & D. The government contribution is planned to be cut further as the government moves away from the support of near-market R & D. This is, however, occurring at a time when the private funding of industrial R & D in the UK is relatively low in international terms.

Non-R & D-based indicators of technological activity are more difficult to locate. Pavitt and Patel (1988) discuss patent data with conclusions that reinforce those above. Work on citation indices has similarly shown a decline in the status of UK science over the last twenty years. Diffusion indicators are very sparse. However, some work (e.g. Northcott *et al.*, 1985, and Nabseth and Ray, 1984), has shown that UK industry has not been particularly laggard in adopting new process technologies, but, on the other hand, a common observation on the UK economy is that it displays a very high incremental capital output ratio (i.e. for any given investment spending it achieves very little extra output). This may imply that UK industry invests in new technology but obtains, for various reasons, only limited effectiveness in its use.

In our view, taking the indicators as a whole, there is cause for concern about technological activity in the UK.

II. Why have technology policies?

There would be little point in having technology policies if unassisted market forces could be expected to lead to the efficient allocation of resources to technological activity. Unfortunately that is not the case. The purpose of this section is to explain the nature of 'market failures' in technological activity, and the next section considers policies to help remedy them.

Technological change is concerned with the production of new information. Information is unlike ordinary commodities (Arrow 1962, and Dasgupta, this volume). Once discovered, a piece of information can usually be made widely available at very little (social) cost. This is an extreme kind of scale economy, it costs virtually no more to produce a given piece of information many times over once the first unit has been produced. Other things being equal it is generally beneficial from the social point of view for information to be widely disseminated. For example, in commercial situations, it allows firms to compete more intensively and resulting benefits are passed on to the consuming public. From the private viewpoint of the innovating firm,

however, dissemination of that information is likely to be very costly. Indeed, the private value of information tends to diminish the more widely it is known. The more that other firms benefit from, or 'free ride' on, the R & D efforts of the first firm, the less incentive is there to engage in R & D activity in the first place. This conflict between the public interest in dissemination and the private interest in exercising exclusive property rights over information—and the tension between static and dynamic efficiency that results—is known as the *appropriability problem*. It is central to the economics of technology policy.

Even where there is perfect appropriability, e.g. watertight and long-lived patents, there are often reasons to expect the private reward from technological activity to be less than the social benefit. For example, a monopolist or oligopolist will have less incentive to cut unit costs than would a benign public enterprise manager setting price equal to marginal cost, because the private firm supplies fewer units of output on which to achieve unit cost savings. (Even in reasonably competitive settings, price typically exceeds marginal cost in R & D intensive industries because a considerable mark-up is needed to recoup R & D expenditures. This is another source of allocative inefficiency.) Furthermore, successful R & D is generally of net benefit to consumers over and above the gain in profits to the innovator. This positive 'externality' to consumers will not be part of private calculations of the marginal benefit of R & D, and is hence another reason why its provision may be socially suboptimal. Mansfield (1977) has actually provided some estimates of the difference between social and private rates of return. Yet another reason is that private discount rates may exceed social discount rates, a point that we shall return to later.

Externalities between firms must also be considered. If there are 'spillovers', so that firm B benefits from the technological activities undertaken by firm A (e.g. because it learns or can partly imitate) then each firm will hold back its technological efforts to some extent, and hope to benefit from the efforts of others. This is the free-rider problem mentioned above.

However, although each firm may have less incentive than socially desirable to engage in technological activity, it is possible that there will be too many firms engaging in such activity. This is the potential problem of *duplication* of, for example, research efforts. It is straightforward to show analytically (see, e.g. Dasgupta and Stiglitz, 1980) that industry R & D expenditure might exceed the socially desirably level of R & D, with too many firms each individually doing too little. In that case there is too much R & D input and too little R & D output, a double inefficiency.

Similarly, in some cases there may be a 'common pool' problem in which the first-past-the-post-takes-all nature of the race to invent induces excessive speed in the process. It is natural to think of policies to promote co-operative R & D in these contexts (see the next section). On the other hand, rivalry in R & D can have advantages. First, it is desirable when independent, as opposed to completely parallel, research strategies are being pursued. Then there is advantage in diversity (though it is questionable whether the market will produce the right type of diversity, see Dasgupta and Maskin, 1987). Second, as noted before, competition between researchers, whether they are in academic or commercial environments, allows reward to be based on priority of discovery. With research inputs and outputs being hard to observe, and the relation between them being unknown, it is difficult to provide incentives for effort in the absence of some rivalry.

As discussed above, technological activity is taking place in an environment of incomplete information and uncertainty. In view of the difficulties of measuring R & D inputs and prospective returns, R & D funding is beset with acute problems of asymmetric information, and the market for R & D finance is likely to be highly imperfect. The problems include ones of adverse selection, moral hazard, performance monitoring, and information flows. The nature of financial institutions can influence how well such problems are overcome, and it has been argued that financing via long-term relationships with banks may be more effective than stock-market financing due to closer monitoring arrangements and better information flows (see Mayer, 1987). Moreover, given asymmetric information, managers anxious to satisfy stock-market opinion may divert resources towards visible signals of corporate health (e.g. high dividends) and away from less tangible activities (e.g. R & D). Such imperfections in the capital market reduce opportunities for risk-shifting, and risk-aversion may become a dominant influence in R & D investment decisions. Problems of this kind are part of what is described as excessive 'short-termism' in financial markets. It is worth noting that only recently has it become a convention in the UK for publicly quoted companies to detail their R & D spending in Annual Reports. Without such information it is difficult to see how capital markets could optimally allocate resources for technological activity across alternative uses. Pavitt and Patel (1988) lay considerable emphasis on the shortcomings of the market for R & D finance in the UK.

Thus there are several reasons—including externalities, scale economies, market power, attitudes to risk, and information asymmetries—to expect that market forces will not result in desirable levels of technological activity and dynamic efficiency if left to themselves. Policy intervention is likely to be necessary to remedy some of these defects. Moreover, there may be other reasons that motivate technology policies by national governments in the context of international competition (see Lyons, 1987 and Yarrow, 1985 for surveys). For example, it is often claimed that Japanese technology policies, in conjunction with trade policies, have been designed to put Japanese firms at a strategic advantage over their international competitors in world markets. It can indeed be shown analytically that a country may have a unilateral incentive to subsidize the technological efforts of its domestic firm or firms in order to shift the 'equilibrium' of oligopolistic international markets to expand their market share and profits. Strategic industrial and trade policies may be used similarly to attempt to influence entry and exit decisions. Competition in the civil aircraft industry between the European Airbus and Boeing and McDonnell-Douglas is often cited as an example of this. Thus, not only are unassisted market forces unlikely to lead to levels and directions of innovative activity that are in the general interest, but governments may also seek to influence the position of their national firms in world markets. This discussion is already complex enough. It is now time to consider what technology policies can do to help.

III. Policy instruments

Many branches of government policy have an influence —actual or potential—on R & D activity. We saw in the last section that externalities between firms, and between firms and consumers, are the principal source of market failure in technological activity, and we highlighted in particular the problem of appropriability. There are four general approaches to externality problems in economics: private property rights, public provision, subsidies/taxes, and co-operation. All four are used in technology policy.

1. The patent system

The patent system and related laws are designed to give discoverers property rights over their new information, at least for a period of years. The advantages of such systems are obvious, they promote dynamic efficiency by providing incentives for R & D effort. The disadvantages are twofold. First, patents do not always succeed in ensuring appropriability of rewards. Other firms may learn a great deal from the filing of a patent, and may be able to innovate by 'inventing around' it. Indeed, it is said that firms sometimes refrain from patenting because of the loss of secrecy that it entails. In addition, there are considerable enforcement costs. Hausman and Mackie-Mason (1988) discuss many of the issues that arise, in the context of international competition. In short patents do not invariably contain spillovers of information to rival firms.

The second difficulty is that, even where patents give appropriability, they do so at a cost. If a patent gives the private reward of market power, then it brings with it the social cost of allocative, and possibly also productive, inefficiency. This is of course the trade-off between static and dynamic efficiency. Furthermore, the competition for that reward may encourage inefficient duplication of effort, also as discussed above. Thus while the enforcement of patents and other intellectual property rights is an important element of overall technology policy, it is usually a very imperfect system even where it is practicable.

2. Public provision

At the other extreme from private property rights lies the public provision of R & D through institutions such as government research labs, research councils, and universities. Public provision overcomes free-rider problems in R & D, avoids competitive duplication of effort, and allows researchers to be motivated other than by the prospective market power conveyed by patents. (The difference in reward schemes between scientists and technologists was discussed above.) However, the difficulties of public provision include the relative lack of commercial information and incentive that firms in industry are more likely to possess. For these reasons, public R & D activity is more appropriate to basic research than near-market research.

3. R & D subsidies

Subsidies to R & D are a way of attempting to improve the terms of the trade-off between static and dynamic efficiency that is at the heart of the appropriability problem. In principle a combination of R & D subsidies and relatively *high* spillovers between firms could promote both kinds of efficiency (Spence, 1984). Innovative efforts would be encouraged by the subsidies, and spillovers would allow the competitive and widespread application of improved technology. The main problem, however, is knowing the appropriate rate and direction of subsidy. Which activities should be subsidized? Should particular firms be singled out for support, or should subsidies be generally available (e.g. via favourable tax treatment of R & D expenditure)? How large should subsidies be? These key questions are enormously difficult to answer. The costs and benefits of R & D are hard enough to measure *ex post*, let alone *ex ante*. And the public authorities who give subsidies are invariably less well-informed about the costs and benefits than those who seek them. (A recent institutional innovation in the UK is designed to overcome this problem, the Centre for the Exploitation of Science and Technology (CEST) has been charged with the formidably difficult task of reporting on those areas of Science and Technology in which the UK should specialize.) In addition, of course, there is the cost of subsidies to public funds. Properly speaking, that cost is the marginal distortion elsewhere in the economy arising from the extra taxation needed to pay for the subsidies. The question of subsidies will be pursued further in the policy discussion in the next section.

4. Co-operative R & D

Like all the other policies considered here, co-operative R & D—in the form of joint ventures or mergers in high technology industries—has pros and cons (see Dasgupta, this volume and Baumol and Ordover, 1988). It 'internalizes' the externalities between firms, and can in principle overcome both free-rider problems and duplication problems in R & D, while also being consistent with product market competition in the case of research joint ventures. However, in practice there is the obvious danger that collaboration in R & D will lead to anticompetitive collaboration in the product market. That necessarily happens in the case of merger (and this was a key issue in the proposed merger between GEC and Plessey, which was stopped on competition grounds). (See Monopolies and Mergers Commission, 1986.)

In addition, there is an equally serious problem when R & D collaboration does not lead to product market collaboration. A research joint venture can greatly diminish the incentive to innovate. For example, if all firms in a competitive industry succeeded in achieving a common cost reduction, they would not enhance their profits much by introducing the same because prices would fall in line with costs; consumers, and not the innovating firms, would be the main beneficiaries from innovation. This point needs to be modified if only a subset of firms in the industry are engaged in

R & D co-operation, but it serves to highlight an important consideration. Market failure in R & D occurs not only because of externalities between firms, but also because of externalities between firms and consumers. This is another awkward tension between the desire to promote innovation and consumer benefit, which requires some competitive stimulus between firms, and the desire to avoid wasteful duplication.

5. Other policy instruments

Many other policies have important effects on technological performance, including the following.

Risk-Sharing: In the absence of perfect markets for shifting risk the Government may intervene as a risk bearer. Also in a world where the Government may be less risk averse than the private sector, the carrying of risk by government is an appropriate policy. In the UK such arguments have been used to support government involvement in for example, Aerospace R & D, via Launch Aid. It is clear, however, that risk carrying policies are subject to problems of adverse selection and moral hazard that makes their design difficult. It should also be made clear that if the risk argument is used to justify government funding of R & D then such policies are bound, on occasion, to involve failures and losses.

Diffusion Policies: We have stressed that diffusion is the stage when new technology affects economic activity and when the benefits arise. It is clear, however, that diffusion policy is the poor relation in technology policy. What diffusion policies there are tend to be of two types—information provision or dissemination policies, and subsidy policies. Information dissemination policies, programmes to promote the awareness of new technologies, are particularly important for diffusion. Increasing returns to scale in information—the one-off cost of information collection and the low marginal cost of its transmission—make centralized policies very appropriate in this context. Subsidy policies are designed to extend the use of or speed the adoption of particular new technologies (past examples include computers, fibre optics, and robotics) by reducing the post subsidy cost of acquisition. Research in this area (see Stoneman, 1987), has explored the welfare consequences of subsidizing the use of new technology in this way. By making comparison with the welfare optimal diffusion path, it is argued that, depending on the price expectations of potential users of the new technology and the market structure of the industry supplying the new technology, the actual diffusion path may be too fast or too slow from a welfare point of view. Thus only in a particular circumstance is a subsidy desirable. Moreover, it is also argued that, with a monopolist supplier of new technology, some of the effects of the subsidy will be offset by compensatory changes in the prices set by the monopolist. Thus the need for and the effectiveness of a subsidy policy is not a simple issue.

Competition Policy: The discussion above on co-operative R & D has indicated the role of competition policy, especially policy on mergers and agreements between firms. Mergers in high technology industries may permit the realization of scale economies and the pooling of incentives in R & D, and avoid duplication of efforts. But, as we have argued above, competition in R & D can have major beneficial consequences. Moreover, even where R & D collaboration is desirable, it should ideally be achieved without undermining product market competition (proper account being taken of international competition) even in high-technology industries. This is consistent with a permissive attitude to many types of R & D agreement in restrictive trade practices policy, provided that such agreements do not lead to product market competition being undermined, and do not blunt the incentive to innovate (see above). R & D agreements are most likely to be beneficial when they involve a subset of firms in the industry. A much fuller account of these and other competition issues is given by Baumol and Ordover (1988).

Trade Policy: We discussed above how R & D policies, e.g. subsidies to R & D, can be used to affect the positions of domestic firms in world markets, including their international rivals. Conversely, trade policies can be used as instruments of technology policy. For example, where there are important learning effects, i.e. technological capability depends on the cumulative output of a firm or industry, measures such as export subsidies or protection from import competition can enhance the output, and hence technological performance of domestic firm(s), and put them at an advantage over foreign rivals (see, for example, Krugman, 1984). This strategy, protection to achieve learning effects followed by aggressive international competition, has sometimes been attributed to the Japanese, for example in the market for TV apparatus. Hausman and MacKie-Mason (1988) examine another aspect of the relationship between R & D and international trade policy—the enforcement of intellectual property rights against foreign competitors, and the emphasis placed in the USA on the protection of industries as against the enforcement of property rights.

Education and Training Policy: Perhaps the most important 'input' to technological activity is trained personnel. An adequate resource of appropriately trained 'human capital' is therefore a prerequisite for successful technology policies. If, for example, there is a restricted supply of scientists and technologists, then the main effect of R & D subsidies could be to drive up their salaries rather than lead to much greater R & D output. (The outcome depends on the elasticity of substitution between labour and other inputs in R & D activity, as well as the elasticity of supply of trained personnel, see Dixit and Grossman, 1986.)

Procurement Policies: These can be oriented towards technological objectives as ways of hidden protectionism (see above), R & D finance, or information dissemination via demonstration effects. However, the costs of deflecting procurement policy from the straightforward objective of cost minimization can be high, albeit hidden from view, and it may often be dominated by other more direct policy instruments.

Defence Policies: Similar comments apply here. Although the technological 'spin-offs' from military projects can be considerable, there is a danger that they will be exaggerated, especially given the large vested interests typically involved. Moreover, the nature of military projects is sometimes such that the technological information gained cannot be made generally available. Another influence of defence policy on civil R & D concerns the supply of scientists and technologists. Depending on the size and flexibility of that supply, defence policy can have undesirable crowding-out effects on the civil sector. If, as seems plausible, the salaries of the individuals involved do not fully reflect their 'shadow values', i.e. potential value added of their contributions elsewhere, then the cost of defence policy to civil R & D is understated by the accounting cost of defence R & D. Any additional cost should be set against the potential value of spin-offs from that R & D.

Policy on Standards and Compatibility: The issue of standards and compatibility arises in many high-technology industries, including telecommunications and electronic data processing. Software and hardware must be able to work together, and complementary pieces of apparatus (e.g. disk drive and processor) must be readily connectable. Standardization, for example of telecommunications protocols, is desirable for two reasons. By minimizing consumer switching costs, it breaks down market segmentation and enhances competition. Second, it allows the full exploitation of scale economies. On the other hand, standardization can have costs. Co-ordination on a suboptimal standard (e.g. the QWERTY typewriter keyboard) has obvious

costs and may be virtually irreversible given the enormous difficulty of changing standards. Moreover, a standard may itself be an object of innovation. The requirement of a given standard could stifle the introduction of new and better standards. There is no guarantee that the market will produce a desirable outcome regarding standards. (Typically there are multiple market equilibria anyway.) The Government can intervene effectively, and at a relatively low direct cost, by laying down requirements on standards. Its ability to influence events is greatest when a new technology is in its infancy, but that is when it is least informed. No general maxims for intervention can be laid down, but standards and compatibility are issues for technology and competition policies that cannot be ignored.

This list of policies could easily be extended, but we shall stop here. To summarize, we have shown how the four direct approaches to externality problems in R & D—intellectual property rights, public provision, subsidies, and co-operation—all have disadvantages as well as advantages. In particular, we hope to have indicated where and why one form of intervention has advantages over another. Several other branches of policy with a bearing on R & D performance have also been discussed. It should, however, be noted that although very thin, the literature on the evaluation of technology policies does not suggest that the use of the various policy instruments in the past has met with particular success. On this point we now turn to consider the recent debates on how, and to what extent, the instruments of technology policy should be used, with particular reference to the UK.

IV. UK technology policy

It is widely believed that the UK's technological performance in the post-war period has fallen short of that of most other industrialized countries, and that this is an important factor in explaining the UK's relatively poor record of economic growth. While it is impossible to draw conclusions from aggregate data the statistical evidence reviewed in section 1 above does suggest a number of problems in the UK, the prime one being the continuing low level of civil R & D, but the overall failure of UK R & D to match the growth of R & D elsewhere and the small share of private finance in industrial R & D are symptomatic of related problems.

It would be natural to consider that the poor R & D performance in the UK is related to the market failures detailed above. However, when basing judgements on international comparisons this raises a problem, for surely those failures also apply in other economies. Differences in the technological performance of economies thus cannot be attributed to the market failures *per se* but must be traced back to the institutional and environmental factors that underlie market conditions. Pursuing this line of argument the poor UK performance could be attributed to several factors, including (a) the economic structure, for example, the UK economy is very different from the US economy in terms of size and external trade relations ('1992' may have important consequences for the UK and EC economies in this regard), (b) entrepreneurial attitudes, e.g. attitudes to risk taking or 'animal spirits' and the nature of the labour market, (c) UK institutions, especially financial institutions that may be excessively short-termist, and (d) UK government policies. It is not our intention here to try to separate out the role of these several different factors in explaining the poor UK performance. Rather we intend to explore here the reaction of the UK government to the problem and the nature of the technology policy that it is currently pursuing.

A useful starting-point is to consider the classification of technology policies as presented by Ergas (1987). He distinguishes between:

(i) 'mission-orientated' countries (UK, US, France) in which science and high technology is applied to big problems (e.g. the space programme, Concorde, and especially defence projects) in the search for international strategic leadership;

(ii) diffusion-orientated countries (e.g. Germany, Switzerland, Sweden) whose policies aim to promote a capacity for adjustment to technological change throughout the industrial structure by the provision of R & D-related public goods, notably in education, product standardization, and co-operative research;

(iii) Japan, where vigorous policies to promote national technological goals have been pursued in tandem with diffusion-oriented policies.

This character of UK policy with its orientation towards high technology and defence is seen by many as the basis of the problem in the UK, the argument often being pursued by comparison with the success of Japan with its much more broadly based policy of intervention. However, the pattern of publicly funded R & D as a whole in the UK is open to question. One can enquire into (a) the level of government R & D spending, (b) its distribution between basic research, applied research and development, (c) its distribution between civil and military, (d) its distribution across industrial sectors and technological opportunities, and (e) its division between in-house and external research. Some information on these issues was presented in section 1 above. In addition, there are questions about policy on research and training in higher education, which are vital to the long-run availability of scientists and technologists. Although it would be possible to discuss in great detail these issues and their relationships to the institutional structure of UK technology policy, we shall approach here what is at one and the same time both a more general and a more specific question. We will address the philosophy that conditions the policy rather than the policies *per se*, and within this we concentrate upon how that philosophy impacts upon government support for private sector industrial R & D.

The philosophy behind current UK government policy can be neatly illustrated by comparing the attitudes of the House of Lords Select Committee on Science and Technology (1986) with the government attitudes as detailed in two policy statements (Department of Trade and Industry, 1988 and HM Government, 1987). In its report on *Civil Research and Development* the House of Lords Select Committee observed 'the gravity of the United Kingdom's prospects in R & D' (p. 66), argued that UK R & D was badly underfunded, and expressed the need for a recognized policy for the public support of R & D. On industrial R & D, the Lords Committee recommended, among other things:

- that more attention, including some public support, be given to the development phase in R & D (para. 7.21);
- that the total amount of DTI support for industrial R & D be increased (7.23);
- that tax incentives for R & D in the UK should be examined (7.24);
- that public purchasing be used more to stimulate R & D in the private sector (7.26);
- that the Government take steps to increase awareness and knowledge of R & D results from overseas (7.27);
- that the provision of information about public and private R & D be greatly improved (7.25 and 7.28); and
- that the Government should do more to meet the R & D needs of small firms (7.29).

The Committee also recommended that a process should be introduced for funding strategic research of particular significance to the country's economic future. It also made recommendations about the research councils and higher education, the civil implications of defence R & D, and administrative structures.

The Government responded to the Lords Committee in a White Paper, *Civil Research and Development* (HM Government, 1987). The conclusions of a review of the DTI's role in technology policy were presented in a White Paper, *DTI—the Department for Enterprise* (Department of Trade and Industry, 1988, chapter 8). In the former document, the Government stated its view that 'the primary problem . . . is the low level of industry's investment in R & D' (para. 4). As to remedying that low level of investment, the Government pointed to the improved economic climate, especially the recovery in corporate profitability, and said that firms were now better placed to invest in R & D than in the past. As to the Government's role, the 1987 White Paper (para. 24) states:

Industry must take the initiative for its R & D programmes. This requires commercial decisions reflecting market forces. Government support is only considered where a worthwhile and viable project is at risk through failure of the market mechanism.

The 1987 White Paper agreed with a number of recommendations of the Lords Committee, and said that its policies (e.g. on helping R & D in small firms) were already in line with them. However, the idea of tax incentives for R & D was rejected, mainly on grounds of cost effectiveness (for a survey of the evidence see Inland Revenue, 1987), and no comment was made on the proposal to increase substantially DTI support for industrial R & D (it is in fact due to decrease through to 1991 in real terms).

The 1988 White Paper announced some changes in the direction, rather than the scale, of DTI support for innovation. The scheme for innovation grant assistance to individual companies is to be ended, as are programmes of support for the microelectronics industry, software products, and fibreoptics. A general move away from 'near-market' R & D support is proposed. Instead, greater emphasis is to be given to collaborative R & D programmes and technology transfer. International collaboration within Europe is highlighted, including programmes such as ESPRIT, RACE, and EUREKA. Research collaboration between industry and institutions of higher education is also emphasized (by, for example, the LINK project). The measures on technology transfer are aimed at improving the transfer of scientific capability into commercial application, which is seen as one of the sources of the UK's weakness in industrial innovation.

Overall, the crux of the Government's strategy is to withdraw from near-market decisions and to try to make the market work better by facilitating collaboration and information provision. The possibility of market failure in R & D is recognized, but seems to be regarded as the exception rather than the rule. Thus: 'There may be exceptional cases of single company projects which offer significant national benefits but which would not be undertaken without financial assistance from the Government' (para. 8.28). As in other areas of economic policy, the Government sees its role primarily as one of creating an appropriate climate, and leaving firms to take the initiative.

However, as was argued in section 2, market failure in R & D is the rule rather than the exception. A number of the Government's policy proposals, for example on dissemination, are welcome so far as they go, but it is partly an act of faith to suppose that the poor record of investment in R & D by UK firms will be radically altered by those proposals (for example, Pavitt and Patel (1988) argue that it is the share of profits devoted to R & D that is the problem in the UK, not total profitability; an improvement in the latter is not the same as an improvement in the former). There is some sense of frustration in the Government's attitude to R & D, and a possible tension between the view that R & D investment decisions should be entirely up to participants in the market, and the evident belief that they continue to underinvest. Better informed and more collaborative *laissez-faire* may work somewhat better than before, but it is far from clear that the Government's response is adequate to the task.

In international terms, as well as in terms of economic theory, one might argue that the UK government with its *laissez-faire* philosophy is somewhat out of step. To give just a few examples, the Australian Government has recently introduced large-scale tax incentives to R & D, the Japanese have for many years helped the development of the technological base of their industries, and the involvement of the French Government in certain civilian high-technology products (e.g. in rail transport and telecommunications) is well known.

V. Conclusions

In this assessment we have examined both the theory and practice of technology policy. It has been argued on theoretical grounds that for numerous reasons one should not expect a free market economy to allocate a socially optimal amount of resources to technological advance and as such there is a role for government to play in correcting such market failures. We have illustrated that, in international terms, the technological performance of the UK economy is not impressive and we have explored the policy stance of the UK government in reaction to this. We find that the Government's relatively *laissez-faire* attitude towards civil R & D is seriously open to question. Theoretical analysis reveals that market failure in R & D is likely to be the norm rather than the exception. The existing institutional and policy framework in the UK is not in practice delivering a technological performance that compares well with that achieved elsewhere, and governments in competitor nations are generally pursuing more active policies. The concerns expressed by the House of Lords Select Committee on Science and Technology appear to be well-founded, and the government's response involves a greater degree of faith in unassisted market forces than we would be prepared to make.

References

Arrow, K. (1962), 'Economic Welfare and the Allocation of Resources for Inventions', in Nelson, R. R. (ed.), *The Rate and Direction of Inventive Activity*, Princeton, Princeton University Press.

Baumol, W., and Ordover, J. (1988), 'Antitrust Policy and High-Technology Industries', *Oxford Review of Economic Policy*, Vol. 4, No. 4, 13–34.

Cabinet Office (1988), *Annual Review of Government Funded Research and Development*, London, HMSO.

Dasgupta, P., and David, P. (1986), 'Information Disclosure and the Economics of Science and Technology', in Feiwel, G. (ed.), *Arrow and the Foundations of the Theory of Economic Policy*, London, Macmillan.

Dasgupta, P., and Maskin, E. (1987), 'The Simple Economics of Research Portfolios', *Economic Journal, 97*, 581–95.

—— and Stiglitz, J. (1980), 'Industrial Structure and the Nature of Innovative Activity', *Economic Journal, 90*, 266–93.

—— and Stoneman, P. (eds.) (1987), *Economic Policy and Technological Performance*, Cambridge, Cambridge University Press.

Department of Trade and Industry (1988), *DTI—the department for enterprise*, Cmnd. 278, London, HMSO.

Dixit, A., and Grossman, G. (1986), 'Targeted Export Promotion with Several Oligopolistic Industries', *Journal of International Economics, 21*, 233–49.

Ergas, H. (1987), 'The Importance of Technology Policy' in Dasgupta, P., and Stoneman, P. (eds.), op. cit.

Hausman, J., and MacKie-Mason, J. (1988), 'Innovation and International Trade Policy: Some Lessons from the US', *Oxford Review of Economic Policy*, Vol. 4, No. 4, 56–72.

HM Government (1987), *Civil Research and Development*, Cmnd. 185, London, HMSO.

House of Lords Select Committee on Science and Technology (1986), *Civil Research and Development*, HL 20 London, HMSO.

Inland Revenue (1987), *Fiscal Incentives for R & D Spending*, London, HM Treasury.

Krugman, P. (1984), 'Import Protection as Export Promotion: International Competition in the Presence of Oligopoly and Economies of Scale', in Kierzkowski, H. (ed.), *Monopolistic Competition and International Trade*, Oxford, Oxford University Press.

Lyons, B. (1987), 'International Trade and Technology Policy', in Dasgupta, P., and Stoneman, P. (eds.), op. cit.

Mansfield, E. (1977), *The Production and Application of New Industrial Technology*, New York, Norton.

Mayer, C. (1987), 'The Assessment: Financial Systems and Corporate Investment', *Oxford Review of Economic Policy*, Vol. 3, No. 4, i–xvi.

Monopolies and Mergers Commission (1986), *The General Electric Company plc and Plessey plc—A Report on the Proposed Merger*, Cmnd. 9867, London, HMSO.

Nabseth, L., and Ray, G. (1984), *The Diffusion of New Industrial Processes: An International Study*, London, Cambridge University Press.

Northcott, J. *et al.* (1985), *Microelectronics in Industry*, London, Policy Studies Institute.

Organization for Economic Co-operation and Development (1984), *OECD Science and Technology Indicators*, Paris, OECD.

Pavitt, K., and Patel, P. (1988), 'The International Distribution and Determinants of Technological Activities', *Oxford Review of Economic Policy*, Vol. 4, No. 4, 35–55.

Spence, M. (1984), 'Cost Reduction, Competition and Industry Performance', *Econometrica, 52*, 101–21.

Stoneman, P. (1987), *The Economic Analysis of Technology Policy*, Oxford, Oxford University Press.

Yarrow, G. (1985), 'Strategic Issues in Industrial Policy', *Oxford Review of Economic Policy*, Vol. 1, No. 3, 95–109.

5

The welfare economics of knowledge production

PARTHA DASGUPTA[1]

University of Cambridge

I. Introduction

Carl Christian von Weizsäcker begins his excellent book on entry barriers by classifying economic activity into three classes, or levels as he calls them: the exchange of goods, the production of material commodities, and the creation of knowledge. (See von Weizsäcker, 1980.) He is prompted into developing this classification, rather than some other, because these three levels are on the whole easy to distinguish, and because they are in an order of increasing distance from the consumption of material goods and services. Von Weizsäcker in fact proceeds to demonstrate in his book that this distance has a marked influence on the organization of the economic activity in question.

Von Weizsäcker's classification is time honoured. But until recently much of the focus of analytical economics had been on the first two levels: those of exchange and production of material goods and services. The analytical economics of knowledge had been on the whole an impoverished sibling. All this has changed over the past decade or so, and the microeconomic analysis of technological change is today an active field of research. But as in all other types of enquiry it would appear rapidly to have acquired an internal history. A number of the early papers in the field (e.g. Kamien and Schwartz, 1978; Levin, 1978; Loury, 1979; Dasgupta and Stiglitz, 1980a,b) analysed the charac-

teristics of strategic behaviour on the part of profit-maximizing firms when they compete not only in the production of goods and services, but also in the development of new products and new ways of manufacturing old products; what one would want to call technological competition. Now, for reasons that are well understood today, the theory of perfect competition is of no use here.[2] Even if technological competition were fierce, the resulting industrial structure would be oligopolistic, as the recent literature on these matters has made clear. Moreover, in order to understand the structure of industries we must trace back to the possibilities facing inventors and developers, to their underlying motivation, and to the background incentive structure. The recent literature on the microeconomics of technological change has clarified a number of these issues. Nevertheless, it is unfortunate that the literature has been dominated by matters concerning patent races, at the expense of pretty much all else.

In this essay I want to redress the balance, even if only by a tiny bit, and talk of other matters. Specifically, I want to study the sorts of social institutions which can, at least in principle, sustain an efficient level of inventive and innovative activity. Plainly, the characteristics of such institutions will depend upon the nature of the produced commodity in question, namely knowledge. It is best then to start with that.

First published in *Oxford Review of Economic Policy*, vol. 4, no. 4 (1988).

[1] Over the years I have gained much from discussions on the matters covered in this essay with Paul David, Eric Maskin, and Joseph Stiglitz, with each of whom I have collaborated on several occasions. The material in Section II is based largely on Dasgupta and David (1988), which also develops a thesis concerning the historical origins of science and technology as social institutions. In writing this essay I have also benefited greatly from the instructions that John Vickers has given me.

[2] See Schumpeter (1976) for an early elaboration of this viewpoint.

II. Knowledge-producing institutions: an argument by design

Knowledge is not a homogeneous commodity. There are different kinds of knowledge and no obvious natural units in which they can be measured. Indeed, each piece of knowledge is a separate commodity. It is indivisible, in the sense that once a certain piece of knowledge has been acquired there is no value to acquiring it again: the wheel does not need to be invented twice. The same piece of information can be used over and over again, at no cost (Marx, 1970; Arrow, 1962). For my purpose here it does not matter whether we think that certain kinds of knowledge possess intrinsic worth in the Aristotelian sense, or whether we value knowledge solely in functional terms.[3] What is of critical importance is that knowledge, and more specifically information, can be jointly consumed and used by as many as care to. Thus, if one person gives another person a piece of information this does not reduce the amount of information held by the first possessor, although of course the benefit to each typically will depend upon whether and in what manner the other makes use of this piece of knowledge. In short, knowledge has the hallmark of a public good, a durable public good.

In what follows I shall for simplicity of exposition assume that the cost of transmitting knowledge is negligible when compared to its production cost. This is not as wild an assumption as it might appear at first blush, especially today, because transmission costs are to be distinguished from the costs incurred in educating people to interpret the knowledge and to make use of it. This latter is what one would call the cost of education, of learning, of absorption, of processing and so forth. Plainly, the greater the number of people who can make use of transmitted knowledge the greater is the social value of that knowledge.[4] Plainly also, not all knowledge can be communicated, especially problem-solving skills, more generally knowledge that is acquired through practice on the part of the researcher.

I am not considering this kind of knowledge here, for they are embodied in the researcher. We would call such knowledge the researcher's skill, or acquired ability. Models of learning (by doing) with incomplete spillover capture this kind of person-specific knowledge. (See Dasgupta and Stiglitz, 1988.)

Given this, one seeks to identify resource allocation mechanisms, more grandly socio-economic institutions, which can *in principle* produce and allocate knowledge in an efficient manner. The qualification should be noted. As in all theories of institutional design, I am here interested in a thought-experiment. So I assume that it is possible costlessly to design and establish an entire socio-economic institution, supporting it with a background of attendant rules, norms, rights, and backing them with the force of the law. As it happens, modern resource-allocation theory suggests that there are three possible institutions. As it also happens, there are analogues of each in the world as we know it. I shall elaborate upon them in turn.

1. The Samuelsonian contrivance

The first consists in the government engaging itself directly in the production of knowledge, allowing free use of it (recall that transmission costs are assumed negligible) and financing the production cost from general taxation. This was at the heart of Professor Samuelson's classic analysis of the efficient production and allocation of public goods (Samuelson, 1954).[5] Government research and development (R & D) laboratories which publicly disclose their findings, such as for example agricultural research establishments, are an approximation of such an arrangement. It is as well to note that the volume of public expenditure for the production of knowledge and the allocation of this expenditure for different kinds of knowledge are in this institutional set-up public decisions.

2. Pigovian public finance

The second resource-allocation mechanism which in principle can produce knowledge in an efficient manner is one where production is undertaken by private agents, who in turn are subsidized for their effort by the public purse. Thus, the subsidies are financed by general taxation. A crucial feature of this arrangement

---

[3] In the context of education policy such a distinction matters greatly, and the education literature has consistently displayed a tension between these two aspects, most especially in debates over the choice of course curricula. This tension has on occasion been diffused, as in the writings of John Dewey, who in his philosophy tried to fuse the two by appealing to a sort of Aristotelian view of the development of a person. Nevertheless, the tension is a real one. But for the most part this distinction does not affect the arguments in this essay.

[4] Throughout, I am thinking of knowledge as a 'good', unlike pollution. Thus I am ignoring the kinds of knowledge that are used for purposes of waging war. This would involve a different set of considerations regarding public policy.

[5] The social cost-benefit rule, it will be recalled, is the equality of the marginal rate of transformation between the public good and a numeraire private good and the *sum* of the private marginal rates of indifferent substitution between these two goods.

is that private producers are denied exclusive rights to the knowledge they produce. Once knowledge is produced under this arrangement it is freely available to all. This is the Pigovian solution to the problem posed by public goods, and more generally, by externalities (see Pigou, 1932; Baumol and Oates, 1975; Dasgupta and Heal, 1979). In albeit imperfect forms this arrangement characterizes much research in public entities, such as state-funded universities, where a good deal of the research output is prohibited from being patented, and where salaries and promotions—the production subsidies—are paid out of public funds.

These two resource allocation mechanisms resemble one another greatly, but there are important differences, at least in theory. I am thinking of the Pigovian solution as a decentralized mechanism, one where production decisions are made by private agents, and whose work is subsidized by the government. (The subsidies are the shadow costs of production.) And I am characterizing the Samuelsonian solution as a command mode of planning: the decision of what to produce and how much to produce is made by the government. Of course, where the second fundamental theorem of welfare economics holds there is no serious difference in the implementability of these two resource allocation mechanisms. Nevertheless, they represent different methods of planning.

3. The Lindahl market mechanism

Each of these institutions reflects a non-market mechanism for resource allocation. The third and final institution to consider is therefore the market mechanism itself. Admittedly, we are discussing the production of a public good, a commodity which can be consumed jointly. But this does not mean that private appropriation of benefits is necessarily impossible. For some types of knowledge, what one might call the output of basic research (see Section III), private appropriation may prove difficult. For other types it may to a large extent be possible. I want to think now of those sorts of knowledge to which private ownership can be legally assigned and whose ownership can be enforced. By ownership I mean the right to control the use of the public good. Suppose then that society grants producers of new knowledge property rights to discoveries and inventions, and allows them to engage in trade should they wish to, via licensing or outright sale. In the world as we know it, patents, trademarks, and copyrights are an embodiment of such ownership.

Clearly, the value of a given piece of knowledge is different for different people. Therefore, if production

under the market mechanism is to be efficient the owner must set different prices for different buyers, since efficiency demands that the marginal cost of production of this knowledge equals the sum of the fees charged by the producer to all buyers. At an efficient market equilibrium the quantity demanded by each buyer equals the total amount which is produced and is on offer. This was Lindahl's proposal for the supply of public goods; to establish a competitive market mechanism for it. (See Musgrave and Peacock, 1968.)

One problem with the suggestion, as Arrow (1971) noted, is this. Since Lindahl prices are 'named' prices, one for each buyer, each of the Lindahl markets for a given piece of knowledge is thin, essentially a bilateral monopoly. This is scarcely a propitious environment for the emergence of efficiency prices. Furthermore, the enforcement of property rights is difficult, particularly on the output of fundamental research, for the findings of such research have possible applications in wide varieties of fields, and it can be exceptionally difficult to detect a violation of property rights. In other words, the economic benefits of knowledge are often difficult to appropriate privately, and therefore to market efficiently. This is so even when patent and copyright protection gives one transferable legal rights to exclude others from using that knowledge. Matters are easier in the case of more narrowly restricted knowledge of new technical processes and practical devices. This partly explains why it is a commonplace today to see A paying B a licence fee for using B's patent on the manufacture of a new product, or on a new process for manufacturing an old product.[6]

There is in fact an additional difficulty in applying Lindahl's theory of public goods directly to the case of knowledge. As we noted earlier each piece of knowledge is a distinct entity. Producing the same piece of knowledge more than once is of no use.[7] Different pieces of knowledge differ from one another in their detailed characteristics, and each piece can be thought of as a unit of the commodity with that characteristic. We are then in the realm of product differentiation, and unless strong assumptions are made, such as for example that the space of product characteristics is closed and bounded, we cannot in general ensure that competitive equilibria with full appropriability is

[6] Private firms often do not rely on patents, which involves disclosure of their discoveries, and they rely instead on secrecy. This involves a different type of risk, in that a rival may at a future date discover the same thing and exploit it with the backing of a patent. I am ignoring the practice of secrecy here only because I am considering Lindahl markets, which by definition cannot be established if firms keep their discoveries secret.

[7] By this I don't of course mean that repeating an experiment to confirm one's own or others' findings is useless. That is a different matter altogether.

efficient.[8] The point is a familiar one, that firms can locate themselves in the 'neighbourhood' of other firms in terms of the characteristics of the knowledge they produce, or more accurately, the characteristics of the research programmes they pursue. We would then expect that firms face downward-sloping demand curves in the market for knowledge, even in a large economy; unless, of course, fairly strong assumptions are made regarding the potential size of firms. I conclude that on *a-priori* grounds there are inefficiencies associated with the market mechanism, even when appropriability poses no problems.[9]

But this is only one side of the ledger. The other side is the fact that if they are to function well the two non-market mechanisms we noted earlier require an enormous quantity of centralized information, not only about private demand for knowledge but also about research possibilities open to individuals and firms. This tension, induced by the fact that the market mechanism and each of the various non-market planning mechanisms suffers from different types of weaknesses, has been a pervasive feature of the literature on science and technology policy.

As noted earlier, each of the three allocation mechanisms we have outlined is to be found in economies we know. They have developed over a long period, traceable in the European context at least, to the Renaissance patronage system. (For a development of this historical thesis, see Dasgupta and David, 1988.) They work in imperfect ways, as the foregoing discussion predicts they would, but they try and capture the essential features of the idealized social constructs. They have not risen and grown out of pure design, they have instead evolved over several hundred years.[10] Nevertheless, it is a useful exercise to study the argument by design, as we have done. It makes clear the central features of the organizations that have evolved over time, and are to be found today. Moreover, the fact that they co-exist requires explanation, and the argument by design gives us a lead as to why they do; why in fact we do not see the dominance of one of them. It has to do with differing characteristics of different kinds of knowledge.[11] I argue this next.

[8] Even in a large economy. For an analysis of the efficiency properties of monopolistic competitive industries, see e.g. Hart, (1979).

[9] There are a number of other problems with this mechanism in the market for knowledge. I do not go into them here. But see Dasgupta, (1988).

[10] For example, the first systematic use of patents began in Venice in 1474, when the Republic promised privileges of ten years to inventors of new arts and machines. The rule of priority in science was institutionalized in the seventeenth century, with the rise of parliaments of scientists, specifically the Royal Society of England (1662).

[11] In an early discussion the late Michael Polanyi, (Polanyi, 1943–4), suggested that the patent system should be abolished, that it should be

III. Basic and applied research

The analysis of Section II suggests that von Weizsäcker's three-level classification of economic activity is too coarse. One would want to classify knowledge into types to see whether there is at least a tendency for the market and non-market mechanisms to produce specific types. As it happens there is a classification which is of use for this purpose: basic and applied knowledge. In his classic article, Arrow (1962), thought of basic research as that kind of activity, the output of which is used only as an informational input into other inventive activities. By way of contrast, applied research is the kind of activity whose informational output is an input in the production of commodities—von Weizsäcker's intermediate level.

There are, of course, other classification schemes that are similar in spirit, though some are misleading. Thus it is a commonplace to think of science as being concerned with basic research and technology with applied research. On occasion one distinguishes abstract from concrete knowledge, and on other occasions the search for principles from the seeking of applications. And so forth. It would be out of place here to discuss connections between these classification schemes. The basic-applied research distinction is adequate enough for my purposes.

The distinction is an analytical one and in actual practice it is not clear cut. Moreover, the intention of a researcher is often quite different from his actual performance. Much basic knowledge has been acquired as an accidental outcome of what is applied research. For example, the immediate motivation behind Pasteur's research around 1870 was to solve certain practical problems connected with fermentation in the local wine industry. He was successful in this. But the by-product of his research is what made him immortal. The history of science and technology is littered with instances of this.

These are happy accidents, a bonus as it were, and although they are not rare, the immediate target of the researcher is in such cases the solution to an applied problem. The fact that there are happy accidents does not rule out the desirability of conducting basic research, that is, where the goal itself is basic knowledge. In his oft-cited essay Arrow (1962) advanced the argument that the more basic the character of the research the more in need it is of public funding. He argued this from two observations. First, the intended

replaced by a system where inventors are rewarded out of public funds and that potential users should have unrestricted access to the inventions. Polanyi was thus arguing (by design) that an imperfect Pigovian solution is superior to an imperfect Lindahl solution.

output of basic research (we are calling it basic knowledge) is more difficult to appropriate than applied knowledge (which is to be taken to mean knowledge applicable directly to the production of material commodities). We have already touched upon this.

The second observation is more controversial. Arrow argued that the value of basic research is more conjectural than that of applied research and is therefore more likely to be undervalued by private individuals and firms. The idea here is that private firms and individuals are likely to be more risk averse than they would be if acting collectively through the government, and so may avoid undertaking basic research to any large extent because of its greater uncertainty. A related idea is that basic research involves on average a longer gestation lag than applied research. If private rates of discount exceed social rates, either because of myopia or because of imperfect capital markets, there is a case for the provision of public assistance to basic research.

These arguments have had an influence on public policy towards basic research, both in Western Europe and in the United States.[12] While the share of basic research expenditure incurred by the Federal Government in the United States has been declining in recent years, it is still about two-thirds of the total. (See National Science Foundation, 1986.) In a recent interesting essay Rosenberg (1988) provides evidence to indicate that these arguments are also correct. For example, he notes that the most successful basic research laboratories in the private sector have been in firms that have strong market positions, such as Bell Labs., IBM, Dupont, Dow Chemical, Eastman Kodak, etc. Being large and enduring they can absorb risk and take the long view. Their research success has been to a large extent due to the close intellectual proximity maintained between the basic research laboratories and the development and production wings of these firms.

It was noted earlier that even though the transmission cost of knowledge may be low, the cost of absorbing the information, of interpreting it and using it fruitfully may well be very high. This is often the case with research output at the frontiers of science and technology. Firms wishing to make use of the latest findings that are publicly available need to have scientists who can make it possible for them to do so. A good portion of the 'technology' of their being able to do so consists in their pursuing basic research! This provides one reason why private firms conduct basic research.[13]

All this is to see basic knowledge as an accidental outcome of applied research, or as being tied to applied research. In fact, of course, many of the most creative leaps that humankind has made have been made by thinkers chasing an intellectual problem thrown up internally by their subjects of specialization. If one had asked the late Professor Paul Dirac what he was doing when attempting to write down the relativistic quantum field equation for the electron, he would have answered that he was attempting just that. The avenues along which basic knowledge grows are many and varied, and typically unpredictable. It is for this reason one hears the argument that a part of the public subsidy for research ought to be earmarked for creative persons rather than projects. Creative people can be relied upon to choose promising problems. That is what makes them creative. One reason behind the astonishing success of the Cavendish Laboratory at Cambridge immediately after the Second World War was that its then Director pursued this policy.

The direction which these considerations point at then is this. Centralized information about promising avenues of research, both applied and basic, is by the nature of things necessarily sparse. Such diverse and specialized knowledge is dispersed among professionals in their fields; scientists, technologists, market analysts, and so on. R & D decisions have to be decentralized. For reasons that we have explored, much basic research needs to be funded publicly, along Pigovian lines, where persons and teams are funded but where the choice of research programmes and strategies are left to the researchers themselves. Of course, the detailed organization of decisions that ought to be established is a complex matter, as current discussion on the subject in the United Kingdom shows. Here I have for obvious reasons been painting the organizational structures in broad strokes, in terms of prototypes.

The matter is different for applied research. Appropriability of applied knowledge is easier. Moreover, a good deal of applied research addresses the development of products and manufacturing processes, involving less in the way of an advancement of one's understanding of basic principles. There is then a supposition that on average applied research, as we have defined it here, is intellectually less enticing. Thus for example the oft-made claim that many scientists hanker after knowledge for its own sake is one made about those who are attracted to basic research. For these reasons as well there is an *a-priori* case for relying in the main on the private sector for applied research by

[12] See Mowery (1983) for a good discussion of the influence these arguments have had on public policy towards basic research in the United States.

[13] A related reason is the large demand of governments for equipment connected with warfare. Private firms conduct basic research in these fields so as to be able to compete against one another for government contracts.

instituting intellectual property rights, such as patents, copyrights, and trademarks.[14] There is then the question of efficient property rights and the desirability of preventing excessive duplication of R & D in the private sector. In the next two sections I go into these issues.

IV. Efficient property rights

At first blush the structure of efficient property rights is obvious. The Arrow-Debreu theory tells us that if it is costless to establish markets, each and every commodity ought to be supported by a competitive market in a private ownership economy. There is then an immediate problem in using the theory when knowledge is treated as a commodity.[15] For suppose that given any knowledge base there are constant returns to scale in the production of commodities. Since R & D involves the expenditure of resources, production of commodities, including knowledge, must involve increasing returns to scale. Thus in particular firms must be allowed to earn profits from their production activities in order to recoup their R & D expenditure. Patents are designed to allow that to happen, to prevent competition in the producer market. But the problem is that it is not clear what a patent means.

We noted in Section II that the right way to think of the production of knowledge is to think about the economics of product differentiation. Inventions and discoveries differ by way of the characteristics of the information associated with them. A statement made with 95 per cent confidence is different from what is verbally the same statement made with 90 per cent confidence. Not by much perhaps, but they are by no means the same. A patent provides a protected sphere around the characteristics of the invention made by the patent holder. We should therefore be interested

not only in the optimal *duration* of patents, but we should also be interested in the optimal *tightness* of patents, or in other words, the size of the protected sphere. In addressing this question I shall elaborate upon an argument put to me by Professor Carl Shapiro of Princeton University.

Purely for the sake of expositional ease I suppose that knowledge characteristics can be aggregated adequately into a scalar number. We then have a natural metric, providing us with a distance measure between any two pieces of information. Without loss of generality I suppose that the state of knowledge at the initial date ($t = 0$) is zero. For simplicity I assume that the cost of producing knowledge of measure y ($y \geq 0$) is k(y). (This cost can be thought of as being the expenditure of a numeraire commodity, say income.) The greater the extent of the invention, the greater is the cost. Thus $k'(y) > 0$.[16] We may think of y as the extent of a cost reducing invention, or an index of the quality improvement of an existing product.

Denote by x the size of the protected sphere around the discovery. The interpretation is that when a discovery is made the discoverer is protected from entry by rivals into the region consisting of points within a distance x from the discovery, y. (It should be remembered that when the discoverer of y announces it rivals can, unless prevented by law, make use of y without having to incur k(y).) Let T be the duration of this protection, the patent length. Let B(x,y) denote the flow of social benefits and P(x,y) the flow of private profits to the discoverer. Making standard assumptions we would conclude that $B_x(x,y) < 0$, $B_y(x,y) > 0$, $P_x(x,y) > 0$, $P_y(x,y) > 0$, and $P(0,y) = 0$ for all y. In what follows I ignore income effects. The government is to choose x, y and T with a view to maximizing the present value of social benefits, subject to the constraint that the present value of profits earned by the inventor is non-negative.[17] Let r (>0) be the social rate of discount, assumed without loss of generality to be equal to the discount rate of the private sector. It follows that the government's problem is: Choose x (≥ 0), y (≥ 0) and T (≥ 0) so as to maximize

$$\int_0^T B(x,y)e^{-rt}dt + (B(o,y)/r)e^{-rT} - k(y) \quad (1)$$

[14] It should be noted that English and American patent laws, as forerunners of modern patent laws elsewhere, expressly forbade patenting a 'fact of nature'. The problem is that it is not clear what is a fact of nature. This was illustrated recently in the litigation over the Stanford University and the University of California at Berkeley patents on recombinant DNA. Under United States Law, a patent can be awarded to cover '. . . any new and useful process, machine, manufacture, or composition of matter, or any new and useful improvement thereof'. The duration of a US patent is 17 years from the date of issue.

[15] I am ignoring oft-cited problems connected with the fact that research often throws up unthought of possibilities, more specifically surprise events, so that the information partition not only becomes finer with discoveries, it contains elements not included previously. These issues are pertinent not only to the Arrow-Debreu theory but to decision theory in particular and economics in general.

[16] As usual, for simplicity of exposition I assume that the discovery is made instantaneously. I ignore uncertainty in the R & D process since this will raise additional matters. For an analysis of this last see Dasgupta (1989). See also Section V.

[17] Thus, the government is a Stackleberg leader. I suppose for simplicity of exposition that competition among potential inventors leads in equilibrium to a single agent carrying out the R & D at a pace which the government can choose so long as it does not yield negative present value profits.

Subject to the constraint

$$\int_0^T P(x, y)e^{-rt}dt \geq k(y).$$

To have a non-trivial problem suppose that it is socially beneficial to have some discovery. It is then a trivial matter to confirm that the optimal values of x and y satisfy the pair of conditions

$$P(x,y) = rk(y) \qquad (2)$$

and
$$P_x(x,y) [B_y(x,y) - rk'(y)]$$
$$= B_x(x,y) [P_y(x,y) - rk'(y)]; \qquad (3)$$

and that the optimal value of T is infinity. In other words, the patent issued should be a permanent one, but the protected sphere defining the patent on y should be of the smallest size consistent with the researcher being willing to undertake the research (condition [2]). Putting it slightly differently, the intellectual property should be a freehold, but the property should be defined as narrowly as is compatible with incentives on the part of the private sector to produce the property.

An immediate implication of conditions (2) and (3) is that the size of the optimum protected sphere is not invariant to the kind of discovery we are studying. This follows at once from the fact that both the social benefit function, B, and the private profit function, P, depend upon the type of knowledge production we are considering. What is invariant is the optimum length of the patent. This invariance result should be contrasted with the results in Nordhaus (1969), Dasgupta and Stiglitz (1980b), Stoneman (1987) and Dasgupta (1989), which argue that the optimum patent length is finite and that it is dependent upon the type of discovery being studied. I shall presently try and explain why we are obtaining such strikingly different results.

Why do we not see the policy implied by (1) put into practice? There are several reasons. Here I want to concentrate on one which brings out quite sharply a feature of knowledge production which is not captured in (1). It has to do with private learning and it carries with it the implication that the solution of (1) is not implementable; in short, it is inconsistent with incentives.

Let x* and y* denote the solution to (1). By hypothesis, the initial state of knowledge is zero. (This, as we noted, is merely a normalization, of no significance.) But y* > 0. Thus the optimum solution envisages a discrete change in the state variable, namely the state of knowledge. Consider the agent who has made the discovery. Assume for the moment that the agent does not disclose his finding. Thus, the state of knowledge of this agent is y*, that of all others is still nil. But now the cost of discovering all pieces of knowledge in the

neighbourhood of y* is tiny for the agent in question and is approximately k(y*) for each of the others. The knowledgeable person has a great advantage over the rest. So then when the discoverer applies for a patent he will seek a patent not only on y*, but on all pieces of knowledge in the neighbourhood of y*, the size of the neighbourhood depending upon how easy it is for the discoverer to scan around the discovery y*. In general when this learning effect is large, the neighbourhood the discoverer can scan pretty much costlessly exceeds x*. One concludes that when a discoverer applies for a patent he applies for a patent on an entire region in the space of knowledge characteristics. It follows that in general x* is not implementable: the protected sphere cannot be made as small as the government might ideally like. From this it follows at once that the optimum patent length is finite.[18]

V. Joint ventures

Research projects have uncertain yields. No one who launches a programme of research can be certain of the outcome. Each project possesses an irreducible element which is specific to the team conducting it; which is another way of saying that in characterizing a project one must include the minds that are directing and conducting it. Thus, a part of the uncertainty concerning output is what one might call 'team-specific'. It follows from this that the uncertainties faced by two research teams can never be fully and positively correlated.[19] They would not be fully and positively correlated even if, acting as separate teams, they were to pursue what is otherwise the same programme of research.

It can be argued that private firms competing for a patent pursue overly correlated projects (Dasgupta and Maskin, 1987). This they tend to do even when they are neutral to risk. The intuition behind this result makes clearer the effect of the institution of patents on R & D races. As we noted earlier, patents aim

---

[18] Nordhaus (1969) and Stoneman (1987) explored the optimum lengths of patents when, as in (1) above, the R & D process involves no uncertainty. This enabled them to postulate that in equilibrium there is a single agent engaged in R & D. Dasgupta and Stiglitz (1980b) explored some of the additional problems that arise if firms face independent uncertainties regarding their R & D technologies. In equilibrium the number of firms in this sort of situation is not unity and one has to correct for the fact that the number of active firms is also affected by the patent length. The result in Dasgupta and Stiglitz (1980b) concerning the length of optimum patents is valid only if the patent holder is a perfectly discriminating monopolist. Dasgupta (1989) corrects the erroneous statement in the earlier paper that it does not depend upon this assumption.

[19] They can, of course, be fully and negatively correlated if they are involved in, say, testing mutually exclusive hypotheses.

at awarding all private profits to the winner of the race, the more comprehensive a patent the greater is the flow of profits to the winner. If a firm were to choose a research project which is less correlated with the project chosen by its rival, it would bestow a positive externality on the rival. Specifically, the likelihood that the rival is successful when the firm in question is not, would increase. This is socially desirable (because cet. par. society does not care who wins the patent, so long as a good discovery is made), but it is not picked up in the firm's private calculation. As our intuitions about externalities would suggest, this means that there is excessive similarity among the research projects pursued by private firms engaged in a patent race.

Entry into patent races can be a cause of waste. If entry is relatively costless there can be a dissipation of expected rents from inventions, as firms chase an invention knowing that there is *some* chance of winning the patent. It is possible to show that under a wide class of cases, patent competition results in firms pursuing an excessive number of parallel research projects. (Loury, 1979; Dasgupta and Stiglitz, 1980*a,b*.) This is another way of saying that the market can sustain excessive duplication.[20]

This is a special kind of market failure, and it is not easy to see how it can be corrected for by R & D taxes. In order to impose such corrective taxes the government needs to be able to monitor a firm's R & D programme in specific details. (How else is the government to judge that it has chosen an overly duplicative programme?) This the firm rightly will not wish to allow, because this would disclose information and would dilute the firm's prospects of appropriating the benefits from its R & D effort. The discussion of Section II is relevant again. Disclosure (of one's R & D project) dilutes the incentives for undertaking R & D in the first place. One concludes that the prescription of an externality tax is incompatible with incentives.

I would argue that these possibilities on their own provide some justification for the encouragement of joint R & D ventures among private firms. They are different from the argument that is most often put forward in popular writings, that joint ventures enable firms to pool their R & D risks and thereby enable them to undertake projects which otherwise would not be undertaken.[21]

The distinction between basic and applied research is somewhat blurred in a joint venture, for the reason that such programmes are highly targeted towards commercial goals. But in principle one can ask about the appropriate mix of co-operation and competition, even at the R & D stage. For example, one can imagine firms co-operating in basic research; that is, pooling their research laboratories and sharing the output of basic research, and then competing at the development stage once the basic research is completed. On the other hand, one often sees in practice an agreement to share the costs and output of R & D (both basic and developmental), to be followed by competition in commodity production. Then there are examples, such as EUREKA, where the venture is joint all the way from research and development to the product market, what I shall call a vertically integrated joint venture.

In a closed economy an analysis of a vertically integrated joint venture may seem in effect an analysis of pure monopoly. But this would not be correct. When firms enter a joint venture they do not become a single firm. Their R & D laboratories will co-operate but they will not become a single laboratory. This makes the analysis of joint ventures difficult even when they are vertically integrated. Nevertheless, many of the ingredients of any such analysis are embedded in the discussions of Sections II and III.

Within joint ventures a distinction should be made between two polar cases: (i) those where the venture not only allows firms to co-ordinate their policies, it also commits them to share their newly discovered knowledge; and (ii) those where the only gain is a co-ordination of policies. The key feature underlying (ii) is that the extent to which knowledge is shared is not subject to control: a certain 'fraction' of each firm's R & D output spills over to the rival firm whether or not they agree on a joint venture. The distinction therefore is based on the extent to which the firms' R & D laboratories are combined by the venture. Underlying (i) is the assumption that the laboratory outputs are common property. Underlying (ii) is the hypothesis that they are kept separate, but that their funding is determined by a joint policy.

Our earlier discussion is directly applicable to (i), and in fact it is (i) which is most often alluded to in the literature. A central gain, both to the firms involved and to society, is the sharing of knowledge. As against this is a possible loss to society, occasioned by the fact that a joint venture implies greater monopoly power. The gain from shared knowledge is absent from (ii),

[20]   We emphasize the use of the term 'excessive' because it is often desirable socially to have several parallel research projects in operation, just as it is desirable to hold a diversified financial portfolio.

[21]   Within the European Economic Community members are engaged in large-scale operations, such as RACE (Research in Advanced Telecommunication Technology for Europe Programme), EUREKA (European Research Coordination Agency), ESPRIT (European Strategic Pro-

gramme for R & D in Information Technologies); and in the United States by MCC (Microelectronics and Computer Technology Corporation).

because by hypothesis the extent to which knowledge is made common is unaffected by the venture, although of course the amount of knowledge each firm produces *is* affected.[22]

In a recent interesting note d'Aspremont and Jacquemin (1987) have analysed the implications of joint ventures with (ii) as the background situation. There is no uncertainty postulated, R & D is directed at process innovations, and the R & D technology is assumed to enjoy no scale economies. It is supposed that a certain amount of knowledge spills across the firms' R & D laboratories in an exogenous manner. (This last is what makes the venture one of pure co-ordination; case [ii].)

Knowledge spillovers are a form of positive externality. So it might be thought that a joint venture must necessarily involve greater R & D expenditure: the venture after all internalizes the externality. But this would be wrong. The point is that if the joint venture were to be restricted to a co-ordination of R & D expenditure, the firms would expect to compete in the product market once R & D were completed. The firms would know in advance that after the completion of R & D there will be no jointly agreed production policy. Given this, they may well choose to agree on a lower R & D expenditure level, lower than, that is, the level that would emerge if they were not to have a joint venture.

Clearly then the answer depends upon the extent of knowledge spillover. If this is large a joint R & D venture would be expected to result in greater R & D expenditure and, indeed, even greater output production. This can be shown to be the case. (See d'Aspremont and Jacquemin, 1987.) In fact it can be shown that if knowledge spillovers are large a vertically integrated joint venture would be expected to sustain even greater R & D expenditure than a mere R & D joint venture. Where a vertically integrated joint venture is restrictive is at the production stage, and consumers can end up paying a higher product price even though production costs are lower because of the integrated nature of the venture. The greater surplus is captured by what is in effect a monopolist and distributed to shareholders. A joint venture, whether restricted to the R & D stage or whether integrated fully, does not produce the first-best efficient outcome. But if spillovers are large an R & D joint venture can be closer to it than unbridled competition.

These results are congenial to intuition. They also indicate that our broad-brush discussion of the welfare economics of knowledge production has probably been along the right lines. The tension we noted earlier in this essay, between the need for co-ordination and sharing of produced knowledge, the paucity of centralized information about R & D possibilities, and dilution of private incentives to produce knowledge if it is to be shared, is at the heart of the basis upon which public policy has to be geared.

References

Arrow, K. J. (1962), 'Economic Welfare and the Allocation of Resources for Inventions', in Nelson, R. R. (ed.), *The Rate and Direction of Inventive Activity: Economic and Social Factors*, Princeton University Press.

—— (1971), 'Political and Economic Evaluation of Social Effects and Externalities', in Intriligator, M. (ed.), *Frontiers of Quantitative Economics*, Vol. I, Amsterdam, North Holland.

d'Aspremont, C., and Jacquemin, A. (1987), 'A Note on Cooperative and Non Cooperative R & D in Duopoly', *American Economic Review*.

Baumol, W. J., and Oates, W. E. (1975), *The Theory of Environmental Policy: Externalities, Public Outlays and the Quality of Life*, Englewood Cliffs, NJ, Prentice Hall.

Dasgupta, P. (1988), 'Patents, Priority and Imitation or, The Economics of Races and Waiting Games', *Economic Journal*, 98.

—— (1989), 'The Economics of Parallel Research', in Hahn, F. (ed.), *The Economic Theory of Information, Games, and Missing Markets*, Oxford University Press.

—— and David, P. (1988), 'Priority, Secrecy, Patents and the Socio-Economics of Science and Technology', CEPR Publication No. 127, Stanford University.

—— and Heal, G. (1979), *Economic Theory and Exhaustible Resources*, Cambridge University Press.

—— and Maskin, E. (1987), 'The Simple Economics of Research Portfolios', *Economic Journal*, 97.

—— and Stiglitz, J. E. (1980*a*), 'Market Structure and the Nature of Innovative Activity', *Economic Journal*, 90.

—— (1980*b*), 'Uncertainty, Industrial Structure and the Speed of R & D', *Bell Journal of Economics*, Spring.

—— (1988), 'Learning-by-Doing, Market Structure and Industrial and Trade Policies', *Oxford Economic Papers*, 40.

Hart, O. (1979), 'Monopolistic Competition in a Large Economy with Differentiated Commodities', *Review of Economic Studies*, 46.

Kamien, M., and Schwartz, N. (1978), 'Potential Rivalry, Monopoly Profits and the Pace of Inventive Activity', *Review of Economic Studies*, 45.

Levin, R. (1978), 'Technical Change, Barriers to Entry and Market Structure', *Economica*, 45.

---

[22] A good deal of the urgency expressed within the EEC and the USA about having joint ventures in R & D, especially in high-technology industries, is the competitive threat from Japan. In the text I shall ignore such gains from joint ventures and ask whether there are gains to a society in having R & D ventures *even* if it were to face no competitive threat from outside.

Loury, G. (1979), 'Market Structure and Innovation', *Quarterly Journal of Economics*, 93.

Marx, K. (1970), *Capital*, London, Lawrence and Wisehart.

Mowery, D. C. (1983), 'Economic Theory and Government Technology Policy', *Policy Sciences*, 16.

Musgrave, R. A., and Peacock, A. T. (eds.) (1968), *Classics in the Theory of Public Finance*, London, Macmillan.

National Science Foundation (1986), 'National Patterns of Science and Technology Resources', NSF, 86–309, Washington DC.

Nordhaus, W. (1969), *Invention, Growth and Welfare*, Cambridge, Mass., MIT Press.

Pigou, A. C. (1932), *The Economics of Welfare*, London, Macmillan.

Polanyi, M. (1943–4), 'Patent Reform', *Review of Economic Studies*.

Rosenberg, N. (1988), 'Why Do Companies Do Basic Research (with their own Money)?', mimeo. Department of Economics, Stanford University.

Samuelson, P. A. (1954), 'The Pure Theory of Public Expenditure', *Review of Economics and Statistics*, 36.

Schumpeter, J. (1976), *Capitalism, Socialism and Democracy*, 5th edn, London, Allen and Unwin.

Stoneman, P. (1987), *The Economic Analysis of Technology Policy*, Oxford, Oxford University Press.

von Weizsäcker, C. C. (1980), *Barriers to Entry: A Theoretical Treatment*, Berlin, Springer-Verlag.

PART III

COMPETITION AND REGULATORY POLICY

6

Competition policy

DONALD HAY

Jesus College and Institute of Economics and Statistics, Oxford[1]

I. Introduction

A precondition for a successful market economy is the existence of an effective competition policy. The need for such a policy was recognized by Adam Smith when he wrote in *The Wealth of Nations* in 1776: 'People of the same trade seldom meet together, even for merriment and diversion, but the conversation ends in a conspiracy against the public, or in some instances to raise prices.' The problem, as many writers since Adam Smith have recognized, is that a market can be manipulated to give some of those involved greater economic power so that competition is distorted and economic efficiency impaired. There may also be ethical and social objections to the absence of competition: it is simply not fair that large firms or cartels should be able to oppress smaller competitors and/or customers by charging prices that greatly exceed the costs of supply. It is perhaps notable that a key piece of UK legislation is called the Fair Trading Act and the main UK competition policy institution is the Office of Fair Trading (OFT). Alternatively, there may be a commitment to competition as the appropriate form of economic organization, either because competition is a good in itself, or because it delivers the goods.

The objective of this paper is to advance four propositions about the purpose, scope, and implementation of competition policy, and to measure existing policies against these theses. The first proposition, that the role of competition policy should be to promote economic efficiency, is explored in section II. Alternative views of the matter are that competition policy should be guided by some broader notion of the public interest, including perhaps non-economic social objectives,

or that competition, *per se*, should be promoted. There is evidence that despite differing objectives at the origination of policy in the USA, European Union (EU), and UK, the growing consensus is that the focus should be on economic efficiency. Papers on competition-policy themes by economists generally make the assumption that economic efficiency is the goal.

The second proposition, discussed in section III, is that economic analysis is generally ambiguous, a priori, about the efficiency effects of particular market structures and conduct. This proposition builds on the considerable advances in industrial organization of the past 20 years, which have enabled theorists to identify the policy issues raised by a wide range of market phenomena. However, the problem for competition policy is that trade-offs are more or less ubiquitous, and only in a few cases (price-fixing or market-sharing are examples) is it possible to reach an unambiguous verdict.

The third proposition, in section IV, builds on the first two. It is that the appropriate design of policy and policy institutions is crucial to a successful competition policy. In particular, given the ambiguity of economic analysis, policy has to identify rules or presumptions to indicate the boundaries between acceptable and unacceptable market conduct and structure, but it has to offer at least some scope for the parties involved in such cases to argue countervailing efficiency benefits. Institutionally, implementation of policy requires a public procedure. We identify an ideal where there is a public competition policy institution empowered to identify, investigate, and propose remedies for failures of competition, with a competition tribunal to review cases where the institution is proposing fines for abuses, or where the firms are unwilling to accept the initial findings.

The final thesis is that international harmonization of competition policies is essential (Graham and

First published in *Oxford Review of Economic Policy*, vol. 9, no. 2 (1993). This version has been updated and revised to incorporate recent developments in UK competition policy.

Richardson, 1997), and probably a supranational competition authority is needed as well. This proposition is the subject of section V of the paper, and reflects the growing internationalization of economic activity, with multinational enterprises supplying markets that extend beyond the boundaries of particular states (and therefore the jurisdiction of competition authorities). A particular example is the development of EU competition policy, and its relation to policies of member states. Another concern is that national governments may use competition policy as an instrument to protect domestic markets against overseas entrants, or to promote the interests of domestic producers in world markets; this suggests the need to harmonize policy in different economies, and to seek international agreements to desist from using policy in a protectionist manner.

In the next four sections we explore these propositions, before using them to evaluate competition policy in the UK in the context of the EU in sections VI and VII.

II. First proposition

The role of competition policy should be to promote economic efficiency.

There are at least three schools of thought about what competition policy is seeking to achieve. Mainstream industrial organization argues that the purpose of the policy is to promote economic efficiency. Competition is not an end in itself. Rather it is to be encouraged as a means to improving economic efficiency, where 'efficiency' is defined in terms of partial equilibrium welfare economics, that is the maximization of the sum of the discounted present value of consumer and producer surpluses (Hay and Morris, 1991, chs. 16 and 17). This definition encompasses the trade-off between static and dynamic efficiency: current welfare losses may be acceptable, if the market structure or conduct which gives rise to the losses will also generate efficiencies in the long run, so long as the prospective benefits are not too delayed in realization and the social discount rate is not too high.

It is important to define quite carefully what is meant by 'competition'. Traditionally, competition has been understood in terms of price competition, with firms pursuing their own self-interest in the setting of prices, not colluding with each other. However, it has been shown that, under a variety of assumptions about information conditions, collusive outcomes are

supportable as perfect Nash equilibria in repeated games (see Tirole, 1989, ch. 6 for a convenient summary), and in any case the Nash–Cournot non-cooperative equilibrium yields a price in excess of the competitive outcome. Furthermore, price-cutting can in some circumstances be anti-competitive: predatory pricing to drive out a rival or an entrant, or low prices seeking to mislead entrants about the efficiency of the incumbent firms are cases in point (Milgrom and Roberts, 1982; Phlips, 1995, ch. IV). Competition can, of course, come in other forms. In differentiated goods markets firms may compete on the number of brands they put on the market, in quality, and in marketing (including advertising). It is not always the case that a partial equilibrium welfare analysis will show unequivocally that more 'competition' in this form is better. For example, brand proliferation may generate a welfare loss through excessive expenditure on fixed costs associated with each brand (Schmalensee, 1978; Salop, 1979). At least some competitive advertising may be wasteful, as firms seek to duplicate each other's expenditures in order to avoid market-share losses (Lambin, 1976; Dixit and Norman, 1978). In the long run firms may compete in physical investment or in R&D, leading to duplication of capacity or innovation expenditures. The outcome of such competition may be that one firm emerges as the 'winner', able to dominate the market and earn monopoly rents (Gilbert and Newbery, 1982). The sunk costs involved in building a strong market position may additionally become a barrier to entry, even if the intention was 'innocent' competition rather than a deliberate strategy to exclude potential competitors. The welfare evaluation of such competition is far from unequivocal. The conclusion is that 'promoting competition' is not sufficient in itself, if the objective of competition policy is to improve economic efficiency. We need to be clear what is meant by competition, and different kinds of competitive behaviour need to be separately evaluated.

A second, smaller but nevertheless vociferous, school of thought argues that competition, in and of itself, is the appropriate objective: this neo-Austrian approach is more concerned with process than with outcomes, and in its extreme statement is not concerned with evaluation of economic efficiency at all. A moderate exposition is that of Littlechild (1986), who argues that it is the process of competition which matters, and that the concept of economic efficiency which emerges from static welfare analysis is at best misleading. The competitive process arises out of disequilibrium in markets giving opportunities for entrepreneurs to exploit their superior information and earn profits. Equilibrium is never achieved, because the market is always changing due to new information, innovation, and shocks. Monopoly profits are (or should be) eroded by the entry of new firms and products, which are able to displace the incumbent firms by offering lower prices or a better product. So monopoly profits are a reward to innovation and entrepreneurship and a signal to competitors rather than a 'welfare loss'. For Littlechild, therefore, the objectives of competition policy should be the promotion of competition, by acting against market conduct designed to inhibit it.

Both the economic efficiency and neo-Austrian schools of thought express concerns about the views of a third school, which either has some fairly broad concept of the public interest as its stated objective, or in practice is motivated by more than a single-minded pursuit of economic efficiency and/or competition. UK competition policy, for example, still does not focus solely on economic efficiency. The Competition Act 1998 does indeed give sole priority to the promotion of competition. But Section 84 of the Fair Trading Act 1973, which has been retained for cases involving scale monopolies, complex monopolies, and mergers, lists five criteria in determining the public interest. The first refers to effective competition between suppliers, the third makes reference to long-run competition through new products, processes, and entry to the market, and the fifth relates to maintaining and promoting competitive activity in markets outside the United Kingdom. The second criterion refers to the promotion of the interests of consumers and purchasers of goods and services via quality and variety. The fourth criterion is 'maintaining and promoting the balanced distribution of industry and employment in the United Kingdom'. This last criterion was applied in the Charter Consolidated Ltd/Anderson Strathclyde Ltd Report (1982), where the concern was for the effects of the merger on employment in an area of Scotland which already had high unemployment. Similarly, in Swedish Match AB/Alleghany International Inc. (1987), one reason adduced for permitting the merger was that a factory in a high-unemployment area of Liverpool would thereby be saved from closure. It is important to note that these criteria are not intended to be an exhaustive definition of the public interest. Indeed, the old Monopolies and Mergers Commission on numerous occasions addressed other public-interest issues. For example, in Lonrho/House of Fraser (1979), it concerned itself with the managerial capacity of a particular individual. In a number of cases it raised a question about a UK company passing into the control of an overseas company. Thus the issue in Shanghai Banking Corporation/Royal Bank of Scotland (1982) was whether it was acceptable for a major UK clearing bank to be controlled from outside the UK, and the likely consequences for the conduct of UK monetary policy. In Government of Kuwait/British Petroleum (1988) the Commission concluded that control of BP by the Kuwaiti government would operate against the public interest. More recently, the question has been raised as to whether it is contrary to the public interest for a private company to be taken over by a foreign state-owned company, given the privatization objectives of the UK government. In Elders IXL/Allied Lyons (1986) the Commission concerned itself with the method by which Elders' bid was to be financed, but came to the view that the issue of leveraged bids was not one on which it should pronounce.

Competition law in the USA is ostensibly focused on competition and economic efficiency. However, historically at least, the origins of US antitrust were somewhat different. Neale (1970, p. 459), for example, noted that:

the rationale for antitrust is essentially a device to provide legal checks to economic power, and is not a pursuit of economic efficiency as such. Consequently the question asked is not whether antitrust decisions lead to the greatest economic efficiency but whether it can be said, given the non-economic reasons for antitrust policy, that these decisions do any serious harm.

According to Neale, the origin of US antitrust legislation, beginning with the Sherman Act in 1890, was a desire to limit the power of big business and trusts, and in particular to protect small business and consumers against their predatory behaviour. George Hay (1987) has shown how this approach to antitrust survived into the post-Second-World-War period with the adverse judgements in the Alcoa and United Shoe Machinery cases, where the companies concerned were condemned for 'monopolization' of their respective markets, despite the fact that they had only employed normal competitive means to acquire and maintain their dominant positions. However, from 1975 consumer surplus became the primary focus of antitrust cases in parallel with an increasing involvement of professional economists in antitrust institutions, and economists began to be used widely as expert witnesses. This was particularly evident in the IBM case, where several academic economists were drafted in to prepare IBM's defence (Fisher *et al.*, 1983), and more recently in the Microsoft case.

Despite these developments, White (1993) still describes US competition policy as 'sloppy', referring particularly to American populism that favours small firms against big business, to a contradictory respect for scale economies, and to the capture of governmental processes by rent-seeking special interests. In his review of the content of US antitrust, he indicates some areas of policy where the decisions are now largely driven by sound economic analysis (horizontal agreements and mergers) and others where the basis for judgements is less satisfactory and the practice sometimes inconsistent (vertical restraints and price discrimination). White also points to conflicts of antitrust policy with other areas of governmental regulation, notably utilities regulation, health–safety–environmental regulations, and incipient import protectionism.

The main objective of EU competition policy has always been the promotion of competition within the single European market, though arguments have sometimes been expressed in favour of industrial policies designed to improve the competitiveness of European firms in international markets (Sapir *et al.*, 1993). The stress on competition has led the competition Directorate of the European Commission (DGIV) to place a particular emphasis on attacking any behaviour which might appear to segment the European market into national markets. Thus in United Brands Co. v. Commission (1978), the Court held that United Brands had abused its dominant position by charging different prices for bananas according to the member state of their destination, where these prices could not be justified on the basis of transport costs. It was as if the Commission was seeking to impose a common market with common prices, rather than to ensure that competition prevailed. The result was that United Brands had to abandon what was generally acknowledged to be a highly efficient distribution system, arguably to the detriment of consumer welfare. While EU competition law has nothing equivalent to a wide 'public-interest' test, Article 81(3)[1] does permit the granting of exemptions for agreements between firms that can be shown to produce beneficial effects. Thus exemptions have been made available for R&D agreements, specialization agreements, and other agreements which seek to improve efficiency in production (Sapir *et al.*, 1993, give examples). There is considerable debate as to whether this category of 'beneficial effects' can be extended to take social objectives into account, for example in the treatment of recession cartels. Article 82, by contrast, has no section 3 to permit exemptions, which has sometimes been thought to be a weakness. Similarly, as Sapir *et al.* note, there is

no provision within the 1989 Merger Regulation for the Commission to consider trade-offs between productive efficiency and reduced competition in assessing mergers.

The comparison of the philosophy of competition policy in the three jurisdictions should serve as a warning against ignoring completely the 'public-interest' dimension. Whatever economists might like to think, economic efficiency is not the only consideration that is motivating policy. A solution might be to accept that while public policy in general cannot be confined to considerations of economic efficiency, it is inappropriate for competition policy to examine wider social costs and benefits. First, a wide definition of the public interest leads to policy implementation that is lacking in transparency: a firm and its advisers will be unable to judge whether or not a proposed course of conduct will be acceptable to the authorities. (This criticism was particularly levelled at the workings of the old Monopolies and Mergers Commission in the UK.)[2] A second reason is that wider economic consequences may be better dealt with by other branches of economic policy: for example, regional policy can be designed specifically to deal with localized unemployment problems, R&D policy to deal with the promotion of R&D and the protection of intellectual property rights. But this doctrine of matching policy instruments to policy variables is unlikely to be effective in all cases: for example, a desire for strategic reasons to protect a domestic defence industry from foreign takeovers, or a desire to maintain a diversity of ownership in the newspaper industry.

III. Second proposition

Economic analysis is often ambiguous, a priori, about the efficiency effects of particular market structures and conduct.

Despite differences of approach in different competition policy jurisdictions, the policy agenda is similar. Competition policy is concerned with agreements between firms, and with monopoly. In respect of monopoly, the concern is generally with the abuse of dominant positions in markets, including charging excessive prices, the practice of price discrimination and vertical restraints, and with the means by which dominant positions are acquired (including mergers)

---

[1] Previously Article 85(3) and often referred to as such in the literature. Similarly Article 82 was previously Article 86. See fn. 6 below.

[2] The Monopolies and Mergers Commission was replaced by the Competition Commission as a result of the Competition Act 1998.

and maintained. The difficulty with all these policy areas is that the effect on economic efficiency is by no means clear cut: there are nearly always benefits and losses that have to be weighed. In this section we will briefly indicate the nature of the trade-offs involved before turning, in the next section, to the implications for the design of competition policy.

1. Agreements between firms

Competition policy in respect of agreements between firms is based on the standard economic analysis of cartels and other collusive agreements (Jacquemin and Slade, 1989; Phlips, 1995, ch. I). The objective of such agreements is to raise prices and reduce output. How this is achieved by the colluding firms varies depending on the circumstances of the market, and the product. In fairly simple markets, agreements may focus on the price of a standardized product (including agreement on exactly what constitutes a standard product, e.g. terms and conditions of sale), or on production quotas for the participating firms. In more complex markets, the agreements may take the form of dividing up the market geographically or according to product type. Where the market is allocated on the basis of tenders, more intricate measures may be needed to ensure that the contracts are shared out, including perhaps 'allocation' of each contract to a particular firm and agreement on how the other firms will rig their bids to ensure that they are not awarded the contract 'by mistake'. The static welfare analysis of such practices is straightforward: price is higher and output lower than it would otherwise have been, so there is a welfare triangle loss. (This, of course, ignores the theory of the second best, where the existence of price distortions in related markets may require a price which exceeds marginal cost in the market under consideration. A counter to that argument is that an effective competition policy will seek to deal with related market price distortions at the same time.) Furthermore, there may also be an X-efficiency loss: high prices and the absence of competition may make firms slack in their use of resources, generating higher costs than would otherwise be the case. Note, however, that if the slack only takes the form of paying out some of the monopoly rents as higher remuneration to factors of production, then there is no efficiency loss implied.

A possible exception to this general conclusion of welfare loss from collusion was provided by Richardson (1965). He argued that in some markets the lumpy nature of demand made it essential that contracts be shared out, to ensure that the competi-

tors were not exposed to the risk of alternating 'feast and famine' in their order books. A similar argument applies to cases where investment is lumpy (e.g. large processing plants): agreements to take turns in investing may be necessary to avoid excess capacity being built (or to avoid insufficient capacity being built as firms are afraid of excess capacity!). In sectors that are suffering long-term or cyclical decline, arguments are often made for 'crisis' or 'recession' cartels, to prevent the scrapping of capacity that will remain viable in the longer term, and to ensure that contraction of the industry occurs in an orderly manner. A sector which faces a monopoly buyer may wish to organize itself to increase its bargaining power: the welfare effects of such a move are ambiguous. Finally, it should be noted that export cartels (to exploit monopoly rents in overseas markets), and import cartels (to increase bargaining power *vis-à-vis* overseas suppliers) improve the terms of trade for the domestic economy and can generate (like optimal tariffs) welfare gains. In practice, export cartels are not pursued by competition authorities in any of the three jurisdictions discussed above, though in the UK export agreements are supposed to be notified to the OFT.

If overt collusion is not permitted, then firms may be able to replicate its effect via tacit collusion (Tirole, 1989, ch. 6; Phlips, 1995, ch. II), which may take the form of 'conscious parallelism', with firms making identical price changes more or less at the same time. This feature of concentrated markets is discussed in the paper by Rees in this volume. He notes that successful collusion requires communication between the firms and that this is made much easier if they are able to exchange information about prices, outputs, and costs. Hence, in most competition policy jurisdictions, agreements to exchange information are frowned upon. But, as Phlips (1987) has pointed out, exchange of information may facilitate the establishment of non-cooperative equilibria, in a situation where demands and costs are changing rapidly. The alternative may be prices that tend to be sticky, unresponsive to shifts in the market. Furthermore, certain commercial practices, such as 'meeting competition clauses', 'most favoured nation' (MFN) clauses, and tie-ins that release the buyer if she can find a lower-price supplier elsewhere, can serve both to ensure information-sharing about discounts and price-cutting and to give (in the case of MFN clauses) an incentive not to cut price (see Salop, 1985). However, Rees also notes that collusion requires a mechanism to enforce agreements. Without such a mechanism, all communication is just 'cheap talk': there is no reason for a firm to believe what the others say. But theoretical analysis suggests that credible punishment strategies may need to be quite subtle and sophisticated, which leads to the conclusion that apparent 'tacit' collusion may involve 'secret' collusion. The implication, according to Rees, is that competition policy in this area should focus on outcomes rather than on market conduct.

As soon as the discussion extends to agreements between firms on other aspects of competition, the welfare analysis becomes even more ambiguous. The seminal analysis of Dixit and Norman (1978) suggested that competitive advertising by oligopolists (which the evidence suggests is mutually cancelling) generates a welfare loss, and that agreements to limit competitive advertising would therefore be beneficial. The difficulty with this result is that advertising is usually only one part of a marketing strategy, and that agreements on advertising are likely to spill over into other elements of that strategy, including prices. A similar difficulty arises with R&D agreements (see Geroski, 1993). The case for R&D agreements is partly that they avoid wasteful duplication of research, and allow complementary skills and risks to be pooled, but mainly that they internalize the information spillovers which mean that a single firm is unable to appropriate all the returns to its R&D efforts. Geroski's review of empirical studies suggests that the effectiveness of patents in ensuring appropriability is generally quite weak, that imitation lags are short, and imitation costs low compared to innovation costs. However, the evidence also suggests that information spillovers are more important in research than in development, and that a firm has to do quite a lot of its own R&D, if it is to be able to absorb information spillovers effectively. These results suggest that R&D agreements will generate the highest social benefits where they concentrate on R rather than D, which will in addition reduce the perceived risk that competition in the markets created by the innovations will be blunted. This risk will also be lessened where the firms involved produce complementary products rather than substitutes, where there are several R&D joint-ventures in the industry, and where joint marketing arrangements are not part of the agreements (joint production may be required for productive efficiency in exploiting the R&D results).

2. Abuse of dominant positions

The most obvious abuses of a dominant position are thought to be excessive pricing, price discrimination, predatory pricing, and vertical restraints. If a firm charges an excessive price, it generates a welfare triangle loss (as in the cartel case). The difficulty is to identify what might be an 'excessive price'. The point is raised most acutely in R&D-intensive sectors. The prices of pharmaceutical products have frequently been reviewed by competition authorities, and at first sight the mark-ups appear to be very large. The response of the companies is that such prices are necessary to recoup the costs of R&D, and to compensate for risk, since only a small proportion of R&D generates innovations that are commercially viable.

Price discrimination can take a number of forms (Phlips, 1983; Varian, 1989). First, it may be spatial in that prices are set to reflect demand conditions in different geographical markets, those prices not reflecting different costs of supply. Second, it may be competitive or 'predatory'—a lower price being charged in markets where actual or potential competition is more active. Third, price discrimination may appear in the guise of loyalty bonuses, rebates, and discounts. Fourth, discounts for 'full line' ordering and commodity bundling are best interpreted as forms of price discrimination. Each of these cases merits a separate welfare analysis. In principle, price discrimination is required for optimal resource allocation: for example, a monopolist practising perfect price discrimination will produce more output than a non-discriminating monopolist. However, Schmalensee (1981) has shown that discrimination allocates output inefficiently across consumers, which is undesirable unless offset by higher total output, e.g. where the discrimination permits additional markets to be served.

So-called 'predatory pricing' has provided a major conundrum for competition authorities. The concern of the authorities is that a dominant firm will price aggressively in those markets where it faces actual or potential competition with the intention of seeing off the competition. There has been much theoretical discussion of this possibility (see Tirole, 1989, ch. 9; Ordover and Saloner, 1989). The argument has to rely either on imperfect information about the predator's costs, so that price-cutting is a means of building a reputation for being efficient, or on a 'deep pocket' story where the predator has access to either internal or external funds to finance its activities (Bolton and Scharfstein, 1990). The defence of a firm accused of predatory pricing is often that it is merely responding to competition: so evidence of its intentions may be quite important in deciding whether a firm's conduct is predatory or not. Unfortunately for competition policy, such evidence will often be lacking, and actual conduct is all that the authorities have to go on. The welfare analysis of predatory pricing is also generally ambiguous. It is necessary to weigh the short-run gains from lower prices against the long-run detriment if the predator does succeed in establishing a monopoly position.

Bonuses, rebates, and discounts related to the buyers' past purchases from the supplier have also been frowned upon by the authorities. These 'loyalty discounts' give rise to switching costs, since a consumer who switches to another supplier loses the discount. Such switching costs can serve to facilitate collusion and to deter competitive entry (Klemperer, 1995). Once again there is a trade-off between lower effective prices in the short run, and the loss of more active price competition in the long run.

The issue of commodity bundling has been central to a number of celebrated competition policy cases, including those involving IBM in both the United States and Europe. The argument against commodity bundling is that by offering a bundle of goods at a lower price than the sum of the prices for the components of the bundle, the supplier is able to prevent competition from producers of individual goods within the bundle. (The situation is even more acute if the existence of intellectual property rights or product design by a dominant firm excludes rivals from supplying products that are compatible with its equipment; Whinston, 1990.) However, Adams and Yellen (1976) have shown that commodity bundling can be a form of price discrimination, which serves to sort consumers into groups with different demand characteristics and thereby to extend the market.

One unresolved issue is the extent to which price discriminatory practices can be taken as evidence of market dominance, since one view is that the authorities should only be concerned about such practices if the firm has a dominant position. Neven and Phlips (1985) show that price discrimination can occur in oligopoly, but that it disappears as the number of competitors increases. However, in a differentiated goods market even a small supplier might use price discrimination as a marketing strategy in its niche of the market, though the adverse effects on welfare will probably be slight.[3]

Another area of firm behaviour that has attracted the attention of competition authorities concerned with the abuse of dominant positions is vertical restraints. Examples of such restraints are exclusive distribution agreements, exclusive purchasing agreements, selective distribution systems and exclusive franchises, tie-ins, and full-line forcing, refusal to supply, and attempts at resale price maintenance (RPM). The consensus of economic analysis is that vertical agreements become a problem only if competition is absent in either the upstream or downstream market.[4] The basic idea is that vertical restraints create vertical structures of firms and distributors, including retailers, which compete in markets. If the markets are competitive, then there are efficiency gains from vertical restraints: vertical coordination in pricing to avoid 'double marginalization', and coordination in the provision of services to overcome incentive and free-rider problems. Vertical agreements may also be important for solving risk sharing and moral-hazard problems between the upstream and downstream firms to mitigate potential efficiency losses.

Waterson (this volume) comments that the welfare analysis of restraints is quite equivocal. They will often combine both pro-competitive and anti-competitive effects, and the net welfare effect is unclear. His analysis also shows that Bork's (1978) position, that there is no reason to interfere with contractual relationships since different firms may adopt different marketing strategies, is not sustainable.

3. The acquisition and maintenance of dominant positions

The acquisition of dominant positions in markets has long been a concern of US antitrust, where section 2 of the Sherman Act 1890 outlaws behaviour to 'monopolize or attempt to monopolize' a market. Article 82 of EU law is *prima facie* only concerned with the abuse of a monopoly position, though the Continental Can judgment implied that an attempt by a firm, which was already dominant, to increase its dominance (e.g. by merger) could be interpreted as an abuse. The UK legislation allows for the scrutiny of mergers, but is generally silent on the acquisition of dominant positions as opposed to the behaviour of firms in maintaining and exploiting these positions once achieved.

These are four means by which firms may achieve dominant positions in markets (Hay and Vickers, 1987):

---

[3] Before leaving the subject of price discrimination, it is worth noting again that actual competition policies on price discrimination are sometimes motivated by a concern to protect small businesses *vis-à-vis* large ones, even though the competitive effects of price discrimination may be beneficial (lower prices to consumers). This is certainly the case with the Robinson Patman Act 1936 in the USA. The same concern was expressed in the investigations of discounts to retailers in the UK (MMC Report on Discounts to Retailers, 1981; OFT, 1985), though these reports argued against a general prohibition of price discriminatory practices in favour of a case-by-case evaluation, and the focus was as much on the monopsony power of the larger retail chains.

[4] See Katz(1989); Dobson and Waterson (1996); Vickers (1996); European Commission (1997, ch.II); and Waterson (this volume).

(i)   The firm is granted market power by a public authority. This is most common in the utility industries—power, water, and telecommunications. In the USA these have always been private-sector firms, but subject to regulation. In the UK the process of privatization over the past 11 years has moved utilities from public to private ownership, again under a regime of regulation (Vickers and Yarrow, 1988; Armstrong *et al.*, 1994). The rationale for retaining at least part of these industries as single units is that they are 'natural monopolies' with subadditive costs, especially where networks are concerned. Regulation is an indication that competition policy cannot provide a solution to the monopolistic behaviour of these sectors.

(ii)   Achieving dominance by 'skill, foresight, and industry'. The problem for competition policy, as stated by Judge Learned Hand in the Alcoa decision (1945) in the USA, is that 'The successful competitor, having been urged to compete, must not be turned upon when he wins' (quoted in Schmalensee, 1987). The problem for competition policy is once again a trade-off. Dynamic competition to establish a dominant position may involve reducing costs, process innovation, and product innovation, which are welfare-enhancing. The resulting market power will generate static welfare losses. The problem is particularly acute where the dynamic competition involves investment in risky R&D: the market power it confers is the incentive for undertaking the investment.

(iii)   There is a further problem of distinguishing fair competition (lower prices, better quality) from anticompetitive behaviour, such as predatory pricing, which is the third means by which firms may come to dominate a market (Ordover and Saloner, 1989; Phlips, 1995, ch. IV). Predatory behaviour was discussed above, in the context of a firm abusing a dominant position. The same problems of interpretation of market behaviour apply in this case.

(iv)   Acquiring a dominant position by merger has been one of the major routes to achieving dominance in recent experience in the UK and USA. Given that merger is the ultimate form of collusion, it might be asked why policy should not take an equally tough stance (Willig, 1991). One reason is that there may be efficiency gains from merger, e.g. owing to scale economies. Williamson (1968) showed that quite modest gains in efficiency could offset a substantial increase in monopoly power. The reason is that efficiency gains accrue across the whole range of a firm's output: the welfare losses only arise from the marginal loss in output as monopoly prices are changed. A second reason is that the market for corporate control is thought to be an important disciplining device, particularly in

those circumstances where competition in product markets is absent. An inefficient management must either improve its performance, or face the consequences of the shareholders selling out to an alternative managerial team. The efficiency of this mechanism has been challenged on both theoretical and empirical grounds. The theoretical argument, stated by Grossman and Hart (1980) (see also Yarrow, 1985), is that shareholders will attempt to free-ride on post-merger improvements in performance by not selling their (small) individual holdings. The consequence is that merger bids aimed at improving performance will tend to fail. The empirical grounds are that studies of post-merger performance are far from unanimous in identifying improved performance. For examples, Jensen and Ruback (1983) and Franks and Harris (1989) report substantial gains to shareholders of target firms, but Meeks (1977) and Ravenscraft and Scherer (1987) fail to identify merger gains from accounting data.

Having acquired a dominant position in a market, a firm will presumably seek to exploit that position, unless it is constrained by the threat of potential competition. The constraint of potential entry on the behaviour of dominant firms lies at the heart of the concept of contestable markets (see Baumol, 1982). In a contestable market, existing firms are vulnerable to entry if they attempt to exploit their market power; there are no sunk costs, and hence exit is costless; and entrants have access to the same technology and factor prices as incumbents. While it may be doubted whether contestability theory is an appropriate benchmark for assessing markets, as claimed by its protagonists (for sceptical views see Schwarz, 1986, and Shepherd, 1984), it has performed a useful role by underlining the significance of sunk costs in the analysis of entry.

The literature on strategic entry deterrence has analysed how firms may be able to use sunk costs to maintain dominant positions (Gilbert, 1989; Sutton, 1991). The basic idea is that sunk costs shift profit outcomes in the post-entry game, so that a potential entrant will be deterred. The costs must be sunk, otherwise the threat would not be credible and, faced with entry, it would be in the incumbent's interest to reverse the decision. Examples of strategic variables that might be used for entry deterrence include physical capital investment or R&D to reduce costs, pre-emptive patenting, and manipulation of demand conditions by advertising or brand proliferation (for a sceptical analysis see Smiley, 1988). The analytic problem, for competition policy, is that these strategies involve both welfare gains and losses. Thus lower costs and prices

arising from R&D or physical investment are beneficial: the loss is that prices might have been even lower
had entry not been deterred. Similarly, an increase in
the number of brands on offer may be a consumer gain,
even though it reduces the probability of new suppliers entering the market in the long run. If we take the
robust view that it is long-run competition which is
important, and therefore entry-deterring strategies are
to be frowned upon, there is the considerable difficulty
of distinguishing 'innocent' from 'strategic' behaviour.
A firm which innocently seeks to lower costs and improve product quality may simultaneously be making it harder for entry to occur. If it passes on lower
costs to its customers in the form of lower prices it may
be open to the accusation of behaving in a predatory
fashion.

There are other means which firms may use to exclude potential rivals from the market. One literature
focuses attention on 'foreclosure': an incumbent may
seek to bar entry by entering into exclusive contracts
with suppliers or customers (Aghion and Bolton,
1987), or by vertical integration upstream or downstream (Ordover and Salop, 1990; Hart and Tirole,
1990; Ordover and Saloner, 1989). A similar strategy,
explored by Salop and Scheffman (1987), is where integration or contracts entered into by the incumbent
have the effect of raising rivals costs, e.g. where a contract with a supplier specifies that an input will only
be supplied to an entrant at a higher price than that
enjoyed by the incumbent.

Finally, there is the theoretical possibility of 'excessive entry' (Mankiw and Whinston, 1986), when firms
compete in quantities rather than prices, or where
products are differentiated. If firms incur fixed costs,
a free-entry zero-profit equilibrium may result in too
many firms operating with high average costs. Entry
deterrence may then be socially optimal, the social
costs of higher prices being offset by lower average costs
(for an example, see Hay and Morris, 1991, pp. 590–2).

The discussion of this section points to the ubiq-
uity of welfare trade-offs in competition policy issues.
This does, of course, greatly complicate the design of
policy—both the substance of competition law, and the
institutional framework for implementing that law. It is
to these questions that we turn in the next section.

IV. Third proposition

**The appropriate design of policy and policy institu-
tions is crucial to a successful competition policy.**

The design of policy has to take into account the ambiguity of the welfare analysis outlined in the previous section. However, it is clearly infeasible to treat
every market situation or example of firm behaviour
as being in principle open to investigation and decision by the competition authorities. For one thing, it
could absorb a lot of expert resources and the policy
gains might not outweigh the costs of investigation in
many cases: it could also encourage rent-seeking behaviour. For another, the main virtue of a market
economy is that firms are able to pursue their objectives and allocate resources without being constantly
subject to scrutiny. If the advantages of decentralization of decision-making are to be preserved, firms
must be able to operate within a set of rules for competition that enable them to identify what strategies
are likely to attract scrutiny, and what strategies they
can pursue without hindrance. It is, therefore, essential that competition policy provides such a set of rules
or guidelines.

Hay and Vickers (1987) identified the following
general principles for the design of policy:

(i)   There are two types of error that competition
policy might make. The first is that desirable behaviour may be condemned or discouraged; the second
is the risk of promoting or permitting undesirable behaviour. Policy should, therefore, be framed with a
view to minimizing these costs, together with the costs
of administering the policy (Hay, 1981). In practice,
this means that rules and guidelines are essential. Two
examples will be briefly reviewed here. The first example is the EU procedure of providing for block exemptions from Articles 81 and 82 (Whish, 1993, ch.
13). Thus Regulation 418/85 provides exemption for
R&D agreements from the effects of Article 81, making it clear that exemptions only apply to agreements
that do not extend to joint marketing and selling. Article 4 of the Regulation provides a list of permitted
restrictions in such agreements. Similarly, franchise
agreements are granted block exemption under Regulation 4087/88. A second example is the US Justice
Department Merger Guidelines, the latest version of
which was published in 1992 (see White (1993) for a
description). One issue is the effect of 'ease of entry'
in the post-merger situation, where there are potential anticompetitive effects. Anticipated entry must be
probable, rapid, and sufficient to counteract these effects. A second issue is the increase in concentration
anticipated in relevant markets, which may be quite
narrowly defined. The guidelines are delineated in
terms of the Herfindahl–Hirschman Index (HHI),
which is the sum of the squares of the market shares,

where the shares are expressed in percentages. A merger with a resulting index between 1,000 and 1,800, and an increase in the index of 100 'potentially' will raise competition concerns; a merger with a resulting index which exceeds 1,800, and an increase over 100, will be presumed anticompetitive, though there is an option for the parties to argue otherwise. The Guidelines also spell out in some detail what anticompetitive effects the Department is concerned about. While the Guidelines are merely informative of how the Justice Department approaches merger situations, and do not bind the Department, the Federal Trade Commission, or private litigants, they are helpful to firms and their advisers in assessing whether a particular merger is likely to be acceptable to the competition authorities. The Justice Department has similar Guidelines setting out the situations in which vertical restraints are likely to attract attention from the authorities.

(ii)   Some rules are likely to generate cases where desirable behaviour is discouraged or condemned. If this is a difficulty, the solution is to allow firms to present a case for exemption from those rules if they can demonstrate that the public interest will be furthered thereby. The reason for putting the onus of proof on the firms is that they have both the incentive to make the case, and access to the detailed information on which the case is to be based. This procedure is quite common in competition policy, but by no means universal. For example, it is possible for firms to apply for exemption for agreements under Chapter I of the Competition Act 1998 (see section VI below) or Article 81(3), even where the agreement is not covered by the block exemptions described above. Similarly, it used to be open to firms to argue for a restrictive agreement before the Restrictive Trade Practices Court, citing one or more of the 'gateways' contained in the Act. This contrasts oddly with the Competition Commission procedure in the case of a merger, where the Commission has to conduct an open inquiry. Obviously it will be in the interests of the firms involved to present evidence favourable to their case. But they do not have to demonstrate that there will be gains. The Commission simply has to be satisfied that the merger is not contrary to the public interest.

(iii)   The competition authorities should concern themselves with firms' conduct only when there is reason to believe that competition is absent (or would be absent were the conduct permitted). This dictum applies particularly to price discrimination and vertical restraints. In the US and EU jurisdictions price discrimination is more or less *per se* illegal: resale price maintenance is also *per se* illegal in all jurisdictions,

though it is difficult to justify separating out RPM from other vertical restraints on the basis of economic analysis. The treatment of other vertical restraints—tie-ins, full-line forcing, and rebates—is more variable, though the general drift of policy is antagonistic. However, it is difficult to see how they might generate significant welfare losses (and, indeed, may involve some welfare gains—see Waterson in this volume), unless practised by firms that have significant market power, in which case they may be used to exploit and sustain a dominant position. There can be no objection in principle to a firm in a competitive environment seeking to differentiate its marketing from its rivals, and this may involve vertical restraints such as exclusive distribution or exclusive purchasing, as well as a package of rebates, loyalty bonuses, and discounts to retailers. It is this type of thinking that lies behind the US Justice Department's Vertical Restraints Guidelines mentioned above, though White (1993) remarks that these 1985 Guidelines have not been particularly successful in clarifying the issues, and vertical restraints remain an unsatisfactory area of US antitrust policy. In principle, applications of Article 82, and the investigation of 'anticompetitive practices' under Chapter II in the UK, are predicated on the existence of market power.

(iv)   It ought to be obvious, but is far from universally acknowledged in competition law, that where policy towards market dominance is in question, prevention is better than seeking remedies after a dominant position has been achieved. Short of drastic action, to split up a major firm (as in the AT&T case in the USA; Evans, 1983), or to order divestment (as in Supply of Beer, 1989), the remedies that can be applied are invariably weak. A major firm has probably sunk cost in such a way that it is unlikely to be successfully challenged by an entrant. Attacks on its conduct (e.g. vertical restraints, price discrimination, etc.) may serve only to decrease its efficiency in extracting monopoly rents, rather than to increase economic efficiency or consumer welfare. Regulation is an option, but creates additional problems of its own, which are unlikely to commend it to the authorities except in exceptional circumstances (e.g. as part of a privatization programme involving natural monopolies). Given these difficulties in dealing with established monopolies, it is surprising that only US antitrust identifies 'attempts to monopolize' a market as a breach of the rules (under the Sherman Act). Article 82 of EU law only deals directly with the abuse of a dominant position, presumably once the firm has achieved that position, and until recently the scope for dealing with mergers which create dominant positions was severely limited. In the

UK, too, it is conduct to exploit a monopoly position which is attacked under the Competition Act 1998, rather than the process of acquiring that position. Mergers that create dominant positions can be referred to the Competition Commission, but there is no presumption against mergers (if anything, the reverse) and general public-interest criteria are applied in their evaluation.

One reason for this reluctance to take action against the process of monopolization is the difficulty of distinguishing acceptable and unacceptable behaviour. As we saw in the previous section, there is an understandable reluctance to move against firms that have competed successfully and won market share. The case history of US antitrust actions against dominant firms (Alcoa, United Shoe, AT&T, and IBM) in the post-war period is a witness to the difficulties that competition authorities face in this area.[5] In both Alcoa and United Shoe the courts acknowledged that the defendants had built their market shares by legal means, but none the less found them guilty because their respective dominant positions were due to conscious choice. In the IBM case, an additional key feature was the question of the relevant market. The Justice Department, and a number of private litigants, argued that attention should be focused on sub-markets of the computer industry, in many of which IBM did indeed have high market shares. IBM argued that the market should be analysed as a whole, in which the IBM share was considerably less (Brock, 1975; Fisher *et al.*, 1983).

(v)   the competition authorities should have powers to impose punishments on firms that engage in anticompetitive practices (e.g. price fixing, and exclusionary or predatory practices), to require firms to enter into binding commitments to desist from conduct that is demonstrably prejudicial to competition, and to propose structural remedies where firms have established a dominant position in a market. In the USA executives of colluding companies have been gaoled for conspiracy, in addition to the levying of substantial fines on their companies; in the EU firms can be fined up to 10 per cent of their worldwide turnover; and in the UK the Director General of Fair Trading is now similarly empowered to impose fines. In all three jurisdictions the authorities can, and do, seek binding undertakings from firms in respect of their market conduct, and can order structural remedies (either formally or as a result of negotiations with the

firms involved). Examples are the splitting up of AT&T in the USA, referred to above, the more stringent conditions put on the BA/BCal merger by the EU authorities, and the Monopolies and Mergers Commission recommendation that the major UK brewers should divest themselves of most of their public houses (Supply of Beer, 1989).

A remaining issue is the shape of institutions that should be given the task of enforcing/applying competition law. First, it clearly requires a public institution that is empowered to seek out and to evaluate possible failures of competition (including powers to collect evidence). Private actions, even class actions, are unlikely to prove effective on their own, because of the free-rider problem, given the costs involved. However, White (1993) argues that private actions have played an important role in the development of more effective antitrust in the USA, and that the recent decline in the number of cases has allayed the fears, expressed in the 1980s, of excessive litigation. Second, it would be appropriate for this institution to emphasize economic analysis of market dominance and conduct, rather than conformity to legal definitions of anticompetitive market situations and/or conduct. However, as explained above, too much emphasis on economic analysis of each situation generates an impossible situation for firms who wish to know what is or is not permitted. Hence it is important for the legislation to spell out the situations and conduct that will be presumed to be anticompetitive, and to provide for the competition policy institution to publish guidelines as to how it proposes to apply the legislation. Furthermore, the institution should be required to listen to representations from the parties as to why the presumption of the legislation should not apply in a particular case, and to evaluate these representations. Having completed its analysis, the institution should then be required to publish a judgment of the matter under consideration, together with a statement of its arguments in arriving at that judgment.

Third, there should be a competition tribunal, which would be involved in two circumstances. The first is where the firms are unwilling to accept the judgment of the competition policy institution, and wish to have the case reviewed. The second is where the institution is proposing the imposition of penalties on the firm for particularly outstanding violations of competition law rules without any mitigating circumstances (e.g. persistent involvement in price-fixing cartels). Then the institution should be required to present the matter before the tribunal: an important role of the tribunal would be to prevent arbitrary ex-

[5] The yet to be concluded (as of March 2000) action against Microsoft may prove to be an exception to the general ineffectiveness of actions against dominant firms in the USA.

ercise of power by the competition policy institution. A further right of appeal to higher Courts on interpretation of the law would also be desirable.

The actual institutions in the UK, USA, and EU, are at first sight quite diverse. In the USA there are two agencies entrusted with the enforcement of antitrust legislation—the Antitrust Division of the Justice Department, and the Federal Trade Commission. The division of labour between them is not entirely clear, but their overall task is to bring actions against infringement of the provisions of the relevant Acts. There are criminal penalties, including fines and imprisonment, for violations. There is also provision for private litigation, whereby private parties can sue for three times the damages inflicted upon them by violations of the law. In the EU responsibility for competition matters rests with Directorate-General IV of the European Commission (DGIV). It is empowered to investigate breaches of Articles 81 and 82 which deal with competition matters, and where an infringement is identified, to require the parties to desist. Fines of up to 10 per cent of the worldwide turnover of the guilty parties may be imposed. The European Court has powers of judicial review over Commission decisions, and there have been many appeals to the Court against the decisions of DGIV. The Court, therefore, has had a considerable impact on the development of policy. As in the USA, there is scope for private parties to bring actions for damages (though not multiple damages) where their interests have been harmed by violations of Articles 81 and 82. In practice, the EU system has attracted considerable criticism. One problem is that appeals to the European Court from decisions of DGIV tend to take a very long time, and there is also some doubt as to whether the Court is an appropriately constituted body to act as a review tribunal in the sense described above. The criticism is that these problems have left DGIV with far too much power to act as both prosecutor and judge in the cases it has pursued. An obvious reform would be to institute a competition tribunal.

In the UK, under the 1998 Competition Act, the procedure is similar to that of the EU with the Director General of Fair Trading in place of DGIV. But firms do have the right of appeal to a special tribunal within the Competition Commission against fines or other penalties proposed by the Director General of Fair Trading under Chapters I or II. In merger cases, the Director General of Fair Trading advises the Secretary of State on a reference to the Competition Commission. In monopoly cases, either the Director General or the Secretary of State can make the reference. In practice, it is almost invariably the Director General who acts,

though the Secretary of State initiated the reference of British Gas to the old Monopolies and Mergers Commission in 1992. The Commission then investigates, and if there is an adverse finding, it makes recommendations to the Secretary of State who is free to accept or reject the recommendations, in whole or in part. The Secretary of State cannot, however, overrule a finding by the Commission that a merger, for example, is not contrary to the public interest. The procedure is administrative (and discretionary): there is no concept of a breach or violation of the relevant competition law, and there is no 'plaintiff' or 'defendant'.

V. Fourth proposition

International harmonization of competition policies is essential and probably a supranational competition authority is as well.

Two further issues for competition policy are becoming increasingly important. One concerns the geographical level at which competition policy should operate, an issue that is arising in the context of EU policy in relation to policy of member states of the EU. The second is the potential for conflict between competition policy and other microeconomic policies, which are often loosely termed 'industrial policies'.

1. The level at which competition policy should operate

The issue to be analysed in this section takes a number of different forms in practice. The most straightforward example is where a firm has a dominant position in the UK national market, but argues before the competition authorities that the relevant market definition is not national, but, for example, the whole EU. A more complex case is where the supplier in the UK national market is a branch of a multinational company, which has made an agreement with other multinationals to share out world markets by allocating different economies to different suppliers. How can the national competition authorities take action against the suppliers? Similarly, the UK national market may be supplied by a group of firms, say American firms, that have (legally) formed an export cartel. Alternatively, consider a case where a UK firm merges with an overseas firm, which was not currently serving the UK market, but which had the potential to enter the UK market. Obviously, potential competition is reduced, though current supplies are not affected. Should the UK competition authorities seek to block the merger?

In principle, once the market has been defined, then it is appropriate to apply competition policy to that market. A sensible division of labour then suggests itself. If a particular market is 'national' in the sense that the good in question is strictly non-tradable, then it is appropriate for the issue to be considered by a national authority. If, however, the market is international, and the good in question widely traded, then a higher level authority is required (or full collaboration between the national authorities affected). The relationship between UK and EU competition policy approximates to this division of labour. Thus UK competition policy is very clearly directed at market behaviour and conduct that affects the supply of goods and services within the United Kingdom. So the behaviour of an overseas firm is not investigated unless its actions and the consequent effects are felt in the domestic market. EU competition policy, by contrast, applies when trade between member states is affected, or potentially affected, by the conduct which is being scrutinized. The rule is that EU competition law takes precedence over UK law, though this has not prevented merger cases being examined by both jurisdictions (e.g. British Airways/British Caledonian, 1987). The 1989 EU Regulation on mergers should help to allocate jurisdiction in these cases.

However, this neat division of labour is predicated on being able to distinguish traded and non-traded goods in a precise fashion. In practice, the problem of market definition remains. Because of transport costs one might expect heavy building materials, such as cement, to be non-traded. However, as UK cement manufacturers discovered to their cost, high prices in the UK market made it worthwhile for low-cost EU and third-country suppliers, located at deep-water ports, to begin supplying the UK market. The basic point is that, in the absence of major tariff or non-tariff barriers to trade, a good becomes more 'traded' (i.e. attracting import competition) the higher the domestic price. Obviously the potential for entry via imports needs to be considered carefully by domestic competition authorities in assessing whether a firm is dominant and whether it is abusing its monopoly position. This emphasizes a further point to which domestic competition authorities need to apply their minds. It is quite possible that a good is in principle tradable, but that the domestic distribution system has been 'captured' by a single supplier in such a way that entry by trade is difficult. But a national authority may find it (politically) difficult to pursue a domestic firm with a view to enabling foreign firms to achieve a greater market share. The EU authorities will need to intervene on the grounds that potential trade is being stifled. However, the EU authorities should not be over-zealous in this matter to the extent of arguing that any territorial division of the EU market, especially the charging of different prices in different countries, is a sign of non-competitive behaviour.

There remains the case where a group of firms in a third country form an export cartel (e.g. a group of United States firms forming an export cartel as permitted by the Webb–Pomerene Act of 1918). The UK maintains a strong doctrine of extraterritoriality which means that UK competition policy cannot be applied in such cases, any more than US antitrust policy would be permitted to pursue a cartel of UK firms exporting to the USA. The EU position remains unclear. In the Wood Pulp case (1985) the Commission held that a concerted practice by non-EU firms fell within the jurisdiction of EU law because of the effects on the EU market. The Court avoided this doctrine by finding that the agreement had been implemented within the EU, and hence fell within the jurisdiction of EU law. Such cases do, however, point to the need for international collaboration to promote competition in global markets.

2. Competition policy and industrial policies

The discussion of export cartels in the previous section has pointed to the possibility that competition policy might be designed and applied to protect domestic markets and to promote domestic producers in export markets (Hay, 1994). Indeed, it is not unusual for business groups to argue that competition policy should be used in this way.

There are a number of ways in which competition policy might be applied (or fail to be applied!) to protect the domestic market. One route is to take a hostile view of takeovers involving the absorption of a domestic firm by a foreign buyer, since takeover is often the best method for a potential competitor to get an initial share in the domestic market. In practice, the Monopolies and Mergers Commission sometimes reported against foreign takeovers as contrary to the public interest, but the reasoning was other than a desire to stifle competition (e.g. the report on Government of Kuwait/British Petroleum, 1988, which decided that it was contrary to the public interest for the government of Kuwait to gain a major shareholding in BP). A second route might be to allow domestic producers to agree on predatory responses to attempts by foreign suppliers to enter the national market. A third route could be to permit vertical relationships and restraints between domestic producers, or domestic producers and distributors, which made it difficult either for a foreign firm to set up production and gain essential supplies, or for a foreign firm to get access to existing distribution networks. None of these possibilities is countenanced by competition policy in any of the three jurisdictions previously discussed, though there have been calls for a more protectionist approach in the USA.

We should also note that there are some trade measures that are protectionist in effect, and have strong links with competition policy. A sector which is under pressure from imports may seek voluntary export restraints on the part of the foreign suppliers (a wide range of Japanese exports to the United States and the EU have been affected by such agreements). Alternatively, a hard-pressed sector may seek to persuade its government to invoke anti-dumping measures. The parallel is with the treatment of predatory pricing in competition policy. Anti-dumping measures are supposed to be a response to 'unfair' competition, but it is difficult to distinguish genuine low-cost entry from predatory entry by foreign suppliers. If all else fails, a sector which is being undermined by imports may successfully apply for exemption from restrictions on the formation of a cartel to enable the decline of the sector to proceed in an orderly manner. A number of such cartels have been permitted, indeed promoted, by the EU authorities.

Industrial policy is usually linked to promotion of exports rather than the protection of the domestic market *per se*. The key insights were provided by Krugman (1984): protection of a market enables domestic producers to realize economies of scale or learning by doing, and to recoup R&D costs, so that when protection is removed, and the firms begin to export, they have cost advantages over foreign producers and can capture larger market shares. Itoh *et al.* (1991) have analysed various industrial policy measures that may achieve these ends, including direct and indirect subsidies to producers as well as standard protectionist measures such as tariffs, quotas, and non-tariff barriers. Our focus here is on the use of competition policy to achieve the same ends.

There are three ways in which competition policy might be used to promote the interests of domestic producers. The first is permitting the creation of 'national champions'. Thus firms may be allowed to grow to dominate their domestic market, by internal growth or by merger, on the pretext of creating firms that will be able to compete on 'equal terms' in world markets.

If these world markets are themselves genuinely competitive, and if the domestic market is open to imports, then there may be little direct harm resulting from the pursuit of large scale (though ideally one would wish there to be some scrutiny of the dominant firm in the context of the world market by a supra-national competition authority). However, the domestic competition authorities should satisfy themselves that the domestic market is genuinely open. Arguments for 'national champions' have sometimes appeared in MMC reports, notably the BA/BCal (1987) Report. Sapir *et al.* (1993) identify a 1990 decision of the European Commission to permit a cooperation agreement on R&D, production, and marketing of electronic components for satellites, on the grounds that the companies otherwise would find it difficult to compete with non-European suppliers.

A second method of promoting the interests of domestic producers is by permitting them to enter into collaborations of various kinds. One kind is the establishment of joint ventures for exporting: the justification is that they can share the fixed costs, and pool expertise, in penetrating foreign markets, and that they can avoid competing against each other for foreign orders. Export cartels are permitted under both UK and US competition law. The justification is that it is undesirable for domestic firms to compete against each other in overseas markets: national welfare is enhanced if they maximize their joint rents. As we have seen, this gain is a loss to the welfare of consumers in the country to which they are exporting, and the cartel would, therefore, presumably be disallowed by an international competition authority.

Other joint ventures are in R&D: once again the gain is the sharing of fixed costs and the avoidance of costly duplication of activities. Another type of collaboration is a specialization agreement where firms agree to specialize in production so that they can achieve scale economies, with commitments to supply each other (on favourable terms) with the products that the other is not producing. All these possibilities are recognized in EU competition policy, and are given exemption from Article 81 so long as certain safeguards are in place.

3. Implications for competition policy jurisdiction

It will be evident that the two issues raised in this section—the appropriate level for competition policy, and the use of competition policy as a tool of industrial policy (whether protectionist or promotional)—

are two sides of the same question. The question is whether competition policy is seeking to raise the welfare of a particular economy, or whether it should be used as an instrument to promote economic efficiency at a supranational (or even international) level. In respect of the EU it should be recalled that Article 3(f) of the Treaty of Rome provides for 'the institution of a system ensuring that competition in the common market is not distorted'. In principle that must imply the abandonment of any attempt by member governments to use competition policy to protect or promote their domestic industry (just as other industrial and trade policy measures have had to be progressively abandoned). At the international level much will depend on whether the OECD countries continue to pursue free trade, or whether protectionist tendencies proliferate. If free trade remains the objective, then agreements on international aspects of competition policy to collaborate in the implementation of competition policy, where more than one economy is affected, will be required.

Neven and Siotis (1993) contrast decentralization of policy to competition authorities in member states with centralization in a strengthened DGIV in Brussels. In favour of decentralization, they appeal to the doctrine of subsidiarity, and additionally argue that a supranational authority is likely to be unduly prone to capture by interest groups. But they recognize that decentralization will only work if there is agreement on the fundamental competition rules to be applied (with little or no discretion), and if there are clear rules for allocating cases across jurisdictions (e.g. where a particular merger will have competition implications in several member states of the EU). There is a particular danger that national competition policies might be used in a protectionist or promotional manner as described above to give advantage to domestic producers. The experience of the EU with member state aids to attract foreign direct investment should serve as a warning that EU rules are not always sufficient to prevent member states from taking unilateral steps to improve their national economies at the expense of others.

VI. The 1998 Competition Act

The 1998 Competition Act completed the legislative process in November 1998, and its main provisions took effect from April 2000. It represented a major reform of UK competition policy, bringing policy into line with Articles 81 and 82 of the Treaty of Amsterdam,[6] which form the basis for EU policy. The key policy institutions under the Act are the OFT (with its Director General), and the Competition Commission (a reformed version of the old Monopoly and Mergers Commission). The respective roles of these institutions will be identified below with respect to various areas of policy.

1. Anticompetitive agreements

Chapter I of the Competition Act 1998 replaces the previous UK legislation on restrictive trade practices with provisions which are drawn more or less in their entirety from Article 81. Section 2 prohibits agreements which 'have as their object or effect the prevention, restriction or distortion of competition within the United Kingdom'. Examples include:

agreements, decisions or practices which –

(a) directly or indirectly fix purchase or selling prices or any other trading conditions;
(b) limit or control production, markets, technical development or investment;
(c) share markets or sources of supply;
(d) apply dissimilar conditions to equivalent transactions with other trading parties, thereby placing them at a competitive disadvantage;
(e) make the conclusion of contracts subject to acceptance by the other parties of supplementary obligations which, by their nature or according to commercial usage, have no connection with the subject of such contracts.

Any agreement is to be judged not on the basis of its form (as in the previous Restrictive Trade Practices legislation) but on the basis of its effects or potential effects on competition. The first three examples are directed at cartel practices of fixing prices, outputs and capacity, and of sharing markets. Examples (d) and (e) are directed at behaviour which, if practised by a dominant firm, might constitute an abuse of a dominant position: the idea is to prevent non-dominant firms agreeing to behave together in an anti-competitive manner.

The Department of Trade and Industry commentary which was published with the draft Bill made clear the intention that the prohibition should only apply to agreements which have a significant or 'appreciable'

---

[6] Previously Articles 85 and 86 of the Treaty of Rome, and often referred to as such in the literature on competition policy. For consistency all references will be to Articles 81 and 82, even though at the time of particular European cases the previous numbers applied.

effect on competition. The Director General of Fair Trading is required to interpret the provisions in the light of European precedents on this issue, to avoid any interpretations developing over time which might diverge from European practice. To this end, the OFT has published guidelines on *Assessment of Market Power* (OFT, 1999d), which indicate how the Office will identify agreements which do not have an 'appreciable effect on competition'. This refers to the precedent established by the European Court: 'an agreement falls outside the prohibition in Article 81(1) where it has only an insignificant effect on the market, taking into account the weak position which the persons concerned have on the market in question.'[7] The suggested guidelines refer both to the market share of the parties to an agreement, and to the nature of the agreement. Where the parties' share does not exceed 25 per cent of the relevant market,[8] the view is that agreements will have no appreciable effect on competition. However the nature of the agreement must also be considered: if the agreement involves price fixing, market sharing, or agreements to impose minimum resale prices, the 25 per cent rule no longer ensures that Chapter I will not be applied. The guidelines also indicate some additional considerations to be taken into account, such as the structure of the market, the conditions of entry, and the structure of the buyers' side of the market. Finally, there is to be limited immunity for small agreements, where the combined annual turnover of the parties is below a threshold. Penalties may not be imposed, and the investigation of such agreements will have a low priority. But the Director General still has the right to investigate, and may subsequently remove immunity from penalties.

The guidelines on *The Chapter I Prohibition* issued by the OFT (1999a) are interesting for what they identify as the main targets of this part of the Act. First, the guidelines are concerned only with horizontal agreements, defined as firms that operate at the same level of the production and distribution chain. Vertical agreements are not discussed. The government's original intention was that vertical agreements, with the exception of RPM, should be dealt with under Chapter II or under the 'complex monopoly' provisions of the Fair Trading Act 1973, but it did not prove possible to draft the Bill explicitly so as to ensure this division of labour.[9] We return to the question of vertical relation-

ships in markets below. The examples of horizontal agreements given in the guidelines contain no surprises: overt collusive agreements, price-fixing, market-sharing, limiting production, limiting or coordinating investment, collusive tendering, agreements between purchasers, and information agreements. All of these are supported by the European experience in applying Article 81.[10]

Less happily the guidelines are drawn into the question of 'concerted practices', which has proved such a contentious issue in Europe. The difficulties with the concept can be identified by reference to two key judgements of the European Court. In the first, the Dyestuffs case,[11] the Court defined a concerted practice as

a form of coordination between undertakings which, without having reached the stage where an agreement properly so-called has been concluded, knowingly substitutes practical cooperation between them for the risks of competition which do not correspond to the normal conditions of the market, having regard to the nature of the products, the importance and number of the undertakings, as well as the size and importance of the said market. Such practical co-operation amounts to a concerted practice.

In the second case, Wood Pulp,[12] the Court ruled that Article 81 does not 'deprive economic operators of the right to adapt themselves intelligently to the existing and anticipated conduct of their competitors'. More recent game theoretic analyses of oligopolistic competition[13] make the issue abundantly clear: in markets which are continuing over time, there is no reason why firms should not successfully collude tacitly without any communication, merely by acting 'intelligently'. The attempt to bring this behaviour within the prohibition of Chapter I is not likely to be very productive. The 'complex monopoly' provisions of the Fair Trading Act 1973, which have been retained in the reforms, are a much more appropriate vehicle for dealing with this situation.

The Act introduces a procedure for exemptions which parallels the provisions of Article 81(3), and enables firms to argue for exemption on the basis of beneficial effects which can be shown to flow from a particular agreement or type of agreement. Specifically, section 9 in Chapter I refers to an agreement which 'contributes to (i) improv-

---

[7] *Volk v. Verwaeke* [1969] ECR 295.

[8] The views of the OFT on market definition are discussed below.

[9] The provisions of Article 81 have been held to apply to vertical agreements since the European Court's decision in *Etablissements Consten and Grundig v. Commission* 56/64, 58/64 [1966] ECR, [1966] CMLR 418.

[10] See the discussion in Whish (1993, ch. 7). A new edition of this excellent text, incorporating the changes arising from the Competition Act 1998, is expected in 2000.

[11] *ICI v. Commission* [1972] ECR 619, [1972] CMLR 557 paragraph 64.

[12] OJ [1985] L 85/1, [1985] 3 CMLR 474, cases C89/85 etc *A Ahlstrom Oy v. Commission* [1993] 4 CMLR 407.

[13] See section IV above.

ing production or distribution, (ii) promoting technical or economic progress, while allowing consumers a fair share of the resulting benefit', so long as the agreement is limited to achieving these desirable effects and does not have wider effects on competition between the parties. Exemptions operate at three levels. The first is firm-specific, where a firm convinces the Director General that there are net beneficial effects from an agreement that might otherwise be prohibited. The second level is block exemptions, such as the exemptions under EU competition policy granted for pure R&D agreements and for pure specialization agreements.[14] The third-level grants parallel exemptions to any already granted as block agreements in Europe: this includes situations which fall within the terms of an existing EU exemption, but are not subject to Article 81 because they do not affect interstate trade. The Act provides for two procedures with respect to the notification of agreements to the Director General. A firm can ask for informal guidance as to whether a particular proposed agreement would infringe the prohibition. Clearance would effectively provide immunity from penalties. But it would be given in confidence without consultation of potentially affected parties, and could not therefore provide contractual certainty. Alternatively, the firm can ask for a formal decision, which involves a much more rigorous investigation by the Director General, including an assessment of the market and the concerns of interested parties. The decision would be published.

The most significant innovation from the point of view of previous UK competition policy is the provision enabling the Director General to levy fines on firms that are found to be breaking the prohibitions. Once again, the legislation follows European precedent in fixing the maximum fine at 10 per cent of UK turnover, recognizing that anti-competitive behaviour in the form of cartels can be very profitable and therefore the penalties need to be large to act as a deterrent. The Director General can also require an agreement to be abandoned by the firms involved. The firms have a right of appeal on both the substance and the penalties to a tribunal which will form part of the Competition Commission. This tribunal will operate entirely independently of government. It will not carry out its own investigations, but rely on the evidence already

prepared by the parties. Should the tribunal decide that further evidence is needed it will be able to refer the matter back to the Director General for further consideration at that stage, or ask that the evidence be provided to it. The tribunal will be able to revise both the findings of the Director General and the proposed fine. It will also be open to third parties to appeal to the tribunal if they can show sufficient interest in the case: such third parties may include general consumer organizations. The Act also includes provisions for third-party actions for damages or interim relief from the effects of a prohibited agreement. These will be heard in the courts rather than in the tribunal. However, a third party will be able to introduce a decision of the Director General or tribunal as evidence that the prohibition has been breached, rather than having to establish the facts anew.

2. Abuse of a dominant position

The core of Chapter II of the Act is section 18. This states that 'any conduct on the part of one or more undertakings which amounts to the abuse of a dominant position is prohibited'. Examples of abuse are then given:

Conduct may, in particular, constitute such an abuse if it consists in—

(a)   directly or indirectly imposing unfair purchase or selling prices or other unfair trading conditions;
(b)   limiting production, markets or technical development to the prejudice of consumers;
(c)   applying dissimilar conditions to equivalent transactions with other trading parties, thereby placing them at a competitive disadvantage;
(d)   making the conclusion of contracts subject to acceptance by the other parties of supplementary obligations which, by their nature or according commercial usage, have no connection with the subject of the contracts.

This is, of course, Article 82. The borrowing is deliberate: the policy is meant to parallel European competition law precisely. The institutional framework is essentially that described in the previous section with respect to agreements between firms. The Director General of Fair Trading has a duty to investigate suspected abuses, and powers to fine firms up to 10 per cent of UK turnover, to halt the conduct which led to the abuse, and to order the firm to behave in specified ways (e.g. to supply a firm which it had previously refused to supply). The firm has a right of appeal to the Competition Commission tribunal against both the finding of an abuse and the punishment imposed by

---

[14] Block exemptions for vertical agreements in place under Article 81(3) include exclusive distribution, exclusive purchasing, franchises, and special arrangements for the retailing of beer, petrol, and motor vehicles. See European Commission (1997, ch. IV) for a summary. These are not discussed in the Chapter I guidelines because of the intention that vertical agreements will be dealt with separately under the Competition Act in a departure from European precedent for Article 81.

the Director General. Small and medium-sized firms are excluded from the prohibition under the rubric of 'conduct of minor significance'. A prior screen based on firm market share and/or turnover is to be applied to ensure that the conduct of small firms is not considered. Apart from that, no other exclusions or exemptions are envisaged, apart from mergers and other situations where other competition rules are more relevant. In particular, there is no procedure for exemptions along the lines of Article 81(3). The Act requires the Director General to publish guidelines to clarify the way in which he or she proposes to apply the prohibition, and European precedent again applies. As in the case of Chapter I above, a firm may apply for negative guidance as to whether a proposed conduct would breach the prohibition. It can ask for informal guidance or for a decision. The former involves a less rigorous analysis, but does not give the same degree of assurance to the firm as the latter, which is given after a full assessment of the matter, including consultation with potentially affected third parties.

Evidently a key feature of policy under Chapter II is the practical definition of 'dominant position'. The OFT has given thought to this issue in guidelines on *Market Definition* (OFT, 1999c). These indicate the use of a 'hypothetical monopolist test: would a hypothetical monopolist of these products maximize its profits by charging higher prices than it would if it faced competition?' The method begins with a narrow market definition and looks at the substitution possibilities on both the demand side and the supply side in response to a price 5–10 per cent above the competitive level. If a hypothetical monopolist in this narrow market would not be able to raise prices because within a year[15] consumers would switch to other products or new suppliers would enter, then these demand and supply substitutes are added to the market and the test is applied again. In evaluating demand-side substitution the Office has indicated that it will use a variety of sources, including surveys of customers and competitors, evidence on switching costs, previous price histories of potential substitutes, and evidence on price elasticities. Supply-side substitution will be assessed by asking potential suppliers about the feasibility (technical and economic) of supplying the market, including the availability of capacity. Within the UK an important issue is the geographic extent of the relevant markets and the degree to which those markets are effectively open to imports from other UK regions or, indeed, from abroad. Particularly interesting issues

arise in the case of products which are intrinsically complementary: for example, cars and car parts, or office equipment and servicing. The focus is on the 'secondary market': once the customer has bought the first product he may be effectively tied in to the purchase of the second product. The main issue is whether potential customers are sufficiently alert to the costs not only of the initial purchase but also the secondary products or services. If they are, then competition in the initial market will be sufficient to prevent the manufacturer trying to exploit captive customers in the secondary market. Having defined the market, it remains to define dominance within that market. The guidelines note that the European competition authorities have a presumption that a business is dominant when it has a market share of 50 per cent, and indicates that the Office of Fair Trading considers 40 per cent to be the appropriate cut-off market share.

Unfortunately, the copying of European policy has brought with it the curious concept of 'joint dominance', which arises from the reference to 'one or more undertakings' in the wording of Article 82, which is reproduced in section 18. Until the Italian Flat Glass case in 1992, the consensus was that this provision was redundant: overt collusive behaviour in oligopoly is caught under Article 81, and tacit collusion under the definition of 'concerted practices'. Clearly the Commission did not feel that this consensus gave it sufficient leverage on oligopolies, and in Italian Flat Glass the Court of First Instance agreed in principle, though not on the facts of the particular case. The judgement was:

There is nothing, in principle, to prevent two or more independent economic entities from being, on a specific market, united by such economic links that, by virtue of that fact, together they hold a dominant position *vis-à-vis* the other operators on the same market.[16]

It would be better for the OFT to issue a self-denying ordinance in respect of this piece of confusion in European policy. The European precedent is a poor one and it would be good to signal that at the beginning of the new regime in the UK. Regrettably, the guidelines envisage circumstances in which the OFT might wish to invoke the doctrine, though without detailing what those circumstances might be.

The economic evaluation of 'abuse of a dominant position' is much less straightforward than that of anticompetitive agreements. First, it is not entirely evident that all the conduct which Chapter II is attacking is

---

[15] This is a rule of thumb: in the circumstances of particular markets it might be appropriate to consider longer or shorter periods than one year.

[16] *Societa Italiano Vetro SpA v. Commission* cases T-68/89 etc. [1992] 5 CMLR 302. For further discussion see Whish (1993), pp. 280–2.

detrimental to economic efficiency. To explore this we need to translate the examples given in section 18 of the Act (Article 82) into the terminology of modern industrial organization economics. Clauses (a) and (b) of the section are primarily directed to the classic monopoly, which exploits its market power, either directly by fixing monopoly prices, or indirectly by restricting supplies to the market and benefiting from the resulting higher market price. The interpretation of 'imposition of unfair trading conditions' remains unclear. Clause (a) apparently applies to cases of predatory pricing, and clause (b) to refusal to supply. Predatory behaviour is not included in the examples of abuse given in section 18, though the section is presumably drafted sufficiently widely to allow the authorities to act where a dominant firm is behaving anti-competitively with respect to existing or potential competitors.

Clause (c) is more problematic. On the face of it, it is referring primarily to price discrimination. An alternative interpretation of (c) is that it is directed at some instances of predatory behaviour: for example, a situation in which a dominant firm is experiencing competition in a part of its market, so it cuts price only in that sub-market to drive off the competitor.

Section (d) may also be applied to vertical restraints such as exclusivity agreements, tie-ins, and full line forcing, and, as previously noted, section (b) to refusal to supply. The evident difficulties of legislating for the regulation of vertical market relationships have been met by introducing a general provision in Chapter V, to permit the Secretary of State to make Orders for any provision of Chapters I and II to apply in relation to vertical agreements, or for explicit exclusions or exemptions. We comment briefly on this below.

When the OFT came to drafting guidelines on *The Chapter II Prohibition* (OFT, 1999*b*), it very sensibly abandoned the attempt to interpret clauses (a)–(d) directly in terms of economic analysis. Instead it distinguishes:

conduct which exploits customers or suppliers through, for example: excessively high prices; and discriminatory prices, or other terms and conditions;

or

conduct which is anti-competitive, because it removes or limits competition from existing competitors, or because it excludes new undertakings from entering the market by, for example: 'predatory' behaviour; vertical restraints; or refusing to supply existing or potential competitors.

Excessively high prices are very obviously inefficient in economic terms—not only is there a loss in welfare, but there is also the distinct possibility that the firm will not achieve productive efficiency. However,

the European precedents do not inspire much confidence, and in fact there have been very few of them. The difficulties are illustrated by the United Brands[17] case, where the Court defined the abuse in the following terms: 'charging a price which is excessive because it has no reasonable relation to the economic value of the product supplied ... is an abuse.' To demonstrate an abuse the Commission first would have to undertake a cost analysis, and then ask

whether the difference between the costs actually incurred and the price actually charged is excessive, and, if the answer to this question is in the affirmative, to consider whether a price has been charged which is either unfair in itself or when compared to other competing products.

It is scarcely surprising that the Commission has not often embarked on such an ill-defined quest, and that the guidelines suggest that the OFT will similarly be cautious. The obvious difficulty is to distinguish abusive prices from prices that are high because of the normal working of the market mechanism. The best the guidelines can do is to point to examples where firms are able to earn supernormal profits without stimulating new entry.

The verdict of economic analysis on price discrimination is very far from negative; in many, if not all, situations it is fairly easy to show that it is actually conducive to economic efficiency.[18] The point is that it generally extends the market: discrimination is what gives the firm the incentive to supply into different markets distinguished by buyer, location, or time. The objection to price discrimination can only be sustained as a general proposition if the sole objective is to maximize consumer welfare (and producer surplus is ignored), or if there are other concerns about equal treatment for all customers. It is, of course, entirely reasonable that the authorities should decide to include these concerns among the objectives of competition policy—the recurrent phrase 'fair trading' is an indication of this broader concern. But the potential loss of efficiency should be noted. For example, if there are high fixed costs involved in producing a product, then price discrimination may be the most efficient way of recouping those costs while supplying the widest possible market: indeed, there may be no single price which enables the firm to break even, so prohibition of price discrimination may mean that the product is not supplied at all. In a series of decisions, the European authorities have moved decisively against such discriminatory practices as loyalty rebates, selec-

[17] *United Brands v. Commission* [1978] ECR 207, [1978] 1 CMLR 429.
[18] See the discussion and references to the literature in section III above.

tive discounting, and delivered pricing. They have been particularly opposed to geographical price discrimination across the markets of the member states of the European Union, as evidenced by the famous United Brands case where the issue was charging different prices for bananas in the Republic of Ireland and Germany!

Much ambiguity is also present in the economic analysis of predatory pricing.[19] In the short term, consumers benefit from low prices, even if in the long term the successful predator can charge higher prices. Moreover, it is not easy to distinguish the normal competitive response in a market in which a firm is experiencing competition, from a predatory response which is seeking the demise of the competitor. The key European cases are AKZO[20] and Tetra Pak II.[21] Both these cases correspond in some degree to the common sense definition of predation, in that in each case a dominant firm moved to counter competition in part of its market by cutting prices. However, the problem of defining a predatory price was never resolved satisfactorily beyond a presumption that a price less than average variable cost is predatory. The Court suggested that some evidence of intent to drive out a competitor was required, if prices exceeded average variable cost. This uncertainty as to what would count as predation is very unsatisfactory, and runs the risk of chilling normal price competition in markets with dominant firms.

The last type of abuse identified in the guidelines is refusal to supply.[22] Here the problem for policy is not so much the economic analysis as the difficulty of distinguishing refusal to supply as an anti-competitive practice and normal commercial decisions. The relevant European cases are the Commercial Solvents and Hugin cases.[23] In both cases, a dominant firm ceased supplies to a firm which was an actual competitor in a downstream market, which the dominant firm was supplying or planning to supply either itself or through a subsidiary. Later decisions of the Commission apparently extended the obligation on a dominant firm to supply even a new entrant. There is a particular concern that dominant firms that have control over a key facility (e.g. a port, a distribution network, a computer network) should not be able to protect a monopoly in services using that facility.

3. Vertical agreements and restraints

The consensus of economic analysis is that vertical agreements become a problem only if competition is absent in either the upstream or downstream market.[24] The European Commission *Green Paper on Vertical Restraints in EC Competition Policy* summarizes its conclusions as follows: 'The fiercer is interbrand competition the more likely are the pro-competitive and efficiency effects to outweigh any anti-competitive effects of vertical restraints. The inverse is true when interbrand competition is weak and there are significant barriers to entry.' The basic idea is that vertical restraints create vertical structures of firms and distributors, including retailers, which compete in markets. If the markets are competitive, then there are efficiency gains from vertical restraints: vertical coordination in pricing to avoid 'double marginalization', and coordination in the provision of services to overcome incentive and free-rider problems. Vertical agreements may also be important for solving risk-sharing and moral-hazard problems between the upstream and downstream firms to mitigate potential efficiency losses.

But if competition is absent, then there are grounds for competition policy. Lack of competition could arise either through a collusive agreement or due to a dominant firm. In the first case, the policy should aim to prevent firms from entering into horizontal agreements to introduce vertical restraints for their downstream buyers: the case of manufacturing firms jointly imposing RPM or territorial restrictions on their retailers comes naturally to mind. The reasoning is that joint imposition of such vertical restraints might help to maintain cartel discipline, or to make the market much less competitive. In the second case, a dominant firm might wish to impose vertical restraints in order to prevent downstream competition among its retailers dissipating monopoly rents, to tie its own hands not to make secret deals with selected retailers which would also undermine its profits, or to make it more difficult for a potential rival to enter (foreclosure). Effectively, the policy should aim to prohibit firms from making horizontal agreements to impose vertical restraints on their retailers, should identify vertical restraints as potential abuses by dominant firms, and in both cases should make provision for exemptions.

European policy has proceeded by making use of exemptions from Article 81, which does not distin-

[19] See Phlips (1995, ch. 4).
[20] *AKZO Chemie BV v Commission* OJ [1993] 5 CMLR 215.
[21] *Tetra Pak II* [1997] 5 CMLR 215.
[22] Note that Chapter II policy with respect to vertical restraints is considered in the next section.
[23] Respectively *Commercial Solvents v. Commission* [1974] ECR 223, [1974] 1 CMLR 309, and *Hugin Kassaregister v. Commission* [1979] ECR 1869, [1979] 3 CMLR 345.

[24] See Dobson and Waterson (1996); Vickers (1996); and European Commission (1997, ch. II).

guish vertical and horizontal, and therefore captures the whole range of vertical agreements. In particular, block exemptions have been issued for exclusive distribution agreements (regulation 1983/83), exclusive purchasing (regulation 1984/83) with special rules for beer and petrol distribution, and franchising (regulation 4087/88). There is no parallel block exemption for selective distribution systems, though there is now a substantial body of cases which indicate what will and will not be allowed under individual exemptions, and there is a special regime for motor vehicle distribution and servicing agreements (regulation 123/84). However, dominant firms (in the terms of Article 82) cannot rely on these exemptions. For example[25] in *BPB Industries plc v. Commission* and *Hoffman-La Roche v. Commission* exclusive purchasing agreements were condemned where the supplier was a dominant firm. However, there have not been many cases in which the issue has been tested by the Commission or before the European Court.

The original intention was that vertical agreements between firms at different levels of the supply chain to final consumers should generally be excluded from the category of anti-competitive agreements prohibited in Chapter I, but it proved impossible to produce a form of words to achieve this without unintentionally excluding some potentially anti-competitive agreements between competitors. Instead, the issue is addressed by section 50, which permits the Secretary of State 'by order [to] provide for any provision [of the Act] to apply in relation to . . . vertical agreements', and goes on to state that 'vertical agreements' may have such meaning as prescribed by an Order. This Order, and the OFT guidelines on *Vertical Agreements and Restraints*,[26] indicate that this matter will be dealt with as follows. First, the Order ('Exclusion Order') aims to exclude vertical agreements from the prohibition of agreements between firms: 'The Chapter I prohibition shall not apply to an agreement to the extent that it is a vertical agreement.' Second, a definition of vertical agreements is provided, reflecting the normal understanding that they are agreements between firms at different levels in the production and distribution chains. The exclusion does not apply in cases where there is more than one firm involved at different levels: for example, an agreement between one manufacturer and six wholesalers would not be exempt. Exempt agreements fall into two categories. First, those that

relate to conditions under which the firms involved may purchase, sell, or resell the goods in question, but agreements that have the effect of RPM are not allowed. Second, agreements in relation to intellectual property rights, where these are directly related to the use, sale, or resale of goods. Moreover, agreements that benefit from a EC individual or block exemption, as noted above, are automatically exempt from the Chapter I prohibition.[27]

These exemptions do not apply to dominant firms (defined as those with market shares in excess of 40 per cent), whose conduct will continue to be scrutinized under Chapter II. The guidelines in *The Chapter II Prohibition* on this subject are quite detailed (OFT, 1999*b*, sections 4.36–4.51). The guidelines provide a list of practices that will come under scrutiny if practised by a dominant firm: RPM, selective distribution, exclusive distribution, exclusive purchasing or dealing, tie-in sales and bundling, full-line forcing, quantity forcing, fidelity discounts, and non-linear pricing. It is noted that, 'These arrangements are common business practices and will be an abuse only if they lead to a reduction in competition.' The possible effects on competition are then explained. RPM can prevent competition in retailing. Exclusive purchasing or dealing, tie-in sales, full-line or quantity forcing, and slotting fees are identified as instruments for market foreclosure at the manufacturing stage. Exclusive or selective distribution, full-line or quantity forcing, non-linear pricing, and franchise fees may foreclose markets to retailers. Even if markets are not effectively foreclosed, these practices still may have the effect of dampening competition between manufacturers or retailers. As we saw in section III, the ambiguity of the economic analysis is perhaps greater here than in any other single competition policy issue. So the absence of an Article 81(3) procedure in Chapter II is a serious gap. The guidelines, very wisely, have sought to infiltrate a rule of reason approach, under the guise of the 'objective justification' doctrine (sections 4.47–4.51).

4. Scale monopolies, complex monopolies, and mergers

An important feature of the new UK competition policy framework is the retention of so-called 'structural' policies to deal with scale monopolies, complex

[25] *BPB Industries plc v Commission* 65/89 [1993] ECR II-389, and *Hoffman-La Roche v Commission* 85/76 [1979] ECR 461, [1979] 3 CMLR 211.
[26] OFT (2000), in draft only at time of writing (January 2000).

[27] The relevant document is the EC Verticals Block Exemption, which applies from 1 June 2000.

monopolies, and mergers. The first two of these have no parallels in European policy; the third is an area where European policy was relatively undeveloped until the Merger Regulation (4064/89) was introduced in 1989. In the UK all three areas are dealt with under the Fair Trading Act 1973, and follow similar procedures. The market situation or merger is investigated first by the OFT (in conjunction with the Mergers Panel in the case of mergers), and if the Director General believes that there should be a full investigation he advises the Secretary of State to refer the matter to the Competition Commission (formerly the Monopolies and Mergers Commission).

In cases of scale monopoly or complex monopoly, the first task of the Commission is to ascertain that a 25 per cent market-share criterion is fulfilled. A 'monopoly' is where a single firm has more than 25 per cent of the market or markets which are the subject of the reference. A 'complex monopoly' is basically a group of firms which has a joint 25 per cent share,[28] where the firms involved are behaving similarly even though there is no evidence of an agreement between them. In a merger case the criterion is again a 25 per cent market share, or a test based on the value of assets involved in the merger. Evidently this raises the same issues of market definition discussed above.

The Competition Commission investigation is guided by a criterion of the public interest, defined to include effective competition, consumer interests, innovation, balanced regional distribution of industry and employment, and the international competitive position of UK producers. The Competition Commission reports to the Secretary of State, giving its findings in respect of the matters referred and making recommendations if the market situation or merger is found to be contrary to the public interest.

Recommendations can include seeking undertakings from a monopolist or oligopoly in respect of business practices, the implementation of price control, and even structural changes such as divestment: in the case of a merger the recommendation can be that the merger be disallowed or that it should be made subject to conditions. There are no penalties for past anti-competitive behaviour. It is for the Secretary of State to decide whether to approve or vary the remedies (if any) recommended in the Competition Commission report. All these policy provisions are carried forward, essentially unchanged, into the new competition policy framework. The old Monopolies and Mergers Commission has become the Competition Commission in its reporting mode, and nothing else has changed.

VII. Conclusions: an evaluation of competition policy in the UK

The paper has argued four propositions concerning competition policy. The first three relate to the objectives and design of policy and institutions and form a logical sequence; the fourth looks at international aspects of policy, particularly the issue of policy jurisdiction between, for example, the member states of the EU and the European Commission in Brussels. We began in section II with the proposition that competition policy should seek to promote economic efficiency. The alternatives are that it should promote competition, *per se*, or that it should operate with fairly broadly defined public-interest criteria. We rejected the former alternative on the grounds that competition can, paradoxically, sometimes be inimical to economic efficiency. The public-interest objective is harder to reject, because it is eminently reasonable that public policy should be concerned with more than just economic efficiency, though it clearly generates considerable uncertainty for firms about what they may and may not do. However, we suggested that this point can be met substantially by the traditional argument about economic policy making, that it is best to assign separate instruments to different targets.

If the first proposition is accepted, it is then necessary to identify market situations and conduct, which are, or are not, conducive to economic efficiency. In section III of the paper, the common policy agenda across different competition policy jurisdictions was identified as (i) agreements between firms, (ii) abuse of dominant positions, and (iii) the acquisition and maintenance of dominant positions. Developments in industrial organization theory in the last 15 years have shown that the effects on economic efficiency in these three areas are seldom entirely clear cut: usually there is a trade-off involved with ambiguous net effects on welfare (price-fixing cartels are an exception). This judgement gives rise to our second proposition: economic analysis is often ambiguous, a priori, about the efficiency effects of particular market structures and conduct. The second proposition generates a considerable difficulty for the design of competition policy. A policy which requires a case-by-case approach would

[28] It is natural to think of oligopolies, but parallel behaviour by a large number of small firms could also be investigated if their combined market share was 25 per cent, as in the MMC medical services case.

not only be extremely expensive, but would also fail to provide firms with a well-defined framework within which to pursue their activities. The third proposition, outlined in section IV, is therefore that institutional design is crucial for competition policy. In particular, policy rules and guidelines are necessary to spell out the presumptions of policy, but there should generally be a procedure by which firms can present a case for exemption if they can demonstrate offsetting efficiency gains. Furthermore, the rules and guidelines should identify situations where there is good reason to believe that competition might be absent, before any investigation of supposed 'anticompetitive practices', such as price discrimination or vertical restraints. Finally, we have argued that an appropriate institutional design must involve giving the competition authorities real 'teeth' to fine firms for abuses of market power, and to order structural remedies or regulation where the circumstances warrant such action.

There remains the question of the optimal shape of the competition policy institutions. We have argued that such institutions should be public (though not ruling out the possibility of a role for private actions, as an additional deterrent to abuses of market power); that there should be a single investigating institution with powers to identify and to investigate cases, and to propose remedies, within a clearly stated framework of rules and guidelines; that firms should be given an opportunity to make representations as to why the competition policy presumptions should not apply in a particular case; and that there should be a competition tribunal with the task of reviewing and monitoring the recommendations of the competition policy institution.

In the following sections we evaluate UK competition policy in the light of the four propositions. Much of this evaluation carries over to EU policy, but a few additional comments are appended in a separate section at the end.

1. Anticompetitive agreements.

It should be evident that Chapter I of the Competition Act 1998 conforms in most respects to the 'ideals' for competition policy set out above. Although the objectives of the legislation have been described by the government in terms of promoting competition and protecting consumer interests rather than the pursuit of economic efficiency, in this case the two coincide. Promoting competition by preventing price or market-sharing agreements between firms is virtually always consistent with economic efficiency.

Furthermore, the presumption against agreements is so strong that a general prohibition is the natural starting point, subject to the appreciability test which includes the precedents created by European decisions, and subject to the exclusion of small agreements (except for price fixing). The duty laid on the Director General to publish guidelines is to be welcomed, since it should reduce the costs of compliance by enabling firms to know the situations in which the prohibitions are likely to be applied. The guidelines produced by the OFT are generally very sensible. The provisions for exemptions also comply with our model of policy in that they recognize the possibility of ambiguity in the economic analysis. The system of block exemptions will reduce the administrative costs of the OFT and the compliance costs of firms, while the provision for individual exemptions will enable special cases to be considered on their merits. The institution of fines for infringements, coupled with the possibility of third party actions for damages, gives firms powerful incentives to comply with the prohibition.

2. Abuse of a dominant position.

As already noted, the objectives of the policy implicit in Chapter II of the Act and in the guidelines, may go beyond economic efficiency to include some notions of equality of treatment for customers and 'fair competition'.[29] Our view is that this introduces a lack of clarity in the analysis of market situations and conduct, and that it runs the risk of inhibiting behaviour which is in fact conducive to economic efficiency.

Whatever one's views on objectives of policy, it is surely essential that a prohibition should be clear as to what is prohibited, and in what circumstances. With respect to circumstances, the definition of dominance proposed by the OFT is entirely sensible, even if a firm might find it difficult to decide whether it is, in fact, dominant within a relevant market. The guidelines interpreting the prohibitions of section 18 of the Act are also perfectly sensible, but inevitably cannot present a clear definition of what constitutes an 'abuse' of a dominant position. The more the Office can do to exemplify 'abuses', the more effective the policy will be, recalling that the primary objective of policy is to educate firms into the rules of the market game that they must follow, and not to 'catch them out'.

[29] It would be difficult to justify a *general* prohibition of price discrimination without some such objectives: and at least some of the popular concern about 'predation' and price discrimination is a desire to protect the little guy against big business.

The provisions for the imposition of fines and other conditions on firms which are found to have abused a dominant position are to be welcomed. If the exercise of monopoly power is profitable, then firms have to be given incentives to comply with the rules. The possibility of third-party actions to recover damages is also important in giving policy the teeth it previously lacked. Under the old policy regime the Director General or the Monopolies and Mergers Commission could condemn certain practices as anti-competitive, but there were no punishments. A firm, therefore, had every incentive to behave anti-competitively until the practices were brought to light and the firm was told not to misbehave in future. After all, there was a reasonable chance it might never be found out!

Very evidently Chapter II of the 1998 Act brings policy in the UK into line with European policy, and the intention is that European experience will be normative for the application of the rules. This harmonization is to be welcomed. But it is not evident that the switch to a policy modelled on Article 82 is in all respects a gain. The problem is, as outlined above, that the evaluation of the 'abuses' identified by the Act and by the draft guidelines cannot be clear cut. In terms of economic efficiency alone, a general prohibition is simply not supported in the same way that a general prohibition of cartels, for example, is supported. It might, nevertheless, be argued that a prohibition is the best way to proceed, but only if there are provisions for firms to argue for exemption on efficiency grounds. The prohibition would make it clear that competition policy is going to be tough, while the possibility of exemption gives firms an incentive to provide the information on which a more favourable evaluation of a particular practice might be based. It might be argued that the Act does permit conduct to be evaluated generally since 'it is the actual or potential effects of a practice or policy which will determine whether it is abusive' (guide to the *Major Provisions of the Competition Act* (OFT, 1999*e*)), reflecting the wording of section 18, which refers to 'any conduct . . . which amounts to the abuse of a dominant position'. However, this is not the same as an exemption, since if the effects are those of the abuse of a dominant position, then the practice should attract condemnation and punishment, whatever its efficiency. The guide to the *Chapter II Prohibition* (OFT, 1999*b*) seeks to soften the impact of the legislation by adopting the European doctrine of 'objective justification'. Thus section 4.15 states, 'In general, price discrimination will not be an abuse in such industries [sc. industries with large fixed costs and low marginal costs e.g. utilities] if it leads to higher levels of output than an undertaking could achieve by charging every customer the same price.' Similarly, in section 4.47, vertical restraints may be objectively justified if there are countervailing efficiency gains. As already noted, this is not as useful as an Article 81(3) clause, with the possibility of block exemptions. Every case will have to be argued on its individual merits.

There is one other respect in which the new policy framework is unfortunate. Effectively the verdict on firm conduct is either 'not guilty', or 'guilty of an abuse and therefore fined': what is missing is an alternative finding of 'not an abuse but not conducive to competition', with the imposition of a structural remedy or order to desist from particular conduct.

3. Vertical agreements and restraints

The detailed attention to vertical agreements and restraints in the new UK policy framework is a significant improvement over previous policy. In particular the Competition Act 1998 and the accompanying OFT guidelines reflect two key conclusions of recent studies of vertical restraints. First, that policy should only be concerned with vertical restraints if competition is absent in either the upstream or the downstream market. Hence the guideline that under Chapter II the policy will normally only concern itself with vertical restraints practised by a dominant firm, defined as a firm with more than 40 per cent of the relevant market. Second, that there is a degree of ambiguity with respect to the efficiency effects of restraints, and a blanket prohibition is not therefore appropriate. Cases should be considered on their merits. Here the policy is somewhat handicapped by the adoption of the Article 82 framework, which lacks an exemption clause similar to Article 81(3). The situation is only partly redeemed by the import of the doctrine of 'objective justification' from EU policy, but it is clear from the *Chapter II Prohibition* guidelines that the OFT will apply a rule of reason to cases. The more awkward problem of 'block exemptions' is dealt with by applying the EC Vertical Block Exemptions which are based legally on Article 81(3). Evidently UK policy has been harmonized with that of the EU, with the helpful addition of guidelines to assist firms in understanding the circumstances in which they need to be careful to avoid behaviour which might be construed as anti-competitive. It would also probably be sensible for the Director General of Fair Trading to eschew the imposition of fines until there are some illustrative cases from the UK as well as from the EU.

4. Scale monopolies, complex monopolies, and mergers

The retention of the provisions of the Fair Trading Act 1973 in respect of scale monopolies and complex monopolies is a definite gain in comparison with European policy. Economic analysis has long recognized that there are market structures and practices which can result in loss of competition and economic efficiency without any obvious abuse of a dominant position by the firm or group of firms involved. In such cases the obvious remedies are structural, or, if that is too difficult to achieve, some degree of regulation (as in the case of the privatized utilities which are also natural monopolies).

An oddity is that the policy framework has retained the former Monopolies and Mergers Commission in the form of the reporting function of the Competition Commission to analyse cases. One wonders why the procedures have not been changed to bring them into line with the procedures proposed for Chapters I and II cases. That is, a system where the initial investigation is undertaken by the OFT. The Director General would issue a report and assessment, including any action that should be taken, such as refusing a merger, requiring a dominant firm to desist from certain market practices, or even some structural changes (e.g. divestment). There would then be a right of appeal to the Competition Commission, as in Chapters I and II cases. This system would remove the role of the Secretary of State in receiving and deciding upon recommendations from the reporting arm of the Competition Commission. If the objective of policy is to promote competition, then it is hard to see any justification for involvement of ministers in implementation, which should be purely administrative. The argument against similar procedures for all competition cases[30] is that there will be a significant difference in 'culture' between cases under Chapters I and II, and the wider-ranging enquiries in structural cases. The concern is that the inevitably legalistic approach of the former would spread to the latter.

Implicitly the public-interest criterion has been retained, despite considerable criticism: and the assurance that references to the Commission will be made primarily on competition grounds is only partly reassuring. It just seems odd to have competition as the

basis for the Chapters I and Chapter II policy, and then have something different for structural policy. There is no point of principle which would support the divergence. (And, of course, an economist would prefer the criterion to be economic efficiency.)[31] In respect of rules, the essence of structural policies is that there is no presumption as to the effect of structure on competition, so prohibitions are not relevant. So a full investigation of particular cases is in order. However, there is much to be said for the development of guidelines, perhaps along the lines of the US Department of Justice (1992) Merger Guidelines, and especially if this were linked to changing the burden of proof (on this more below).

We consider briefly an aspect of competition policy which is neglected by both the UK and European policy regimes. If one is concerned about competition (either for its own sake or as a means to economic efficiency), then there is much to be said for a policy which aims to prevent potentially anti-competitive market situations emerging. The antitrust legislation of the United States in section 2 of the Sherman Act 1890 recognizes this in measures to prevent 'attempting to monopolize a market'. In principle, dominant positions in markets can arise in a number of different circumstances. The first is public grant, as in the privatization of utilities in the UK in recent years. A government which is serious about competition should ensure that the market structure created by privatization is as competitive as possible, given the circumstances of the industry. Where competition is not possible, as in the case of natural monopolies, then some regulatory framework will have to be put in place from the beginning. The 1998 Act strengthens the hand of the regulators by bringing the regulated utilities within its scope. In particular, regulators will now be able to apply Chapter II to counter any abuse of a dominant position, including the power to impose a fine for anti-competitive behaviour.

The second route to market dominance is 'skill, foresight, and industry'. This is when a firm has competed vigorously and successfully in terms of products, quality, and price, and has seen off the competition in

---

[30] Apart from the adage 'if it ain't broke, don't fix it' (attributed to Bert Lance, an American government official, in *The Nation's Business*, May 1977): after all the Monopolies and Mergers Commission system appeared to be working well enough. Moreover, the 1998 reforms had the undoubted advantage of legislative simplicity for the government.

[31] It can be argued that, in practice, the public-interest criterion will continue to be interpreted by the first three criteria of Section 84 of the Fair Trade Act, which are competition, consumer benefit, and innovation—the last two criteria (exports and regional employment) having hardly ever been used. In which case there is no substantive difference from Chapters I and II. However, in the past there have been cases where matters that have no connection to competition have been considered—e.g. the MMC reports on Lonrho/House of Fraser (1979) or Elders IXL/Allied Lyons (1986)—and there is no guarantee that such cases will not occur in future if the public-interest criterion is retained.

the process. This is the defence that has been advanced in a number of recent antitrust cases in high technology sectors: it was argued by IBM in the 1970s and by Microsoft in the late 1990s. The concern is, of course, that such firms having achieved dominance by acceptable means may resort to anti-competitive actions to preserve that dominance, and that they may abuse their dominant position by charging monopoly prices. It would not be sensible to try to stop firms achieving dominance by this route: but, once they have achieved it, there is every reason for the competition authorities to keep a very close eye on their continuing activities to prevent abuse (under Article 82 or Chapter II).

The third route is by anti-competitive market practices. The focus here is on predation and vertical restraints. Under the UK framework for policy, such behaviour cannot be contested by the competition authorities unless the firm is already dominant in the relevant market. However, it is not difficult to envisage circumstances in which a multidivisional firm has a relatively small market share in one of the markets in which it operates, but is able to use resources from other divisions to conduct a predatory campaign to gain market share in that market.[32] Once it has passed the threshold for market dominance it may then modify its behaviour to avoid being attacked under the provisions of Chapter II. One way of dealing with this possibility would be to allow the provisions of Chapter II to be applied to the conduct of very large firms (defined on an asset basis, as in the merger policy) even if in the particular market in question the firm is not dominant (yet).

The final route is that of mergers and acquisitions. In principle, this route to dominance is well covered by the provisions of current policy. But it would perhaps be wise to consider again the burden of proof in assessing the public interest in mergers which will potentially create dominant positions. If the objective of policy, as reiterated by the government, is to maintain competitive markets, then it surely should be a privilege to be permitted to build a dominant position in a market by merger, and a privilege which should be granted only after the firm has shown net public benefits therefrom.[33] After all mergers are the ultimate 'collusive agreements', and such agreements are rigorously opposed under Chapter I. There is a distinct possibility that a tougher policy regime in respect of horizontal agreements will simply increase the incentives for merger. Reversing the burden of proof (in cases where *de minimis* rules do not apply) would also assist in arriving at an accurate evaluation of a proposed merger, since the firms involved would have every incentive to provide the evidence that the competition authorities required.

5. EU policy

Given our generally favourable assessment of UK policy after the 1998 Competition Act, our evaluation of EU policy should also be generally positive. However, there are a number of concerns, some equivalent to our concerns about UK policy, others not. One such concern is that while Article 81 has a section 3, which permits both block and individual exemptions to be granted on the basis of beneficial affects of particular agreements, there are no corresponding sections in either Article 82 or the Merger Regulation. This denies market participants the opportunity to argue that a particular merger or dominant firm practice does offer efficiency gains. A danger in giving such an opportunity might be that it would give greater scope for industrial policy ('European champions') proponents, not least within the European Commission: however, that is not a reason for preventing DGIV from considering the point in a particular case, however sceptically. A second concern, noted by Sapir *et al.* (1993) and by Neven *et al.* (1993), is that EU merger policy, even since the introduction of the Merger Regulation, has been seen to be ineffective. Tougher policy rules, and tougher implementation are required. A third concern is that Article 82 does not provide for remedies where a market situation is not conducive to economic efficiency but the actual conduct of dominant firms is 'innocent'. A fourth concern is that the rules on price discrimination and vertical restraints, for example, do not reflect the ambiguity of economic analysis with respect to the welfare consequences of these practices. A fifth concern is the absence of a specialized competition tribunal to review the decisions of DGIV. The European Court procedure is too slow and cumbersome. The effect has been to leave DGIV acting as both prosecutor and judge in competition cases, which is unacceptable.

6. Harmonization of UK and EU policies

Our fourth proposition is that harmonization of national competition policies, and possibly a supra-

---

[32] This point has been persuasively argued by Newton (1998) in a perceptive comment on the Act.

[33] The argument that the authorities should not interfere in the takeover market, because shareholders know best, is besides the point. Shareholders should indeed support takeovers which create market power for their companies, but that is clearly not in the public interest!

national competition policy authority, are essential. The obvious application of this proposition is to relationships between European policy and DGIV on the one hand, and policy and institutions in the UK (or any other member state of the EU) on the other hand. This is not just for administrative tidiness: lack of coordination generates significant problems. The first is where the relevant market or markets being examined in a competition case are genuinely multinational, and the issue of extraterritoriality is raised. A particular example is where a merger wholly overseas affects the level of competition, or potential competition, in a domestic market. The question is whether domestic competition-policy authorities have the capacity to pursue the issue. Either there have to be bilateral agreements between the competition-policy authorities in different economies, or they have to cede the authority to act to a supranational body. Obviously there will have to be agreements on the division of labour between national authorities and the supranational agency. The EU Merger Regulation spells out some rules, mainly relating to the degree to which the parties are operating in more than one member state, and the overall size of the merger. In other policy areas, as noted previously, all EU policy rules take precedence over national policy, though DGIV is unlikely to get involved with competition in national domestic markets unless trade within the Union is potentially affected.

The second problem is that a lax competition policy might be used by a member state as a substitute for trade policy or industrial policy, to protect domestic producers or to promote export sectors. The solution here, as in trade policy (the World Trade Organization), is for international agreements to harmonize policies. It is a moot point whether a supranational authority is also required. Obviously, consistency in competition policy is going to be easier to achieve with a central authority. In the EU context, the ability of DGIV to override member-state interests is probably crucial for full integration of the European market.

If this fourth proposition is accepted, the UK should press for reform of EU policy to deal with the weaknesses identified above. The major practical difficulty is decisions on whether the EU or UK authorities should handle a particular case. As in the case of the EU Merger Regulation, published rules for assignment are probably the best method, with negotiation between the authorities to decide borderline cases.

References

Adams, W. J., and Yellen, J. (1976), 'Commodity Bundling and the Burden of Monopoly', *Quarterly Journal of Economics*, **90**, 475–98.

Aghion, P., and Bolton, P. (1987), 'Contracts as a Barrier to Entry', *American Economic Review*, **77**, 388–401.

Armstrong, M., Cowan, S., and Vickers, J. S. (1994), *Regulatory Reform: Economic Analysis and British Experience*, Cambridge, MA, MIT Press.

Baumol, W. J. (1982), 'Contestable Markets: An Uprising in the Theory of Industry Structure', *American Economic Review*, **72**, 1–15.

Bolton, P., and Scharfstein, D. (1990), 'A Theory of Predation Based on Agency Problems in Financial Contracting', *American Economic Review*, **80**, 93–106.

Bork, R. H. (1978), *The Antitrust Paradox*, New York, Basic Books.

Brock, G. W. (1975), *The US Computer Industry: A Study of Market Power*, Cambridge MA, Harvard University Press.

Dixit, A. K., and Norman, V. (1978), 'Advertising and Welfare', *Bell Journal*, **9**, 1–17.

Dobson P. W., and Waterson M. (1996), 'Vertical Restraints and Competition Policy', Office of Fair Trading, Research Paper 12, London.

European Commission (1997), *Green Paper on Vertical Restraints in EC Competition Policy*, COM (96) 721, Brussels

Evans, D. S. (ed.) (1983), *Breaking up Bell*, New York, North Holland.

Fisher, F., McGowan, J., and Greenwood, J. (1983), *Folded, Spindled and Mutilated: Economic Analysis and US vs. IBM*, Cambridge MA, MIT Press.

Franks, J., and Harris, R. (1989), 'Shareholder Wealth Effects of UK Takeovers', in J. A. Fairburn and J. A. Kay (eds), *Mergers and Merger Policy*, 148–74, Oxford, Oxford University Press.

Geroski, P. A. (1993), 'Antitrust Policy towards Cooperative R&D Ventures', *Oxford Review of Economic Policy*, **9**(2), 58–71.

Gilbert, R. J. (1989), 'Mobility Barriers and the Value of Incumbency', ch. 8 in R. Schmalensee and R. Willig (eds), *Handbook of Industrial Organisation*, Amsterdam, North Holland.

——— Newbery, D. M. G. (1982), 'Pre-emptive Patenting and the Persistence of Monopoly', *American Economic Review*, **72**, 514–25.

Graham E. M., and Richardson J. D. (eds) (1997), *Global Competition Policy*, Institute for International Economics, Washington DC

Grossman, S., and Hart, O. D. (1980), 'Takeover Bids, the Free-rider Problem and the Theory of the Corporation', *Bell Journal*, **11**, 42–64.

Hart, O., and Tirole, J. (1990), 'Vertical Integration and Market Foreclosure', *Brookings Papers on Economic Activity*, Microeconomics, 205–86.

Hay, D. A. (1994), 'International aspects of competition policy in the United Kingdom', University of Oxford Institute of Economics and Statistics Applied Economics Discussion Paper Series No. 160.

—— Vickers, J. S. (1987), 'The Economics of Market Dominance', in D. A. Hay and J. S. Vickers (eds), *The Economics of Market Dominance*, Oxford, Blackwell.

—— Morris, D. J. (1991), *Industrial Economics and Organization*, Oxford, Oxford University Press.

Hay, G. A. (1981), 'A Confused Lawyer's Guide to the Predatory Pricing Literature', in S. Salop (ed.), *Strategy, Predation and Antitrust Analysis*, Washington DC, Federal Trade Commission.

—— (1987), 'The Interaction of Market Structure and Conduct', ch. 4 in D. A. Hay and J. S. Vickers (eds.), *The Economics of Market Dominance*, Oxford, Blackwell.

Itoh, M., Kiyono, K., Okuno-Fugiwara, M., and Suzumura, K. (1991), *Economic Analysis of Industrial Policy*, San Diego, Academic Press.

Jacquemin, A., and Slade, M. E. (1989), 'Cartels, Collusion and Horizontal Merger', ch. 7 in R. Schmalensee and R. Willig (eds.), *Handbook of Industrial Organisation*, Amsterdam, North Holland.

Jensen, M. C., and Ruback, R. (1983), 'The Market for Corporate Control: The Scientific Evidence', *Journal of Financial Economics*, **11**, 5–50.

Katz, M. L. (1989), 'Vertical Contractual Relations', ch. 11 in R. Schmalensee and R. Willig (eds.), *Handbook of Industrial Organisation*, Amsterdam, North Holland.

Klemperer, P. (1995), 'Competition when Consumers have Switching Costs: An Overview with Applications to Industrial Organization, Macroeconomics and International Trade', *Review of Economic Studies*, 62, 515–39.

Krugman, P. R. (1984), 'Import Protection as Export Promotion: International Competition in the Presence of Oligopoly and Scale Economies', in H. Kierzkowski (ed.), *Monopolistic Competition and International Trade*, Oxford, Oxford University Press.

Lambin, J. J. (1976), *Advertising, Competition and Market Conduct in Oligopoly over Time*, Amsterdam, North-Holland.

Littlechild, S. C. (1986), *The Fallacy of the Mixed Economy*, 2nd edn, London, IEA.

Mankiw, N. G., and Whinston, M. D. (1986), 'Free Entry and Social Inefficiency', *Rand Journal of Economics*, **17**, 48–58.

Meeks, G. (1977), *Disappointing Marriage: A Study of the Gains from Merger*, Cambridge, Cambridge University Press.

Milgrom, P., and Roberts, J. (1982), 'Limit Pricing and Entry under Incomplete Information', *Econometrica*, **50**, 443–60.

Neale, A. D. (1970), *The Antitrust Laws of the USA: A Study of Competition Enforced by Law*, 2nd edn, Cambridge, Cambridge University Press (a third edition with D. G. Goyder as an additional author, was published in 1980).

Neven, D., and Phlips, L. (1985), 'Discriminating Oligopolists and Common Markets', *Journal of Industrial Economics*, **34**, 133–50.

—— Siotis, G. (1993), 'Foreign Direct Investment in the European Community: Some Policy Issues', *Oxford Review of Economic Policy*, 9(2), 72–93.

—— Nuttall, R., and Seabright, P. (1993), *Merger in Daylight*, London, CEPR.

Newton C. (1998), 'Do Predators Need to be Dominant?', *Competition and Regulation Bulletin*, 9 July, London Economics, London.

OFT (1985), *Competition and Retailing*, London.

—— (1999a), *The Chapter I Prohibition*, OFT 401, London

—— (1999b), *The Chapter II Prohibition*, OFT 402, London

—— (1999c), *Market Definition*, OFT 403, London

—— (1999d), *Assessment of Market Power*, OFT 415, London.

—— (1999e), *The Major Provisions of the Competition Act*, OFT 400, London.

—— (2000), 'Vertical Agreements and Restraints', draft, OFT 419, London

Ordover, J. A., and Saloner, G. (1989), 'Predation, Monopolization and Antitrust', ch. 9 in R. Schmalensee and R. Willig (eds), *Handbook of Industrial Organisation*, Amsterdam, North Holland.

—— and Salop, S. (1990), 'Equilibrium Vertical Foreclosure', *American Economic Review*, **80**, 127–42.

Phlips, L. (1983), *The Economics of Price Discrimination*, Cambridge, Cambridge University Press.

—— (1987), 'Information and Collusion', ch. 4 of D. A. Hay and J. S. Vickers (eds), *The Economics of Market Dominance*, Oxford, Blackwell.

—— (1995), *Competition Policy: A Game Theoretic Perspective*, Cambridge, Cambridge University Press.

Ravenscraft, D., and Scherer, F. M. (1987), *Mergers, Sell-Offs and Economic Efficiency*, Washington, The Brookings Institution.

Richardson, G. B. (1965), 'The Theory of Restrictive Practices', *Oxford Economic Papers*, **19**, 432–49.

Salop, S. (1979), 'Monopolistic Competition with Outside Goods', *Bell Journal*, **10**, 141-56.

—— (1985), 'Practices that (Credibly) Facilitate Oligopoly Coordination', in F. Mathewson and J. E. Stiglitz (eds), *New Developments in the Analysis of Market Structure*, London, Macmillan.

—— Scheffman, D. (1987), 'Cost Raising Strategies', *Journal of Industrial Economics*, **36**, 19–34.

Sapir, A., Buigues, P., and Jacquemin, A. (1993), 'European Competition Policy in Manufacturing and Services: a two speed approach?', *Oxford Review of Economic Policy*, 9(2), 113–32.

Schmalensee, R. (1978), 'Entry Deterrence in the Ready to Eat Breakfast Cereal Industry', *Bell Journal*, **9**, 305–27.

—— (1981), 'Output and Welfare Implications of Monopolistic Third Degree Price Discrimination', *American Economic Review*, **71**, 242-7.

—— (1987), 'Standards for Dominant Firms' Conduct: What can Economics Contribute?', ch. 2 of D. A. Hay and J. S. Vickers (eds), *The Economics of Market Dominance*, Oxford, Blackwell.

Schwarz, M. (1986), 'The Nature and Scope of Contestability Theory', *Oxford Economic Papers*, **38**, 37–57.

Shepherd, W. (1984), 'Contestability vs. Competition', *American Economic Review*, **74**, 572–87.

Smiley, R. (1988), 'Empirical Evidence on Strategic Entry Deterrence', *International Journal of Industrial Organisation*, **16**, 167–80.

Smith, A. (1776), *The Wealth of Nations*, available in a Penguin Classics edition, 1986.

Sutton, J. (1991), *Sunk Costs and Market Structure*, London, MIT Press.

Tirole, J. (1989), *The Theory of Industrial Organization*, Cambridge, MA, MIT Press.

US Department of Justice and Federal Trade Commission (1992), *Horizontal Merger Guidelines*, Washington DC.

Varian, H. (1989), 'Price Discrimination', ch. 10 in R. Schmalensee and R. Willig (eds), *Handbook of Industrial Organisation*, Amsterdam, North Holland.

Vickers, J. S. (1996), 'Market Power and Inefficiency: A Contracts Perspective', *Oxford Review of Economic Policy*, **12**(4), 11-26

—— Yarrow, G. K. (1988), *Privatization: An Economic Analysis*, Cambridge, MA, MIT Press.

Whinston, M. D. (1990), 'Tying, Foreclosure and Exclusion', *American Economic Review*, **80**, 837–59.

Whish, R. (1993), *Competition Law*, 3rd edn, London, Butterworths. [A revised edition of this excellent text, incorporating the changes arising from the Competition Act 1998 is due in 2000.]

White, L. J. (1993), 'Competition Policy in the United States: An Overview', *Oxford Review of Economic Policy*, **9**(2), 133–53.

Williamson, O. E. (1968), 'Economies as an Antitrust Defence', *American Economic Review*, **58**, 18–31.

Willig, R. D. (1991), 'Merger Analysis, Industrial Organisation Theory and Merger Guidelines', *Brookings Papers on Economic Activity*, 281–331.

Yarrow, G. K. (1985), 'Shareholder Protection, Compulsory Acquisition and the Efficiency of the Takeover Process', *Journal of Industrial Economics*, **34**, 3–16.

7

Introducing competition into regulated industries

DIETER HELM

New College, Oxford

TIM JENKINSON[1]

Keble College, Oxford

I. Introduction

For most of the post-war period it has been a conventional wisdom that the market failures in the utility industries were so great as to merit state ownership, vertical integration, and monopoly. State ownership 'resolved' the conflict of interests between the private and public good; vertical integration ensured that customers bore the risk of upstream sunk investments; and monopoly prevented the destructive competition which was widely thought to have pervaded the industries in the 1920s and 1930s.

For a variety of reasons—some ideological, some budgetary and some grounded in economics—state ownership was abandoned as the preferred option in the 1980s. In Britain, assets with a current market value in excess of £100 billion[1] have been transferred to the private sector in the course of the extensive privatization programme.

As privatization got under way, the merits of vertical integration and monopoly were increasingly questioned, and the possibility of introducing competition actively considered. In the early 1980s, Mercury was

created as a competitor to British Telecom (BT). For certain companies in the state sector, the 1980 Competition Act abandoned the statutory monopoly, the 1982 Oil and Gas (Enterprise) Act limited British Gas's vertical integration into the North Sea, and the 1983 Energy Act provided for private purchase tariffs and network access in the electricity industry.

From these early tentative steps, bolder plans emerged, leading eventually to the idea of retail customer choice for all gas and electricity customers, the arrival of cable to rival BT, and even plans to introduce competition into the supply of water. The electricity and (eventually) the gas industries have been broken up, and the railways have been split along vertical and horizontal lines.

The concept of supply competition has caught on in Europe and the USA. Following the Single European Act in 1987, and the programme for completing the internal market by 1 January 1993, the European Commission turned its attentions to the utility sectors, with initiatives in telecoms, energy, and postal services. Draft directives in these areas have had a difficult history, but the general direction of European utility policy is now well-established as a process of gradually prising open the utility markets. In the USA the 1996 Telecoms Act further liberalized the telecommunications market, while the 1992 Energy Act and the subsequent order 888 by the Federal Energy Regulatory Commission (FERC, 1996) provided for the transition to a more competitive electricity supply

First published in *Oxford Review of Economic Policy*, vol. 13, no. 1 (1997). This version has been updated.

[1] It is increasingly difficult to estimate the market value of privatized companies as a result of the large number of takeovers that have occurred. However, Jenkinson and Mayer (1994) estimated that in July 1992, before the recent takeover wave, the market capitalization of the listed privatized companies was over £80 billion. Subsequent privatizations and general stock-market movements suggest that this figure would now be over £100 billion.

market, at least at the wholesale level. Numerous other countries have also begun the process of introducing competition, notably New Zealand, Chile, Australia, and Sweden.

As with privatization, the idea of competition has driven politicians frequently to embrace policies without sufficient attention to the details of implementation. The simple political rhetoric extolling the virtues of competition belies the complexities in its application. Too often the public debate fails to distinguish the different kinds of competition and the particular characteristics of each industry. Competition is not an end in itself, but rather a means to higher economic welfare. Its applicability to particular circumstances depends upon the relevant costs and benefits. While there are frequently considerable gains, regulated monopoly may in some circumstances be preferable. Even where competition is both feasible and desirable, the transitional arrangements may have profound effects on the type and degree of competition that emerges, and the political acceptability of the outcome.

In this chapter, a number of these complexities are considered. In section II, we discuss the types of competition and the necessary conditions which must be met to make competition work. In section III, the transitional issues are considered, including the problem of stranded assets, the impact of technology, and cross-subsidies. Finally, in section IV, we examine the regulatory implications. Contrary to the views of some of the early exponents of competition, there is little evidence (and little reason to imagine) that as competition rises, regulation will 'wither away'.

II. The structure of competitive markets

In order to design a policy to introduce competition, there are a number of conceptual issues which need to be addressed. The utilities comprise different elements, each of which displays different kinds of market failure. All utilities contain networks, and most of these have significant elements of natural monopoly. Access to the network is essential for producers to get their products to customers. It follows that not all parts of utilities are open to production and supply competition, though there may be other kinds of competition which can be applied to the core network.

Thus, we need to distinguish the different kinds of competition which can be applied to utilities and the underlying structural components to which these may be appropriate. We also need to consider the linkages between stages of production, and therefore the forms and degrees of vertical integration which maximize efficiency.

1. Types of competition

When the advocates of competition discuss utilities, they typically distinguish between natural monopoly and potentially competitive activities, and focus on the latter. This distinction is useful, and we return to it below. The competition they have in mind is *output* (or commodity) *competition*, and the traditional models of competitive markets are used to elicit the conditions under which it can be promoted.

Within the domain of output competition, a number of distinctions can be made. These focus on two dimensions: *the definition of the output* and *the time period*. In the utility sector, the boundaries between production and transmission, and between supply and distribution are uncertain. For example, in the electricity industry, generation of electricity is a fairly well-defined activity, but the boundary between generation and the related dispatch and Pool activities is not. In addition, electricity generation provides not only the commodity itself, but the stand-by capacity which ensures that, whatever time of day we turn on a light, the power is instantly available.

Downstream, at the customer interface, there are a variety of services which lie on the boundary between supply and distribution. Customers buy electricity with associated services, such as meter reading, energy advice, credit facilities, and payment options. If competition is confined to the commodity (which is, after all, homogeneous), it focuses on purchasing strategy, financial risk management, and marketing, and, as such, may be highly competitive with small margins. Financial failures of suppliers are quite possible and mechanisms have to be put in place to deal with customers stranded by a failed supplier. If, however, the other services are added in, supply competition is a much broader activity.

The strategy many policy-makers and regulators have adopted is to begin with the core supply activities, and gradually extend competition to the ancillary services. There is much to commend this approach, as we discuss in section III below. However, in a number of utilities, a prior decision has been made to widen the initial definition of outputs. In gas, for example, supply is given a wide scope, to include social obligations. The consequence has been a form of quasi-franchise competition.[2]

Turning to the second dimension of output competition, the time period, very little economic activity is governed purely by spot transactions, even where there are spot markets. Competition also arises in contract markets and between vertically integrated firms. Economic theory suggests that the term structure of contracts will be determined in part by the project characteristics of upstream production and the lives of associated infrastructure assets. Again, the electricity industry provides a good example. Virtually all new entrants' combined-cycle gas-turbine power stations (CCGTs), built by independent power producers (IPPs), were based upon 10–15-year power purchase contracts with regional electricity companies (Helm, 1994a).

These time-period distinctions matter in designing policies to promote competition. Regulators have considerable control over the structure of contracts with final customers. If these customers are inhibited in signing long-term contracts with suppliers, risks cannot be assigned downstream. This will influence the type and amount of upstream investment. Similarly, if all electricity has to be dispatched through the Pool, and bilateral contracting outside the Pool is prohibited, then the structure of investment will be affected. (These issues are discussed further in section III(1) below.)

Output competition is not the only option in the utilities. Competition can also be applied to *inputs*. The usual mechanism is competitive tendering, whereby the utility is required to test its own production costs against the market. The uses of such mechanisms stretch from the reduction of the core areas of natural monopoly, through to a mechanism for overcoming the informational asymmetries between utilities and regulators when prices are set at periodic reviews.

It is not surprising that competitive tendering has been used most extensively as a regulatory tool in the water industry, where the scope for output competition is limited and, therefore, the pressure on costs to prevent the loss of market share is very weak. Although the theory of price-cap regulation stresses the incentives created to minimize costs, the severity of the problems associated with defining the starting cost base for periods, and the frequent inter-period interventions have reduced these incentives.[3] The role of input com-

petition has been further refined in the case of multi-utilities (notably Hyder, United Utilities, and ScottishPower) where the creation of facilities management companies, providing services to a number of utilities, has brought additional cost-allocation problems.

Most utilities operate under licences. These are granted for a period of time, and they can be open to competitive bidding. The competition in this case is for a monopoly right and, in theory, bidding should transfer the potential monopoly rent to customers or government. Such *franchise competition* has been applied most extensively in the railway privatization, where train-operating companies were required to provide a minimum standard of service, and then to bid for the right to a 7-year (or in some cases longer) monopoly. Where subsidies are involved, the bids were aimed at minimizing the Treasury contribution.

The final form of competition is provided by the *capital market*. Competing sets of owners and managers can take over the assets and licences of utilities and, given a price cap, attempt to reduce costs to maximize profits. Indeed, Professor Stephen Littlechild (former Director General of Electricity Supply) placed very considerable faith in this form of competition, arguing, for example, that the capital market pressure could be relied upon to play a significant role in the water industry in enforcing efficiency (Littlechild, 1988). Such competition has, however, been limited in many privatized utilities by golden shares put in place by government[4] and regulatory and political uncertainty as to references to the Competition Commission (formerly the Monopolies and Mergers Commission (MMC)) and subsequent decisions. Nevertheless, following the expiry of golden shares in the regional electricity companies and water companies in 1995, a large number of takeovers occurred, ironically mainly by US utilities whose claimed inefficiencies (as a result of the rate-of-return regulation) had been the main motive for adopting the superior price-cap incentives.[5]

These various types of competition—outputs, inputs, franchises, and takeovers—set in various time horizons provide a much more complex set of considerations for the design of competition initiatives. As we shall see below, politicians have rarely paid much

---

[2] In the pilot phases of domestic gas competition, participants were required to designate supply areas which contained a balanced socio-economic range of domestic customers (see Waddams Price, 1997).

[3] See Helm and Rajah (1994) for a discussion of the erosion of these incentives in the water industry.

[4] See Jenkinson and Ljungqvist (1996, ch. 7) for a discussion of golden shares and the conflicting objectives often faced by governments in conducting a privatization programme.

[5] See Beesley and Littlechild (1989) for a critique of US regulation. It has been suggested that the difference between US and UK costs of capital in utilities in part explains the valuation differences.

attention to these distinctions, preferring a crude catch-all concept.

2. Separating out the natural monopoly

While the previous section noted that input and output competition has, to a considerable extent, blurred the definition of what activities we would expect the operator of a set of natural monopoly assets to perform, it is still clear that it is typically the networks of pipes, wires, and rails that constitute the natural monopoly assets. A clear trend in UK regulatory policy has been to attempt to separate the operation (and increasingly the ownership) of these assets from the upstream or downstream activities (where competition may be possible). Some have seen this separation as a necessary condition for the development of competition.

Early privatizations, such as BT and British Gas, maintained horizontally and vertically integrated monopolies having *de jure* or *de facto* franchise areas that consisted of most UK customers. In such integrated businesses, definitions of costs for the various vertical stages of the businesses were ill-defined and, as a result, cross-subsidies were rife.[6] Indeed, in many of the early privatizations there was no proper cost allocation between the various businesses, let alone a realistic set of transfer prices.

As governments attempted to introduce competition into the sectors, it became apparent that cross-subsidization might well stifle entry, with new entrants potentially being at a competitive disadvantage to the integrated incumbent, who was able to cross-subsidize the competitive part of the business with profits from the natural monopoly element. There were also fears that if the network operator also operated in one of the potentially competitive upstream or downstream markets (such as generation or supply) they would be tempted to favour their associated business over competitors, whether in quality of service or in the prices charged for using the system. Even where such anticompetitive conduct did not, in fact, take place, the expectation that it *might* provided a powerful entry deterrent.

These concerns led, in the case of the gas industry, to the MMC (1993*a*) recommending that *prior to the introduction of competition* British Gas should be split up, with the operation of the pipeline network being the responsibility of a separate company, legally distinct from both the upstream exploration and the downstream supply business. The government rejected this recommendation. Accounting separation between the pipeline business and the other parts of British Gas was introduced, and the company itself eventually chose, in 1997, to split itself into two separate legal entities, BG plc and Centrica. However, from a regulatory perspective, the way the company was split was not ideal: the pipeline business was bundled together with most of the upstream exploration and production business (BG plc), while the downstream supply business was bundled together with the servicing company and the large Morecambe gas field (Centrica). The reasons for including a gas field with the supply company revolve around the impact of the introduction of competition on existing contracts (essentially a serious contracting problem was internalized within one company) and the need to make Centrica financially viable. We return to this issue of 'stranded contracts' in section III(1).

In the later privatizations of electricity and rail, attempts were made to introduce vertical separation between ownership of the network assets and the other markets into which competition was to be introduced. In the case of rail, the vertical separation has gone to its logical extreme, with the rail network being operated by Railtrack (which is barred from running train services), and train-operating companies competing for the right to run particular services and leasing trains from separate rolling-stock companies. In the electricity supply industry, two networks exist: the high voltage transmission network (operated by the National Grid Company) and the local distribution networks operated by the regional electricity companies. The latter, however, are also involved in the supply of electricity to the final households and many have also made significant investments in electricity generation. The logic of separating out the natural monopoly implied the separation of the distribution businesses from the supply and generation businesses, which has recently occurred.

The encouragement of entry and competition is clearly one important motivation for separating out the natural monopoly. However, a further justification for such a policy is that it improves the information upon which regulators make their decisions. While 'ring-fence' accounting of regulated assets is possible, the task of regulators would certainly become easier if all data—both accounting and market-related, such as share prices, credit ratings, and dividends—referred solely to the regulated company. This issue has become especially important as utilities have di-

---

[6] In addition to cost uncertainties, a further cause of cross-subsidy was deliberate social policy. This is discussed more extensively in section III(2) below.

versified into unregulated businesses, or have been acquired by other companies.

By mid-1997, for example, 11 of the 12 original UK regional electricity companies (privatized in 1990) had been taken over. The majority were acquired by US utilities keen to diversify overseas. Some were acquired by water companies to form 'multi-utilities'. One (Manweb) was acquired by the vertically integrated ScottishPower. Another (Eastern Electricity, later the Eastern Group) was acquired by Hanson and then spun off into an integrated energy company (the Energy Group), after acquiring divested coal generation assets from National Power and PowerGen. The Energy Group was then subject to bids by the US utilities, PacifiCorp and Texas Utilities. These bids were referred, by the new Labour government, to the MMC, despite the fact that the original takeover by Hanson was not subjected to MMC scrutiny. Eventually, the bids were cleared by the MMC and Texas Utilities won control of Eastern. Water companies, themselves protected to a considerable extent from takeover, have also been acquisitive, moving into both unregulated businesses (such as waste management) and other regulated sectors (for example, North West Water acquired its local electricity distribution company, Norweb, and renamed the merged group United Utilities, while Welsh Water similarly acquired SWALEC and became Hyder).

While accounting information on the core regulated company has been retained (and in some cases ringfencing has been reinforced) such acquisitions inevitably raise questions about abuses of transfer pricing and cross-subsidy, as well as denying the regulator potentially valuable market information about the performance of the regulated companies.

These regulatory concerns motivate the calls for the separate listing of the core utility businesses (see, for example, Byatt, 1997; Jenkinson and Mayer, 1997) that have, so far, been vigorously opposed by the companies themselves. On the one hand, separate listing represents one substantive way in which the information flowing to regulators could be improved, and is, in many ways, the logical extension of the policy to separate out the core natural monopoly from the potentially competitive businesses. On the other, it can be argued that changes in the underlying cost structure dictate a more market-based approach.

3. Vertical integration and contracts

When utilities face no competition for final customers they are able to enter into all sorts of contracts—for supply, fuel, assets, and services—with very limited

risk, provided they are allowed to pass on the costs to final customers. In the case of vertically integrated monopolies many of these contracts are internalized within the firm and may not even be formally defined. The utility may be able to cross-subsidize between customers, and invest in assets that may not be economic (or are too risky) since it can earn supernormal returns on other assets to compensate.

Two important characteristics of utility industries are the relatively long asset lives and the fact that a large proportion of the investment is sunk, with few alternative uses. Given these asset characteristics it is quite rational for companies to want to sign long-term contracts with customers in order to reduce the risk of investing. In particular, long-term contracts may be needed in order to prevent the hold-up problem (see Williamson, 1985; Lyons, 1996) whereby customers may act opportunistically, once the investment has been sunk, and renegotiate terms to their own advantage. A lack of competition in large parts of the final market essentially allowed such long-term contracts to be written.

When the core natural monopoly is separated (either legally or by ring-fencing) from the upstream and downstream businesses, contracts are typically put in place between companies at different vertical positions in the production chain. These contracts reproduce many of the characteristics of vertical ownership. Before privatization they were frequently put in place by the government. For example, in the case of the UK electricity industry, the generators were required to sign contracts with coal suppliers which were linked to 'back-to-back' contracts to sell power on to regional electricity companies. The regional electricity companies in turn had a monopoly franchise in their domestic markets which guaranteed a market for the final electricity. The (high) cost of coal was thus passed down the contract chain to the final consumer with few risks to any of the parties concerned. Arguably, the industry was more vertically integrated in the early years after privatization than before, despite the vertical separation of formal ownership.

Similarly, British Gas could enter into long-term gas supply contracts with North Sea producers to meet its supply obligations in the expectation that it would continue to have a monopoly franchise over the residential market into which the gas could be sold. Of course, such expectations have, in the event, been overly optimistic, and we explore in the next section the implications of unanticipated changes in policy on the incumbent and potential entrants.

Hence, franchise markets for the final product provide an end point in the contracting chain. Even if there is extensive vertical separation of the various parts of the chain, the existence of a monopoly market into which the product can ultimately be sold allows long-term contracts to be written between firms at various stages of production. Competition for final customers undermines this chain. Thus, in introducing competition, a significant shift in risk allocation takes place. It is to the problems of this transition that we now turn.

III. The transition to competitive markets

The design of a competitive market will vary from industry to industry, according to the kinds of market failure identified. However, design is only a necessary condition for a competition policy for the utilities. It is practically impossible instantaneously to translate a monopolistic, state-owned industry into a competitive one. Although there may be much debate concerning a relatively fast versus a slower transition, in the UK all the main transitions have taken at least 7 years to liberalize formally, and all will, in practice, take more than a decade to complete.

There are several reasons why transitions are complex. Some of these are primarily distributional, related to the property rights the affected parties hold at privatization. Those held by producers may give rise to stranded assets. Consumers, too, have typically experienced widespread cross-subsidies in the state sector, and the unwinding of these under competition creates losers as well as winners. In addition, there are important technical constraints on the form and speed of the transition. We now consider each of these constraints in turn.

1. Contracting problems

In the previous section we argued that the introduction of competition can have significant implications for the whole vertical chain of contracts in utility industries. In the absence of such contracts (or even if they are written, because they are likely to be of a much shorter duration) uncertainty is increased. This increased uncertainty has two major implications. First, the required rates of return to investment are likely to increase. Since many investments in the utility sector are partially, or completely, irreversible, increased uncertainty is likely to result in higher required rates of return for investment. As Dixit and Pindyck (1994)

show, when the capital stock can be adjusted upwards by investment, but cannot be adjusted downwards other than through depreciation, expansion today may leave the firm with surplus assets over a prolonged period should future conditions turn out to be less favourable than currently expected. By *not* investing today, the firm retains an *option* to expand later, should investment indeed be warranted. This option is more valuable as uncertainty increases, and the loss of the option can be considered an important part of the cost of investing. While it is difficult to value such options, this approach suggests that increased uncertainty is likely to increase significantly the cost of capital and hence the 'hurdle rates' that firms use to evaluate investment projects. Ultimately, of course, the effect of an increase in the cost of capital is likely to be borne by the consumer in the form of higher prices.

Second, the increased level of uncertainty helps to explain the general desire to reintegrate vertically in some sectors, such as electricity. It is well known that there are potential benefits and costs from such integration. If the upstream is not competitive then vertical integration can be welfare-enhancing under certain circumstances (see Waterson, 1996). On the other hand, vertical integration may act as a barrier to entry and lead to foreclosure problems. In the UK, the Conservative government lacked consistency in its treatment of vertical reintegration, waving through some early vertical takeovers, and allowing Eastern Group (an electricity distribution and supply company) to acquire a substantial amount of generating capacity from PowerGen and National Power, while blocking bids by the latter two companies to acquire regional distribution and supply companies themselves.[7] The Labour government's position shows no signs of any greater level of consistency.

In theory, there are solutions to these contracting problems. Markets can develop to replace the long-term implicit or explicit contracts that previously existed. In theory, once spot markets develop, derivative markets should soon follow, such as options and futures markets. It should, in principle, be possible to spread risks and transact in such markets, just like any other competitive industry.

However, in practice, the emergence of such markets is not spontaneous or straightforward. In the case of electricity, it is necessary to define precisely what the market refers to. A megawatt-hour of electricity produced at 5 p.m. is worth much more than one pro-

---

[7] See MMC (1996*a,b*). In this case the government went against the majority recommendation of the MMC.

duced at 3 a.m., and one produced in the summer is worth less than one produced in the winter. Electricity is not storable[8] and so such issues matter. In addition, there have been long-standing concerns related to market power in the Pool. These have led to planned implementation of new trading arrangements, to replace the existing Pool, in autumn 2000. Gas markets have only developed since the mid-1990s. While a sizeable proportion of gas is traded in bilateral deals,[9] the first formal physical gas spot market was only introduced at the end of January 1997 by the International Petroleum Exchange. The contracts traded are for delivery of physical natural gas to a notional point in the pipeline network. Volumes have gradually built up and the market prices are beginning to be used as reference points for longer-term gas supply contracts.[10]

Thus, although markets can be used, in theory, to hedge many of the risks introduced by competition, to date the development of such spot, forward, and derivative markets has been inadequate to solve such problems. Furthermore, it is unlikely that these problems will be solved in the short to medium term, and the traditional risk-spreading mechanism—vertical integration—is likely to remain a substantive objective of firms in utility markets for some time to come.

The introduction of competition not only makes it more difficult to write new contracts but can also result in existing contracts being *stranded*. This is especially a problem when there is a change in policy regarding the introduction of competition.

For example, in the 1980s and early 1990s British Gas had signed a portfolio of long-term contracts with upstream gas producers (including its own exploration and production division) in the expectation that it would retain a monopoly over residential (although not industrial) gas supply. During its investigation into the gas industry in 1993, the MMC considered how competition should be introduced and concluded that such competition should be phased in cautiously with most residential customers being offered a choice of supplier by 2002. In the event, in exchange for rejecting the MMC's recommendation for structural break-up (discussed above), the government chose to ignore this caution and announced that the market would be completely liberalized by 1998 (in line with electricity).

Of course, had British Gas anticipated such a policy change, its optimal portfolio of supply contracts would, in all likelihood, have looked very different. It would have known that, after 1998, it would be exposed to substantial price risk, as there would no longer be a guaranteed market for its contracted supplies. Hence, it is unlikely that British Gas would have agreed to contracts extending beyond 1998 that were not referenced, in some way, on the post-1998 spot price of gas. This is especially important as many gas supply contracts are of the 'take-or-pay' variety, specifying both price and quantity.

In the event, the stranded contracts problem for British Gas resulting from the change in government policy was exacerbated by the large falls in the spot price of gas in the run-up to liberalization. British Gas entered the new competitive era with a portfolio of supply contracts committing it to purchase gas at an average of around 20p per therm, while gas could in 1995 (when new entrants were first entering into supply contracts) be bought for as little as 8–10p per therm. New entrants, unencumbered with such contracts, were thus able to enter the market and undercut the incumbent with ease. While such stranded contracts certainly make entry easier and may further the cause of reducing the incumbent's market share (as discussed below), they result in large distributional issues that governments should take into account.

Such problems are not isolated. There have been enormous problems of stranded assets and contracts in US energy markets as states have sought to introduce competition in supply. There are similarly large problems for many European utilities as the European Union progressively moves towards creating integrated networks and encouraging competition in utilities.[11]

Such problems can be dealt with much more easily under public ownership as the government can effectively write off any losses and decide on their distribution (for example, as between the general taxpayer or consumers of the product). However, when the contracts are between private-sector companies, the allocation of contract losses is a matter for negotiation between the parties concerned. Of course, the govern-

---

[8] The pumped storage facilities in North Wales, now owned by First Hydro, owned in turn by Edison Mission Energy, are an exception.

[9] Typically for delivery to the beach-head, although also for delivery to a notional point in the gas pipeline network.

[10] There is also the 'flexibility mechanism' introduced recently to allow the pipeline operator to balance the demands on the system with the overall supply of gas. However, although this system generates a spot price for buying and selling additional gas, it is not intended to act as a formalized mass market for gas trading.

[11] The long delay in the Directive to liberalize the European Union electricity market (finally agreed in a watered-down form in December 1996) can be in part explained by the potential stranding of France's nuclear power stations, and of both nuclear and coal power stations in Germany. Objections to the draft gas Directive have focused on the problem of signing new long-term gas supply contracts.

ment could step in and cover such losses by imposing a levy on all competitive suppliers (as with the Fossil-fuel Levy in the UK to contribute towards nuclear costs), or recover costs through the transmission system charges (as has happened in the US transition; see FERC, 1996). In the case of gas in the UK, no such intervention was forthcoming. In the absence of such action, the cost of the stranded contracts inevitably ends up being borne in part by the shareholders of the incumbent.

It is worth stressing that while stranded assets and contracts resulting from changes in government policy are (or should be) a major distributional issue, their existence will greatly encourage entry. For example, the ease with which rival UK gas suppliers entered the market probably had less to do with their superior efficiency compared to British Gas than with their ability to write contracts based upon a low spot market price of gas. It would be quite wrong to think of the large price reductions observed in the UK residential gas market as simply reflecting the impact of increased competition on efficiency.[12]

2. Cross-subsidies

The second distributional problem for transitions is cross-subsidies. When the main utilities were being nationalized by the Labour government in 1945–51, these industries were regarded as merit goods—part of the more general welfare state (see Dilnot and Helm, 1987). Each citizen was entitled to these basic social primary goods, regardless of income or location. Thus education and health were to be universally provided, and the provision of electricity and mains water and sewerage were to be extended to marginal areas without the recovery of the full costs. Water had never been metered at the domestic level, and electricity customers in remote areas have not paid for the full infrastructure costs or transmission costs. With the advent of telephone services and natural gas, a similar policy of cross-subsidy was employed.

Though this approach was strictly economically inefficient, its objective was distributional. It could be sustained indefinitely as long as the utility service providers were statutory monopolies. Revenue collection was, in effect, a form of taxation. Customers, faced with distorted prices, invested in capital goods to consume the utility services, and the choice of housing location

was similarly distorted. House prices capitalized the actual rather than optimal utility prices.

As noted in section II(2), the effect of competition is to undermine cross-subsidies. Unless other policies are adjusted, there will be losers. Although there will also be gainers, it is likely that the former will be politically far more important than the latter. In practice, it may be possible to disguise these losses if exogenous costs drive down the real cost of services (such as in the case of gas). However, it is likely that the cross-subsidies across each of the industries are concentrated in the same geographical areas, and hence concentrated in their effects on household income, as many of the cross-subsidies are simultaneously unbundled.

The clearest example of this geographical distributional effect is perhaps the south-west, which has been affected by the unbundling of water, gas, and electricity tariffs. The biggest effect is in water, where the contributions from other areas and government to the higher regional water and sewerage costs have ceased. Around one and half million people in Cornwall and Devon have to meet the full costs of cleaning up around 30 per cent of Britain's bathing waters, improving water quality standards, and dealing with water shortages. Bills have risen sharply as a result and it has become a major local political issue (see the MMC report on SWW (MMC, 1995a)).

There are several possible policy responses. These fall into four broad categories:

• allowing a slow enough transition to permit adjustments in the capital stock and housing markets;

• adjusting the natural monopoly prices to deal with social costs;

• adjusting social security policy; and

• relying on the efficiency gains to offset the cross-subsidies.

The first has been pursued most notably in the electricity industry, where an initial 8-year period was established at privatization for a phased reduction in the franchise. In gas, the transition was only provided for less than 3 years, following the 1995 Gas Act. The second has been partially adopted for gas, where rebalancing of the transmission and distributional tariffs has been slowed. The third has not been adopted for any of the main utilities. Indeed, the unwinding of cross-subsidies has actually coincided with a number of reductions in social security provisions (and the introduction of VAT on domestic electricity and gas).

[12] Indeed, in the pilot for domestic gas competition in 1996, customers in the south-west were offered discounts of up to 22 per cent on British Gas's price by entrants (see Waddams Price 1997).

Finally, the efficiency gains have only gradually been passed on to customers. For the period 1990–5, water prices were rising in real terms, as were some electricity distribution prices. Only after 1995 did real price cuts begin to provide a cushion in these industries. The exceptions were gas and telecoms.

3. Technology

A third factor in implementing competition is technology. For many utility industries, competition requires complex information technology to facilitate customer switching. This may comprise data-handling, metering, billing, and system balancing. Unlike the monopoly situation, where errors in meter reading and estimations can be carried from one period to the next, switching requires accurate readings at the switch point. The development of remote reading and smart meters has, therefore, been important for the practical implementation of competition. In addition, billing systems need a substantial information technology resource. Finally, as customers switch, modelling the demands and supplies on systems which must be quickly balanced becomes more complex, and here again information technology is critical.

Until the 1980s such technology was largely confined to the telecommunications industry, and even here issues such as itemized billing and number portability were only beginning to be developed at the time of privatization, and in the latter case were only introduced in the late 1990s (see MMC, 1995*b*). In electricity and gas, metering proved a significant impediment to meeting the 1998 timetable. In water, the absence of metering for many households makes competition at the domestic level practically impossible.

Thus, the necessary conditions for the implementation of competition vary over time and include not only the technical facilitation of competition, but also the political constraints. The latter reflect the distributional impacts on producers and consumers. In the UK, scant regard has been paid to these issues in the original proposals, and it is hardly surprising that the results in managing transitions have been at best mixed. Indeed, regulators have had to step in to fill in the details of the transitions. But, far from the expectation held out for the earliest utility privatization—telecoms—that after a transitionary period of just 7 years, regulation would wither away (Littlechild, 1983), regulation has in fact increased as competition has developed. Regulating for competition has proved much more difficult than regulation of monopoly.

IV. Regulating for competition

Partly in recognition of the difficulties in prescribing a complete transitionary plan—and, indeed, in having a full model of competition—the regulators were given general duties to promote, facilitate, or secure competition. This general competition duty is usually a primary one, along with the duty to ensure that the utility functions can be financed. (The exception is water.) In practice, the regulator has considerable scope to follow his or her own preferred course to achieve the competition objective. The discretion is great, and has resulted in some regulators pursuing market-share targets, while others have attacked structure and entry conditions.[13]

1. Regulatory control over transitions

The mechanisms available to regulators are both direct and indirect. A regulator can propose licence changes in pursuit of the competition duty. The regulatee can either accept such changes, or request a reference to the Competition Commission. Usually the Competition Commission reports back to the regulator, who then 'takes account of' its findings. The Secretary of State sometimes has powers in this regard, for example to veto licence amendments.

But, in many circumstances, the regulator need not confine his or her actions to direct licence amendments. The *threat of regulation* can prove a powerful tool in gaining compliance. A good example was the 'voluntary undertakings' entered into by the two main electricity generators, National Power and PowerGen, to divest a total of 6,000 MW of plant (in the event, ironically, to Eastern Electricity which, as noted above, thereby integrated vertically) and to price in the Pool so as to meet an average price over a 2-year period. The divestment arose in the context of an investigation by the regulator into the separate matter of the costs and margins in contracts between the generators and the RECs for the period 1993–8. Since these were fixed, a change in their value had virtually nothing to do with

---

[13] See Helm (1994*b*) and Hansard Society (1997) for a discussion of the discretion issue.

competition. Yet the regulator, in effect, bargained for a divestment instead of a reference to the MMC over the contracts. The threat of action in one domain forced compliance in another.

In addition to the general duties, regulators also set price caps for utilities, both with respect to natural monopoly activities and those activities which are in transition to competition. Examples of the latter include caps on electricity and gas supply, and overall caps in telecommunications. In fixing the level, structure, and duration of these caps, regulators have considerable scope to influence the development of competition. If prices are set close to costs, and therefore with tight margins, customers benefit immediately, but the incentive to enter the market is blunted. Thus, the regulator trades off short-term price benefits against longer-term competition.

In some cases, the regulator can influence entry directly by adjudicating on the cost pass-through of specific entrants' costs. Thus, the electricity regulator allowed RECs to pass through the costs of their contracts with new independent power producers' CCGTs in the price caps on supply, without competitive tender against existing incumbents (see Helm, 1994a). These new entrants have turned out to be expensive, not only against conventional coal stations, but also against subsequent gas stations.

Regulators also adjudicate on the input costs to be included in price caps. Comparative efficiency evidence is used to inform on best practice, but, in addition, regulators can specify rules for the use of competitive tendering. As noted above, these rules have been most significant in the water industry.

2. Anti-competitive practices

Some regulators have argued that even the powers mentioned above do not give sufficient control over the transition to competition. In particular, the Director General of Telecommunications successfully proposed the granting of anti-competitive practices (ACP) powers which enabled him to intervene and adjudicate over BT's conduct without BT being able to appeal to the MMC but only to judicial appeal (see Oftel, 1996b).

As part of the wide-ranging reform of competition policy introduced in the 1998 Competition Act (see the chapter by Hay in this volume), all utilities regulators now have powers (concurrently with the Office of Fair Trading) to investigate ACP and possible abuses

of a dominant position. In each case, the interpretation of the requirement is likely to depend upon the incumbent regulator, and may add to the discretion inherent in the British approach to regulation.

3. Regulatory reform

Progress toward competition has been fraught with regulatory conflict in all the main utility industries. The introduction of number portability and the granting of ACP powers in telecommunications led to an MMC inquiry and a judicial review, respectively. The proposals for competition in water have been subject to major criticism by the industry. The introduction of gas competition has witnessed major controversies over some entrants' conduct, and acrimonious exchanges between Ofgas and British Gas over the systems and support for the implementation of competition. (Indeed, dispute over the costs was a component of the appeal to the MMC triggered in late 1996 over TransCo's price formula.) In electricity, some of the companies were accused of dragging their feet in preparing for 1998, and the earlier deregulation of the over 100 kW market in 1994 was described by some participants as a 'shambles', with customers left without proper billing and metering for some considerable period, and subsequent widespread disputes. In the case of electricity, the costs of the necessary information technology increased enormously during the transition.

It is apparent that the regulatory aspects of the transitions in many of the utility industries have not been carried out as well as they might. There are two major faults: that the objectives and market design have not been properly specified; and that the exercise of regulatory powers has been subject to too much discretion and hence lack of predictability.

Objectives and market design

The discussion in section II indicated that the design of the competitive market comprised several dimensions, and that this specification would determine in large part the type of competition which resulted. Too often, this design has been vague. Sometimes this has been deliberate, in order to facilitate privatization. In the case of rail, the model of competition (open access) was deliberately subverted to provide sufficient transitional monopoly to enable franchises to be let to train-operating companies. Sometimes the vagueness has been by omission, and sometimes the result of genuine ignorance as to how competition will evolve.

In general, the greater the extent of specification of market design, and hence the objective of the transition, the less the subsequent controversy on matters other than those of detail. Furthermore, to the extent that stranded assets are the inevitable consequence of a move towards competition, pre-specification of the method of recovery has greatly assisted the subsequent process.

Specification does not, however, mean a determined path. Rather, the specification should deal with how such matters as stranded assets and the cost-allocation rules will be handled as a result of the inevitable changes as the path unfolds. Where, for example, new information technology is required by the natural monopoly to facilitate competition, these costs may be subject to cost pass-through. The assignment of risk between the parties reduces the extent of *ex-post* conflict. When these risks are not properly assigned, then appeals to the Competition Commission and public disputes are likely.

Limiting regulatory discretion

The experience of the UK suggests that the main regulatory failures derived from the way in which the regulators were left to implement competition, together with the discretion granted to them through the general powers noted above. The exercise of these powers was not easy for investors or entrants to predict, with the result that the cost of capital may have increased, and competition may have been reduced.

The lessons learnt from the UK suggest the following steps are essential in order to allow competition to develop:

- limiting the degree of regulatory discretion, by specifying the nature of the transition in greater detail;
- requiring regulators to give reasons for their actions, together with the supporting analysis and evidence, thereby opening the exercise of discretion to public scrutiny and challenge;
- specifying responsibility for implementation, and encouraging proper project management;
- providing for pilots which properly test systems, and allowing time for consultation and modification of the transition.

V. Conclusions

The UK's experience in attempting to introduce competition into the utility industries provides important insights for other countries in considering liberalization policies and implications for the completion of the transition to competition in the UK.

At the policy design stage, it needs to be recognized that competition is a means not an end, and that each industry displays unique elements. In addition, there are different kinds of competition, and the type of competition which best meets the efficiency criterion depends upon the market failures and government failures which arise in each industry.

On structure, there is a general preference for the separation of natural monopoly from the potentially competitive activities. There is, however, no presumption in favour of spot over contract relationships, and the pros and cons of vertical integration between production and supply depend upon the industry characteristics. There should similarly, given technological changes, be no general presumption against integration along multi-utility lines.

The widespread prevalence of upstream sunk costs in the potentially competitive parts of the utilities gives rise to two related problems: stranded assets in relation to past investments, and contracting failures and risk assignment with respect to new investments. Stranded assets, in turn, create two related problems in designing the transition to competition. Without prior arrangements, those holding these assets are likely to block liberalization, as has happened in Europe in most utility industries. Where they are held by the state, they can be written off as part of the privatization package. Alternatively, the natural monopoly can carry a levy to finance these past costs. This is the model for nuclear stranded assets in the UK and the USA. In the former case these accrue to the state, in the latter to private shareholders.

An additional distributional problem in the transition to competition is the position of those who lose when cross-subsidies are unwound. The preferred solution here is adjustment to social security policy or a social levy on the natural monopoly.

The transition to competition in several British utility industries was hindered by significant regulatory failure: in failing to assign the costs and risks of the transitional period, in failing to define the end-state type of competition, and in the exercise of regulatory discretion. Those countries considering the introduction of competition into their utility industries will find many useful lessons contained within the UK casebook.

References

Beesley, M. E., and Littlechild, S. C. (1989), 'The Regulation of Privatized Monopolies in the United Kingdom', *RAND Journal of Economics*, 20(3), 454–72.

Byatt, I. (1997), 'Taking a View on Price Review. A Perspective on Economic Regulation in the Water Industry', *National Institute Economic Review*, January, 77–81

Dilnot, A., and Helm, D. R. (1987), 'Energy Policy, Merit Goods and Social Security', *Fiscal Studies*, 8(3), 29–48.

Dixit, A. K., and Pindyck, R. S. (1994), *Investment under Uncertainty*, Princeton, Princeton University Press.

FERC (1996), '*Order 888*', Washington DC, Federal Energy Regulatory Commission.

Hansard Society (1997), *The Report of the Commission on the Regulation of Privatised Utilities*, London, The Hansard Society for Parliamentary Government.

Helm, D. R. (1994*a*), 'Regulating the Transition to the Competitive Electricity Market', in M. E. Beesley (ed.), *Regulating Utilities: The Way Forward*, IEA Readings 41, Institute of Economic Affairs in association with the London Business School.

—— (1994*b*), 'British Utility Regulation: Theory, Practice, and Reform', *Oxford Review of Economic Policy*, 10(3), 17–39.

—— Rajah, N. (1994), 'Water Regulation: The Periodic Review', *Fiscal Studies*, 15(2), 74–94.

Jenkinson, T. J., and Ljungqvist (1996), *Going Public*, Oxford, Oxford University Press.

—— Mayer, C. P. (1994), 'The Costs of Privatisation in the UK and France', in M. Bishop, J. Kay, and C. P. Mayer, *Privatisation and Economic Performance*, Oxford, Oxford University Press.

—— —— (1997), 'Regulation, Diversification, and the Separate Listing of Utilities', in M. E. Beesley (ed.), forthcoming.

Littlechild, S. C. (1983), *Regulation of British Telecommunications' Profitability*, London, Department of Industry.

—— (1988), 'Economic Regulation of Privatised Water Authorities and Some Further Reflections', *Oxford Review of Economic Policy*, 4(2), 40–67.

Lyons, B. R. (1996), 'Empirical Relevance of Efficient Contract Theory: Inter-firm Contracts', *Oxford Review of Economic Policy*, 12(4), 27–52.

MMC (1993), *Gas: Volume 1 of Reports Under the Fair Trading Act 1973 on the Supply Within Great Britain of Gas Through Pipes to Tariff and Non-tariff Customers, and the Supply Within Great Britain of the Conveyance or Storage of Gas by Public Gas Supplies*, London, HMSO.

—— (1995*a*), *South West Water Services Ltd: A Report on the Determination of Adjustment Factors and Infrastructure Charges for South West Water Services Ltd*, London, HMSO.

—— (1995*b*), *Telephone Number Portability: A Report on the Reference Under Section 13 of the Telecommunications Act 1984*, London, HMSO.

—— (1996*a*), *National Power Plc and Southern Electric Plc: A Report on the Proposed Merger*, London, HMSO.

—— (1996*b*), *PowerGen Plc and Midland Electricity Plc: A Report on the Proposed Merger,* London, HMSO.

Offer (1996), *Statement by the Director General of Electricity Supply About the Arrangements for Opening the Electricity Market in 1998*, Birmingham, Office of Electricity Regulation.

Offer NI (1996), *Price Control Reviews for Northern Ireland Electricity Plc: Director General's Proposals,* Belfast, Office of Electricity Regulation Northern Ireland.

Oftel (1996), *Pricing of Telecommunications Services from 1997*, London, Office of Telecommunications.

Waddams Price, C. (1997), 'Competition and Regulation in the UK Gas Industry', *Oxford Review of Economic Policy*, 13(1), 47–63.

Waterson, M. (1996), 'Vertical Integration and Vertical Restraints', in T. J. Jenkinson (ed.) *Readings in Microeconomics*, Oxford, Oxford University Press.

Williamson, O. E. (1985), *The Economic Institutions of Capitalism*, New York, Free Press.

PART IV

EXTERNALITIES AND THE ENVIRONMENT

8

The problem of global environmental protection

SCOTT BARRETT

London Business School

Suppose that land is communally owned. Every person has the right to hunt, till, or mine the land. This form of ownership fails to concentrate the cost associated with any person's exercise of his communal right on that person. If a person seeks to maximize the value of his communal rights, he will tend to overhunt and overwork the land because some of the costs of his doing so are borne by others. The stock of game and the richness of the soil will be diminished too quickly. It is conceivable that those who own these rights, i.e. every member of the community, can agree to curtail the rate at which they work the lands if negotiating and policing costs are zero . . . [However,] negotiating costs will be large because it is difficult for many persons to reach a mutually satisfactory agreement, especially when each holdout has the right to work the land as fast as he pleases. [Furthermore,] even if an agreement among all can be reached, we must yet take account of the costs of policing the agreement, and these may be large, also.

Demsetz (1967, pp. 354–5)

I. Introduction

Demsetz's influential paper on the development of private property rights makes depressing reading for anyone concerned about global common property resources such as the oceans and atmosphere. Demsetz's view—and it is one that is shared by many others—is that users of a communally owned resource will fail to come to an agreement on managing the resource even though it is in the interest of all users to cooperate and reduce their rates of use of the resource. The

First published in *Oxford Review of Economic Policy*, vol. 6, no. 1 (1990). This version has been up dated and revised to incorporate recent developments.

reason is that if this improved situation is attained, every user will earn even higher returns by free-riding on the virtuous behaviour of the remaining cooperators. As a consequence, united action on the part of users can be expected to be unstable; cooperative agreements, even if they are reached, will not persist. The only way out of the common property dilemma, as Demsetz makes clear, is intervention by '*the* state, *the* courts, or the leaders of *the* community' (emphasis added). In Demsetz's example, the intervention manifests itself in the development of private property rights to the resource, but the intervention could just as easily involve regulation.

The reason this view is disquieting is that for global common property resources there is no World Government empowered to intervene for the good of all. To be sure, there do exist international institutions—most notably the United Nations Environment Programme—which have been given the mandate to coordinate international environmental protection efforts. But none of these institutions can dictate what is to be done; that requires agreement by the parties concerned. The problem is perhaps best exemplified by the International Whaling Commission (IWC), which was established to conserve whale stocks, but whose best efforts in this regard have been repeatedly foiled. IWC membership is open to any country, and this leaves open the possibility that the whales could be protected for the global good. But any member can object to a majority decision, and hence render that decision meaningless. For example, a 1954 proposal to prohibit the taking of blue whales in the North Pacific was rejected by the only members who hunted blue whales in this ocean—Canada, Japan, the US, and the USSR—and hence did nothing to protect this species. In 1981 the IWC sought to ban the use of the non-explosive harpoon for killing minke whales. The ban was objected to by Brazil, Iceland, Japan, Norway, and the USSR. Since these were the only countries that hunted minke whales, the ban had no effect.[1]

Because national sovereignty must be respected, the problem of conserving global common property resources is no different from that described by Demsetz. The only way out of the global common property dilemma is agreement. Yet, just as in the situation Demsetz describes, there are strong incentives for governments not to cooperate, or to defect from an agreement should one be reached. This is the crux of the problem of managing global common property, and what distinguishes this problem from the long studied one of common property management under the jurisdictional control of a central authority.

Attempts to correct global, unidirectional externalities will encounter similar difficulties. Consider the problem where certain activities by one country harm all others. A good example is deforestation of Amazonia by Brazil. The rain forests play a crucial role in the protection of biological diversity and in the functioning of the carbon cycle. When standing, the rain forests serve as habitat to about a half of all wildlife species and absorb carbon dioxide, one of the so-called greenhouse gases. When the forests are burned, masses of species can become extinct and substantial quantities of greenhouse gases are emitted. If the rights to generate these externalities are vested in the one country, as indeed they are in the case of Brazilian deforestation, then the others will have to pay this nation to cease its destructive activities. If the externality affected only one other country, then bargaining might be possible; the externalities might be internalized without outside intervention.[2] But in the case of global externalities, all countries except the generator suffer. All sufferers might be willing to bribe the generator to cease its harmful activities. But a contribution by any one country would confer benefits on all others and not just the one making the compensating payment. The others could therefore do better by free-riding. But then so too could the one that contemplated making the payment. Cooperation would again be foiled.[3]

Mechanisms exist that can lead countries to reveal their preferences for global public goods truthfully (see, e.g. Groves and Ledyard, 1977), and hence for correcting global externalities. But in the absence of a World Government these mechanisms cannot be employed without the consent of the sovereign nations themselves. Every country would be better off if it agreed to participate in the revelation exercise. But each would do even better if others participated and it did not. All will therefore choose not to participate. The crux of the problem of correcting global externalities, like that of managing global common property, is that global optimality demands global cooperation, and yet the incentives facing individual countries work in the opposite direction.

The theoretical arguments for supposing that cooperation will not develop are compelling. But they can hardly be complete. Cooperation does take place and is often codified in international agreements. Some of these are woefully ineffective—a famous example being the International Convention for the Regulation of Whaling (1946) which established the IWC. Others do appear to have achieved a great deal. Of these last, the Montreal Protocol on Substances that Deplete the Ozone Layer (1987) seems the most impressive, because it demands that its many signatories undertake substantial reductions in their emissions of ozone-depleting chlorofluorocarbons (CFCs) and halons. Though agreements dealing with unidirectional externalities are rare and almost invariably toothless, there is one—the World Heritage Convention—that at least holds some promise. This agreement places responsibility for safeguarding natural environments like the Serengeti and the Galapagos Islands on a community of nations, and could be invoked to protect the remaining tropical rain forests. There is clearly a need to explore why international cooperation might develop, and what the significance of particular forms of cooperation might be.

To make any progress we will need a basis from which to assess whether cooperation can in fact be expected to achieve much. Contrary to Hardin's (1968) famous allegory of the commons, the absence of cooperation need not lead to tragedy. Section II discusses some of the parameters that are important in determining the potential gains to cooperation. Having drawn the boundaries, we then consider how we might move closer to the full cooperative solution, the global optimum. Non-cooperation may sometimes wear the disguise of cooperation, and section III shows that an outcome better than the purely nationalistic one

---

[1] See Lyster (1985).
[2] See Coase (1960). Bargaining has in fact taken place at the bilateral level. A famous example is the Trail Smelter case. The Canadian smelter emitted pollutants that crossed the US border. The case was arbitrated by an international tribunal comprised of an American, a Canadian, and a Belgian. The tribunal found that Canada was liable for damages, and also established emission regulations for the plant. The judicial decisions on this case make fascinating reading. See Trail Smelter Arbitral Tribunal (1939, 1941).
[3] Demsetz (1967, p. 357) argues that in the large numbers case, 'it may be too costly to internalize effects through the market-place'. Elsewhere, Demsetz (1964) argues that it might in fact be optimal for the externality not to be internalized since the costs of internalization should include the costs of transacting the agreement. But even then the free-rider problem would prevail; intervention, were it possible, might still be desired.

can emerge even where binding agreements are absent. Effective management of global environmental resources does however seem to rely on the more formal institution of international law. Section IV discusses the rudiments of a model that explains why countries would cooperate when the free-rider problem must surely bite, and what international agreements mean for global social welfare and the welfare of citizens of individual countries. Just as failure to cooperate may not lead to tragedy, so cooperation may not buy us very much. Indeed, combining the analysis of the potential gains to cooperation with this model of formal agreements, it can be shown that cooperation is sometimes hardest to obtain when it is most needed.

II. The potential gains to cooperation

Where a global externality is unidirectional, the country causing the externality will, in the absence of a negotiated settlement, ignore the damages its activities impose on other countries. This is the full *non-cooperative* outcome. The full *cooperative* outcome is found by internalizing the externality. In this case the country inflicting the externality chooses its actions so as to maximize the net benefits of all countries, including itself. Global net benefits will of course be higher in this case. The difference between the global net benefits for the cooperative and non-cooperative outcomes defines the potential gains to cooperation.

Where the externalities of concern are reciprocal in nature, every country has some incentive to take unilateral action even in the absence of a binding agreement. Furthermore, the strength of this incentive will depend on the actions taken by all other countries. An example of a reciprocal externality is the emission of a global pollutant. If one country reduces its emissions, it will benefit from the improved environmental quality, provided other countries do not increase their emissions so as to fully offset the one country's action. The other countries will benefit partly by being able to increase their emissions somewhat and partly by enjoying a cleaner environment (again, provided their increase in emissions does not entirely offset the one country's extra abatement). The extent of the benefit enjoyed by the conserving country will clearly depend on the actions taken by the other countries, and of course all countries are subject to a similar calculus. It is this interdependence which makes calculation of the

potential gains to cooperative management of global common property more difficult. It is better, then, that we work with a specific model.

To fix ideas, reconsider the problem of global pollution. Suppose that the relevant number of countries is N. One might think that N would include all the world's countries, but that need not be so, a point we return to later. Let us however suppose for simplicity that N does include all countries and that each is identical. Each, therefore, emits the same quantity of a pollutant ex ante—that is, before the game is played—and each faces the same abatement cost and benefit functions. The problem is then perfectly symmetric. To simplify the analysis further, assume that the marginal abatement cost and benefit functions are linear. Clearly, the marginal abatement cost schedule for each country must depend on its own abatement level, while each country's marginal abatement benefit function must depend on *world-wide* abatement.

In the absence of any cooperation, each country will maximize its own net benefits of abatement and in so doing will choose a level of abatement at which its own marginal abatement cost equals its own marginal abatement benefit.[4] This is the non-cooperative (Nash equilibrium) solution to this game, and it is shown as abatement level Q^* in Figure 8.1. Were countries to cooperate fully, they would seek to maximize the global net benefits of abatement. Since we have assumed that all countries are identical, the global net benefits of abatement can be defined as the sum of every country's net benefits of abatement. In maximizing the global net benefits of abatement, each country will choose a level of abatement at which its own marginal costs of abatement equal the global marginal benefits of abatement, or the sum of the marginal abatement benefits enjoyed by all countries.[5] The full cooperative solution to this game is shown as abatement level Q^{**} in Figure 8.1.

One sees immediately that the full cooperative solution demands greater abatement but, equally, gives to every country a greater net benefit. For a given size

---

[4] I am assuming here that every country believes that its choice of an abatement level will not alter the choices of the other countries; that is, I am assuming zero conjectural variations. One can impose positive or negative conjectures, but these assumptions would be *ad hoc*. Alternatively, we could determine a consistent conjectures equilibrium—that is, one in whose neighbourhood every country's conjectures are confirmed by the responses of the other countries. Cornes and Sandler (1983) find that consistent conjectures can lead to even greater overuse of the resource compared with the Nash equilibrium.

[5] This is of course nothing but a restatement of Samuelson's (1954) rule for the optimal provision of public goods. For an alternative presentation of these principles, see Dasgupta's (1982) model of a global fishery.

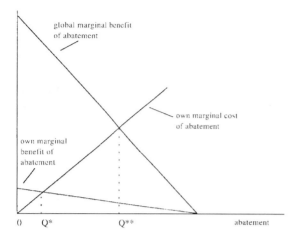

Figure 8.1. The potential gains to cooperation

of N, the difference between Q^* and Q^{**} can be shown to depend on the slopes of the marginal abatement benefit and cost curves. Denote the (absolute value of the) slope of each country's marginal abatement benefit curve by the letter b, and the slope of each country's marginal abatement cost curve by the letter c. Then it can be shown that the discrepancy will tend to be small whenever c/b is either 'large' or 'small' (see Barrett, 1994). The approximate implication of this result is that fairly innocuous pollutants (that is, pollutants for which b is small) that are very costly to control (that is, that have a large c) do not cause too great a problem. Nor do extremely hazardous pollutants (that is, pollutants associated with a large b) that are cheap to control (that is, pollutants that have a small c). In the former case, even collective action will not call for large abatement levels. In the latter, countries will want to abate substantial quantities of emissions unilaterally. The real problem is with pollutants whose marginal abatement benefit and cost curves are both either steep or flat—that is, hazardous pollutants that are costly to control, and mildly offensive pollutants that can be controlled at little cost. Of these, the former type naturally causes the greatest concern, for the cost of failing to cooperate in this case is very, very high.

Unidirectional and reciprocal externalities are plainly different in their effects. A country has no incentive to abate its emissions if the externality is unidirectional (provided side payments are ruled out), unless negotiations on this one issue are linked to another issue in which, in some sense, the tables are turned. Not so if the externality is reciprocal in nature. For then the emitting country will have private incentives to control its emissions.

III. Non-cooperative environmental protection

The politics of global environmental protection are not as sterile as the above models would imply. Once we permit alternative strategies to be chosen, widen the choice sets themselves, and allow motivations other than self-interest (narrowly defined) to guide decision-making, global environmental protection can be enhanced.

1. Supergames

In the above games, strategies are chosen once, and the games are never repeated. But in the common property game countries are unavoidably locked in a continuing relationship, and this leaves open the possibility that they may retaliate and hence that cooperative strategies may be countenanced. Suppose then that all countries choose one of two strategies: they either choose the full cooperative abatement level Q^{**} initially, and continue to choose Q^{**} in every future period provided all other countries chose Q^{**} in every previous period; or they choose not to cooperate in any period.[6] Then the cooperative trigger strategy will constitute an equilibrium to this supergame provided the rate of discount is sufficiently low (for then the gains to choosing the non-cooperative strategy will be low, too; see Friedman, 1986). Although this supergame equilibrium entails cooperation, the cooperation is tacit and is enforced by means of a non-cooperative mechanism, retaliation; there is no explicit agreement, no open negotiation.[7]

One variant of this game involves countries adopting a convention that says that a subset of countries should cooperate in the face of free-riding by the others (see Sugden, 1986). It may, for example, be believed that the industrialized countries should cooperate to reduce emissions of CFCs or greenhouse gases (because it was their emissions that caused the environmental reservoirs to be filled in the first place), and that the poor countries should be allowed to free ride. In this game, each of the members of the subset could adopt the trigger strategy with respect to the subset, and each of the

[6] If countries choose not to cooperate in the initial period, they need not choose Q^* in this period. The reason for this is that the optimal non-cooperative abatement level is contingent on the abatement levels chosen by the other countries.

[7] Axelrod's (1984) tournaments of the repeated prisoners' dilemma game suggest that behaviour in the disguise of cooperation may well emerge. Whether his findings carry over to the common property game with many players, however, is as yet unknown.

others could simply choose their optimal non-cooperative responses. This latter possibility may be fragile, because different countries may have different views about which should cooperate and which should not. This ambiguity may help explain why unilateral action to reduce CFC emissions was limited (US Environmental Protection Agency, 1988, p. 30576):

In 1978 the United States restricted the use of CFCs in aerosols. While several nations adopted similar restrictions (e.g. Sweden, Canada, Norway) and others partially cut back their use (European nations, Japan), there was no widespread movement to follow the United States' lead. Concerns existed then that other nations had failed to act because the United States and a few other nations were making the reductions thought necessary to protect the ozone layer. Similar concerns exist today that unilateral action could result in 'free riding' by some other nations.

It is not obvious how sufferers of a unidirectional externality could punish the offending nation. But so long as the countries are engaged in some form of exchange, potent weapons may be at the sufferers' disposal. The Packwood–Magnuson Amendment to the US Fishery Conservation and Management Act (1976) requires the US government to retaliate whenever foreign nationals compromise the effectiveness of the IWC. An offending nation automatically loses half its allocation of fish products taken from US waters, and if the country refuses to improve its behaviour within a year, its right to fish in US waters is revoked.

2. Matching

In the one-shot common property game, each country chooses an abatement level and nothing else. There is no reason why a country's choices need be limited in this way. We could, for example, allow countries to choose a 'base' abatement level—that is, a level of abatement which is not explicitly contingent on the abatement levels chosen by other countries—and a 'matching rate'—in our example, a fraction of the sum of all countries' base abatement levels. In effect, countries would then voluntarily subsidize each other's abatement levels. In the original game, one unit of abatement by country i buys country i one unit less of global emission (assuming that the emissions of all other countries are held fixed). In the matching game, one unit of abatement by country i may yield a much greater reduction in global emission. Matching might improve matters—Guttman (1978) shows that under certain conditions matching can sustain the full cooperative solution. But in the management of global

common property, matching is rarely invoked. Recently, Norway announced that it would allocate one-tenth of one per cent of its GDP each year to a fund on climate change if other industrial countries matched its contribution (on a GDP percentage basis). The offer has yet to be taken up. Environmental groups in the United States have argued that the US should unilaterally surpass the reductions specified in the Montreal Protocol and at the same time impose restrictions on imports of products containing or made with CFCs from countries that fail to agree to make the same reductions. Their plea was rejected by the authorities (US Environmental Protection Agency, 1988, p. 30574).

3. Morality

In the models discussed thus far, the welfare of every country is assumed to depend solely on its own net benefits. An alternative way of looking at the problem is to assume that countries act according to some moral principle which requires that they take stock of the effect their actions have on the welfare of other countries. For example, suppose every country but one reduces its emissions of some global pollutant by at least x tonnes. Let us further suppose that the recalcitrant nation would like all others to reduce their emissions by y tonnes each. Then the leaders of the recalcitrant nation might feel compelled to obey the rule: if y > x then we are morally obligated to reduce our emissions by at least x tonnes. If countries obey this rule, then the free-rider problem can be mitigated (see Sugden, 1984). That moral principles may guide non-cooperative abatement is suggested by the following remarks made by the House of Commons Environment Committee (1984, p. lxxi) in its report recommending that the UK join the Thirty Per Cent Club:[8]

As our inquiry has progressed the stance of the United Kingdom has become increasingly isolated by its refusal to legislate to reduce SO2 and NOx emissions. Since our work began three West European countries have joined those already in the 30 per cent club, and several Eastern European countries have committed themselves to reduce transfrontier emissions by 30 per cent. SO2 emissions in the United Kingdom have indeed fallen by 37 per cent since 1970, but the levels of high-stack emissions which affect remote areas have not fallen. In 1970, when the 37 per cent fall began, we were the largest

[8] The Thirty Per Cent Club consists of the countries that have signed the Protocol to the 1979 Convention on Long-Range Transboundary Air Pollution on the Reduction of Sulphur Emissions or their Transboundary Fluxes by at least 30 Per Cent (1985). The UK has not joined this 'club' but it has committed itself to substantial reductions in sulphur dioxide and nitrogen oxides emissions by agreeing to comply with the European Community Large Combustion Plant Directive.

emitter in Western Europe. In 1984, we are still the largest emitter. NO$_x$ emissions have not fallen. In Western Europe only West Germany deposits more SO$_2$ in other countries than does the United Kingdom, and further significant reductions cannot be achieved by either without controls.

The Committee's concern in this passage lies less with the net benefits to the UK of reducing emissions than with how UK abatement has lagged behind the rest of Europe. Indeed, the Committee's evaluation did not even consider whether the other European countries were abating more simply because it was in their own self interest to do so. The argument seems to be: 'The other European nations are reducing their emissions, so we should, too.' Compared with the supergame problem, cooperation in this case is not instrumentally important—the Environment Committee did not seek to reduce UK emissions so that others would reduce theirs even further—but intrinsically important. Concerns about fairness have been shown to militate against the free-rider problem in experimental tests (Marwell and Ames, 1981). However, in the next section we shall see that in a bargaining situation, obeying moral principles may serve only to undermine the cause of environmental protection.

IV. Cooperative environmental protection

In the absence of cooperation, outcomes better than the full non-cooperative one can sometimes develop, at least in principle. But such instances seem to be rare. Even two close neighbours with strong trading ties can fail to arrive at a preferred solution, as the disagreement between the United States and Canada over the exploitation of the North Pacific fur seal illustrates. Following an initial conflict between the two nations over the pelagic seal hunt, a Tribunal Arbitration was convened at the request of the two parties (with Great Britain acting for Canada). In late 1893 the Tribunal decided that the United States did not have territorial jurisdiction over the Bering Sea, and hence could not keep Canadian sealing vessels out of these waters. This effectively sanctioned open-access harvesting of the species, and cooperation proved impossible to secure (Paterson and Wilen, 1977, p. 94):

Following the decision of the Tribunal, the diplomatic efforts of both Great Britain and the United States had been directed to convincing the other to reduce its sealing in order to allow the herd to recover from earlier depradations. No agreement could be reached and in 1897 the United States unilaterally forbade its citizens to engage in pelagic sealing in the North

Pacific. At the same time quota adjustments were made as the herd diminished in size. So strong was the reaction to the declining herd size and the continued Canadian pelagic hunt that a bill reached the [United States] Senate which called for the complete destruction of the herd. It did not pass . . .

Better management of the population had to await the signing of the North Pacific Fur Seal Treaty by Great Britain, the United States, Japan, and Russia in 1911—a remarkable agreement that remains in force today.[9] Effective management of global environmental resources seems to demand that countries cooperate openly and put their signatures on international agreements, treaties, and conventions. Explanations for why cooperation of this kind might emerge are offered below.

1. International environmental agreements

Consider the following modification to the common property game described earlier. Suppose a subset of the N identical countries 'collude' by signing an international environmental agreement and that the remaining countries continue to act non-cooperatively. Suppose further that the signatories to the agreement choose their collective abatement level while taking as given the abatement decision functions of the non-signatories, while the latter countries continue to behave atomistically and choose their abatement levels on the assumption that the abatement levels of all other countries are fixed. That is, the signatories act as 'abatement leaders', and the non-signatories as 'abatement followers'. Quite clearly, we would like the number of signatories, the terms of the agreement, and the abatement levels of all non-signatories to be determined jointly. We also require that the agreement itself is stable. A stable agreement is one where non-signatories do not wish to sign the agreement and signatories do not wish to renege on their commitment. Then it can be shown that for identical countries with linear marginal abatement benefit and cost functions a stable international environmental agreement always exists (Barrett, 1994).

The solution to this problem exhibits many of the features of actual agreements. The net benefits realized by both signatories and non-signatories are higher than in the earlier problem where negotiation was ruled out. What is more, the signatories would like the non-cooperators to sign the agreement. However, non-signatories do better by free-riding.

[9] For legal background on this treaty and its successors, see Lyster (1985).

It is important to emphasize that the agreement is *self-enforcing*. Any signatory that renounces its commitment can reduce its abatement level and hence its costs. However, in pulling out of the agreement, the number of cooperators is reduced and the agreement itself is weakened; the remaining cooperators reduce their abatement levels, too. A signatory will want to pull out of an agreement only if the saving in abatement costs exceeds the resulting loss in benefits. Similarly, a country that joins an agreement will have to abate more and hence incur higher costs. But the very act of joining will strengthen the agreement; the other cooperators will also increase their abatement levels. Joining appears attractive if the resulting increase in benefits realized by the new signatory exceeds the increase in costs that this country must incur in committing itself to the terms of the agreement.

Real treaties are not rewritten with every defection or accession, but mechanisms are at work that have a similar effect. It is common for treaties to come into force only after being ratified by a minimum number of signatories. The Montreal Protocol did not come into force until it had been ratified by at least eleven countries representing at least two-thirds of global consumption of the controlled substances. It is also common for treaties to be reviewed and altered when necessary and often at regular intervals. Over the last few years the Montreal Protocol has been amended three times. On each occasion the requirements of the agreement were significantly strengthened. That this agreement is self-enforcing is suggested by a comment made by the US Environmental Protection Agency (EPA) (1988, p. 30573):

EPA judged that the obvious need for broad international adherence to the Protocol counselled against the United States' deviating from the Protocol, because any significant deviation could lessen other countries' motivation to participate.

Self-enforcement is essential in any model of international environmental agreements because nation states cannot be forced to perform their legal obligations. A country can be taken to the International Court of Justice for failing to comply with the terms of a treaty, but only with the defendant's permission. Even then, the disputing countries cannot be forced to comply with the Court's decision.[10]

What are the gains to having international environmental agreements? The answer depends partly on the number of relevant and potential signatories. When N is large, international environmental agreements can achieve very little no matter the number of signatories.

The reason, quite simply, is that when N is large, defection or accession by any country has only a negligible effect on the abatement of the other cooperators.

Determination of N is not always a trivial matter. Some treaties do not restrict participation, but in these cases many of the signatories may have no effective say in environmental protection. Over 100 countries have signed the 1963 Partial Nuclear Test Ban Treaty, but only a few signatories possess nuclear weapons technology. The 1967 United Nations Treaty on Principles Governing the Activities of States in the Exploration and Use of Outer Space including the Moon and Other Celestial Bodies has been ratified by scores of countries but not by the two with space technology capabilities— the US and USSR. Other treaties explicitly restrict participation. The Agreement on the Conservation of Polar Bears can only be signed by five circumpolar countries (Canada, Denmark (including Greenland), Norway, the US, and the USSR). To become a signatory to the Antarctic Treaty of 1959 a country must maintain a scientific research station in the Antarctic and be unanimously accepted by existing parties to the agreement. In these cases non-signatories may quite clearly be affected by how the signatories manage the resource. Signatories to the Antarctic treaty voted recently to allow mineral exploration, despite appeals by non-signatories to designate Antarctica a nature reserve.

In the above model, N was assumed to represent both the number of countries that emit a (uniformly mixed) pollutant into the environment and the number harmed as a consequence. However, for some problems the number of emitters may be less than the number of sufferers (for global pollutants, all countries). When the number of emitters is small, an international environmental agreement signed by a subset of emitters may well have a significant effect on the welfare of these countries. However, the effect on global welfare may still be small because the emitters have no incentive to take into account the welfare losses suffered by non-emitting nations. The appropriate way to account for countries that do not emit the pollutant but nevertheless suffer the consequences of others' emissions is to admit side payments—payments which induce emitting nations to undertake greater abatement but which leave all parties no worse off compared to the situation where side payments are forbidden. We return to the side payments issue later.

The gains to international cooperation can also be shown to depend on c, the slope of each country's marginal abatement cost curve; and b, the (absolute value of the) slope of each country's marginal abatement benefit curve. For a given size of N, the number of signatories to a treaty increases as c/b falls. This suggests

---

[10] See Lyster (1985) for a discussion of other compliance mechanisms.

Table 8.1. Estimates of the reduction in percentage ozone depletion effected by the Montreal Protocol

Case	2000	2025	2050	2075
No controls	1.0	4.6	15.7	50.0
Montreal Protocol	0.8	1.5	1.9	1.9

Source: US EPA (1988), Table 3, p. 30575.

that we should expect to observe a large number of signatories (in absolute terms) when N is 'large', the marginal abatement cost curve is flat, and the marginal abatement benefit curve steep. However, we already know that when c/b is 'small' the benefit of having an agreement is diminished. It is commonly asserted that treaties signed by a large number of countries accomplish little of substance: 'The greater the number of participants in the formulation of a treaty, the weaker or more ambiguous its provisions are likely to be since they have to reflect compromises making them acceptable to every State involved' (Lyster, 1985, p. 4). This analysis suggests that the reason treaties signed by a large number of countries appear to effect little additional abatement is not that the signatories are heterogeneous—although that may be a contributing factor. Nor is the reason solely that in these cases N is also large. A major insight of the model is that a large subset of N will sign an agreement only when the non-cooperative and full cooperative outcomes are already close.

This latter observation may not seem consistent with all the evidence. The Montreal Protocol, for example, demands of its signatories significant reductions in the production and consumption of the hard CFCs and halons, and about 150 countries have already signed the agreement—a fairly large number by any standard. As Table 8.1 shows, the effect of the agreement on ozone depletion is estimated to be very significant. Percentage ozone depletion is estimated to be reduced from 50 to 2 per cent in 2075 as a result of the agreement. But of course each country has some incentive to take unilateral action in reducing emissions; in doing so all other countries will benefit, but so too will the country taking the action. Furthermore, non-signatories to the agreement may well face an incentive to abate less than they would otherwise for the simple reason that greater abatement on the part of signatories improves the environment for non-signatories as well. Hence it is by no means clear that the agreement necessarily means that the environment and global welfare will be significantly better off, contrary to what the figures in Table 8.1 imply. What the model does suggest is that so many countries would not have committed themselves to the agreement in

the first place unless they already intended to take substantial unilateral action. In other words, although the agreement itself may effect only little additional abatement, the very fact that so many countries have signed the agreement suggests that the potential gains to cooperation were in this instance not very great.

What does the model predict about the prospects of an agreement being reached on global warming? N will again be large, and this will militate against significant united action. However, in this case c will be large, too; the marginal costs of abating carbon dioxide emissions will rise very steeply as fossil fuels must be substituted for and energy is conserved. This suggests that the number of signatories to an agreement would be small, and that little additional abatement could be effected by cooperation. Whether or not this should be of concern depends on whether b is large or small. If b is small, as Nordhaus (1994) suggests, then the potential gains to cooperation will be small, too. If, however, b, is large, as Cline (1992) believes, then the potential gains to cooperation would be large. Failure to cooperate would, indeed, be a tragedy in this case.

2. Leadership

It is sometimes asserted that countries should, on their own, do more than the non-cooperative solution demands of them. US environmental groups, for example, have argued that the US should have taken greater unilateral action before the Montreal Protocol was drafted, that it should now comply with the terms of the Protocol in advance of the deadlines, and that it should exceed the agreed emission reductions and phase out production and consumption of these chemicals entirely. The House of Commons Energy Committee (1989, p. xvii), in its investigation on the greenhouse effect, recommended 'that the UK should . . . consider setting an example to the world by seriously tackling its own emission problems in advance of international action, especially where it is economically prudent to do so'.

We have already seen that such 'unselfish' unilateral actions need not be matched by other countries. The United States, Canada, Sweden, and Norway banned the use of CFCs in non-essential aerosols in the late 1970s, and yet other countries did not reciprocate.[11] Unilateral restrictions on pelagic sealing in the North Pacific by the US were not duplicated by

---

[11] Reciprocity was certainly not full. The European Community, for example, passed two decisions limiting production capacity of the so-called hard CFCs (CFC-11 and -12) and reducing their use in aerosols by 30 per cent.

Canada. We have also seen that countries may wish to give in to their moral beliefs and embrace a less insular view of their responsibilities. An important question is whether 'unselfish' unilateral action can be expected to have a positive influence on international negotiations. If one country (or group of countries) abates more than the Nash non-cooperative solution demands, and all others choose the abatement levels that are optimal for them in a non-cooperative setting, will the environment be any better protected when international treaties are later negotiated?

In a two-country analysis, Hoel (1991) shows that the answer depends on whether the unilateral action is taken before agreement is reached and is not contingent on that agreement or whether the action is a commitment to abate more than the negotiated agreement requires. Hoel shows that in the former case, 'unselfish' unilateral action may compromise negotiations and lead, ultimately, to *greater* emissions than would have occurred had both countries behaved 'selfishly'. In the latter case, however, the country's announced commitment to overfulfil its negotiated abatement level can be expected to reduce total emissions.

There is an obvious incentive compatibility problem with this tactic, for the 'unselfish' country could do better by reneging on its commitment (the agreement is therefore *not* self-enforcing). Nevertheless, the analysis shows that the desire by environmentalists and others to reduce total emissions may not be well served by their calls for 'unselfish' unilateral action, a point that the EPA stressed in defending its ozone depletion policy (1988, p. 30574): 'Unilateral action by the United States would not significantly add to efforts to protect the ozone layer and could even be counter productive by undermining other nations' incentive to participate in the Protocol.'

It is important to note that the US and the European Community announced their intentions to phase out production and consumption of the ozone-depleting chemicals by the end of the century *after* the Montreal Protocol came into force but before renegotiation talks had started. It would be wrong, however, to ascribe these developments simply to 'unselfish' behaviour. After all, the world's largest manufacturer of CFCs, US-based Du Pont, announced its intention to phase out production of CFCs by the end of the century *before* the phase-out decisions were taken by the US and EC. Three days after the EC decided to phase out CFCs, the chairman of the leading European producer of CFCs, ICI, declared that production of CFCs should cease 'as soon after 1998 as is practicable'. Much more is at work here.

3. Efficient cooperation

Signatories to an international environmental agreement are assumed to maximize the net benefits accruing to the *group*. This means, among other things, that the marginal abatement costs of every signatory must be equal; the abatement undertaken by the group must be achieved at minimum total cost.

How realistic is this assumption? In the case of the Montreal Protocol, the assumption is not very wide of the mark. The Protocol imposes on every industrial country signatory an obligation to reduce its production and consumption of CFCs by an equal percentage. This requirement on its own is inefficient because at the margin the costs of complying with the Protocol will surely vary. For example, the UK can apparently meet its obligations by simply prohibiting the use of CFCs in aerosols—an action that is nearly costless. The US banned the use of CFCs in aerosols many years ago, and hence can meet the terms of the Protocol only by instituting more costly measures. However, the Protocol allows limited international trading in emission reductions. For any signatory, CFC production through mid-1998 can be 10 per cent, and from mid-1998 onwards 15 per cent, higher than it would have been without trading provided the increase in production by this signatory is offset by a decrease in production by another signatory. Furthermore, trades of consumption (but, strangely, not production) quotas are permitted by the Protocol within the European Community. These provisions will help increase the efficiency of attaining the total emission reduction implicit in the agreement, although they almost certainly do not go far enough.

4. Side payments

The equilibrium in the model of international environmental agreements is determined by a concept of stability that prohibits side payments. An important question is whether side payments might effect a Pareto improvement. To investigate this issue, reconsider the concept of stability employed in the model. In equilibrium, non-signatories do better than signatories, but no country can do better by changing its status. Signatories want non-cooperators to sign the agreement, because their net benefits would then increase. But non-signatories do worse by signing. Hence, without compensating payments, non-signatories will not want to sign the agreement. It is in this sense that the agreement is stable.

However, the very fact that signatories do better if non-cooperators sign the agreement suggests that trade might be possible. In particular, it might be possible for signatories to make side payments to a subset of non-cooperators to encourage them to sign the agreement. All might be made better off. It is in fact very easy to show that this can happen, that an international environmental agreement that specifies abatement levels *and* side payments can manage the global common property resource better than one that prohibits side payments.

An important feature of the World Heritage Convention is that it does admit side payments. The Convention established a World Heritage Fund that is used to help protect natural environments of 'outstanding universal value'. Each party to the Convention (there are over 90 signatories) is required to provide the Fund every two years with at least one per cent of its contribution to the regular budget of UNESCO.[12] In practice this means that the Fund is almost entirely financed by the industrial countries. Clearly, both the industrial and poor countries benefit from the Convention—otherwise they would not have signed it—but the poor countries may not have signed the Convention were it not for the Fund. Though the Fund is small, the mechanism could prove instrumental in protecting many of the world's remaining natural environments, including the tropical rain forests.

The World Heritage Convention is not unique among international environmental agreements for incorporating side payments. The success of the Montreal Protocol, for example, ultimately hinged on the accession of poor countries, such as China and India. This was effected by amendments to the Protocol negotiated in London in 1990. These amendments created a fund, the purpose of which was to compensate poor countries for the 'incremental costs' of complying with the agreement. It was this 'carrot', coupled with the 'stick' of threatened trade sanctions, which has sustained nearly full participation in this agreement. The question this example raises is whether this apparent success can be replicated for other global environmental problems. The analysis presented here does not provide a ready answer to this important question. It does, however, provide a basis for formulating an answer.

References

Axelrod, R. (1984), *The Evolution of Cooperation*, New York, Basic Books.

Barrett, S. (1994), 'Self-enforcing International Environmental Agreements', *Oxford Economic Papers*, **46**, 878–94.

Cline, W. R. (1992), *The Economics of Global Warming*, Washington, DC, Institute for International Economics.

Coase, R. H. (1960), 'The Problem of Social Cost', *Journal of Law and Economics*, **3**, 1–44.

Cornes, R., and Sandler, T. (1983), 'On Commons and Tragedies', *American Economic Review*, **73**, 787–92.

Dasgupta, P. (1982), *The Control of Resources*, Cambridge, MA, Harvard University.

Demsetz, H. (1964), 'The Exchange and Enforcement of Property Rights', *Journal of Law and Economics*, **7**, 11–26.

—— (1967), 'Toward a Theory of Property Rights', *American Economic Review*, **57**, 347–59.

Friedman, J. W. (1986), *Game Theory with Applications to Economics*, Oxford, Oxford University Press.

Groves, T., and Ledyard, J. (1977), 'Optimal Allocation of Public Goods: A Solution to the "Free Rider" Problem', *Econometrica*, **45**, 783–809.

Guttman, J. M. (1978), 'Understanding Collective Action: Matching Behavior', *American Economic Review Papers and Proceedings*, **68**, 251–5.

Hardin, G. (1968), 'The Tragedy of the Commons', *Science*, **162**, 1243–8.

Hoel, M. (1991), 'Global Environmental Problems: The Effects of Unilateral Actions Taken by One Country', *Journal of Environmental Economics and Management*, **20**, 55–70.

House of Commons Energy Committee (1989), *Energy Policy Implications of the Greenhouse Effect*, vol. 1, London, HMSO.

House of Commons Environment Committee (1984), *Acid Rain*, vol. 1, London, HMSO.

Lyster, S. (1985), *International Wildlife Law*, Cambridge, Grotius.

Marwell, G. E., and Ames, R. E. (1981), 'Economists Free Ride, Does Anyone Else?', *Journal of Public Economics*, **15**, 295–310.

Nordhaus, W. D. (1994), *Managing the Global Commons*, Cambridge, MA, MIT Press.

Paterson, D. G., and Wilen, J. (1977), 'Depletion and Diplomacy: The North Pacific Seal Hunt, 1886–1910', *Research in Economic History*, **2**, 81–139.

Samuelson, P. (1954), 'The Pure Theory of Public Expenditure', *Review of Economics and Statistics*, 36, 387–9.

Sugden, R. (1984), 'Reciprocity: The Supply of Public Goods through Voluntary Contributions', *Economic Journal*, **94**, 772–87.

—— (1986), *The Economics of Rights, Co-operation and Welfare*, Oxford, Basil Blackwell.

Trail Smelter Arbitral Tribunal (1939), 'Decision', *American Journal of International Law*, **33**, 182–212.

—— (1941), 'Decision', *American Journal of International Law*, **35**, 684–736.

US Environmental Protection Agency (1988), 'Protection of Stratospheric Ozone; Final Rule', *Federal Register*, **53**, 30566–602.

---

[12] The United States and the UK continued to contribute to the Fund even after withdrawing their funding from UNESCO.

9

Pricing and congestion: economic principles relevant to pricing roads

DAVID M. NEWBERY

Department of Applied Economics, University of Cambridge

I. Introduction

The road network is a costly and increasingly scarce resource. For the UK the Department of Transport (1994a) calculates that total road expenditures (capital and current) or 'road costs' averaged £7.07 billion per year at 1995/6 prices for the period 1992/3–1994/5. Public expenditure on roads increased sharply from 1988/9 to 1992/3 but has since fallen, and over the decade from 1984/5 has risen by just 15 per cent, less than the increase in private car ownership (of 28 per cent), or vehicle km travelled (39 per cent). Capital expenditure on roads doubled between 1988/9 and 1992/3 and increased by 56 per cent over the whole decade. (Department of Transport, 1995, Tables 1.17, 1.20, 1.22, 3.2, 4.7.) From the 26.1 million vehicles registered, road taxes of £19.0 billion were collected, or 2.9 times the Department's figures for 'road costs'. In 1993 15.6 per cent of consumers' expenditure was on transport and vehicles, and 13 per cent was on motor vehicles alone. Clearly, road transport is of major economic significance. Car ownership per 1,000 population in the UK appears to be catching up on the rates in the larger European countries and is now about 83 per cent of French and Italian levels, 73 per cent of West German levels. Over the decade 1984–94 the number of private cars increased from 16.1 to 20.5 million, or by 28 per cent. From 1978 to 1988, the total vehicle-km driven rose from 303 to 422 billion or by 39 per cent. As the length of the road network increased by only 5

First published in *Oxford Review of Economic Policy*, vol. 6, no. 2 (1990). This version is the 1995 update published in the first edition of *Readings in Microeconomics* and has been left unchanged except for the addition of an Appendix that updates the story to the end of 1999. The interested reader can update the cost and revenue data presented in Table 9.1 from the latest issue of *Transport Statistics Great Britain* (DETR).

per cent, the average daily traffic on each km of road rose by 34 per cent over the same decade on all roads and by 62 per cent on motorways. Traffic on major roads in built-up areas (i.e. those with a speed limit of 40 mph or less) increased by 25 per cent. (Department of Transport, 1995, Tables 3.17, 4.10.)

As road space is a valuable and scarce resource, it is natural that economists should argue that it should be rationed by price—road-users should pay the marginal social cost of using the road network if they are to be induced to make the right decisions about whether (and by which means) to take a particular journey, and, more generally, to ensure that they make the correct allocative decisions between transport and other activities. If road-users paid the true social cost of transport, perhaps urban geography, commuting patterns, and even the sizes of towns would be radically different from the present. The modest aim here is to identify these social costs, provide rough estimates of their magnitude for Britain, and hence identify the major policy issues.

One way to focus the discussion is to ask how to design a system of charges for road use. The problem of designing road charges can be broken down into various sub-problems. First, what is the marginal social cost (that is, the extra cost to society) of allowing a particular vehicle to make a particular trip? Part will be the direct cost of using the vehicle (fuel, wear and tear, driver's time, and so forth) and will be paid for by the owner. This is the private cost of road use. Other costs are social: some will be borne by other road-users (delays, for example); some by the highway authority (extra road maintenance); and some by the society at large (pollution and risk of accidents). These are called the *road-use costs*—the social costs (excluding the private costs) arising from vehicles using roads. It seems logical to attempt to charge vehicles for these road-use costs, in order to discourage them from making journeys where the benefits are less than the total social costs (private costs plus road-use costs). The first task, therefore, is to measure these road-use costs.

The second question is whether road-users should pay additional taxes above these road-use costs. One argument is that road-users should pay the whole cost of the highway system, not just the extra cost of road use, either to be 'fair' in an absolute sense or to achieve parity or equity with, say, rail-users (in those rare countries where the railway is required to cover its total costs without subsidy). Another argument is that the government needs to raise revenues and some part of this revenue should be collected from road-users, since to exempt them would be to give them an unreasonable advantage over the rest of the population. Both arguments appeal either to the desire for equity or fairness, or to the need for efficiency in the allocation of resources (road versus rail), or both.

1. Relevant principles of taxation

The modern theory of public finance provides a powerful organizing principle for taxing and pricing. Under certain assumptions policies should be designed to achieve production efficiency, with all distortionary taxes falling on final consumers. Broadly, the conditions for this result, set out formally in Diamond and Mirrlees (1971), are (a) that production efficiency is feasible, and (b) that any resulting private profits are either negligible or can be taxed away. The feasibility condition would be satisfied if the economy were competitive and externalities could be corrected or internalized.

The theory has immediate implications for road charges and taxes. Road-users can be divided into two groups: those who transport freight, which is an intermediate service used in production, and those who drive their own cars or transport passengers, who enjoy final consumption. Freight transport, which is roughly and conveniently synonymous with diesel-using vehicles, should pay the road-use costs to correct externalities and to pay for the marginal costs of maintenance. Additional taxes (comprising the *pure tax element*) on (largely gasoline-using) passenger transport can be set, using the same principles that guide the design of other indirect taxes. We shall show below that one would expect a close relationship between road-use costs and total road expenditures. There is no logical reason to attribute the taxation of passenger transport to the highway budget, since it is a component of general tax revenue. But if all road taxes and charges are taken together, there are good reasons to expect that they will exceed total highway expenditure. In short, in a well-run country no conflict need arise between the goals of designing an equitable and efficient system of road-use charges and taxes and the desire to cover the highway system's costs.

The theory provides a useful framework for the study of road-user charges. The first step is to identify the road-use costs. The second is to see what methods are available for levying charges and how finely they can be adjusted to match these costs. The third step is to examine how far these methods have repercussions outside the transport sector and, where these occur, how to take them into account. These three steps will suffice for freight transport. For passenger transport, one other step is needed: to determine the appropriate level of (and method of levying) the pure tax element.

II. Quantifying the social costs of road use

Vehicles impose four main costs on the rest of society—accident externalities, environmental pollution, road damage, and congestion. Accident externalities arise whenever extra vehicles on the road increase the probability that other road-users will be involved in an accident. To the extent that accidents depend on distance driven and other traffic these accident costs can be treated rather like congestion costs. Newbery (1988a) argued that accident externalities could be as large as all other externality costs taken together, and are thus possibly of first order importance. There are two reasons for this high estimate, both disputed. The first is that the figure critically depends on the value of a life saved or the cost of a life lost. If one bases this on apparent willingness to pay to reduce risks, then the cost per life saved might be between £650,000 and £2 million at 1989 prices, based on the survey results of Jones-Lee (1990). The lower figure is over double that originally used by the Department of Transport, who based their earlier estimates on the expected loss of future earnings of a representative victim. Apparently the Department of Transport has been persuaded of the logic behind the willingness-to-pay approach, and now uses a figure of £500,000 (Jones-Lee, 1990).

The second reason is that in the absence of convincing evidence, the estimate assumed that the number of accidents increased with the traffic flow as the 1.25 power of that flow. (That is, if the traffic is twice as heavy, the risk of an accident happening to each car is increased by 19 per cent. Compare this with the number of pairwise encounters between vehicles, which rises as the square of the flow.) This in turn means that a quarter of the cost of mutually caused accidents is an uncharged externality, even if each driver pays the full cost of the accident to him. (To the extent that society pays through the NHS, these individual costs are borne by society and attributable as part of 'road costs'. The Department of Transport includes direct costs. It might argue that their earlier valuation of life was based on the loss of earnings which might have to be made good through the social security system to survivors.) Note that it is important to relate the accident rate to traffic levels in order to identify the size of the externality. Indeed, one might argue from the fact that the accident rate has fallen as traffic has increased that this 1.25 power law is invalid, and that at best there is no relationship between traffic and the accident rate. If so, then there would be no externality between motor vehicles (other than that already counted in the cost falling on the NHS). This would be the case if one took seriously the explanation of 'risk compensation', according to which road-users choose a desired level of perceived risk with which they are comfortable—too little risk is boring, too much is frightening. Improvements in road safety then induce compensating increases in risk taking, while deteriorating road conditions (ice, snow, heavier traffic) induce more caution. Of course, one should be wary of using time series information about accident rates as road improvements are continuously undertaken to improve road safety. The relationship between accident rate and traffic should be derived from a properly estimated cross-section analysis.

Jones-Lee (1990) does indeed assume that the accident *rate* (i.e. the risk of an accident per km driven) is independent of the traffic flow, from which it follows that there is no externality between motor vehicles (except those caused by the system of social and health insurance). He also assumes that the probability of any vehicle having an accident involving a pedestrian or cyclist is constant per km driven, in which case it follows that the accident rate experienced by cyclists and pedestrians is proportional to the number of vehicle km driven. If this is the case, then motor vehicles do impose an externality on non-motorized road-users (though not on other motorists), which Jones-Lee calculates to be quite large—perhaps 10–20 per cent of total road costs. Of course, we remain relatively uncertain about the relationship between accidents to other road-users and traffic. It has been remarked that not so long ago children were allowed to play in the street, and cycle or walk unaccompanied to school. The

number of accidents to such children was quite high. Now it is so obviously insane to allow such activities that the number of accidents may have fallen with the increase in traffic. Of course, that accident externality is still there, though hidden in the form of the extra costs of ferrying children to school, and not allowing them to play or cycle unsupervised.

The main problem therefore lies in identifying the relationship between traffic and accidents—in the words of the US Federal Highway Cost Allocation Study 'Quantitative estimation of accident cost and vehicle volume relationships, however, has not yet proved satisfactory . . .' (US Federal Highway Authority, 1982). Given the huge costs involved and the potential gains from lowering accident rates, identifying such relationships should have overwhelming research priority.

Similarly, pollution costs share many of the same features as congestion costs (and tend to occur in the same places). Where they have been quantified (for the US) they appear to contribute less than 10 per cent of total road costs. They are normally dealt with by mandating emission standards, and by differential taxes on the more polluting fuels (for example, by having higher taxes on leaded petrol). A new European Directive on vehicle emissions, known as the Luxembourg Agreement, will be implemented in the UK. This mandates NO_x levels of half the current limit, and reductions in hydrocarbon releases of three-quarters, at an estimated cost to the motorist of £800 million or about 4 per cent of motoring costs (Department of the Environment, 1989). Provided the pollution costs are reflected in fuel taxes, and the requirement to meet emissions standards, these costs will have been satisfactorily inter-nalized. One should, however, be rather cautious about mandating stringent emissions standards without a careful cost–benefit analysis. Crandall *et al.* (1986, pp. 114–15) estimate that the programme costs for the US of the more stringent 1984 emissions standards might be about $20 billion per year with a replacement rate of 10.5 million cars, which is several times greater than rather optimistic estimates of the potential benefits of reducing pollution. (Safety regulations in contrast, though expensive, seem to have been justified on cost–benefit criteria.) Some of these issues are discussed further in Newbery (1990).

1. Road damage costs

These are the costs borne by the highway authority of repairing roads damaged by the passage of vehicles, and the extra vehicle operating costs caused by this road damage. The damage a vehicle does to the road pave-

Table 9.1. Road costs in 1993/4 prices (£ million)

Cost category	Annual average	
	5% TDR	8% TDR
Interest on capital	4500	7200
(Capital expenditure)	(3060)	
Maintenance *less* costs attrib		
to pedestrians	3252	3252
Policing and traffic wardens	408	408
Total road costs	8160	10860
of which attributable to		
road damage costs	446	446
Gross vehicle mass	683	683
VKT	479	479
Balance attributable to PCU	6552	9252
PCU km (billion)	456 billion km	
Cost per PCUkm pence/km	(1.33p/km)	(1.92p/km)
Cost per PCUkm incl.		
VKT costs pence/km	(1.44p/km)	(2.03p/km)

Source: Department of Transport (1994 *a, b*).
Notes: Figures are annual averages for the years 1991/2 to 1993/4 at 1993/4 prices TDR: Test Discount Rate; VKT: vehicle km travelled. Costs attributable to Gross Vehicle Mass taken from Department of Transport (1994 *a*), entirely allocated. VKT costs from same source adjusted in the same proportion as in Newbery (1988, Table 2).

ment increases as the fourth power of the axle load, which means that almost all damage is done by heavy vehicles such as trucks. Increasing the number of axles is a potent method of reducing the damaging effect of a vehicle—doubling the number of equally loaded axles reduces the damage to an eighth of its previous level. Consequently most highway authorities closely regulate the axle configuration and maximum legal axle loads. Increasing the road thickness dramatically increases the number of vehicles that can be carried before major repairs are required—doubling the thickness increases this number by 2 to the power 6.5 or so (Paterson, 1987). Consequently the most damaging and therefore costly combination is a heavy vehicle on a thin road.

The theory which allows these costs to be quantified is set out in Newbery (1988a, b). The road-damage costs of a vehicle will be proportional to its damaging power (and will be measured in terms of Equivalent Standard Axles, or ESAs). Britain, in common with most advanced countries, follows a condition-responsive maintenance strategy in which the road is repaired when its condition reaches a predetermined state. In such cases, the road-damage costs will be equal to the average annual costs of maintaining the road network in a stable state, multiplied by the fraction of the road deterioration caused by vehicles, as opposed to weather, allocated in proportion to ESA-miles driven.

The fraction of total costs allocated to vehicles will depend on the climate, the strength of the road, and the interval between major repairs, and the formula is given in Newbery (1988a,b). In hot, dry climates it will be between 60 and 80 per cent, while in freezing temperate climates the proportion will be between 20 and 60 per cent, the lower figures corresponding to more stringent maintenance criteria or lower traffic volumes. For Britain, Newbery (1988a) argued that the appropriate fraction was 40 per cent. If maintenance is condition-responsive then it is not necessary to charge vehicles for the damage they do indirectly to subsequent vehicles which experience increased operating costs on the damaged pavement—on average the condition of the pavement will remain unchanged.

It is simple to update the road-damage costs given in Newbery (1988a) using the latest estimates of road-track costs provided in Department of Transport (1994a, Table 2.5). The total cost identified is £1,114 million, or 12.07 pence/ESAkm. The allocable fraction is 0.4, giving £446 million or 4.83 pence/ESAkm. As such, road-damage costs are a small fraction of total road costs. To provide a quick estimate of how large a fraction, Table 9.1 above updates the results from 1986 to 1993 from Newbery (1988a, Table 2). There the value of the road network was estimated at £50 billion excluding land. Updating to 1993 (Newbery, 1995) and adding the cost of land brings it to £90 billion. In Newbery (1988a) the rate of interest on this capital value was taken to be the then Test Discount Rate of 5 per cent real, and if this figure is again used, then interest on the value of the road network would be £4,500 million, compared to the actual capital expenditure of £3,060 million. Recently, the Test Discount Rate has been revised upward to 8 per cent real (presumably reflecting the perceived higher real rate of return in the rest of the economy), and at this rate the interest costs would rise to £7,200 million.

There is little logic in combining current and capital expenditures as the Department of Transport does in estimating 'road costs', and Table 9.1 only includes imputed interest at the two different rates of 5 per cent and 8 per cent. It will be seen that allocable road-damage costs amount to 4–5.3 per cent of total road costs, and are thus essentially negligible (which is not to deny that it is important to charge them appropriately to heavy goods vehicles).

This estimate is quite close to that for 1986 of 3.5 per cent given in Newbery (1988a). Even if repair costs currently allocated by the UK Department of Transport in proportion to gross vehicle weight are included (and the theoretical justification for so doing is rather unclear) the figure only rises to 10–14 per cent (depending on the choice of the TDR). Small *et al.* (1988) estimate that pavement costs, including construction and periodic resurfacing, are less than 16 per cent of road costs in their simulations of an optimized US road system, and road-damage charges would only account for 2 per cent of total charges. Far and away the largest element (again ignoring accident costs, which might also be very large) are the congestion costs.

2. Congestion costs

These arise because additional vehicles reduce the speed of other vehicles, and hence increase their journey time. The standard way of calculating the short-run marginal congestion cost (MCC) of an extra vehicle in the traffic stream starts by postulating a relationship between speed (v kph) and flow (q vehicles or PCU/h) where PCU are passenger car units, a measure of the congestive effect of different vehicles in different circumstances (e.g. higher for heavy lorries on steep hills than on the level). If the travel cost per km of a representative vehicle is

$$c = a + b/v, \tag{1}$$

where b is the cost per vehicle hour, including the opportunity cost of the driver and occupants, then the total cost of a flow of q vehicles per hour is $C = cq$. If an additional vehicle is added to the flow, the total social cost is increased by

$$dC/dq = c + q.dc/dq. \tag{2}$$

The first term is the private cost borne by the vehicle and the second is the marginal externality cost borne by other road-users.

The next step is to establish the speed–flow relationship, $v = v(q)$ and here one must be careful to pose the right question. Engineers designing particular sections of the road network are concerned with flow at each point, and most of the relationships estimated are of this form. They show that traffic flow is heavily influenced by junctions, where additional traffic enters or disrupts the smooth flow, and it is possible for the speed–flow relationship to be backward bending, as in Figure 9.1.

The curve is to be interpreted as follows. As traffic increases above q the speed is given by points such as A, B. As traffic nears the capacity of the link, k, at the point C, the flow changes to a condition of stop-start, and traffic flow through the bottleneck drops, to a point such as D, associated with a lower speed. This is an unstable situation, and as flow falls, so the traffic leaving the bottleneck will accelerate, and eventually

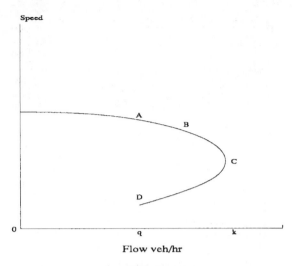

Figure 9.1. Speed flow relationship for a link

clear the blockage. At that time, the speed will jump back up to point A. (Further details are given in Newbery, 1987, and Hall *et al.*, 1986.)

Useful though this relation is for road design, it is not what is wanted for estimating the cost of congestion, where we need a measure of the total extra time taken by the remaining traffic to complete their planned journeys, not their speed at a particular point on the road network. The Department of Transport, when planning roads to alleviate congestion, uses formulas estimated by the Transport and Road Research Laboratory, and reported in Department of Transport (1987). These are based on 'floating car' methods, in which the observing vehicle remains in the traffic stream for a period of time, and hence give a better estimate of the average relationship between speed and flow. They find a reasonably stable linear relationship of the form

$$v = \alpha - \beta q, \tag{3}$$

where q is measured in PCU/lane/hr. The estimated value of β for urban traffic is 0.035. This agrees closely with a careful study of traffic flows within zones of Hong Kong, reported in Harrison *et al.* (1986), itself commissioned as part of Hong Kong's road-pricing experiment.

This linear relationship can be used to quantify the average and marginal costs of traffic and hence to determine the MCC. Figure 9.2 below gives this relationship for suburban roads at 1990 prices, based on the estimated COBA 9 formula. The left-hand scale gives the speed associated with the traffic flow, and on such roads average speeds rarely fall below 25 kph, so the

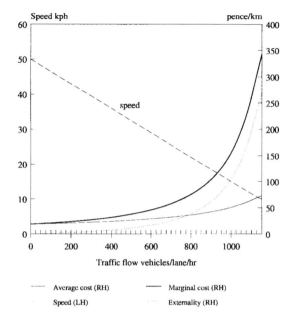

Legend:
- — — — Average cost (RH)
- ——— Marginal cost (RH)
- Speed (LH)
- ········ Externality (RH)

Urban non-central roads, 1990 prices

Figure 9.2. Average and marginal cost of trips

multiplied by the current value of the time use of the vehicle, b in (1). From (3), the MTC is just $\beta q/v^2$. Given data for q and v, the MTC can be estimated.

Newbery (1988a, Table 1) estimated these costs for Britain for the year 1985. Rather than repeat the rather time-consuming calculations reported there, the following short-cut has been adopted. If m is the MCC as a function of q, and if Δq is the increase in traffic over some period, then the revised estimate of the MCC is $m + dm/dq.\Delta q$. The factor by which to scale up the original estimates of MCC can be found from the above equations and is

$$\{1 + (2\beta q/v)\}(\Delta q/q). \tag{4}$$

The results of this updating procedure are given in Table 9.2. If anything, the estimate will be on the low side, as the relationship is very non-linear. If some roads have an above-average increase in traffic while others have a below-average increase, then taking the average increase q/q will underestimate the average of the costs on each road.

Table 9.2 shows in a vivid way the great variation in marginal congestion costs by time of day and location. Urban central areas at the peak have an *average* congestion cost of 10 times the average over all roads, and more than 100 times that the average motorway or rural road.

The table shows that the average congestion cost is 4.2 pence/PCUkm, and, given the 456 billion PCUkm driven from Table 9.1, if road-users were to be charged for congestion, the revenue collected would have been £19,000 million. If we add to this sum the road-damage costs (£446 m), the amounts allocated according to gross vehicle mass (£683 m), and VKT (£479 m),

relevant part of the diagram is to the left of that speed level. Another, quite useful way of representing this limitation is to suppose that the demand for using suburban roads becomes highly elastic at this level, an idea pursued further below.

In some ways a better measure of the congestion relationship is given by the marginal time cost (MTC) in vehicle-hours per vehicle-km, which can then be

Table 9.2. Marginal time costs of congestion in Great Britain, 1993

	MTC (veh h/ 100 PCUkm)	VKT per cent	MCC p/PCUkm	Congest cost share %	Index of MCC
Motorway	0.05	17	0.32	1	8
Urban central peak	5.41	1	44.74	13	1071
Urban central off-peak	4.35	3	35.95	27	861
Non-central peak	2.36	4	19.51	17	467
Non-central off-peak	1.30	10	10.75	26	257
Small town peak	1.03	3	8.47	6	203
Small town off-peak	0.63	7	5.17	9	124
Other urban	0.01	14	0.08	0	2
Rural dual carriageway	0.01	12	0.06	0	1
Other trunk and principal	0.04	18	0.23	1	6
Other rural	0.01	12	0.06	0	1
Weighted average			4.18		100

Source: Updated from Newbery (1990, Table 2)

all taken from Table 9.1, then the appropriate level of road charges should yield £20,700 million. Total road taxes were £19,000 million, or 92 per cent of the required level. Congestion charges would amount to 92 per cent of the total appropriate road charge.

It is interesting to compare these estimates with those given in Newbery (1988*a*). The estimated congestion charges for Britain for 1986 were £6,203 million out of the total appropriate charge (excluding accident costs) of £7,033 million, or 88 per cent. The figures are high as the amount of time wasted is so high, though the costs are frequently ignored by highway authorities, as they are entirely borne by highway-users. The Confederation of British Industries has calculated that traffic congestion costs the nation £15 billion a year in 1989 prices, or £10 a week on each household's shopping bill (*The Times*, 19 May 1989). Uprating the CBI figure by the increase in family expenditure gives a 1993 value of nearly £19 billion, comparable to the £19 billion for the appropriate congestion charge calculated above, though the question of how best to measure the true social cost of congestion is discussed more fully below.

Small *et al.* (1988) cite evidence that suggests congestion costs are also high in the US. Thus average peak-hour delays in crossing the Hudson River to Manhattan have roughly doubled in the past ten years, while congestion delays in the San Francisco Bay Area grew by more than 50 per cent in just two years. In 1987, 63 per cent of vehicle-miles were driven on Interstate Highways at volume to capacity ratios exceeding 0.8, and 42 per cent on other arterials. Although their study does not quantify the congestion costs they suggest figures of some tens of billions of dollars annually—a figure which squares with the evidence in the next paragraph.

The correct charge to levy on vehicles is equal to the congestion costs they cause (in addition to other social costs like damage costs). If roads experience constant returns to scale, in that doubling the capital expenditure on the road creates a road able to carry twice the number of vehicles at the same speed, and if roads are optimally designed and adjusted to the traffic, then it can be shown that the optimal congestion charge would recover all of the non-damage road costs. (Newbery, 1989). These include interest on the original capital stock, as well as the weather-induced road-damage costs not directly attributable to vehicles, and other maintenance expenditures, collectively identified as 'road costs attributable to PCU' in Table 9.1. The available evidence supports constant returns to scale or possibly rather mildly increasing returns, of the order of 1.03–1.19. (This always surprises highway engineers, who *know* that it does not cost twice as much to double the capacity of a highway, as many costs—embankments, etc.—are fixed, and the capacity of a two-lane divided highway is considerably greater than of a one-lane divided highway. But most capacity increases are needed in congested urban areas where the costs of land acquisition can be extremely high. The econometric estimates pick this factor up. See Keeler and Small, 1977, and Kraus, 1981.) If we take the estimates as supporting constant returns, then the result is directly applicable, and provides a useful benchmark against which to judge the estimated congestion charges. If we assume increasing returns to scale, then road charges would not cover road costs of an optimal road network.

In 1986 the estimated average congestion charge was 1.42 times as high as the road costs attributable to PCU, suggesting either that the road network was inadequate for the level of traffic, or that the correct rate of interest to charge was higher than 5 per cent real. (At 8 per cent the ratio was only 1.0.) The corresponding ratio for 1993 is 2.90 (or 2.06 at 8 per cent interest). In short, if roads were undersupplied in 1986, they are becoming critically scarce as traffic volumes increase faster than road space is supplied. Notice that assuming that there are increasing returns to capacity, expansion strengthens the conclusion that roads are undersupplied.

III. Charging for road use

Ideally, vehicles should be charged for the road-use cost of each trip, so that only cost-justified trips are undertaken. In practice it is not too difficult to charge for road damage, which is largely a function of the type of vehicle and the extent to which it is loaded. Ton-mile taxes as charged by some of the states of the US can ap-proximate the damage charge quite closely, provided they are made specific to the type of vehicle. Vehicle-specific distance taxes would be almost as good, provided axle loading restrictions were enforced. Fuel taxes are moderately good in that they charge trucks in proportion to ton-miles. As they charge different types of vehicles at (almost) the same ton-mile rate, they must be supplemented by vehicle-specific purchase taxes or licence fees and combined with careful regulation of allowable axle configurations and loadings (Newbery *et al.*, 1988; Newbery 1988*c*).

The more difficult task is to charge for congestion, which varies enormously depending on the level of traffic, which in turn varies across roads and with the time of day, as Table 9.2 shows dramatically. The most direct way is to charge an amount specific to the road and time of day, using an 'electronic number plate' which signals to the recording computer the presence of the vehicle. The computer then acts like a telephone exchange billing system, recording the user, the time and place, and hence the appropriate charge, and issuing monthly bills. The cost per number plate is of the order of $100, or perhaps a quarter of the cost of catalytic converters which are now mandatory for pollution control in many countries. Such systems have been successfully tested in Hong Kong (Dawson and Catling, 1986) but there was initially some pessimism at the political likelihood that they would ever be introduced (Borins, 1988). The stated objection was that the electronic detectors could monitor the location of vehicles and hence would violate the right to privacy. This objection may be valid in a society suspicious of (and not represented by) its government, though evidence suggests that this is not likely to be much of a problem in Europe (ECMT, 1989). The objection could be levied against telephone subscribers once itemized bills are introduced, and the objection can be overcome in much the same way by the use of 'smart cards', rather like magnetic telephone cards. The electronic licence plate would be loaded with the smart card and would debit payments until exhausted. Only thereafter would the central computer monitor and bill for road use.

A more plausible explanation for the lack of success in Hong Kong may have been that it was not clear to car owners that the new charges (which were quite high, of the order of $2–3 per day) would replace the existing and very high annual licence fee. Faced with a doubling of the cost of road use, commuters understandably objected. But the whole point of charging for road use by electronic licence plates is to replace less well-designed road charging schemes, such as fuel taxes and licence fees. The proposition that needs to be put to the public is that in exchange for the entire system of current road taxes (fuel taxes in excess of the rate of VAT, the special car purchase tax, and the licence fee), road-users will be charged according to their use of congested road space, at a rate which for the average road-user will be roughly the same. (For the UK this is still just about feasible on the figures given above, at least if the pure tax element on private motorists is allowed to fall to zero.) As more than half the road-using population drives less than the average number of miles in congested areas, this should command majority support.

An alternative method of selling the use of electronic licence plates might be to offer rebates for tax on fuel used (at the estimated rate per km, or on production of receipts) and to waive the licence fee for those installing the licence plates. This might be necessary as an interim measure when their use is confined to major urban centres, notably London. It is noticeable that despite the claim by Channon as Minister of Transport that the Government had no plans to introduce road pricing because of the perceived public hostility, that hostility seems to be diminishing, at least in London. An opinion survey conducted by the Metropolitan Transport Research Unit showed 87 per cent in favour of some form of traffic restraint, and 53 per cent in favour of a fixed charge to drive into Central London. Charging per mile was widely supported, and 48 per cent said they would use public transport if such charges were introduced (*Independent*, 26 January 1990).

Until road pricing is introduced, alternative and less satisfactory methods of charging are necessary. One such is selling area licences which grant access to congested zones such as city centres during rush hours. This solution has been used in Singapore for over a decade, with considerable success. Heavy parking charges and restricted access may also be effective to varying degrees (World Bank, 1986). At the moment, however, the only way to charge vehicles for the congestion they cause is in proportion to the distance they drive, by fuel taxes and/or vehicle purchase taxes (which approximate reasonably well to distance charges for heavily used vehicles, but less well for automobiles). Such taxes, combined with access charges (area licences, or even annual licences) achieve the desired effect of charging road-users on average for congestion, but do little to encourage them to drive on less congested roads or at less busy times of the day (or, indeed, to take public transport instead). In Britain, the estimates above suggest that road taxes might usefully be increased somewhat. It is worth remarking that there are clear advantages in raising such corrective taxes to their efficient level, as they allow other distortionary taxes, which incur deadweight losses, to be reduced.

IV. Measuring the costs of congestion

So far we have avoided discussing the actual cost of congestion in Britain, and instead calculated the revenue that would be generated if vehicles were to be charged for the congestion they caused. Figure 9.3 shows how the equilibrium demand for trips is estab-

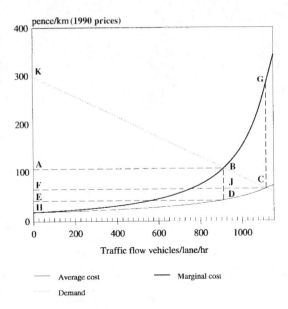

Figure 9.3. Costs of congestion: urban non-central roads

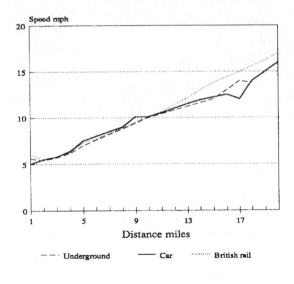

Figure 9.4. Equilibrium trip speed: average door-to-door speed, Central London

lished in the absence of such charges. If road-users pay only the private costs of the trip, their costs are given by the average cost schedule, which meets the demand schedule at point C. At that point the willingness to pay by the marginal road-user is equal to the cost of the trip. The efficient congestion charge would be an amount BD, which, if levied, would cause demand to fall to the level associated with point B. The revenue then raised would be $ABDE$, and this is the amount referred to above as the revenue attributable to the congestion charge. In the figure it would amount to £600 per lane-hour. But is this the correct measure of the congestion cost? Consider various alternative measures. One measure frequently cited in newspaper accounts of the cost of congestion is the extra costs in-volved in travelling on congested rather than uncon-gested roads. This might be measured by FC times FH, the excess of the average actual cost over the cost on a road with zero traffic. On the figure this would amount to £530 (per lane-hour). But this is an unre-alistic comparison, as it would be uneconomic to build roads to be totally uncongested. Instead one might compare the extra costs of the excessive congestion at point C above that which would be efficient, at point D. These extra costs might be measured as CF times EF, or £270. This is not satisfactory either, as fewer trips would be taken at the efficient level of charges. A bet-ter alternative is the loss in social surplus associated with excessive road use. The efficient total social sur-

plus associated with point B is the consumer surplus triangle KBA, plus the tax revenue $ABDE$. The social surplus associated with point C is just the triangle KCF, and the difference is the rectangle $FJDE$ less the trian-gle BCJ, or £198. This is also equal to the area of the standard deadweight loss triangle BCG. In this case the deadweight loss is equal to one-third of the revenue measure.

There is one important case in which the revenue measure accurately measures the deadweight loss, and that is where the demand for trips becomes perfectly elastic beyond its intersection with the marginal so-cial cost schedule at point B. In this case there is no gain in consumer surplus in moving from the efficient level of traffic to the equilibrium level, and hence the loss is just equal to the forgone tax revenue. Put an-other way, by not charging the efficient toll in this per-fectly elastic case, the government forgoes revenue but the consumer makes no gain. In crowded urban areas this is a plausible situation. The equilibrium level of traffic is found where the marginal road-user is indif-ferent between using a car or some alternative—pub-lic transport or walking. Thus traffic speeds in London are about the same as they were in the nineteenth cen-tury, and the time taken to get to work (or, more prop-erly, the total perceived cost) for many commuters is no better by road than alternatives. Figure 9. 4, which is taken from a graph in *The Times*, 5 December 1988, itself based on work by Martin Mogridge, illustrates

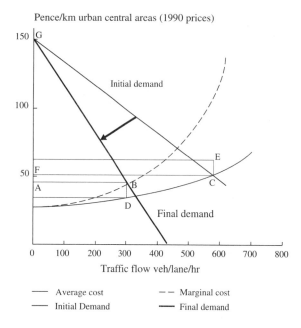

Figure 9.5. Congestion with public transport

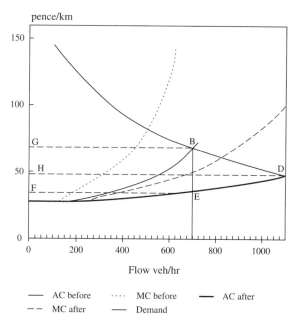

Figure 9.6. Cost–benefit of road improvements

this graphically for central London. The average door-to-door time taken between points in central London is remarkably similar for all three modes of transport, so car speeds in equilibrium are determined by the speeds of alternative public transport.

In such circumstances, the social costs of congestion may even be understated by the revenue measure. Consider the situation portrayed in Figure 9.5. Initially demand is *GC* and equilibrium is established at *C* with commuting costs of 0*F*. But if road-users were charged an amount *BD* = *CE* (the equilibrium efficient toll, less the short run external cost), then some road-users would switch to public transport, reducing demand for private road use. This increased demand for public transport would, after appropriate investment and expansion, lead to an improved frequency of service, while the reduced traffic would lead to a faster public transport service, lowering the costs of travel. Given this lower public transport cost, the demand for private transport would fall from *GC* to *GD*, and the willingness to pay for private commuting would fall, from the level 0*F* to 0*A* for the marginal commuter. In this case charging the congestion tax would yield tax revenue (a social gain) while reducing the cost of commuting (an additional consumer gain). The tax forgone thus understates the cost of the congestion.

V. Cost–benefit analysis of road improvements

The average road tax paid by vehicles per km is roughly the same as the average efficient level. On roads of below average congestion, vehicles may be overcharged, but in urban areas they are certainly undercharged, in many cases by a large margin. Faced with growing congestion, one natural response is to increase road capacity. Figure 9.6 illustrates the pitfalls in simple-minded cost–benefit analysis. If the road capacity is doubled, then the average and marginal cost schedules will move from 'before' to 'after'. The initial equilibrium will be at *B*, where demand is equal to the initial average cost (*AC*), and traffic will be *BG*. If the *AC* is lowered to *E*, then the apparent cost-saving is *GBEF*, to be compared with the cost of the improvement. But the lower *AC* will induce increased traffic and the new equilibrium will be at point *D*, not *E*. The benefit will be *GBDH*, which may be significantly lower.

Figure 9.7 shows that where traffic increases come from previous users of public transport the effect of the road 'improvement' may be to increase traffic volumes but to raise average costs, making everyone worse off, and adding negative value. It is hard to escape the

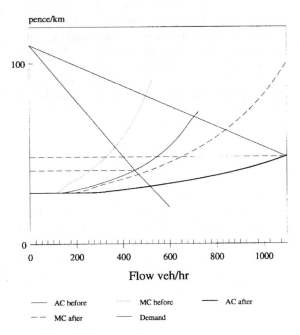

Figure 9.7. Perverse road improvement

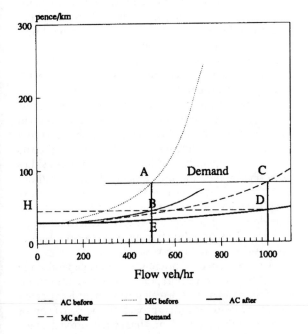

Figure 9.8. Road improvements with charges

conclusion that as journey speeds in London are now below their level at the turn of the century, before the introduction of the car, much of the road investment has been self-defeating.

The situation is radically changed when road-users pay the efficient congestion charge. Consider Figure 9.8, in which the demand for trips is perfectly elastic along *AC*, and congestion charges at the rate *AB* (marginal cost *less* average cost) are levied by means of an electronic number plate. If road capacity is expanded, but the charge maintained, then the social gain is the increase in the revenue collected, *ACDB*, which can be compared with the cost. If there are constant returns to capacity expansion and the road improvement is self-financing, it is justified. This is another application of the proposition that with constant returns to road expansion, congestion charges will recover the costs of the road investment. If there are increasing returns to expansion, then expansion may still be justified even if it is not self-financing—one should compare the marginal expansion costs with the marginal benefit measured by the increased revenue.

The implications of this are clear—without road pricing, road improvements may yield low or even negative returns, but with efficient pricing, not only are improvements easy to evaluate, they should also be self-financing, at least if there are constant or diminishing returns to expansion, as is likely in congested areas.

VI. Pricing public transport

If private road-users are significantly undercharged for using the road in urban areas, then commuters face the wrong relative prices when choosing between public and private transport. If it is hard to raise the price of private driving, why not lower the price of public transport to improve the relative price ratios? There are a number of problems with this proposal. First, it is hard to compute the second-best public transport subsidies given the great variation of congestion costs by time of day and location. Second, the subsidies have to be financed by taxes which have distortionary costs elsewhere. (Note that congestion charges would reduce the distortionary costs of the tax system.) Third, subsidies to public transport appear to be rather cost-ineffective. Few motorists are attracted off the road into private transport, with much of the increase in public transport use coming from those previously not using either mode.

There are also political economic problems with operating public bus companies at a loss—there is a temptation to ration them and lower the quality, thus defeating the purpose of making them more attractive to commuters. It becomes more difficult to gain the benefits of deregulation and privatization. It may just lead to rent-dissipation by the supplier of public transport—as seems to have happened to some extent when the London Underground was heavily subsidized. The same applies to subsidizing rail travel—it becomes unattractive to expand capacity if this just increases the size of the loss.

A more promising approach is to make private transport relatively less attractive and public transport more attractive, by improving the quality of the latter, possibly at the expense of the former. Bus lanes which reduce road space to other road-users have this effect, as would electronic signalling to give priority to public transport at traffic lights. Banning private cars from congested streets during the working day has a similar effect. Arguably the greatest obstacle to overcome is that of making private road-users aware of the true social costs of their road use. Table 9.2 reveals that *average* congestion charges of 44 pence/km would be appropriate in urban centres at the peak, and 36 pence/km during the off-peak, with higher charges appropriate on roads with higher volume and/or lower speeds. Figure 9.2, which is plotted for 1990 costs for suburban areas, shows that when traffic speeds have fallen to 20 kph, then congestion charges of 50 pence/km are in order. It is hard to make public transport 50 pence/km cheaper than its unsubsidized level, and thus it is more productive to think of ways of raising the cost of private transport at congested periods, or directly reducing its level.

It was argued above that road pricing gives rise to sensible cost–benefit rules for road improvements. The same is also true for other transport investments, especially in public transport and that most capital intensive form, rail transport. If road-users paid the full social cost of road use, then there would be every reason to charge users of public transport the full social marginal cost, including congestion. It is unlikely that there are economies of scale in peak-period road or rail use in London, or in peak-period bus use in other cities, and this would lead to fares that would cover the full operating costs, including interest on capital. It would therefore again be easier to apply commercial criteria to investment in public transport, and, indeed, there would no longer be a strong case for keeping these services in the public sector.

VII. Conclusion

Road pricing is the best method of dealing with congestion, and would have far-reaching implications for the viability and quality of public transport, for the finance of urban infrastructure, and ultimately for the quality of life. The average road charge might not need to increase above current levels, for if roads were correctly priced, demand for the use of the most congested streets would fall, and with it the efficient charge to levy. Current road taxes are heavy and yield revenue substantially greater than the average cost of the current road system. In equilibrium, with efficient road pricing and an adequate road network, one would expect road charges to be roughly equal to road costs, so either road charges would fall below current tax levels, or substantial road investment would be justified, and possibly both.

A shift to road pricing would cause a fall in the cost of driving in non-urban areas, and an increase in the cost of urban driving. In the medium run the quality of urban public transport would improve, and the average cost of urban travel by both public and private transport might fall below current levels. Energy consumption would increase, as there would no longer be any reason to have heavy fuel taxes (other than those needed to reflect the costs of pollution, and this problem is arguably better addressed by mandatory emissions standards). A shift to road pricing matched by offsetting adjustments to other taxes to raise the same total tax revenue is unlikely to be inflationary, both because the average road tax/charge would be almost unchanged, and because any increase in charge leading to higher travel costs could be matched by lower taxes on other goods, leading to a fall in those elements of consumer expenditure.

Similarly, the impact on the distribution of income is likely to be slight and probably favourable. Urban private travel costs would rise, at least in the short run, and urban public transport quality-adjusted costs might fall (depending on how rapidly any subsidies were phased out, and how quickly the increased demand for public transport were translated into more supply at higher average quality). Rural transport costs would fall. As urban car-owners are richer than average, and users of public transport are poorer, the redistribution should be favourable.

The subject of road pricing and, more generally, the management of transport policy has moved firmly into the policy arena. The British government is attracted to a more commercial approach to the provision of transport infrastructure, and has restructured the railways with the intention of privatizing the rail track, which would charge train operating companies for the use of the track. Parity would suggest that road users should also be charged for using specific roads, and the government has indicated that charges should not only cover maintenance and operating costs, but also the capital value of the road network and the wider costs such as noise and other environmental costs—consistent with the approach set out in this reprinted article. The Department of Transport published a Green Paper, *Paying for Better Motorways* (HMSO, 1993), suggesting that road pricing should be introduced for motorways, while the British government is keen to introduce private-sector finance into road building. The idea of commercializing the road network is discussed in Newbery (1994), where the particular suggestions of motorway charges and private toll roads are criticized. The House of Commons Transport Committee studied the government proposals on *Charging for the Use of Motorways* (House of Commons, 1994), and subsequently investigated *Urban Road Pricing* (House of Commons, 1995).

The environmental impact of road transport was examined by the Royal Commission on Environmental Pollution (1994), and various estimates of the social costs are provided in Newbery (1995).

Cambridge County Council has been experimenting with a simple form of congestion meter, which is activated when a vehicle enters the city, and which can then charge the vehicle (deducting from a prepaid magnetic card similar to a phone card). It may be programmed to charge for distance travelled, time elapsed, or speed (or any combination of these). The original idea was to charge for time spent travelling below a pre-determined speed (reasoning that this would be because of congestion), but there were considerable doubts about the safety implications and unpredictability of this otherwise attractively decentralized system. What emerges clearly to any participant in the experiments is that the simple speed-flow models described above deal poorly with delays to traffic waiting at junctions and traffic lights. The best design for a system of charging for urban congestion remains unclear, though the Department of Transport has now published the results of its extensive study of road pricing in London based on traffic simulation models that attempt to deal with the longer-run impacts on the location of commuters and business.

Appendix: Update to 1999

This article was first published in 1990 and updated in 1995. Since then, road taxes have substantially increased as a result of the fuel tax escalator. This was originally introduced by the Conservative government and increased the rate of duty on motor fuels by 5 per cent above the rate of inflation each year. The original defence was that increasing fuel taxes were required to control vehicle emissions, particularly carbon dioxide, in order to meet the countries' targets for total carbon emissions. The labour government committed itself to raise the fuel tax escalator to 6 per cent in real terms each year while at the same time freezing or reducing expenditure on new roads. Expenditure on road maintenance has only increased slightly, despite the substantial increase in traffic, and as a result the road quality has deteriorated (as measured by the defects index of road conditions published in the DETR *Transport Statistics Great Britain*).

By 1997/98, road tax revenue was £24 billion, compared with total road costs of £11 billion, measuring the interest on the infrastructure at 6 per cent). With road traffic growing at just over 2 per cent per annum, and the real duty rising at 6 per cent per annum, real tax revenue will rise at about 8 per cent per annum, rapidly raising the excess of road tax revenue over road costs.

Given the emphasis placed by the government on sustainable development, the obvious questions to ask are what does one mean by sustainability for transport, and what implications does that have for the taxation of transport. In its document on *Sustainable Development* (HMSO, 1994, p.169), sustainability is taken to mean that 'users pay the full social and environmental cost of their transport decisions, so improving the overall efficiency of these decisions for the economy as a whole and bringing environmental benefits.' Newbery (1998a) reviewed the evidence on social and environmental costs to assess what sum should be added to road costs to give the total costs of road transport. His estimates were somewhat lower than some other sources, at £2–8 billion per year, mainly because he attached a lower cost to the mortality effects of air pollution. Some commentators have valued the mortality from air pollution at the same rate per person as accidents (£2 million per person), but the overwhelming medical evidence is that pollution shortens lives by weeks or possibly months rather than the expected value of forty years for a road accident. If one adjusts for life years lost as a result of pollution, the figures are dramatically reduced. Nevertheless, the degree of uncertainty about these social and environmental costs remains high, as indicated by the factor of 4 to 1 in the range from the low to the high figure.

Even if the high figure is added to the road costs, and even if road maintenance currently understates the depreciation of the network (as the quality is dete-

riorating), making the necessary adjustments to give
the total social cost of road use results in costs substantially less than current road taxes.

The present debate on road pricing has two strands.
The first and more fundamental question is whether
the charges that road users pay should be related to
the costs of the road system, as with other public utilities. The case for separately identifying these road costs
is that they could be levied as road charges with the
revenue allocated to one or more agencies charged to
provide road services. These agencies would be the
road counterpart of Railtrack, the privatised owner of
the railway infrastructure, and would be subject to
regulation to ensure that road charges were set at the
efficient level and to ensure that the agencies delivered
an acceptable quality of service. Environmental
('green') taxes could then be levied on road fuel as on
other fuels to reflect the environmental costs of various emissions. Both road charges and environmental
charges would be subject to VAT, just as the current
road fuel excise tax is subject to VAT.

The second issue is how best to levy the road charges.
Road pricing implies that different roads charge different prices depending on their scarcity and congestion. Sophisticated road pricing would require
electronic equipment, and would only be justified if
the improvement in the efficiency of road use were
greater than the costs of installing the system. Until
that time, the road charge could continue to be collected by fuel charges and vehicle excise duties. When
the technology is sufficiently mature and the cost-benefit analysis indicates that the time is ripe, these road
charges can be reduced and replaced by road prices
yielding the same total revenue. The regulator of
Roadtrack would ensure that total revenues did not
exceed the regulated level of costs. The regulator would
therefore give road users the assurance that road pricing was not intended as an additional charge but as a
more efficient way of collecting the amount deemed
appropriate.

A decade after the original article, there is growing
acceptance that transport policy is in disarray, that road
taxes can no longer be defended as reflecting road costs
including environmental costs, and that the system of
financing transport investments is deeply unsatisfactory. Newbery (1998b) discusses various solutions to
these problems, but other countries such as Australia
and New Zealand are further advanced in contemplating the proper financing of the road system.

Economic principles continue to be relevant for the
design of transport policy and these principles have
not changed. What has changed are the magnitudes
of the costs, and the more interesting problems of the

design of institutions to manage investment and maintenance and mechanisms to improve the efficiency of
road use. No doubt the next decade will provide more
evidence to guide practical policy making.

References

Borins, S. F. (1988), 'Electronic Road Pricing: An Idea whose Time may Never Come', *Transportation Research*, **22A**(1): 37–44.

Crandall, R. W., Gruenspecht, H. K., Keeler, T. E., and Lave, L. B. (1986), *Regulating the Automobile*, Brookings, Washington DC.

Dawson, J. A. L., and Catling, I. (1986), 'Electronic Road Pricing in Hong Kong', *Transportation Research*, **20A** (March): 129–34.

Department of the Environment (1989), *Environment in Trust: Air Quality*.

Department of Transport (1987), *COBA 9*, Department of Transport, London.

—— (1989a), *The Allocation of Road Track Costs 1989/90*, Department of Transport, London.

—— (1989b), *Transport Statistic Great Britain 1978–88*, Department of Transport, London.

—— (1994a), *The Allocation of Road Track Costs 1994/95*, Department of Transport, London.

—— (1994b), *Transport Statistics Great Britain 1994*, Department of Transport, London.

—— (1995), *Transport Statistics Great Britain 1995*, Department of Transport, London.

Diamond, P. A., and Mirrlees, J. A. (1971), 'Optimal Taxation and Public Production, I: Productive Efficiency', *American Economic Review*, **61**: 8–27.

ECMT (1989), European Conference of Ministers of Transport Round Table 80, *Systems of Infrastructure Cost Coverage*, Economic Research Centre, OECD, Paris.

Hall, F. L., Allen, B. L., and Gunter, M. A. (1986), 'Empirical Analysis of Freeway Flow-Density Relationships', *Transportation Research*, **20A**: 197–210.

Harrison, W. J., Pell, C., Jones, P. M., and Ashton, H. (1986), 'Some Advances in Model Design Developed for the Practical Assessment of Road Pricing in Hong Kong', *Transportation Research*, **20A**: 135–44.

HMSO (1993), *Paying for Better Motorways*, CM 2200, London, HMSO.

—— (1994) *Sustainable Development: the UK Strategy*, London: HMSO Cm 2426.

House of Commons (1994), *Charging for the Use of Motorways*, Fifth Report of the Transport Committee, Session 1993–94, Cm 376, London, HMSO.

—— (1995), *Urban Road Pricing*, Third Report of the Transport Committee, Session 1994–95, Cm 104–1, London, HMSO.

Jones-Lee, M. W. (1990), 'The Value of Transport Safety', *Oxford Review of Economic Policy*, **6**(2).

Keeler, T. E., and Small, K. (1977), 'Optimal Peak-Load Pricing, Investment and Service Levels on Urban Expressways', *Journal of Political Economy*, **85**(1): 1–25.

Kraus, Marvin (1981), 'Scale Economies Analysis for Urban Highway Networks', *Journal of Urban Economics*, **9**(1): 1–22.

Newbery, D. M. G. (1987), 'Road User Charges and the Taxation of Road Transport', *IMF Working Paper WP/87/5*, International Monetary Fund, Washington DC.

—— (1988a), 'Road User Charges in Britain', *The Economic Journal*, **98** (Conference 1988): 161–76.

—— (1988b), 'Road Damage Externalities and Road User Charges', *Econometrica*, **56**(2): 295–316.

—— (1988c), 'Charging for Roads', *Research Observer*, **3**(2): 119–38.

—— (1989), 'Cost Recovery from Optimally Designed Roads', *Economica*, **56**: 165–85.

—— (1990), 'Acid Rain', *Economic Policy*, **11**, October.

—— (1994), 'The Case for a Public Road Authority', *Journal of Transport Economics and Policy*, **28**(3), 325–54; also in *Minutes of Evidence*, Transport Committee Fifth Report, *Charging for the Use of Motorways*, Vol. II, 74–87 HC 376-(II).

—— (1995), 'Royal Commission *Report on Transport and the Environment*—Economic Effects of Recommendations', *The Economic Journal*, **105**, 1258–72.

—— (1998a) *Fair payment from road-users: A review of the evidence on social and environmental costs*, Report published by Automobile Association, February

—— (1998b) 'Fair and efficient pricing and the finance of roads', (The 53rd Henry Spurrier Memorial Lecture), *The Proceedings of the Chartered Institute of Transport in the UK*, **7**(3), October, 3-19

—— Hughes, G. A., Paterson, W. D. O., and Bennathan, E. (1988), *Road Transport Taxation in Developing Countries: The Design of User Charges and Taxes for Tunisia*, World Bank Discussion Papers, 26, Washington, DC.

Paterson, W. D. O. (1987), *Road Deterioration and Maintenance Effects: Models for Planning and Management*, Johns Hopkins University Press for World Bank, Baltimore.

Royal Commission on Environmental Pollution (1994), *Transport and the Environment*, 18th Report, Cm 2674, London, HMSO.

Small, K. A., Winston C., and Evans, C. A. (1988), *Road Work: A New Highway Policy*, Brookings, Washington DC (In Press).

US Federal Highway Authority (1982), *Final Report to the Federal Highway Cost Allocation Study*, US Government Printing Office, Washington, DC.

World Bank (1986), *Urban Transport*, Washington DC.

10

Economic policy towards the environment

DIETER HELM

New College, Oxford

DAVID PEARCE[1]

University College, London

I. Introduction

When Mrs Thatcher declared that the challenge of the 1990s will be to preserve the environment for the next generation she was highlighting a perceptual change in the nature of environmental problems. What had hitherto been viewed as a local and, at best, national issue, became in the 1980s an international and global one. The fate of natural environments was suddenly everyone's concern. The globalization of environmental degradation had been anticipated in the 1970s with warnings about ocean pollution, ozone layer damage, and climate change. But the popular focus was misdirected: resources were running out; the world was getting colder, not warmer; and the ozone layer was under threat from supersonic air transport. A mixture of poor and incomplete science combined with alarmism to produce *Limits to Growth* (Meadows *et al.*, 1972) and *Blueprint for Survival* (Goldsmith *et al.*, 1972).

Global concerns remain subject to scientific uncertainty: rates of loss of biological diversity are not known, the greenhouse effect is not yet a scientific fact, and the precise functioning of global and regional ecosystems is ill-understood. But the scientific base is clearer and, above all, the manifestations of environmental neglect are now conspicuous.

While scientific evidence is essential to identify the extent of the problem, the policy questions are largely ones for social science. The problem can only be addressed through changing human behaviour—altering the demand for environmental services and changing and controlling their supply. Indeed, a major feature of the modern environmental debate is the widespread acceptance of the role which economics must play in analysing the causal processes of environmental decay and in formulating policy. In the 1970s the economic voice was heard, often in critical response to alarmist environmentalism, in defence of economic growth and in favour of the use of economic policy instruments.[2] But it seems fair to say that, with exceptions, economists then were transfixed by a presumption that environmental issues were localized examples of externalities, fairly minor deviations from the reasonably efficient workings of market and quasi-market economies. Transboundary pollution (acid rain, ocean pollution) and mutual destruction of the global commons (ozone layer holes over the Antarctic and Arctic, tropical deforestation, biodiversity loss) soon ended the misconception, backed by demonstrations of the theoretical foundations of the pervasiveness of the environment in economic life.[3]

In order to construct a viable environmental policy, it is necessary to start with a proper analysis of environmental problems. It is a task to which economic theory is well suited. To an extent, the relevant literature already exists. Environmental effects are externalities—effects of which the costs and benefits are not

First published in *Oxford Review of Economic Policy*, vol. 6, no. 1. (1990).

[1] The authors are grateful for detailed comments on early drafts from Christopher Allsopp, Patrick Lane, Derek Morris, and Mark Pearson. The usual disclaimers apply.

[2] See for example, Beckerman (1974).
[3] See, notably, Ayres and Kneese (1969).

fully reflected in potential or actual market exchanges. They represent incomplete or missing markets. A huge literature exists on the nature of these market failures and on theoretical solutions.[4] In part, the objective of this paper is to highlight the relevance of some of the major results to current policy problems.

However, much of the existing literature focuses on externalities as special cases in otherwise perfect markets. In practice, market failures rarely arise in neatly segmented boxes. Externalities arise in oligopolistic and monopoly markets, where there is risk and uncertainty, in conjunction with public goods, and in areas where the state is already involved. Indeed, a distinctive feature of global externalities is the requirement for international cooperative solutions. The conventional economic approach to externalities is therefore unlikely to prove sufficient to define the policy options. The institutional context and the associated market structure matter.

Complexity also arises from the fact that most environmental assets are not marketed. There is no explicit market in clear air, in unpolluted bathing beaches, in forest views, and in the carbon-fixing properties of tropical rain-forests. Though many regard these assets as priceless, such an approach is devoid of policy implications unless it is to leave the existing structure of environments untouched. Practical policy responses require trade-offs, and these in turn necessitate that values are placed on non-market goods in order to construct the appropriate policy interventions.

The task of environmental economics is therefore to adapt theoretical tools to provide an integrated framework of analysis and to develop existing tools to place valuations on environmental assets and consequences and, thereby, to develop appropriate policies. No doubt this task will take decades to perfect. However, since the lags are long and the effects may be irreversible, there is a substantial expected pay-off to early imperfect policy initiatives. The global nature of many environmental problems exacerbates the scale of the pay-offs. Investing in sea defences, inland water supplies, drainage, and flood control schemes now yields potentially very large benefits in the future in the form of avoided risks of massive sea-water inundation in, say, Bangladesh or Guyana. Moreover, the first steps in a cost-effective ladder of investments to combat global warming would, in any event, yield

other benefits. Energy conservation reduces acid rain and saves foreign exchange costs in resource-impoverished economies.

Many of the policies will, no doubt, of necessity be crude, but they must be evaluated against the do-nothing option, not against an idealized solution. The purpose of this paper is to provide an overview of progress to date in constructing an analytical framework, and to suggest a number of policy conclusions which follow.

The structure of the paper is as follows. Following the Introduction, section II provides a classification of environmental externalities differentiated by their institutional contexts. Section III considers the conventional economic theory approaches, based upon relatively strong informational assumptions. Section IV then introduces the informational problems and indicates why cooperative solutions to global externalities may prove particularly hard to achieve. Section V concentrates on valuation of the future, and indicates a number of issues that arise with conventional discounting procedures. Section VI looks at the potential role of the market in environment policy and in particular the consequences of privatization, taxes, and marketable permits. Finally section VII sets out some tentative suggestions for the way forward.

II. The context of externalities

Recognizing environmental problems as externalities is essential in framing economic policy. It is however important to note that there are many different contexts within which they arise. These may be classified according to the number of parties respectively causing and suffering the consequences of pollution, the jurisdictions, and the economic systems within which the externalities arise.

1. The number of generators and affected parties

The numbers involved in producing and receiving an externality have an important effect on the ability of different institutions to deal with the consequences. The classic textbook examples of externalities which arise between two identified parties are in fact special cases. Though these one-to-one cases are easiest to

[4] See for recent surveys Cornes and Sandler (1986) and Baumol and Oates (1988). Other definitions, based on different conceptual approaches are provided by Buchanan and Stubblebine (1962), Arrow (1970), and Heller and Starrett (1976).

model and hence are the ones on which the literature concentrates most heavily, nearly all pollution problems are more general. Indeed the distinctive feature of the current environmental agenda is its global nature. Results which hold in the bilateral case do not necessarily carry over to the global one.

In these simple one-to-one cases, the parties are easily identified, and the costs of pollution can typically be evaluated. These cases can often be tackled either through taxes and subsidies or through negotiation and bargaining. For example, neighbours can often resolve problems of smoke, waste disposal, and noise through direct discussions and complaints, use of police, and through the legal process, whilst the Pollution Inspectorate can relatively straightforwardly regulate and if necessary prosecute individuals and firms.

Greater complexity is introduced when a large number of individuals and firms are affected. Many standard pollution problems fall into this one-to-many category: chemical spillages into water systems and oil tanker disasters, for example. In this case it remains relatively easy to identify the source of the pollution, but the affected parties are usually each too small to warrant the expense of solving the problem as in the one-to-one case above. The major new features introduced are the complexity of measuring environmental damage and the problems of establishing cooperative action amongst the affected parties where the costs to each are small relative to the costs of taking effective action against the polluter. The free-riding incentives for some affected parties on others are typically strong given the costs of enforcement. Class actions and the use of the political and regulatory process are typically required, introducing their own transactions costs and the burden of associated government failures.

The most persuasive externalities combine many generators with many recipients. These many-to-many cases include a number of new problems which have arisen in the 1980s, most noticeably the increasing concentration of greenhouse gases (carbon dioxide, methane, nitrous oxide), ozone depletion, and biodiversity losses. They can be called global mutual externalities. They also include the range of household and industrial wastes, including sewage, paper, and plastics. Measurement problems are much more pressing with multiple pollution generators. Their identification can itself pose difficulties and detailed emissions data is typically costly to collect. Greater reliance on the polluters to provide information is necessitated, increasing the chances of regulatory bias and even capture.

Distributional considerations can also arise in this category. Many of the associated products, especially energy and transport, are inelastic in demand, and have strong income effects.

2. Jurisdictions

Since, as we shall see in section III.2 below, property rights play an important role in the defining and solving of externalities, the legal system matters greatly in framing economic policies towards the environment. In cases where externalities are within nations, the legal base is co-extensive with the externality, and existing taxation and regulatory systems can typically be adapted for environmental policy. Environmental consequences do not, however, always respect national boundaries. Hence the domain of the externality and judicial boundaries do not always coincide. National law and national regulation provide weak methods of control, while general international law is usually too weak to provide adequate remedies. For example, the UN Convention on the International Law of the Sea in 1982 has yet to be signed by the US and the UK, and the UN International Whaling Convention has not yet been signed by the major whaling countries. In these circumstances, the benefits to the polluters from the polluting activity frequently exceed the costs of resisting international pressure from the affected parties, or indeed, in some cases, of breaking signed agreements.

3. Economic systems

All these problems are common to different types of economic regime, from free market through to planned. Nevertheless the type of economic system is likely to affect the extent of externalities and the efficiency of environmental policy. Planned economies reduce the likelihood of bargaining between the polluters and pollutees to internalize externalities, and the emphasis on production rather than consumption in many planned systems is likely to result in less weight being placed on the consequences of environmental degradation. Where planning is associated with single party dominance of the political process, the growth of regulation via the political process is also likely to be hindered. It is widely agreed that pollution problems in Eastern Europe and the USSR are more severe than in the West European market-based economies.

The policy options are also constrained by the type of economic system. The creation of marketable pollution permits does assume a market system, as does the wider use of property rights. The impact of taxes rather than direct controls also presumes a price system.

The emergence in the last decade of regulatory activity and privatization in the developed and developing world has further highlighted the relationship between environmental concerns and free market activity. The shift of emphasis towards markets in Eastern Europe and in the Soviet Union can only increase this focus.

Whatever the economic system, the distribution and incidence of pollution, and the burden of environmental policy is unlikely to be even. The developing world faces particular concerns over environmental quality owing to its much greater direct reliance on natural resources—e.g. wood for fuel, direct abstraction of water, and the use of marginal lands for subsistence crops—and its extensive sensitivity to ecosystem shocks and stresses (droughts, wars, and floods). Hence the emergence of an environmental economics applied to the Third World.

III. Conventional economic approaches

Having established the salient institutional characteristics, the range of possible economic instruments can then be considered. The conventional economic approaches to externalities provide the framework of environmental policy. The models are simplistic, and deliberately so, to illustrate the fundamental theoretical characteristics which pervade both simple and complex practical examples. We examine first the early ideas for using taxes and subsidies to modify imperfect markets—to alter costs and incentives. These pragmatic tax/subsidy interventions are then contrasted with the more full-blooded free market approaches, associated with Coase and the Chicago school. Together they provide a number of quite general results and a framework for assessing the extent to which markets, regulation, and planning are appropriate policy regimes. More complex global problems require the addition of cooperative models, and therefore can be analysed through models of collusion and games.[5]

1. Pragmatic solutions to market failures: Pigouvian taxes and subsidies

The standard economic approach to externalities is typically ascribed to Pigou (Pigou, 1920). While regarding externalities as a minor problem (compared, for example, to monopoly), Pigou devised a system of taxes and subsidies to correct for the social costs which were not incorporated in private decision-making. Crudely, a tax is placed on the polluter to bring his cost function into line with what it would have been had he faced the true social costs of production. The polluter pays, and therefore reduces his output to the socially optimal level. Conversely, a subsidy can be paid to the pollutee, to compensate for the damage done.[6]

The government provides the mechanism to force the polluter to pay the full costs of his activities. The tax may or may not be exactly offset by the subsidy, depending on whether the tax revenue is transferred to the victim or not, and on demand and supply elasticities. Clearly, if, for example, the revenue from an energy tax were spent on energy conservation, as opposed to reducing income tax, the impact on energy demand and supply would be much more marked.

This problem corresponds to the simple one-to-one case identified in the previous section. The model provides a number of insights into the policy problems besetting governments. Indeed it is this Pigouvian model which remains the basis of the taxation proposals currently being actively discussed. It provides a simple benchmark, and its shortcomings have provided much of the research agenda in the literature.

The following points are particularly important. First, there is no suggestion that any level of pollution is *per se* bad. It is, after all, the by-product of an activity which is economically valuable. Rather, its full cost needs to be reflected in decision-making. The problem of the market is not the creation of pollution, but rather the wrong amount of it. The optimal level of pollution is only zero in the extreme case that the externality costs require a tax so great that the firm stops production altogether.

Second, it is assumed that, after the tax, firms face the true marginal costs of production. There is therefore no distortion of competition between polluting firms. Thus it is assumed in this simple analysis that an externality arises in a context in which there are no other market failures. In particular, there is no oligopoly or monopoly, no uncertainty, no coordination problems, or other public goods. However, since

---

[5] Accessible texts surveying the literature include Mäler (1974), Tietenberg (1988), Baumol and Oates (1988), and Pearce and Turner (1990). See also Greuenspecht and Lave (1989).

[6] The payment of subsidy does not however reduce the level of pollution in this case. It is purely compensatory.

externalities in practice always arise in markets riddled with other failures, models with joint-failures are of great importance. The design of more complex optimal Pigouvian taxes must therefore take these into account.

Third, it is assumed that the costs of the polluting firm and the damage function of the polluted firm or consumer are known. In particular, there is no private information unavailable to the regulator, no strategic revelation of information by the affected parties, and there is no uncertainty about the pollution impacts. Thus, this approach is informationally very demanding.

Finally, there are no regulatory failures associated with the incentives of authorities. Regulators are concerned only with maximizing economic efficiency. Other social objectives—such as distribution and rights —are ignored. There is no regulatory capture.

These assumptions provide a menu of issues which the policy-maker needs to evaluate empirically in designing optimal interventions. The presence of monopoly or of substantial distributional consequences will modify the optimal form of intervention. Only if all the assumptions of the model are met will simple tax/subsidy solutions be the obvious first-best solution. Nevertheless, the Pigouvian model does carry a number of policy presumptions. The most important basic insight is that environmental damage has a cost, and that this should be reflected in economic decisions by facing the participants with a price. Furthermore, to the extent that taxes rather than subsidies are utilized, there is a presumption in favour of the *polluter pays principle*. There is certainly no role for the *victim pays principle*. Furthermore, since social costs are uniquely defined for each case of pollution, the Pigouvian model points inevitably towards pragmatism in the uses of taxes and subsidies to regulate markets, and provides the basis for the piecemeal case-by-case approach which is the hallmark of UK environmental policy.[7]

2. Laissez-faire approaches: Coase and property rights

The pragmatic approach to externalities has been directly challenged by the more full-blooded market theorists. This challenge is associated most closely with Coase's seminal article (1960).

The free-market approach identifies the problem of externalities as the absence of markets and the associated property rights. An economy in which every asset is owned would internalize all externalities. On this view, over-grazing of pastures and pollution of the oceans and atmosphere result from the fact that common land, seas, and air are not owned. If they were, then the resolution of damage levels and payments would be organized through the valuation and enforcement of the relevant property rights. These are determined either through the market or through the legal system. Crudely, if a chemical firm pollutes a river, the river owner, if he owns the right to clean water, will demand compensation, or sue. Alternatively, if he does not own the right to clean water, it will be in his interest to bribe the chemical firm to reduce pollution.

In Coase's original model, the externality problem is one-to-one.[8] The parties bargain with each other, with the result that the equilibrium is determined irrespective of the allocation of the property rights between polluter and polluted. Thus, whether the polluter pays compensation for the damage done, or the affected party bribes the polluter to reduce emissions is irrelevant to the efficiency of the outcome, being only of distributional concern.

If correct, Coase's bargaining model would have quite radical implications for policy. First, emphasis on the polluter pays principle would be invalid, or, at least, an equity judgement with no foundation in economic efficiency. It would be equally appropriate for the injured party or the government itself to bribe polluters with subsidies.[9] Second, the assignment of property rights to 'free' assets—such as air and water— would solve externalities. Finally, the fact that most environmental assets are not owned by identified individuals creates a very strong presumption against 'do nothing' policies.

The simple Coasean model inevitably suffers many deficiencies. First, Coase tends to assume that markets exist. In practice, the major global environmental problems arise in circumstances where property rights are impossible to define. The essential feature—excludability—is not present. Second, like the Pigouvian tax solution, it, too, assumes well-functioning markets. Yet, if there is monopolistic competition, the

---

[7] See Vogel (1986) for a contrast between US and UK policy approaches. It should be noted that European Community regulation typically pursues a rule-based approach in contrast to that of the UK.

[8] See Farrell (1987) for an exposition and critique.
[9] There are other reasons why the polluter pays principle might be suboptimal. Affected parties may have little incentive to minimize their exposure to pollution—there may be moral hazard. See on this Olson and Zeckhauser (1970).

bargain becomes more complex, involving polluter, polluted, and consumer (Buchanan, 1969). Third, when there are many parties involved, there may be significant free-ride incentives and transactions costs reducing the efficiency of the bargaining process. Finally, in the intergenerational context, bargains take on a new meaning because it is not clear who is bargaining on behalf of the next generation. (We return to this aspect in section V.)

Yet, despite the unreality of the examples frequently cited in support of the Coasean argument, the idea that the optimality of the outcome is unaffected by whether the polluter or pollutee pays is much exploited in international problems. The notion that the victim should pay the polluter is a stark reality in the context of international environmental policy. This is the import of Mäler's (1990) exposition of the underlying principles of international environmental negotiations. The reality of global or regional environmental problems is that they are a game in which those who gain by cooperation must devise incentives to make those who lose play the game. Game theory predicts that this requires side payments—inducements to participate to those who stand to gain little by cooperation, but whose cooperation is essential to the objective. Inducements are all the more essential when the polluter is poor and therefore lacks the economic resources to tackle control.

3. Comparing the Pigouvian and Coasean approaches

A fundamental difference between the two approaches lies in the mechanisms proposed for resolving externalities. The Pigouvian approach creates a presumption in favour of pragmatism with civil servants and government agencies evaluating each case on its individual merits. The official identifies the parties and then attempts to estimate the marginal costs and benefits to each. Information is gathered from the parties, and demand and cost functions are estimated. The 'optimal' tax is then imposed.

The Coasean approach, by contrast, relies on the market itself to facilitate bargaining between the affected parties. If they cannot agree, the dispute is viewed as one about the definition of their respective property rights. The appropriate forum is then the courts, with the legal process providing for the resolution of the differences between the parties. Lawyers and judges calculate the costs and benefits to the parties of the externality, and in practice conduct a simi-

lar enquiry to that of the Pigouvian civil servant. In deciding the rival claims, and in assigning compensation, the legal process requires the same information as government regulation. The differences therefore lie less in the specification of the problem than in the costs of each method of resolution—the relative transaction costs of legal and government failure. It is by no means obvious that the legal approach is the more cost-effective. We turn now to the common problem—information.

IV. Imperfect information, strategic behaviour, and global cooperation

Both the Pigouvian and Coasean approaches assume that markets function well. The associated assumptions, as we saw above, rule out precisely those aspects of environmental problems which are so endemic in practical examples. The analysis of cases where these assumptions have been relaxed has provided the subsequent research agenda. We shall concentrate on two related aspects—imperfect information and the problems of global cooperation.

1. Imperfect information and the assessment of environmental risks

In contrast to the case of the simple full-information models, we typically lack precise information on the nature of externalities and the costs and benefits of alternative methods of dealing with them.[10] Uncertainty is a pervasive characteristic of environmental problems.

The first question to be addressed is that of the appropriate method of scientifically modelling uncertainty. Second, there is the incentive problem of individuals, firms, and countries revealing private information, and negotiating cooperative agreements. Many of the major environmental externalities are uncertain in their effect. For example, it will be at least a decade before we can be certain whether global warming is really occurring, or whether it is merely a climatic cycle caused by non-greenhouse-gas phenomena. Although the increases in carbon can be measured and predicted relatively accurately, the proc-

---

[10] See Johansson (1990) for a survey of the major measurement problems.

ess of climatic change is very poorly understood. Furthermore, the impact of carbon is complex. Its effects are not limited to simply increasing pro rata the total greenhouse ability to absorb and retain solar energy; carbon has effects on other gas impacts, on cloud cover, and water vapour content.[11]

Our degree of uncertainty can be reduced by further research. The question is: should we take action now on the basis of very imperfect information, given that if we do not and the problem turns out to be serious, it may be very much worse to start later? Alternatively, should we engage in research now in the hope of better-designed policies later and indeed better technologies for tackling the problem? The answer must be pragmatic: the expected costs and benefits must be evaluated and a balanced decision taken.

Cost–benefit analysis, however, requires a method for measuring uncertainty. Conventional economic approaches assume that we at least know the subjective expected utility loss to individuals of the environmental damage, their risk preference, and the marginal costs of pollution control to firms. These assumptions are always questionable. They are increasingly so where the environmental problems are global, requiring the aggregation of individuals' preferences, and where uncertainty about costs and consequences is great. In these circumstances, it is often appropriate to consider a series of scenarios: what would happen if the probabilities were some assumed set? Crudely, a worst and best case scenario maps the range of possible outcomes. This kind of approach has the added advantage of helping to specify the bounds within which particular problems are nested, and may be extremely useful in providing a framework for considering the gains from cooperative solutions, to which we now turn.

2. Global cooperation

Many modern environmental problems are instances of the 'tragedy of the commons' (see Hardin, 1968). Essentially, the atmosphere, the oceans outside exclusive economic zones, and the stratosphere are open-access resources, res nullius—owned by no one. Biological models predict a steady-state equilibrium for open-access resources, but one that may be perilously close to the carrying capacity of the habitat (see Pearce and Turner, 1990). Put another way, the risk of extinction of the resource—the tragedy—is potentially

high under open-access. Common property—res communes—on the other hand, relates to resources held in common by a reasonably well-defined group of owners who, typically, establish rules of use. The distinction helps to characterize modern international environmental agreements as attempts to modify property rights away from open-access towards common property rights.

But even common property agreements risk breakdown because of the essential internal contradiction between the maximization of individual gains and the maximization of the collective good. This is the essence of the 'Prisoners' Dilemma' characterization of the common property problem.[12] Each player in the game stands to gain by not cooperating with other players, but all players would be better off if they did cooperate. Non-cooperative equilibria are inefficient and cooperative solutions require binding agreements. Any agreement that is not wholly binding risks individual defection by free-riders.

Are environmental agreements in the global sphere subject to the Prisoners' Dilemma? Many would argue that they are and that binding agreements require incentive systems in the form of side payments, cash or technology or in-kind transfers, to potential defectors. As Mäler (1990) notes, such side payments can easily turn the morality of the polluter pays principle upside down, so that victims pay polluters not to pollute—the victim pays principle. Examples of the victim pays principle are already evident, as with Sweden's technical assistance to reduce acid emissions from Poland, and the currently negotiated technology transfers to China and India with respect to chlorofluorocarbons (CFCs) emission reductions. The issue of 'side payments' dominated the 1992 United Nations Environment Conference in Brazil.

Global environmental negotiation and agreement need not be as bleak a prospect as the Prisoners' Dilemma suggests. In game theory pay-offs tend to be characterized by single-dimensions—time spent in jail or monetary fines in the original Prisoners' Dilemma example, profits or utility in the generalized case. In the real world, however, multiple objectives characterize the game. Countries may be prepared to act counter-preferentially for a greater good, out of obligation, fairness, or out of environmental stewardship motives. A second feature of real-world games, familiar in game theory as well, is that they are repeated. If one player defects in the first game, he may face a coalition to his disadvantage in a second game, and so on. *Sequential games* may not face the Prisoners' Dilemma

---

[11] See House of Commons Select Committee on Energy (1989) for a survey of the evidence.

[12] On the Prisoners' Dilemma, see Taylor (1976).

syndrome, particularly if the time period over which games are played is a long one.[13]

The weapons at the disposal of cooperative coalitions are familiar, including international disapprobation, as Britain has learned from its uncooperative stance on European Community environmental legislation.

Game theory models suggest that the incentives to cooperate depend critically on the analysis of the counterfactual—what happens if the parties do not agree? In particular, if the two parties are differentially affected so that, for example, one country experiences large-scale destruction before others, or if the parties take different views of the probability of significant damage, they may have differential incentives to pay the pollution costs. Bankruptcy—in the sense of inability to pay—may also be highly significant. Many developing countries simply cannot meet the costs of environmental degradation.

In environmental problems, the end-game can at least be sketched in outline. If increasing concentrations of greenhouse gases lead to rising temperatures, and if these raise sea level, then those countries with low-lying, densely populated areas will face major population displacement and increased sea defence and drainage costs. Furthermore, agricultural areas sensitive to temperature change would experience depopulation. Large scale population movements, adverse food production trends, and higher population levels are likely to create instability in international relations and ultimately these may become security issues.[14]

Although such an analysis is, of course, conjectural, it indicates which countries face the greatest costs if repeated games fail to produce a cooperative outcome and which countries are likely to gain little by cooperation. Bangladesh would face very high costs but lacks the resources to build appropriate sea defences. The UK, by contrast, might even benefit from an improved climate, and the costs of sea defences might be manageable.

A further important consideration in appraising the prospects for international cooperation is noted in Barrett's article in this volume. Global environmental agreements are not homogeneous in nature. An agreement on CFCs was feasible, first because of the small number of players in the game (the CFC producers of USA, Europe, and the Eastern bloc) and the small number of potentially interested parties (industrializing developing countries). Second, the costs of substituting for CFCs in several major uses are small. No such conditions apply to greenhouse gases. All the world becomes the set of players and the costs of carbon cutbacks are formidable for some of the players. Offsetting this is the potential for some major emitters to cooperate in the initial stages and use demonstrated reductions in carbon dioxide as a bargaining instrument.

International environmental issues represent very fruitful ground for economic analysis in terms of game theory. For example, Mäler (1990) and Barrett in this volume, reveal some of the potential and some of the insights.

V. Valuing the future

Most of the major consequences of global externalities will fall on the next generation and beyond. Almost all environmental externalities have an intertemporal dimension. Nuclear waste generated now imposes a cost on future generations in terms of disposal costs and hazards; greenhouse gas emissions now may commit the future to irreversible global warming; a species lost now imposes a user cost on future generations in terms of foregone benefits from that species.

Intertemporal resource allocations are incorporated into economic analysis by discounting the future. The value of £100 now is greater than £100 in a year's time because of the return between now and a year's time if the money is invested, or because consumption now is certain, whereas consumption in one year's time depends on being alive to consume it.[15] Discounting allows for the lower weight that individuals place on the future—their myopia —compared to the present. But discounting in the environmental context is contentious precisely because it justifies the forward shifting of environmental costs to future generations. Although it may be rational for individuals to value the future consumption at a discount to present consumption, it is by no means obvious that society should make the same trade-off.[16] Although technical progress may enhance the consumption possibilities of future generations over the present, environmental damage may have the opposite effect.

---

[13] See for example Axelrod (1984) for an exposition of tit-for-tat rules. For a formal treatment of sequential games, see Kreps and Wilson (1982).

[14] See Grubb (1989) for an extensive discussion of the role of international negotiations in framing agreements on greenhouse gas emissions.

[15] Respectively, we consider the cost to society of waiting as the social opportunity cost, and the demand valuation as the social time preference rate. Only in competitive equilibrium will the two approaches yield the same answer.

[16] See Parfit (1984, Annex F).

The first-best solution to this intertemporal bias is the downwards adjustment of discount rates, perhaps to zero to reflect indifference about the temporal incidence of costs and benefits.[17] Indeed, if society is risk averse concerning the environment, and wishes to hand on to future generations environmental assets at least as good as it inherited, it may even be negative.

In practice, however, the optimal policy towards future generations is not so straightforward. Again, the treatment of one aspect of the environmental problem—valuing the future—cannot be considered in isolation from other market failures. There are, in consequence, a number of additional factors which should be borne in mind. First, by altering the normative balance between aggregate investment and consumption, lowering discount rates across the board could accelerate environmental degradation if investment is more materials/energy intensive.[18] This effect is of particular importance in considering the impact of privatization. As we argue below, privatization typically raises the discount rate and may consequently have the environmentally beneficial effect of providing a premium to small, less capital-intensive production techniques. Second, the impact of lowering the discount rate may be affected by the size of the errors in calculating the costs and benefits of projects. If, for example, the benefits of a project are overstated and the environmental consequences undervalued, a lower discount rate may exacerbate the total effect. It is therefore important to incorporate externality costs fully before applying a discount rate.

It is therefore not surprising that the discount rate debate remains unresolved. One suggestion is that discounting is permissible only within an ecological constraint which sets limits on the degradation that would be permitted and which would protect future generations' capability to enjoy an undegraded environment.[19]

VI. Market-orientated solutions

It is currently fashionable to advocate the use of markets to solve environmental problems. This approach draws upon the basic Pigouvian insight, noted above in section III, that individuals and firms should be explicitly faced with the costs of environmental damage resulting from their activities. It also fits neatly with the trend towards expanding the role of markets in traditional production areas and in the provision of welfare services. The collapse of state planning in Eastern Europe has given powerful impetus to this trend, while the continuing world debt crisis has encouraged developing countries to sell assets.

Environmentalists have, however, typically argued for greater state intervention. It has often been assumed that, since environmental problems result from market failures, state intervention is necessitated. This simplistic approach is not, however, supported by evidence from the planned economies of Eastern Europe. It ignores the costs of intervention: market failure only justifies intervention if the costs of that failure are greater than the resultant costs of government failure consequent upon the intervention. The latter are often at least as important as the former.

Furthermore, there are typically a number of different responses to market failure: the options are, broadly, to replace the market; to make it work better by altering the incentives and costs; or to extend the market by the application of property rights.[20] These strategies are exemplified by a number of practical policy suggestions which are currently the focus of debate: introducing private ownership; utilizing the taxation system; and creating a market in pollution permits.

1. Privatization

Privatization in the narrow sense involves the transfer of assets from one set of owners (the government) to another (private shareholders). It does not introduce new property rights (à la Coase). Rather it changes the nature of existing property rights. Its impact thus depends upon the incentives and constraints faced by the two sets of owners. Despite almost a decade of privatization, the efficiency consequence of changing incentives and the replacement of government control by shareholders remains poorly understood. Nevertheless, since the sectors which have been privatized are frequently those which are most environmentally sensitive—water, energy, and transport—the consequences of this policy are important.

Government objectives in operating firms reflect wider considerations than profit maximization. Recent models have focused on the maximization of output (Rees, 1984, 1989) rather than profit, leading to over- rather than under-provision. In the public sector in

[17] For a survey of environmental concerns about discount rates see Markandya and Pearce (1988).

[18] Markandya and Pearce (1988).

[19] See, for example, Page (1977).

[20] See Helm (1986) for an overview of these strategies and Helm (ed.) (1989) for applications to a range of economic activities.

the UK, electricity witnessed substantial over-capacity, and coal output was maintained beyond profit maximization. This trend towards output rather than profit was reinforced by the lower cost of capital to government compared with private ownership. In this sense, if output and pollution are correlated, public ownership may result in higher pollution.

Privatization can, in these models, be assumed to reduce output and investment at the margin, given the profit objective and a higher cost of capital. A higher discount rate induces shorter-term investment horizons and therefore the assignment of lower valuations to the future. In the case of electricity investments, for example, Sizewell B nuclear power station passed the critical 5 per cent real rate of return requirement laid down in the 1978 White Paper. In the private sector, Hinkley B would face at least 11 per cent, and therefore not be viable (Dimson, 1989). Choice of technique for long-term utility industries will, therefore, on this argument, be profoundly affected by privatization. Paradoxically, this change in discount rates may actually be environmentally beneficial in the electricity case. It will raise the price of electricity, reducing consumption at the margin. It will also place a premium on small generating units, and especially favour combined heat and power plants.[21]

Some commentators have argued that the efficiency of the resources controlled in the private sector will be greater, thereby economizing on environmental damage. These effects fall into three categories: that more output will be produced from given inputs (thereby reducing the demands on natural resources); that the ratio of capital to labour will be closer to the optimum (correcting for labour bias in the public sector) and hence reduce costs of production of environmental improvements; and finally that prices and hence outputs will be more closely related to costs, thereby eliminating over-production.[22]

Since the magnitude of these factors will vary on a case-by-case basis, the dynamic effects on investment will need to be compared with static efficiency gains. The more substantial the environmental impact of longer-term investments—as for example in the electricity and water industries—the greater the impact of privatization. When investment is environmentally benign—as in the water industry—privatization may only be beneficial if the static efficiency gains are large. When investment is environmentally damaging, the balance goes the other way.

Private firms do not, however, operate in a vacuum. In developed countries virtually all firms are subject to environmental regulation. The final and perhaps most important aspect of privatization is its impact on regulation. Is regulation likely to be tougher and easier to impose and monitor in the private or the public sector? The intuitive and conventional answer that greater control is engendered through ownership is highly misleading. It may be much better not to own the regulatee. The problem can be modelled through 'principal–agent' analysis.[23] The incentives of government regulators need first to be assessed. If they also own the polluter, they are likely to be susceptible to its financial performance. In the public sector, a politician is answerable for the performance of the firm, and will inevitably want to defend its record. In the UK water industry, Government Ministers frequently acted as de facto apologists for the low standards of water quality. Now that the industry is privatized, Ministers are still answerable for water quality, but have no financial responsibility to the shareholders of the water companies. There is an incentive gain through privatization.

On the other hand, access to the relevant information to monitor performance is much reduced and there may be an offsetting cost created by the strategic behaviour of regulatees. This provides another opportunity for regulatory capture.[24] On balance, UK evidence suggests that privatization has significantly improved regulation. The establishment of the National Rivers Authority and the Office of Water Supply have provided an opportunity to create a programme of sustained environmental improvement.

2. Taxes

As we noted in section III above, the Pigouvian approach to externalities suggests that the tax system may provide a mechanism by which the incentives of polluters can be brought closer to a position reflecting the costs of environmental damage. Its attractions to government are considerable. Environmental taxes raise revenue, they elicit widespread acceptance and therefore compliance, and they leave the market to sort out the most efficient methods of pollution production and control. Once the desired level of pollution is set, the need for further complex regulatory oversight is minimal.

---

[21] In the case of water, the effects may go the other way.
[22] See Bishop and Kay (1988) for some early efficiency estimates.

[23] See Rees (1985) for a survey of the principal–agent literature.
[24] See Helm, this volume, for a summary of the major problems in regulating utilities.

As we saw in section III.1 above, the ideal tax from an efficiency point of view is one which exactly reflects the costs of pollution at the margin. However it is often impractical to tax the pollution precisely, and therefore a number of proxy solutions are often adopted. The options can be illustrated by considering the example of carbon emissions from power stations.

The first option is to tax carbon-producing fuels, on the basis of their approximate carbon pollution potential. This alters the polluting input price and encourages substitution towards fuels with lower pollution potential (gas for coal, for example) and towards non-fossil fuels, like nuclear, water (barrages), and wind (windmills). The disadvantage of this method is that it treats all coal plants alike, and therefore penalizes coal plants with higher efficiency levels and hence fails to match actual pollution. A second option is to tax power station emissions, on a plant-by-plant basis. On this approach, each station is regarded as a unit converting inputs into two outputs, e.g. electricity and pollution. The tax exactly penalizes plants according to pollution emission.[25]

The third option is to tax the output of electricity: to tax final consumers. This could be achieved through the imposition of VAT. This would, however, be a crude measure, creating no incentive to substitute cleaner technology at the margin because it taxes all inputs equally, with no account being taken of their different carbon contents. It is also unlikely to achieve the desired effect of significant reductions in emissions since the price elasticity of demand is very low.[26] Very substantial price increases would be required, illustrating the point that careful case-by-case empirical studies are required if policy is not to be misdirected.

Thus far, taxes have been considered in terms of their substitution effects. Income effects are also likely to be important. Income effects from taxes may at least partially offset the substitution effect. Many goods produced by polluting technologies are merit goods. Electricity, transport, and water are obvious examples and the resulting demand behaviour from taxes may conflict with distributional objectives. Indeed, in the case of a tax on electricity, the substitution effect is very small, while the income effect is very large.[27] On an international scale, environmental taxes would require

a compensating redistribution to developing countries. Taxes may also be non-neutral at the national level, adversely affecting aggregate demand, and thus requiring compensatory expenditure or reductions in other taxes.

The latter point raises the question of the use to which additional revenues are put. For example, the low electricity price effect discussed above would not be so much of a problem if the resulting revenues were spent on energy conservation measures—i.e. if the tax funded a subsidy. This would create a double effect, and have the attractive feature of avoiding an extra call on the exchequer. Similarly, an environmental tax on rich countries (perhaps on energy consumption) may provide a politically more acceptable method of funding a transfer to developing countries to provide side payments for reducing their pollution.

Taxes on a national scale may therefore provide an attractive policy option to reduce national pollution and to fund subsidies. In isolation, however, the impact may induce perverse substitution effects between countries. A unilateral tax on energy users in the UK would disadvantage the competitiveness of some UK traded goods. The competitors without the tax would gain market share, and hence increase total pollution. This is another example of the Prisoners' Dilemma, discussed above in section IV.2. The policy implication is clear: tax based solutions of international externalities are best dealt with consistently at the international level. Unilateral action may have a considerable demonstration effect, but it may be counterproductive.[28]

3. Marketing pollution rights

Pollution taxes seek to regulate waste, effluent, and ambient emissions through prices. But economists have long debated the merits of price incentives compared to quantity incentives. The idea of regulating the environment through emission quotas which are then traded, was first espoused in the 1960s.[29] The environmental quality objective can be translated into an emissions target. Suppose the target is 100 units of pollution. Permits allowing the emission of 100 units can be issued to polluters. The initial allocation rule is important. Typically, the historical pattern of emissions will form the basis of the allocation: polluters will each receive permits according to their emissions at

[25] The optimal ranking of the electricity merit order is then, given the inputs, a function of the two efficiency parameters (electricity and pollution) considered jointly.

[26] See Department of Energy (1989).

[27] See Baker *et al.* (1990) for micro disaggregated consumption patterns for electricity, and Pearson and Smith (1990) for estimates of the impact of electricity taxes on different consumer groups. See also Dilnot and Helm (1987) on energy as a merit good.

[28] In this context, it is interesting to note that UK discussion of the possibility of carbon taxes has stressed the international discussion. See Ridley (1989).

[29] See Dales (1968).

some agreed baseline date—'grandfathering'. Polluters are then free to trade the permits which then command a market price. For some polluters with low abatement costs, the market price (P) will exceed the abatement cost (A). As long as $P > A$, such polluters have an incentive to sell permits, thus surrendering the right to pollute, and to abate pollution. High cost polluters will face a context in which $P < A$, giving them an incentive to acquire permits in the market. The attraction of tradable permits is that the concentration of abatement in low cost polluters will minimize the compliance costs.

Tietenberg (1990) shows how this result can be achieved in addition to environmental quality being improved. Any polluter able to emit pollutants below the initial allocation will secure certified emission reduction credits. It is these credits that become the currency of the emissions trading programme. A new source of pollution can be allowed only if it acquires adequate credits, thus offsetting the initial gain in quality. By allowing trade only if credits exceed debits, the regulating authority can actually improve environmental quality. Some debate exists as to whether emissions trading under the US Clean Air Act has achieved improvements in air quality. Certainly it appears not to have deteriorated, so that trading has fared no worse than the alternative of command and control and has certainly achieved cost compliance benefits of several billion dollars (see Hahn and Hester, 1987, 1989).

The potential for using the tradable permit as an incentive system is enormous. It does, however, require imaginative administration. Most of the cost-savings under the US legislation have come from within-plant (internal) trading (see again Hahn and Hester, 1987, 1989). The greatest potential almost certainly lies with inter-firm trading. Moreover, trading offers a means of handling international environmental agreements. A carbon convention, for example, will have to function via emission targets allocated to individual countries. Grandfathering with some initial discount—e.g. carbon dioxide emissions in 1990 less, say, 20 per cent—is the most likely initial allocation. Emissions trading options are then twofold. At the very least, within-country trading can occur, just as the US proposes for compliance with the Montreal Protocol on the protection of the ozone layer.

More imaginatively, permits could be traded between nations. A country that is able to secure carbon dioxide reductions of more than the initial discount can secure credits which can be traded with other countries. The obvious problem with this solution lies with the grandfathering clause, since developing countries will acquire a fairly low initial allocation if rights are allocated on the basis of base year emissions, and will be unable to afford traded permits. One solution is to bias the initial allocation to developing countries according, say, to population. Trade will then be from developing countries to the richer world, with a consequent significant transfer of funds to the Third World.

Such a prospect opens up imaginative possibilities. Permit trading could be subject to its own form of conditionality. For example, sales might be contingent upon agreed proportions of permit revenues being used for energy conservation expenditure in the Third World. Offsets would also be permitted in the form of carbon-fixing investments such as afforestation. New additions to carbon dioxide emitting capacity would be allowed if the potential permit holder agreed to fund tree-planting, anywhere in the world. Tietenberg's enthusiasm for permits is therefore warranted at least in terms of the potential for tradable permit solutions to major environmental problems. Moreover, the quantity solution avoids a major pitfall of tax policy—the political difficulty of getting new taxes accepted. This difficulty might be significantly reduced by aligning green taxes with reductions in taxes on labour and capital. The advantage here is that the incentive effects of green taxes are preserved in a revenue-neutral budget, and the excess burden of the supply-side disincentive taxes is reduced. None the less, the psychology of tax burdens is likely to remain an obstacle to pricing solutions. Tradable permits thus have considerable attractions.

VII. Conclusions

The prospect for the 1990s will be one of movements towards green economies. Both planned and free markets have failed lamentably to provide adequate environmental protection. Moreover, green market phenomena, in the form of green consumerism and, potentially more important, the green investor, cannot be relied upon to solve environmental problems. Major new policy initiatives will be required.

Environmental economics offers a number of important insights into the appropriate economic policies. The Pigouvian framework provides a strong presumption in favour of market-based approaches which utilize the price mechanism to confront individuals and firms with the real costs of environmental damage. The Coasean approach suggests that policy should be pragmatic between the polluter and the victim paying. Much, however, depends on the number of parties involved, and the institutional and legal framework.

The presumption in favour of market-based policies does not, however, imply the unfettered operation of market forces. Rather, the market should be harnessed to generate the most efficient method of achieving desired pollution reductions. The role of the state is to regulate through command and control procedures, in setting maximum pollution levels. The role of the market is to find the best method of achieving them. Although it may be possible in some cases to create property rights, the scope is limited. None of the current major environmental concerns falls into the pure Coase category.

The type of intervention will vary on a case-by-case basis. There is no general first-best solution. The pursuit of single instrument solutions is naïve and possibly even dangerous. The universal pursuit of taxes or command-and-control regulations is suboptimal and sometimes perverse. There is no escape from pragmatism: the application of empirically based cost–benefit analysis to the evaluation of alternative policies. Market and government failures vary on a case-by-case basis, and so inevitably must the solutions.

The balance of the argument will, however, generally favour the exploitation of the market's mechanisms for revealing information, as compared with the excess costs and bureaucracy associated with total reliance on the command-and-control approach. Governments will be forced to search out cost-minimizing procedures to lower the projected costs of future environmental policy. The way forward lies with market-based incentives—taxes, charges, deposit-refund systems, tradable permits, and off-set policies.

References

Axelrod, R. (1984), *The Evolution of Cooperation*, New York, Basic Books.

Arrow, K. (1970), 'The Organisation of Economic Activity', in R. Haverman and J. Margolis (eds.), *Public Expenditures and Policy Analysis*, Chicago.

Ayres, R. V., and Kneese, A. (1969), 'Production, Consumption and Externality', *American Economic Review*.

Baker, P., Blundell, R. McKay, S., Symons, E., and Walker, I. (1990), 'A Simulation Programme of Consumer Expenditure', Institute for Fiscal Studies Working Paper.

Baumol, W., and Oates, W. (1988), *The Theory of Environmental Policy*, 2nd edn., Cambridge, Cambridge University Press.

Beckerman, W. (1974), *In Defence of Economic Growth*, Jonathan Cape, London.

Bishop, M., and Kay, J. A. (1988), *Does Privatisation Work? Lessons from the UK*, London Business School, Centre for Business Strategy.

Buchanan, J. M. (1969), 'External Diseconomies, Corrective Taxes and Market Structure', *American Economic Review*, March.

—— Stubblebine, W. C. (1962), 'Externality', *Economica*, **29**: 371–84.

Coase, R. H. (1960), 'The Problem of Social Cost', *Journal of Law and Economics*, **3**: 1–44.

Cornes, R., and Sandler, T. (1986), *The Theory of Externalities, Public Goods, and Club Goods*, Cambridge, Cambridge University Press.

Dales, J. H. (1968), *Pollution, Property and Prices*, Toronto, University of Toronto Press.

Department of Energy (1989), 'The Demand for Energy', in D. R. Helm, J. A. Kay, and D. Thompson (eds.), *The Market for Energy*, Oxford, Oxford University Press.

Dilnot, A., and Helm, D. R. (1987), 'Energy Policy, Merit Goods and Social Security', *Fiscal Studies*, (reprinted in Helm *et al.*, 1989).

Dimson, E. (1989), 'The Discount Rate for a Power Station', *Energy Economics*, 11.

Farrell, J. (1987), 'Information and the Coase Theorem', *Journal of Economic Perspectives*.

Goldsmith, E. *et al.* (1972), *Blueprint for Survival*, Penguin Books, London.

Grubb, M. (1989), *The Greenhouse Effect: Negotiating Targets*, London, Royal Institute of International Affairs.

Gruenspecht, H. K., and Lave, L. B. (1989), 'The Economics of Health, Safety and Environmental Regulation', in R. Schmalensee and R. D. Willig (eds.) (1989), *Handbook of Industrial Organisation*, Amsterdam, North-Holland, Vol. 2, 1507–50.

Hahn, R., and Hester, G. (1987), 'The Market for Bads', *Regulation*, 3–4.

—— (1989) 'Where did all the Markets Go? An Analysis of EPA's Emissions Trading Program', *Yale Journal of Regulation*, **6**(1): 109–53.

Hardin, G. (1968), 'The Tragedy of the Commons', *Science*, **162**: 1243–8.

Heller, W. P., and Starrett, D. A. (1976), 'On the Nature of Externalities', in S. A. Lin (ed.), *Theory and Measurement of Economic Externalities*, New York, Academic Press.

Helm, D. R. (1986), 'The Economic Borders of the State', *Oxford Review of Economic Policy*, **2**(2).

—— (ed.) (1989), *The Economic Borders of the State*, Oxford, Oxford University Press.

—— Yarrow, G. (1988), 'The Regulation of Utilities', *Oxford Review of Economic Policy*, **4**(2).

Helm, D. R., Kay, J. A., and Thompson, D. (eds.) (1989), *The Market for Energy*, Oxford, Oxford University Press.

House of Commons Select Committee on Energy (1989), 6th Report, *Implications of the Greenhouse Effect*, HMSO.

Kreps, D., and Wilson, R. (1982), 'Reputation and Imperfect Information', *Journal of Economic Theory*, **27**: 253–79.

Mäler, K.-G. (1974), *Environmental Economics: a Theoretical Inquiry*, Baltimore, Johns Hopkins University Press.

—— (1990), 'International Environmental Problems', *Oxford Review of Economic Policy*, **6**(1), 80–108.

Markandya, A., and Pearce, D. W. (1988), 'Environmental Considerations and the Choice of the Discount Rates in Developing Countries', Environment Department, World Bank Working Paper No. 3, Washington DC.

Meadows, D. H., Meadows, D. L., Randers, J., and Behrens, W. (1972), *Limits to Growth*, New York, Earth Island.

Olson, M., and Zeckhauser, R. (1970), 'The Efficient Production of External Economies', *American Economic Review*, LX: 512–17.

Page, T. (1977), *Conservation and Efficiency*, Baltimore, Johns Hopkins University Press.

Parfit, D. (1984), *Reasons and Persons*, Oxford, Oxford University Press.

Pearce, D. W., and Turner, R. K. (1990), *The Economics of Natural Resources and the Environment*, London, Harvester-Wheatsheaf.

Pearson, M., and Smith, S. (1990), 'Taxation and Environmental Policy: Some Initial Evidence', IFS Commentary, No. 19, Institute for Fiscal Studies.

Pigou, A. (1920), The Economics of Welfare, London, Macmillan.

Rees, R. (1984), 'A Positive Theory of Public Enterprise', in M. Marchand, D. Pestieau, and H. Tulkens (eds.), *The Performance of Public Enterprises*, Amsterdam, North-Holland.

—— (1985), 'The Theory of Principal and Agent, Parts 1 and 2', *Bulletin of Economic Research*.

—— (1989), 'Modelling Public Enterprise Performance', in Helm *et al.,* 1989 (op. cit.).

Ridley, N. (1989), *Policies Against Pollution*, London, Centre for Policy Studies.

Taylor, M. (1976), *Anarchy and Cooperation*, Chichester, John Wiley.

Tietenberg, T. (1988), *Environmental and Natural Resource Economics*, 2nd edn., Glenville, Illinois, Scott Foresman.

—— (1990), 'Economic Instruments for Environmental Regulation', *Oxford Review of Economic Policy*, **6**(1), 17–33.

Vogel, D. (1986), *National Styles of Regulation: Environmental Policy in Great Britain and the United States*, Ithaca and London, Cornell University Press.

PART V

INTERNATIONAL TRADE

Recent advances in international trade theory: a selective survey

HENRYK KIERZKOWSKI[1]

Graduate Institute of International Studies, Geneva

I. Introduction

International trade theorists have lived for many decades in a blissful state of accepting a common set of assumptions on which to construct the edifice of their theory. While macro-economists drew fine distinctions between Keynesians and neo-Keynesians; monetarists Mark I and monetarists Mark II, the fundamentals of the trade theory were rock hard. The outcome of this consensus was a very solid theory which has come to be known as the Heckscher-Ohlin-Samuelson model.

Research progress in the field of international trade tended to add continuously to the stock of knowledge and build on previous achievements. It is interesting to note that this research consensus and continuity could be observed in, among other things, the reference lists of articles and books. Even today it is not unusual to find citations of trade literature from the 1950s, 1940s or even 1930s, in sharp contrast with macroeconomics and international finance, where occasionally one gets the impression that only articles written during the last six months seem to count.

But all was not well with the theory of international trade. While trade theorists looked with a great deal of pride on the results of their intellectual efforts, policy makers, businessmen and the public at large regarded the policy conclusions of the Heckscher-Ohlin-Samuelson model with considerable scepticism, if not disbelief. When, some thirty years ago, Max Corden (1965) surveyed the field of international trade, he

made the following observation: 'It must be confessed, in conclusion, that the pure theory of international trade has suffered from bad public relations. Some of its main conclusions are often misunderstood, and, even when understood, very often disagreed with. There are two reasons for this. Firstly, the models of the pure theory usually make a large number of assumptions, some of which when stated explicitly sound so unrealistic as to discredit the whole model from the start, while others tend to be forgotten. . . . The second reason for the poor image in some countries of trade theory is the commitment to free-trade liberalism of many of the leading theorists.'

Indeed the assumptions of the Heckscher-Ohlin model are rather stringent. The theory assumes in particular that:

1. There are only two countries and two goods.
2. Production functions involve only two factors of production (usually called labour and capital) and are homogeneous of degree one.
3. Countries have access to the same production functions which are however different for each good.
4. Perfect competition prevails in commodity as well as in factor markets.
5. Tastes are identical within and between countries.
6. Factors of production are perfectly mobile between industries in each country but not mobile at all between countries.
7. No transportation costs or other impediments to trade exist.

The above assumptions practically eliminate all differences between countries except with regard to factor endowments. Thus relative factor endowments become the sole explanation of trade patterns in the

First published in *Oxford Review of Economic Policy*, vol. 3, no. 1 (1987). This version has been updated and revised to incorporate recent developments.

[1] I wish to thank Ronald Jones, Andre Sapir, and Ethan Weisman for helpful comments.

Heckscher-Ohlin model. The country relatively well-endowed with capital, exports the relatively capital-intensive good and imports the labour-intensive commodity. A set of very restrictive assumptions leads to a very powerful prediction. The three other basic theorems of the Heckscher-Ohlin-Samuelson model are: (1) the factor-price equalization theorem, demonstrating that under non-specialization free trade evens factor rewards between countries; (2) the Stolper-Samuelson theorem, showing how a factor intensively used in the import-competing sector gains from protection; (3) the Rybczynski theorem, explaining that with constant commodity prices factor accumulation results in an expansion of the sector employing this factor intensively and a contraction of the other sector.

The critics of the Heckscher-Ohlin model have focused on the realism of the above assumptions as the basis of their discontent. Although I am in sympathy with the general logic of the argument, I find this criticism somewhat misplaced when applied only (and the word only needs to be stressed) to trade theory. For better or worse, the economics profession has accepted the 'as if' methodology of Milton Friedman expressed in his Essays in Positive Economics. The proper test of a theory should be, it was claimed, the accuracy of its predictions rather than the realism of its simplifying assumptions. Given this methodology, the appropriate evaluation of the Heckscher-Ohlin theory should be done in the light of its empirical test. Alas, here is where the real problem started.

The most famous test of the Heckscher-Ohlin model was carried out by W. Leontief as early as 1953. The outcome of this test was that the United States was found to be a net exporter of labour-intensive goods and a net importer of capital-intensive commodities and was taken to contradict the Heckscher-Ohlin theory. Interestingly enough, the result has come to be known as the Leontief paradox, where it should, more correctly, be called the Leontief falsification, if it was a correct test of the theory. If Newton, in an attempt to verify his theory, threw an apple into the air and it went higher and higher instead of falling to the ground, he would not have called the result a paradox. The christening of the Leontief test revealed that not only the minds but also the hearts of trade theorists were with the Heckscher-Ohlin model.

Reversing the Leontief paradox became, for almost three decades, a growth industry in international economics. Many ingenious and painstaking empirical studies have been done which greatly enriched the field. Possibly, or even probably, the biggest contribution has been made by Leamer (1980, 1984) who

pointed out that the data used by Leontief revealed the United States to be both a net exporter of capital services and a net exporter of labour. This could happen in a situation of unbalanced trade. Leamer then went on to demonstrate that, with unbalanced trade the relationship between the capital/labour ratio used in exports and imports, and the overall relative factor endowment breaks down. Under unbalanced trade it is quite consistent with the Heckscher-Ohlin theory for a capital-rich country to have a higher capital/labour ratio in imports than in exports. The valid test is a comparison of the capital/labour ratio in production against the capital/labour ratio embodied in consumption. Applying the relevant test, Leamer found that indeed the capital/labour ratio embodied in US production exceeds that contained in consumption. Leamer (1984) could thus conclude that 'the paradox rests on a simple conceptual misunderstanding . . . If the correct calculations are done, the United States is revealed by trade to be relatively abundant in capital compared with labour . . . The impropriety of the Leontief inference is a consequence of the fact that the inference is made without benefit of a fully articulated theory.'

Nevertheless, the controversy surrounding the Leontief paradox turned out to be a stimulating influence in the field of international trade. It helped to articulate the basic paradigm and improve the quality of empirical work. For example, more factors, and in particular natural resources and human capital, have been brought into the standard model. Trade patterns in a multi-country and multi-commodity world have been investigated. Transportation costs and other barriers to trade have been formally introduced into analysis. This list could go on and on.

In fact, it would be accurate to described theoretical research in international trade over the past 20 years as systematic attempts to relax the basic assumptions of the Heckscher-Ohlin model and test its robustness. Of course, not all of this was done because of the existence of the Leontief paradox. Other stylized facts and empirical regularities, in addition to sheer intellectual curiosity, have played a role in this process. In particular, the existence of multinationals and intra-industry trade led trade theorists to expand the framework of their analysis.

This paper reviews some of these developments. Naturally, one must be very selective in a field as vast as international trade theory. I focus, in Section II, on some extensions of the basic trade model. In Section III models of monopolistic competition are discussed. Finally, in Section IV, I take up some issues related to modelling of trade in services. Although the survey

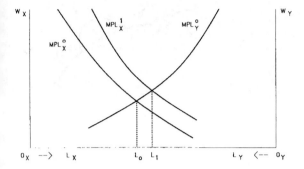

Figure 11.1. Equilibrium in the specific-factor model

deals with positive analysis, some basic welfare questions cannot be escaped when discussing monopolistic competition in international trade.

II. Extensions of the basic model

I propose to review in this section some of the work and issues which go beyond the 2 ∞ 2 ∞ 2 (two goods, two factors, two countries) format. Some of the models which will be discussed here have a very specific and tight structure, while others are very general. However, they all share the basic feature of altering the 'twoness' of the standard model in one way or another.

1. The specific-factor model

The first major departure in this direction was the so-called specific-factor model. The model has been developed by Jones (1971), Mayer (1974), Mussa (1974) and Neary (1978) among others. The basic structure is rather simple: there are only two goods, (X and Y), and three factors of production (labour and two types of capital). Labour moves freely and costlessly between the industries in response to the wage rate differential, while capital is specific to each sector (immobile between industries).

The specific-factor model has a number of interesting properties which are worth flushing out. This can be accomplished with the help of Figure 11.1. The total amount of labour available in the economy is given by the distance $O_X O_Y$. The wage rates are measured along the two vertical axes. The curves MPL_X and MPL_Y denote the value of the marginal product of labour in the two industries and are drawn with reference to O_X

and O_Y respectively. The position of these curves depends on the commodity prices and the amount of the specific capital in each industry. Assume that initially the value of the marginal product of labour curves are located at MPL_X^0 and MPL_Y^0. The equilibrium allocation of labour must be given by the point directly below the intersection of the two curves. Any other sectoral distribution of employment would imply that wages would not be equalised between the industries. Perfect labour mobility assures, however, that this cannot happen.

Figure 11.1 also shows that equalization of commodity prices through free trade will in general not lead to equalization of factor rewards. If there were two identical countries, except that one had more capital specific to the X industry than the other, the value of the marginal product of labour curve would be situated above the MPL_X curve in the capital rich country. As a result, the wage rate would be higher and the two rental rates lower in the latter country. In the model containing three factors but only two goods, commodity prices do not suffice to determine factor prices, and factor endowments exert an independent role. This result lends itself to an immediate generalization (discussed below).

The second attractive feature of the specific-factor model shows the response of factor rewards to changes in commodity prices to be markedly different from the Stolper-Samuelson theorem. As is well known, this theorem states that an increase in the price of X, say, through the imposition of a tariff, will benefit the factor intensively used in the production of X and lower the return of the other factor. The effects of a tariff in the specific-factor model can be analysed in terms of Figure 11.1 by noting that a tariff of 20 per cent will shift the MPL_X curve upwards by an equiproportionate distance to, say, MPL_X^1. The new equilibrium shows more labour ($O_X L_1$ instead of $O_X L_0$) employed in the industry being protected and hence a greater output of X. In order to induce reallocation of labour, the wage rate must increase. Note, however, that as long as the MPL_Y curve is not vertical, the wage rate increases by less than the rise in the domestic price of the protected sector. Since the wage rate increased by less than the price of X, it follows that the rental on capital specific to the protected industry, r_x, must increase proportionally more than P_X. Furthermore, with P_Y remaining constant, r_y must necessarily decline.

It is useful to contrast the patterns of responses of factor prices to changes in commodity prices in the Heckscher-Ohlin-Samuelson and the specific-factor models. These patterns are respectively given by inequalities (1) and (2):

$$\hat{w} > \hat{P}_X > \hat{P}_Y > \hat{r} \text{ or } \hat{r} > \hat{P}_X > \hat{P}_Y > \hat{w} \quad (1)$$

$$\hat{r}_X > \hat{P}_X > \hat{w} > \hat{P}_Y > \hat{r}_Y \quad (2)$$

While the Stolper-Samuelson result depends crucially on the relative factor intensity assumption, inequality (2) holds regardless of this presupposition. One appealing element of the specific-factor model is that it can possibly explain why, in so many countries, both labour and capital employed in the same industries demand tariff protection.

In spite of the fact that the Heckscher-Ohlin-Samuelson and specific-factor models give different comparative static results, they need not contradict each other. The latter is a better description of short-run behaviour, whereas the former may be seen as focusing on long-run responses. Even though capital specificity is clearly observed in reality, the existence of rental rate differentials should encourage investment in some industries, and lead to capital depletion in others. This process is likely to be slow and costly but it should be expected to occur. As the degree of capital mobility increases, the specific-factor model produces responses which become increasingly similar, and in the limit identical, to the predictions of the Heckscher-Ohlin-Samuelson model.

Generalization of the specific-factor model to allow for n industries, n specific factors and one perfectly mobile factor that can be employed in any sector presents no special problem. Jones (1975) has shown that in such a model an increase in the price of commodity i, P_i, will reduce rewards to n - 1 specific factors outside the favoured industry. The reward to the mobile factor and to one specific factor goes up as a result of the price increase. The specific factor gains proportionally more and the mobile factor proportionally less than the price rise. An implication of this generalization is that an expansion of one sector provoked by a slight price increase must be accompanied by a contraction of n - 1 sectors.

The assumption that certain factors are trapped in certain industries may go too far, even as a description of short-run reality. It could be plausibly argued that there is always some degree of factor mobility in the economy. On the other hand, it may also be plausible to postulate that no factor is perfectly mobile across industries. A Ph.D. in physics can easily transfer from employment in a personal computer company in the Silicon Valley, California to the Space Research Centre in Houston, Texas or to the Research Laboratory of Boeing in Seattle, Washington, but he

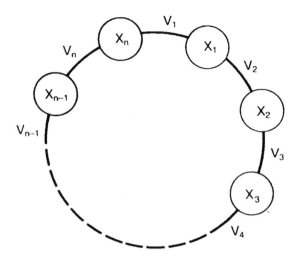

Figure 11.2. Neighbourhood production structure

cannot easily become a heart surgeon or even a hospital nurse.

Limited factor specificity is the focus of attention in the model of neighbourhood production structures developed by Jones and Kierzkowski (1986). The model is quite general in that it allows for any number of goods and factors: however, the number of commodities is assumed to be equal to the number of factors. Production of any good requires only two factors of production and each and every factor has two alternative sectors where it can be employed. For the ease of presentation one can arrange the industries (and the factors) along a circle. Thus each sector (and factor) has two neighbours, as shown in Figure 11.2.

Factor V_i (i = 1, . . . n) can be employed in the neighbour sectors, X_{i-1} or X_i. Every pair of neighbours shares one factor and this feature of the model makes the whole economy interdependent. A disturbance such as a price increase or factor endowment expansion spreads through the whole system.

Consider, for instance, an increase in price in the last sector, P_n, and assume that n is an even number. The two factors employed in this sector are V_1 and V_n, with corresponding rates of return w_1 and w_n. Suppose that it is w_1 which increases as the result of the disturbance. Since all the other prices remain constant, w_2 must decline to assure that the zero profit condition continues to hold in the sector producing X_1. The decline in w_2, however, allows w_3 to go up and so on until the 'ripple' effect has come back full circle to X_n. Since w_1 was assumed to increase, w_n must decline. Of course, in the case of an initial decline of w_1, w_n would

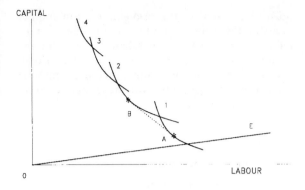

Figure 11.3. Unit-value isoquants

The position and the shape of each unit-value iso-quant is determined by technology and the world price of the commodity in question. The isoquants show combinations of labour and capital required to produce one dollar's worth of output under zero profit conditions. Goods 4 and 1 can be seen to be the most capital-intensive and labour-intensive, respectively. Figure 11.3 is useful in describing the trade patterns of a small country in static as well as dynamic contexts.

A labour-rich country can have a factor-endowment ray such as OE which cuts the unit-value isoquant to the right and below point A. The wage-rental ratio in this country is uniquely determined by its factor endowment. As capital accumulation takes place, the factor-endowment ray rotates counter-clockwise.

Capital accumulation leads to a continuous rise in the relative wage rate until point A is reached. When the relative factor endowment ray falls between A and B, commodities 1 and 2 are being produced. For a small country with exogenously given commodity prices, factor prices become locked, within the AB chord, and independent of factor endowment. Under non-specialization it is commodity prices and not factor endowment that determine factor rewards.

As factor accumulation continues, this process repeats itself. The country traverses the commodity space moving to more and more capital-intensive products and, in the process, abandons the production of labour-intensive goods. The relative wage rate rises but not in a strictly monotonic fashion.

Figure 11.3 also brings out the point that a country in a multi-commodity world is likely to produce only a small subset of goods. It also shows that free trade should not be expected to equalise wages and rentals across the world. Even countries at a similar stage of economic development may have different factor prices. For example, two similarly endowed countries with overlapping production structures may employ different techniques in the production of the same good. This can be seen in the case where one country produces only good 1 but another country with slightly more capital, produces commodity 2 in addition to 1. The latter country will use labour more sparingly in the production of good 1 than the former.

Anne Krueger (1977), who developed a model quite similar to Jones (1974), pointed out that the Heckscher-Ohlin explanation of trade will manifest itself, in a multi-commodity world, in the pattern of production and specialization rather than relative factor intensities of exports and imports. 'Countries in the middle of the factor-endowment ranking will tend to specialise in producing commodities in the middle

rise. Which of these two outcomes actually occurs depends on relative factor intensities. However, the relevant measure of factor intensity becomes a multi-lateral concept in this model; every single sector of the economy will have a share in it.

As long as n is an even number, the rewards to any pair of factors employed in the same industry move in the opposite directions. 'Even' models produce 'non-cooperative' results. The simplest case of an even model with 'non-cooperative' outcomes is the Heckscher-Ohlin-Samuelson model.

It can be readily established that when the number of sectors, and factors, is an odd number, both factors employed in an industry favoured by a price rise will gain at least in nominal terms. Thus the 'odd' model produces 'cooperative' outcomes. Of course, the specific-factor model is just a simple version of an 'odd' model, but with the number of factors greater than the number of goods.

2. Specialised production models

The usual assumption, in the context of the Heckscher-Ohlin model, is that specialization in production does not occur, which means that relative factor endowments of the trading countries are not too dissimilar. In the $3 \infty 2 \infty 2$ specific-factor model specialization cannot occur, and therefore each country produces both goods. I now wish to turn to models which are specifically designed to allow only a small subset of goods to be produced by an individual country. The first of these models, due to Jones (1974), looks at a small country in a world of many commodities. Figure 11.3 shows unit-value isoquants for four different commodities in the Lerner diagram.

of factor-intensity ranking. They will import labour-intensive commodities from more labour-abundant countries and capital-intensive commodities from countries with relatively higher capital-labour endowments. The implications of these propositions for empirical testing of the factor-proportions explanation of trade are immediate.'

It was also noted by Krueger (1977) that distortions in commodity and factor markets have an important bearing on the pattern of specialization and the composition of trade. In the $2 \infty 2 \infty 2$ model, market distortions divulge themselves through departures of factor rentals from their free-trade values. In the framework under discussion, on the other hand, a tariff on a previously unproduced good can make production of this good justifiable from the perspective of private interests, and at the same time lead to the elimination of production of a good that was produced under an efficient allocation of resources. Other policy measures can also result in a distorted production mix. Of course, that may be exactly what policy measures are sometimes designed to accomplish. It may be recalled that, several years ago, Singapore's authorities embarked on a policy of rapid wage increases which, until the late 1970s, had not been allowed to exceed the pace of inflation. One of the main justifications for engineering this wage explosion was to force domestic and foreign firms to move up the ladder of comparative advantage and undertake production of more sophisticated goods while abandoning labour-intensive commodities. This particular episode clearly shows that higher dimensions of the trade model are of keen interest not only to trade theorists but also to policy makers.

3. Other higher-dimensional findings

So far I have discussed specific departures from the Heckscher-Ohlin model. I wish to conclude this section by briefly mentioning several important studies and, in particular, Deardorff (1980, 1982) and Dixit and Norman (1980). The essence of their contribution is that, in higher dimensions, correlation between autarkic commodity price differences and import volumes, and between autarkic factor-price differentials and the factor content of imports, holds only on average. For example, a capital-rich country only tends to import labour-intensive goods; it could happen that its imports also contain some capital-intensive goods. Stated in other words, this means that a country may import some goods in which it actually has a comparative advantage.

Another important generalization is due to Ethier (1974), who demonstrated that if the price of one produced good goes up, the real return to some factor

must rise. If this factor is also employed in another industry, the real return on some other factor must fall. This result is very general and it holds for any number of goods and any number of factors. To identify the loser(s) and the winner(s) requires imposing some restrictive assumptions on the productive structure of the economy.

III. International trade under imperfect competition

It has been recognised for a long time that the world economy does not consist of small and powerless countries nor is any single economy a collection of atomistic firms. A substantial literature on the optimal tariff in the presence of monopoly power and numerous writings on tariff wars testify to the willingness of trade theorists to depart from the competitive paradigm. Yet, it is only during the last few years that monopolistic competition has become one of the central subjects of trade theory.

The most immediate reason for this increased interest in non-competitive market structures can be attributed to the alleged failure of the Heckscher-Ohlin model to explain the existence of intra-industry trade. Reality has not borne out the prediction of the standard model that trade flows should be most intensive between countries with substantial differences in factor endowments. As Grubel and Lloyd (1975) demonstrated in their pioneering study, the bulk of international trade occurs between countries with similar factor endowments and particularly among the highly developed economies. Furthermore, this trade is not inter- but intra-industry. Thus the UK, for instance, exports cars to France, Germany, Italy, Sweden and the United States and at the same time imports motor vehicles from the same destinations. The same is true for just about any industrial product. Intra-industry trade consists of flows in similar but not identical goods. Jaguar, BMW, Mercedes, Volvo and Cadillac, to pick only one segment of the car industry, are sold to customers with similar incomes, yet they have their distinctive characteristics. This fact is often underlined by the producers.

1. Trade in one good

I intend to give a short exposition of several models which aim to explain intra-industry trade and then discuss some general issues related to monopolistic competition in international trade. Let me start off with the simplest model comprising two countries and a single good. The model has been developed by Brander (1981), Brander and Spencer (1984) and Brander and Krugman (1983) and it establishes that market structure alone (independent of technology, taste and endowment differences), suffices to generate international trade. In this one-good model all trade has, of course, an intra-industry character.

Assume that under autarky the domestic market in each country is supplied by a monopolist. The familiar condition equating the marginal cost with marginal revenue establishes equilibrium prices and quantities. For the time being suppose that the marginal cost, c, is constant. Now, what happens when free trade is allowed between the two countries? It would seem that there is no apparent reason for trade because there is just one good. To make trade even more difficult, introduce international transportation costs, à la Samuelson. As the good is shipped abroad a fraction, g (where $0 < g < 1$) of it melts on its way, like an iceberg. In spite of these difficulties, the Brander model does generate trade, as will be seen shortly.

In order to complete the specification, the demand conditions have to be spelled out. This is done in equations (3) and (4)

$$P_1 = a - b(X_{11} + X_{21}) \qquad (3)$$
$$P_2 = a - b(X_{12} + X_{22}) \qquad (4)$$

The demand functions are taken to be linear and are written in an inverted form. X_{ij} denotes the quantity of the good sold by the producer located in country i and selling in market j (i,j = 1,2). The expressions in the parentheses of equations (3) and (4) denote the aggregate quantity of the good made available in each market.

Given the above equations, the profit functions for each of the duopolists can be written as:

$$\pi_1 = P_1 X_{11} + P_2 X_{12} - c(X_{11} + 1/g\, X_{12}) - F \qquad (5)$$
$$\pi_2 = P_1 X_{21} + P_2 X_{22} - c(X_{22} + 1/g\, X_{21}) - F \qquad (6)$$

The profit functions also contain fixed costs, F, in addition to variable costs.

Now enter the crucial assumption of the Brander model: the producers are said to play a Cournot strategy. Each producer decides how much to supply to each market believing that his competitor's behaviour will not alter as a result of his actions. Differentiating equations (5) and (6) with respect to X_{11}, X_{12}, X_{21}, and X_{22} gives four reaction functions (two for each market) which determine the equilibria of the system. The

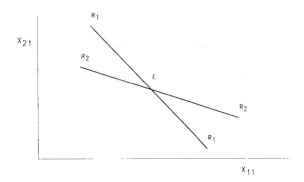

Figure 11.4. The Brander model

assumption of constant marginal costs permits a look at each market separately.

Figure 11.4 illustrates the results of the model for country 1. The reaction function of the domestic product is represented by $R_1 R_1$ and that of the foreign producer by $R_2 R_2$. (The picture for the market of country 2 is symmetric). Equilibrium is established at E and it is stable given the slopes of the two reaction functions. It can be readily seen that the market is split between the two duopolists, with the domestic firm enjoying a bigger share of sales. (A 50–50 split would occur if transportation costs were zero).

The driving force behind this model is the desire of each producer to invade the foreign market. Trade increases the degree of competition, indeed there are now two competing duopolists rather than two separate monopolistic systems. As a result, prices tend to fall and consumers in both countries are better off. Gains from competition may more than compensate social losses involved in sending the same good back and forth across the border.

One possible and very interesting extension of this model is to assume decreasing rather than constant marginal costs. As a firm produces more, it does so more cheaply. Krugman (1984) showed that under these circumstances protection of the domestic market allows the local producer to become more efficient and, hence, more competitive abroad. Tariffs can thus serve as a double-edged instrument for protection of the domestic market and for export promotion.

2. Characteristic approach to differentiated products

As I pointed out earlier, intra-industry trade seems to involve similar but not identical products and, therefore, considerable efforts have been made to develop

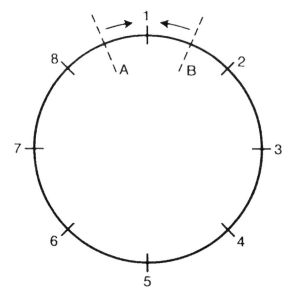

Figure 11.5. Equilibrium in the Helpman model

an appropriate model. Lancaster (1979) developed the so-called characteristics approach to demand for variety. Helpman (1981) and Lancaster (1980) have shown how the interaction of demand for variety with in-creasing-returns-to-scale technology results in intra-industry trade. Their models are cast in terms of general equilibrium.

Assume that there are two industries: one producing a standard good and another producing differentiated products. Both sectors use labour and capital as the factors of production. The production function for the homogenous good is characterised by constant returns, while in the differentiated goods sector production of each model offers economies of scale. Models can be distinguished by a characteristic defined for simplicity along a unit circle, such as Figure 11.5.

With regard to the demand side, each consumer is assumed to have a preferred model of the differentiated good. Imagine now that in a closed economy the consumers are uniformly distributed along the unit circle. Each point on it represents the desired model for some individuals. The individual utility function favours consumption of the desired model, however the consumer can do with a less-than-ideal specification if that's what is available. In fact, a sufficiently lower price of an alternative model would make him give up the desired model.

If an infinite number of models of the differentiated good are demanded, why not produce them? The existence of increasing returns to scale prevents this outcome happening. Only a limited number of models will be produced. The exact number depends on the demand functions, production technology and the size of the market. Every model will be produced by only one firm. In Figure 11.5, the equilibrium in the closed economy is shown with eight different specifications. As cost functions are assumed identical and the consumers are uniformly distributed along the circumference of the circle, the prices of these models will be the same. Furthermore, the producers will be spaced equidistant between themselves, each capturing the same fraction of the total market. Thus producer of model 1, for instance, will attract all consumers in the AB segment of the market. Points A and B are located exactly half-distance in between 1 and 8 and 1 and 2, respectively. The marginal consumers at A and B are indifferent between neighbouring models. Of course, the consumers whose preferred specification is given by point 1 are better off, in the absence of price discrimination, than those whose preferences are located some distance from it.

The consequence of opening to foreign trade can now be analysed readily. When the market expands, more models can be produced. So the new equilibrium must involve greater variety. Each model can be produced by only one firm, either domestic or foreign. The expansion of the market also allows producers to increase output of each variety. Hence, the gains to the consumers in this model involve greater choice and lower prices. Of course, distributional effects are likely to be present as well, but this model has too much symmetry built into it to pin down the actual location of firms either in the closed or open economy equilibrium.

A powerful feature of the Helpman-Lancaster model is that it allows countries to trade differentiated and homogeneous goods and hence inter- and intra-industry trade can co-exist. If the differentiated products are relatively capital-intensive, the capital rich country can be shown to export more of them than it imports. The country well-endowed with labour runs a deficit in differentiated products which it covers by exporting the standard good. This shows that factor endowments do matter but other things matter as well. It is clear, however, that to explain the co-existence of inter- and intra-industry trade one needs two independent reasons for trade. The combination of

Heckscher-Ohlin and monopolistic competition is only one alternative.

3. Love of variety approach to differentiated products

Dixit and Stiglitz (1977) developed a different approach to modelling demand for differentiated products. The approach was applied to international trade by Krugman (1979, 1981, 1982) and Dixit and Norman (1980). In their formulation, every individual loves variety and would like to consume as many types of differentiated products as possible. Assume for simplicity, that there is no outside good and that the individual utility function is of the following form:

$$U = \Sigma v(C_i) \qquad v' > 0, \quad v'' > 0 \qquad (7)$$

where C_i denotes consumption of the ith good by the representative consumer. An important property of this function is that if n goods were available, all of them would be demanded by every individual. Furthermore, if an individual consumer were offered additional goods, ceteris paribus, he would gladly buy them and his welfare would increase. In contrast with the Helpman-Lancaster approach, demand for variety already exists at the micro-level.

In modelling the supply side, assume that labour is the only factor of production and write the production functions in inverted form:

$$L_i = \alpha + \beta x_i \qquad (8)$$

where L_i stands for the amount of labour required to produce the ith commodity. Equation (8) reveals the existence of increasing returns to scale. For a large fixed labour cost, α, one would expect only a small number of goods to be produced.

In determining the equilibrium number of products in the closed economy one needs to invoke the condition equating marginal cost and marginal revenue in every sub-market:

$$P_i(x_i)(1 - 1/e_i) = \beta w \qquad (9)$$

where e_i is the elasticity of demand facing the ith producer. The elasticity depends on the specification of the utility function of the representative consumer. In the Chamberlinian world of monopolistic competition, each producer attempts to create pure profits, yet free entry leads to the equality of the total revenue with the total cost of production of the good.

$$P_i x_i = (\alpha + \beta x_i) w \qquad (10)$$

Equations (9) and (10) suffice to determine the level of output of each firm as well as the real wage rate. The full employment condition for labour then gives the number of firms in the closed economy.

Introduction of trade implies that more products can be produced in the integrated market than in either of the two countries in isolation. Once again, gains from trade may involve not only greater variety but also lower prices as economies of scale are realised when every firm increases output.

The model can be modified to analyse North-South trade issues. Dixit (1984) focused on the question of North-South terms of trade. Production of differentiated products requires an intermediate good which is produced in developing countries under constant-returns-to-scale technology. Developed countries produce differentiated goods and enjoy monopoly power. Growth in the North increases demand for intermediate goods and improves the South's terms of trade. Labour expansion in developing countries has the opposite effect, but even then, welfare losses stemming from adverse price changes can be more than compensated by increased variety.

Dynamic effects are pursued in Krugman (1979). New products can be introduced in the market, not instantaneously, as in the basic model, but only over time. Product innovation takes place in the North. However, the South eventually learns how to produce new goods and can do it more cheaply. A technological gap gives the North certain monopoly power and is responsible for trade. Developing countries export 'old' products and developed countries specialise in 'new' products, with the division between the old and the new shifting continuously. Product innovation can also explain why per capita incomes differ between countries. However, in order to maintain an income differential the North has to keep innovating.

Product innovation, technological competition and dynamic economies of scale are becoming a central issue in the new trade literature. In particular, the concept of the so-called learning curve developed by Spence (1981) has found application in several trade models. It is assumed that in certain industries large current output can help to reduce production costs in the future. If this is indeed the case, then protection of the domestic market (or export subsidies) today can make the home industry more competitive later on in foreign markets. The mechanism is really quite similar to that evoked in the Brander model with decreasing marginal costs, except that the effects are spread over time.

4. New trade models and commercial policy

I have attempted to convey the flavour of the new trade literature by singling out several important contributions. Should these new models give rise to new thinking about commercial policy? While in the traditional framework free trade tended to be the best solution, the recent wave of research produced numerous examples where government intervention can dominate laissez-faire policy. This should not after all be a surprising finding. Non-competitive market situations usually call for some policy intervention. However, this need not imply that the case for free trade is buried. As a general methodological issue, it is not enough to demonstrate that a commercial policy measure can improve welfare. One has to show that trade interference is the best form of intervention. So far, I have not seen this accomplished frequently in a convincing way.

A case for intervention can be made where monopoly profits can be shared between the home and the foreign country as in the Brander model. However, one has to remember that this model is based on the Cournot strategy. It is hard to find an example of a monopolistic industry where firms decide on quantities and not on prices. Once firms are allowed to compete in prices, the case for intervention goes by the board. Equally disconcerting is the assumption that firms totally lack anticipation of some response from competitors when they made their strategic decisions. Alternative assumptions regarding firms' conjectural variations produce vastly different outcomes with vastly different optimal policies. But even within the rules of the game of the Cournot model, Dixit (1984) demonstrated that the justification for an export subsidy loses its power when the number of firms is even moderately increased.

In the Helpman-Lancaster and Dixit-Krugman models, profits are driven to zero so the argument for intervention needs to be based on the ability to affect the terms of trade. But this is, of course, an old argument and product differentiation does not bring in new elements. I should add, however, that this strand of literature has greatly enriched welfare analysis by identifying a new and, possibly, a very important source of gains from trade. There is, of course, a larger issue of socially optimal product diversity.

It would seem that the strongest case for trade policy intervention arises in the context of technological spillovers generated by some sectors for the rest of the economy. Those 'strategic' sectors, if they indeed exist, could clearly have special value for the economy.

But as Krugman (1986) put it 'Are there "strategic" activities in the economy, where labour and capital either directly receive a higher return than they could elsewhere or generate special benefits for the rest of the economy? This is the question on which old and new thinking about trade differs.'

The identification of 'strategic' sectors becomes a formidable task. Unfortunately, they are not listed in the Yellow Pages, nor can they be readily spotted based on available market information. Furthermore, it is not really 'strategic' industries that the policy makers would wish to single out for a special treatment but individual firms, small or large, with great market potential. I, for one, would be willing to accept that policy makers in Washington, DC could have had enough wisdom to realise at an early stage that the personal-computer industry was such a strategic activity. But even this is not certain. I am much less certain that a small firm run out of a garage—it will be realised that I am making a reference to the Apple company—could have been identified as a future market leader. New industrial (rather than commercial) policy towards 'strategic' industries would involve many policy misses, just like betting on horses. Furthermore, helping some firms or sectors bids up the rental of factors jointly shared with other producers and this constitutes a form of reverse protection.

In entertaining new commercial strategies, one should not forget a valuable lesson from an area of international trade theory which I do not have enough space to discuss here, namely the political economy of protection. Prospects of government hand-outs are likely to encourage firms to invest resources in seeking them. This process would create unproductive activities and further cloud the economic landscape from which to pick winners.

Having said all this, I wish to counter the view that questions the research value of new trade theories. It would be a pity if trade economists refrained from exploring alternative models because their work can be misused by policy makers and others. What needs to be stressed is the very tentative nature of these models, the fragility of their results and the difficulties of formulating and implementing new policies.

IV. A new challenge: trade in services

Let me now turn to a topic which is, in my view, on the point of attracting a great deal of attention from trade theorists, i.e., international trade in services. The

	Traded	Non-traded
Goods	1	2
Services	3	4

Figure 11.6. Trade classification

issue of trade in services has been very much in the minds of international trade negotiators as they strive to launch a new round of negotiations. But deregulation of certain industries, most notably banking and insurance, also has important international aspects which have not escaped the attention of policy makers.

It may be useful to start off with a brief classification of the effects of human economic activities and their status with regard to international transactions. This is done in the figure below.

We use resources to produce goods or services which can be either consumed domestically or traded internationally. Perhaps quite naturally, international trade theorists put most of their research efforts into square one. (The pun is not intended). Yet, at one stage, it was also important to bring non-traded goods into the analysis and see how their existence affected the basic trade theorems. Curiously enough there was a basic consensus that most services are in square four. Perhaps for this reason the field of services became a *chasse gardee* of development economists. The main themes of their investigations have been the role of services in the development process, the relative share of tertiary production in national income, and productivity in service sectors.

There have been some notable exceptions to the general neglect of services by trade theorists. Bhagwati (1984), for instance, provided an explanation for the well-established fact that the relative price of services is higher in the developed than in the developing countries. The explanation can be related to the models of Jones (1974) and Krueger (1977) discussed earlier. The basic argument is that factor endowments differ substantially between countries and hence the factor-price equalization theorem does not hold. If service industries employ labour intensively, production costs should be higher in the countries well endowed with capital.

What determines the line of demarcation between traded and non-traded goods, and services? And, why is it that the latter seem to be produced to a greater extent for the domestic market? In both cases the key may lie in obstacles to trade, such as high transporta-

tion costs, tariffs and quotas which prevent international exchange from materializing. In addition, certain physical characteristics of goods and services may render them non-tradable. To elaborate on the last point, it will be useful to refer to the classification of service transactions suggested by Bhagwati (1985) and Sampson and Snape (1985). They distinguish various groups of transactions according to the physical proximity of the suppliers and the receivers of services:

1. Transactions which can be executed at arm's length, i.e. suppliers and receivers of services can be geographically separated. An individual living in New York can obtain an insurance policy from Lloyd's of London without having to be in London or without the insurance company being present in New York.

2. Transactions which require the receiver to move, at least temporarily, to the country where a particular service is provided. International tourism is a case in point.

3. Transactions involving movement of factors of production to the country where a service is provided. Development of a coal mine in Brazil requires a foreign constructor to be on the site.

4. Transactions occurring in a third country where neither the supplier not the receiver reside. An American bank established in London can undertake financial operations for, say, an Australian customer.

I find this classification illuminating because it shows that many so-called trade transactions actually involve no trade but international movements of factors of production. Only the first category of service transactions is comparable with trade in goods. The obstacles to the exchange of services between countries, thus consist not only of trade measures but also of limits to foreign investment, rights of establishment, visa requirements and so on. It is quite clear that complete liberalization of the international exchange of services would also, or even primarily, involve removal of obstacles to factor movements. Bhagwati (1984) pointed out that technological progress allows more and more services to be traded, just like goods, by relaxing the requirement of physical proximity. Advances in telecommunications and information sectors rendered many banking and insurance services tradeable at long distances. But in other sectors, the natural barriers will continue to limit direct trade in services for a long time to come.

Explanation of trade in services calls for application of the theoretical apparatus of international trade theory. The question can be asked whether the existing models are suitable for the problem at hand. Hindley and Smith (1984) argued forcefully that the theory of comparative advantage is equally applicable to goods and services. The fact that services differ from goods does not imply a need to construct new theoretical models. Indeed some researchers used the standard Heckscher-Ohlin model to provide an explanation for the existing trade patterns in services. In particular, Sapir and Lutz (1981) attempted to explain net service trade flows in freight, insurance and passenger services of developed and developing countries by using variables related to factor endowments. Their results suggest that the Heckscher-Ohlin model has some explanatory power but quite a lot of trade remains unexplained.

One of the challenges facing trade economists is to fully incorporate services into Heckscher-Ohlin and other models. The task is not as trivial as it may seem because it demands careful articulation of the characteristics of the service and its market conditions. To explain this point more fully let me turn to the model developed by Findlay and Kierzkowski (1983).

The Findlay-Kierzkowski model investigates the formation of human capital through educational services. Its structure is relatively simple; it involves two goods-producing industries, and an educational sector. The goods, X and Y, are produced with neo-classical functions, each using two factors of production—skilled and unskilled labour. No physical capital is required in the X and Y industries but this simplifying assumption is of no great importance and it could be relaxed. The total population is stationary, however, N individuals are born every period and N die. All individuals are alike and they all live T periods.

Each individual has a choice of either entering the labour force immediately and working as an unskilled worker with the wage rate w_u, or acquiring education to be employed later as skilled labour at the wage rate of w_s. It takes n periods to pass through the educational system.

Turning to the educational system, assume that it is located in Oxford and consists of a large number of colleges. The colleges with their fellows, rich libraries and beautiful buildings constitute a specific factor of production, K, which cannot be used elsewhere in the economy. The total amount of human capital produced in Oxford is governed by the neo-classical production function: $Q = F(K,E)$ where E is the number of students enrolled in the educational system. This production function has the normal properties. With K historically given, an increase in E causes Q to rise. However, as the number of students expands, the system gets overcrowded so the amount of human capital generated per student, Q/E, is reduced.

Let us assume that each college behaves like a perfectly competitive firm charging the students a tuition fee. No entry restrictions exist, so as many individuals as wish to can acquire education. The three important questions to ask at this stage are: How many students will want to come to Oxford every year? What is the total stock of skilled labour in the economy? Finally, how high are the tuition fees? The tuition fees charged by a competitive college should be equal to the contribution of K to the future earning power of an individual, that is:

$$\int_n^T w_s \, F_K(K,E)(K/E)e^{-rt}dt \qquad (11)$$

where r is the discount rate. Tuition fees are only one element of total individual costs of acquiring education, the other being lost income during the period when a person is in Oxford and also foregone future income as an unskilled worker. The benefit of having obtained education is the discounted stream of w_s to be earned during the period from n to T. An individual will decide to invest in education if the benefits at least cover the costs. However, given the fact that the colleges in Oxford are assumed to be competitive and there are no enrolment limits, the equilibrium requires that property discounted costs and benefits are equal for each and every individual. This can be shown to happen when:

$$w_u/w_s = F_K (e^{-rn} - e^{-rT})/(1 - e^{-rT}) \qquad (12)$$

Now the system can be closed by noting that w_u and w_s are known, once the prices of X and Y are given. Consequently the above condition determines the number of new entrants into the colleges. The total number of educated people must be equal to nE.

It becomes a rather simple matter to demonstrate that, *ceteris paribus*, a country with a larger stock of educational capital or a lower discount rate, will end up having more skilled labour. Consequently, when trade in goods is allowed this country will specialise in exporting the skill-intensive commodity X and importing Y. The relative factor endowment has been endogenised in this model. The pattern of trade is based on the Heckscher-Ohlin mechanism.

Returning to the proximity classification of international transactions in services discussed earlier, it is clear that the first type of exchange cannot occur in the industry under discussion. However, any of the remaining types of transactions are, in principle, possible. Educational services cannot be traded (at least not yet), so liberalization of educational services would have to involve eliminating restrictions on international movement of the educational capital, K, or the international movement of students. The important question to ask is whether such a liberalization would be welfare increasing. Note first of all that even with free trade in goods, factor prices will not be equalized between countries because the world stock of K is unequally distributed. The return on K in England should be lower than in the countries poorly endowed with this factor. Free movement of K would thus increase world welfare by improving the allocation of resources.

It is, of course, true that although Oxford fellows may be internationally mobile, the Bodleian Library cannot be displaced. Under these circumstances, international mobility of students would be a perfect substitute for movement of the educational composite factor. One way or another, England would be earning income from foreign countries by exporting educational services. One implication of this analysis is that the UK would have a deficit in goods trade. Another would be that the average amount of human capital per British citizen would be lowered. It is interesting to note that some general implications of this model are similar to the predictions of the consequences of Big Bang.

A conclusion to be drawn at this point is that services can be incorporated into the traditional trade framework by articulation of the Heckscher-Ohlin model. But as I stated before this requires some care in specifying the nature of a particular service and of demand and supply conditions. Furthermore, given the nature of some services transactions, the standard trade model has to be combined with the theory of foreign investment. Similar attempts could be made with regard to such services as banking and insurance. Quite clearly, however, risk would have to be introduced into the analysis.

There are, however, alternative ways of modelling services well worth pursuing. Many service sectors are non-competitive and therefore the insight of the 'new' trade models discussed in Section III can prove very valuable in this context. Telecommunications, shipping and computer services are clear examples of oligopolistic market structures. Furthermore, it seems that the nature of certain services requires a variant of the Lancasterian characteristic specification of demand and not the traditional approach. All this remains to be done.

V. Conclusion

In conclusion, let me cite again from Corden's (1965) critical review of the international trade theory. 'The pure-theory models usually assume "perfect competition"; in fact this could be restated as an assumption of equal degrees of monopoly, and when restated in this way is a reasonable first approximation which then requires modification for particular circumstances. Other assumptions—such as two factors, two products, two countries, internal factor mobility and international immobility—are not always necessary to sustain the main conclusions, though they are often necessary to provide simple but rigorous proofs'. If nothing else, international trade economists have demonstrated in the course of the last three decades their willingness to explore alternative assumptions. In doing so they have provided a greater variety of models and—in a curious way—strengthened the basic framework which they had been so reluctant to abandon.

The emergence of a large number of international trade models means different predictions and policy conclusions. As a result, the international trade economist of today, and most likely tomorrow, would be well advised to be cautious in giving policy advice or analysing consequences of an economic change. Perhaps paradoxically, I see this development as strengthening rather than weakening the position of the theorist vis-à-vis the policy-maker.

Finally, the rapid expansion of the field of international trade and the emergence of alternative theories call for an intensification of empirical research. Alternative models need to be tested to help further development of the theory and to provide guidance in making policy recommendations.

Postscript

The above essay, originally written in the fall of 1986, showed the field of international trade theory as it was entering a new stage of its development. It was an exciting time to do research, exploring new theoretical possibilities and looking for surprising results. The 'new' trade theory has now come of age and is more complete in that its original focus on imperfect competition, product differentiation and intra-industry trade has been considerably widened. I can only briefly indicate the main directions of research and cite important writings. For a very thorough and masterly overview of recent developments and their integration with the traditional trade theory the reader can do no better than consult Ronald Findlay (1995).

The new growth theory and the new trade theory have come to prominence at about the same time and it was only natural for the latter to incorporate insights of the former. We knew and appreciated the importance of technological progress as a source of economic growth at least since the late 1950s when Denison, Kendrick and Solow begun their search for explanation of the so-called growth residual. However, bringing in imperfect competition and increasing returns to scale has given the modern growth theory a completely new dimension. And trade theorists were quick to incorporate an endogenous process of technological change and product innovation into their models. The work of Grossman and Helpman, 1992) focused on economic determinants of technical progress and showed how comparative advantage can evolve over time. While the trade theorists borrowed from others they also gave others something back in return, namely an analysis which is general equilibrium in its scope.

It is interesting to note that the growth theorists went on to explore the question of economic convergence in time and space while the trade theorists (re)discovered the importance of geography in explaining the location of production in different regions and inter-regional flows of goods. Paul Krugman has, once again, led the way and 'new economic geography' has come into being. (See Krugman, 1991.) The basic result of geography/trade models is that economic divergence may often occur under sufficiently strong increasing returns to scale and low transportation costs. Certain regions emerge as industrial hubs and, once in that position, they tend to dominate industrial production for a long time to come. Do we observe economic divergence or convergence in the real world? Think of possible scenarios for ex-East Germany or reforming countries of Eastern Europe. Surely, this question is of utmost importance and it calls for solid empirical work to be carried out.

Unfortunately, I cannot report outstanding empirical results obtained as a result of new theoretical work of the last ten years or so. Perhaps this is so because it is no longer possible to make as powerful predictions as within the Heckscher-Ohlin or Ricardian models.

References

Bhagwati, J. (1985), 'International Trade in Services and its relevance for Economic Development', Xth Annual Lecture of the Geneva Association held at the London School of Economics, November, London.

—— (1984), 'Why are Services Cheaper in the Poor Countries', *Economic Journal*, June, 279–286.

Brander, J. (1981), 'Intra-industry Trade in Identical Commodities', *Journal of International Economics*, Vol. 11, 1–14.

—— and P. Krugman (1983), 'A Reciprocal Dumping Model of International Trade', *Journal of International Economics*.

—— and B. Spencer (1984), 'Tariff Protection and Imperfect Competition', in H. Kierzkowski, ed., *Monopolistic Competition and International Trade*, Oxford University Press, Oxford, 313–321.

Corden, W. M. (1965), *Recent Developments in the Theory of International Trade*, Special Papers in International Economics, Princeton University.

Deardorff, A. (1980), 'The General Validity of the Law of Comparative Advantage', *Journal of Political Economy*, Vol. 80, October, 941–957.

—— (1982), 'The General Validity of the Beckscher-Ohlin Theorem', *American Economic Review*, Vol. 72, 683–694.

Dixit, A., and J. Stiglitz (1977), 'Monopolistic Competition and Optimum Product Variety', *American Economic Review*, Vol. 67, 297–308.

—— and V. Norman (1980), *Theory of International Trade*, Cambridge University Press, Cambridge.

—— (1984), 'International Trade Policy for Oligopolistic Industries', *Economic Journal*, Supplement, 1–15.

—— (1984), 'Growth and Terms of Trade under Imperfect Competition', in H. Kierzkowski, ed., *Monopolistic Competition and International Trade*, Oxford University Press, Oxford.

Ethier, H. (1974), 'Some of the Theorems of International Trade with many Goods and Factors', *Journal of International Economics*, Vol. 4, May, 199–206.

Findlay, R. (1995), *Factor Proportions, Trade and Growth*, MIT Press.

—— and H. Kierzkowski (1983), 'International Trade and Human Capital: A Simple General Equilibrium Model', *Journal of Political Economy*, Vol. 91, December, 957–978.

Grossman, G., and Helpman, E. (1992), *Innovation and Growth in the Global Economy*, MIT Press.

Grubel, H., and P. Lloyd (1975), *Intra-industry Trade: The Theory and Measurement of International Trade in Differentiated Products*, Macmillan, London.

Helpman, E. (1981), 'International Trade in the Presence of Product Differentiation, Economies of Scale, and

Monopolistic Competition', *Journal of International Economics*, Vol. 11, 305–340.

Hindley, B., and A. Smith (1984), 'Comparative Advantage and Trade in Services', *The World Economy*, Vol. 7, December, 369–389.

Jones, R. W. (1971), 'A Three-Factor Model in Theory, Trade and History', in J. Bhagwati *et al.*, eds., *Trade, Balance of Payments, and Growth: Essays in Honor of Charles P. Kindleberger*, North-Holland, Amsterdam.

—— (1974), 'The Small Country in a Multi-Commodity World', *Australian Economic Papers*, Vol. 13, December, 225–236.

—— (1975), 'Income Distribution and Effective Protection in a Multi-Commodity Trade Model', *Journal of Economic Theory*, Vol. 11, 1–15.

—— and H. Kierzkowski (1986), 'Neighbourhood Production Structures, with an Application to the Theory of International Trade', *Oxford Economic Papers*, **38**, 59–76.

Krueger, A. (1977), *Growth, Distortions and Patterns of Trade Among Many Countries*, Princeton Studies in International Finance, No. 40, Princeton University.

Krugman, P. (1979), 'A Model of Innovation, Technology Transfer and the World Distribution of Income', *Journal of Political Economy*, Vol. 87, 253–266.

—— (1984), 'Import Protection as Export Promotion: International Competition in the Presence of Oligopoly and Economies of Scale', in H. Kierzkowski, ed., *Monopolistic Competition and International Trade*, Oxford University Press, Oxford.

—— (1986), 'Introduction: New Thinking about Trade Policy', in P. Krugman, ed., *Strategic Trade Policy and New International Economics*, MIT Press, Cambridge, MA.

—— (1991), *Geography and Trade*, MIT Press.

Lancaster, K. (1979), *Variety, Equity and Efficiency*, Blackwell, Oxford.

—— (1980), 'Intra-industry Trade under Monopolistic Competition', *Journal of International Economics*, Vol. 10, 151–175.

Leamer, E. (1980), 'The Leontief Paradox Reconsidered', *Journal of Political Economy*, June, 495–503.

—— (1984), *Sources of International Comparative Advantage*, MIT Press, Cambridge, Massachusetts.

Leontief, H. (1953), 'Domestic Production and Foreign Trade: The American Capital Position Re-examined', *Proceedings of the American Philosophical Society*, September, 322–349.

Mayer, W. (1974), 'Short-run and Long-run Equilibrium for a Small Open Economy', *Journal of Political Economy*, Vol. 82, 955–967.

Mussa, M. (1974), 'Tariffs and the Distribution of Income: The Importance of Factor Specificity; Substitutability, and Intensity in the Short and Long Run', *Journal of Political Economy*, Vol. 82, 1191–1204.

Neary, J. P. (1978), 'Short-run Capital Specificity and the Pure Theory of International Trade', *Economic Journal*, Vol. 88, 488–510.

Sampson, G., and R. Snape (1985), 'Identifying the Issues in Trade in Services', *The World Economy*, Vol. 8, June, 171–182.

Sapir, A., and E. Lutz (1981), 'Trade in Services: Economic Determinants and Development-related Issues', World Bank Staff Working Paper, World Bank, Washington.

Spence, M. (1981), 'The Learning Curve and Competition', *Bell Journal of Economics*, Vol. 12, 49–70.

The new trade theory and economic policy

CHRISTOPHER BLISS[1]

Nuffield College, Oxford

I. Trade theory and experience

In recent years trade theory has enjoyed a great revival. Ten years ago I would tell a student who enquired what to read on trade theory to look at Bhagwati and Corden, certainly, and best of all, if he could manage it, Chipman.[2] Even at that time these works were many years old, but they still contained excellent expositions of most of the pure trade theory that a student needed to know. In 1980 there appeared a book which insisted on its inclusion in my core reading list. Dixit & Norman (1980) provided a fresh approach to trade theory, treated several topics at a higher level of generality than had been usual previously, and did more than any other work to establish the duality approach. However, much of what Dixit & Norman offered was already present, although differently exposited, in those older sources.

These works catalogued a trade theory and brought its presentation to a point of high perfection. However, a trade theorist who fell asleep in 1960 and woke up in 1980 would have found himself, once he had decoded some new terminology and mastered new approaches, in a rather familiar world. The same would not have been the case for a similarly comatose balance-of-payments theorist, still less for a macroeconomic theorist, who would have awoken to find their fields transformed.

Historians of thought, including economic thought, tend to explain periods of relative intellectual stagnation in terms of a lack of the stimulus provided by new problems and new questions. Thus one could argue that almost any economic theory, and particularly a beautiful one, will command acceptance provided that it is neither in clear conflict with current observations nor wholly unable to address questions to which people would like answers.[3] The theory may well develop and enrich itself under its own momentum, but it usually takes new observations or anomalous findings to generate exciting new departures.

The pure trade theory which had matured by the 1960s really had two branches between which it is important to distinguish. To put it crudely, there was a high-brow version and a low-brow version. In the high-brow version there were many different goods and factors and a more general mathematical specification. The low-brow version always had smooth production functions and just two factors (called labour, and capital or land). The high-brow version was superior in terms of generality and elegance, but the low-brow version nearly always came out on top because it could obtain definite results where the high-brow version often lead to ambiguity.[4] We shall refer to these two versions of the theory as respectively the general model and the standard model.

First published in *Oxford Review of Economic Policy*, vol. 3, no. 1 (1987).

[1] Before completing this article I was fortunate to have access to Henryk Kierzkowski's paper (also included in this volume). He therefore deserves both a genuine acknowledgment for help received and a total acquittal from blame for any errors in my own piece.

[2] The references are to: Bhagwtai (1969), Corden (1965) and Chipman (1965–66).

[3] Thomas Kuhn (1962) has described the origin of a paradigm change in science as being partly the inability of existing science to explain current observations.

[4] There was a deep mathematical reason for this. Some of the underlying concepts of the standard model did not generalize beyond the two by two case. With two goods and two factors, for example, each good must use a particular factor intensively relative to the other good. With three goods and three factors this pairing of goods and factors may not occur.

Broadly speaking, events of the 1960s and 1970s did not pose great difficulties for received trade theory. Trade was increasing at an unprecedented rate in a fairly liberal environment. Most trading nations seemed to gain from trade. The successful development of the European Common Market (ECM) gave pause for thought, as it plainly involved a great deal of trade diversion, but as the standard model could be extended to treat customs unions and to illustrate trade diversion, this development did not seem particularly threatening to received theory. Above all, economic theorists and policy makers took more or less the same view: that trade was beneficial and protection harmful, and that some customs unions could be a good thing.

It is true that difficulties associated with trade seemed to increase during the period. Certain countries, among them Britain, suffered from chronic balance of payments difficulties, the Bretton Woods system collapsed under the strains caused by inflation and profligate expenditure by the United States, and trade did not involve the less developed countries in a manner which was always felt to be beneficial and successful. However, none of these problems seemed to arise from sources which had to be identified as shortcomings of the pure trade model. The difficulties with the Bretton Woods system surely arose from the system itself, or from the inflationary policies adopted by governments. If the *raison d'etre* of the ECM was not factor-endowment based comparative advantage, the ECM was at least consistent with other kinds of comparative advantage. Moreover economies of scale were widely felt to be important and were used to justify Britain's entry to the ECM. True they were not included in the pure trade model in either its general or its standard versions, but they seemed intuitively to reinforce the case for specialization. Finally, the experience of the less developed countries could be seen as providing an object lesson in the benefits of comparative advantage and of the costs of ignoring it as recklessly as many developing countries did.

It is instructive to contrast the way in which developments in trade left mainstream theory more or less untouched with what happened to macroeconomics. There, as with trade theory, the 1960s was a period of consensus and what can now only be seen as complacency. The majority of economists in the Anglo-Saxon world adhered to some form of the Keynesian model, and a number of relationships seemed to be established and solid, among them the consumption function, the demand for money function and, most important for our present concerns, the Phillips curve. At the time of course the agreement did not always appear to be impressive. A great deal of controversy was generated by Milton Friedman, who promulgated a version of the Keynesian model which he claimed to be fundamentally different from the orthodox version, and which went under the name of monetarism. These differences were not unimportant and in them lay the roots of later and far more fundamental changes in the views of macroeconomic theorists. However, they disguised a very considerable amount of consensus. Certainly policy makers in the Anglo-Saxon countries were broadly in agreement with the Keynesian model and believed themselves to be regulating their economies by means of Keynesian demand management. It was a happy time for economic theorists and, as with trade theory, the same material was taught to students year after year, and old references were still relevant, indeed sometimes the best references were years old.

Then came the 1970s[5] and within the space of a few years the whole structure collapsed. The Phillips curve broke down, double-digit inflation arrived in the company of the highest levels of unemployment since the end of the Second World War, a new and ugly word was coined, 'stagflation', and macroeconomic theory was pitched into the most radical revision of its assumptions and arguments since Keynes' *General Theory*. In revising their views theorists and econometricians were only doing the same as the policy makers, who likewise radically revised their understanding of how the economy functions. These changes were the inevitable result of new observations which did not fit the old theory.

Nothing similar happened to pure trade theory. The problems for trade, which were considerable, did not, as I have argued, seem to come from that direction. Also trade theory had developed much less than macroeconomics in the direction of well-established econometric relations. Trade theory had no Phillips curve for experience to demolish. There had been attempts to test the theory empirically, most notably by Leontief in his study of the effect on the factor requirements of the US economy that would follow from displacing some international exchange.[6] This study seemed to show that US exports were more labour intensive than US imports, which was in contradiction to what the standard version of the trade model would lead one to expect. This result came to be known as the Leontief paradox, in recognition of the fact that it represented an anomaly in terms of the standard

---

[5] I am dividing the period into decades which provides a convenient short-hand for various time-spans. In fact stagflation began in the late 1960s. However, the response of theory and policy to this new phenomenon belongs largely to the 1970s.

[6] See Leontief (1954).

theory. However, pure trade theory had several lines of defence available, the most interesting of which was Leontief's own suggestion that when allowance was made for the greater efficiency of US labour, the United States was really a labour-abundant capital-scarce economy.[7] As there was no alternative theory that did explain the Leontief paradox, most people were more or less satisfied. This is typical. It takes theory to beat theory and a model never falls before its own negation.

Another observation that appeared to be damaging to received trade theory was provided by the European Common Market and the rapid growth in trade that followed upon its establishment. If trade was based on comparative advantage and comparative advantage was due to differences in factor endowments, as the standard model at least maintained, then what was the source of so much exchange between countries that seemed to have somewhat similar factor endowments? The consideration of this question did generate new theory, the product cycle model,[8] in which countries were allowed to have different technical possibilities in the short or medium term, due to the recent development in one or another country of a new product, although in the long-run no country could enjoy a technical advantage over any other in the production of a good.

Other developments in the new theory can also be attributed to experience. There was for example the observation that a large proportion of international trade came to be accounted for by large multinational companies. Regardless of the explanation for this fact, and an obvious one was the existence of economies of scale, it plainly carried the implication that the assumption of perfect competition which had been a feature of nearly all pure trade theory had to be dispensed with.

Another example of observation moving theory was provided by the study of the commodity composition of the high volume of trade between industrial countries. This revealed that even when detailed categories of goods were used, a great deal of two-way exchange was revealed. By two-way exchange is meant here that one country exported to another goods in a category from which it also imported from the same country. An obvious example was provided by passenger cars which were exported from most producing countries into all the same countries. Was this simply evidence that even after detailed classification of goods important differences remain, and if so what were the implications of that for a trade model?

It is not my intention to argue that all the recent advances in trade theory are due to observations that have called for a theoretical explanation. The relation between theory and observation is more subtle than that account would suggest, and theory sometimes moves forward 'under its own steam'. Trade theory has in part been the passive beneficiary of developments in other areas of economic theory, in industrial economics and game theory for example. However it probably is the case that the need for models to deal with new problems is what has enlivened trade theory and brought into it a new generation of theorists. It is the implication of their work for economic policy that will be considered in the following sections.

II. Theory and policy

No one can doubt that the old trade theory was elegant or that it absorbed the minds of a large number of outstanding economists. However most of its practitioners saw it, not as a game, but as a tool to use in understanding the world, and particularly as a means to making policy recommendations. What were the policy implications of the old theory? It is useful to divide these policy recommendations into those that were implied by nearly every version of the theory, and which were therefore implications of the general model, and those which were specific to the standard model.

The general policy implications of the trade model follow from the fact that the trade model is an instance of the allocation of economic resources, and as such is subject to the welfare economic principles which apply to all examples of resource allocation. The most powerful principle concerned goes under the name of *the fundamental theorem of welfare economics*.[9] This result states that any efficient allocation of resources may be supported by a price system. That means that all goods and factors will have prices, producers will maximize profit at those prices, and consumers will maximize (choose the best available consumption) given those prices and their incomes. The incomes of consumers will need to be adjusted to suit the particular allocation, so that each consumer can just afford the welfare level that the allocation assigns to him. As

---

[7] Another suggestion, that the role of natural resources, including climate, would explain the paradox was really an implicit criticism of the two goods and factors model. One reason why Leontief's findings had a relatively mild impact is that what had been tested was a particular version of a more general theory.

[8] See Vernon (1966).

[9] See Koopmans (1957).

the income level assigned to a particular consumer may not correspond to the value of his resources and labour at the prices which support the allocation, this process may be interpreted as including lump-sum transfers of income between consumers.[10]

We shall return to the implications of not allowing lump-sum transfers. However it is appropriate to postpone the consideration of that important issue because to a remarkable extent the policy implications of the pure trade model were developed under assumptions which amounted to the same thing as admitting lump-sum transfers. The most usual way in which the equivalent of lump-sum transfers gained admittance to the analysis was by the use of community indifference curves.[11] A community indifference curve has the same affect as reducing the preferences of the community to preferences exactly like those of a single maximizing individual. As the preferences of the community, which are manifested in its final demand for goods, depend upon how income is distributed between its members, assuming community indifference curves clearly sets aside issues of income distribution between consumers. In general this cannot be justified[12] and results derived from that assumption are always limited in their application.

What follows for trade policy from the fundamental theorem? We note some leading results and then show how the fundamental theorem implies them. Important implications include:

(i) trade is gainful. In particular, free trade is superior to autarky (no trade);

(ii) for a small country, tariffs are inefficient. They impose a burden in the sense that they are a more costly way of redistributing income than are lump-sum transfers;

(iii) when a tariff is imposed on a good this can improve the welfare of a group only if it worsens the welfare level of another group.

To see how these results follow from the fundamental theorem, consider them in turn. First consider trade and whether it constitutes an improvement on no trade. We suppose an allocation without trade and ask whether it can be supported by some price system. If it cannot, we know that it is inefficient,[13] as every efficient allocation can be supported by a price system. If trade were permitted feasible allocations would include exchanges through international trade and normally some of these would allow a welfare improvement. Certainly allowing the use of international exchange can only make things better, never worse. Hence no trade can be inefficient and optimal trade can never make things worse. Hence trade is gainful, strictly not pernicious. This result is rather trivial once one understands what it claims. Notice that it says that trade normally permits a better allocation. For that allocation to be a price equilibrium we shall usually need lump-sum transfers of income.

To see the potential[14] inefficiency of tariffs for a small country, notice that an allocation with tariffs is supported by prices which do not constitute a price system as the term is intended by the fundamental theorem. This is because a price system implies that all agents face the same prices and producers maximize at those prices. However with tariffs prices for goods in the home market differ from world prices, so that the notional agents responsible for importing and exporting would not be maximizing. Such an agent could transfer 1 unit of steel into 100 units of wheat, say, in international exchange, but a domestic producer might make a loss from the same transformation. Hence normally a tariff-bound allocation cannot be supported by any price system and so is inefficient. Another allocation would improve and could be supported by a price system.[15]

The statement of this last result has had to be somewhat complicated because of the possibility that an efficient allocation might be an equilibrium with tariffs, because the tariffs might make no difference to resource allocation. A Simpler result to state is the following. Every efficient allocation can be supported by a price system, hence can be an equilibrium without tariffs.

---

[10] The transfers are lump-sum because they cannot be related to many economic variables, such as income or labour supplied, without changing the optimizing decision of the household.

[11] Community indifference curves are meant to show the preferences of the community over the total of resources allocated to consumption in the same way that ordinary indifference curves show the preferences of a consumer over various consumption bundles.

[12] The single exception is when income may be distributed between consumers without affecting the final demand of the collectivity. This requires linear parallel Engle curves, which may be interpreted as the poor having the demands of the rich scaled down to their smaller incomes. As this excludes any interesting income effects it only underlines how special are community indifference curves.

[13] An allocation is efficient if no alternative feasible allocation would make one consumer better off and no consumer worse off.

[14] The inefficiency is potential because it could happen that a tariff made no difference whatsoever to resource allocation in which case it would of course be benign.

[15] The assumption that this is a small country plays an essential role in the argument, as transformation possibilities in trade are assumed fixed and constant. If the terms of trade vary with the extent of trade, as in the optimum tariff model, an efficient allocation may be supported by a price system in which marginal transformation rates at home and in trade are equalized and all agents maximize at prices different from average exchange rates in trade. The allocation is efficient, and is supported by a price system, but prices are not the terms of international trade.

The last result provides a simple opportunity to illustrate the difference between the general and the standard model. In the standard model it is a theorem that a tariff always makes one group, specifically the owners of one factor, better off.[16] For the general model we suppose the imposition of a tariff and a distribution of its revenue which makes some group better off. As the initial position is without tariffs it is supported by a price system, from which it follows that it is efficient. This is the converse of the fundamental theorem and is also true. But if the reallocation corresponding to the imposition of the tariff has made one group better off, and if no group has been made worse off, the original allocation was not efficient, which contradicts the fact that it was supported by a price system.

Notice that all the results that have just been rehearsed are implications of the general trade model. They do not depend upon two-good, two-factor or two-country assumptions. Stronger results are available from the standard model, mainly because of its assumption of a smooth technology and continuous substitution. In this case, for example, one can be more definite concerning the effects of a tariff. The movement of prices away from world prices always introduces a production distortion, as even a small price change causes substitution in domestic production towards goods that have risen in price; and this production distortion always entails inefficiency. There is an additional distortion on the consumption side. All this is equally true of the general model when its functions are smooth and responses to price changes non-zero.

How useful are these results for a policy maker? At first sight it appears that they are not useful at all. The trade model, whether in its general or in its standard formulation, and the results derived from it, depend on assumptions that in the eyes of most policy makers would disqualify it from serious consideration. In particular:

(i) perfect markets are assumed, so that prices change to ensure that resources are fully employed, and agents act competitively taking the prices that they face as fixed;

(ii) there are no externalities or increasing returns to scale; and

(iii) lump-sum transfers of income are available to adjust the distribution of income, or to compensate those who have lost from a reform.

It is true that these restrictions underline the need for a broader analysis and we shall shortly consider such an analysis, but the theory should not be dismissed simply because it makes a number of strong assumptions.

First, by laying out its assumptions, the argument puts the onus on someone who wants to claim that trade is not gainful, or to argue that a tariff might be good for everyone, to say which of the assumptions he would like to change. We shall see that the argument is not vulnerable to every change in its assumptions, but even where it is vulnerable, conducting the argument against the background of a strong result will only help to advance understanding.

Second, the assumption of lump-sum transfers appears to be particularly unsatisfactory, as no real system of taxation or subsidy corresponds to a lump-sum transfer. We shall shortly see that we do not need such an implausible form of taxation to show that tariffs lead to distortion. But leaving that point aside for the moment, compensation systems that are not strictly lump-sum transfers may nevertheless do the trick. Suppose, for example, that a tariff on the import of wheat is distorting the British economy.[17] However, if the tariff is removed landlords or farmers will lose. Suppose we compensate the losers from general taxation. The results already stated show that if these transfers could be achieved by the lump-sum method, everyone, farmers included, could be made better off.

The problem seems to be that the revenue to pay the compensation cannot be collected without itself causing further distortions. An income tax for example may discourage effort. However the distortion caused by an income tax might be small compared with the distortion caused by the tariff. Economists like to be able to *demonstrate* that an improvement will follow from a certain policy and this is difficult to do if offsetting effects are involved. However to assume that the result of offsetting effects always nets out as unfavourable to reform is an unduly pessimistic approach.

Transfers in the form of compensation are not always infeasible. For example, so large is the distortion caused by the protection of domestic sugar production in temperate countries, that it is probable that farmers growing sugar (that is sugar beet) in the EEC,

---

[16] This result depends upon how the tariff revenue is distributed between the factors. If we assume that it provides a uniform subsidy on all expenditure then it is the case that a tariff must help the owners of one factor. This is the Stolper-Samuelson result.

[17] This hypothetical assumption was satisfied in the early Nineteenth Century, when Ricardo attacked the Corn Laws, and is satisfied again today, when the Common Agricultural Policy of the European Community raises the domestic wheat price above the world price.

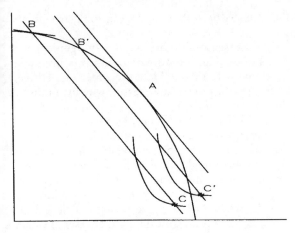

Figure 12.1. The effects of tariffs and taxes on trade

could be paid enough to set aside the land presently growing sugar without income loss, and the consumers still gain.[18]

As an example of the analysis of policy conducted without the assumption of lump-sum transfers, we consider a result due to Diamond and Mirrlees as it applies to international trade.[19] We show this result for the standard two-good model, as this allows a simple diagrammatic representation of the result. However the same result applies in the general model, provided that there are constant returns to scale in production,[20] and the method of proof is the same.

The theorem states that if the value of production at world prices is not being maximized, say because a tariff has been imposed, then an improvement is possible which will make all consumers better off. This improvement does not require lump-sum transfers but may be implemented by means of consumption, production and factor-use subsidies.

In Figure 12.1 the curved frontier is the production possibility curve. World prices are given by the slope of the line that is tangential to the frontier at A, so that A is the value maximizing production. However, due to a tariff, production is at B, and domestic goods prices

are the slope of the tangent to the production possibility frontier at B. Factor prices are not illustrated, but we should bear in mind that they have been determined by the goods prices at B and are thus determining individual incomes. Consumption is at C which has the same value at world prices as B so the movement from B to C is attainable by international exchange at world prices.

The idea is to proceed as follows. We move along the production possibility frontier to a point such as B′ which has a higher value at world prices. To do this we change producer prices, for goods and factors, so that the new production becomes profit maximizing. However we keep the prices, for goods and factors again, that consumers pay and receive constant.

To maintain the separation of producer prices from consumer prices we employ indirect taxes and/or subsidies.

As consumer prices and incomes are unchanged, consumers continue to consume at C. The indifference curve through C is illustrated. Now however the value of production at world prices is higher. We may therefore cut all goods prices to consumers somewhat, relative to the factor prices that consumers receive, hence relatively to their incomes. Aggregate consumption moves to C′. This makes every consumer better off. So we have achieved an unambiguous improvement without recourse to lump-sum transfers.

The Diamond–Mirrlees result shows that the assumption of lump-sum transfers in the orthodox argument for efficient allocation in trade is not really required. However this particular line of argument cannot settle the case for and against protection. For that purpose we need to consider alterations to the standard model, particularly the effect of distortions of various kinds, and their implications for optimal economic policy. This is the task of the next section.

III. Policy rankings and the second-best

We have seen in the previous section that trade theory can have strong implications for economic policy. However so far these implications seem to be compromised by the extremely restrictive assumptions on which they depend. The particular assumption which we shall examine in this section is the requirement that, apart from some distortion, such as a tariff, which is being examined, everything else in the economy is ideal. To put it another way, we have been consider-

---

[18] This is not the usual type of resource reallocation following the removal of protection, as in that case resources released are assumed to migrate to their next best alternative use. With land set-aside the land released is unused.

[19] See Diamond & Mirrlees (1971) and Dasgupta & Stiglitz (1974).

[20] The reason why constant returns to scale is required is that it ensures that no productive activity will make a surplus of revenue over costs of inputs, with the consequence that changes in producer prices do not change the pure profits associated with the ownership of firms. If these profits can be taxed away, constant returns to scale is not required. See Dasgupta & Stiglitz (1974).

ing policy for an undistorted economy, or 'first-best'[21] theory as it is sometimes called. However most real cases of intervention, it will be argued, concern, or are perceived to concern, the 'second-best'. To take a tariff as an example, most justifications for tariffs really depend upon the assertion of a distortion which the tariff is meant to correct. To understand the arguments concerning policy which will eventually settle the issue, we need to look at distortions and the second-best.

It goes without saying that a distortion is a good reason for intervention, we would hardly call it a distortion otherwise. The question is, what will be the consequences of various interventions, and can some be shown to be better than others. This line of enquiry has given rise to a large field of trade theory from which some definite conclusions emerge.[22] These conclusions may be summarized as follows:

(i)   a distortion calls for an intervention of some kind, in the sense that policy interventions in the form of taxes, subsidies, tariffs, etc. can improve on the laissez-faire outcome;

(ii)   not all interventions have equally good results, and typically a policy ranking emerges from the comparison of different types of intervention in which the best of one type of intervention may be shown to dominate the best of another type;

(iii)   the best intervention in the policy ranking is usually directed closely at the source of the mis-allocation, where inferior interventions are indirect and affect changes not relevant to the original distortion.

These rather vague and sweeping statements may be illustrated by means of an example. We consider one of the oldest arguments for intervention in the form of tariff or quota protection, the infant industry,[23] which was considered by Adam Smith and the classical economists, and which frequently reappears in contemporary discussions, not always bearing the title used here. The infant industry is supposed to be an industry presently uncompetitive in the face of foreign competition, but which will become competitive in due course if provided with a period of protection during which its costs will fall until it eventually can compete. The idea of the classic argument is to give

this industry protection until it can compete without it.[24]

To make sense of the infant industry argument one needs more than the story of an industry presently uncompetitive that will later become competitive. First, there has to be some reason why the industry should not wait its time until it is competitive. The reason will usually be that only by operating now and gaining experience, or economies of learning by doing, can the industry prove competitive later. Even that alone is not enough. It has to be explained why private investors cannot foresee that present operation at a loss will be rewarded by profits later and why, if they do, they do not arrive at socially efficient decisions, as they presumably do in other cases in which present costs are offset by future benefits. Why are the losses of an infant industry not simply an investment cost, like any other investment cost, and if they are, where is the presumption that private decisions will be improved by intervention?

It is important to understand the force of these questions and to see how the case for protecting an infant industry depends on the answers to them. However this is not to say that answers cannot be provided. The most plausible and important case arises when the efficiency of an industry improves with operation, not in a manner which producers cannot foresee but policy makers can, an assumption hard to credit, but in a manner which the producers cannot capture and keep outsiders from sharing the benefit. Suppose, for example, that an industry will enjoy an international comparative advantage once local labour has been trained in the operation of its processes. However this labour is footloose, it cannot be tied by contract to a particular employer. Hence if investors borrow money to train labour and take operating losses during this period, they will reap no benefit. The labour can be attracted away by late-arriving employers who have not bothered to suffer the investment costs of training labour. This seems to provide a genuine case for infant protection.

This is the case that we shall examine in more detail. It needs a little more filling out of the example just to describe the situation. Since workers benefit from the training, one way of supporting the optimum in this case would be to have the workers finance their training, say by working unpaid and using borrowed money to see them through the training period. So we

[21]   This illogical terminology gained currency after the term 'second-best' was used to describe an allocation in which not all the welfare conditions for a full optimum could be satisfied. The so-called 'first-best' is simply the best, the optimum. See Lipsey & Lancaster (1956).

[22]   For more thorough treatments, see Bhagwati (1971), Corden (1974) and (1984), and Michaely (1977).

[23]   See Johnson (1970).

[24]   In the past the argument was largely theoretical, a counter-example to what was seen as a general case for free trade. However in modern times policies based in part on the infant industry case have been influential in practice, particularly in developing countries.

have to tell a story according to which this solution is impossible. However we shall not go into too much detail but simply suppose that that method is infeasible. We may call it an imperfection of the capital market that workers cannot borrow against future earnings.[25] We have now provided an example of the infant industry argument in which the case can be spelt out in detail and withstand obvious objections.

We now consider some policies which will achieve the end of allowing the infant industry to operate during its period of growing-up and we then derive a policy ranking. Policies which would allow the infant industry to operate include:

(a) a limited period of tariff protection;[26]
(b) a limited period of investment subsidy;
(c) a limited period of production subsidy;
(d) a state-sponsored loan scheme to enable workers to finance their own training.

There may well be further interventions which would enable the infant industry to get going but the above will serve our need for an example of a policy ranking. Notice that in regard to directness or indirectness, the policies are ranked above in order of increasing directness. Thus a tariff is furthest from the source of the problem, which is the mobility of labour and the employer's difficulty in attaching the benefits of his training. An investment subsidy is closer in that the employer is compensated for the fact that his investment shows a return below the social return. A production subsidy is closer still in that the employer is rewarded for doing the action which provides an external social benefit, namely producing and training labour. A training loan scheme goes directly to the heart of the problem. In fact it overcomes the imperfection of the capital market and supports the best outcome.

The same ordering above is in order of increasing efficiency. Thus any policy high on the list may be dominated by a policy lower on the list. As usual, this requires lump-sum transfers. The reason why this should be so is that each of policies (a), (b) and (c) correct the distortion caused by the imperfection of the capital market only at the cost of introducing another distortion which is not introduced by a policy lower on the list.

[25] Such an imperfection may be quite explicable. As collateral, earnings have the property that they are difficult to attack if repayment of the loan is not forthcoming. Mortgaged property for example provides better collateral.
[26] Or another kind of protection such as a quota on imports. We ignore differences between different kinds of protection in the present argument.

Consider the tariff for example. This allows the infant industry to operate but does this by raising the price in the domestic market. It thus distorts the level of production, which is lower than in the optimum solution, so that the infant takes longer to grow up than it should, and it distorts consumption in that consumers pay more than the true social opportunity cost of the product and end up consuming less of it. An investment subsidy overcomes the problem that the scale of operation of the industry is too small but at the cost of introducing another distortion. It is investment which is encouraged and hence production, but this leads to production which is too capital intensive. A production subsidy partly avoids that difficulty, and also the contraction of the industry which would be caused by a tariff. However to the employer labour is still more expensive than it really is from the social point of view, and so production is still too capital intensive (but not as capital intensive as it would be with an investment subsidy). Finally, with the labour training loan scheme we remove all distortions and attain the 'first-best'.

In the case of the infant industry example protection came high in the list of policies, that is low in terms of desirability. How typical is this? A little thought will reveal what conditions have to be satisfied for protection to rank high in terms of desirability. We need only to apply the principle that direct intervention, that is intervention targeted at the source of any misallocation, is superior to indirect intervention. From this it follows that protection will be an optimal intervention when protection is similarly targeted. But what would that mean?

Protection is targeted at trade as such and it therefore follows that it will be the optimal intervention only when trade is itself the source of the misallocation. Two examples illustrate this point. First, we know that a tariff is optimal, not surprisingly, in the case of an optimal tariff. But this is precisely a case in which trade is the source of misallocation. From the point of view of the home country, for an individual agent to engage a little more in trade, whether as exporter or importer, is an action to which an external diseconomy attaches. The diseconomy arises because the terms of trade vary slightly with a small change in the quantity traded, and this affects the intra-marginal trades, an effect which the agent does not take into account. The optimal tariff simply faces the individual agent with the true social shadow price that attaches to his action. It is a direct intervention and it is therefore not surprising that it supports the optimum.

Secondly, consider the case in which national self-sufficiency is itself an objective. This may be for good reasons, a prudent need to survive a possible crisis, or bad, simple xenophobia. In either case trade as such enters into the national objective function with a negative weight. This will mean, of course, that an individual agent deciding on an action which leads to more trade generates an external economy from the point of view of the national objective function. With tariffs the same agent may be faced with the exact correct shadow prices. Once again a tariff is the direct targeted intervention and once again the 'first-best' may be supported with a tariff.[27]

It should now be clear why, in the received theory of policy design and policy rankings, protection is seldom an optimal intervention. On the whole, instances in which protection is the correctly targeted intervention are unusual. This is not the same as saying that they are unimportant. However it is significant that the advocates of protection are usually not content to rely on variable terms of trade or xenophobia, although both of these are encountered. However without relying on these arguments the advocate of protection always runs up against the difficulty that his policy proposal can be trumped by a more direct intervention.

It is important to bear in mind that while the theory of policy design is an impressive apparatus, it has relied more than it ought to on lump-sum transfers or community indifference curves. This is unfortunate because those assumptions are often not required to make the point. We saw in section II above that a tariff-bound equilibrium could be improved using only indirect taxes and subsidies. However in other cases an analysis which employs lump-sum transfers leads to too complacent a view of non-intervention.

Anand & Joshi (1979) consider an example in which the distortion is inequality of incomes between the same factor according to where it is employed. The correction of this situation by means of taxes and subsidies is supposed to be impossible.[28] What happens is that under free trade the industrial sector of the economy expands too much. In a sense the expansion is excessive because there is an external diseconomy from the advanced sector, rather like pollution, but in this case the pollutant is mal-distribution of income. Intervention is required in this case, however a tariff is not optimal, as it plainly is not targeted and may distort consumption.

Another example which illustrates the difficulties that may arise when we cannot make use of lump-sum transfers follows from a subtle feature of the Diamond-Mirrlees result. We presented that result above as showing that commodity and factor taxes or subsidies could improve on a tariff. It was pointed out that the argument assumed either constant returns to scale or that pure profits were taxed away. Neither of these conditions is satisfied in the example which follows. The example is fanciful, but it illustrates a serious point.

We imagine a man who owns some land which he can devote to rearing sheep, and his own labour, which is of poor quality, so that if he sells it on the market he will earn very little. However valued at world prices his output is more in industry than on his farm. Presumably his country has no comparative advantage in rearing sheep. How can policy help this man? Nothing that is done to consumer prices, by subsidy for example, will help, because he earns so little.[29] Producer prices are meant to reflect comparative advantage, and lump-sum transfers are not permitted. However if a large tariff is placed on the import of mutton or wool, their prices will rise in the home market, and our hypothetical man may make a much better living following his comparative disadvantage as a sheep farmer. As in the Anand-Joshi example, so in this case, a distorting policy intervention is the only way to produce a favourable redistribution of income.

We have covered enough ground to see what kind of results the theory of optimal policy and policy rankings can establish. The argument has been conducted so far in terms of the long-established general and standard models of trade. What difference does it make when we come to consider the recent advances in trade theory? That is the question that will be addressed in the next two sections.

IV. What does the new theory imply for policy?

The new theory is reviewed in the paper in this volume by Henryk Kierzkowski in a contribution which he explicitly calls a selective survey. Despite its modest designation that paper covers most of the new theoretical departures that we shall need to consider in order to see what new theory has done to policy. However before embarking on the consideration of the

[27] It is worth noting how this is consistent with the fundamental theorem of welfare economics. The 'first-best' is clearly an efficient allocation. However the example includes an externality where these are not included in the framework within which the fundamental theorem is valid.

[28] That would be the case if workers in the industrial sector can press for and maintain higher wages because of their greater political 'muscle'.

[29] As he supplies little effective labour, subsidizing sales of labour will not work.

models included in the Kierzkowski paper, it is worth mentioning a contribution which has profoundly affected the way that economists think about protection and allied topics: the theory of rent seeking.[30]

To understand the importance of rent seeking one needs to consider the quantitative importance of distortions. So far our assessment of distortions and non-optimal interventions has been qualitative—subsidies are better than tariffs, etc. However economists obviously tried to assess the quantitative importance of tariffs and, at least for modest tariffs, they tended to find that the costs were small, the equivalent of some tiny fraction of national income. This was not surprising when one considers that the analysis was based on the implicit assumption that lump-sum taxes could redistribute income as necessary. Only the efficiency cost, or excess burden, of tariffs was being measured. So it was perhaps not surprising that the costs turned out to be small.

The idea behind rent seeking is that the redistributive consequences of protection and other intervention are not neutral, because real resources are diverted into trying to steer these rents in the direction of particular agents. Businessmen, for example, will spend time and money to lobby politicians to obtain tariff protection for their industry.[31] Hence the transfers of income consequent upon tariff protection are not neutral transfers that may be costlessly reversed by opposing transfers. They use real resources.[32]

The development of the theory of rent seeking has coincided with a world wide movement away from interventionist theories and policies, and the growth in influence of the idea that trade promoting 'open' economic policies are superior to the 'closed', import substituting, policies that characterized the developing countries in the 1950s and 1960s. It is too soon now to say whether this represents a permanent shift of opinion, or whether there will be a reaction in due course back towards interventionism.

We turn now to the new theories included in the Kierzkowski survey and their consequences for policy. We consider here extensions that are such by virtue of going beyond the standard model, which are not necessarily extensions of the general model. Included are

the specific factors model in its various versions, specialized production models, other higher dimension models, and trade in services. We postpone until the next section the consideration of increasing returns and imperfect competition.

Consider first the specific factors model. This has a number of important theoretical implications but they are not particularly relevant to policy design. Thus with the specific factors model there is no factor price equalization result. This is hardly surprising, as the model has essentially more factors than goods. However the factor price equalization result is not required, and is not used, in developing the theory of economic policy. The model implies a different response of factor prices to commodity prices and this should have implications for the design of policy, although they will be of a particular nature rather than general points. Perhaps the most important conclusion for the policy maker is that he cannot expect to divide and rule along factor divisions when trade liberalization proposals are concerned. In the Heckscher-Ohlin-Samuelson (HOS) model the Stopler-Samuelson result applies. One factor gains and one factor loses from a tariff cut unaccompanied by income transfers. Empirically this always looked dubious, as typically labour and capital from a particular industry line up together to oppose a cut in the protection of that industry. The specific factors model explains that fact but does not unseat the fundamental result that with a tariff reduction and transfers all parties could gain, and that an all round gain could also be achieved with optimal commodity and factor taxes and subsidies.

What is true for the basic two-sector specific factors model is equally applicable to its elegant n-dimensional extensions. It would be easy to dismiss the importance of the specific factors model where policy is concerned, but this would be a mistake. The model points to an important policy issue which, as is often the case, is of a quantitative and not a qualitative nature.

We have seen that the theory of optimal economic policy is importantly dependent on the use of compensation and transfer mechanisms. This provides a reference point for the assessment of real-life policy decisions in which the transfers to a great extent will not be made and the implied consequences for income distribution will simply have to be suffered by the parties concerned. The old theory made it appear that these unfortunate consequences of reform were perhaps not very serious. A change in the relative earning and income levels of different factor groups would follow from trade liberalization. However this would be dispersed throughout the economy and should not

[30] See Bhagwati & Srinivasan (1980), Buchanan, Tollison and Tullock (1980), Collander (1984) and Krueger (1974).
[31] Bhagwati noted that because the allocation of rationed inputs in India was related to capacity, producers tended to overinvest in capacity so as to gain favourable allocations.
[32] Under the assumption that rent seeking is a constant returns to scale activity, costs will equal revenue, in which case the resource cost of rent seeking will be equal to total tariff revenue. This contrasts with the much smaller triangles of lump-sum burden theory.

perhaps be of catastrophic importance when compared, for example, with the consequences for factor incomes of a few years' technical progress.

The specific factors approach paints a much less rosy picture. The impact of a cut in protection will be concentrated in a few sharp reductions in income or, if their prices are inflexible, unemployment. What emerges then is sharp redistributions of income. From the theoretical point of view this is somewhat reassuring, because it has always been something of a problem for the received theory with its lump-sum transfers to explain the strength of pressures for protection that one observes, and which now become much more understandable.

We next consider specialized production models. The assumption that equilibrium does not result in a country producing only one good was always a feature of the HOS model, and it was long ago pointed out by Chipman (1965–66) that this assumption is not independent of the differences in factor endowments between countries, nor of the form of the production functions, nor even of the factor intensity reversal condition itself. Specialization seems to be an important feature of reality, although reality might be held to include less specialization than theory predicts, and for this reason the existence of specialized solutions in the trade model should be welcomed.

What difference does specialization make to policy? Once again the basic results are unaffected but some quantitative conclusions are affected. With non-specialization a small tariff will typically not be large enough to lead to specialization. True a change in factor prices is induced, and this leads to an alteration in factor input proportions and hence to a change in the quantities of the outputs produced. However the menu of goods produced is unaffected. In the Jones-Krueger model[33] a small tariff frequently induces a change in the pattern of specialization but this difference is of less moment than may at first appear. The shifts in specialization only involve local movements along the spectrum of many goods that a country may produce. Hence the welfare costs of a misallocation that results in the precise goods produced being slightly wrong will not be very large. This point is an example of a more general point. Closeness is a relative concept, it depends on the metric at issue. Thus it may happen that a large change in production may be a small change in welfare level or conversely.

Other higher dimension models bring few new policy implications with them. This is largely because the policy framework never required most of the specific properties of the HOS model. Of course the HOS model was so popular that its recitation became like a creed of trade theorists, and it was frequently employed to illustrate policy conclusions that did not in fact depend on it.

Finally we come to trade in services. It is probable that the most important single way in which services differ from goods is that the greater difficulty of standardizing services makes the competitive case even less usual than it is where goods trade is concerned. That consideration belongs to the next section, so for the time being we assume competitive markets.

The problem, as Kierzkowski's discussion shows, is to isolate the characteristic differences between goods and services. It is intuitively obvious that the export of a car is very different from the export of an insurance service, but are the differences that strike us as obvious germane to trade theory? It is after all an implication of the HOS model that trade in goods, assumed possible, substitutes for trade in factors, assumed impossible. That is how factor price equalization comes about. With many services the factors move to the customer, but this is not always so, indeed it is not always the case that the factors and the customer need meet. Thus tourism requires the customer to visit the factors. However an insurance service may require no more than a telex message and an international money transfer. The factors and the customer both stay put.

From the point of view of the welfare economics that lies at the base of the theory of commercial policy the most important issue raised by services surely concerns information and assessment of quality. No doubt it is often the case that the producer of a good is in a particularly advantageous position compared with the buyer when it comes to assessing the quality of what he is selling. However these difficulties are greatly increased where services are concerned. Very often if the buyer could assess the quality of the service that he is receiving he would not need the service. This is plainly the case where the service is medicine or education. The student who can fully assess and evaluate the education that he receives is probably already educated. These ideas point to intervention to improve information and quality assessment. Unfortunately, this is one of the disguises that protection is quick to adopt.

We have remarked on the close relation between the consequences of trade and the consequence of factor mobility. In the special case of the HOS model the former is a perfect substitute for the latter, but more generally there is scope for gains from factor mobility even after trade has been fully exploited.[34] In the light

---

[33] See Jones (1974) and Krueger (1977).

[34] This would be the case in the Jones-Krueger model for example.

of this observation it is surprising that economists, who have been vocal in support of free trade, have been rather hushed when it comes to advocating greater international mobility of labour. This contrasts with a firmer advocacy of the removal of restrictions on capital mobility.

V. Policy with variety, increasing returns and imperfect competition

In this section we come to probably the most interesting implications of the new trade theories for policy. Previously there was a certain sameness about our argument. We reviewed a model and concluded that, while it was not the HOS model, it was nevertheless more or less covered by existing commercial policy theory. Of course we could find some things to say about these models and policy, but even so the ground was more or less familiar once one viewed it in the right way. With the topics of this section we come to areas in which the theory of economic policy can require radical reconsideration and extension.

Let us begin with the love of variety. The appeal of this concept in trade theory is the possibility that it might explain the intra-industry trade which is such a marked feature of contemporary trading patterns. Notice that love of variety by itself carries few interesting implications. In the formal general equilibrium model we treat goods as different goods if consumers distinguish between them and we allow as many goods as necessary. An international trade equilibrium might be a special case of that model and standard policy conclusions will apply.

Of course this model will fail to explain why goods with similar production conditions are produced in various countries but not in all countries. This is because the general equilibrium model cannot admit non-convexities of production sets and cannot therefore explain why a good of a particular detailed type will tend to be produced in one country only, with intra-industry trade resulting. This suggests the conclusion that the importance of love of variety arises from its natural association with non-convexities, that is increasing returns, and not from variety as such which only leads to many more goods than factors.[35]

Increasing returns is a more fundamental change in assumptions, particularly as it requires us to aban-don the assumption of perfect competition, and the introduction of imperfect competition is itself of interest, as presumably one could imagine a monopolized industry with constant costs. We consider first in fact a simple model without increasing returns in production but with imperfect competition due to the fewness of the sellers. This is the model we shall refer to as the Brander model.[36]

The Brander model generates trade, in fact crosshauling in one good, from market structure, that is imperfect competition. The interesting thing about this starting point is that, unlike the usual one, we begin from a situation which is plainly non-optimal, and in which it is sure that some kind of intervention can do good. This contrasts with standard trade theory, in which we start from an equilibrium in which it is far from obvious that intervention would help, the intervention concerned usually has a minimal direct effect on trade.[37]

What is the optimal intervention in the Brander model? To answer that question we need to specify both the model and the policy interventions available. We shall take the case of constant costs of production of the one tradeable good and consider decreasing costs later. We assume that lump-sum transfers of income may be used so that our conclusions will be comparable with the usual trade theory.

The optimal trade policy would be the policy adopted by a single agent acting in full knowledge of trading conditions including the Cournot behaviour of the foreign producer. Such a hypothetical agent would import the good only if its price was below home marginal cost and would export it as long as marginal revenue exceeded marginal cost. These marginal costs are the same as average cost, which is constant. As the foreign producer will not export at a price below domestic average cost, as this is the same as his own average cost, this implies that prices will stop the inflow of the good. However this does not require a prohibitive import tariff. If the domestic price is set at average cost of production there will be no imports, the transport costs guarantee that.

Hence the following prices support the optimum. The domestic price is equal to average cost and the export price maximizes profit from exports. How can this price system function when the producer is a monopolist as keen to exploit the domestic market as

---

[35] Which is another example of a change which is important from the point of view of the standard model but not important from the point of view of the theory of policy.

[36] We refer to it as the Brander model for the sake of brevity although Spencer and Krugman are also associated with it. See Brander (1981), Krugman (1984) and further references in Kierzkowski above.

[37] For example lump-sum transfers may be the only optimal interventions and of course by redistributing income they affect trade flows. However they do not act directly on trade.

he is keen to exploit the foreign market? The answer must be a subsidy of sales in the domestic market financed by a tax on the monopolist's profit. This is better than a tariff, as the domestic consumers get the good at a price equal to social opportunity cost. However a tariff is better than no intervention.

What happens when there are decreasing costs in domestic production? This is the case for which Krugman (1984) showed that a tariff, by protecting the domestic market and leading to a decline in domestic costs of production, promotes exports. We should again ask what is the optimal policy intervention, and this will once more give us prices that will support what a maximizing and comprehending single agent would do. Consumers should again get the good at marginal cost, which is now variable. Exports should again maximize profit with output charged at marginal cost. The difference is that with decreasing costs these conditions may not automatically imply the optimum. They may not even exclude exports.

Suppose we start at a point at which our output is low, and let foreign output be high. The foreign producer has low costs and may export profitably into our market. His prices in his market may be below our own marginal cost, which is high, and so we do not export. However if the two countries are symmetrical, there must exist a similar equilibrium in which we are big and our trading partner is small. The question is not what equilibria can be supported by locally reasonable price systems, but rather how we leap from one equilibrium to another better, from our point of view, equilibrium some distance away. Clearly a tariff will do the trick as it enables the domestic market to enlarge and this eventually allows exports.

Notice that the role of a tariff in this example is quite different from its usual role in the theory of economic policy. It is only needed temporarily and it functions by shifting the system from one equilibrium to another. The case is reminiscent of the infant industry, but his is an infant which grows due to a scale effect. To a certain extent it is misleading to regard this argument as an argument for protection. The tariff is basically a second-best intervention. Taxing the monopolist's profit and subsidizing domestic sales is always better. However even with the best type of policy we may get stuck in the wrong equilibrium and need a jolt to move us to a better one. And a tariff will serve well in this regard.

If we look back at the earlier discussion of policy intervention we can see why this was likely to be the case. The new trade models introduce important new considerations but they do not demolish the principle of policy rankings, and they do not negate the very

solid rule that interventions are best when targeted. If we look at the Brander model and ask where misallocations are arising we find them in the exploitation of domestic consumers by a monopolist. The wasteful imports are an incidental consequence of this exploitation. Hence the targeted intervention removes the monopolistic exploitation, by a subsidy of sales in this case. A tariff is inferior for a reason which is the same as would apply in the old theory—it is not targeted.

Lastly consider differentiated products. Once again the important new principles which these introduce come from their association with decreasing costs and imperfect competition. These as we have seen do introduce fundamentally new possibilities, particularly local optima that are not global optima. They do not however, and could not, upset the notion of a policy ranking and they do not introduce new arguments for tariffs, although a tariff might be used to jolt the system as with the Brander model.

VI. Concluding remarks

For a paper concerned with the implications of the new trade theories for policy this piece has devoted a remarkable amount of space to the old theories and the old trade policy. There are two reasons why this imbalance may be justified. First, it is important to put the new theories in a proper perspective. Of course this typically shows that the new theories are not all new. It is true that trade theory was never exclusively the HOS model, and that indeed higher dimension models have been around and have been discussed for the last 25 years. Yet they were always the preserve of a few specialists, mainly an untypically mathematical subset of trade theorists. The HOS model did used to dominate the subject, and it certainly dominates it less now as a result of the recent advances.

The second reason why the careful consideration of old commercial policy theory may be right is that the new theories have made much less of a dent in the normative theory than they have in the positive theory. This is partly because the old normative theory never used or needed all the assumptions that were commonly used in the positive theory. It is also because the basic ideas of the old normative theory, the notion of policy rankings, the idea of targeting interventions, really are particularly solid and robust ideas. They could not be easily displaced. However despite the difficulty of injecting new principles into the field of commercial policy theory, the new trade models have succeeded in doing just that. By drawing attention to the fact that, once we abandon the convexity assumption, an optimum may be only local, and noting that a discrete policy intervention might shift the system to a higher solution in such a case, the new theories have presented policy theorists with a challenging new idea. As trade theory develops further in the future it may be expected to produce further genuine novelties regarding economic policy design.

References

Anand, S., and Joshi, V. R. (1979), 'Domestic distortions, income distribution and the theory of optimum subsidy', *Economic Journal*.

Bhagwati, J. N. (1964), 'The pure theory of international trade: A survey', *Economic Journal*, **74**.

—— (1971), 'The generalised theory of distortions and welfare', in J. N. Bhagwati and others, eds., *Trade, balance of payments and growth* (North-Holland: Amsterdam).

—— (1982), 'Directly unproductive profit-seeking (DUP) activities: A welfare-theoretic synthesis and generalisation', *Journal of Political Economy*, **90**.

—— and Srinivasan, T. N. (1980), 'Revenue-seeking: A generalisation of the theory of tariffs', *Journal of Political Economy*, **88**.

Brander, J. (1981), 'Intra-industry trade in identical commodities', *Journal of International Economics*, **11**.

Buchanan, J. M., Tollison, R. D., and Tullock, G. (1980), *Towards a theory of the rent-seeking society* (Texas A&M University Press: College Station).

Chipman, J. S. (1965–66), 'A survey of the theory of international trade', *Econometrica*, **33, 34**.

Collander, D. (1984), *Neoclassical political economy: The analysis of rent-seeking and DUP activities* (Ballinger Publishing Company).

Corden, W. M. (1965), *Recent developments in the theory of international trade*. Special papers in international economics, Princeton University.

—— (1974), *Trade policy and economic welfare* (Clarendon Press: Oxford).

Dasgupta, P. S., and Stiglitz, J. E. (1974), 'Benefit-cost analysis and trade policies', *Journal of Political Economy*, **82**, 1–33.

Diamond, P. A., and Mirrlees, J. A. (1971), 'Optimal taxation and public production', *American Economic Review*, **61**, Mar. and June.

Dixit, A. K., and Norman, V. D. (1980), *Theory of International Trade* (Cambridge University Press: Cambridge).

Johnson, H. G. (1970), 'A new view of the infant-industry argument', in I. A. MacDougall and R. H. Snape, eds., *Studies in International Economics:* Monash Conference Papers (North-Holland: Amsterdam).

Jones, R. W. (1974), 'The small country in a multi-commodity world', *Australian Economic Papers*, 13.

Koopmans, T. S. (1957), *Three essays in the state of economic science*, McGraw Hill.

Krueger, A. O. (1974), 'The political economy of the rent-seeking society', *American Economic Review*, **64**.

—— (1977), *Growth, distortions and patterns of trade among many countries*, Princeton Studies in International Finance 40.

Krugman, P. (1984), 'Import protection as export promotion', in H. Kierzkowski (ed.) *Monopolistic competition and international trade*, Oxford University Press.

Kuhn, T. S. (1962), *The structure of scientific revolutions*, Chicago.

Leontief, W. W. (1954), 'Domestic production and foreign trade: the American capital position re-examined', *Economica Internazionale*, 7, Feb.

Lipsey. R. G., and Lancaster, K. (1956), 'The general theory of the second-best', *Review of Economic Studies*, **24**.

Michaely, M. (1977), *Theory of Commercial Policy*, Phillip Alan: Oxford.

Vernon, R. (1966), 'International investment and international trade in the product cycle', *Quarterly Journal of Economics*, **80**.

What's new about the new economic geography?

PAUL KRUGMAN

Massachusetts Institute of Technology

I. Introduction

The study of spatial economics—of the location of production—has a long if somewhat thin history. Von Thünen's (1826) analysis of land rent and use around an isolated city was roughly contemporaneous with Ricardo's statement of comparative advantage; the location analysis of Weber (1909), the central-place theory of Christaller (1933) and Lösch (1940), the regional science of Isard (1956), and the urban systems theory of Henderson (1974) are all old and well-established ideas.

None the less, the simple model developed in Krugman (1991) is widely regarded as having given birth to something called the 'new economic geography', and has certainly stimulated the emergence of a new wave of theorizing and (to a lesser extent) empirical work. This approach inevitably has much in common with older approaches. Nevertheless, it also has a number of distinctive features that do qualify as a new departure. The purpose of this article is to review briefly the distinctive aspects of the 'new economic geography' as a theoretical construct, describe the main lines of work within the genre, and assess its contribution to economic theory.

First published in *Oxford Review of Economic Policy*, vol. 14, no. 2 (1998).

II. The new economic geography: distinctive aspects

1. Modelling strategy

Many economic activities are markedly concentrated geographically. Yet we do not all live in one big city, nor does the world economy concentrate production of each good in a single location. Obviously there is a tug of war between forces that tend to promote geographical concentration and those that tend to oppose it—between 'centripetal' and 'centrifugal' forces.

What are these forces? We may represent them in terms of a menu, of the type shown in Table 13.1. The menu should not be viewed as comprehensive; it is a selection of *some* forces that may be important in practice. It shows two columns: one of centripetal forces, one of centrifugal forces.

The centripetal forces listed on the left side of Table 13.1 are the three classic Marshallian sources of external economies. A large local market creates both 'backward linkages'—sites with good access to large markets are preferred locations for the production of goods subject to economies of scale—and 'forward linkages'—a large local market supports the local production of intermediate goods, lowering costs for downstream producers. An industrial concentration supports a thick local labour market, especially for spe-

Table 13.1. Forces affecting geographical concentration

Centripetal forces	Centrifugal forces
Market-size effects (linkages)	Immobile factors
Thick labour markets	Land rents
Pure external economies	Pure external diseconomies

cialized skills, so that employees find it easier to find employers and vice versa. And a local concentration of economic activity may create more or less pure external economies via information spillovers. (In Marshall's words: 'The mysteries of the trade become no mystery, but are, as it were, in the air.')

The centrifugal forces listed on the right-hand side of the table are a bit less standard, but represent a useful breakdown. Immobile factors—certainly land and natural resources, and, in an international context, people as well—militate against concentration of production, both from the supply side (some production must go to where the workers are) and from the demand side (dispersed factors create a dispersed market, and some production will have an incentive to locate close to the consumers). Concentrations of economic activity generate increased demand for local land, driving up land rents and thereby providing a disincentive for further concentration. And concentrations of activity can generate more or less pure external diseconomies such as congestion.

In the real world not only agglomeration in general, but any particular example of agglomeration, typically reflects *all* items on the menu. Why is the financial services industry concentrated in London? Partly because the sheer size of London itself makes it an attractive place to do business, and the concentration of the financial industry itself means that many clients and many ancillary services are located there; but a thick market for special skills, such as securities lawyers, and the general importance of being in the midst of the buzz are also important. Why doesn't all financial business concentrate in London? Partly because many clients are *not* there, partly because renting office space in London is expensive, and partly because dealing with the city's traffic, crime, etc. is such a nuisance.

To conduct analytical work on economic geography, however, it is necessary to cut through the complexities of the real world and focus on a more limited set of forces. In fact, the natural thing is to pick one from the first column and one from the second: to focus on the tension between just one centripetal and one centrifugal force. One way to summarize the distinctive character of the 'new economic geography' is

in terms of its choice, namely the first item in each column: linkages as the force for concentration, immobile resources creating the tension necessary to keep the model interesting.

These choices are dictated less by empirical judgement than by two strategic modelling considerations. First, it is desirable to put some distance between the assumptions and the conclusions—to avoid something that looks too much like the assertion that agglomeration takes place because of agglomeration economies. This is especially true because much of the analysis we will want to undertake involves asking how a changing economic environment alters economic geography. This will be an ill-defined task if the forces producing that geography are inside a black box labelled 'external effects'. So the pure external economies and diseconomies are put on one side, in favour of forces that are more amenable to analysis.

Second, if location is the issue, it is helpful to be able to deal with models in which distance enters in a natural way. Linkage effects, which are mediated by transportation costs, are naturally tied to distance; so is access to immobile factors. On the other hand, thickness of the labour market, while it must have something to do with distance, does not lend itself quite so easily to being placed in a spatial setting. And land rents as a centrifugal force turn out to pose a tricky conceptual issue: why don't we simply get an immense conurbation, in which the suburbs of each city blend into that of the next? (I sometimes refer to this as the 'infinite Los Angeles problem'.)

The central thrust of the 'new economic geography' work to date, in short, has been driven by considerations of modelling strategy toward an approach that concentrates on the role of market-size effects in generating linkages that foster geographical concentration, on one side, and the opposing force of immobile factors working against such concentration on the other.

2. Modelling principles

If one had to define the philosophical difference between the 'new' economic geography and the location theory that preceded it, it would be this: the new literature insists on models that are *general equilibrium*, and in which spatial structure emerges from *invisible-hand* processes. Both of these aspects need some discussion.

First, most traditional analysis in location theory is partial equilibrium, or not even that. Weber (1909) framed the problem of location in terms of an individual producer who took not only the locations of other producers but all prices (including his own) as given. Subsequent work has enlarged on this, notably by letting prices be endogenous, and by considering strategic interaction among location decisions of different firms. But typically the geographical distribution of demand, the location of input sources outside the industry in question, and so forth were taken as given. And adding-up constraints for the economy as a whole tended to be ignored. By contrast, the new economic geography consists of full general-equilibrium models, in which budget constraints on both money and resources are carefully specified and honoured; the geographical distributions of population, demand, and supply are endogenous, and it is, indeed, the two-way feedback between location decisions by individual agents and these distributions that is the main source of interesting stories.

Second, some of the most influential strains of thought in location theory—especially the central place theory of Christaller (1933) and Lösch (1940)—appear to be describing planning solutions rather than market outcomes. Or at least they fail to explain how the spatial structures they describe would be either created or maintained by the actions of self-interested individuals. Again by contrast, the new economic geography is all about what spatial equilibria might exist—and perhaps emerge through a dynamic process—when individuals are choosing locations to maximize their welfare given what other individuals are doing.

Of course, the failure of traditional location theory to be based on internally consistent maximization-and-equilibrium models was not the result of a moral failing on the part of the theorists; most location theorists have understood quite well that they were engaged in some kind of partial exercise. What makes it possible for the newer models to do something different is the development of a useful menu of modelling tricks.

3. Modelling tricks

The idea that there may be a circular process, in which individual producers choose locations with good access to markets and suppliers, but in which the decision of each individual producer to choose a location improves the market and/or supply access of other producers in that location, is hardly a new one. Indeed, it was the central theme of well-known (among geographers) studies by Harris (1954) and Pred (1966). Why, then, did this idea not become widely known in economics until the 1990s?

The most likely answer is that underlying all such stories is the implicit assumption that there are substantial economies of scale at the level of the plant. In the absence of such scale economies, producers would have no incentive to concentrate their activity at all: they would simply supply consumers from many local plants. And expansion of a regional market would not predictably lead to any increase in the range of goods produced within that region. Increasing returns, in other words, are central to the story.

The same may be said of spatial economics in general. Almost all of the interesting ideas in location theory rely implicitly or explicitly on the assumption that there are important economies of scale enforcing the geographic concentration of some activities. Thus Weber's (1909) analysis of the location decisions of an individual producer trying to minimize the combined costs of producing and delivering his product assumes that there can be only one production site; Christaller's (1933) suggestion that cities form a hierarchy of central places depends on the assumption that larger cities can support a wider range of activities; Lösch's (1940) famous demonstration that an efficient pattern of central places would imply hexagonal market areas assumes that there are economic activities that can be undertaken only at a limited number of sites. (The main example of a location model that does not rely on some form of scale economies, the land-rent analysis of von Thünen (1826), in effect hides the role of increasing returns by simply assuming the existence of a central city.) But unexhausted economies of scale at the level of the firm necessarily undermine perfect competition.

The key reason for the emergence of the new economic geography is therefore technical: imperfect competition is no longer regarded as impossible to model, and so stories that crucially involve unexhausted scale economies are no longer out of bounds. Indeed, the new interest in geography may be regarded as the fourth (and final?) wave of the increasing returns/imperfect competition revolution that has swept through economics over the past two decades. First came the 'new industrial organization', which created a tool-box of tractable if implausible models of imperfect competition; then the 'new trade theory', which used that tool-box to build models of international trade in the presence of increasing returns; then the 'new growth theory', which did much the same for economic growth. Like these earlier movements, the new economic geography might be best described as a 'genre': a style of economic analysis which tries to explain the spatial structure of the economy using certain technical tricks to produce models in which there are increasing returns and markets are characterized by imperfect competition. These tricks are summarized in Fujita *et al.* (1999) with the slogan 'Dixit–Stiglitz, icebergs, evolution, and the computer'. Let us consider each part of that slogan in turn.

Dixit–Stiglitz

The remarkable model of monopolistic competition developed by Dixit and Stiglitz (1977) has become a workhorse in many areas of economics. In the new economic geography, it has one especially appealing feature: because it assumes a continuum of goods, it lets the modeller respect the integer nature of many location decisions—no fractional plants allowed—yet analyse the model in terms of the behaviour of continuous variables such as the share of manufacturing in a particular region. In effect, Dixit–Stiglitz lets us have our cake and cut it into arbitrarily small pieces, too.

Icebergs

This is a less familiar technical trick. In location theory, transportation costs are of the essence; yet any attempt to develop a general-equilibrium model of economic geography would be substantially complicated by the need to model the transportation as well as the goods-producing sectors. Worse yet, transportation costs can undermine the constant-demand elasticity that is one of the crucial simplifying assumptions of the Dixit–Stiglitz model. Both problems can be sidestepped with an assumption first introduced by Paul Samuelson (1954) in international trade theory: that a fraction of any good shipped simply 'melts away' in transit, so that transport costs are in effect incurred in the good shipped. (In the new geography models, melting is usually assumed to take place at a constant rate per distance covered—e.g. 1 per cent of the cargo melts away per mile.) In terms of modelling convenience, there turns out to be a spectacular synergy between Dixit–Stiglitz market structure and 'iceberg' transport costs: not only can one avoid the need to model an additional industry, but because the transport cost between any two locations is always a constant fraction of the free-on-board price, the constant elasticity of demand is preserved.

Evolution

Interesting stories about economic geography often seem to imply multiple equilibria. Suppose, for exam-

ple, that producers want to locate where other producers choose to locate; this immediately suggests some arbitrariness about where they actually end up. But which equilibrium does the economy select? New economic geography models typically assume an *ad-hoc* process of adjustment in which factors of production move gradually toward locations that offer higher current real returns. This sort of dynamic process was initially proposed apologetically, since it neglects the role of expectations. But it is possible to regard models of geography as games in which actors choose locations rather than strategies—or rather in which locations *are* strategies—in which case one is engaged not in old-fashioned static expectations analysis but rather in state-of-the-art evolutionary game theory! (To middlebrow modellers like myself, it sometimes seems that the main contribution of evolutionary game theory has been to re-legitimize those little arrows we always wanted to draw on our diagrams.)

The computer

Finally, despite the best efforts of the theorist, all but the simplest models of economic geography usually turn out to be a bit beyond the reach of paper-and-pencil analysis. As a result, the genre relies to an unusual extent on numerical examples—on the exploration of models using both static calculations and dynamic simulations.

4. Dynamics of geographical change

Suppose that, for some reason, some economic activity has a slightly larger initial concentration in one location than in another. Will that concentration be self-reinforcing, with a growing disparity between the locations, or will they tend back toward a symmetric state? The answer presumably depends on the relative strength of centripetal and centrifugal forces.

Suppose, on the other hand, that a concentration of economic activity already exists, but that some of that activity for some reason moves elsewhere. Will the activity move back, or will the concentration unravel? The answer to this question similarly depends on the relative strength of centripetal and centrifugal forces.

As these generic questions suggest, models of economic geography will typically exhibit a pattern in which the qualitative behaviour of the model changes abruptly when the quantitative balance of forces passes some critical level. That is, the models are characterized by bifurcations. And bifurcation diagrams are therefore a central analytical tool in this literature.

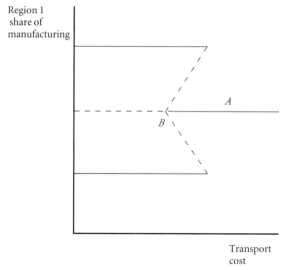

Region 1
share of
manufacturing

A

B

Transport
cost

Figure 13.1.

The typical form of these bifurcations may be illustrated by Figure 13.1, which summarizes the dynamics implied by the model originally introduced in Krugman (1991). That paper was, in effect, an attempt to formalize the story suggested by Harris and Pred. The model envisaged an economy consisting of two symmetric regions with two industries: immobile, perfectly competitive agriculture and mobile, imperfectly competitive (Dixit–Stiglitz) manufacturing. The backward and forward linkages in manufacturing generate centripetal forces; the pull of the immobile farmers the centrifugal force.

In that model, the difference in real wages between regions depends on the allocation of manufacturing between those regions—but the nature of that dependence in turn depends on the parameters of the model, including the level of transport costs. The rough intuition behind this dependence runs as follows. In the case of high transport costs, there is relatively little inter-regional trade; so the wages workers can earn depend mainly on the amount of local competition, and are thus decreasing in the number of other workers in the same region. On the other hand, when transport costs are low, a typical firm sells extensively in both regions; but since it has better access to markets if it is located in the region with the larger population, it can afford to pay higher wages—and the purchasing power of these wages is also higher because workers have better access to consumer goods. So in that case real wages are increasing in a region's population.

Since workers are assumed to move to whichever region offers the higher real wage, in the case of high

transport costs there is a unique equilibrium with workers evenly divided between the regions. In the case of low transport costs there are three equilibria—an unstable equilibrium with workers evenly divided, and two with workers concentrated in either region. And it turns out (in what is essentially an artifact of the particular functional forms) that there is an intermediate range in which there are five equilibria: a locally stable equilibrium with equal division, two unstable flanking equilibria in which there is some manufacturing in one region but more in the other, and finally two in which all manufacturing is concentrated in one region.

These equilibria are summarized in Figure 13.1, which shows how the set of equilibria (as measured by the share of the manufacturing labour force in region 1) depend on transport costs, with solid lines indicating stable and broken lines unstable equilibria. The figure illustrates nicely one of the appealing features of the new economic geography: it easily allows one to work through interesting 'imaginary histories'. Suppose, for example, that we imagine an economy that starts with high transport costs and therefore with an even division of manufacturing between regions, a situation illustrated by the point labelled *A*. Then suppose that transport costs were gradually to fall. When the economy reached *B*, it would begin a cumulative process, in which a growing concentration of manufacturing in one region would lead to a still larger concentration of manufacturing in that region. That is, the economy would spontaneously organize itself into a core–periphery geography.

This example is, of course, only illustrative. None the less, it gives a sense of the typical dynamics of new geography models: multiple equilibria; spontaneous self-organization of the economy into some kind of spatial structure, often one with very uneven distribution of activity among locations with more or less identical natural endowments; and qualitative, often discontinuous change as a result of quantitative changes in underlying parameters.

III. Modelling themes

1. Core and periphery

What is Figure 13.1 a model of? Its most natural interpretation is as a model of the spontaneous organization of a single country into a manufacturing 'core' and an agricultural 'periphery', along the lines of the division of the United States into manufacturing belt and farm belt in the middle of the 19th century, or perhaps the emergence of Italy's industrial north and Mezzogiorno some decades later.

Since its original statement in Krugman (1991), this core–periphery model has become to the new economic geography more or less what, say, the two-by-two-by-two model is in international trade: not so much a model that everyone believes, as the simplest model that illustrates all the main principles of the genre, and therefore the model one teaches first to show how this sort of thing works. This is not to say that the evolution of core–periphery patterns within nations is an unimportant question in itself. On the contrary, it is such a striking feature of modern economic history that one must view it as nearly scandalous that economists have ignored it until now. But it remains true that much, perhaps most, of the usefulness of the core–periphery model is that it opens the door to the study of a much wider range of issues.

2. Regions, cities, and nations

Broadly speaking, post-core–periphery theoretical work in the new economic geography has moved in two directions. One direction has been an effort to build links from the new genre to traditional questions of location theory. The other has been an effort to use the genre as the basis for a new, 'spatial' view of international trade.

If you want to use the new economic geography to bring the grand tradition of location theory into the economic mainstream, you are likely to be unsatisfied with a two-region model, which does not have much spatial content. What you really want is a multi-location model, or even better a model with continuous space. As long as you are willing to rely on numerical examples, however, the new economic geography style of model can easily handle any number of regions, with whatever 'geometry' of transport costs one likes.

An interesting aspect of such multi-regional models is that they provide a justification for a version of the 'market potential' function used by Harris (1954). In this case, market potential can be defined as the real wage manufacturing firms can afford to pay in any given location; it is a function of access to markets, although not quite as simple a function as Harris used. And the dynamics of the economy can, if one likes, be viewed as the co-evolution of two landscapes: a landscape of current distribution of economic activity, which determines a second landscape of market po-

tential, which in turn determines how that first landscape changes over time.

The results of multi-region simulations depend, of course, not only on parameters but on the geometry of the economy. An interesting if artificial special case has turned out to be the 'racetrack' economy: an economy whose regions are laid out around a circle, with transportation possible only along that circle's circumference. In such an economy a uniform distribution of manufacturing is always an equilibrium, referred to in Fujita *et al.* (1999) as the Flat Earth. However, the Flat Earth may be unstable: the circular logic of concentration can cause an even slightly perturbed Flat Earth spontaneously to develop one or more local concentrations of manufacturing. One might expect the resulting structures to have a high degree of arbitrariness; but simulation results show a surprising tendency toward highly regular structures, in which concentrations of economic activity are evenly spaced across the landscape.

The reasons for this regularity, it turns out, can be understood using an approach originally suggested by none other than the mathematician, Alan Turing (1952). Turing was interested in the interacting effects of chemical signals diffusing around a ring of cells, but his approach works equally well for the distribution of manufacturing around a ring of regions. It involves linearizing the model in the vicinity of the Flat Earth, then representing the initial distribution of manufacturing (or whatever) as a Fourier series. It turns out that the components of that Fourier representation are also eigenvectors of the linearized model, so that you can in effect think of the components of that series as growing independently—and of the distribution becoming increasingly dominated by a fluctuation at some 'preferred frequency' that depends on the parameters of the model, but *not* on the initial conditions. And it is this preferred frequency that determines the eventual number of agglomerations that emerge. (This is only one example of the tantalizing affinity that one often finds between the new economic geography and fashionable scientific trends such as 'complexity' theory.)

An alternative way to go beyond two-region modelling is to use the new economic geography to revisit some of the questions of traditional location theory. In a series of papers, Masahisa Fujita and his students have in essence tried to take the German tradition of urban modelling that began with von Thünen and give it a true microeconomic foundation. (In Fujita's models all labour is mobile; thus the location of agriculture as well as manufacturing is endogenous.) In Fujita and Krugman (1995) a version of the original von Thünen model is offered in which the existence of a central city is no longer simply assumed: instead, manufacturing concentrates in the city because of the forward and backward linkages generated by that very concentration. Or, looking at the issue another way, the concentration of economic mass at the city generates a self-validating cusp at that point in the market potential function that determines where manufacturing locates. Agriculture is then spread around that centre, with land rents declining to zero at the agricultural frontier. Such a monocentric equilibrium, however, turns out to be sustainable only if the population is sufficiently small. Fujita and Mori (1996*a*) take the same basic model, but envision a gradually rising population which leads to the periodic emergence of new cities in a 'long, narrow' economy that gradually spreads along a line; the resulting multi-city spatial economy may be regarded as a (one-dimensional) version of Lösch's central place theory. (Nobody has yet managed to produce a model with Lösch's famous hexagonal market areas.) Fujita *et al.* (1997) consider an economy with multiple manufacturing industries, differing in transport costs and/or scale economies; such an economy spontaneously develops a system of central places that finally provides a justification (again in only one dimension) for Christaller's (1933) hierarchical model of central places. Finally, Fujita and Mori (1996*b*) address an issue that, astonishingly, appears never to have been formally modelled before: the reasons why ports and other transportation nodes so often become the sites of major cities. What they show is that such transport nodes generate cusps in the market potential function, even in the absence of a city, and therefore tend to serve as the seeds for city growth.

Moving from the local to the global, Anthony Venables and his students have tried to use new economic geography models as the basis for a new style of international trade model. What is the difference between regions and countries? One answer is that factors of production are far less mobile between countries than between regions of the same country; and in Venables-type models they are normally assumed to be completely immobile. None the less, Venables (1996) shows that a circular process leading to economic differentiation between nations can still result if there are intermediate goods produced with economies of scale and subject to transport costs: in that case a country with a large manufacturing sector offers a large market for intermediates; this leads to a concentration of intermediate production in that country, which gives it a cost advantage in downstream production, which further reinforces its advantage, and so on. In Krugman and Venables (1995) this story is used as the basis for a 'history of the world', in which gradually declining transport costs lead first to the spontaneous differentiation of the world into a high-wage industrial 'core' and a low-wage agricultural 'periphery', then to a later convergence of wages as the periphery industrializes. Puga and Venables (1997) offer an alternative version of this story in which the driving force is the growing size of the market rather than growing economic integration. And Krugman and Venables (1997) use the 'racetrack' geometry to model global international trade and specialization in a world in which borders are irrelevant, and in which even economic regions are left unspecified; none the less, the world spontaneously organizes itself into manufacturing zones surrounded by agricultural hinterlands.

Most recently, Baldwin and Forslid (1996) have developed an alternative version of geography and trade analysis, this time relying on tools borrowed from the endogenous growth literature. In these models the circular process involves not the movement of factors but their accumulation: countries with large markets invest more, which further enlarges those markets.

It is also possible to mix trade and urban economics using the new genre. Krugman and Livas (1996), for example, develop a model suggested by the relative decline of Mexico City as Mexico has opened itself to trade; the basic idea is that the importance of access to domestic consumers and suppliers, which was crucial as long as Mexico pursued a policy of inward-looking industrialization, has become much less relevant now that it exports more of its output, and imports more of its intermediate goods.

As this partial survey of the theory indicates, the new economic geography has opened the door for analytical discussion of interesting and important issues that were previously pretty much ignored by economists. That in itself is something of an achievement. Moreover, partly because of the novelty, partly because of the inherent sexiness of the stories—geography models naturally produce multiple equilibria, dramatically 'catastrophic' changes in outcomes from small changes in parameters, large effects from small differences in initial conditions, and spontaneous emergence of unexpected order from randomness—these models are a lot of fun to work with.

But are they really relevant?

IV. Empirical work

It has been an unfortunate feature of much of the 'new' theorizing since the 1970s that it has failed to lead to much validating empirical work. The new industrial organization has been notoriously better at creating interesting models than at generating empirical predictions; the new growth theory gave rise to a massive industry of cross-country growth regressions, but with few exceptions these regressions have neither been closely tied to the theory nor provided clear evidence in its support. Under the combined influence of the new growth and new geography movements, there has been a parallel effort to extract insight from cross-sectional regressions on the growth of metropolitan areas; with only a few exceptions like Ades and Glaser (1995), however, these studies have similarly failed to offer much direct testing of the specifics of the models.

Perhaps the closest thing to a direct test of the models has been the recent work of Davis and Weinstein (1996, 1997 a,b), who have used international and inter-regional production and consumption data to test for the 'home market effect': the prediction, made by the underlying models of new geography, that a larger demand for the products of an industry in any given region will lead, other things being the same, to a more than one-for-one increase in the regional production of that industry. (Their results are generally negative for international comparisons, but generally positive at the regional level.)

It would not be surprising if it turns out that the market-size effects emphasized by the current generation of new-geography models are a less important source of agglomeration, at least at the level of urban areas, than other kinds of external economies. It is, for example, a well-documented empirical regularity that both plants and firms in large cities tend to be *smaller* than those in small cities (see, for example, Hoover and Vernon, 1959); this suggests that big cities may be sustained by increasing returns that are due to thick labour markets, or to localized knowledge spillovers, rather than those that emerge from the interaction of transport costs and scale economies at the plant level. However, serious empirical work—which will probably require detailed micro studies of particular industries—still remains to be carried out.

Eventually, one might hope to develop 'computable geographical equilibrium' models, which can be used to predict the effects of policy changes, technological shocks, etc. on the economy's spatial structure in the same way that computable general equilibrium models are currently used to predict the effects of changes in taxes and trade policy on the economy's industrial structure. However, preliminary efforts in this direction by several researchers, myself included, have found that such models are not at all easy to calibrate to actual data; in general, the tendency toward agglomeration is stronger in the models than it seems to be in the real economy!

At this point, then, the new economic geography—like its sister genre the new growth theory—has been more successful at raising questions than at answering them, better at creating a language with which to discuss issues than at creating the tools to resolve those discussions.

V. The new economic geography and economic theory

Even the most recent edition of Mark Blaug's *Economic Theory in Retrospect* (1997) speaks of a 'curious disdain of location theory on the part of mainstream economics', and asserts that 'this neglect largely continues to this day'. Blaug is a bit behind the times, and is surely wrong in supposing that the main reason for historical neglect lies in the accident that von Thünen wrote in German. 'Disdain' for location theory surely has mainly to do with the more fundamental issue of market structure—and the not incidental point that too much of the classical tradition in that field seemed not to understand that increasing returns and perfect competition do not mix. Still, Blaug's comments serve to indicate the remarkable extent to which an economic subject of considerable *prima facie* importance has been marginalized.

The most obvious contribution of the new economic geography, then, is that it has helped to end that marginalization. The characteristic modelling tricks of the genre do not represent a general solution to the market structure problems that have historically prevented economists from saying much about spatial structure, but they provide *a* solution—and thus make spatial structure an issue safe for mainstream economic respectability. Since economic geography clearly is important in the real world, this in itself justifies the genre—even if empirical research may eventually lead us to a somewhat different emphasis than that of the currently most popular theoretical models.

In addition, however, one might argue that the new economic geography has some broader implications,

implications about how economic theory as a whole is conducted.

The first of these involves increasing returns. It has been a long time since economic theorizing was restricted to constant-returns settings; increasing returns in one form or another are central to modern theory in industrial organization, international trade, and economic growth. However, in each of these cases it is still possible for sceptics to question the importance of increasing returns to the relevant issues: for example, while Romer (1986) may have created a great deal of excitement with his suggestion that increasing returns and growth are intimately linked, constant-returns Solow-type models remain the workhorses of the field. In the case of geography, however, it is impossible even to discuss the important phenomena sensibly without assigning a key role to increasing returns (which is why, as Blaug noted, for the past century and a half most economists have shown a surprising ability *not* to discuss anything involving space or location). By making geography a field that is safe for mainstream economists, then, we also firmly nail down the place of increasing returns in that mainstream.

The second implication is a related one: geography turns out to be perhaps the most naturally 'non-linear' area of economics. Over the decades a series of critics of economics have argued that the field takes too little account of a set of interrelated possibilities, such as the existence of cumulative processes of change involving 'circular causation', the persistent effects of historical accident via 'path dependence', the occasional emergence of discontinuous change (maybe even 'punctuated equilibrium'), and so on. And from time to time mainstream economists have attempted to make allowance for all these exotic possibilities. For the most part, however, such efforts have been forced and relatively unconvincing. In the new economic geography, however, such non-linear phenomena emerge absolutely naturally from the most basic models (indeed, most of them are on view in Figure 13.1). And they have plausible, if not rigorously proven, empirical relevance. So the new economic geography, in addition to legitimizing the specific issue of location, may help to make economic theory in general a more friendly place for ideas that are exciting but have lacked a natural home in the field.

In the end, of course, while the achievements of new economic geography to date certainly justify the work involved, a theory must survive or be discarded based on its empirical relevance. So empirical and quantitative work is clearly the next geographical frontier.

References

Ades, A., and Glaser, E. (1995), 'Trade and Circuses: Explaining Urban Giants', *Quarterly Journal of Economics*, 110, 195–227.

Baldwin, R., and Forslid, R. (1996), 'Trade Liberalization and Endogenous Growth: A q-Theory Approach', Centre for Economic Policy Research, Discussion Paper 1397.

Blaug, M. (1997), *Economic Theory in Retrospect*, 5th edn, Cambridge, New York, and Melbourne, Cambridge University Press.

Christaller, W. (1933), *Central Places in Southern Germany*, Jena, Fischer.

Davis, D. R., and Weinstein, D. E. (1996), 'Does Economic Geography Matter for International Specialization?', NBER Working Paper No. 5706, August.

——, and ——(1997a), 'Increasing Returns and International Trade: An Empirical Confirmation', mimeo, Harvard University, October.

——, and ——(1997b), 'Empirical Testing of Economic Geography: Evidence from Regional Data', mimeo, Harvard University.

Dixit, A., and Stiglitz, J. (1977), 'Monopolistic Competition and Optimum Product Diversity', *American Economic Review*, 67, 297–308.

Fujita, M., and Krugman, P. (1995), 'When is the Economy Monocentric: Von Thünen and Christaller Unified', *Regional Studies and Urban Economics*, 25, 505–28.

—— Mori, T. (1996a), 'Structural Stability and Evolution of Urban Systems', *Regional Science and Urban Economics*.

——, and ——(1996b), 'The Role of Ports in the Making of Major Cities: Self-agglomeration and Hub-effect', *Journal of Development Economics*, 49, 93–120.

—— Krugman, P., and Venables, A. J. (1999), *The Spatial Economy; Cities, Regions, and International Trade*, Cambridge, MA, MIT Press.

—— Mori, T., and Krugman, P. (1997), 'On the Evolution of Hierarchical Urban Systems', mimeo, Kyoto.

Harris, C. D. (1954), 'The Market as a Factor in the Localization of Production', *Annals of the Association of American Geographers*, 44, 315–48.

Henderson, J. V. (1974), 'The Sizes and Types of Cities', *American Economic Review*, 64(4), 640–56.

Hoover, E., and Vernon, R. (1959), *Anatomy of a Metropolis*, Cambridge, MA, Harvard.

Isard, W. (1956), *Location and Space-economy*, Cambridge, MA, MIT Press.

Krugman, P. (1991), 'Increasing Returns and Economic Geography', *Journal of Political Economy*, 99, 483–99.

—— Livas Elizondo, R. (1996), 'Trade Policy and the Third World Metropolis', *Journal of Development Economics*, 49, 137–50.

—— Venables, A. J. (1995), 'Globalization and the Inequality of Nations', *Quarterly Journal of Economics*, 110(4), 857–80.

——, and ——(1997), 'The Seamless World: A Spatial Model of International Specialization and Trade', mimeo, MIT.

Lösch, A. (1940), *The Economics of Location*, Jena, Fischer.

Pred, A. R. (1966), *The Spatial Dynamics of US Urban-industrial Growth, 1800–1914*, Cambridge, MA, MIT Press.

Puga, D., and Venables, A. J. (1997), 'The Spread of Industry: Spatial Agglomeration in Economic Development', CEPR Working Paper No. 1354.

Romer, P. M. (1986), 'Increasing Returns and Long-run Growth', *Journal of Political Economy*, **94**(5), 1002–37.

Samuelson, P. (1954), 'The Transfer Problem and Transport Costs', *The Economic Journal*, **64**, 264–89.

von Thünen, J. (1826), *The Isolated State*, English edn, London, Pergamon Press.

Turing, A. (1952), 'The Chemical Basis of Morphogenesis', *Philosophical Transactions of the Royal Society of London*, **237**(37).

Venables, A. J. (1996), 'Equilibrium Locations of Vertically Linked Industries', *International Economic Review*, **37**, 341–59.

Weber, A. (1909), *Theory of the Location of Industries*, Chicago, IL, University of Chicago Press.

PART VI

EDUCATION AND TRAINING

14

The failure of training in Britain: analysis and prescription

DAVID FINEGOLD

Pembroke College, Oxford

DAVID SOSKICE[1]

Wissenschaftszentrum, Berlin

I. Introduction

In the last decade, education and training (ET) reform has become a major issue in many of the world's industrial powers. One theme which runs throughout these reform initiatives is the need to adapt ET systems to the changing economic environment. These changes include: the increasing integration of world markets, the shift in mass manufacturing towards newly developed nations and the rapid development of new technologies, most notably information technologies. Education and training are seen to play a crucial role in restoring or maintaining international competitiveness, both on the macro-level by easing the transition of the work force into new industries, and at the micro-level, where firms producing high quality, specialized goods and services require a well-qualified workforce capable of rapid adjustment in the work process and continual product innovation.

This paper will highlight the need for policy-makers and academics to take account of the two-way nature of the relationship between ET and the economy. We will argue that Britain's failure to educate and train

its workforce to the same levels as its international competitors has been both a product and a cause of the nation's poor relative economic performance: a product, because the ET system evolved to meet the needs of the world's first industrialized economy, whose large, mass-production manufacturing sector required only a small number of skilled workers and university graduates; and a cause, because the absence of a well educated and trained workforce has made it difficult for industry to respond to new economic conditions.

The best way to visualize this argument is to see Britain as trapped in a low-skills equilibrium, in which the majority of enterprises staffed by poorly trained managers and workers produce low-quality goods and services.[2] The term 'equilibrium' is used to connote a self-reinforcing network of societal and state institutions which interact to stifle the demand for improvements in skill levels. This set of political-economic institutions will be shown to include: the organization of industry, firms and the work process, the industrial relations system, financial markets, the state and political structure, as well as the operation of the ET system. A change in any one of these factors without corresponding shifts in the other institutional variables may result in only small long-term shifts in the equilibrium position. For example, a company which de-

First published in *Oxford Review of Economic Policy*, vol. 4, no. 3 (1988). The postscript to this chapter introduces material from David Finegold's article in *Oxford Review of Economic Policy*, vol. 15, no. 1 (1999).

[1] The authors would like to thank Kay Andrews, Geoffrey Garrett, Ken Mayhew, Derek Morris, John Muellbauer and Len Schoppa for helpful comments; and to acknowledge intellectual indebtedness to Chris Hayes and Prof. S. Prais. Research on comparative aspects of training was financed in part by a grant to Soskice from the ESRC Corporatist and Accountability Research Programme.

[2] 'Equilibrium' is not meant to imply that all British firms produce low-quality products or services, or that all individuals are poorly educated and trained. A number of companies (often foreign-owned multinationals) have succeeded in recruiting the educational élite and offering good training programmes.

cides to recruit better-educated workers and then invest more funds in training them will not realize the full potential of that investment if it does not make parallel changes in style and quality of management, work design, promotion structures and the way it implements new technologies.[3] The same logic applies on a national scale to a state which invests in improving its ET system, while ignoring the surrounding industrial structure.

The argument is organized as follows: section two uses international statistical comparisons to show that Britain's ET system turns out less-qualified individuals than its major competitors and that this relative ET failure has contributed to Britain's poor economic record. Section three explores the historical reasons for Britain's ET problem and analyses the institutional constraints which have prevented the state from reforming ET. Section four argues that the economic crisis of the 1970s and early 1980s and the centralization of ET power undertaken by the Thatcher Administration increased the possibility of restructuring ET, but that the Conservative Government's ET reforms will not significantly improve Britain's relative ET and economic performance. The fifth section proposes an alternative set of ET and related policies which could help Britain to break out of the low-skill equilibrium.

II. International comparisons

1. Britain's failure to train

Comparative education and training statistics are even less reliable than cross-national studies in economics; there are few generally agreed statistical categories, wide variations in the quality of ET provision and qualifications and a notable lack of data on training within companies. Despite these caveats, there is a consensus in the growing body of comparative ET research that Britain provides significantly poorer ET for its workforce than its major international competitors. Our focus will be on differences in ET provision for the majority of the population, concentrating in particular on the normal ET routes for skilled and semiskilled workers. This need not be technical courses, but may—as in Japan or the US—constitute a long

course of general education followed by company-based training.

The baseline comparison for ET effectiveness begins with how students in different countries perform during compulsory schooling. Prais and Wagner (1983) compared mathematics test results of West German and English secondary schools and found that the level of attainment of the lower half of German pupils was higher than the average level of attainment in England, while Lynn (1988, p. 6) reviewed thirteen-year-olds' scores on international mathematics achievement tests from the early 1980s and found that 'approximately 79 per cent of Japanese children obtained a higher score than the average English child'. The results are equally disturbing in the sciences, where English fourteen year-olds scored lower than their peers in all seventeen countries in a recent study (Postlethwaite, 1988).

This education shortfall is compounded by the fact that England is the only one of the world's major industrial nations in which a majority of students leave full-time education or training at the age of sixteen. The contrast is particularly striking with the US, Canada, Sweden and Japan, where more than 85 per cent of sixteen year-olds remain in full-time education. In Germany, Austria and Switzerland, similar proportions are either in full-time education or in highly structured three or four-year apprenticeships. Britain has done little to improve its relative position. It was, for example, the only member of the OECD to experience a decline in the participation rate of the sixteen–nineteen age group in the latter half of the 1970s. (OECD, 1985, p. 17) Although staying-on rates have improved in the 1980s—due to falling rolls and falling job prospects—Britain's relative position in the OECD rankings has not.

The combination of poor performance during the compulsory schooling years and a high percentage of students leaving school at sixteen has meant that the average English worker enters employment with a relatively low level of qualifications.

Workers' lack of initial qualifications is not compensated for by increased employer-based training; on the contrary, British firms offer a lower quality and quantity of training than their counterparts on the Continent. A joint MSC/NEDO study (1984, p. 90) found that employers in Germany were spending approximately three times more on training than their British rivals, while Steedman's analysis (1986) of comparable construction firms in France and Britain revealed that French workers' training was more extensive and less firm-specific. Overall, British firms have been estimated to be devoting 0.15 per cent of turnover to training compared with 1–2 per cent in Japan, France and West Germany (Anderson, 1987, p. 69). And, as we will show in section IV, neither individuals nor the Government have compensated for employers' lack of investment in adult training.

2. Why train? The link between ET and economic performance

Britain's relative failure to educate and train its workforce has contributed to its poor economic growth record in the postwar period. While it is difficult to demonstrate this relationship empirically, given the numerous other factors which affect labour productivity, no one is likely to dispute the claim that ET provision can improve economic performance in extreme cases, i.e. a certified engineer will be more productive working with a complex piece of industrial machinery than an unskilled employee. Our concern, however, is whether marginal differences in the quality and quantity of ET are related to performance. We will divide the evidence on this relationship in two parts: first, that the short-term expansion of British industry has been hindered by the failure of the ET system to produce sufficient quantities of skilled labour; and second, that the ability of the British economy and individual firms to adapt to the longer-term shifts in international competition has been impeded by the dearth of qualified manpower.

A survey of the literature reveals that skill shortages in key sectors such as engineering and information technology have been a recurring problem for UK industry, even during times of high unemployment. The Donovan Commission (1968, p. 92) maintained that 'lack of skilled labour has constantly applied a brake to our economic expansion since the war', a decade later, a NEDO study (1978, p. 2) found that 68 per cent of mechanical engineering companies reported that output was restricted by an absence of qualified workers. The problem remains acute, as the MSC's first *Skills Monitoring Report* (May, 1986, p. 1) stated: 'Shortages of professional engineers have continued to grow and there are indications that such shortages will remain for some time, particularly of engineers with electronics and other IT skills.'

The shortages are not confined to manufacturing. Public sector professions, i.e. teaching, nursing and social work, which rely heavily on recruiting from the limited group of young people with at least five O-levels, are facing a skilled (wo)manpower crisis as the number of school-leavers declines by 25 per cent between 1985 and 1995. In the case of maths and science teachers, the shortages tend to be self-perpetuating, as the absence of qualified specialists makes it harder to attract the next generation of students into these fields (Gow, 1988, p. 4; Keep, 1987, p. 12).

The main argument of this paper, however, is that the evidence of skill shortages both understates and oversimplifies the consequences Britain's ET failure has on its economic performance. Skill shortages reflect the unsatisfied demand for trained individuals within the limits of existing industrial organization, but they say nothing about the negative effect poor ET may have on how efficiently enterprises organize work or their ability to restructure. Indeed, there is a growing recognition among industry leaders and the major accounting firms that their traditional method of calculating firms' costs, particularly labour costs, fails to quantify the less tangible benefits of training, such as better product quality and increased customer satisfaction (*Business Week*, 1988, p. 49).

There are, however, a number of recent studies which show the strong positive correlation between industry productivity and skill levels. Daly (1984, pp. 41–2) compared several US and UK manufacturing industries and found that a shift of 1 per cent of the labour force from the unskilled to the skilled category raised productivity by about 2 per cent, concluding that British firms suffered because 'they lacked a large intermediate group with either educational or vocational qualifications'. The specific ways in which training can harm firm performance were spelled out in a comparison of West German and British manufacturing plants (Worswick, 1985, p. 91): 'Because of their relative deficiency in shop-floor skills, equivalent British plants had to carry more overhead labour in the form of quality controllers, production planners . . . the comparative shortage of maintenance skills in British plants might be associated with longer equipment downtime and hence lower capital productivity.'

Likewise, employee productivity levels in the French construction industry were found to be one-third higher than in Britain and the main explanation was the greater breadth and quality of French training provision (Steedman, 1986).

While these studies have all centred on relatively comparable companies producing similar goods and services, a high level of ET is also a crucial element in enabling firms to reorganize the work process in pursuit of new product markets, what Reich has called 'flexible-system' production strategies (Reich, 1983, pp. 135–6). 'Flexible-system' companies are geared to respond rapidly to change, with non-hierarchical management structures, few job demarcations and an emphasis on teamwork and maintaining product quality. They can be located in new industries, i.e. biotechnology, fibre optics, or market niches within old industries, such as speciality steels and custom machine tools.

A number of recent studies have highlighted the role of training in 'flexible-system' production: in Japanese firms, Shirai (1983, p. 46) found that employees in 'small, relatively independent work groups . . . grasped the total production process, thus making them more adaptable when jobs have to be redesigned'. Streeck (1985) took the analysis one step further in his study of the European car industry, arguing that the high-quality training programmes of German automakers have acted as a driving force behind product innovation, as firms have developed more sophisticated models to better utilize the talents of their employees. Even in relatively low-tech industries, such as kitchen manufacturing, German companies are, according to Steedman and Wagner (1987), able to offer their customers more customized, better-quality units than their British competitors because of the greater flexibility of their production process—a flexibility that is contingent on workers with a broad skill base.

III. Why has Britain failed to train?

Economists' normal diagnosis of the undersupply of training is that it is a public good or free ride problem: firms do not invest in sufficient training because it is cheaper for them to hire already skilled workers than to train their own and risk them being poached by other companies. While the public good explanation may account for the general tendency to underinvest in training, it does not explain the significant variations between countries' levels of training nor does it address the key public policy question: Given the market's inability to provide enough skilled workers, why hasn't the British Government taken corrective action? To answer this question we will look first at why political parties were long reluctant to intervene in the ET field, and then, at the two major obstacles which policy-makers faced when they did push for ET change: a state apparatus ill-equipped for centrally-led reform and a complex web of institutional constraints which kept Britain in a low-skills equilibrium.

1. Political parties

Through most of the postwar period, the use of ET to improve economic performance failed to emerge on the political agenda, as a consensus formed among the two major parties on the merits of gradually expanding educational provision and leaving training to industry. Underlying this consensus was an economy producing full employment and sustained growth, which covered any deficiencies in the ET system. The broad consensus, however, masked significant differences in the reasons for the parties' positions: For Labour, vocational and technical education were seen as incompatible with the drive for comprehensive schooling, while the Party's heavy dependence on trade unions for financial and electoral support prevented any attempts to infringe on union's control over training within industry (Hall, 1986, p. 85). In the case of the Conservatives, preserving the grammar school track was the main educational priority, while intervening in the training sphere would have violated their belief in the free market (Wiener, 1981, p. 110). An exception to the principle of non-intervention came during the war, when the Coalition Government responded to the manpower crisis by erecting makeshift centres that trained more than 500,000 people. When the war ended, however, these training centres were dismantled.

2. The state structure

One of the main factors which hindered politicians from taking a more active ET role was the weakness of the central bureaucracy in both the education and training fields. On the training side, it was not until the creation of the Manpower Services Commission (MSC) in 1973 (discussed in section four) that the state developed the capacity for implementing an active labour market policy. The staff of the primary economic policy-making body, the Treasury, 'had virtually no familiarity with, or direct concern for, the progress of British industry' (Hall, 1986, p. 62) and none of the other departments (Environment, Trade and Industry, Employment or Education and Science) assumed clear responsibility for overseeing training. There was, for example, a dearth of accurate labour market statistics, which made projections of future skill requirements a virtual impossibility (Reid, 1980, p. 30). Even if the state had come up with the bureaucratic capability to develop a coherent training policy, it lacked the capacity to implement it. Wilensky and Turner (1987, pp. 62–3) compared the state structure and corporatist bargaining arrangements of eight major industrialized nations and ranked the UK last in its ability to execute manpower policy.

While responsibility over education policy in the central state was more clearly defined, resting with the Department of Education and Science (DES), the historical decentralization of power within the educational world made it impossible for the DES to exercise effective control (Howell, 1980; OECD, 1975). Those groups responsible for delivering education, local authorities (Jennings, 1974) and teachers (Dale, 1983), were able to block reforms they opposed, such as vocationalism. The lack of central control was particularly apparent in the further education sector, an area accorded low priority by the DES until the 1970s (Salter and Tapper, 1981).

The main obstacle to ET reform, however, was not the weakness of the central state, which could be remedied given the right external circumstances and sufficient political will, but the interlocking network of societal institutions which will be explored in the following sections, beginning with the structure, or lack of it, for technical and vocational education and entry-level training.

3. The ET system

Technical and work-related subjects have long suffered from a second-class status in relation to academic courses in the British education system (Wiener, 1981). The Norwood Report of 1943 recommended a tri-partite system of secondary education, with technical schools to channel the second-quarter of the ability range into skilled jobs; but while the grammar schools and secondary moderns flourished, the technical track never accommodated more than 4 per cent of the student population. In the mid-1960s two programmes, the Schools Council's 'Project Technology' and the Association for Science Education's 'Applied Science and the Schools', attempted to build an 'alternative road' of engineering and practical courses to rival pure sciences in the secondary curriculum (McCulloch et al. 1985, pp. 139–55). These pilot experiments were short-lived due to: 1) conflicts between and within the relevant interest groups, 2) minimal co-ordination of the initiatives and 3) the absence of clearly defined objectives and strategies for implementing them (ibid., pp. 209–12).

The efforts to boost technical education were marginal to the main educational tranformations of the postwar period: the gradual shift from division at eleven-plus to comprehensives and the raising of the school-leaving age to fifteen, and eventually sixteen in 1972. The education establishment, however, was slow to come up with a relevant curriculum for the more than 85 per cent of each age cohort who were now staying longer in school, but could not qualify for a place in higher education. Success for the new comprehensives continued to be defined by students' performance in academic examinations (O- and A-levels), which were designed for only the top 20 per cent of the ability range (Fenwick, 1976) and allowed many students to drop subjects, such as mathematics and science, at the age of fourteen. The academic/university bias of the secondary system was reinforced by the powerful influence of the public schools, which while catering for less than 6 per cent of students produced 73 per cent of the directors of industrial corporations (Giddens, 1979), as well as a majority of Oxbridge graduates, MPs and top education officials; thus, a large percentage of those charged with formulating ET policy, both for government and firms, had no personal experience of state education, much less technical or vocational courses.

The responsibility for vocational education and training (VET) fell by default to the further education (FE) sector. The 1944 Education Act attempted to provide a statutory basis for this provision, declaring that county colleges should be set up in each LEA to offer compulsory day-release schemes for fifteen–eighteen year-olds in employment. The money was never provided to build these colleges, however, with the result that 'a jungle' of different FE institutions, courses and qualifications developed (Locke and Bloomfield, 1982). There were three main paths through this 'jungle': the academic sixth form, the technical courses certified by independent bodies, such as City & Guilds, BTEC or the RSA, and 'the new sixth form' or 'young stayers on', who remain in full-time education without committing to an A-level or specific training course (MacFarlane Report, 1980). A host of factors curtailed the numbers pursuing the intermediate route: the relatively few careers requiring these qualifications, the lack of maintenance support for FE students and the high status of the academic sixth, which was reinforced by the almost total exclusion of technical students from higher education.

The majority of individuals left education for jobs which offered no formal training. Those who did receive training were almost exclusively in apprenticeships. The shortcomings of many of these old-style training programmes, which trained 240,000 school-leavers in 1964, were well known: age and gender barriers to entry, qualifications based on time-served (up to seven years) rather than a national standard of proficiency and no guarantee of off-the-job training (Page, 1967). The equation of apprenticeships with training also had the effect of stifling training for positions below skilled level and for older employees whose skills had become redundant or needed updating.

In the early 1960s the combination of declining industrial competitiveness, a dramatic expansion in the number of school-leavers and growing evidence of skill shortages and 'poaching' prompted the Government to attempt to reform apprenticeships and other forms of training (Perry, 1976). The route the state chose was one of corporatist compromise and minimal intervention, erecting a network of training boards (ITBs) in the major industries staffed by union, employer and government representatives (Industrial Training Act, 1964). The ITBs' main means of overcoming the free-rider problem was the levy/grant system, which placed a training tax on all the companies within an industry and then distributed the funds to those firms that were training to an acceptable standard, defined by each board (Page, 1970).

The boards created a fairer apportionment of training costs and raised awareness of skill shortages, but they failed to raise substantially the overall training level because they did not challenge the short-term perspective of most companies. The state contributed no new funds to training and each board assessed only its industry's training needs, taking as given the existing firm organization, industrial relations system and management practices and thus perpetuating the low-skill equilibrium. Despite the Engineering ITB's pioneering work in developing new, more flexible training courses, craft apprenticeships remained the main supply of skilled labour until Mrs Thatcher came to power in 1979.

4. Industrial/firm structure

Industry Type.   One of the main reasons that British industry has failed to update its training programmes is the concentration of the country's firms in those product markets which have the lowest skill requirements, goods manufactured with continuous, rather than batch or unit production processes (Reich, 1983). An analysis of international trade in the 1970s by NEDO found that the UK performed better than average in 'standardized, price-sensitive products' and

below average in 'the skill and innovation-intensive products' (Greenhalgh, 1988, p. 15). New and Myers' 1986 study of two hundred and forty large export-oriented plants confirmed that only a minority of these firms had experimented with the most advanced technologies and that management's future plans were focused on traditional, mass-production market segments.

Training has also been adversely effected by the long-term shift in British employment from manufacturing to low-skill, low-quality services. Manufacturing now accounts for less than one-third of British employment and its share of the labour market has been declining. The largest growth in employment is in the part-time service sector where jobs typically require and offer little or no training. The concentration of British service providers on the low-skill end of the labour market was highlighted in a recent study of the tourist industry (Gapper, 1988).

While the type of goods or services which a company produces sets limits on the skills required, it does not determine the necessary level of training. Recent international comparisons of firms in similar product markets (i.e. Maurice *et al.*, 1986; Streeck, 1985) have revealed significant variations in training provision depending on how a company is organized and the way in which this organizational structure shapes the implementation of new technologies. In the retail trade, for instance, 75 per cent of German employees have at least an apprenticeship qualification compared with just two percent in the UK. The brief sections which follow will outline how, in the British case, the many, integrally-related components of firms' organizational structures and practices have combined to discourage training.

Recruitment.   British firms have traditionally provided two routes of entry for young workers: the majority are hired at the end of compulsory schooling, either to begin an apprenticeship or to start a semi- or unskilled job, while a select few are recruited from higher education (HE) for management posts (Crowther Report, 1959). (Nursing is one of the rare careers which has sought students leaving further education (FE) at the age of 18.) As a result, there is little incentive for those unlikely to gain admittance to HE to stay on in school or FE. Indeed, Raffe (1984, Ch. 9) found that Scottish males who opted for post-compulsory education actually had a harder time finding work than their peers who left school at sixteen. Vocational education is perceived as a low status route because it provides little opportunity for career advancement and because managers, who themselves typically enter employment without practical experience or technical training, focus on academic examinations as the best means of assessing the potential of trainees.

Job design and scope.   After joining a company, employees' training will depend upon the array of tasks they are asked to perform. Tipton's study (1985, p. 33) of the British labour market found that 'the bulk of existing jobs are of a routine, undemanding variety' requiring little or no training. The failure to broaden individuals' jobs and skill base, i.e. through job rotation and work teams, has historically been linked to craft unions' insistence on rigid demarcations between jobs, but there is some evidence that these restrictive practices have diminished in the last decade. The decline in union resistance, however, has been counterbalanced by two negative trends for training: subcontracting out skilled maintenance work (Brady, 1984) and using new technologies to deskill work (Streeck, 1985). The latter practice is particularly well documented in the automobile industry, where British firms, unlike their Swedish, Japanese and German rivals, have structured new automated factories to minimize the skill content of production jobs, instead of utilizing the new technology to increase flexibility and expand job definitions (Scarbrough, 1986). Tipton concludes (p. 27): 'the key to improving the quality of training is the design of work and a much needed spur to the movement for the redesign of work . . . may lie in training policies and practice'.

Authority Structure.   In the previous section we used job design to refer to the range of tasks within one level of a firm's job hierarchy (horizontal scope); how that hierarchy is structured—number of levels, location of decision-making power, forms of control—will also affect training provision (vertical scope). *A Challenge to Complacency* (Coopers and Lybrand, 1985, pp. 4–5) discovered that in a majority of the firms surveyed, line managers, rather than top executives, are generally responsible for training decisions, thereby hindering long-term manpower planning. British firms also lack structures, like German work councils, which enable employees to exercise control over their own training.

Career/Wage Structure.   A company's reward system, how wages and promotion are determined, shapes employees' incentives to pursue training. While education levels are crucial in deciding where an employee enters a firm's job structure, these incentives are low after workers have taken a job because pay and career advancement are determined by seniority not skill levels (George and Shorey, 1985). This disincentive is particularly strong for the growing number of workers trapped in the periphery sector of the labour market (Mayhew, 1986), which features part-time or temporary work, low wages and little or no chance for promotion.

Management.   Linking all of the preceding elements of firm organization is the role of management in determining training levels. The poor preparation of British managers, resulting from a dearth of technical HE or management schools and a focus on accounting rather than production, is often cited as a reason for the lack of priority attached to training in Britain. A recent survey of over 2,500 British firms found that less than half made any provision at all for management training (Anderson, 1987, p. 68). In those firms which do train, managers tend to treat training as an operating expense to be pared during economic downturns and fail to incorporate manpower planning into the firm's overall competitive strategy. For managers interested in career advancement, the training department is generally seen as a low-status option (Coopers and Lybrand, 1985, pp. 4–5). And for poorly qualified line managers, training may be perceived as a threat to their authority rather than a means of improving productivity. It is important, however, to distinguish between bad managers, and able ones who are forced into decisions by the institutional structure in which they are operating. We will explore two of the major forces impacting on their decisions, industrial relations and financial markets, in the following sections.

5. Financial markets

The short-term perspective of most British managers is reinforced by the pressure to maximize immediate profits and shareholder value. The historical separation of financial and industrial capital (Hall, 1986, p. 59) has made it harder for British firms to invest in training, with its deferred benefits, than their West German or Japanese competitors, particularly since the City has neglected training in its analysis of companies' performance (Coopers and Lybrand, 1985). Without access to large industry-oriented investment banks, British firms have been forced to finance more investment from retained profits than companies in the other G5 nations (Mayer, 1987).

6. Industrial relations

Just as the operation of financial markets has discouraged training efforts, so too the structure, traditions, and common practices of British industrial relations have undermined attempts to improve the skills of the work force. The problem must be analysed at two levels: a) the inability of the central union and employer organizations to combine with government to form a co-ordinated national training policy; and b) the historical neglect of training in the collective bargaining process.

Employer Organizations.   The strength of the CBI derives from its virtual monopoly status—its members employ a majority of Britain's workers and there is no competing national federation. But while this membership base has given the CBI a role in national training policy formulation, the CBI lacks the sanctions necessary to ensure that employers implement the agreements which it negotiates with the Government. The power lies not in the central federation, nor in industry-wide employers' associations, but in individual firms. The CBI's views on training reflect its lack of control, as Keep (1986, p. 8), a former member of the CBI's Education, Training and Technology Directorate, observes: 'The CBI's stance on training policy . . . was strongly anti-interventionist and centred on a voluntary, market-based approach. Legislation to compel changes in training policy . . . was perceived as constituting an intolerable financial burden on industry.'

This free-market approach, combined with the absence of strong local employer groups, like the West German Chambers of Commerce, has left British industry without an effective mechanism for overcoming the 'poaching' problem. Among the worst offenders are the small and medium-sized firms, poorly represented in the CBI, which lack the resources to provide broad-based training.

Trade Unions.   There are four key, closely connected variables which determine the effectiveness of a central union federation in the training field (Woodall, 1985, p. 26). They are: degree of centralization, financial membership and organization resources, degree of youth organisation and structure and practice of collective bargaining. Woodall compared the TUC with European central union federations and found it weak along all of these axes. Like the CBI, it could exert a limited influence on government policy, but it lacked the means to enforce centrally negotiated initiatives on its members.

The TUC has had to deal with 'the most complex trade union structure in the world', (Clegg, 1972, p. 57) while having little control over its affiliated unions. And whereas the German central union federation, the DGB, claims 12 per cent of its member unions' total receipts, the TUC has received less than 2 per cent and devotes only a small fraction of these resources to training. This inattention to education and training is reflected in unions' lack of involvement in the transition from school to work. Britain's major youth organizations, the National Unions of Students and Youthaid, grew outside the formal union structure and have often criticized the labour movement for failing to address the needs of the nation's school-leavers, particularly the unemployed. The unco-ordinated nature of British collective bargaining, with agreements varying from coverage of whole industries to small portions of a particular factory, and the lack of central input in the negotiations further hinder TUC efforts to improve training provision. The combination of these factors prompted Taylor (1980, p. 91) to observe that 'by the standards of other Western industrialised nations, Britain provides the worst education services of any trade union movement.'

Although we have broken down this analysis into separate sections for conceptual clarity, it is essential to view each element as part of a historically evolved institutional structure which has limited British ET. In the next part we will examine how the economic crisis of the 1970s destabilized this structure, creating the opportunity for the Thatcher Government's ET reforms.

IV. Mrs Thatcher's education and training policies

During the 1970s a confluence of events brought an end to the reluctance of central government to take the lead in ET policy-making. The prolonged recession which followed the 1973 oil shock forced the Labour Government to cut public expenditure, necessitating a re-examination of educational priorities. This reassessment came at a time when the education system was drawing mounting criticism in the popular press and the far Right's 'Black Papers' for allegedly falling standards and unchecked teacher progressivism (CCCS, 1981). The response of the then Prime Minister, Callaghan, was to launch the 'Great Debate' on education in a now famous speech at Ruskin College, Oxford in October 1976, where he called on the ET sector to make a greater contribution towards the nation's economic performance (*TES* 22/10/76, p. 72).

The increase in bipartisan political support for vocational and technical education was matched by a strengthening of the central state's capacity to formulate ET policy. The Manpower Services Commission

Table 14.1. Mrs Thatcher's education and training policies

Phase/Date	Characteristics	Education	Programmes Youth Training	Adult Training
I. Preparation 1979–81	Market orientation Weaken resistance Lack overall strategy	Budget cuts	Apprenticeship collapse	Dismantle ITBs
II. NTI 1982–86	Focus on 14–18s Concern with youth unemployment Enterprise economy Increase central control	TVEI Pilot–National Programme in 4 yrs	YTS/ITeCs NCVQ YOP; 1 yr YTS; 2 yr YTS YTS apprentice route	TOPS/JTS/CP TOPS–new JTS Focus on adult unemployment
III. Expansion 1987–	Education–new priorities Adults–first attempt at coherence	GERBIL/CTCs TVEI extension or extinction?	Weaken MSC Compulsory YTS NCVQ finish in 1991.	Weaken MSC Training for employment 600,000 places; no new money.

(MSC), a tripartite quango funded by the Department of Employment, was established in 1973 to provide the strong central organization needed to co-ordinate training across industrial sectors which was missing from the industrial training board structure. In practice, however, the ITBs were left to themselves, while the MSC concentrated on the immediate problem of growing youth unemployment. The Commission supervised the first substantial injection of government funds into training, beginning with TOPS (Training Opportunities Scheme) and later through YOP (Youth Opportunities Programme). The rapid increase in government spending—the MSC budget rose from £125 million in 1974–5 to £641 million in 1978–9—did little to improve skills, however, since the funds were concentrated on temporary employment, work experience and short-course training measures and the demands for quick action precluded any long-term manpower planning.

Spurred on by its new rival, the MSC, the DES set up the Further Education Unit (FEU) in 1978, which produced a steady stream of reports that helped shift educational opinion in favour of the 'new vocationalism', (i.e. *A Basis for Choice*, 1979). The Department teamed up with the MSC for the first time in 1976 to launch the Unified Vocational Preparation (UVP) scheme for school-leavers entering jobs which previously offered no training. Although this initiative never advanced beyond the early pilot phase, it set a precedent for subsequent reform efforts.

The state structure was in place for the new Thatcher Government to transform the ET system. The first half of this section will outline three distinct phases in the Conservatives' ET reform efforts (see Table 14.1), examining how the Government has avoided many of the pitfalls which plagued past efforts at change, while the latter portion will argue that these reforms, while leading to significant shifts in control over ET, will not raise Britain's relative ET performance.

1. Phase 1: preparation

It is only in retrospect that the first few years of the Thatcher Administration can be seen as an effective continuation of the movement towards greater centralization of ET power. At the time, Government economic policy was dominated by the belief that controlling the money supply and public expenditure were the keys to reducing inflation and restoring competitiveness. Education and training accounted for approximately 15 per cent of the budget and thus needed to be cut if spending was to be curtailed. The cuts included: across the board reductions in education funding, a drop in state subsidies for apprenticeships and the abolition of seventeen of the twenty-four training boards (one new one was created), despite the opposition of the MSC. The financial rationale for the cuts was underpinned by the then strongly held view of the Government that training decisions were better left to market forces.

The net effect of these cuts, coming at the start of a severe recession in which industry was already cutting back on training, was the collapse of the apprenticeship system. The number of engineering craft and technician trainees, for example, declined from 21,000 to 12,000 between 1979 and 1981, while construction apprentice recruitment fell by 53 per cent during the same period (from EITB and CITB in TUC Annual Report, 1981, pp. 434–5). The destruction of old-style apprenticeships, combined with the Government's attacks on trade unions' restrictive practices through industrial relations legislation, meant that when the state eventually chose to reform initial training within companies, there was only minimal resistance from organized labour and employers.

2. Phase II: 'the new training initiative'

By 1981 the deepening recession and the dramatic rise in youth unemployment which it caused compelled the Government to reassess its non-interventionist training stance. While the Conservative's neo-liberal economic philosophy offered no immediate cure for mass unemployment, it was politically essential to make some effort to combat a problem which the polls consistently showed to be the voters' primary concern (Moon and Richardson, 1985, p. 61). This electoral need was highlighted in a Downing Street Policy Unit paper from early 1981:

We all know that there is no prospect of getting unemployment down to acceptable levels within the next few years. (Consequently) we must show that we have some political imagination, that we are willing to salvage something—albeit second-best—from the sheer waste involved. (Riddell, 1985, p. 50.)

What this 'political imagination' produced was the New Training Initiative (NTI) (1981), whose centrepiece, the Youth Training Scheme (YTS), was the first permanent national training programme for Britain's school-leavers. YTS replaced YOP, which had begun as a temporary scheme in 1978 to offer a year's work experience and training to the young unemployed. In just four years, however, YOP had swelled to more than 550,000 places, and as the numbers grew so did the criticism of the programme for its falling job-placement rates and poor quality training. YTS attempted to improve YOP's image by upgrading the training content, 'guaranteeing' a year's placement with at least thirteen weeks off-the-job training to every minimum age school-leaver and most unemployed seventeen year-olds and more than doubling the programme's annual budget, from £400 to £1,000 million.

Despite these improvements, the scheme got off to a difficult start, with a national surplus of close to 100,000 places, as school-leavers proved reluctant to enter the new programme. In response, the MSC implemented a constant stream of YTS reforms: the scheme was lengthened from one to two years, with off-the-job training extended to twenty weeks, all sixteen and seventeen year-olds, not just the unemployed,

were made eligible, some form of qualification was to be made available to each trainee, and monitoring and evaluation were increased by requiring all training providers to attain Approved Training Organisation (ATO) status. While the majority of YTS places continue to offer trainees a broad sampling of basic skills ('foundation training') and socialization into a work environment, some industries, such as construction, engineering and hairdressing, have used the scheme to finance the first two years of modernized apprenticeships.

The other major ET reform originating in this period was the Technical and Vocational Education Initiative (TVEI), launched by the Prime Minister in November 1982. TVEI marked the Thatcher Administration's first attempt to increase the industrial relevance of what is taught in secondary schools, through the development of new forms of teacher training, curriculum organization and assessment for the fourteen–eighteen age group. Under the direction of MSC Chairman David (now Lord) Young, the Initiative grew extremely rapidly, from fourteen local authority pilot projects in 1983 to the start of a nationwide, £1 billion extension just four years later. Lord Young conceived TVEI as a means of fostering Britain's 'enterprise economy', by motivating the vast majority of students who were not progressing to higher education: 'The curriculum in English schools is too academic and leads towards the universities. What I am trying to show is that there is another line of development that is equally respectable and desirable which leads to vocational qualifications . . .' (*Education*, 19 Nov. 1982, p. 386).

This line of development was extended into the FE sector in 1985 with the introduction of the Certificate of Pre-Vocational Education (CPVE), a one-year programme of broad, work-related subjects for students who wished to stay on in full-time education, but were not prepared for A-levels or a specific career path. In 1985 the Government set up a working group to review Britain's increasingly diverse array of vocational qualifications. The De Ville Committee's Report (1986) led to the establishment of the National Council for Vocational Qualifications (NCVQ) which has the task of rationalizing all of the country's training qualifications into five levels, ranging from YTS to engineering professionals, with clear paths of progression between stages and national standards of proficiency. The Council, which is scheduled to complete its review in 1991, will be defining broad guidelines for training qualifications into which the courses of the independent certification bodies (i.e. RSA, BTEC, City and Guilds) can be slotted.

Taken together these initiatives represent a dramatic reversal in the Government's approach to ET. The scope and pace of reform was made possible by the centralization of power in the hands of the MSC, an institution which has proved adept at securing the co-operation required to implement these controversial changes. In the case of YTS, the MSC has thus far retained trade union support, despite protests from over one-third of the TUC's membership that the schemes lead to job substitution and poor-quality training (*TUC Annual Reports*, 1983–86), because the TUC leadership has refused to give up one of its last remaining channels for input into national policy-making.

The MSC has also become a major power in the educational world because it offered the Conservatives a means of bypassing the cumbersome DES bureaucracy (Dale, 1985, p. 50). The Commission was able to convince teachers and local authorities, who had in the past resisted central government's efforts to reform the curriculum, to go along with TVEI through the enticement of generous funding during a period of fiscal austerity and the use of techniques normally associated with the private sector, such as competitive bidding and contractual relationships (Harland, 1987). Its influence over education increased still further in 1985, when it was given control over 25 per cent of non-advanced further education (NAFE) funding, previously controlled by the LEAs. This change has, in effect, meant that the MSC has the power to review all NAFE provision.

3. Phase III: expanding the focus

The constantly changing nature of ET policy under Mrs Thatcher makes it hazardous to predict future developments, but early indications are that education and training reform will continue to accelerate in her third term. The combination of a successful economy (low inflation, high growth and falling unemployment) and a solid electoral majority has enabled the Conservatives to turn their focus toward fundamental social reform. As a result, the narrow concentration of ET policy on the fourteen–eighteen age group appears to be broadening to include both general education (The Great Education Reform Bill (GERBIL), 1987) and adult training (Training for Employment, 1988).

The 1987 Conservative Election Manifesto signalled the emergence of education reform as a major political issue. While GERBIL is primarily an attempt to raise standards by increasing competition and the account-

ability of the educational establishment, a number of its provisions will impact on the vocational education and training (VET) area: the National Curriculum, which will ensure that all students take mathematics and science until they reach sixteen; City Technical Colleges, which may signal the beginning of an alternative secondary school track, funded directly by the DES with substantial contributions from industry; the removal of the larger Colleges of Further Education (CFEs) and Polytechnics from LEA control, freeing them to compete for students and strengthening their ties with employers; and increased industry representation on the new governing body for universities, the UFC (University Funding Council).

At the same time, the Government has begun restructuring adult training provision. Over the previous eight years, the MSC concentrated on reducing youth unemployment, while financing a succession of short-duration training and work experience programmes for the long-term unemployed: TOPS (Training Opportunities Scheme—short courses normally based in CFEs), JTS, and new-JTS (Job Training Scheme—work placement with minimal off-the-job training for eighteen-to-twenty-fours), and the CP (Community Programme—state-funded public work projects). In February 1988 the Government's White Paper, *Training for Employment*, introduced a plan to combine all of these adult initiatives into a new £1.5 billion programme that will provide 600,000 training places, with initial preference given to the eighteen-to-twenty-four age group. To attract the long-run unemployed into the scheme the Government is using both carrot and stick: a training allowance at least £10 above the benefit level, along with increases in claimant advisors and fraud investigators to ensure that all those receiving benefit are actively pursuing work.

The new scheme will be administered by the Training Commission, the heir to the MSC. The Employment Secretary surprised both critics and supporters when he announced that the Government's most effective quango would come to an end in 1988. The new Training Commission lacks the MSC's employment functions, which have been transferred to the DoE, and its governing board structure has been altered to give industry representatives, some now appointed directly rather than by the CBI, effective control. The changes seem to indicate that the Thatcher Government no longer feels the need to consult trade unions and wants to play down the role of the CBI in order to push forward its training reforms.

The Government has also started to devote a limited amount of resources to broadening access to ET for those already in employment. The DES is expanding its PICKUP (Professional, Industrial and Commercial Updating) Programme, which is now spending £12.5 million a year to help colleges, polytechnics and universities tailor their courses more closely to employers' needs. And in 1987, the MSC provided start-up money for the Open College, which along with Open Tech uses open-learning techniques to offer individuals and employers the chance to acquire new skills or update old ones.

4. Problems with Mrs Thatcher's ET policies

While Mrs. Thatcher brought about more radical and rapid changes in the ET system than any British leader in the postwar period, there are a number reasons to doubt whether her reforms will succeed in closing the skills gap which has grown between Britain and its major competitors. Rather than detail the shortcomings of specific programmes, we will focus on two major flaws in the Government's ET policy: the lack of coherence and weakness in the many initiatives designed to change the transition from school to FE or employment (reforms for the fourteen–eighteen age group) and the absence of an adult training strategy and sufficient funding to facilitate industrial restructuring.

The Transition from School to Work.   Oxford's local education authority has coined a new term, 'GONOT'. GONOT is the name of a committee set up to coordinate GCSE, OES, NLI, OCEA and TVEI,[4] just some of the reforms introduced by the Government since 1981 for the fourteen–eighteen age group. The need to create abbreviations for abbreviations is symptomatic of the strains which the Conservatives' scatter-shot approach to ET policy has placed on those charged with implementing the reforms. The case of TVEI provides a clear illustration of the difficulties created by this incoherence.

When TVEI was first announced one of its primary objectives was to improve staying-on rates. This goal has since been de-emphasized, however, because TVEI's sixteen–eighteen phase comes into direct conflict with YTS. Students have a dual incentive to opt for the narrower training option: first, because YTS offers an allowance, while TVEI does not, and second,

because access to skilled jobs is increasingly limited to YTS apprenticeships. The failure of the MSC to coordinate these programmes is evident at all organizational levels, from the national, where the headquarters are based in different cities, to the local, where the coordinators of the two initiatives rarely, if ever, come into contact.

The success of individual TVEI pilot schemes is also threatened by recent national developments. Local TVEI consortia, for example, have built closer ties between schools and the FE sector to rationalize provision at sixteen-plus, a crucial need during a period of falling student numbers. But these consortia are in jeopardy due to GERBIL's proposals for opting out, open enrolment and the removal of the larger Colleges of Further Education (CFEs) from LEA control, which would foster competition rather than co-operation among institutions. Likewise, TVEI's efforts to bridge traditional subject boundaries and the divide between academic and vocational subjects are in danger of being undermined by the proposed national curriculum with its individual subject testing and the failure to include academic examinations (GCSE and A-level) in the National Review of Vocational Qualifications (DeVille Report, 1986, p. 4).

These contradictions stem from divisions within the Conservative Party itself. Dale (1983) identifies five separate factions, industrial trainers, populists, privatizers, old-style Tories and moral educationalists, all exercising an influence on Thatcher's ET policies. Do the Conservatives, for instance, want to spread technical and vocational subjects across the comprehensive curriculum (the TVEI strategy) or resurrect the old tripartite system's technical school track (the City Technical College route)? Another conflict has emerged in the examination sphere, where modular forms of assessment pioneered under TVEI and GCSE, which are already improving student motivation and practical skills (HMI, 1988), have been stifled by Conservative traditionalists, such as the Minister of State at the DES Angela Rumbold, insisting on preserving the narrow, exclusively academic focus of A-levels and university admissions (Gow, 1988, p. 1). The splits within the Party were highlighted in a leaked letter from the Prime Minister's secretary to Kenneth Baker's secretary, indicating Mrs Thatcher's reservations concerning the forms of assessment proposed by the Black Committee to accompany the National Curriculum (Travis, 1988, p. 1).

Emerging from this unco-ordinated series of reforms appears to be a three-tiered, post-compulsory ET system (Ranson, 1985, p. 63) which will not significantly raise the qualifications of those entering the work force: At the top, higher education will continue to be confined to an academic élite, as the White Paper 'Higher Education—Meeting the Challenge' (1987) projects no additional funds for HE in the next decade, despite growing evidence of graduate shortages; the middle rung of technical and vocational courses in full-time FE seems equally unlikely to expand, given that the Government refuses to consider educational maintenance allowances (EMAs) and that the extension funding for TVEI appears inadequate to sustain its early successes (Dale, 1986); the basic training route, then, will remain YTS, a low-cost option which has not succeeded in solving the skills problem (Deakin and Pratten, 1987). As of May 1987, more than half of all YTS providers had failed to meet the quality standards laid down by the MSC (Leadbeater, 1987). And though the quality of training may since have improved, organizations are finding it increasingly difficult to attract school-leavers on to the scheme, as falling rolls lead to increased competition among employers for sixteen year-olds to fill low-skill jobs (Jackson, 1988).

Restructuring/Adult Training.   As we have shown (section II.2), the capacity for continuously updating the skills of the work force is a key factor in the process of industrial restructuring, either at firm or national level. But in the rush to develop new ET initiatives for the fourteen–eighteen sector, the Conservatives have neglected the largest potential pool of trainees: adults in employment. The Government has not secured sufficient extra resources from any of the three basic sources of funding for post-compulsory ET, the state, individuals or companies, to finance a major improvement in British ET performance.

The largest increase in expenditure has come in the state sector, but it is crucial to examine where the money was spent. Although the MSC's budget tripled (to £2.3 billion) during the Conservatives' first two terms, only just over 10 per cent of these funds were spent on adult training, the vast majority on the long-term unemployed. Those courses, like TOPS, which did offer high-quality training geared to the local labour market, have been phased out in favour of the much-criticized JTS and new-JTS, which offer less costly, lower-skill training (Payne, 1988). This emphasis on quantity over quality was continued in the new 'Training for Employment' package, which proposes to expand the number of training places still further without allocating any new resources. Mrs Thatcher's efforts to improve training within companies have been largely confined to a public relations exercise designed to increase 'national awareness' of training needs (*Training for Jobs*, 1984). Former MSC Chair-

man Bryan Nicholson made the Government's position clear: 'The state is responsible for education until an individual reaches sixteen. From sixteen to eighteen, education and training are the joint responsibility of industry and government. But from eighteen on, training should be up to the individual and his employer.' (Press Conference at People and Technology Conference, London, November, 1986.)

The Conservatives, however, have had little success in convincing the private sector to assume its share of responsibility for training. While the MSC has been gradually placing a greater portion of YTS funding on employers, the bulk of the cost is still met by the state. In fact, an NAHE study (1987) revealed that private training organizations were making a profit off the MSC's training grants. The Government may be regretting its decision to do away with the one legislative means of increasing employers' funding for training, as this remark made by Nicholson indicates: 'Those industries who have made little effort to keep the grand promises they made when the majority of ITBs were abolished should not be allowed to shirk forever.' (Clement, 1986, p. 3)

Mrs Thatcher has made somewhat more progress in her attempts to shift the ET burden on to individuals, who can fund their own ET either through direct payments (course fees, living expenses) or by accepting a lower wage in exchange for training. The state has compelled more school-leavers to pay for training by removing sixteen and seventeen year-olds from eligibility for benefits and then setting the trainee allowance at a level well below the old apprenticeship wage. It has also forced individuals staying on in full-time education to make a greater financial contribution to their own maintenance costs through the reduction of student grants, a policy which seems certain to accelerate with the introduction of student loans.

These measures, however, are not matched by policies to encourage adults to invest their time and money towards intermediate or higher-level qualifications. This failure can be traced to three sources: lack of opportunity, capital and motivation. The state's assumption of the full costs of higher education (HE), among the most expensive per pupil in the world, has resulted in a strictly limited supply of places. Those individuals who wish to finance courses below HE level suffer both from limited access to capital and a tax system which, unlike most European countries, offers employees no deductions for training costs (DES, 1988). But the main reason for workers' reluctance to invest in their own training is that the Government has done nothing to alter the basic operation of British firms which, as we saw in section III, are not structured to reward improvements in skill levels.

This underinvestment in ET raises the question: If it is true that training is critical to economic restructuring and that Mrs Thatcher has failed to improve Britain's poor ET record, why has the UK grown faster than all the major industrial nations, except Japan, over the last eight years? Part of the answer lies in the Conservatives' success in creating more efficient low-cost production and services economy. A series of supply-side measures, weakening Wage Councils and employment security legislation, subsidizing the creation of low-wage jobs (the Young Workers Scheme) and attacking trade unions, have improved labour mobility and company profitability. Training programmes, like YTS, have played a pivotal role in this process, providing employers with a cheap means of screening large numbers of low-skilled, but well-socialized young workers (Chapman and Tooze, 1986). The liberalization of financial markets, with the resultant pressure on firms to maximize short-term profits, and the explosion of accountancy-based management consultancy (*Business Week*, June 1988) have further reinforced industry's cost-cutting approach. The irony is that while Britain is striving to compete more effectively with low-cost producers such as South Korea and Singapore, these nations are investing heavily in general education and training to enable their industries to move into flexible, high technology production.

V. Policies for the future

This section suggests in broad terms what policies could remedy the insufficiencies of our system of education and training. It covers both those in the sixteen to twenty age group and the (far larger) adult labour force. We take the quantitative goal to be the broad level which the Japanese, Germans, and Swedes have achieved, namely where about 90 per cent of young people are in full-time highly-structured education and training until nineteen or twenty. And, less precisely, that major improvements take place in the training of those already in the workforce, both by the employer and externally. Training of managers, in particular of supervisors, is treated in relation to these goals.

What type of education and training? There is broad agreement about the need to raise ET standards and levels, but less about its content. This reflects the failure of the (opposed) ET methodologies of the post-

war decades: manpower planning, on the one hand, and human capital theory, on the other. Manpower planning has proved too inflexible in a world in which long-run predictions about occupational needs can seldom be made. And the rate of return calculations underlying human capital approaches to optimal training provision have foundered on the difference between social and market valuations. While both approaches have a role to play when used sensibly, few practitioners would see either as sufficient to determine the content of ET.

Reform of education and training is seen in this section as part of the process of 'managing change'. This context argues for three general criteria as determining the content of education and training.

First, the uncertainty of occupational needs in the future requires *adaptability*. Many people in the labour force will have to make significant career changes in their working lives, which will require retraining. There is some agreement that successful retraining depends on a high level of general education and also on previous vocational training. Moreover, as much training for new occupations covers skills already acquired in previous ET (e.g. computing skills), a modular approach to training is efficient.

Second, ET needs to equip workers with the skills required for *innovation in products and processes* and the *production of high quality goods and services*. One implication is that participation in higher education will have to steadily increase. And there is a more radical implication: effective innovation and quality production requires participation; that means that workers and managers should acquire not just technical competence, but also the social and managerial skills involved in working together. We may need increasingly to blur the distinction between management ET and worker ET. The implications are various: a high level of general education, sufficiently broad that young people are both technically competent and educated in the humanities and arts; strong emphasis on projects, working together and interdisciplinary work; vocational education and training which provides management skills as well as technical understanding. More generally, ET should be designed to reduce class barriers (not only as a good in itself, but also) because of the requirements of innovation and high-quality production.

Third, ET must be *recognizable* and *useful*, so that employers want to employ the graduates of the ET system and young people and adults want to undertake ET. There is a potential tension here with the previous paragraph. For the abilities stressed there are at present only demanded by a minority of companies. Vocational education is thus a compromise between the characteristics needed in the longer term and the skills and knowledge which companies can see as immediately useful to them. A second implication of the need for recognition and usefulness is that there be a widely agreed and understood system of certification, based on acceptable assessment.

Much policy discussion, sensibly, concerns potential improvements within the broad context of the existing framework of ET provision within the UK. As a result less thought has been given to the wider transformations which we believe the management of change and the move to a high skills equilibrium imply. The discussion of this section thus takes a longer-term perspective.

There are five interdependent parts to these recommendations for reform: reforming ET provision for the sixteen to twenty age group; training by companies; individual access to training; the external infrastructure of ET; and the macroeconomic implications of a major ET expansion.

1. The education and training of sixteen to twenty year-olds

The focus of this section is on how incentives, attitudes, institutions and options can be changed so that young people will choose to remain in full-time education and training until the age of nineteen or twenty, rather than entering the labour market or YTS at age sixteen.

For two reasons the next decade offers a window for reform which was not previously open. First, the demographic decline in the sixteen-plus age cohort will mean a drop of nearly a third over the next ten years in the numbers of young people aged between sixteen and nineteen. It will therefore be an ideal period for bringing our system into line with that of other advanced countries. For the resource cost, although considerable, of a substantial increase in the ET participation ratio of sixteen to nineteen year-olds will be significantly less than in the past decade.

The second reason was spelt out in section IV. The institutional constraints against change are in two ways significantly weaker now than a decade or two decades ago. Unions at national level, far from seeking to frustrate change, would support it in this area; they would see it as a means of regaining membership, rather than a threat to the bargaining position of existing skilled workers. The education system (teachers, LEAs, educationalists, teachers unions) no longer sees itself as having the right to determine education policy alone;

central government has far stronger control over it than in the past, and this will increase over the next decade as opting out develops; the larger CFEs will no longer be run by LEAs; teachers unions are moving away from the belief that they can successfully oppose government to the view that they need to cultivate wider alliances, including industry; and educationalists today are far more aware of the role which schools can play in helping children to get employment. In addition political parties are no longer constrained as they were (say) two decades ago in formulating policy in these areas.

What basic requirements are implied for a sixteen to twenty ET system by the discussion in the introduction above? Five should be stressed:

— good general education, covering both technical subjects and the humanities;
— this should be designed to encourage interaction (project etc.) and reduce social class differences;
— rising percentage over time going into HE, and ease of switching between more vocational and more academic routes;
— structured vocational training for those not going on to HE, with acquisition of broad skills, including communications and decision-making competences;
— modularization and certification.

Despite the 'window of opportunity' how feasible is the sort of major change envisaged? Aside from the question of financing, formidable problems will need to be resolved:

(a)   Young people have the option at sixteen to remain in full-time education. About 65 per cent choose not to. Raising the legal minimum school leaving age to eighteen is politically not a possibility, and in any case it is desirable that young people should choose to stay on. How are incentives to be structured and attitudes changed to raise the staying-on rate to above 80 per cent?

(b)   Relatively few businesses are currently capable of providing high-quality training. And, while employer organizations are becoming more committed to involvement in ET, effective action on their part will require a co-ordinating capacity which is beyond their present power or resources.

(c)   In comparison to other countries with well-developed vocational training systems the UK lacks an effective administrative structure and a major research and development capacity.

Of these constraints the first must be overcome. It will be argued in this section that the involvement of employers and their organizations and a proper state infrastructure will be needed to achieve both this and the ET desiderata set out above. To see why this is the case, we look first at why sixteen year-olds choose to leave education and training, and with this in mind, examine the experience of sixteen–twenty ET in other countries.

Why do such a large proportion of young people choose to join the labour market or YTS at sixteen? There are two main reasons. The first is financial. On YTS or social security young people get a small income. If they remain in full-time education they receive nothing (their parents receiving child benefit). There are therefore strong inducements to leave full-time education at sixteen. The demographic shrinking of the sixteen-plus age group (while it will make reform easier) will, in the absence of reform, strengthen the incentive to leave; this is because employers are accustomed to recruiting from this age group, directly or nowadays through YTS, since it provides relatively cheap and pliable labour, so that relative earnings at sixteen-plus may be expected to rise.

In the second place, staying on in full-time ET has not been seen as a bridge to stable employment. The best route to employment for most sixteen year-olds today is via YTS, which is used by many employers as a screening device for the choice of permanent employees. YTS trainees who show themselves to be co-operative have a high probability of securing permanent employment; and that probability will rise as the demographic decline in the sixteen-plus cohort sets in.

Foreign experience can give an idea of different possible systems of sixteen–twenty ET, as well as alerting to some of the problems.

— One country often cited as an exemplar is the US. About 75 per cent of the relevant age group graduates from high school by age eighteen after a broadly based course, more academically geared for those going on to HE, more vocational for those going directly into the labour market. Over 40 per cent go on to two year junior colleges or university, producing a remarkably educated population. But there are problems with the education and training of those who do not go on to HE. In many areas, lack of co-ordinated employer involvement has meant there is no clear bridge between education and employment. The 'Boston compact', under which a group of companies guaranteed training and employment for those with good high school performance, acknowledged this need. And lack of involvement by companies in sixteen to twenty ET has

limited firms' provision of training for manual workers and low-level white collar workers.

— France has a more highly structured system of initial vocational training. Less able children can go to vocational schools from fourteen to eighteen, and end with craft-level qualifications. More emphasis in the future is being placed on the various higher-level vocational baccalaureat courses, from sixteen to nineteen, which turn out technician engineers with managerial skills. Compared with the UK, both routes are impressive, especially the second. But, as in the US, there is limited employer involvement. One consequence is staying-on rates at sixteen-plus well below the Northern European and Japanese, and a higher rate of youth unemployment. A second is limited training for manual workers in companies.

— In the Germanic (Germany, Austria, Switzerland) system, those going on to higher education spend two years from sixteen to eighteen in a high school before taking the *abitur*. Those working for vocational qualifications become apprenticed at sixteen for three or four years and follow a highly structured, carefully monitored system of on-the-job and off-the-job training and education, with external exams on both practical and theoretical subjects.

— In the Scandinavian (Norway, Sweden) system, young people remain in the same college between sixteen and eighteen, specializing in vocational or academic areas; vocational education is then completed in vocational centres post-eighteen.

— Denmark has been actively experimenting with post-sixteen ET in the last two decades. The Danes have been moving towards a system in which all young people remain within the same educational institution between sixteen and eighteen, more or less a tertiary college. If they choose the vocational route, they move into a two year apprenticeship at eighteen, for which much work will have already been covered in the college.

Both the Germanic and Scandinavian systems succeed in attaining very high participation rates for the sixteen–eighteen age groups, and in delivering high-quality vocational training as well as good general education. There are, however, arguments against both Germanic and Scandinavian systems as the optimal model for the UK, despite the fact that both systems are greatly superior to our own. The main argument against applying the Scandinavian system to the British context is that Britain lacks the infrastructure to make it work: the close involvement of employer organizations with the public system of vocational education. Moreover, there is powerful union and state pressure on companies to maintain training standards.

The Germanic system also has disadvantages, in part because it would be based too strongly on employers if transplanted to the UK. There are four reasons why we should be wary of advocating a German-type division at sixteen between academic education and an employer-based three or four-year apprenticeship:

— The greater the employer involvement (unless restrained by powerful employer organizations and unions as in Germany), the more the apprenticeship will reflect the short-term needs of the employer. This is illustrated by the otherwise excellent EITB engineering apprenticeship scheme in the UK: broken into modules, employers select those modules most relevant to their own needs, rather than to the longer-term needs of the trainee.

— Few UK employers are in a position to run quality three or four year apprenticeships; but these would be needed across the board in public and private sectors, and in industry and services.

— If young people were to move into employer-based apprenticeships at sixteen, it would *de facto* close them off from higher education.

— Equally, by dividing the population at sixteen, the opportunity to reduce class distinctions would not be taken.

How, then, should sixteen–twenty ET evolve in the future? We believe a system very roughly along Danish lines is the most feasible model to aim for, given the current UK position.

(1) *A common educational institution from sixteen to eighteen.* Apart from the Germanic countries, the US and Scandinavia, as well as Japan (more or less), have a common institution from sixteen to eighteen. France and Denmark have both been moving towards it as a matter of conscious choice. It is an obvious vehicle for encouraging a rising percentage of young people to go on to higher education at eighteen. Equally it has a necessary part to play in reducing class differences.

(2) *Accelerated apprenticeships post-eighteen: the bridge to employment.* The Germanic and Scandinavian systems, and Japan and South Korea, provide at least four years of ET post-sixteen. This could be done in the UK by short, highly structured apprenticeships, which would at the same time build clear bridges to employment. If further training was carried out mainly in vocational schools post-eighteen, this bridging perception would be less clear; of course, vocational schools would be important post-

eighteen, since UK companies would require considerable help if they were to provide high-quality training. The next section discusses how companies could develop high-quality training capacities: it is evident that if they can the benefits would go beyond sixteen–twenty ET; the need for companies in both public and private sectors to develop effective training capacities is central to the management of change.

(3) *Linking post-eighteen apprenticeships with pre-eighteen ET.* In order for two-year apprenticeships to be of high quality, considerable preparatory work towards them will need to have been completed pre-eighteen. It is also important to make clear to students the link between what is expected from them in the sixteen–eighteen period and their subsequent training opportunities. Preparatory work covers both general and vocational education. The role of a good general education, covering technical subjects and the humanities, has already been stressed, as has the parallel need for vocational education to include the acquisition of broad skills including communications and decision-making competences, with emphasis on developing individual initiative and team-work through projects. Vocational education will also be focused in part on the chosen apprenticeship area. Thus, for those who choose it at sixteen, there will be a 'vocational' route, with specific and general requirements for particular apprenticeship areas.

(4) *Modules and certification.* Vocational qualifications would be awarded and HE entrance requirements satisfied by successfully completed modules. In the case of HE the modules would all be taken in the common institution; it would be natural to think of AS levels as module-based (the original intention), and that the major part of the most common route to satisfying HE entrance requirements would consist in completing the modules needed to gain so many AS levels. To gain a vocational qualification, and to fulfil the condition for entry to an apprenticeship, a substantial proportion of the necessary modules could and should be completed pre-eighteen. A modular system in a single institution provides considerable flexibility. Most students would choose early on a vocational or an HE route; but if some proportion of AS modules were allowed for vocational qualification purposes and some proportion of vocational modules for entry into HE, those students who wished to do so could keep their options open for longer. Modules could also be used to broaden HE entry requirements, and to increase the general education component in vocational qualification. There might in addition be a case for a college graduation diploma, as in many countries, based on successful completion of modules.

(5) *Employer co-ordination and involvement.* A high degree of employer co-ordination and involvement will be needed to make this system work. That is the positive lesson of Northern Europe. Local co-ordination is necessary to link 'training' employers with educational institutions and with students. At a regional and national level, employer involvement is needed to help develop curricula, monitoring of 'trainers', assessment procedures, and so on. This will require more powerful employer organizations, nationally, sectorally and locally than the UK has now. How this might be achieved is further discussed below.

(6) *Role of unions.* Many 'training' employers, especially in the public sector, are unionized, so that union co-operation will be needed. Union involvement in curriculum development and the like will also be important in balancing the power of employer organizations. This again is a lesson from the experience of Sweden and Germany.

(7) *Local and national government.* Government has played a key role in providing a coherent framework for the sixteen–twenty ET system at local, regional and national level in each of the countries discussed, with the exception of the US. The UK lacks institutional coherence in this area, and has only a limited research and policy-making capacity.

(8) *Education maintenance allowance and financial incentives.* A central purpose of the reform strategy suggested above has been to construct a clear bridge from education to employment so that young people stay within a well-structured ET system from the age of sixteen to nineteen or twenty. This is in line with the instrumental view of education taken by most young people who leave at sixteen (Brown, 1987). But to be successful in raising the sixteen-plus participation rate, it is also necessary to ensure that leaving at sixteen is less attractive than staying on. This will require, first, an educational maintenance allowance for those who stay on, at least equal to state payments for those who leave. More fundamentally, it raises the question of reducing employer incentives to hire sixteen year olds, and convincing them to stop seeing the sixteen-plus age group as its main recruiting ground for unskilled and semi-skilled labour (Ashton and Maguire, 1988). This is discussed in the next section.

2. Developing the training capacity of employers

International comparisons suggest that UK employers devote a smaller share of value added to training expenditures than any other major advanced country.

For radical reform to be successful, the attitude of employers will have to change, as has been seen in the discussion in the last section of post-sixteen ET and restructuring: specifically, the development by employers of a training capacity is necessary for a system of accelerated apprenticeships. In addition to sixteen–twenty ET, a training capacity is needed for restructuring within organizations for training and retraining existing employees.

In looking at restructuring, it is useful to distinguish between retraining by the existing employer, which will be referred to as internal retraining, and retraining elsewhere, primarily in state/union/employer-organization or private vocational training centres. This will be referred to as external retraining and will be discussed below. Roughly the internal/external retraining distinction corresponds to that between internal (e.g. changing product composition within a company) and external (e.g. closures/running down an industry) restructuring.

With internal restructuring companies meet declining demand by product innovation. In countries where product innovation strategies are emphasized they are associated with reliable sources of long-term finance, and long-term relations with suppliers which the company does not wish to disrupt. More important, they are associated with internal training capacities in companies, a retrainable workforce with on-the-job flexibility and a high perceived cost to making workers redundant (Streeck *et al.*, 1985; Sorge and Streeck, 1988; Hotz-Hart, 1988). The high perceived cost may arise from legal requirements, as in Germany, or collective bargaining power, as in Sweden, or from a basic communitarian view of the enterprise, as in Japan (Dore, 1987). Cost reduction strategies under these circumstances will tend to focus on reducing capital or material or financing costs, rather than labour saving changes. Again, retraining capacities are critical.

In the UK much more use has been made of external restructuring. This reflects the lack of the characteristics described in the last paragraph as associated with internal restructuring in countries such as Germany, Japan and Sweden. Instead the UK is characterized by:

(i)   The organization of production around relatively standardized goods and services, with low skill requirements and cost-cutting rather than technically competent management; aggravated by:

— the public goods problem; and
— the pressure of financial institutions and, in the public sector, cash limits against long-term investment activity.

(ii)   The lack of pressure from employees to maintain training; and the ease with which companies can make workers redundant without being required to consider product innovation and retraining as alternative ways of maintaining employment.

(iii)   The lack of an effective infrastucture. Few sectors of the economy have well developed training structures, with worked out systems of certification, training schools, and information and counselling for companies. Employers organizations are weak, and unions are seldom equipped to provide good training services to their members.

The difficulties involved in increasing company expenditure on training and ensuring it is of the right quality are thus substantial. In a longish-term perspective two general points may be made. First, the increase in the educational level of young people entering the labour force and a different attitude to adult education and training will make it easier for companies to move to a higher skills equilibrium. Second, policies to change company behaviour on training should be one part of a co-ordinated strategy to help companies focus on marketing, product innovation, new technology, high-quality production, and provision of long-term finance. Education and training policies should be closely linked to industrial and regional policies; but to trace out these links would be beyond the scope of this paper. Four main policy directions are set out here: how they might be financed, where not implicit, is discussed below.

(1) *Financial incentives.*   There is little question that companies in both public and private sectors need financial incentives (positive or negative) if they are significantly to increase their training activities. This is because, for the foreseeable future, there will be a divergence between private and public returns because of the public good problem and the low-skills equilibrium. (The general strategy advocated in this paper is designed to reduce the divergence over time, but specific incentives will be necessary until then.)

The form of the incentives is critical. A minimum legal requirement is unlikely to be productive, at least by itself. It might take one of two forms: a requirement to spend a certain minimum percentage of value added or payroll on training; and/or a requirement to carry out certain types of training, e.g. to take so many apprentices, with a significant enough penalty to gain compliance. One problem with both approaches is that some companies may be better placed to carry out effective training than others. In addition, the minimum percentage approach (by itself) says nothing about

who gets trained: in France this approach led to senior managers being sent to expensive hotels in the French Pacific to learn English. And the 'minimum number of apprentices' approach poses formidable quality problems.

A sensible approach, at least to start with, is to give financial incentives to companies (private and public) who are prepared to train and undergo the monitoring and other conditions necessary to ensure both quality and coverage (i.e. that training covers apprenticeships and semi-skilled workers as well as managers, etc.). The further conditions are discussed in the next paragraph. These incentives would not need to be uniform across industries, regions or types of training.

(2) *Meisters and certification.*   How are we to ensure that companies train to the right quality and over the desired coverage? In Japan, Germany and similar countries, the role of the supervisor in both industry and services is different to the UK supervisor, (see e.g. Prais and Wagner, 1988). In those countries supervisors (in German '*meister*') are technically skilled as well as playing a management role; moreover they have major responsibility for training. In the German system, they have themselves to pass a rigorous training after having gained a technician or craft-level qualification. The above suggests ideas along the following lines:

(a)   A distinction should be drawn between certified skills and non-certified skills. This would be similar to the distinction between marketable and firm-specific skills. In practical terms it would reflect those that the NCVQ included as certifiable.

(b)   Companies wishing to participate in the training of employees for certified skills would be required to employ certified 'training supervisors', i.e. similar to German *meisters*.

(c)   The Government could then negotiate with employer organizations tariffs for different certified skills, and use this as one means of influencing the size and distribution of training. Those companies would then get automatic payments for certified training, subject to periodic inspections and subject to satisfactory results of trainees in external assessment.

In summary, financial incentives should be used, not just to produce a desired amount of training, but also to ensure that companies acquire a training capacity and supervisory staff with a professional commitment to training.

(3)   *Changing the age structure of hiring.* Specific disincentives will be needed to dissuade businesses from hiring sixteen–eighteen year olds over the next decade.

(4) *Employee representation.* Again, as in Northern Europe, it is sensible to give employees a role in decision-making on training within companies. They have an interest in the acquisition of certified skills. For this role to be effective, decisions on training would need to be co-determined between management and employees. In addition, continental experience suggests that employee representatives need union expertise if they are to challenge low-spending management with any chance of success.

In particular, it is important to enable employees to challenge management decisions on redundancies. In the German model, management is required to reach an agreement with the works council on how redundancies are to be dealt with. The cost to management of not reaching an agreement means that managers emphasize innovation and retraining in their long-term planning.

(5) *External infrastructure.*   Both (2) and (3) impose strong demands on an external infrastructure. Companies will in practice rely heavily on the advice of employer organizations, whom they can trust at least to give advice in the interest of the sector they represent, if not in the interest of the individual company. Employees need the advice of unions if they are to challenge company decisions on training and redundancies. Public or tripartite bodies will be required to provide R & D on training technology and labour market developments (e.g. skill shortages); to run a system of certification; and to provide training where it is needed to complement company training. How this can be done is discussed in V.4.

3. A culture of lifetime education and training

There is an apparent lack of interest by adults in the UK in continuing education and training. In countries with good training systems, a strong belief by individuals in the benefits of ET reinforces the system: parents can see the value of education and training for their children; employees put pressure on laggardly employers to provide training; the public good problem which companies face is reduced by individuals paying for the acquisition of marketable skills. Yet in the UK little adult training takes place which is not paid for by the employer; this is in particular the case for unskilled and semi-skilled employees and for the unemployed. Why is human capital theory wrong in asserting that individuals will be prepared to pay for the acquisition of marketable skills? Why especially is this the case when vacancies for skilled jobs coexist with high unemployment and insecure semi-skilled employment?

In the first place, individuals seldom have access to financial resources sufficient to finance any extended period of vocational training:

(1)   Financial institutions are reticent about lending without security for training, except for a few cases where returns from the training are high. This is not particular to UK financial institutions. Banks in most countries will not lend for ET purposes to individuals, unless the loans are guaranteed or subsidized or unless the bank has close connections and knowledge of a community. This likely reflects both moral hazard and adverse selection problems.

(2)   There is limited access to state subsidy for most adult vocational training, particularly for maintenance, but also for tuition. Individual expenditure on training is in general not tax deductible. The unemployed likewise have limited access to funds: their retraining possibilities seldom relate to those areas in which there are vacancies.

(3)   Major reductions in income are seldom feasible for those who are employed; *a fortiori* for those who are unemployed.

Secondly, the individual return from much vocational training is not high. There are several reasons for this:

(1)   The low-skills equilibrium organization of work means that the marginal productivity of skills for individual workers is below what it would be in an economy where a large enough proportion of the work-force was skilled to permit a high-skills pattern of work organization.

(2)   For a large proportion of the workforce (manual and low-level white-collar) there reflects the organization of work discussed. Second, differentials for skilled workers were heavily compressed in the 1970s, and though they have widened since, they are still not high in comparison to high-skill countries. (Prais and Wagner, 1988.)

(3)   A large proportion of the workforce does not have the basic education required to proceed to craft-level vocational training; so a major prior investment is necessary.

(4)   The existing system of certification is unhelpful, as the NCVQ has emphasized. Aside from being confusing, it fails to give employers real guarantees in many areas as to the competences of the certified employee, because of the lack of proper assessment procedures. In addition, and more important, portability is limited. In the modern economy skills obsolesce. The acquisition of new skills should not involve returning to square one, as it frequently does today.

(5)   Finally, for those who are currently employed, and wish independently to take leave to pursue education or training, there is seldom a guarantee that they will be able to keep their job.

This means that major self-financed training or retraining is not seen as a realistic possibility, if it is considered at all, by most unskilled or semi-skilled workers or those who are unemployed. Moreover, with the exceptions of a few unions who provide good counselling services, little advice is available.

A comprehensive external training system

Those who seek, or might be persuaded to seek, external training fall into two categories with some overlapping: people with clear goals and courses in mind, adequate previous education and training, but held back by unavailability of finance or employment insecurity; and the unskilled, semi-skilled and unemployed with little belief in the possibility of effective retraining. For both groups adequate financing is necessary. There is a strong case for formalizing a system of education credits for adults. These credits would be intended for training not covered by companies. The general question of financing is considered below, but it should be noted here that if individuals had their own 'training accounts', into which education credits were put, these credits could be added to by saving, perhaps topped-up by public funding. For most people in the second group, additional financing will be necessary, since it will not be reasonable to expect them to save enough. It is of great importance that those threatened by redundancy or made redundant are given sufficient resources for long periods of ET. Along Swedish lines, a reasonable income might be conditioned on in effect a contract to train for a given range of skills in which there are vacancies or in which employment is likely.

For this group, much more is required than financing. Also needed are counselling, an information system covering vacancies and future areas of demand, structured basic education if necessary, training and retraining facilities (though they might be in the private sector and hired by the state), and a support system to facilitate mobility if needed. How an external retraining system might be set up is discussed in the next section.

Returns to skills

This is an important problem to which there are few easy solutions. We argued above for policies to encourage the development of a supervisory grade with technical qualifications: if successful, that would help the concept of a career ladder based on skills. It is harder for the government to intervene in the process of wage determination, and widen skill differentials even if there is case for doing so. In our view, the more sensible approach is to give incentives to employers to increase training, on the one hand, and to develop an external training policy to help redundant and potentially redundant workers, who have less need of incentives to acquire skills, on the other.

4. Institutional infrastructure

Radical reform of ET requires a more effective institutional infrastructure than presently exists. Our view is that radical reform is not a simple political option, but one requiring major institutional changes which will be difficult to bring about in the UK, at least if reform is to realize its full potential. This returns the argument to those economic historians that our basic economic problems lie in our institutions.

It was argued in section IV that the old constraining infrastructure has broken down; and that the Government has substituted increased centralized control via the MSC (as was) and the DES, combined with the use of contracts with training agencies. The centralization of policy-making has not been accompanied by a significant expansion of the very limited research and information-gathering capacities of the MSC and the DES. A parallel can be drawn between this system and large conglomerates controlled by a small financially-oriented headquarters. The new system will become more pronounced as: (a) local education authorities have a diminished role in post-sixteen ET, with the removal of polytechnics and the larger CFEs from their control, with the decline in importance of TVEI, and with the possible opting out of secondary schools; (b) the wide variety of course-development, assessment and accreditation bodies are encouraged to behave more competitively; and (c) the NCVQ becomes more a body carrying out government instructions, especially in relation to certification of YTS trainees, than a forum in which different points of view, of the business community, of unions and of educationalists and trainers can be expressed.

The new system is hardly adequate for dealing with YTS and ATS; it has major drawbacks if it is to carry through radical reform. We will argue that a different system needs to be developed in which employers organizations, unions, educationalists and the regions should all ideally play a more important part; and in which the role of government should be more concerned with the provision of information, research and development, and coordination, than with unilateral policy-making.

The need for better information, R & D, and co-ordination

The reforms discussed in the preceding sub-sections involve major course developments: for sixteen–eighteen year olds; for accelerated apprenticeships; for those at work; for meisters; for those undertaking external retraining; together with development of assessment procedures, certification and accreditation of examining bodies. It will be necessary to co-ordinate academic examining boards with vocational training institutions such as BTEC; and to co-ordinate the activities of the vocational institutions themselves. Also, it is important to allow experimentation and thus course development by individual teachers or trainers, and a mechanism is needed to permit the diffusion of best-practice innovations. All this demands a much greater role of government in the R & D and co-ordination process. This might perhaps be on the lines of regional labour market and regional education boards in Sweden.

For two broad reasons, a more effective ET system also requires involvement by the social partners (employers' organizations and unions) as well as educational institutions and the Government. The first is to ensure that policy-making is conducted in a balanced way. The second is to bring about the participation of companies (3), and employees (4).

Multilateral participation in ET governance

Running a complex ET system is a principal-agent problem. However clear the ideas of the Government (the principal) and however effective its own research and development activities, the co-operation of teachers and trainers as agents is essential to efficient course development, assessment, etc. But educators will have their own interests. (Japan is a case in point, where educationalists dominate the development of sixteen–eighteen education, business has no influence, and where rote learning still plays a major role.) A tempting solution is for governments to use expert civil servants as additional agents; of course it is important that government experts should be involved, but there is a danger: if detailed policy-making is left to government experts and educationalists, the former may assimilate over time the goals of the latter, particularly if governments change.

A more effective solution is to balance the interests of educators against the interests of employers and those of employees. Hence the case for involving their representatives as additional agents, to bring about more balanced objectives. If this is to be successful, both employers' organizations and unions need expertise; here again Northern European experience, where the social partners have their own research institutions, in some cases financed by the state, is suggestive. Moreover, as employers' organizations and unions acquire expertise, so a common culture of understanding and agreement on a range of training issues gets built up by professionals on all sides. Thus the agents, with their different interests but shared culture, become players in a co-operative game over time in which compromise and flexibility are available to meet changing conditions. (For a broader use of this type of approach, see the insightful Lange, 1987.)

A similar case can be made for involving representatives of regions in addition to central government. For individual regions will have their own economic goals, and more political stability than central government. Again, effective involvement requires expertise. This reinforces the argument for regional labour market and regional education boards.

Employers' organizations and the participation of companies

Most companies see no gain in participating in training in marketable skills and associated activities to a socially optimal degree. This is both because of the standard prisoner's dilemma problem and the low skills equilibrium. As a partial solution to both problems we suggested the use of financial incentives to encourage the building up of a training capacity within companies. Important though that is by itself, its effectiveness can be greatly enhanced through employers' organizations. First, getting companies to train in the right way is difficult for government, because of an asymmetry of information: the company knows much more about how good its training is than the Government. Companies are often loathe to be monitored by, or give detailed information to, government, because they distrust the use to which the information will be put. Employers' organizations are in a better position to engage the co-operation of companies, because they are seen to be on the side of companies as a whole. Secondly, powerful employers' organizations, as in Germany, can sanction free-riders more cheaply than the Government. This is the case where employers' organizations distribute a range of valued services to companies, not necessarily just in the training area; and have a degree of discretion over their distribution. One of these services may be training advice; others might be in, say, export marketing. This gives the organization potential sanctions, which might enable it, for instance, to organize local co-ordination of companies with respect to the bridge between education and employment; or to prod companies into increasing training activities.

Employees and unions

Unions have several important roles to play in an effective ET system, as mentioned above. Here we want to stress the role of unions in promoting employee involvement in training decision-making. Such involvement is a critical component of high-skill economies. If it is to be effective, employees must be properly backed up by union advice and expertise.

Much of the argument of this sub-section is influenced by the study of why the Scandinavian and Germanic ET systems have been successful. There is an important research agenda here for the UK. We do not want to suggest the type of powerful employers organizations or union confederations in those countries, or regional government as in Germany is transplantable, it is not. But there is a strong case for giving muscle to employers' organizations and unions, and to regions and perhaps metropolitan areas, in the training field. Unions are moving in the UK (some much faster than others) to consider training as a core area of their interests. Business organizations are moving less fast, but in the right direction. Radical reform of ET will need a push by government. One possibility, for a radical reforming government, is to give the social partners the resources to develop major expertise in training. A second is to consider whether chambers of commerce can play a more significant role at local level, so as to enable them to develop local employer networks. Third, to consider the possibilities of regional labour market and regional education boards as quadripartite institutions, with educationalists and regional representatives as well as the social partners.

5. Macroeconomic and financing implications

The preceding four sub-sections have looked at the micro aspects of policies needed for transforming the post-sixteen education and training system. They have suggested how to change incentives facing individuals and organizations; how co-ordinating and providing institutions could be built up; and how training policies should be seen as part of a broader microeconomic strategy directed at changing ways in which companies operate. If successful these changes carry great benefits in terms of macroeconomic performance. But to be successful they require a major injection of resources.

In a steady-state, the benefits can be assumed to outweigh the resource cost. But in the process of transforming the system, resource costs would be likely to precede the benefits of additional resources. There is not the space in this article to discuss in detail the financing of this gap. But we want to make some brief points to indicate why we believe that increased expenditures in this area can be more easily managed than in many others.

The increased resources devoted to ET can be met in one or more of three ways:

— an increase in GDP;
— a reduction in other expenditures;
— an increase in imports.

There are two reasons why some part of the resource cost can be met by reduction in other expenditures. First, specific forms of taxation or quasi-taxation can be exploited with minimal economic damage.

— A training levy on companies who do not undertake certified training. It will be difficult for these companies to pass on the levy in the form of higher prices if some competitors are undertaking certified training and hence not paying the levy. And since most of the non-training companies are likely to be in the sheltered sector of the economy, any reduction in their activity levels as a result of the levy will have the beneficial effect of transferring business to training competitors.

— Individual training accounts. If individuals choose to contribute to an individual training account, it will come from a voluntary reduction in consumers expenditure.

Second, other government expenditures will be reduced:

— Reduction in government expenditures on YTS and other MSC related activities which would be phased out as a new system of sixteen–twenty ET developed.

— Reduction in government expenditures on education and training post-sixteen as a result of demographic decline.

Thus some part of the necessary resources can be met from reduced expenditure elsewhere but without relying on an increase in general taxation. The damage caused by the latter is not only political, but also, via its inflationary potential, economic. But there are limits beyond which it may be unwise or impossible to push these reductions.

This means that the resources to finance a training programme will have to come in part from increased GDP and increased imports. The point to be made here is that the standard problems associated with an expansionary policy can be more easily handled within the context of a training programme than in other cases.

The first problem is that of inflation caused by the increased bargaining power of employees as employment rises. Appropriate increases in the skilled workforce can reduce inflationary pressures in two ways. Directly, it reduces skilled labour bottlenecks and the power of 'insiders' relative to outsiders. Indirectly, it facilitates wage restraint especially if unions are involved in the training institutions.

The second problem is financing the external deficit and the public sector deficit, at least without a fall in the exchange rate or a rise in the interest rate. Avoiding these consequences requires that inflation does not increase and that the increase in the PSBR and the external deficit are seen as eventually self-correcting. The last paragraph was concerned with inflation. A training programme can, more easily than most programmes involving increased government expenditure, be credibly seen as self-correcting in its effect on the PSBR and the external deficit.

VI. Concluding remarks

The UK has long suffered from a low-skills equilibrium in which the ET system has delivered badly educated and minimally trained sixteen year-old school-leavers to an economy which has been geared to operate—albeit today more efficiently—with a relatively unskilled labour force. Some companies have broken out of this equilibrium with the aid of strategic managers, to see training and innovation as core activities. Most have not.

Despite the much-vaunted reforms of the ET system of the last few years, major improvements are unlikely to be brought about:

— The majority of children will still leave school at sixteen, and will gain a low-level training in YTS; referring to the certification of YTS by the NCVQ, Jarvis and Prais argued that it would lead to 'a certificated semi-literate under-class—a section of the workforce inhibited in job-flexibility, and inhibited in the possibility of progression'. (*Financial Times*, 1/7/88, quoting Jarvis and Prais, 1988.)

— There are no substantive policies to remedy the vacuum in training in most companies.

— There are no measures to undertake the depth of education and training frequently needed in a rapidly restructuring world economy to enable those made redundant to acquire relevant skills.

We have argued the case in section V for: full-time education to eighteen, with 'accelerated' apprenticeships thereafter, for those not going on to higher education; building up training capacities within companies; and an external retraining system to deal with restructuring between companies and industries.

Instead of summarizing these proposals, we want to underline certain points which have not always been adequately brought out in discussions of reform:

— It is important to think in terms of the incentives which face individuals, rather than make the mistake of some educators of just talking about institutions or educational innovations. But equally the economist's mistake, of treating incentives as only financial, must be avoided. We lay stress on the idea of enabling individuals to see career progressions: thus importance is attached to the bridge from education to employment for sixteen to twenty year-olds.

— Companies should be seen not as profit-maximizing black boxes, but as coalitions of interests, particularly among managers. We argue that, rather than incentives being used to increase the amount of training as such, they can more effectively be used if they increase a company's training capacity, by giving companies an incentive to train or hire meisters, or training supervisors. This produces a stake in training as a company activity.

— Along similar lines, employees should be given a role in training decision-making within the company. Here, there are lessons to be learned from industrial democracy procedures in Germany and Sweden. This reinforces the idea of groups within the company with a stake in training.

— More generally, the problem of moving companies from a low-skill to a high-skill equilibrium involves much more than training and education. It requires changes in management style, R & D, financing, marketing, etc. so training policy should be seen as part of a wider industrial strategy.

— Countries with successful ET systems devote substantial resources to research on education and training and labour market developments. In the UK today policy-making has become highly centralized but based on limited information and research.

— Successful countries also place great reliance on employers' organizations and unions. In the UK their role in the governance of training has been progressively reduced. If radical reform is to be successful, it will be important to build up the expertise and involvement of the social partners.

To conclude, the UK is becoming isolated among advanced industrialized countries. They have either attained or are targeting a far higher level of generalized education and training than is being considered here. This should be worrying enough in itself. What makes it more so, is the progress made by other countries with substantially lower labour costs: South Korea has currently 85 per cent in full-time education to the age of seventeen or eighteen, and over 30 per cent in higher education. (*Financial Times*, 30 June 1988.)

Postscript

A decade ago we described Britain as trapped in a *low-skill equilibrium*: 'a self-reinforcing network of societal and state institutions which interact to stifle the demand for improvement in skill levels . . . [resulting in] the majority of enterprises staffed by poorly trained managers and workers produc[ing] low quality goods and services'.

Prior to that, the prevailing explanation for the low skill levels of the British work-force was cultural—that the British class structure had instilled a set of anti-education and anti-industry attitudes that discouraged investment in the skills needed for a modern economy (Wiener, 1981). We argued instead that the decision by most British young people to leave school at 16 with no recognized qualification (still the case in the mid-1980s) could be seen as a rational response to the set of incentives they faced. These incentives were shaped by an education system that offered few opportunities for the majority who could not qualify for higher education, and a youth labour market that offered no premium for additional years of educational investment that did not lead to a degree. Likewise, we showed that most managers' decisions to adopt a low-skill form of work organization, even if it hurt the performance of the British economy as a whole, could be seen as a rational response to the institutional conditions—e.g. short-term financial markets, an adversarial industrial relations system, and a low supply of skills in the labour market—in which they operated.

One advantage of an institutional over a cultural explanation of Britain's skills shortfall was that it suggested that if the incentives facing firms and individuals could be altered, then Britain might be able to break out of the low-skill equilibrium. Britain, however, has historically lacked effective corporatist institutions, such as strong employer organizations, capable of overcoming the market-failure problems associated with convincing firms to invest in transferable skills; past government efforts to remedy this deficiency (the Industrial Training Boards and Manpower Services Commission) did not prove very successful. Hence, we (Finegold *et al.*, 1990, 1992; Soskice, 1993) have argued for a focus on greatly increasing the participation in full-time further and higher education as a first step toward making the shift toward a higher-skill economy.

This is, in fact, exactly what has begun to occur in Britain over the last decade, in part by accident and in part by design. Britain entered the 1980s with just 7 per cent of the working population possessing a university degree and one of the lowest levels of participation in post-compulsory education in the OECD (Hayes *et al.*, 1984); by 1995, there had been a dramatic increase in staying-on rates, with close to 25 per cent of young people obtaining a bachelor's degree, a level comparable to the USA's mass higher education system. However, while Britain has been improving its education participation rates, so too have most of the advanced industrial countries; as Table 14.2 illustrates, Britain continues to trail some of its top competitors in the percentage of young people staying on in education until the age of 18 and obtaining economically vital intermediate (craft or technical) qualifications.

A key factor contributing to an improvement in the supply of skills leaving the education system was higher-education reform (for a more complete discussion of the factors leading to improved education participation rates, see Finegold, 1991). In the late 1980s, the government merged the polytechnics and universities into a unified higher-education sector and overhauled the funding formulas for post-compulsory education. This channelled additional resources to those institutions that were able to expand student enrolments most significantly at the lowest unit cost. While the competition among providers for a smaller cohort of young people[5] led to a major increase in the percentage of individuals participating in higher education, the reorientation of the higher education system to expanding undergraduate enrolment may have

---

[5] Between 1985 and 1995 the number of young people leaving the school system in Britain dropped by approximately 25 per cent.

Table 14.2. OECD Education Participation Rates (%, selected countries, 1995)

Site	Age 17	Age 18			Age 19		
	A	A	B	C	A	B	C
North America							
Canada	69	34	11	17	10	17	25
United States	75	22	14	19	4	17	21
Pacific area							
Australia	77	32	10	24	20	10	24
Japan	94	2	—	—	1	—	—
Korea	90	23	13	18	3	16	23
New Zealand	74	33	6	18	17	7	24
EU							
Austria	88	56	1	6	22	2	12
Belgium	99	54	14	19	31	23	21
Denmark	82	71	—	—	52	—	3
Finland	90	80	1	—	28	4	10
France	91	60	—	—	34	—	—
Germany	93	82	2	1	57	3	6
Greece	56	14	12	22	6	10	29
Ireland	74	46	—	27	12	—	35
Italy	—	—	—	—	—	—	—
Luxembourg	78	70	—	—	54	—	—
Netherlands	91	69	—	13	47	—	23
Portugal	71	45	2	8	27	4	13
Spain	75	43	—	19	26	1	26
Sweden	96	87	—	1	24	—	11
United Kingdom	73	31	4	18	15	6	24

Notes: A is secondary education; B is non-university tertiary education; C is university-level education.
Source: OECD, *Education at a Glance* (1997).

inadvertently contributed to a further weakening in the other vital role that universities play in creating a high-skill economy: generating research that is a key enabler of new high-technology enterprises. There was a steady decline (17 per cent in real terms) in UK government spending on R&D between 1986 and 1997 (DTI, 1998).[6]

From equilibria to ecosystems

The low/high-skill equilibrium approach remains useful for understanding why Britain suffered from a skills deficit and the set of institutional changes required to address this problem. The original formulation of the framework, however, did have several related shortcomings. First, while the stark categorization of a national economy as either a predominantly high- or

low-skill equilibrium was useful for theoretical purposes in illustrating the self-reinforcing nature of institutions and the interactions between the supply and demand side of the skill equation, it entailed a major over-simplification of reality. Not only are there significant high-skill regions or industries existing within otherwise relatively low-skill economies (e.g. in the Third Italy or UK's pharmaceutical and aerospace sectors), but the classification of sectors or regional economies as either high- or low-skill may itself be misleading. International comparisons of economic performance suggest that there are at least three meaningful skill segments in most countries (intermediate or medium, as well as high- and low-skill) and that the requirements for success in each skill segment may be very different (Crouch *et al.*, 1999).

Second, like much political economy work of the 1980s, our examples tended to over-emphasize the strengths of the Japanese and German approaches to skill creation and economic decision-making, and underestimate the potential of the more market-based systems of the USA and UK to compete successfully in high-skill markets. Despite their recent economic

---

[6] Most of this decline came in military R&D, which, as noted later in the case of Silicon Valley, can have important spin-off effects in launching new commercial technologies.

difficulties, Japan's state education system and large-company-driven networks, and Germany's corporatist dual system continue to be world leaders in solving one of the key skill problems facing industrialized countries: how to get a large majority of the population to a high foundation level of skills for entering the work-force. And they have created companies that effectively use and continue to develop this large supply of workers with intermediate skills to compete successfully in global markets (see Crouch *et al.*, 1999).[7] Where they have been less successful, however, is in generating major new research breakthroughs and new forms of business services and the flexible, high-technology start-ups that can turn these ideas into successful enterprises. Japan and Germany's relative failure in the highest-skill markets is a product of the very same set of institutions that has made them successful in generating supply and demand for intermediate skills.

A third shortcoming with the low/high-skill equilibrium framework is, as suggested by the term 'equilibrium', that the analysis was more static than dynamic. Although there are very strong inertial forces slowing any change in the skill composition of a national economy, the rapid pace of change in technology and global competition reduces the value of static frameworks. This is particularly the case for the highest-skill, most knowledge-intensive portions of the economy. Hence, the decision to change the focus from *equilibria* to *ecosystems*. Both concepts highlight the interdependence of actors in a system, but in the study of ecosystems the focus is on continual evolution; in these high-skill systems equilibrium is typically associated with stagnation or death of a sector.

The dense concentrations of biomedical and computer hardware and software firms clustered in Northern and Southern California,[8] for example, have become self-sustaining *high-skill ecosystems* (HSEs), that once started, generate a positive, mutually reinforcing dynamic that fuels ongoing knowledge creation and growth and adaptation to changing competitive conditions. An HSE is a geographic cluster of organizations (both firms and research institutions) employing staff with advanced, specialized skills in a particular industry and/or technology. The basic

concepts of the firm, individuals' careers, and skill development operate differently in these HSEs than in the traditional economy.

It is important to note that HSEs do not constitute a general solution to the problem of the low-skill equilibrium. While they can play a vital role in generating growth in high-wage jobs for advanced manpower in exposed sectors of the economy, they will inevitably exclude a high percentage of individuals who lack the minimum skills or live outside these regions. Putting in place the elements necessary to foster HSEs, however, does not preclude the development of distinct education and training and other policy options for other parts of the economy.

References

Anderson, A. (1987), 'Adult Training: Private Industry and the Nicholson Letter', in Education & Training UK 1987, Harrison, A., and Gretton, J. (eds.), *Policy Journals*, pp. 67–73.

Brady, T. (1984), *New Technology and Skills in British Industry*, Science Policy Research Unit. *Business Week* (1988), 'How the New Math of Productivity Adds Up', pp. 49–55, June 6.

Callaghan, J. (1976), Ruskin College Speech, *Times Educational Supplement*, 22 October, p. 72.

Centre for Contemporary Cultural Studies (1981), *Unpopular Education*, London, Hutchinson.

Chapman, P., and Tooze, M. (1987), *The Youth Training Scheme in the UK*, Aldershot, Avebury.

Clegg, H. (1972), *The System of Industrial Relations in Great Britain*, Oxford, Basil Blackwell.

Clement, B. (1986), 'Industry Threatened over Training Lapses', *Independent*, p. 3, 29 November.

Coopers and Lybrand Associates (1985), *A Challenge to Complacency: Changing Attitudes to Training*, MSC/NEDO, Moorfoot, Sheffield.

Crouch, C., Finegold, D., and Sako, M. (1999), *The Political Economy of Skill Creation in Advanced Industrial Societies*, Oxford, Oxford University Press.

Crowther Commission (1959), *15 to 18*, Report to the DES, HMSO.

Dale, R. (1983), 'The Politics of Education in England 1970–1983: State, Capital and Civil Society', Open University, unpublished.

—— (1983), Thatcherism and Education, In Ahier, J., and Flude, M. (eds.), *Contemporary Education Policy*, London, Croom Helm.

—— (1985), The Background and Inception of TVEI, in Dale (ed.), *Education, Training and Employment*, Milton Keynes, Open University.

Daly, A. (1984), 'Education, Training and Productivity in the U.S. and Great Britain', NIESR no. 63, London.

---

[7] It is important to note that, at least in the Japanese case, highly productive organizations appear to be generally confined to certain exposed sectors of the economy, with much lower productivity in non-traded services.

[8] The Northern California region consists of Santa Clara County (Silicon Valley) that has a high concentration of both computer and biotech firms, while there is a second cluster of biomedical firms in Southern California, from San Diego to Santa Barbara.

Deakin, B. M., and Pratten, C. F. (1987), Economic Effects of YTS, *Department of Employment Gazette*, **95**, 491–7.

Department of Education and Science (1987), Education Reform Bill, 20 November.

—— (1988), *Tax Concessions for Training*, HMSO, May.

Department of Employment (1988), *Training for Employment*, HMSO no. 316, February.

Department of Education and Department of Education and Science, *Training for Jobs*, HMSO, Jan.

De Ville, H. G. *et al.* (1986), *Review of Vocational Qualifications in England and Wales*, Report to MSC and DES, April.

Donovan, Lord (1968), *Royal Commission on Trade Unions and Employers' Associations 1965–1968* Report, HMSO, London.

Dore, R. (1987), *Taking Japan Seriously*, Athlone Press, London.

DTI (1998), *Science, Education and Technology Statistics*, Department of Trade and Industry, London, HMSO.

Fenwick, I. G. K. (1976), *The Comprehensive School 1944–1970*, London, Methuen.

Finegold, D. (1991), 'Institutional Incentives and Skill Creation: Preconditions for a High-Skill Equilibrium', in P. Ryan (ed.), *International Comparisons of Vocational Education and Training for Intermediate Skills*, London, Falmer.

—— Keep, E., Miliband, D., Raffe, D., Spours, K., and Young, M. (1990), 'A British Baccalaureat', Institute for Public Policy Research, July.

——, ——, ——, Robertson, D., Sisson, K., and Ziman, J. (1992), *Higher Education: Expansion and Reform*, Institute for Public Policy Research, September.

Gapper, J. (1987), '£500,000 scheme to boost training in tourist sector', *Financial Times*, 17 March.

George, K. D., and Shorey, J. (1985), 'Manual Workers, Good Jobs and Structured Internal Labour Markets', *British Journal of Industrial Relations*, 23:3, pp. 425–47, November.

Giddens, A. (1979), 'An Anatomy of the British Ruling Class', *New Society*, 4 October, pp. 8–10.

Gow, D. (1988), 'Fury at A-Level Rejection', *Guardian*, p. 1, 8 June.

—— (1988), 'Teaching Shortage Catastrophe Feared', *Guardian*, p. 4, 16 June.

—— and Travis, A. (1988), 'Leak Exposes Thatcher Rift with Baker', *Guardian*, p. 1, 10 March.

Greenhalgh, C. (1988), *Employment and Structural Change: Trends and Policy Options*, mimeo, Oxford.

Hall, P. (1986), *Governing the Economy*, Oxford, Polity Press.

Harland, J. (1987), 'The TVEI Experience', in Gleeson, D. (ed.) *TVEI and Secondary Education*, Milton Keynes, Open University.

Hayes, C. *et al.* (1984), *Competence and Competition: Training and Education in the Federal Republic of Germany, the US and Japan*, London, NEDO/MSC.

Hotz-Hart, B. (1988), 'Comparative Research and New Technology: Modernisation in Three Industrial Relations Systems', in Hyman, R. and Streeck, W. (eds.) *New Technology and Industrial Relations*.

Howell, D. A. (1980), 'The Department of Education and Science: its critics and defenders', *Educational Administration*, 9, pp. 108–33.

Hyman, R., and Streeck, W. (eds.) (1988), *New Technology and Industrial Relations*, Oxford, Blackwells.

Independent (1986), 'Managers "a Decade Out of Date"', 11 December.

Jackson, M. (1988), 'More leavers shun youth training scheme', *Times Educational Supplement*, 19 February, p. 13.

Jennings, R. E. (1977), *Education and Politics: Policy-Making in Local Education Authorities*, London, Batsford.

Keep, E. (1986), *Designing the Stable Door: A Study of how the Youth Training Scheme was Planned*, Warwick Papers in Industrial Relations No. 8, May.

—— (1987), *Britain's Attempts to Create a National Vocational Educational and Training System: A Review of Progress*, Warwick Papers in Industrial Relations no. 16, Coventry.

Lane, C. (1988), 'Industrial Change in Europe: the Pursuit of Flexible Specialisation', in *Work, Employment and Society*.

Lange, P. (1987), *The Institutionalisation of Concertation. International Political Economy*, WP no. 26, Duke University.

Leadbeater, C. (1987), 'MSC criticises standard of youth training', *Financial Times*, 13 May, p. 1.

Lynn, R. (1988), *Educational Achievement in Japan*, Basingstoke, MacMillan.

MSC (1981), *A New Training Initiative, a Consultative Document*, HMSO, May.

—— (1986), *Skills Monitoring Report*, MSC Evaluation and Research Unit, Sheffield.

Maurice, M., Sellier, F., and Silvestre, J. J. (1986), *The Social Foundations of Industrial Power: A Comparison of France and West Germany*, Cambridge, MIT Press.

Mayer, C. (1987), 'The Assessment: Financial Systems and Corporate Investment', *Oxford Review of Economic Policy*, Winter.

Mayhew, K. (1986), 'Reforming the Labour Market', *Oxford Review of Economic Policy*, Summer.

McArthur, A., and McGregor, A. (1986), 'Training and Economic Development: National versus Local Perspectives', *Political Quarterly*, **57**, 3, July–September, pp. 246–55.

McCulloch, G. *et al.* (1985), *Technological Revolution? The Politics of School Science and Technology in England and Wales since 1945*, London, Falmer.

Macfarlane, N. (1980), Education for 16–19 Year Olds, report to the DES and Local Authority Associations, HMSO, December.

Moon, J., and Richardson, J. (1985), *Unemployment in the UK*, Aldershot, Gower.

Morton, K. (1980), *The Education Services of the TGWU*, Oxford University, Ruskin College Project Report.

National Economic Development Council (1984), *Competence and Competition: Training in the Federal Republic of*

Germany, the United States and Japan, London, NEDO/MSC.

—— (1978), *Engineering Craftsmen: Shortages and Related Problems*, London, NEDO.

New, C., and Myers, A. (1986), *Managing Manufacturing Operations in the UK, 1975–85*. Institute of Manpower Studies.

Nicholson, B. (1986), Press Conference at People and Technology Conference, London, November.

OECD (1975), *Educational Development Strategy in England and Wales*, Paris.

—— (1985), *Educational and Training After Basic Schooling*, Paris.

Page, G. (1967), *The Industrial Training Act and After*, London, Andre Deutsch.

Perry, P. J. C. (1976), *The Evolution of British Manpower Policy*, London, BACIE.

Postlethwaite, N. (1988), 'English Last in Science', *Guardian*, 1 March.

Prais, S. J., and Wagner, K. (1983), Schooling Standards in Britain and Germany, London, NIESR Discussion Paper no. 60.

Raffe, D. (1984), *Fourteen to Eighteen*, Aberdeen University Press.

Rajan, A., and Pearson, R. (eds.) (1986), *UK Occupational and Employment Trends*, IMS, London, Butterworths.

Ranson, S. (1985), 'Contradictions in the Government of Educational Change', *Political Studies*, 33, 1, pp. 56–72.

Reich, R. (1983), *The Next American Frontier*, Middlesex, Penguin.

Reid, G. L. (1980), 'The Research Needs of British Policy-Makers', in McIntosh, A., *Employment Policy in the UK and the US*, London, John Martin.

Riddell, P. (1983), *The Thatcher Government*, Oxford, Martin Robertson.

Salter, B., and Tapper, T. (1981), *Education, Politics and the State*, London, Grant McIntyre.

Scarbrough, H. (1986), 'The Politics of Technological Change at BL.', in Jacobi, O. et al. (eds.), *Technological Change, Rationalisation and Industrial Relations*.

Sorge, A., and Streeck, W. (1988), 'Industrial Relations and Technological Change', in Hyman and Streeck (1988).

Soskice, D. (1993), 'Social Skills From Mass Higher Education: Rethinking the Company-based Initial Training Paradigm', *Oxford Review of Economic Policy*, 9(3), 101–13.

Steedman, H. (1986), 'Vocational Training in France and Britain: the Construction Industry', *NI Economic Review*, May.

Steedman, H., and Wagner, K. (1987), 'A Second Look at Productivity, Machinery and Skills in Britain and Germany', *NI Economic Review*, November.

Streeck, W. (1985), 'Industrial Change and Industrial Relations in the Motor Industry: An International Overview', Lecture at University of Warwick, 23/10/85.

Streeck *et al.* (1985), 'Industrial Relations and Technical Change in the British, Italian and German Automobile Industry'. IIM discussion paper 85–5, Berlin.

Taylor, R. (1980), *The Fifth Estate*, London, Pan.

Tipton, B. (1982), 'The Quality of Training and the Design of Work', *Industrial Relations Journal*, pp. 27–42, Spring.

TUC Annual Reports, 1980–1986.

Wiener, M. (1981), *English Culture and the Decline of the Industrial Spirit*, Cambridge, Cambridge University Press.

Wilensky, H., and Turner, L. (1987), *Democratic Corporatism and Policy Linkages*, Berkeley, Institute of International Studies.

Woodall, J. (1985), 'European Trade Unions and Youth Unemployment', unpublished Kingston Polytechnic Mimeograph, London.

Worswick, G. D. (1985), *Education and Economic Performance*, Gower, Aldershot.

15

Higher education: expansion and reform

MARTIN CAVE

Brunel University

MARTIN WEALE

National Institute for Economic and Social Research

I. The development of mass higher education

Wide availability of higher education in the United Kingdom is a new phenomenon. The 1981 Census showed the fraction of the population educated at post-secondary level declining sharply with age. It was lower for women than for men in all age groups. The fraction of the population educated to degree level declined even more rapidly with increasing age, reflecting the fact that, for professions such as teaching, there has been a shift from sub-degree to degree-level qualifications.

There was a major increase in the availability of higher education beginning in the 1960s after the publication of the Robbins Report (HMSO, 1963a) in 1963. In response to the report, the government stated:

The basic assumption of the Report is that courses of higher education should be available for all those who are qualified by ability and attainment to pursue them, and who wish to do so. The Government accepts this assumption. (HMSO, 1963b)

A related expansion of the polytechnic sector was announced in 1966 (HMSO, 1966) and the whole system was made financially practical from the students' point of view by means of a system of student grants introduced following a report published in 1960 (HMSO, 1960).

First published in *Oxford Review of Economic Policy*, vol. 8, no. 2 (1992). This version has been updated and revised to incorporate recent developments.

Over the 10-year period from 1965 to 1975 the number of university students almost doubled, and the number of polytechnic students rose by over 50 per cent, raising the fraction of the female 25–9 age cohort with degrees in 1981 to 8.1 per cent from the level of 4.6 per cent 10 years earlier and raising the male proportion from 10.1 per cent to 12.1 per cent.

Since 1975 there has been a further expansion which has been particularly rapid in the early 1990s following the conversion of the polytechnics into 'new' universities. Figures 15.1 to 15.4 show the expansion since the mid-1980s. Until 1993/4 the data showed students only in 'old' universities. From 1994/5 students at all Higher Education Funding Council for England (HEFCE)-funded institutions are included. This makes it impossible to chart the expansion of the university system across this break. But it is plain that the number of students has expanded rapidly throughout the 1990s and, as Figure 15.4 shows, the number of women has now overtaken the number of men.

In 1987 the government restated its commitment that higher education should be available to all suitable candidates who wish to take it up (HMSO, 1987). The White Paper noted that the demand for qualified manpower was unlikely to fall in line with the reduction in the size of the 18–19-year-old cohort, and that this in itself implies a further rise in participation rates. The traditional concern that there was a shortage of scientists and engineers was restated. It should, however, be noted that data on graduate salaries are more suggestive of a shortage of engineers than of other types of scientists. At this stage the government's plan was for a 5 per cent increase in student numbers between 1985 and 1990 with a reduction to 1985 levels in absolute numbers by the mid-1990s.

In fact student numbers increased by over 20 per cent between 1985 and 1990 and in 1991 the decision was taken to place the polytechnics on the same footing as the existing universities. At the same time financing methods were changed so that universities faced incentives to expand their student intake, particularly if they were relatively weak at research (HMSO, 1990). The result was a further sharp increase in student numbers which continued until 1993 when the government became alarmed at the costs of the expansion. For a moment it seemed that it decided to limit further growth, but, as indicated above, steady growth seems to have continued until the late 1990s, and the government in 1999 signalled plans further to increase participation rates, though with a greater emphasis on further than on higher education. Bennett *et al.* (1992) point to an increase in the return to higher education as a possible factor behind increased participation.

At the same time as fostering an expansion of higher education, the government took the view that there should be better value for money from the public funds made available to higher education and this has led to wide-ranging reforms in the provision of student finance and in the manner in which higher education institutions (HEIs) are funded.

The system of student grants was changed radically from 1990. A system of loans was introduced to top up the grants to an amount believed necessary for student support. The grant was frozen in nominal terms so that, as inflation eroded its real value, the gap was made up by increasing the size of the loan available. These changes were justified on the grounds that the grant system was regressive and also on the simple argument that increased participation meant that the government could not afford to be as generous as it had been in the past (HMSO, 1988).

In 1996 the government became concerned again about the rising costs of the system and appointed Lord Dearing to report on various options for paying for higher education. His report was produced after the 1997 election (Dearing, 1997) and suggested that a fee system should be introduced. The government did not follow his proposals exactly, but introduced a fee of £1,000 p.a. charged to each student from 1998 onwards (raised to £1,025 in 1999/2000 in line with the general rise in prices). The residual grants were abolished in 1999 and the loan scheme was extended slightly. At the time of writing the Scottish Parliament is likely to abolish the fee for Scottish students studying in Scotland.

In parallel with changing the system of student funding, the government is developing a market structure for higher education. This is being done with the aims of improving efficiency and providing incentives for the system to expand. We discuss this in section III of this survey.

International comparison of higher education provision and attainment is notoriously difficult, because different countries adopt different definitions of higher education, while course structures differ considerably. Many other European countries have traditionally had higher enrolment rates than the United Kingdom. These do not necessarily translate into higher graduation rates but, in assessing this, one should not fall into the trap of assuming that time spent on a course partially completed is time wasted. High participation rates quoted for the United States often include courses which would be labelled as further education in the United Kingdom.

Williams (1992) argued that participation rates in degree courses were still low in the UK in comparison with France, Germany, Japan, and the USA; however, the UK has relatively more non-degree students in higher education. Public expenditure per student year is similar to that of other countries, but degree courses are shorter in the UK than elsewhere so that the cost per graduate (as a percentage of GNP) is lower than anywhere except France.

We can identify three main issues concerning higher education in the UK. First of all there is the question of how much there should be and of what type. Second, should there be a further shift away from public provision toward charging the consumer? Third, can one identify any institutional structure which will lead to the most efficient provision of both teaching and research functions of higher education?

II. Costs and efficiency

1. Measuring performance

Until the last 15 years or so, decisions relating to resource allocation in higher education and the monitoring of outcomes were left largely to academics in individual higher education institutions. This was especially true of the universities, whose funding body, the University Grants Committee (UGC), allocated resources to institutions on the basis of opaque judgements concerning academic merit. The universities were then free to use these resources as broadly as they thought fit. As the UGC observed in 1984, the result-

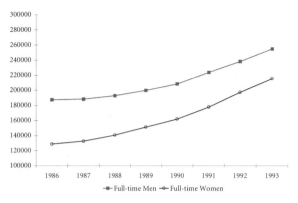

Figure 15.1. Full-time students at old universities

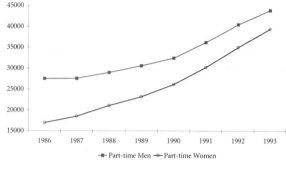

Figure 15.2. Part-time students at old universities

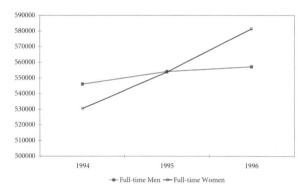

Figure 15.3. Full-time students at all higher education institutions

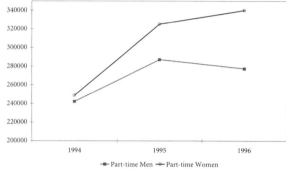

Figure 15.4. Part-time students at all higher education institutions

ing system was one of deficiency grants. The grant was raised in cases of what were believed to be high-cost institutions, and lowered to take account of universities' other income. Polytechnics and colleges, then under the control of local authorities, were subject to a variety of monitoring and accounting procedures.

This system changed considerably throughout the 1980s as part of the Conservative government's general attempts to introduce accountability and performance measurement within the public sector. Over this period, the higher education funding bodies increasingly sought to impose transparent resource-allocation mechanisms and uniform measurement procedures upon the institutions which they funded. In the case of the universities in particular, the new measures were resisted. But the government was able to use the threat of withdrawal of funding to enforce its will.

This process was most transparent in 1986, when the Secretary of State for Education and Science told the House of Commons that the government's willingness to make further financial provision for the universities in 1987/8 and subsequently depended crucially on evidence of real progress on implementing and building upon the changes that were needed. The areas identified were selectivity in the distribution of resources, the rationalization and, where appropriate, the closure of small departments, better financial management, and improved standards of teaching (Cave *et al.*, 1996, pp. 9–10). As part of the agreement then struck, the university sector began to prepare and publish volumes of performance indicators.

Some of these are reviewed in Johnes (1992). If performance measures are to be effective, they must satisfy a number of criteria. First, and most importantly, they must accurately capture whatever attribute of the activity of the unit in question is considered to be desirable. As a corollary of this, in order that the indicator can properly be interpreted, it is necessary to have a view of the desired level or rate of change of the variable in question. These characteristics may sound easy to satisfy, but experience teaches otherwise. As an example, cost per student is often proposed as a performance indicator for higher education institutions. One of the obvious difficulties with it is that, without further information about quality of outcomes and other matters, one cannot say whether an increase or a decrease in unit cost is preferable.

A further desirable characteristic of performance indicators is that they should not be manipulable by the organization whose performance is being measured. There are numerous examples of this, but one taken from the field of research may suffice. Research output is sometimes measured in terms of the number of articles published by an individual or a department. Anecdotal evidence suggests that this leads to publishing inflation—i.e. maximization of the number of articles produced through repetition, the lowering of quality standards, or the breakdown of research into publishable units of minimal size. This phenomenon has echoes of the substantial literature on problems with physical success indicators in centrally planned economies and their manipulation.

The aim of performance measurement is to capture a variety of attributes of the higher education process in circumstances when a monetary valuation of the output is not readily available. If this approach is going to succeed, it is essential that all relevant aspects of the activity in question should be measured, to avoid the well-known problem of the measurable driving out the unmeasurable. Thus, in the case of higher education, it will be necessary to collect measures on students' preferences for entry into particular institutions, their experience while undergoing the educational process reflected in cost data and the quality of the teaching process, and outcomes, in terms of such variables as employability. It will, in addition, be necessary to measure research outputs when the institution in question is engaged in research.

In terms of teaching-performance measures, arguably the best measure of the educational process is value added, defined as the difference between a student's knowledge and ability on entering the institution and capacities on leaving it. Several attempts have been made to devise indices of value added using a weighted measure of students' qualifications on entry (based, for example, on A-level scores) and a weighted measure of qualifications on exit (based on degree clas-

sifications, completion rates of intermediate years, etc.). Simple approaches of this kind are vulnerable to the objection that they depend crucially upon the weighting ascribed to entry and exit qualifications. This is, of course, in addition to the objection that the institutions themselves in many cases award degree classes, so that exit qualifications may be subject to manipulation.

One way of avoiding the former problem is to adopt an approach based upon the so-called comparative method proposed in the final report of a joint PCFC/CNAA (1990) project to test different approaches to the calculation of value added. The method involves comparing the performance of a particular unit in generating exit qualifications for entrants of a particular type with the national average of exit qualifications for equivalently qualified entrants:

The expected degree class is derived from the national relationship between degree results and entry qualifications ... The value added score of a course is thus a function of the difference between the degree result achieved and the result predicted from entry qualifications. (ibid., para 3.7)

The method thus takes national average performance as the yardstick against which the value added for a particular unit will be judged. In effect, the comparative method eliminates the need to weight entry qualifications, but still requires the weighting of exit qualifications. It thus solves half the problem of arbitrariness in scaling, but not all of it. Indeed, the presence of some arbitrariness of this kind is inevitable when units differ from the national average in the composition of both their inputs and their outputs. None the less, it is an approach which deserves attention, although current prospects for value-added measures are not good (Cave et al., 1995). Instead, attention has focused on highly particular indicators of institutional performance, where attempts have been made to compare performance with some 'expected' or normalized level; this takes into account such things as an institution's funding level or the social class composition of the student body (HEFCE, 1999).

2. Economies of scale and scope

Performance measures for higher education are designed to monitor, normally on a comparative basis, the performance of HEIs in various aspects of their work. But what do we know, in terms of rather more fundamental analysis, about the processes by which inputs are turned into outputs in higher education?

To what extent do they exhibit economies of scale, or decreasing unit cost as output expands? How significant are economies of scope between teaching and research, so that the two activities are more cheaply performed together? These issues have an obvious bearing not merely upon the efficient organization of higher education but also upon the costs associated with the government's current expansion.

Evidence of economies of scale in UK higher education institutions is extremely sparse. Perhaps this is hardly surprising, given the basis upon which higher education has been controlled in the post-war period. For the USA, Bowen (1980) formulated the interesting hypothesis that spending in any higher education institution is basically determined by its revenue: because HEIs do not maximize profits or surplus, their managements spend what they get, rather than cut costs. On this basis, we would expect that a well-provided large institution would increase its unit costs with as much vigour as an equally well-endowed small institution. Observations of the underlying technology would thus be muddied by the peculiar nature of the incentives. It is reasonable to suppose that this problem afflicts estimates of the cost functions of UK institutions.

One of the most original studies of economies of scale in HEIs was carried out by Verry and Davies (1976) using UK data. This study was path-breaking in its use of quality and other adjustments. The authors found that marginal costs for both graduate and undergraduate students in the UK were generally constant over enrolment levels. These views were consistent with many of the earlier US studies (for example, Radner and Miller, 1975) which found that economies of scale in undergraduate-only institutions were fully exploited at enrolment levels of about 3,000 students.

Other studies (Cohn et al., 1989; de Groot et al., 1991) have used a more sophisticated theoretical apparatus to examine the data. In particular, they have adopted multi-input, multi-output cost-modelling to estimate not only economies of scale in undergraduate and graduate tuition but also economies of scope between teaching and research. Both studies find cost reduction in average universities continuing at output levels substantially in excess of 3,000 students. They also find economies of scope between teaching and research.

More recently, Johnes (1997) suggests that there are some benefits to be gained from concentrating research in only 40 or so of the universities in the UK. He finds more impressive gains from concentrating postgraduate teaching and also suggests that efficiency would be improved if undergraduate teaching were concentrated on a subject-by-subject basis.

However, another study by Getz and Siegfried (1991) draws attention to the difference in estimates of economies of scale between institutions which are expanding their enrolments and those which are not. Institutions with declining enrolments tend to exhibit higher operating costs, while those with increasing enrolments tend to have lower costs per student. This implies that US HEIs appear to be slow in adjusting their operations to changing enrolment levels. One possible implication is that the quality of instruction declines during periods of expansion.

3. The costs of expansion

The extent of economies of scale is important for the pattern of costs arising from the government's intended expansion of higher education in recent years. The number of students enrolled, in terms of full-time equivalents (FTEs) doubled between 1979 and 1994, and by 1994 the age participation index reached about 30 per cent, the target set for 2000.

Not surprisingly, the expansion had major consequences for total unit costs. Unit public funding in universities remained constant throughout the 1980s, while unit costs in polytechnics fell by about 20 per cent from 1980/1 to 1988/9. In the 3 years following 1988/9, unit public funding in universities is estimated to have fallen by 16 per cent, while polytechnics and colleges have experienced a decline of 20 per cent. Data for the two sectors were not fully comparable for a number of reasons. However, the data suggest that the Polytechnics and Colleges Funding Council (PCFC) and the Universities Funding Council (UFC) at that time provided their institutions with broadly the same level of funding per student for teaching purposes, after allowance has been made for differences in subject mix.

Following the amalgamation of the funding of all higher education institutions by HEFCE, unit public funding data and projections are now available for all English institutions. These are shown in Table 15.1, which demonstrates that a reduction in unit costs of approximately 30 per cent took place over the 8-year period to 1997/8. The fall in unit costs can be broken down into productivity gains and the effects of changes in input prices. (In addition, unit costs are affected by changes in subject mix, and data show that in the 1980s this factor reduced costs by about 3 per cent over the decade as a whole, as a result of shifts to cheaper subjects.) Productivity changes depend themselves upon static improvements and on the effects of economies

Table 15.1. Costs per student in Higher Education (£ p.a. at 1998 prices)

	Universities	Polytechnics	All HEIs
1990/1	7,790	4,480	6,520
1993/4			5,404
1994/5			5,270
1995/6			5,010
1996/7			4,690
1997/8			4,600

Source: Education and Training Statistics for the United Kingdom, 1997, 1999.

of scale. Changes in input prices depend critically upon academic salaries. As Keep and Sissons (1992) show, academic salaries have lagged behind average earnings of non-manual workers by about 2 per cent per year in recent years. Largely as a consequence of this, input prices in universities grew more slowly than the GDP deflator. However, it is unlikely that such a trend can be maintained permanently. As a consequence input prices are likely to rise in real terms.

III. Funding

1. Funding tuition

The previous section highlighted the costs associated with the development of higher education. This section considers some of the funding implications. As Williams (1992) reported, UK higher education was characterized until the mid-1980s by a relatively low level of participation in degree-level studies, comparatively short durations of first degrees, and generous public funding. In addition to the payment of tuition fees for qualified home and EC students, the government also made available parental means-tested maintenance grants. Indeed, a higher proportion of GNP was devoted to student maintenance in the UK than in all but one of the 10 countries for which data were provided in an OECD report (OECD, 1990). These circumstances combined to generate the relatively high private rates of return to higher education reported below. However, returns in the mid-1990s after the removal of this support remained buoyant (Dutta *et al.*, 1999).

As far as tuition is concerned, the government and the funding councils made attempts during the period of expansion up to 1994 to introduce a degree of competition among institutions for student places. This replaced the previous system whereby student places

were funded in quantities determined by the funding council at a standard rate, with some adjustment for special factors.

In 1989, the bulk of public funds for teaching and research in higher education institutions was allocated through two parallel bodies:

- the Universities Funding Council or UFC (which replaced the earlier University Grants Committee (or UGC);

- the Polytechnics and Colleges Funding Council or PCFC (for further details, see Cave *et al.*, 1992).

The latter body in particular experimented with competitive methods for funding teaching places at the margin, and the UFC later came under pressure to introduce a more ambitious tendering system for the allocation of places. The arrangements thus had the characteristics of a quasi-market: institutions competed with one another not to sell their services directly to students, but for funding from an agency acting on behalf of final consumers. Places were then allocated to individual students in accordance with criteria established by individual institutions.

In relation to the allocation of funding for student places, the PCFC explicitly introduced a form of quality evaluation: institutions seeking to provide additional places in programmes deemed to be of above average quality were specially favoured in the tendering arrangements. The UFC also proposed to adopt a quality threshold, rather than a handicapping system, in its proposed system for the competitive allocation of funding. In the event, however, the UFC's plans were aborted as a result of lack of competition among the universities.

When the funding of HEIs in Great Britain was unified between universities and polytechnics, and conducted through separate Higher Education Funding Councils for England, Scotland and Wales, institutions still enjoyed substantial incentives to expand, on the basis of marginal student fee levels which were less than the average unit of funding, but still quite substantial. The result of all these changes was a massive expansion in enrolments in higher education, accompanied by a substantial decline in public funding of each student as Table 15.1 indicates. From 1994, however, the Department for Education, concerned at the increasing cost to the Exchequer of higher education places and also—possibly—about the deterioration of quality, introduced a new system designed to stabilize student numbers. This system establishes for each institution a MASN (Maximum Aggregate Student Number), deviations from which (beyond a permitted threshold of 1 per cent) in either direction are punished by withdrawal of funds. This has meant that competition among institutions for additional student numbers has been replaced by competition for the best students to fill given student places. It might be expected that this major funding change would alter the incentives to improve quality, provided that the student targets can be met, thus strengthening the potential importance of performance indicators. In practice, however, the effect has been less marked. As a generalization, institutions enjoying high student demand for places have been unwilling to expand student numbers, perhaps from a fear that the resulting decline in unit public funding would dent their perceived quality. Institutions which have expanded numbers substantially in the past few years may still have difficulty in meeting their MASN, and thus have strong incentives to gain a reputation for higher quality.

Although arrangements in Scotland and Wales are slightly different, the Higher Education Funding Council for England (HEFCE) has pursued a policy of causing the (subject-adjusted) level of funding in its institutions to converge to within 5 per cent of the national average. This has involved some re-allocation of funding and of student numbers.

2. Quality regulation in a competitive system

Price competition among institutions and declining public funding immediately raise the issue of quality regulation. Traditionally, the universities have relied upon the professional independence of their staff to maintain quality standards, and the system has been supported by external examiners from other institutions whose task is to maintain comparability. The polytechnics and colleges sector, by contrast, had more formal validation procedures provided by the Council for National Academic Awards.

Anxieties about the effects of competitive tendering and observed declines in unit costs have refocused attention on quality. Higher education has a number of stake-holders: the staff of the institution, the students themselves, their employers, and the government which funds much of the system. Each is likely to have its own understanding of quality. The academics may emphasize the acquisition of specialist knowledge in their disciplines; students, the quality of their learning experience and its subsequent value in the labour market; and employers, the acquisition of 'transferable' skills. For these reasons, defining and

regulating quality standards is peculiarly difficult. Cave *et al.* (1992) describe the two approaches now in use.

There have been two strands to quality assurance in higher education since 1992. The first has focused on institutional procedures. The process, known as 'audit' and now 'continuation audit' or 'institutional audit', was initiated by the Higher Education Quality Council, a body set up by the HEIs themselves, and is now carried out by the independent Quality Assurance Agency (QAA). Trained groups of auditors, drawn from HEIs in the main, visit each institution for 3–4 days, meeting staff and students to evaluate the rigour of the procedures as described in material provided by the institution.

The second strand has been evaluation of teaching quality. Assessments are conducted on a subject-by-subject basis by a chief assessor and some three subject assessors (drawn from HEIs), who undertake visits of 3 days or so. The visits involve attendance in teaching sessions, and interviews with staff, students, graduates, and employers. Quality is determined by reference to a self-assessment document which includes a statement of the aims and objectives for the teaching provision. The methodology has evolved from one in which three grades were assigned ('excellent', 'satisfactory', and 'unsatisfactory') to a four-point scale which is applied to six separate aspects of provision. Since 1997, the process has been undertaken by the QAA. All subject reviews in England will be completed by the end of 2001. The methodology of teaching quality assessments or subject reviews has been much criticized because of the alleged duplication between aspects of the process and the work of professional bodies.

The QAA has been seeking to develop a lighter touch, which consists of the same two strands—institutional audit and subject review. The latter will examine individual departments against benchmarks, devised by subject experts, and evaluate the quality of the student experience.

The introduction of a specific focus on standards, in addition to quality, is a major change to the system. Again the HEIs have lobbied hard about the way in which results of visits (no longer a 3-day block, but spaced over a year) will be published. Three summary grades will be used for the quality judgements. Standards will not be graded. Intensive external quality regulation of this kind normally characterizes markets with low levels of competition or severe information problems. Its persistence says something about the government's limited degree of trust in ordinary market forces to maintain quality.

Although the British system is likely to become increasingly competitive and, as we argue in the next section, private funding will account for an increasing amount of total expenditure on higher education, the proposed reforms will keep British higher education significantly different from the system in the USA, in terms of use of market forces. The US system contains significant elements of private production (although by not-for-profit organizations) and explicit price differentiation. In the UK, by contrast, private universities are still insignificant, and proposals for price differentiation, with fees paid by students varying either by institution or subject, have been strenuously resisted by the government.

The development of an efficient market in higher education, in which consumers (or purchasers) make informed decisions among alternative price and quality combinations, faces many difficulties. Information is asymmetric, as students often have little knowledge of courses available. Moreover, higher education is a long-term experience good: its effects only become apparent over a long period after graduation, and only limited information about it can be acquired through *ex ante* searching.

The current and proposed system of finance seeks to enforce a uniform price for what is intended at least to be a uniform quality. But the pressures of competition and increased private funding may make this unsustainable. As variation across institutions increases, better information will be required. This may take the direct form of consumers guides or the indirect form of the development of brand names, or other commitments to high quality through investment in reputation. The process of overcoming informational market failures is likely to be a long and painful one.

3. Additional funding sources

The expansion of student numbers has created extra demands on maintenance as well as on tuition expenditure. Government expenditure on student maintenance in the United Kingdom amounted in 1997/8 to about £1.25 billion—a higher proportion of its GDP than most OECD countries. The UK government had already taken steps to limit expenditures on student maintenance by the introduction of the student loan scheme. Maintenance grants were abolished by the academic year 1999/2000. Students have access to loans at a zero real rate of interest, but the loans cover only a part of the cost of student maintenance plus the tuition fee. There is nevertheless an element of means-testing built in to the system. Students from families

Table 15.2. Student loans versus graduate taxes: contrasts and similarities

Mortgage loan	Income-contingent loan	Graduate tax
Government provides student loans to pay fees or living costs	Government provides student loans to pay fees or living costs	Government acquires share in human capital equity
Government recovery of costs	Government recovery of costs	Government shares in benefits
Loan pays fees (tuition or living)	Loan pays fees (tuition or living)	Tax applies to subsidized education
Payments accrue to loan fund	Payments accrue to loan fund	Taxes accrue to the Treasury
Level of annual payments fixed	Level of payment contingent on annual income	Level of tax payments contingent on annual income
Annual payments: a declining proportion of income	Annual payments: a fixed proportion of income	Tax payments: a fixed proportion of income
Fixed term payment obligation	Payment obligation until loan repaid	Tax obligation within employment
Loan disbursement institutions	Loan disbursement institutions	No disbursement
Need to maintain individual accounts	Need to maintain individual accounts	No individual accounts

whose income after various deductions is less than £17,370 in 1999/2000 receive the maximum loan of £3,635 outside London or £4,480 in London and are exempted from the fee. As their parents' income rises, an increasing parental contribution is expected, first towards the fee and then in place of the student loan. Finally the contribution is used to reduced travel grants and other entitlements, so that the maximum parental contribution, from a household with an income of £68,110 or more, is £6,280.

Loans are not the only form of deferred payment for maintenance and tuition. Many countries have experimented with alternative methods of deferred payment of student tuition and maintenance expenditures. The options fall broadly into the following categories: a loan repayable over a fixed period, an income-contingent loan (whereby the rate of repayment depends upon the graduate's attained level of income in any year), or a graduate tax (whereby graduates pay over their lifetime an additional and possibly progressive income tax). The main features of the alternatives are laid out in Table 15.2, taken from Albrecht and Ziderman (1992).

The current UK scheme lies somewhere between the first and second types of loan, with the full debt being repayable, but with repayments set at 9 per cent of salary above a base of £10,000 p.a. in 1998 prices. The merits of these alternative schemes naturally depend upon the government's objectives as well as upon estimates of their costs in terms of administration costs, default rates, etc. Many countries introducing deferred payment schemes have seen advantages in terms of equity in linking repayments to graduates' subsequent income.

To the extent that the interest rate in an income contingent repayment scheme is subsidized, deferment of repayment by lower earners reduces their overall costs. One of the most interesting recent experiments with an income-contingent scheme has recently been conducted in Australia. The Australian experience suggests that one of the main objections to such schemes—a fear that they will reduce access to higher education for disadvantaged groups in the community—has not materialized (Chapman, 1992).

The mortgage loan and the income-contingent loan have the advantage that, in one form or another, students can be charged for what their higher education actually costs; the mortgage loan is a simple charge while the income-contingent loan has the advantage over the mortgage loan that it reduces the post-repayment income uncertainty of the borrower in the same way that equity finance offers lower risk than loan finance for an entrepreneur. The graduate tax gains over both of these in terms of simplicity. The imposition of a higher rate of tax on graduates (and not just on new graduates) is quite straightforward.

But it is doubtful that one could operate a pure tax system which charged different people at different rates for differing types of higher education. As a consequence individuals' choices would not be influenced by price differentials and this would entail a loss of efficiency purchased by greater simplicity. Thus the income-contingent repayment system which the government has introduced in the UK offers a helpful degree of flexibility. It is unfortunate that, at present, the government is reluctant to take advantage of this by allowing differential charging regimes.

4. Funding of research

Funding of research in UK universities has become increasingly selective over the past 15 years. The UFC carried out three evaluations of research in university departments, and HEFCE is now carrying out a fourth. An institution's research funding in a particular sub-

ject depends upon its level of activity (largely reflected in staff members submitted) and its rating on a seven-point scale. The principal basis for the evaluation is peer review of outputs, supplemented by a limited amount of bibliographic information and (in some subjects) by input data relating to research and contract income. No systematic attempt has been made to apply some of the more elaborate bibliometric performance indicators, such as output or citation measures, discussed by Johnes (1992). *Ex-post* analysis of assessments has, however, suggested that a high proportion of the variation in assessment is accounted for by a handful of explanatory variables, which differ among broad groups of subjects (Taylor, 1995).

Hare and Wyatt (1992) investigated some of the implications of higher education institutions participation in both teaching and research. Their model suggests that institutions may have different capacities and different propensities to engage in the two activities. If true, this would lead to polarization of institutions into those which are teaching-based and those which are research-based. The funding councils are apparently encouraging this specialization on a subject-by-subject basis through their current peer review arrangements. Over the past decade, funding has been increasingly directed to those departments which are seen to be best in research. As a consequence, research funding per staff member in such departments is many times higher than funding allocated to departments judged to be inferior. In the current round of evaluations, the apparent yardstick employed is research output per staff member rather than per unit of research funding. This approach naturally extends the polarization of funding.

The trend in research funding in UK higher education is to reduce automatic allocations and introduce more competition. It has sometimes been proposed that research resources should increasingly be channelled to the research councils for distribution on a project-by-project basis, rather than the via Higher Education Funding Councils for more general research purposes. If this route were followed, teaching and research might be funded by entirely separate bodies. Although this solution appears logical it was not recommended by Dearing (1997) and is not under active consideration.

IV. Outturns

The most obvious way of measuring the consequence of higher education is by looking at the effect on the incomes of those who have experienced higher education. One has to consider both the return to the individual (private return) and the return to society (social return). The private rate of return exceeds the social rate of return in the UK because most students do not pay full tuition fees and some receive a grant to cover part of their living expenses. Against that must be offset the fact that society benefits from increases in income gross of income tax, while individuals only benefit from post-tax enhancement of their incomes. The calculations do not take into account the possibility that the social benefit of some types of work may not be fully reflected in rates of pay, and it is difficult to see how they could.

Estimates of private rates of return produced by the Department for Education and Science (HMSO, 1988) suggested that the social return to education was of the order of 5 per cent p.a. with the private return being over 20 per cent p.a. Nevertheless, there was considerable variation by subject. Social science degrees showed the highest return at 26 per cent private return and 8 per cent p.a. social return. Arts degrees were found to have a private return of under 10 per cent and a negative social return. Evidence submitted more recently to the Dearing Committee found a social return of about 9 per cent and private returns of about 14 per cent (Dearing, 1997, Report 7). An even more recent study by Dutta *et al.* (1999) suggested rather higher average social rates of return of 11.4 per cent p.a. to graduates in agriculture, physical sciences, maths and computing, social and business studies, design, and general courses. Returns were estimated at 7.5 per cent for engineering, architecture, mass communication, and education graduates. Graduates in the biological sciences and humanities had an average return of –3.5 per cent p.a. Unlike the Department of Education and Science (DES) estimates, these figures were calculated assuming that students earn £1,000 p.a. (in 1995 prices) while studying. They were also enhanced because the earnings of people with A levels but no degree seem to have fallen relative to the average population between the mid-1980s and 1995. Private rates of return were higher for the first two groups of subjects and lower for the last group, and the estimates suggested that they would be little affected even if the tuition fee were doubled to £2,000 p.a. in 1997 values.

Bennett *et al.* (1992) argue that the DES figures, and, implicitly, those of Dutta *et al.*, overstate true returns once one corrects for the benefits of family background; people from professional/managerial backgrounds form a disproportionate number of university students but would have enhanced earning power even if they did not go to university. The private rate of return which they identify, in the region of 6–7 per cent p.a. post tax, should be compared with the long-term return on equity capital which is probably around 6 per cent pre-tax.

These figures do not take account of the fact that research is, at least to some extent, a joint product of higher education, or that education may have external benefits. We discuss these later in this section. They do not affect the private return but obviously raise estimates of the social return to education.

While there is, then, an element of uncertainty over the rate of return to undergraduate degrees, the evidence against there being a positive private return to postgraduate study is rather firmer. Rudd (1990) describes in detail the results of a survey looking at the benefit of a social science Ph.D. He found that, for a male social scientist with a first-class degree, graduating between 1972 and 1977, the median salary in 1987 was £13,100. For a social scientist who failed to complete a Ph.D. or took a research-based Masters degree, the median salary was £18,100, while for those with a taught Masters degree the median salary was £18,000. For those with no postgraduate qualification the median salary was £20,900. Similar patterns are found for men with 2.1 degrees and for women with both firsts and 2.1s.

Rudd offers two explanations of this. First of all, while postgraduate university training may be useful, employers seem to regard on-the-job training as more useful (see Booth, 1992). Second, the poor return to Ph.Ds arises substantially because many Ph.Ds become teachers in higher education, where they face a monopsonist employer who pays them badly. This raises a second important issue. Is the route of Masters degree followed by Ph.D. the best method of producing higher education teachers? We do not discuss the point here, although it certainly merits wide debate in view of these figures. One should add that Rudd's figures are calculated from simple cross-tabulations. Dolton *et al.* (1990) use regression analysis to show postgraduate education in a more positive light, but there is no suggestion that the returns approach those associated with undergraduate education. Nor is there any reason to think that the situation has changed a great deal during the 1990s.

Financial benefit is an important aspect of an assessment of higher education. But there are a number of others. An international comparison (OECD, 1999) of the chance of unemployment for graduates as compared to other types of workers suggests that it is generally lower. In the UK in 1996 a man who had left school at the earliest opportunity was over three times as likely to be unemployed as a graduate. Only Korea and Greece had higher unemployment among graduates than among early school-leavers.

A third point which has to be borne in mind in assessing different courses is the extent to which degree courses match jobs. In 1981 8 per cent of science and engineering graduates became accountants. This fraction had risen to 12.8 per cent in 1988. There is no point in gearing higher education to meet supposed manpower needs if graduates tend to take jobs for which their degrees are unsuited or unnecessary. Dolton (1992) presents entropy scores for the 1980 cohort of graduates. These show that students of more vocational subjects, such as education and law, are more likely to choose relevant jobs, but physical scientists are well dispersed. Of course, this may reflect the importance of a physical science degree as offering mental training.

The effects of higher education should ideally be considered jointly with those of employer-provided training. Booth (1992) finds that men are more likely than women to be offered further training. In the case of men it is reasonably clear that the benefits of this training are portable from one job to the next, although long periods of training appear worse than short periods in this respect. As far as training offered by current employment is concerned, only courses taken outside the firm appear to have a significant effect on graduate earnings. A week of training seems to raise income by 1 per cent, suggesting that the effects are of the order of three times as great as those of higher education. Since training is likely to be tightly focused, this should come as no great surprise.

The other side of this coin to be explored is the role of the higher education sector in offering short training courses or retraining to people with considerable work experience. This is a departure from their traditional market, but it is likely to become important in the future.

In addition to these effects of higher education and training, there are, of course, other intangible benefits of higher education which may be important despite the fact that they are difficult to measure. Graduates may be able to make more of their leisure as well as their work. There may be spill-over influences on other people. One particular aspect of this is the possibility of an external benefit of education on economic activity: we look at this next.

1. Externalities

The idea that there may be external benefits from education has returned to the fore with the work of Lucas (1988). His argument was that a high level of education is likely to accelerate the rate of technical progress, perhaps because the extent to which a country can catch up with others through the import of technical knowledge is likely to depend on the level of education and training.

Since the benefits of technical progress are typically going to be passed on from one generation to the next, education benefits future generations as well as the current generation, creating an external benefit (and, incidentally, a good reason for financing education partly from public borrowing) quite separate from the possibility that education may raise the productivity of the uneducated as well as the educated.

While these externalities may be present, they are very difficult to quantify, particularly with respect to higher education. Barro (1991), looking at a large sample of developed and underdeveloped countries, found school enrolments in 1960 were a significant factor explaining growth between 1960 and 1985. One should not attribute all of this to externalities. If one assumes that access to education rose sharply between 1945 and 1960, then the countries with high enrolments in 1960 will also have a sharply increasing level of educational attainment of their working population. This will lead to an increase in human capital and economic growth even in the absence of an externality. Indeed Matthews *et al.* (1982) suggest that, out of a total increase in labour productivity of 1.2 per cent p.a. between 1856 and 1973, half can be directly attributed to increased attainment, without any externality being present.

Nevertheless, some evidence for external benefits of education can be found. Weale (1992) suggested that a part of the growth residual of OECD countries for the years 1973–85, calculated after adjustment for changes in effective labour and capital input as well as catch-up, could be explained by educational attainment of the work-force in 1974. The results are open to the objection that they rely on the inclusion of Mediterranean countries in the sample, but they suggest an increase in the rate of growth of 0.14 per cent p.a. for one extra year of education of the work-force as a whole, and the magnitude of this at least seems plausible.

It should be noted that, if the external benefits of higher education are of this magnitude, it is most unreasonable to expect a sharp increase in the take-up of higher education to have much effect on economic growth. An increase in the take-up from 30 per cent to 50 per cent of the work-force would raise the attainment level of the work-force by 0.6 years per worker, and would raise the growth rate by 0.08 per cent p.a. But it would take the full working life of a graduate, nearly 45 years, for the growth rate to rise to its full extent.

Mankiw *et al.* (1992) describe a different framework, in which output is a function of inputs of labour and two forms of capital, physical and human capital. They suggest that the production structure can be represented by a Cobb–Douglas utility function in which each of these inputs has a coefficient of 1/3. They, almost like Barro, measure human capital by secondary-school enrolments, an approach much criticized by Gemmell (1996) and Temple (1999). More generally, while evidence for the role of education, and specifically higher education, as a source of economic growth remains unclear, links between skills and technical progress are increasingly understood. It is, however, not obvious whether the skills needed to take advantage of the information revolution are those provided by university education (Mason, 2000).

While there may be external benefits from higher education, and while they are almost certainly extremely important in assessing the case for public finance of higher education, their macroeconomic effects take a very long time to appear. We should not expect an increase in the resources devoted to higher education to have a visible effect on the UK's economic performance in the short term. The converse is also true. It will be a long time before any neglect of higher education, or of any other part of the education system starts to show in the country's macroeconomic performance.

2. Benefits of research

The benefits of research expenditures are much harder to assess. There is one argument that any prosperous, self-respecting country ought to have a viable research community, for much the same reason as it ought to have a national opera; but, even for those areas of research which are *prima facie* quite unrelated to scientific progress, it is possible to be more specific than this. First of all, it is hard to imagine the provision of higher education taking place in an atmosphere completely divorced from research. Research-training is seen as an important ingredient of preparation for teaching in higher education and, even if teachers do

not do much subsequent research, the skills they have learnt are likely to be helpful in deciding what to teach and how it should be taught. Second, the UK attracts a large number of students from overseas who study a wide range of subjects. It is probable that what attracts them to the UK is, among other things, the academic reputation of the higher education sector. This reputation is maintained by research. Third, there is a general argument, which cannot be dismissed simply because it is rather vague, that the utility of the public at large may be enhanced by discoveries, broadly defined, even though these discoveries have no specific economic application.

In the case of scientific research one can be much more precise, because many, but not all, types of scientific research lead either to new goods and services which can be marketed, or to results which impinge directly on people's welfare even if they are not directly marketed. Patents are often used as a way of measuring discoveries, and Griliches *et al.* (1987) argue that they are a good measure of inventive activity. Narin and Frame (1989) argue that the number of publications cited by US patents has risen from 0.2 in 1975 to somewhere between 0.4 and 0.9 in 1986, depending on the origin of the patent. Since around 80 per cent of academic papers describe the results of publicly supported research, the implication is clearly that scientific research is useful, and perhaps increasingly useful in the development of new technologies. Jaffe (1989) found corporate patent activity associated with spillovers from academic research, and Acs *et al.* (1992) reported that his conclusions were strengthened if one looked at innovations rather than patent activity.

But, whatever the difficulties of measurement of the effects of basic research on patenting, it is important to note the links between patenting and economic performance. Archibugi and Pianta (1992) observe that, among the major industrial countries, patenting performance is related to specialization in research, suggesting that economies of scale are present (see Dasgupta, 1987). In the 1980s there was a correlation between economic growth and the growth in the number of patents granted in the USA. This provides some evidence that scientific research has economic benefits. On the other hand Jones (1995) points out that an increase in research spending in the OECD after the Second World War has not led to any upturn in growth rates, a conclusion which might, with greater hindsight be contradicted by the experience of the US economy in the mid- and late 1990s.

There is also the suggestion that working on academic research projects provides useful skills for non-academic work (Irvine and Martin, 1980) and there may be other spill-over effects present. But can one actually calculate a social rate of return to basic scientific research? Although such calculations are possible, Pavitt (1990) is sceptical. His worry is that it is not possible to take account of the way in which the results of basic research feed through into subsequent applied research, and it is therefore not possible to measure the full benefits of such research.

V. Conclusions

There is good evidence that investment in higher education offers a social return at least as good as that on physical capital, and this provides a strong justification for expansion of the system in the 1990s. Since students with good A levels are already well represented at university, the expansion has taken place by increasing the participation of students with poor A levels or of part-time and mature students. The benefits of higher education are subject specific, but the difference between old and new universities is much less important than it was. It remains to be seen what the employment experience in the aftermath of the expansion in the mid-1990s turns out to be. There are good arguments, based on principles of equity, to say that those who receive the education should meet its costs. This points to an increase in the student tuition fee; such a change would not have a major impact on the private return to education. The UK system is a cross between a simple loan and a graduate tax; its defect is that it does not allow differential charging by subject or by institution.

In performing these calculations one should not ignore two points. First of all, externalities may mean that social returns to education exceed those thrown up by conventional rate of return estimates. Second, the research activity of the higher education sector has benefits which are more tangible in the case of science subjects than arts subjects. These benefits should not be ignored simply because they are difficult to measure.

Could the universities offer better value for money? The shift towards a system whereby the income of institutions depends on numbers of students recruited and research performance, and the efforts to end cross-subsidies between research and teaching funds, are moves in this direction. But these policies are likely to lead to a larger part of the burden falling on the student rather than the tax-payer. The issues in the next decade will be increasingly those of combating not government, but market failure, and of finding ways by which institutions can appropriately combine the professional commitment of their staffs with their customers' growing market power.

References

Acs, Z. J., Andretsch, D. B., and Feldman, M. P. (1992), 'Real Effects of Academic Research: Comment', *American Economic Review*, **82**, 363–7.

Albrecht, D., and Ziderman, A. (1992): 'Student Loans and Their Alternatives: Improving the Performance of Deferred Payment Programmes', *Higher Education*, **23**(4), June.

Archibugi, D., and Pianta, M. (1992), *European Technological Specialisation*, Report for Commission of the European Communities, DG. XII.

Barro, R. J. (1991), 'Economic Growth in a Cross Section of Countries', *Quarterly Journal of Economics*, **104**(2), 407–44.

Bennett, R., Glennerster, H., and Nevison, D. (1992), 'Investing in Skill: To Stay on or Not to Stay On', *Oxford Review of Economic Policy*, **8**(2), 130–45.

Booth, A. (1992), 'Private Sector Training and Graduate Earnings', *Review of Economics and Statistics*.

Bowen, H. R. (1980) *The Cost of Higher Education: How Much do Colleges and Universities Spend Per Student and How Much Should They Spend?*, San Francisco, Jossey Bass.

Cave, M., Dodsworth, R., and Thompson, D. (1992), 'Regulatory Reform in Higher Education: Incentives for Efficiency and Product Quality', *Oxford Review of Economic Policy*, **8**(2), 79–102.

—— , Hanney, S., and Henkel, M. (1995), 'Performance Measurement in Higher Education Revisited', *Public Money and Management*, October–December, 17–25.

—— , —— , —— , and Kogan, M (1996) Performance Indicators in Higher Education (3rd edn), Jessica Kingsley.

Chapman, B. (1992), *AUSTUDY: Towards a More Flexible Approach*, Canberra, AGPS.

Cohn, E., Rhine, S., and Santos, M. (1989), 'Institutions of Higher Education as Market Products: Economies of Scale and Scope', *Review of Economics and Statistics*, **71** (May), 284–390.

Dasgupta, P. (1987), 'The Economic Theory of Technology Policy', in P. Dasgupta and P. Stoneman (eds.), *Economic Policy and Technological Performance*, Cambridge, Cambridge University Press, 7–23.

Dearing R. (1997). *Report of the National Committee of Enquiry into Higher Education*. www.leeds.ac.uk/educol/ncihe.

de Groot, H., McMahon, W. W., and Volkwein, J. F. (1991), 'The Cost Structure of American Research Universities', *Review of Economics and Statistics*, **73**, 424–31.

Dolton, P. (1992), 'The Market for Qualified Manpower in the UK', *Oxford Review of Economic Policy*, **8**(2), 103–29.

—— Makepeace, G. H., and Inchley, G. D. (1990), *The Early Careers of 1980 Graduates*, Department of Employment Research Paper No. 78.

Dutta, J., Sefton, J., and Weale, M. R. (1999). 'Education and Public Policy'. *Fiscal Studies*, **20**(4), 351–86.

Education and Training Statistics for the United Kingdom (1997, 1999). Department for Education and Employment.

Gemmell, N. (1996), 'Evaluating the Impacts of Human Capital Stocks and Accumulation on Economic Growth: some New Evidence', *Oxford Bulletin of Economics and Statistics*, **58**, 9–28.

Getz, M., and Siegfried, J. J. (1991), 'Costs and Productivity in American Colleges and Universities', in C. T. Clotfelter *et al.* (eds), *Economic Challenges in Higher Education*, University of Chicago Press.

Griliches, Z., Pakes, A., and Hall, B. H. (1987), 'Patents as Indicators of Inventive Activity', in P. Dasgupta and P. Stoneman (eds), *Economic Policy and Technological Performance*, Cambridge, Cambridge University Press, 97–124.

Hare, P., and Wyatt, G. (1992), 'Economies of Academic Research and its Implication for Higher Education', *Oxford Review of Economic Policy*, **8**(2), 48–66.

HEFCE (1999) Performance Indicators in Higher Education, Bristol

HMSO (1960), *Grants to Students*, Cmnd 1051, HMSO.

—— (1963*a*), *Higher Education: Report of the Committee Appointed by the Prime Minister under the Chairmanship of Lord Robbins*, Cmnd 2154, HMSO.

—— (1963*b*), *Higher Education: Government Statement on the Report of the Committee under the Chairmanship of Lord Robbins*, Cmnd 2165, HMSO.

—— (1966), *A Plan for Polytechnics and Other Colleges. Higher Education in the Further Education Sector*, Cmnd 3006, HMSO.

—— (1987), *Higher Education: Meeting the Challenge*, Cm 114, HMSO.

—— (1988), *Top-up Loans for Students*, Cm 520, HMSO.

—— (1990), *Higher Education: a New Framework*. Cm 1514, HMSO.

Irvine, J., and Martin, B. (1980), *The Economic Effects of Big Science: the Case of Radio-Astronomy*, Proceedings of the International Colloquium on Economic Effects of Space and Other Advanced Technologies, European Space Agency.

Jaffe, A. B. (1989), 'Real Effects of Academic Research', *American Economic Review*, **79**, 957–70.

Johnes, G. (1992), 'Bidding for Students in Britain: Why the UFC Auction Failed', *Higher Education*, **23**, 173–92.

—— (1992), 'Performance Indicators in Higher Education: A Survey of Recent Work', *Oxford Review of Economic Policy*, **8**(2), 19–34.

—— (1997). 'Costs and Industrial Structure in Contemporary British Higher Education'. *Economic Journal*, **107**, 727–37.

Jones, C. I. (1995), 'R&D-based Models of Economic Growth', *Journal of Political Economy*, **103**, 759–84.

Keep, E., and Sissons, K. (1992), 'Owning the Problem: Personnel Issues in Higher Education Policy Making in the 1990s', *Oxford Review of Economic Policy*, **8**(2), 67–78.

Lucas, R. E. (1988), 'On the Mechanics of Economic Development', *Journal of Monetary Economics*, **22**, 3–42.

Mankiw, G, Romer, D., and Weil, D. N. (1992), 'A Contribution to the Empirics of Economic Growth', *Quarterly Journal of Economics*, **107**, 407–37.

Mason, G. (2000), 'The Mix of Graduate and Intermediate-level Skills in Britain: What should the Balance Be?', *Journal of Education and Work*, forthcoming. Also National Institute of Economic and Social Research Discussion Paper.

Matthews, R. C. O., Feinstein, C. H., and Odling-Smee, J. (1982), *British Economic Growth 1856–1973*, Oxford, Clarendon Press.

Narin, F., and Frame, J. (1989), 'The Growth of Japanese Science and Technology', *Science*, No. 245, 600–4.

OECD (1990), *Financing Higher Education: Current Patterns*, Paris, OECD.

—— (1999), *Employment Outlook*, Paris, OECD, Table D, 237.

Pavitt, K. (1990), 'What Makes Basic Research Economically Useful?', *Research Policy*, **19**, 110–21.

PCFC/CNAA (1990), *The Measurement of Value-Added in Higher Education*.

PCFC/UFC (1992), *A Funding Methodology for Teaching in Higher Education: Report from the Joint Working Group*.

Radner, R., and Miller, J. (1975), *Demand and Supply in US Higher Education*, New York, McGraw-Hill.

Rudd, E. (1990), 'The Early Careers of Social Science Graduates and the Value of a PhD', *Journal of the Royal Statistical Society*, Series A, **153**, 203–32.

Taylor, J. (1995), 'A Statistical Analysis of the 1992 Research Assessment Exercise', *Journal of the Royal Statistical Society*, **158**(2), 241–61.

Temple, J. (1999), 'The New Growth Evidence'. *Journal of Economic Literature*, **37**, 112–56.

Verry, D., and Davies, B. (1976), *University Costs and Outputs*, Amsterdam, Elsevier.

Weale, M. R. (1992), 'Externalities from Education', in F. Hahn (ed.), *The Market: Practice and Policy*, Macmillan.

Williams, G. (1992), 'British Higher Education in the World League', *Oxford Review of Economic Policy*, **8**(2), 146–58.

Understanding Sociological Theory for Educational Practices

Second edition

Understanding Sociological Theory for Educational Practices introduces readers to the contemporary classroom through the lens of sociological theory. By compelling readers to think critically and reflexively, this book helps future teachers create a welcoming and equitable learning environment for all students.

This edition has been updated to include the latest research and resources, including links to the Australian Professional Standards for Teachers (APST) to help readers connect the theory with their practice. Learning is supported through pedagogical features including key term definitions, and end-of-chapter reflection questions and recommended resources. A new instructor website features a curated suite of questions and links to informative videos.

Understanding Sociological Theory for Educational Practices is an essential resource that enables teachers to confidently navigate the topics of diversity, disadvantage, discrimination and marginalisation in a range of educational contexts.

Tania Ferfolja is Associate Professor in Social and Cultural Diversity in the School of Education at Western Sydney University.

Criss Jones Díaz is Senior Lecturer in Diversity Studies and Language Education at Western Sydney University.

Jacqueline Ullman is Senior Lecturer in Adolescent Development, Behaviour and Wellbeing at Western Sydney University.

Understanding Sociological Theory for Educational Practices

Second edition

Edited by

Tania Ferfolja

Criss Jones Díaz

Jacqueline Ullman

CAMBRIDGE
UNIVERSITY PRESS

CAMBRIDGE
UNIVERSITY PRESS

University Printing House, Cambridge CB2 8BS, United Kingdom

One Liberty Plaza, 20th Floor, New York, NY 10006, USA

477 Williamstown Road, Port Melbourne, VIC 3207, Australia

314–321, 3rd Floor, Plot 3, Splendor Forum, Jasola District Centre, New Delhi – 110025, India

79 Anson Road, #06–04/06, Singapore 079906

Cambridge University Press is part of the University of Cambridge.

It furthers the University's mission by disseminating knowledge in the pursuit of education, learning and research at the highest international levels of excellence.

www.cambridge.org
Information on this title: www.cambridge.org/9781108434409

© Cambridge University Press 2015, 2018

First published 2015
Second edition 2018

Cover designed by eggplant communications
Typeset by Integra Software Services Pvt. Ltd
Printed in Singapore by Markono Print Media Pte Ltd, April 2018

A catalogue record for this publication is available from the British Library

A catalogue record for this book is available from the National Library of Australia

ISBN 978-1-108-43440-9 Paperback

Additional resources for this publication at www.cambridge.edu.au/academic/sociological

Please be aware that this publication may contain several variations of Aboriginal and Torres Strait Islander terms and spellings; no disrespect is intended. Please note that the terms 'Indigenous Australians' and 'Aboriginal and Torres Strait Islander peoples' may be used interchangeably in this publication.

Education is the most powerful weapon which you can use
to change the world.

Nelson Mandela, former president of South Africa,
1993 Nobel Peace Prize laureate

Foreword

The overarching message of the second edition of *Understanding Sociological Theory for Educational Practices* is that teachers *can* and *do* make a difference to the lives of young people and, through them, to the broader community. However, it is clear that this is most powerful and positive when they develop nuanced understandings of the complex socio-cultural contexts within which teaching and learning take place. This requires sophisticated understandings of educational sites as institutions where power circulates, where it is produced and contested and where certain ways of being in the world are made possible while others may be precluded. Therefore, education can be understood as producing particular subjects with specific needs, aspirations and desires that are inflected in complex ways by location, class, language background, belief systems, indigeneity, ethnicity, gender, sexuality, mobility, dis/ability, family structures and histories and other factors. These insights are just as relevant to the teaching and learning that occur in informal or flexible sites of education, including volunteer and community locations, as they are in more familiar and formal sites, such as schools and universities.

Classrooms, playgrounds and other diverse sites of learning are the everyday material spaces within which our diverse subjectivities come into collision, where we express and learn about difference and are shaped and influenced by others with their own constellations of differences. At worst, as Connell, Ashenden, Kessler and Dowsett pointed out in their groundbreaking sociological study of Australian schooling, *Making the Difference: Schools, Families and Social Division* (1982), they can be sites that actively produce and exacerbate disadvantage for many students, and that shore up social advantage for others. More productively, educational sites are where we learn to create community, and begin to understand and contribute to democracy.

Creating equitable educational spaces does not mean naïvely treating everyone the same, repeating normative practices and reproducing oppressive ways of thinking and behaving. Rather, promoting an equity agenda means that, as educators, we learn to recognise, to name and to disrupt oppressions, particularly where that means catching ourselves out in moments or habits of thinking that may be unjust to some of our students or their families or communities. It means developing pedagogical practices that are nuanced by complex understandings of cultural, social and linguistic diversity. It means that we must be committed to equitable outcomes for all children and young people. It means that we will assist our students to recognise, critique and challenge oppressions. It means reiterating education as a social justice project and reshaping its institutional structures to achieve this, from the minute details of our classroom and centre routines, through how we talk about children in staffrooms, through to school-wide policies, and to policy contexts beyond individual schools. This is a career-long commitment, requiring ongoing critical reflexivity and awareness. There is no better place to start than in pre-service teacher education.

Understanding Sociological Theory for Educational Practices provides the critical toolbox that beginning educators need to develop their understandings of the socio-cultural contexts of education. The principal tools are theoretical – sophisticated concepts and ways of thinking that can help us to think about education differently; that is, beyond the prejudices and habits of thought that we have formed through our own experiences. Although we may feel that schools and other educational settings are the most familiar places, where each of us has spent most of our childhood for at least 12 years, and where many of us are also involved as parents, what is certain is that the particular educational sites that each of us knows so intimately are not representative of all such sites. We cannot generalise from those schools or centres, or those students or teachers, to all schools, all centres, all students, all teachers. Nor is it fair to generalise about communities or sectors. Rather, we need conceptual tools, tools for critical thinking, that are versatile and useful and that we can take with us into any of the very particular educational sites where we may find ourselves throughout our careers. This book both provides these tools and, most importantly, in a range of case studies set in diverse educational sites, it shows us how they can be put to use.

Since Connell et al.'s *Making the Difference: Schools, Families and Social Division*, which revolutionised the sociology of education in Australia during my postgraduate teacher training, the theoretical toolbox has been considerably expanded. Connell et al.'s book introduced the notion of 'socio-economic status' as a way of thinking about class and poverty in Australian society, and how it contributed to tiered systems of schooling in Australia and educational practices that instantiated 'deficit' discourses about particular groups of students, and their intellectual and educational potential. The reproduction theory that their book drew upon was the most powerful available at the time to investigate the social contexts of schooling, particularly in terms of class, but it also began to address issues of gender in education. More than 30 years later, we have developed more complex ways of thinking about the multiplicities of factors impacting on education, the intersections of categories of identity, and the fluidity of student and teacher subjectivities, and we have expanded our notions of educational sites worthy of analysis. With a recent upsurge in context-free pre-packaged 'solutions', and government policies that seem to position students primarily as 'data points' for measurement, we risk losing sight of the complexities of socio-cultural effects on learning, and the capacities to design research-informed local responses. It is more important than ever to develop a critical sociological gaze on schooling.

Understanding Sociological Theory for Educational Practices presents a very sophisticated and practical toolbox to draw from, filled with concise and powerful precision tools to help you pry open all sorts of taken-for-granted assumptions and practices in education.

Associate Professor Susanne Gannon
School of Education
Western Sydney University

Reference

Connell, R. W., Ashenden, D., Kessler, S. & Dowsett, G. (1982). *Making the difference: Schools, families and social division.* Sydney: Allen & Unwin.

Contents

Contributors

....

Tania Ferfolja is Associate Professor in Social and Cultural Diversity in the School of Education at Western Sydney University. Tania is an experienced pre-service teacher educator who is passionate about equity issues and the need to create change for more sustainable and equitable futures; as a result, her teaching focuses on the areas of in/equity, discrimination, social justice and critical social and cultural inclusion in education. She has received national and university teaching awards for her work in the area.

Tania's teaching is complemented by her research interests, which focus on gender and sexuality–diverse subjectivities in education, policy and curriculum, and the education of pre-service teachers for marginalised communities. She has recently been awarded Australian Research Council funding to conduct a three-year research project with colleagues Jacqueline Ullman and Tara Goldstein which will examine parental attitudes and beliefs about the inclusion of sexuality and gender diversity education in school classrooms. Tania has presented at many local and international conferences, including the American Education Research Association and World Education Research Association meetings. She is on the editorial board for several journals and book series and is a founding member of the Australia Forum on Sexuality, Education and Health – NSW arm. Tania is the lead author of *Crossing Borders: African Refugees, Teachers and Schools* (2011) and co-editor of *'From Here to Diversity': The Social Impact of Lesbian and Gay Issues in Education in Australia and New Zealand* (2002). She is currently lead author on a book she is writing with Jacqueline Ullman entitled *Sexuality and Gender Diversity in a Culture of Limitation: Student and Teacher Experiences in Schools* (Routledge, UK).

Criss Jones Díaz has been a teacher educator for over 20 years. Prior to her work as Senior Lecturer at Western Sydney University, she taught English as an additional language in Central America and the Caribbean, where she learned Spanish as a second language. Her professional background is in education and community contexts, where she actively promotes equity and social justice for children and families from diverse social and cultural backgrounds. She continues to collaborate with educators in prior-to-school and school settings, providing professional development on bi/multilingualism, languages learning, literacy learning and diversity and difference. She also works closely with the NSW Department of Education and Communities (DEC), providing professional development to Community Language and EAL teachers. She is the Principal and Treasurer of a not-for-profit Community Language Spanish School, affiliated with the DEC (NSW), which offers Latin American Spanish to primary-aged children in the Inner West of Sydney.

Her research and publication interests investigate the complex articulation between languages, identity, power and education in bi/multilingual children and families. Her work is informed by critical and cultural studies, with an emphasis on languages, literacies and identity negotiation in contexts of diversity and difference. In 2009, she was awarded the Beth Southwell Research Award for outstanding thesis by the NSW Institute for Educational Research. She has recently served as Chief Investigator in the UTS/DOCs ARC study investigating early literacy in informal settings in Pacific, Indigenous and culturally and linguistically diverse communities. She has co-authored and co-edited texts entitled *One Childhood, Many Languages: Guidelines for Early Childhood Education in Australia* (1995) and *Literacies in Childhood: Changing Views, Challenging Practice* (2nd edition, 2007). She is also co-author of *Diversity and Difference in Childhood: Implications for Educators, Children and Community Services, Policy and Practice* (2nd edition, 2016). She is currently investigating issues of diversity, difference and social justice in early childhood settings with national and international colleagues, and also working with Western Sydney University colleagues on projects relating to bi/multilingualism in childhood.

Jacqueline Ullman is Senior Lecturer in Adolescent Development, Behaviour and Wellbeing in the School of Education, Western Sydney University. Her commitment to addressing inequities in the school setting began through her work as a secondary school teacher in a New York City public school. Since then, Jacqueline has earned degrees in sociology and education (MA) and research methods (MEd) and a PhD in educational psychology, providing her the opportunity to investigate school climate, curricular and institutional marginalisation, self-concept, belonging and pedagogies of equity. She has served as a primary investigator on a number of competitive funded research projects in these areas, with particular interest in sexuality and gender diversity in schooling. Her 2015 *Free2Be?* project, a national survey of sexuality and gender–diverse high school students, investigated the relationship between students' reported school climate and school wellbeing, including academic self-concept, motivation, attendance behaviours and intentions for future study. Her Australian Research Council (ARC) project (2018–20), with A/P Tania Ferfolja and Tara Goldstein, will explore parents' attitudes towards sexuality and gender–diversity education in K–12 classrooms to better inform teachers' work in this space. Jacqueline brings her research findings back to the classroom as a pre-service teacher educator, where she lectures on social justice, critical pedagogy, classroom climate and the intersection of theory and teaching practice.

Jacqueline is a founding member of the Australia Forum on Sexuality, Education and Health, an associate editor of the *Journal of LGBT Youth* and a regular peer reviewer for a number of journals in education. Further, she is a member of the Queer Studies and Stress and Coping special interest groups of the American Educational Research Association, where she has presented regularly. Jacqueline has published widely, including journal articles in *Sex Education, Teaching Education* and the *Journal of Youth Studies.* Jackie is currently working on a co-authored book alongside Tania Ferfolja titled *Sexuality and Gender Diversity in a Culture of Limitation: Student and Teacher Experiences in Schools* (Routledge, UK; forthcoming).

Bruce Burnett is Professor of Education at Australian Catholic University and co-founder and current director of the National Exceptional Teaching for Disadvantaged Schools (NETDS) program, now offered at seven universities across Australia. He has a background in sociology, cultural diversity and leadership.

Karen Dooley is Associate Professor in English Curriculum at Queensland University of Technology. She taught in Australian schools with substantial refugee populations. She is interested in pedagogy both in school and beyond and in formal and informal contexts. Karen's sociological research investigates pedagogy for language and literacy education in conditions of economic disparity and cultural and linguistic diversity.

Jacqueline D'warte is Senior Lecturer in English language and literacy curriculum and pedagogy in the School of Education at Western Sydney University and is a Senior Researcher in the Centre for Educational Research. Her research interests include exploring connections between language, identity and learning in culturally and linguistically diverse educational settings.

Kate Huppatz is Senior Lecturer in Sociology at Western Sydney University. Her recent research projects have examined gendered embodiments and inequalities within households and the labour market. Kate's publications include the books *The Good Mother: Contemporary Motherhoods in Australia* (2010), *Gender Capital at Work: Intersections of Femininity, Masculinity, Class and Occupation* (2012), *Identity and Belonging* (2016) and *Gender, Work and Social Theory* (forthcoming). She is joint Editor-in-Chief of the *Journal of Sociology*.

Jo Lampert is Professor in Education at La Trobe University and has a long history of teaching, publication and research in Aboriginal and Torres Strait Islander education and equity. She is co-founder of the National Exceptional Teaching for Disadvantaged Schools program.

Mohamed Moustakim is Senior Lecturer in Education at Western Sydney University. His career in education began as a teacher in the early 1980s and subsequently a youth worker in London for several years. Prior to joining Western Sydney University, Mohamed taught Youth and Community and Education Studies at a number of universities in the United Kingdom. Equity and diversity issues in education and alternative forms of schooling have been central to his teaching and his research interests, which are specifically focused on identifying the barriers that prevent young people from marginalised groups from making successful transitions through education and employment.

Marnee Shay is an Aboriginal education educator and researcher. She is Senior Lecturer in the School of Education and senior research fellow in the Centre for Policy Futures, University of Queensland. Marnee teaches and researches in the fields of Indigenous Studies, Aboriginal education, flexi schooling and Indigenous research methodologies. Marnee is passionate about undertaking ethical, participant-driven research with young people and Indigenous communities in addressing critical social justice issues.

Son Truong (PhD, University of Alberta) is Senior Lecturer in Health and Physical Education in the School of Education, and is a member of the Sustainability Research Team in the Centre for Educational Research, at Western Sydney University. Son also leads the school's Overseas Professional Experience Program. He has extensive experience working with children and young people in diverse settings. For the past 15 years, Son has led international engagement and intercultural service-learning projects in the global South, with a particular focus in the Asia-Pacific region. Son is a recognised educator, currently teaching in the Master of Teaching Primary School and Early Childhood programs. He has presented and published in the areas of children's wellbeing and environments, participatory methodologies, and teacher education. His current research projects examine tertiary students' participation in outbound mobility programs, and the impact of community and school gardens on subjective wellbeing.

Megan Watkins is Associate Professor in the School of Education and Institute for Culture and Society at Western Sydney University. Her research interests lie in the cultural analysis of education and the formation of human subjectivities. These interests mesh with her exploration of the impact of cultural diversity on education and the ways in which different cultural practices can engender divergent habits and dispositions to learning. Megan has written extensively in these areas, including *Discipline and Learn: Bodies, Pedagogy and Writing* (Sense, 2012), *Disposed to Learn: Schooling, Ethnicity and the Scholarly Habitus* (Bloomsbury, 2013), the latter with Greg Noble, with whom she is currently co-authoring the book *Multicultural Education for a Culturally Complex World: Doing Diversity Differently* (Bloomsbury).

Preface

....

The dynamic nature of school populations, impacted by globalisation and constant socio-cultural change, has implications for educational policy, pedagogy, classroom practices, early childhood settings and school–community relations. Thus, to work as an equitable educator with today's children and youth, one requires a sociological understanding of schooling from early childhood through to secondary completion. It is critical that educators see how education intersects with a range of diverse subjectivities, the power relations inherent in these intersections, and the inequities that are apparent – including the visible and invisible, the voiced and silenced.

Thus, pre-service educators require knowledge about a range of sociological theoretical concepts to critically unpack the complexities of education in relation to the lives of young people, their families and communities. Such knowledge should be fostered during the pre-service stages of an educator's career to provide a foundation from which to appreciate more deeply their potential impact on future generations. Additionally, the changing expectations of educators, as reflected in the Australian context, demand a greater focus on the teacher–researcher nexus. This has been institutionally inscribed through changes to the Australian Qualifications Framework at Level 9, which calls for teacher education courses to produce graduates capable of researching and applying theory to their work. This enhances the imperative for pre-service educators to embrace theoretical understandings during their pre-service teacher education to develop the capacity to use this knowledge to analyse and critique praxis.

This book, based squarely on the research of its contributors, provides an accessible theoretical and research-based reader for upper-level and postgraduate pre-service educators. Each chapter reports upon current, topical research in the sociology of education. Through explanation and analysis, key theoretical concepts are applied to critically interrogate, inform and challenge many taken-for-granted knowledges and practices in education. The chapters are generally grounded in the Australian context; however, some chapters are linked to international research demonstrating widespread relevance of the issue under discussion. Wherever possible, the implications of the theory and research are made relevant to early childhood, primary and secondary contexts; as a result, the book resonates with a variety of audiences.

This second edition, at the beginning of each chapter, articulates how the work reflects the relevant Australian Professional Standards for Teachers (APST). Provision of the pertinent Standards helps readers to connect the theoretical and research-based content with the requirements of their everyday practice. We have not included APST Standard 6 'Engage in Professional Learning' at the start of each chapter as we believe that *all* of the chapters in the book contribute, directly and indirectly, to this Standard.

For ease of use, while each chapter can stand alone as a discrete research paper, all chapters follow a similar format, enabling the reader to focus on a particular area and/or move within and between chapters for comparison and contrast. Consequently, the book may be used according to the reader's requirements and does not need to be read from front to back. Readers who are seeking greater theoretical understandings, however, should read Chapter 1 first, as it provides a useful explanation of key theoretical concepts in the sociology of education.

Understanding Sociological Theory for Educational Practices addresses important issues while aiming to enable readers to become more comfortable with using theory to frame, enhance and extend their comprehension of key social and cultural phenomena impacting on classrooms and teacher practices. We hope you enjoy the book.

Tania Ferfolja

Criss Jones Díaz

Jacqueline Ullman

Acknowledgements

We would like to thank Cambridge University Press for supporting the publication of the second edition of this book and for the organisation's unwavering positivity throughout the publishing process. We would also like to thank the various anonymous reviewers who contributed their time and expertise in the spirit of collegiality and appreciation of academic work.

Further, we would like to acknowledge Associate Professor Susanne Gannon for her ongoing support of our work and for her wonderful words that appear in the Foreword of this book.

We would like to express our sincere gratitude to each of the authors for their invaluable contributions to this project and for their daily commitment to exposing and eliminating social and academic inequities in Australia and beyond. Likewise, we would like to thank participants across each of the studies reported upon herein, for their generosity of time, their trust and their faith in the power of research, even in these dark political times.

Last, but never least, we would like to thank our partners, children, friends and pets who have offered their kind words, their hugs and cuddles and their resolute support (even when they had no idea what we were on about). Our love for you is boundless.

The authors and Cambridge University Press would like to thank the following for permission to reproduce material in this book.

Extract from *Superdimensions in globalisation and education*, Growing up Bilingual and Negotiating Identity in Globalised and Multicultural Australia, Vol 5, 2016, 37–53, Criss Jones-Díaz, © Springer Science+Business Media Singapore 2016, with permission of Springer.

Every effort has been made to trace and acknowledge copyright. The publisher apologises for any accidental infringement and welcomes information that would redress this situation.

CHAPTER 1

The unseen half

Theories for educational practices

Tania Ferfolja, Criss Jones Díaz and Jacqueline Ullman

....

AUSTRALIAN PROFESSIONAL STANDARDS FOR TEACHERS

Standard 7: Engage professionally with colleagues, parents/carers and the community

Through an enhanced understanding of theory and reflexivity and their relationship to teaching as a profession, this chapter enables readers to more meaningfully engage with school professionals and communities through a critically aware and socially cognisant lens.

....

[M]y students' desire to learn about issues related to social justice seems to have been limited to those issues that did not confront them with their own complicity with oppression ... Many of my students acknowledged and condemned the ways schools perpetuate various forms of oppression, but asserted that, as teachers, their jobs will be to teach academics, not disrupt oppression. By separating the school's function from the individual teacher's role, they were able to maintain their belief that they do not – and, as future teachers, will not – contribute to these problems. (Kumashiro, 2002, pp. 1–2, on pre-service teachers)

Introduction

In today's world, teachers' work is more complex than ever before. This is due to: changes within the last 50 years in global economic forces and highly competitive production modes; the merging of finance, trade and communication knowledges; rapidly advancing technologies; political instability; and environmental concerns. There has been an intensification of migration and labour markets, bringing into contact diverse languages, cultures and identities in ways never before experienced (Romain, 2011). Those living in the Antipodes have not been untouched by changing global forces. These both result in and coincide with a local range of social, cultural and political complexities. These include, but are not limited to: economic disparities in and between postcodes; continued social disadvantage of Indigenous Australians; intolerance towards religious and other forms of diversity; changing mores in relation to gender and sexuality–diverse people; the rise of single-parent and same-sex-headed families as well as changing family constellations; and a political imperative that reduces access to social services, which have been increasingly privatised.

The increase in privatisation is one element of neoliberalism. Neoliberalism, an economic theory that gained popularity in the late 1970s, has considerable influence on schooling. Claiming to offer individuals greater choice and freedoms, neoliberal educational policies have significantly impacted on the functioning and intent of education, requiring schools to produce particular kinds of work-ready subjects. Neoliberalism has resulted in, among other things: curriculum standardisation; top-down school management practices (Giroux, 2010); the introduction of teacher 'performance indicators'; the redefinition and surveillance of official knowledge in terms of 'skills and competence', which is evaluated through high-stakes standardised testing regimes; and the publication of school league tables (Apple, 2001; Connell, 2011). Deeply rooted in neoliberal philosophy is the discourse of individualism, self-responsibility and blame (Jones & Calafel, 2012), and a resistance to social justice education. Children who succeed in environments based on these measurements are constructed as competent and capable. Those who fall below standardised score counts, typically minority students, are constructed as being in deficit (Robinson & Jones Díaz, 2016) and their families and communities as liable for their 'problems'. This manifests as inequality in the classroom, marginalising students from diverse backgrounds because of the limited understandings of how students are positioned depending on their subjectivities and the discourses that shape them.

The above realities are reflected in a complex web of social and cultural relations in educational settings, which not only affect learning, teaching and professional interactions, but question the efficacy of pre-service teachers' common claims that to teach equitably simply involves 'treating all students the same' regardless of diversity and that if an individual student 'just tried harder' then they would undoubtedly 'succeed'. Although in our experience pre-service teachers believe that this position is right and just, as Kumashiro alludes to in the above quote, it fails to recognise the impact of broader social and economic policy on individuals and communities, the inevitable diversities apparent in twenty-first-century class-rooms and, as a result, the pre-service teacher's potential 'complicity with oppression' (Kumashiro, 2002, p. 1). Treating all students the same fails to consider: the ways that, for example, they, their families and communities differentially experience advantage or disadvantage; the extent to which they are able to access and/ or activate power in various contexts; how technologies of surveillance, silencing, in/visibility and/or resistance shape their everyday experience; and whether they are able to give voice to their experience. Often taken for granted and therefore unquestioned is the reality that those with greater access to power and privilege, even the privilege of not being seen as 'different' or 'marked', are Anglo, English-speaking, Christian, heterosexual, middle-class, adult and male identities – or what is constituted in Western societies as the 'normal' person and the standard by which all others are judged. This is the person to whom education most often caters and is reflected in curriculum knowledges, pedagogical practices and educational policy.

A metaphor in teaching: The 'unseen half'

Although diversity is apparent in all educational settings, it is often undervalued, positioned as deficit or difficult, and rendered invisible (Mills & Keddie, 2012). Thus, diversity within an educational community, or the different ways that social categorisations of diversity intersect and the implications that this intersectionality has on people, may be metaphorically understood as constituting an 'unseen half'. This metaphor is central to this chapter and in less explicit ways is a concept depicted throughout this book. It carries multiple meanings. First, it refers to the individuals or communities who are present in educational settings but are rendered invisible by the day-to-day practices of schooling. Thus, the unseen half reflects the diversity of children and families who are in many ways insufficiently catered for by educational curricula; institutional and government policy; teacher pedagogies; and classroom, centre and playground practices. These individuals are marked by their 'difference' from the 'mainstream' and, as such, are often constructed as problematic. Ironically and contradictorily, despite being overlooked, their difference from the socially constructed norm renders them visible in particular ways, scrutinised and under surveillance. As they consciously or unconsciously challenge, contradict or resist society's taken-for-granted truths about who and what one should be, how one should act and what one should think, they are positioned by others as problems requiring policing and regulation.

Second, the unseen half is a metaphor for that which is taken for granted and, thus, is often neither interrogated nor challenged. This unseen half lies in the unquestioned privilege inherent in certain identity positions that are so naturalised as 'normal' that they simply 'are' (Mills & Keddie, 2012). Being considered 'normal' provides them with the licence to live a largely unscrutinised life where they are not required to justify, hide or explain their identity, or fight for equal rights; nor are they expected to speak for all others in their community.

The constructed normality of their identity graces them with an embodied, uncontested space in which to function; however, its socially fabricated superiority contributes to and sustains the disadvantage and inequity experienced by those who are considered Other. That is, the positioning of normalised identities as central, right and acceptable means that all who are 'different' from this norm are marginalised in manifold ways. Education caters to these normalised identities who, ironically, are visible but are, as a result of their identity categories, unmarked. In this way, the lack of interrogation of the normalised subject and their privileged position is another unseen half.

It is critical for pre-service teachers to understand the unseen half in educational settings because, having attended school themselves, they draw on their personal knowledge and experience of education. Their admission to tertiary studies also highlights their personal success in negotiating the educational context, suggesting that 'it worked for them' and is therefore unproblematic. Teaching is positioned as 'known' or familiar territory (Britzman, 1998; Kervan & Turnbill, 2003) as virtually all have witnessed, and interacted with, a range of teacher pedagogies, practices and routines over many years. Thus, nearly everyone has experienced the role of teacher, albeit vicariously, and many believe they have some knowledge of education although this is not necessarily accurate. Traditional and publicly recycled understandings of what teaching encompasses reinforce the imperative of content knowledge, the 'three Rs' (reading, (w)riting and (a)rithmetic) and the centrality of classroom management and good discipline. These foci, however, engender little understanding of the complexities of teaching, learning and student interactions and all but ignore the pastoral and emotional (Connell, 2011).

This half-formed perspective fails to recognise, acknowledge or understand the impact of broader social, political and cultural dynamics on education and how future teachers need to be cognisant of the implications of these dynamics in relation to in/equity, access and social justice (Apple, 2012). Theoretical knowledge, in the form of sociological theories, can provide tools to help one recognise and interpret how external forces affect education; with insight comes opportunities to enact change. Theory is the unseen half of teaching; and ironically it is the half that many pre-service teachers fail to acknowledge, as practice is perceived to be the raison d'être of the teacher's world. As Deng (2004, p. 145) states: 'The role of theory is not only to assist in the training of pre-service teachers in skills and procedures, but more importantly, to educate them more widely about the complexities, intellectual and moral dimensions of classroom practice'. Simply stated, theory can assist with teachers' work.

Theory equals value adding

Many beginning teachers experience difficulties relating the theories learned during their tertiary teacher education to professional practices within educational settings (Allen & Wright, 2014; Kervin & Turnbill, 2003). This book's goal of incorporating sociological theory into pre-service teacher education is to enhance future teachers' ability to identify, confront, challenge and unpack beliefs about students, parents and the broader community. Thus, sociological theories become more than simply a set of historical signposts, marking shifts and advances in ways of thinking about the world and how people function within it. Rather, the incorporation of sociological theories into pre-service teacher education has the potential to illuminate the ways in which individuals' perspectives function to shape the social phenomena around them.

Learning about sociological theories and applying them to education may be challenging but also enlightening. Such learning can be inspirational and purposive and help pre-service teachers see how their individual teaching transforms society (Holland, Evans & Hawksley, 2011). Theoretical considerations are intellectually stimulating, rewarding and as much a part of teaching practice as syllabus considerations and classroom management, since they are fundamentally woven into teachers' understanding of their students, their school or centre community and the institution of education itself.

Interestingly, as society and educational settings become increasingly diversified and the inequities across educational communities grow wider and more entrenched, independent organisations have attempted to respond with shifts towards 'on-the-job' training of potential teachers, particularly in underfunded or high-need schools. This phenomenon, epitomised by 'Teach for America' in the United States, 'Teach First' in the United Kingdom (Holland et al., 2011) and, as of 2008, 'Teach for Australia', has meant that recent university graduates with little to no explicit teacher education are brought into 'disadvantaged' classrooms, where students are positioned as 'at-risk', with an apparent assurance that skill building is best done 'in the field'. The implication is that the theoretical frames that might influence or direct effective teaching practices are positioned as dispensable, rather than fundamental to the daily work of teachers. At the root of this assumption, as Sellars and Stevens (1983) outline in their seminal work on theory and pedagogical practice, are three ongoing issues in education: the lack of communication between educational research and teacher decision making; the (mis)perception that teaching has a shallow knowledge base; and the belief that teaching does not require a theoretical knowledge base at all. Such beliefs are acknowledged in more recent work (Hennissen, Beckers & Moerkerke, 2017).

This sentiment lives on in the present, passed down like some kind of teaching folklore. In our collective experiences teaching early childhood, primary and secondary pre-service teachers, we have found that many approach theory with a sense of affective disconnect and as an unpleasant hurdle that must be overcome to cross the finish line of the degree. Many approach sociological theory in fear that it will be challenging, abstract and disconnected from both their personal reality and the realities of classroom practice.

This could not be further from the truth. Exposure to theory enables pre-service teachers to ask questions of the text, to reflect on the applicability of the theory to their own lives, personally and professionally, and to consider the lives of their future students and the social organisation of the world around them. Perhaps the biggest intellectual challenge of sociological theory for pre-service teachers is at once its greatest strength: such writing does not begin and end with the text itself. Rather, theoretical frameworks applied to teaching practice are, by their nature and purpose, provocative. They are the beginning, rather than the end point – constantly shifting rather than being static. It is to a review of some key sociological theories that this chapter now turns.

Poststructuralist theories

Poststructuralism refers to a philosophical movement that originated in the 1960s and whose key theorists include thinkers such as Derrida, Deleuze, Lyotard, Foucault and Kristeva (Williams, 2014). Poststructuralism arose as a critique of structuralism, which posits that human societies operate in terms of overarching social systems. Although it is near impossible to define what poststructuralist theories 'are', simplistically, poststructuralist theories disrupt taken for granted understandings of the world; they reject grand narratives or comprehensive systems that endeavour to explain social or historical realities, identity knowledge or experience. Poststructuralist theories criticise attempts to neatly box society into fixed, bounded categories. Rather, they consider our social realities and their manifestations as affected by many dynamic and intangible factors, which include the situational, contextual, historical, temporal, cultural, social and political. There is no single truth and no absolutes; therefore, there is no 'right' way to explain any particular phenomenon or event (Dumont, 2008). Poststructuralist theories consider that meaning is plural, diverse, complex and unstable, and that what is perceived as knowledge is socially and culturally constructed and political.

Many theories may be defined as 'poststructuralist', and several of these, including feminist poststructuralism, critical theory, cultural studies, Critical Race Theory and postcolonial theory, are applied in the chapters of this book. As space precludes a detailed analysis, the following section outlines some key concepts arising from these theories, beginning with feminist poststructuralism.

Feminist poststructuralism
Conceiving the subject

Feminist postructuralism a theory of how subjectivity is socially constructed and constituted within discourse. It explores how language, power and discourse intersect, impacting in particular on gendered subjects. It understands that subjectivities are fluid, contextual and dynamic.

Feminist poststructuralism is a feminist theory that employs aspects of poststructural thinking and has been informed by Davis, Weedon, Butler and Walkerdine, among others. Drawing on the work of Foucault (but not limited to or by it), feminist poststructuralism sees our subjectivity (that is, who we are both consciously and subconsciously) as socially constructed and contingent on discourse, a term explored in greater detail below. Feminist poststructuralism breaks from dominant structuralist traditions that posit subjectivity as encompassing a 'real', coherent, unchangeable or authentic self, presumed to be a fundamental part of our 'essence'. In some ways, having an essence is an appealing explanation of the self. Humans enjoy consistency and predictability, and as Weedon (1997, p. 109) astutely points out, 'To be inconsistent in our society is to be unstable'. However, our subjectivity is complex, messy, multiple, fluid and contextually influenced; produced by the society and culture in which it is located and the multiple histories that precede it. Rejecting an essentialised subjectivity more readily explains this instability and flexibility. Language is critical to subjectivity, in that 'we learn to give voice – meaning – to our experience and to understand it according to particular ways of thinking, particular discourses, which pre-date our entry into language' (Weedon, 1997, p. 32).

Positioning and discourse

Foucault's concept of discourse is central to feminist poststructuralism's understanding of subjectivity. Discourse may be understood as:

> What can be said and thought, but also about who can speak, when, and with what authority. Discourses embody meaning and social relationships, they constitute both subjectivity and power relations. Discourses are 'practices that systematically form the objects of which they speak … Discourses are not about objects; they do not identify objects, they constitute them and in the practice of doing so conceal their own invention'. (Foucault, 1974, p. 49, as cited in Ball 1990, pp. 2, 5)

Importantly, both the stated and unstated contribute to the formation of discourse. As Foucault (1978/1998, p. 27) articulates, silence 'functions alongside the things said, with them and in relation to them within over-all strategies'. Discourse may have to do with words or texts, but it is also constitutive of the broader social, political and cultural contexts and the power inherent in institutions (McLaren, 2002). These institutions include, but are not limited to, medicine, the law, education, the church and the family, which together construct dominant discourses that are taken for granted as truths about the world.

For example, a dominant educational discourse constructs schooling as positive for individuals through its contribution to a skilled labour force and upward mobility. Politicians who espouse education's ability to create a more equal society for all broadcast its advantages. As such, mandating school attendance legally reinforces the importance of education. There are penalties for adults who fail to send their children to school and teachers are officially required to keep records of students' participation and results. There is political retribution and media denigration of schools that do not adequately provide what is constructed as a valuable education or where children are 'falling behind' in national testing. Thus, political, educational, legal and media institutions reinforce the discourse that formal schooling is of benefit to the individual. This discourse holds great sway because these institutions all promote this same position and its pervasiveness deflects en masse reflection of the inequality in outcomes that formal education produces.

However, counter-discourses simultaneously operate. For example, many argue that school education reproduces social inequalities and does not guarantee worthwhile employment and upward mobility as the dominant discourse promotes. Although the dominant discourse is powerful, it does not mean it is not challenged or resisted. The fact that there is a 'lack of discursive unity and uniformity' (Weedon, 1997, p. 106) around education means that people potentially have available other discursive locations in which to position themselves. Discourse can be resisted, different discourses can ascend and new discourses can develop, although less powerful discourses do not necessarily possess the degree of social power located in dominant discourse through institutions. It is critical to understand that discourse is political; it constitutes knowledges about people, groups and phenomena. As such, some discourses have more power than others, resulting in unequal power relations among people, benefitting some while disadvantaging others.

An examination of power

Foucault argues that power is constituted in discourse and as such it is unstable and contextual. Discourse produces and reinforces power, but may also challenge, impede, reveal and weaken it (Weedon, 1997). Importantly, power can be executed from various positions and levels (Foucault, 1978/1998). It is simplistic to consider power as all-encompassing, where one person or entity 'from the top' is able to carry out their wishes or 'control' another unchallenged or without resistance. Rather than emanating from a central location or being distributed from the top in what may be considered a repressive manner, power is apparent at all levels and may even originate at the bottom of a hierarchy. Power does not require force, violence or constraint to render individuals obedient or to have effect.

For example, dominant discourses of schooling identify the teacher as the authority who possesses greatest power in the classroom. The teacher is not only constructed as 'in control', but also possesses institutional power and power apportioned to adult subjects. These forms of authority are not available to students, who are positioned in Western discourses of childhood that construct them in opposition to adults – as innocent, irrational, ignorant and in need of adult direction. Despite these seemingly binary positions, the teacher is not 'all-powerful', nor are they able to force students into compliant obedience. Students, too, have power and may choose to exercise it. They may, for instance, 'act out' or refuse to cooperate with the teacher's request; or they may be less confrontational and simply disengage from an activity or absent themselves from class; alternatively, they may choose to acquiesce. Because humans have agency, they may comply with, resist and challenge the discourses in operation. These are some key tenets used by feminist poststructuralists.

Key tenets of feminist poststructuralism may include the employment of the above concepts of subjectivity, discourse and power to inform new ways of conceiving of, gathering and analysing data, including data from educational contexts. Feminist poststructural discourse analysis, as employed by key thinkers in the field, suggests that individuals perform their own identities through language by drawing on various, sometimes competing, discourses about their subjectivities. This analytical framework acknowledges that power is often fluid yet contradictory – no one individual is always in a position of power or subordination – and that these differential constructions are due to varied discursive frameworks which influence individual subjectivities in any given social situation.

Intersections of critical theoretical paradigms

Within the broad paradigm of **critical theory** there are intersecting frames that together share a critical approach to lived experience. These frames incorporate poststructuralist perspectives of subjectivity and identity with a transformative agenda that addresses the production of inequality in daily life at micro and macro levels of society. Critical theory's concern is driven by emancipatory principles committed to the examination of the complexities of diversity and difference in how individuals and groups experience marginalisation, oppression and inequality with a focus on how material and cultural practices create structures of coercion and domination (Denzin & Lincoln, 2013). Hence, critical paradigms are concerned with social justice in society in which people have political, economic and cultural control of their lives (Aliakbari & Faraji, 2011). The discussion below outlines critical theories, including key concepts from cultural studies, Critical Race Theory and postcolonialism, drawing on their similarities and differences in their applicability to their particular concerns around identities of class, 'race', ethnicity, gender and, more recently, sexuality, language and age. It also presents a précis of Bourdieu's theory of social practice in articulating how reproductions of power operate within social processes and structures in our society.

Critical theory an examination of the complexities of diversity and difference and their impact on marginalised communities in view of how material and cultural practices construct inequality in society. In education, it explores how pedagogical practices can reproduce existing regimes of privilege and social control.

Cultural studies

There are two distinct traditions in **cultural studies** informed by critical theory. The first tradition, inspired by the Brazilian educator and activist Paulo Freire (1982), questions whether education functions as an instrument of oppression of minority groups through its socialisation processes or has the potential for liberation and emancipation in 'the practice of freedom' in which individuals critically and creatively participate in the transformation of the world (p. 14). Notable scholars associated with Freirean approaches to critical theory and pedagogy include bell hooks, Henry Giroux, Michael Apple and Joe L. Kincheloe. Their contributions to **critical pedagogy** involve critical thinking and the deconstruction of taken-for-granted dominant ways of thinking about how minorities are often marginalised and subordinated in education. As argued by Giroux (2011), educators theoretically engage with, are shaped by,

Cultural studies the exploration of how knowledge and representation define and construct identities through language, discourse and ideology. It provides an analysis of representation in historical and political fields and media contexts. Concepts of hybridity and diaspora are used to critically inform understandings of identity negotiation, mediated by 'race', language, ethnicity and class.

Critical pedagogy a teaching approach that seeks to challenge and resist educational practices that reinforce privilege for particular groups while maintaining the subordination of minority groups.

and are responsive to, the social, cultural, economic, political and global realities that shape people's daily lives. Thus, teacher educators must support pre-service teachers to make critical connections between the theory and practice.

The second tradition is concerned with how identity is represented in the media, literature, cinema, dance, music and theatre. Scholars associated with this include Stuart Hall, Homi Bhabha and Gayatri Chakravorty Spivak, just to name a few. These scholars adopt a cultural analysis of the construction of identity in relation to historical, cultural and political contexts. Both traditions have much to offer educators and pre-service teachers in their applications to critical pedagogy and everyday teaching practice, policy and relationships, equipping future teachers with forms of critical consciousness and a 'language of critique' to produce equitable educational outcomes for their students.

Conceptualisations of cultural identity

Traditionally situated within a neo-Marxist frame which applied an analysis of class relations to cultural representation, the most notable scholar, Stuart Hall, has advanced conceptualisations of cultural identity beyond the context of class, to include immigration, representation and political economy. Hall (1993, 1996) conceptualises identity in terms of the relationship between cultural practices and representation. His first position is related to the role of culture in building solidarity with, and belonging and allegiance to, individuals or groups. Notions of belonging are based on shared cultural practices, mutual histories and imagined homogeneity. His second position builds on the concept of imagined homogeneity to exemplify how identity can exclude and leave out. Through processes of exclusion, imagined homogeneity forms the basis of collective identities and fixed boundaries through which power relations between the 'insiders' and 'outsiders' are reproduced (Bhabha, 1994; Hall, 1993).

The third position highlighted by Hall describes identity as transformative and situational, which is subject to negotiation and change. This negotiation, often contradictory, is influenced by historical, social, linguistic and political complexity. Hall critiques the notion of a fixed identity and argues that the construction of identity in itself is fluid, seamless and unstable. Therefore, identity powerfully shapes the diverse lived experiences of all stakeholders in education, including children and their families. Finally, Hall's fourth position on identity recognises that within shared cultural discourses, practices and social processes there are points of difference, which are fragmented and contingent upon historical, contemporary power relations. His 1996 claim that identities are constantly changing – particularly due to globalisation, population flux and political instability – holds currency in today's ever-increasingly complex and dynamic global multicultural societies in which identities are produced in specific historical, cultural, global and institutional sites.

Diaspora and hybridity

Diaspora and hybridity are two key concepts in cultural studies, central to understandings of the shifting and transformative aspects of identity work. Diaspora is the voluntary or forced disbursement of cultural or 'racial' groups over different historical time periods and geographic locations. Within a contemporary context, the term 'diaspora' denotes transnational migration movements linked to globalisation, embedded in a social condition entailing a particular form of consciousness and sense of identity (Anthias, 1998; Vertovec & Cohen, 1999). Hybridity, on the other hand, is the borrowing, blending and lending between cultures that involves fusion and recreation of something anew, informed and influenced by the old of which it is partially made (Rosaldo, 1995; Young, 1995). Hybridity comes into existence at the moment of cultural, linguistic and social practice where meaning is articulated from within both past and present cultural histories, languages and trajectories. Papastergiadis (1998) argues that contemporary and politicised notions of hybridity have the potential to acknowledge the construction of identity through the negotiation of difference. Therefore, by examining diaspora and hybridity through a cultural studies lens, identities constructed through difference go beyond fixed notions of 'race', ethnicity, linguistic and gendered categories, to the recognition that lived experience of difference is also intersected across these categories.

Postcolonial studies, whiteness and Critical Race Theory (CRT)

Australia is a postcolonial nation state and, like other postcolonial societies, it continues to be subjected to colonial domination in which there are power relations and internal divisions based on ethnic, racial, linguistic and religious identities, including, most importantly, unequal power relations with Indigenous peoples. Therefore, the meanings and consequences of colonisation are influenced by social, political, linguistic, economic and historical domination due to slavery, migration, and oppression of Indigenous communities. Postcolonial theory problematises and challenges colonial representation and domination in its discursive and material forms and its historical legacies to reverse the effects of the colonial impact on Indigenous and immigrant peoples. As Giroux (1992) argues, the challenge that postcolonial theory presents to educators is the call for new ideas, pedagogical strategies and social movements that construct a politics of difference forged in the struggle to achieve cultural democracy.

Over the last 20 years, sociologists, cultural theorists and poststructural feminists have begun to interrogate whiteness as a social construction (Frankenberg, 1997; Gillborn & Ladson-Billings, 2010; Kincheloe & Steinberg, 1998). Defining whiteness is not easy or clear-cut. As an unmarked identity, it constantly evades scrutiny while maintaining social privilege. It is a refusal to acknowledge white power, and those who are white are often unknowingly implicated in social relations of privilege, domination and subordination (McLaren, 1998). As a result, the structural and subjective constructions of normative whiteness as universal, homogenised and essential remain underexamined. Still, Kincheloe and Steinberg (1998) point out that whiteness, like other racial, social and cultural identities, is a socio-historical construction. From this perspective, whiteness is not only subject to political, social, economic and cultural histories but also influenced by contemporary shifts and changes in a globalised and diverse world.

Critical Race Theory
(CRT) an interrogation of
invisible historical and social
constructions of whiteness. It
draws on postcolonial theory
and cultural studies to focus
on the relationships that
exist between race, racism
and power. CRT in education
challenges accepted practice
and provides a critical lens
through which it is possible
to identify normative white
privilege and interpret racial
inequality.

Scholars and researchers investigating the lived experiences of racialised minorities define **Critical Race Theory (CRT)** as a framework for unravelling how the supremacy of whiteness has continued to subordinate and marginalise people of colour (Villenas & Deyhle, 1999; Zues, 2015). CRT draws on cultural studies to critically analyse the positions of dominant white identity. The social category of 'white' is often unnamed and, as a result, it evades interrogation and scrutiny, which serves to reinforce its social privilege, power and normativity (Ashcroft, Griffiths & Tiffin, 2013; Robinson & Jones Díaz, 2016). Therefore, CRT examines issues of power and identity to reveal how normalising discourses of whiteness are often legitimised in institutional policies, politics, procedures, discourses and everyday social practices.

Bourdieu's theory of social practice

Of central importance to Bourdieu's theory are three key tenets: capital, habitus and field (Bourdieu, 1977, 1990). His framework is useful to educators in understanding how relations of power, which operate at both macro and micro levels, are also reproduced in education. His concern is directed at the manifestation of inequality within educational discourses, policies and pedagogies and, in this regard, his work enables educators to understand how they are positioned within contexts that can inhibit or promote equitable opportunities for learning.

Bourdieu's emphasis on capital incorporates various human forms of capital, including cultural, social and economic capital, through processes of transfer and conversion of one kind of capital into another. This may or may not yield social, political and economic power across different social institutions and social practices. Cultural capital is accumulated through knowledge, language, skills, family background and taste, which are transferred into privilege that some people acquire as part of their life experiences. It constitutes various forms of linguistic capital, including various language resources that make up the different human dispositions that influence the way we act, think and carry out our daily lives.

Social and economic capital are connected to the broader societal distributions of economic and social resources. Economic capital is accrued in monetary wealth that enables the conversion into material goods, such as property and resources. However, as Bourdieu (1993) points out, economic capital does not necessarily operate in isolation and a conversion process based on social capital is necessary, which also depends on the laws governing that conversion. For example, wealth does not necessarily bring about prestige, reputation and social status within a group, unless the individual has undergone a process of social recognition. Social capital involves access to social networks, institutions, relationships, recognition and resources that are accrued to individuals or groups as a result of group membership and mutual acquaintance (Bourdieu & Wacquant, 1992).

Bourdieu's notion of habitus is equally important in understanding that conversion processes do not exist in isolation. Habitus involves the resilient incorporation of dispositions, practices and perceptions expressed in moments of everyday social practices within social contexts or cultural fields (Bourdieu, 1990). He argues that the habitus produces individual and collective practices, thoughts, perceptions and dispositions. While the term 'habitus' is suggested by the idea of habit, Bourdieu (1993) argues that it does not imply mechanical and automotive behaviour. Rather, his use of the term denotes the durable and generative incorporation of a 'system of schemes for generating and perceiving practices' (p. 87). This involves the combination of dispositions, practices and perceptions expressed both subconsciously and consciously, 'set by the historically and socially situated conditions of its production' (p. 55). Ways in which the habitus can operate can be random and unpredictable: a direct reflection of the social context in which it is produced. Hence, the conditions that generate and organise social practices form the dispositions that in turn can be adapted to suit the outcome, event or social situation in which the habitus operates. For example, children growing up in middle-class English-speaking households where book-based literacy practices are highly valued develop reading dispositions and practices congruent with schooled literacy practices in education. Therefore, in education, 'a schooled literacy habitus is required by children in literacy learning' (Jones Díaz, 2007, p. 37).

The third important concept in Bourdieu's (1977, 1990, 1991) theory of conversion is his notion of social fields, constituted in broader institutions, such as education, law, family, health, the arts, media and popular culture. Fields also exist in relationships, events, topics, social situations and interactions through which the circulation and consumption of cultural and material practices mediate the relationship between social structure and cultural practice (Swartz, 1997). Given that Bourdieu is concerned with the production of power relations in fields, he argues that those who construct the field have the greatest power within that field. As a result of their monopoly of the power invested in their habitus, their play and ownership of the 'rules of the game' afford them positions of advantage. In this analysis of the field, the link between playing the game (habitus) and the game itself (field) is apparent. Added to this important nexus is the role of capital. Positions of advantage in playing the game are driven by the acquisition and accumulation of resources or goods that are deemed valuable and that are necessary in assigning positions of prestige or privilege within the field.

What does this mean for future teachers? Concepts of praxis, reflexivity and critical pedagogy

Praxis is a relational concept that draws together theory and practice. As Giroux (2011) argues, educators are not isolated from the social, cultural, economic, political and global realities impacting educational settings. Therefore, for teachers to make critical connections between theory and practice, their work requires reflection that is informed by a language of theory grounded in the everyday. This enables them to respond in equitable, just and sensitive ways as they are able to incorporate a variety of perspectives to reflect on their pedagogy, practices and how these relate to children, parents, colleagues and the broader community. Being reflective requires the challenging of assumptions and belief systems in terms of their implications in pedagogical practice, and peeling away deeply embedded normative assumptions about the world. This involves a process of critical inquiry in which the power relationships between the teacher and student are interrogated; for example, understanding how educational discourses construct gender, sexuality, 'race', class, ability, language and so forth, to position children's subjectivities in certain ways that reinforce inequality in education; or, appreciating how neoliberalism impacts on pedagogical practices and students' learning rather than blaming the individual for perceived 'failures'.

Reflexivity, however, transcends mere reflection; it involves a critical awareness of the 'self' in relation to Others (McNay, 2013). Schirato and Webb (2002) refer to reflexivity as the 'practical sense away from automatic or habituated practice to a more aware and evaluative relation to oneself and one's contexts' (p. 255). They argue that such knowledge allows us to make sense of what is happening in social practice, to assist in determining which practices can be deployed at the appropriate moment. Reflexivity is not just a matter of being sensitive to and aware of one's own standpoint, but recognises that language, assumptions, social practices and discursive positionings are embedded; these inform the relationships and knowledge production central to teachers' work.

Critical pedagogy is concerned with the knowledge–power nexus in education that privileges dominant or grand narratives constructed in discourses of Western history, patriarchy, monoculturalism, monolingualism and heteronormativity, privileging particular kinds of knowledge and experiences 'centered on the power/knowledge relations of the academy and largely on white, male, heterosexual [and monolingual] assumptions' (Apple, 1999, p. 171). Its aim is to address how unequal relations of power are sustained and reproduced in pedagogical relationships between 'teacher' and 'student'. Within this power relationship, teachers teach 'official knowledge' (curriculum) that is deemed appropriate by the state, the academy and, more recently, through neoliberal, economic rationalism. As Apple (2001) argues, what counts as legitimate knowledge represents the grand narratives (history, disposition, epistemology and discourses) of dominant cultural groups.

As critical pedagogy is concerned with transforming the relations of power to bring about a more just and equitable world for marginal and minority communities, it also forms part of the metaphor of the 'unseen half' in terms of how it is often silenced, invisible and risky work in teacher education. As its agenda is to critique and deconstruct dominant oppressive narratives and practices, produced at both global and local levels, it is often silenced and viewed as dangerous and potentially subversive. Thus, teachers who actively challenge and disrupt everyday relations of social power that produce forms of educational inequality often take risks as they question normalising assumptions around controversial and contemporary issues, particularly in relation to sexuality and gender diversity, refugees, immigration and racism. Their practices may be scrutinised by parents, principals, supervisors and, indeed, colleagues who themselves are challenged. Furthermore,

teacher educators adopting critical pedagogical approaches in their work experience resistance from pre-service teachers (hooks, 1994; Kumashiro, 2002; Mills &
Keddie, 2012). Working with forms of resistance is also part of the unseen half as
teacher educators confront new issues attributed to the complexities of new times.
When this work is informed by sociological theory, educators, including pre-service
teachers, are equipped with vital tools that enable transformative and reflexive
approaches.

Theory in practice: An overview of the chapters

Pre-service teachers are most likely to connect with theoretical work when such
content is framed by particular social issues and introduced via students' pre-
existing perceptions regarding social phenomena. Korthagen and Kessels (1999)
contend that, while pre-service teacher educators often hinge the act of teaching
theory on efforts to 'bridge the gap between the theory presented and teaching
practice' (p. 6), educators' choice of theoretical concepts a priori creates this gap,
while the line of thought that there is a gap to be bridged at all helps to entrench
that gap. We stand in agreement with this position: that theoretical thinking is
more likely to find fertile ground where the social and practical issues of education – issues that stimulate affective responses, concern and attention – are foregrounded, situating theory as a tool for their enhanced understanding. Hence, this
book examines theoretical application to real issues experienced in educational
settings.

Chapter 2 begins Part 1: Applying Poststructuralism(s). In this chapter, Son Truong
examines the diverse experiences of childhood as explored via Western pre-service
teachers' experiences of travelling abroad to work with children in diverse settings,
including schools, orphanages and community centres. Poststructural theoretical
concepts are employed to highlight the learning experiences of the university students specifically around destabilising dominant images of childhood.

In Chapter 3, Tania Ferfolja examines the critical notion of subjectivity and how
this is constructed in policy and other official documents. Ferfolja demonstrates
how particular understandings of gender and sexuality–diverse subjects are discursively constituted and the implications of these constructions. Feminist poststructuralist and Foucauldian theoretical tools guide the analysis and provide a
more nuanced understanding of the potential effects of policy.

Chapter 4 explores the experiences of gender and sexuality–diverse students
located in regional and rural locations across Australia. In this chapter, Ullman
works with the theory of social constructionism to explore concepts relevant to
the sociological study of gender and sexuality in educational settings, including
hegemonic masculinity and emphasised/hegemonic femininity, binary classifications of gender and sexuality, and gender performativity. These frames help guide
the analysis of students' reported 'gender climate', implicating teachers, peers,

curricular and institutional factors in the co-construction of gender and sexualities in school.

Chapter 5 marks the start of Part 2: Intersecting Theories for Meaning. In this chapter, Jo Lampert and Bruce Burnett focus on the journey of a pre-service teacher as she grapples with tensions generated by reflecting on her white, middle-class, privileged background while engaging in field experience within a high-poverty school. The authors employ CRT to enhance understanding of the deep and profound personal reactions of this student, and others like her, through a discursive analysis of the student's personal reflections.

In Chapter 6, Marnee Shay presents an interrogation of Australian 'flexi schools', which Indigenous students attend in disproportionally high numbers, and the Indigenous cultural considerations therein, as reported by principals in these locations. She discusses the tensions of a multicultural pedagogy that is inclusive of Indigenous people's cultures and histories and problematises the reductive 'dots and boomerangs' approach taken by some schools. Shay uses CRT to explore the institutionalised, deficit discourses of Indigenous 'race' and difference that remain entrenched in the Australian context and the ways in which deficit is reconstructed through school curriculum, policy and, ultimately, pedagogical framing.

Chapter 7 explores children's and their families' experiences of bi/multilingualism as they negotiate minority language and identity constructions. Drawing on frameworks of cultural studies, Criss Jones Díaz uses concepts of hybridity, diaspora and Bhabha's (1994) 'third space' to understand interracial/interethnic families' negotiation and use of languages and constructions of identity where English dominates social institutions, cultural discourses and linguistic practices. By drawing on concepts of discourse, subjectivity and power, Jones Díaz contrasts these views against educators' awareness of children's experiences to critically highlight language ideology in relation to constructions of identity.

In Chapter 8, Mohamed Moustakim uses Bourdieu's forms of capital, coupled with resistance theory, to analyse the counter-narratives of disaffection from young people who have experienced difficult relations with schooling. He positions the phenomenon of early school leaving as a rational reaction to students' low sense of connectedness and lack of perceived respect and solidarity with their peer group.

Chapter 9 begins Part 3: Using Critical Theory. Megan Watkins begins this section by exploring the changing face of multiculturalism in Australian education, using the Australian National Curriculum capability 'Intercultural Understanding' as a starting point from which to explore notions of 'culture' and 'ethnicity'. Drawing on her research, Watkins provides comparative accounts of teacher-led action research and models of how socio-cultural theory can be used to effect change, prompting readers to reassess their own understanding of culture and ethnicity.

In Chapter 10, Kate Huppatz explores the role of education in the production and reproduction of disadvantage and privilege. Working with the theories of Bourdieu, this chapter explores the classed dimensions of school choice in an analysis of Australian mothers' orientations to 'private' and 'public' schooling. Huppatz applies Bourdieu's concepts of cultural capital, habitus and field to interview data, exploring mothers' negotiation of school choice, assumptions about the

value of 'private' education, 'public' schooling as a form of resistance and the negotiation of the family–school relationship.

In Chapter 11, Karen Dooley examines the challenge of English literacy experienced by some refugee students new to Australia. She draws on Bourdieu's concepts
of field, habitus and capital to gain a better understanding of these challenges, presenting a critique of the reproductive work of schooling for groups of students who
experience educational disadvantage. Dooley presents data from an after-school
digital media club to explore literate practices of refugee students, outlining implications for teachers of literacy in culturally and linguistically diverse contexts.

Chapter 12 continues the exploration of the literacy practices of students from
diverse backgrounds, drawing attention to the ways in which schools are increasingly constrained by societal and institutional requirements that promote singular
language and literacy. Here, Jacqueline D'warte examines Bourdieu's concepts of
social and cultural capital and applies these to a consideration of 'linguistic capital' in the context of education. The chapter stresses the importance of agency
and voice for groups and individuals who have traditionally been marginalised in
educational practice and social life.

Chapter 13 explores how theory may unpack the complexities and multifaceted
nature of education and assist in gaining a more informed and critical perspective on the institution. The potential of theoretically informed practice to deepen
pre-service teachers' comprehension of the complex socio-cultural and political
contexts inherent in policy, praxis, pedagogy, school and community relationships
is discussed. The chapter explores the pitfalls of pedagogical practice without this
theoretical base. Theory is situated as an integral feature of educators' reflexive
practices and, further, as a protective factor for teacher burnout.

Conclusion

This chapter has explored the metaphor of the 'unseen half' in teachers' work and
educational settings from multiple perspectives. This includes how diversity and
social justice issues are often underacknowledged, undervalued and, as a result,
rendered problematic and invisible. Building on this notion of invisibility within
this metaphor, minority groups are present but invisible, marked by their 'difference' from the mainstream and often viewed as problematic. This positioning constructs diversity as a problem and diverse communities as somehow deficient – in
need of intervention, policing and regulation. On the other hand, normalised identities are visible but also unmarked and unscrutinised, afforded social, cultural
and political privileges without their marginalisation and Othering. This chapter
has also examined how teachers' lack of awareness of diversity, difference and
social justice issues, including their understanding of broader social processes and
structures in society, impacts on minority groups.

When teachers make critical connections between theory and practice, this
informs their practice, enabling equitable, sensitive and responsive pedagogies.
Such pedagogies embrace 'difference' and challenge the inequities arising out of

unequal power relations in society and represented in education. Finally, this chapter has provided a synopsis of the chapters in this book, to highlight the important contribution contemporary sociological theories have in drawing together theory and practice in educational contexts.

Considerations

- Reflect on your experiences of early childhood, primary or secondary education in terms of how issues of difference, diversity and social justice were addressed within the school/setting in terms of policy, pedagogy and practice. After reading this chapter, what recommendations would you offer this school/setting that incorporate a critical pedagogical approach informed by sociological theories?
- Identify key theoretical concepts presented in this chapter that resonate with you as a pre-service teacher and that you believe would inform your work in making the 'unseen half' visible.

Of interest

For further reading in critical, cultural and poststructural feminist theory, we encourage you to read the work of Foucault, Butler, Giroux, hooks, Freire, Apple, Weedon, Bourdieu, Hall, Bhabha and Ball. We have cited some of this seminal work in the reference list below and have marked particularly useful texts with an asterisk (*).

References

Aliakbari, M. & Faraji, E. (2011). Basic principles of critical pedagogy, 2nd International Conference on Humanities, Historical and Social Sciences, 2011. IPEDR, 17. Singapore: IACSIT Press.

Allen, J. M. & Wright, S. E. (2014). Integrating theory and practice in the pre-service teacher education practicum. *Teachers and Teaching: Theory and Practice*, 20(2), 136–51.

Anthias, F. (1998). Evaluating 'diaspora': Beyond ethnicity? *Sociology*, 32(3), 557–80.

*Apple, M. W. (1999). *Power, meaning and identity: Essays in critical educational studies*. New York: Peter Lang.

—— (2001). *Educating the 'right' way: Markets, standards, God and inequality*. New York: Routledge.

—— (2012). *Education and power* (2nd ed.). New York: Routledge.

Ashcroft, B., Griffiths, G. & Tiffin, H. (2013). *Postcolonial Studies: The Key Concepts*. Oxon: Routledge.

*Ball, S. J. (1990). Introducing Monsieur Foucault. In S. J. Ball (Ed.), *Foucault and education: Disciplines and knowledge* (pp. 1–8). London: Routledge.

*Bhabha, H. (1994). *The location of culture*. London: Routledge.

*Bourdieu, P. (1977). *Outline of a theory of practice*. Cambridge: Cambridge University Press. doi:10.1017/CBO9780511812507

——— (1990). *The logic of practice* (R. Nice, Trans.). Cambridge: Polity Press.

——— (1991). *Language and symbolic power*. Cambridge, MA: Harvard University Press.

——— (1993). *Sociology in question*. London: Sage Publications.

*Bourdieu, P. & Wacquant, L. (1992). *An invitation to reflexive sociology*. Cambridge: Blackwell.

Britzman, D. P. (1998). *Lost subjects, contested objects: Toward a psychoanalytic inquiry of learning*. Albany: State University of New York Press.

Connell, R. (2011). *Confronting inequality: Gender, knowledge and global change*. Sydney: Allen & Unwin.

Deng, Z. (2004). The role of theory in teacher preparation: An analysis of the concept of theory application. *Asia-Pacific Journal of Teacher Education, 32*(2), 143–57. doi:10.1080/1359866042000234232

Denzin, N. K. & Lincoln, Y. S. (Eds.). (2013). *Collecting and interpreting qualitative materials*. Thousand Oaks, CA: Sage Publications.

Dumont Jr C. W. (2008). *The promise of poststructuralist sociology: Marginalized peoples and the problem of knowledge*. Albany: State University of New York Press.

*Foucault, M. (1978/1998). *The will to knowledge: The history of sexuality: Vol. 1. An introduction* (R. Hurley, Trans.). New York: Penguin Books.

Frankenberg, R. E. (1997). *Displacing whiteness: Essays in social and cultural criticism*. Durham, NC: Duke University Press. doi:10.1215/9780822382270

*Freire, P. (1982). *Pedagogy of the oppressed*. Middlesex, England: Penguin Education.

Gillborn, D. & Ladson-Billings, G. (2010). Education and critical race theory. In M. W. Apple, S. T. Ball and L. A. Gandin (Eds.), *The Routledge international handbook of the sociology* (pp. 37–47). Oxon: Routledge.

Giroux, H. (1992). *Border crossings: Cultural workers and the politics of education*. London: Routledge.

——— (2010, November). Public values, higher education and the scourge of neoliberalism: Politics at the limits of the social. *Culture Machine – Interzone*, 1–18. Retrieved from http://www.culturemachine.net/index.php/cm/article/view/426/444

——— (2011). *On critical pedagogy*. New York: The Continuum International Publishing Group.

*Hall, S. (1993). Cultural identity in question. In S. Hall, D. Held & T. McGrew (Eds.), *Modernity and its futures* (pp. 274–316). Cambridge: Polity.

—— (1996). Who needs 'identity'? In S. Hall & P. du Gay (Eds.), *Questions of cultural identity* (pp. 1–17). London: Sage Publications.

Hennissen, P., Beckers, H. & Moerkerke, G. (2017). Linking practice to theory in teacher education: A growth in cognitive structures. *Teaching and Teacher Education*, 63, 314–25.

Holland, M., Evans, A. & Hawksley, F. (2011, August). International perspectives on the theory–practice divide in secondary initial teacher education. Paper presented at the Annual Meeting of the Association of Teacher Educators, University of Latvia, Riga, Latvia.

*hooks, b. (1994). *Teaching to transgress: Education as the practice of freedom*. New York: Routledge.

Jones, R. G. & Calafel, B. M. (2012). Contesting neoliberalism through critical pedagogy, intersectional reflexivity, and personal narrative: Queer tales of academia. *Journal of Homosexuality*, 59, 957–81. doi:10.1080/00918369.2012.699835

Jones Díaz, C. (2007). Literacy as social practice. In L. Makin, C. Jones Díaz & C. McLachlan (Eds.), *Literacies in childhood: Challenging views, challenging practice* (2nd ed., pp. 31–42). Sydney: Elsevier.

Kervan, L. K. & Turnbill, J. (2003). Teaching as a craft: Making links between pre-service training and professional practice. *English Teaching: Practice and Critique*, 2(3), 22–34.

Kincheloe, J. L. & Steinberg, S. R. (1998). *Addressing the crisis of whiteness: Reconfiguring white identity in a pedagogy of whiteness*. London: Macmillan.

Korthagen, F. A. J. & Kessels, J. P. A. M. (1999). Linking theory and practice: Changing the pedagogy of teacher education. *Educational Researcher*, 28(4), 4–17. doi:10.3102/0013189X028004004

Kumashiro, K. K. (2002). *Troubling education*. New York: Routledge.

McLaren, M. A. (2002). *Feminism, Foucault, and embodied subjectivity*. Albany, NY: State University of New York Press.

McLaren, P. (1998). Whiteness is … The struggle for postcolonial hybridity. In J. L. Kincheloe, S. E. Steinberg, N. M. Rodriquez & R. E. Chennault (Eds.), *White reign: Deploying whiteness in America* (pp. 63–75). London: Macmillan.

McNay, L. (2013). *Foucault: A critical introduction*. Maldan, MA: Polity Press.

Mills, C. & Keddie, A. (2012). 'Fixing' student deficit in contexts of diversity: Another cautionary tale for pre-service teacher education. *International Journal of Pedagogies and Learning*, 7(1), 9–19. doi:10.5172/ijpl.2012.7.1.9

Papastergiadis, N. (1998). *Dialogues in the diasporas: Essays and conversations on cultural identity*. London: Rivers Oram Press.

Robinson, K. H. & Jones Díaz, C. (2016). *Diversity and difference in childhood: Issues for theory and practice*. London: Open University Press.

Romain, S. (2011). Identity and multilingualism. In K. Potowski & J. Rothman (Eds.), *Bilingual youth: Spanish in English-speaking societies* (pp. 7–10). Amsterdam: John Benjamins.

Rosaldo, R. (1995). *Hybrid cultures: Strategies for entering and leaving modernity.* Minneapolis: University of Minnesota Press.

Schirato, T. & Webb, J. (2002). Bourdieu's notion of reflexive knowledge. *Social Semiotics*, 12(3), 255–68. doi:10.1080/10350330216373

Sellars, N. & Stevens, K. J. (1983). Three problems in the relationship of educational theory and teaching. *Australian Journal of Teaching Practice*, 3(2).

Swartz, D. (1997). *Culture and power: Sociology of Pierre Bourdieu.* Chicago: The University of Chicago Press.

Vertovec, S. & Cohen, R. (1999). Introduction. In S. Vertovec & R. Cohen (Eds.), *Migration, diasporas and transnationalism* (pp. xiii–xxviii). Aldershot, UK: Edward Elgar.

Villenas, S. & Deyhle, D. (1999). Critical race theory and ethnographies challenging the stereotypes: Latino families, schooling, resilience and resistance. *Curriculum Enquiry*, 29(4), 413–45. doi.org/10.1111/0362-6784.00140

Weedon, C. (1997). *Feminist practice and poststructuralist theory* (2nd ed.). Oxford: Blackwell.

Williams, J. (2014). *Understanding poststructuralism.* Hoboken: Taylor & Francis.

Young, R. J. C. (1995). *Colonial desire: Hybridity in theory, culture and race.* London: Routledge.

Zues, L. (2015). Poverty in education and the social sciences: Three definitions. In W. Tierney (Ed.), *Rethinking education and poverty* (pp. 77–96). Balitmore, MD: John Hopkins University Press.

Part 1

Applying Poststructuralism(s)

CHAPTER 2

Pre-service teacher identities and the social construction of childhood

Son Truong

AUSTRALIAN PROFESSIONAL STANDARDS FOR TEACHERS

Standard 1: Know students and how they learn

This chapter encourages readers to think more critically about child development, and the importance of questioning the universality of particular truth claims. Contextualist approaches help us to understand the relations between culture and human development and to consider alternative perspectives and question taken-for-granted assumptions about human development.

Standard 4: Create and maintain supportive and safe learning environments

This chapter highlights the importance of deconstructing dominant images of childhood to create inclusive learning environments in diverse educational settings. In particular, inclusive play practices begin with the recognition that children's play is a culturally structured activity.

> I guess just always being ready to question yourself. Like why things are done the way they are and not making assumptions of where those actions or behaviours are coming from. And constantly being self-aware of where your values and beliefs are coming from versus theirs, I think is a major part of working in a cross-cultural experience. Yeah, just trying your best to understand the context and the situation that the children and the community members are living in so that what you do is relevant for their lives. (Sam, undergraduate student, reflecting on what it means to teach in a cross-cultural context)

Introduction

In the contemporary global context of social, cultural, technological, political and economic integration, schools have become increasingly complex and diverse settings. Many Western countries, including Australia, have continued to see an increase of new immigrants, particularly from non-European-heritage countries (Organisation for Economic Co-operation and Development [OECD], 2013). Within these culturally diverse societies, schools, and in particular teachers, are tasked with the challenge of not only fostering an environment of respect for diversity, but also nurturing a sense of global citizenship through their teaching. However, given these responsibilities, it is essential to consider how we as educators develop or question our own perspectives and how this informs our approach to teaching children in culturally diverse educational settings. Fundamental to this process is a critical awareness of our own constructions of childhood and culture.

This chapter examines the experiences of a small group of undergraduate students from a Canadian university during an overseas cross-cultural service-learning placement in Thailand in relation to the ways in which the experience became a catalyst towards a more emergent understanding of childhood and culture. As an ethnographic researcher, I was a participant-observer with the students during their placement and conducted interviews with them to facilitate reflection on their experiences. The opening quote illustrates how the placement became a meaningful learning experience for Sam, and speaks to the messy, entangled and at times self-contradictory process of engaging in critical reflection. Sam shares about teaching in a cross-cultural context and the importance of questioning our ideologies, such as our values and beliefs about the world. For Sam, this self-awareness also involved understanding the different context of the children's lives and teaching in a way that was relevant to them.

In this chapter, I will draw specifically from four of the students' experiences of teaching in primary schools, orphanages and social centres. The objective of focusing on their reflections is not to generalise them, but rather to consider how their experiences of encountering childhoods and cultures, different from the dominant Western European–heritage culture, challenged them to think more critically about how they viewed the social world. Each individual student entered into the placement with their own set of beliefs, experiences and perspectives, informing their world view. Similarly, each student took something different from the experience and to an extent expressed how they learned about themselves, their identity and their work with children. Importantly, the participants shared stories of how they came to view different images of childhood and negotiated power and privilege while teaching overseas. These fundamental experiences help inform more culturally relevant teaching, particularly as classrooms become increasingly diverse and global citizenship advances as a prominent feature in the curriculum in countries such as Canada and Australia.

It is essential to highlight, however, that there is also a danger that these cross-cultural experiences can perpetuate, rather than challenge, dominant images of childhood and unequal relationships of power and privilege. This has become increasingly apparent to me as a pre-service teacher educator who has taught and led overseas placements with tertiary students from Canada and Australia. For example, through my own teaching, as well as work with children in a number of geographic and cultural contexts, I have witnessed how my position as a male academic coming from a large Western university has resulted in my ways of knowing being privileged. This can become a highly comfortable position and it is imperative to understand that it is also a precarious one, which must be questioned with regard to the complex interplay between power, knowledge and colonial legacies. Thus, regardless of our ethno-cultural background or whether we teach locally or overseas, ongoing critical reflexivity is imperative at all levels. Therefore, central to the discussion on childhood and culture in this chapter is the sociology of childhood and poststructuralist concepts of discourse and power. These theoretical concepts will be employed in the analysis of the students' experiences, and will be considered in more detail following a brief background discussion on cultural diversity and global education in Australia.

Background

Cultural diversity and global education in Australian classrooms

In highly industrialised nations, such as Canada and Australia, both past and present migration flows coupled with First Nations and Indigenous peoples mean that ethno-cultural diversity has become the rule rather than the exception. For Australia, this means that it is inevitable that teachers will need to work with cultural diversity, since 'the range of cultural backgrounds in Australian schools is considerable and extends from remote schools with Indigenous children to urban settings with children from Asian, Middle-Eastern, South American, African or European backgrounds' (Synott, 2009, p. 134). It can also be argued that in major urban centres these geographic boundaries become blurred even further. The impact of globalisation and the ways in which it has brought cultures into contact with each other in unprecedented ways places new demands on teachers. For example, teachers are expected to have an openness to other cultures, an ability to understand different cultural contexts and an awareness of global issues. This is exemplified by the *Melbourne Declaration on Educational Goals for Young Australians*, published by the Ministerial Council on Education, Employment, Training and Youth Affairs (MCEETYA, 2008). The declaration acknowledges the demands that globalisation has placed on Australian education, stating: 'As a consequence, new and exciting opportunities for Australians are emerging. This heightens the need to nurture an appreciation of and respect for social, cultural and religious diversity, and a sense of global citizenship' (p. 4). The document itself is reflective of globalised educational policy that increasingly emphasises notions of global citizenship.

Global education a term generally referring to curriculum content and materials that support the teaching of topics related to the interconnectedness of local and global issues, including globalisation, human rights, social justice, diversity and environmental sustainability.

The term '**global education**' has become commonplace in most curriculum discourse. Education Services Australia (ESA, 2008), a not-for-profit company owned by all Australian education ministers, explains that 'Global education promotes open-mindeness leading to new thinking about the world and a predisposition to take action for change' (p. 2). In relation to teaching about identity and cultural diversity, this includes identifying and critically analysing ethnocentric views, identifying stereotypes that obstruct understanding of peoples and cultures, and analysing and discussing the assumptions and underlying causes of stereotypical perceptions of other cultures based on colonialism, racism, ethnocentrism and sexism. However, the question remains as to what extent teachers themselves are positioned to engage with global education and, in particular, around issues of cultural diversity, especially at a time when research suggests conflicting results in relation to attitudes towards multiculturalism, immigration and diversity (see Dandy & Pe-Pua, 2010; Vedder, Horenczyk, Liebkind & Nickmans, 2006).

In response to these changing demands, many universities have turned their attention towards internationalisation, which is a multidimensional approach that often includes as one of its strategies opportunities for students to study and/ or work overseas. However, the mere act of occupying a different geographic space does not consequentially result in challenging ethnocentric viewpoints. There is also the danger that these experiences can result in maintaining cultural stereotypes and in constructing and perpetuating dominant and subordinate cultural identities (see Epprecht, 2004; Jorgensen, 2010; Razack, 2005), which accentuates the importance of considering the underlying principles that guide such programs. Equally, with the diversity of today's societies we do not need to travel overseas to have cross-cultural experiences. For example, the OECD *International Migration Outlook* states that the United Kingdom, which has traditionally been the top country of origin of selected migrants in Australia, is being overtaken by India and China, and seven of the top 10 origin countries in 2011–12 were in Asia (OECD, 2013). Research suggests that Australian public schools in large urban centres, such as Sydney and Melbourne, reflect the country's cultural diversity. Ho (2011, p. 606) found that two-thirds of children in Australia attend public schools, and across Sydney, 50% or more are from language backgrounds other than English. This underpins the important work **pre-service teachers and educators** must embark upon to think more critically about intercultural engagement and cultural difference in the classroom.

Pre-service teacher education the tertiary education and training required to enter into the teaching profession. Pre-service teachers are tertiary students studying to become early childhood, primary or secondary teachers.

In this study, the students were encouraged to move beyond reflection to be reflexive in their practice. Reflexivity, as described in Chapter 1, involves not only being critically aware of one's viewpoint, but being able to situate it within relationships of power, discourse and knowledge. Understanding these key theoretical concepts, which are introduced and discussed in Chapter 1, are critical for developing a deeper awareness of one's world view and view of self in relation to others. In this case, the students were studying in the fields of education and child development; thus, a relevant entry point into the process of reflexivity was questioning dominant images of, and understandings about, childhood. It is to a discussion of childhood, discourse and power that we now turn.

Key theoretical concepts

The new sociology of **childhood** and poststructuralist concepts of discourse and power are used in this chapter to analyse the tertiary students' overseas professional placement. At the core of this experience was teaching children in a **cross-cultural** context, thus highlighting the need to engage with notions of childhood and culture. This section examines the critical perspectives in the sociology of childhood before turning to a discussion on cultural representation. These concepts, as well as Said's (1978) 'Orientalism', illustrate how images of childhood and culture are constructed and help us to understand the need to reconceptualise these representations when working in diverse educational settings, whether local or abroad.

Childhood the period of life that is distinct from adulthood. Childhood has been studied across numerous academic disciplines and has been described by biological age, by development stages and as a social construct.

Cross-cultural a term referring to interactions or comparisons between two or more cultures. Cross-cultural engagement may occur locally, but may also be used to refer to overseas experiences, which result in more immersive learning for students.

Reconceptualising images of childhood

Critical theorists of the sociology of childhood attempt to analyse the dominant discourses of the child. Drawing on the work of Foucault (1971), discourse can be understood as a bounded system of social knowledge that establishes what is accepted as reality within a given society. Ashcroft, Griffiths and Tiffin (2000) explain that this system of statements informs the ways in which the world is known. The concept of discourse helps us to understand a particular way of meaning-making within specific contexts and power relations. For example, viewing dominant discourses such as childhood as a particular system of statements that have been made about the child helps us to see how these statements are made up of 'certain assumptions, prejudices, blindnesses and insights, all of which have a historical provenance, but exclude other, possibly equally valid statements. All these statements and all that can be included within the discourse thus become protected by the assertion of "truth"' (p. 73). These assertions of truth perpetuate a very particular, universal image of childhood and the child.

Discourses of children and childhood have been shaped by scholars across many fields, including history, sociology, geography and psychology. Steinberg and Kincheloe (2004) contend that the dominant construct is informed by a positivist paradigm – the belief in an objective, knowable reality – where children are viewed as naturally compliant and dependent upon adults. Positivists defend this position by drawing on the physical biological immaturity of children. This image of the child as innocent is a dominant construction that positions children as incapable and in need of protection. The underlying assumptions of this view are rooted in developmental psychology's child development discourse, which is attributed with the positivist authority of neutral and objective knowledge. However, this 'truth' is based almost entirely on a decontextualised view of childhood and ignores the social, cultural and political context of other children's realities. For example, many studies of children's play and development that have influenced the dominant discourses of developmental psychology were conducted in Western contexts and/or controlled experimental environments. These studies position play, childhood and development as independent of culture and provide little insight into the play and development of children in non-Western contexts (Göncü, Jain & Tuermer, 2007).

Among the seminal works that have influenced a sociological approach to the study of childhood is *Centuries of Childhood: A Social History of Family Life*, in which Philippe Ariès argues that the notion of childhood did not exist in medieval society (Ariès, 1962). Ariès' thesis prompted new possibilities for the concept of childhood as a social construction. While it must be acknowledged that many scholars have contributed to reframing childhood studies, it is the work of Allison James, Chris Jenks and Alan Prout, starting in the early 1990s, which is credited with instigating the new sociology of childhood.

James, Jenks and Prout (1998) describe how historical observations about childhood suggest that it is 'less a fact of nature and more an interpretation of it' (p. 62). Therefore, within the new sociology of childhood, childhood is a social construction 'depicted as the complex interweaving of social structures, political and economic institutions, beliefs, cultural mores, laws, policies and the everyday actions of both adults and children, in the home and on the street' (James & James, 2004, p. 13). While there are differing streams of thought, Corsaro (2015) elucidates that there are two central concepts in the new sociology of childhood. First, children are active, creative social agents who produce their own cultures and simultaneously contribute to the production of adult societies. Second, childhood is a structural form that is socially constructed. This concept recognises that children are a part of society and are affected by its structural arrangements, including but not limited to social class, gender and age groups. Therefore, the new sociology of childhood is a field of inquiry that seeks to understand children's lived experiences and how social structures constrain or shape their lives. This has relevance for educators across all fields and years because the ways in which we view children and our expectations about childhood affect the ways in which we carry out research and how we teach and interact with them and their families on a daily basis. As educators teaching in diverse settings, we must consider the children and families in our classrooms whose everyday lives are not reflected in the images and ideologies that are informed solely by dominant Western discourses.

Deconstructing dominant images of childhood involves reconceptualising our understanding of children as different from adults based upon age and generation, but not as inferior. For Cannella (1997), this requires an analysis of our work as educators to uncover who has been privileged or oppressed by the dominant perspectives in the field, and reconceptualisation encompasses new images, new constructions and new possibilities for education. This will require continued pluralism rather than a universalist truth. Therefore, reconceptualisation requires us as educators to question knowledge claims about children and childhood. When working with children from diverse backgrounds, this could lead us to ask questions such as: Whose knowledge counts when we seek to understand children and culture?

Understanding cultural representation

Understanding the relationship between power and knowledge is central to our understanding of childhood and cultural representation. For example, as a pre-service teacher observing a child's interactions with teachers, peers or their parents, are we making interpretations through our own cultural lens or seeking first to understand their behaviours through their cultural context? Furthermore, when we formulate our understanding of other cultures, what language is used when encountering different cultural groups, how is knowledge constructed about these groups, and whose knowledge counts? In his influential book *Orientalism*, Edward Said (1978) examines the process in which representations of the Orient were produced by European colonial powers, legitimised as valid ways of knowing, and served to establish and maintain imperial control over the colonised. Said (1978) refers to Orientalism as the way in which the Orient came to be known within the European Western experience, and contributed to defining Europe (or the West) as its contrasting image. Thus, in constructing cultural identity, the colonisers' representations produce knowledge of the Other and alternative forms of knowledge become subjugated. For Said (1995), the construction of identity 'involves establishing opposites and "others" whose actuality is always subject to the continuous interpretation and re-interpretation of their differences from "us". Each age and society re-creates its "Others"' (p. 332).

This 'us'/'them' system of binary logic contributes to an unequal relationship of power by creating hierarchies in the way we make sense of the world. Ashcroft et al. (2000) explain that the problem with binary thinking is that it creates categories of opposition, but suppresses any ambiguous spaces between them. Therefore, the binary logic of imperialism perpetuates a relation of dominance in colonial discourse (e.g. coloniser/colonised, white/black, civilised/primitive, advanced/backward, good/ evil, beautiful/ugly). The concept of Orientalism continues to have relevance in today's postcolonial or neocolonial world as we think about how we view, encounter and represent culture (and especially cultural differences) through language. This could be in our everyday lives, in our educational settings or when travelling overseas. How do we represent 'us' and 'them', how does this contribute to perpetuating cultural stereotypes, and how do we construct our understanding of culture? Any attempts to define culture are fraught with limitations. Drawing from the work of postcolonial theorists, namely Homi Bhabha (see Bhabha, 1994), Yazdiha (2010) states, 'The contemporary cultural landscape is an amalgam of cross-cultural influences, blended, patch-worked, and layered upon one another. Unbound and fluid, culture is hybrid and interstitial, moving between spaces of meaning' (p. 31). Therefore, culture cannot be conceptualised in binaries, nor can it be viewed as fixed, rigid and unchanging. Rather, the work of scholars in the field of cultural studies (see Chapter 1) reveals that culture is hybrid and cultural identity is continually being negotiated. These theoretical concepts contribute to the analysis that shortly follows examining how the Canadian tertiary students challenged and/or maintained ethnocentric viewpoints about children and Thailand through their overseas teaching experiences.

Methodology

The purpose of the research was to gain critical insight into the Canadian university students' experiences teaching in schools, orphanages and social centres in Thailand. Within this context, an ethnographic case study was the methodology best suited for this aim, as it allowed me, as a researcher, to spend an extended period of time to become acquainted with the participants, understand the dynamics of their interaction and elicit the meanings attached to their experiences (LeCompte & Schensul, 1999). In practice, this meant that I was a participant-observer who travelled overseas with a group of seven university students, and was both a volunteer and a researcher throughout their three-month placement in Thailand. The four students whose reflections are included in this chapter were all senior-level undergraduate students from a large Canadian university, studying in the fields of education and child development. The students, three female and one male, were in their early twenties with varying international travel experience. Their overseas

Service-learning an educational approach that integrates community volunteer work within a facilitated or guided learning experience. The learning experience includes reflection on personal and professional growth, as well as civic engagement.

placement was a part of their coursework and involved a semester of preparation prior to the three-month **service-learning** experience, which included approximately 35 hours per week of structured and unstructured teaching. The preparation included elements of pedagogical content, discussions on the social construction of childhood, cross-cultural preparation and fundraising activities. The study received appropriate ethical approvals and all students voluntarily gave informed consent to take part in the research.

The data collection methods included researcher field notes and a reflective journal, as well as informal discussions and semi-structured interviews with the students. The students were interviewed early in the placement, where they were asked to discuss their motivations for taking part in the program; their initial reactions and experiences upon arrival; the relationship-building process with the various organisations, teachers and children; and their personal learning experiences. The students also participated in final interviews, where many of the preceding topics were revisited, with a particular focus on how the students encountered and responded to cultural differences in their everyday activities.

All of the interviews were audio-recorded and transcribed verbatim. The data analysis was completed using the constant comparative method for coding qualitative data (Strauss & Corbin, 1998). This involved comparing segments of data to explore similarities and differences, in order to identify patterns, which were eventually grouped into themes. The analysis for this discussion is guided by the theoretical framework outlined in the previous section and, within the tradition of critical inquiry, seeks not only to increase understanding but also to initiate reflexivity and action. I must also recognise my voice and interpretation within the analysis of the students' experiences. As with all interpretive research, I acknowledge that the responses and stories shared are situated in space and time, and that the students' identities and views are fluid and continually shaped by their lived experiences. In this study, the participants shared stories of how they started to view childhood and themselves in relation to others in new ways. Therefore, the following discussion is organised into two parts: encountering childhoods and encountering the self.

Analysis and discussion

Encountering childhoods: Challenging dominant images of childhood

Researchers in children's geographies and development have highlighted the importance of understanding the socio-cultural context, including the everyday environments, of children's lives. It is this 'stuff' of everyday life that is a main explanatory variable for understanding childhood (Tudge, 2008), and yet is often overlooked in a 'culture-free' view of childhood. In one of the pre-departure sessions with the students, we found ourselves looking at images often associated with children and childhood. Photographs of children running in parks, playing with various materials and playthings, sitting at their desks at school and eating with their families in grassy tree-lined yards flashed across the screen. While seemingly neutral, these images were selected because they portray a very particular Western childhood; in other words, a childhood that is experienced by a minority of the world's children. These images become normalised on a global scale through popular media, advertisements, and even teaching materials and curriculum that are exported around the world. The purpose of the activity was not to create a binary between Western and non-Western childhoods, but rather to draw attention to the ways in which we construct our own images of childhood and may come to view, or judge, other childhoods through these frames of reference.

Working outside of the students' own dominant cultural environment brought a new level of awareness of the importance of contextualising their understandings. After arriving in Thailand and getting started in their placements, the students were asked to create a timeline of events and then reflect on their initial observations and responses to their placement sites. During the interviews, there was reflection on how the physical environment was an initial stimulus towards disrupting Western views of childhood. For example, while thinking about her first visit to one of the schools, Jamie stated:

> I just remember the school was a lot different from what I thought it would be like. I thought it was going to be, well, appearance-wise just one big building, but it's actually like a collection of buildings, so that was neat. And also seeing what kind of opportunity we had here. Because I expected them not to have very good facilities, not very good equipment, not very many opportunities.

Within this context, Jamie was coming to see the diversity of children's everyday environments. Moreover, beyond the recognition of the physical differences of place, this also initiated reflection on a preconceived image of the Other (i.e. Thailand as a less economically developed country) and the meanings attached to that representation (i.e. not very good facilities or many opportunities). Immediately following the above statements, Jamie went on to say:

> Maybe I even sort of expected there not to be as many staff and not the quality of staff that they have. Then I realised that it's a really good school and then seeing that they have art, they have computers, they have occupational therapy, they've got like that playground.

During similar discussions with the other six students there was reflection on the assumptions that were made about a less economically developed country, in terms of not only the teaching environment, but also the quality of the teaching. Some students also reflected on how they had not realised there would be a range of disparity in resources among the organisations or the communities in which they were working. Their initial encounters with the various organisations started to pull apart some of their preconceived views of a less economically developed country and challenged possible developed/undeveloped, rich/poor, advanced/backward binary thinking, which can lead to broad generalisations such as, in this case, views of the quality of educational experience. Upon completion of the placement, Jamie shared in an exit interview how the experience helped her to view different teaching methods within their context rather than within a hierarchy, prompting her to 'think twice about some of the things that I have learned' and to question 'well, that's not what I was taught, but maybe what would the benefits be of doing it this way?' This was a significant lesson, as it is an example of how Jamie as a pre-service teacher started to critique and contextualise the teaching practices expounded in her Western education. In the case of early childhood education, taking this critical analysis of educational practices further involves identifying and evaluating the forms of discourse that have dominated the field, including, according to Cannella (1997), developmentally appropriate practice, child-centred, play-based perspectives, among other privileged knowledges. This represented an initial step towards engaging in deeper reflexivity about the assumptions informing pedagogical practice.

There were many other encounters with diverse childhoods over the course of the placement. For example, many of the placements involved teaching physical education and after-school activities; therefore, the students were asked to reflect on their observations about children's play. In another interview, Kelly shared her initial response and interpretation that the children's play was too rough; however, upon discussion with the teachers, she learned that it was an accepted, 'normal' form of play within the local context. In a post-placement interview, Kelly reflected on learning about the cultural dimensions of play:

> We never really figured out what play was for them. So we kind of assumed that it was the same kind of play. I don't know what they consider play, but I think it's neat to be able to bounce off ideas … it's very beneficial.

Kelly's statement alludes to the recognition that play must be defined within its own cultural context. This is significant, especially since play has become a dom-inant discourse in the field of early childhood education; however, like childhood, it has been largely viewed in dominant discourses as culture-free and universal (Kirova, 2010), rather than recognising that play is 'a culturally structured activity that varies widely across cultures (as well as within them) as a result of differences in childrearing beliefs, values, and practices' (Gaskins, Haight & Lancy, 2007, p. 179), among other social structures.

Working outside of their own dominant cultural environment also brought a new level of awareness to the students' constructions of children's roles and capabilities. For example, there were many discussions focused on observations of the children's behaviours, such as how the children looked after one another and how older children were responsible for younger children. Additionally, there were observations of the different roles the children had within their everyday activities and routines, including contributing to the running of households and possibly income. This challenged some of the pre-service teachers' notions of childhood and constructions of competency associated with age, which are usually informed by dominant discourses that have designated those who are younger as simple, immature and lacking (Cannella, 2002). For example, while reflecting on the topic of child development, Jordan stated:

> I think this has definitely opened me to cultural differences and how certain aspects of development that I've learned, like in classes, as being steps in a process, are maybe not as present in a different culture. So maybe some of these things are being able to distinguish things that are maybe more related to actual steps towards development and the things that are more related to culture and society that they live in and how that relates to development.

This statement shows how Jordan was starting to think more critically about child development, and the importance of questioning the universality of partic-ular truth claims. Contextualist approaches help us to understand the relations between culture and human development by focusing on everyday life and the complex interconnections within it (Tudge, 2008). Additionally, while it is import-ant for educators to have an understanding of child development and develop-mental psychology, it is equally important to consider alternative perspectives and question taken-for-granted assumptions about human development (see Bradley, 1989; Burman, 2008). Through these experiences, the students had brief glimpses into different interconnections between child, family, school and broader social structures, which initiated for some of them a reconceptualisation of their images of childhood.

Encountering the self in relation to Others: Questioning identity and privilege

In addition to viewing childhood in new ways, the experience was also a catalyst towards viewing themselves differently. In particular, the participants were confronted with questions of privilege in relation to their identity as Canadian students, pre-service teachers or future professionals. For some of the students, this reflexivity was initiated through being viewed as 'experts'. For example, Kelly shared that she was surprised to teach classes without a supervising teacher or director being present, and Sam commented on how the group felt they were being treated as 'professionals' and 'experts', which made them uncomfortable, as it was not a perception they were trying to perpetuate. There are various factors that may have come into play in this situation, including a lack of staff members to supervise, language barriers, and the students' own interpretations; however, the privileging of Western knowledge and subsequent subjugation of other ways of knowing is an important consideration, which Sam also reflected upon:

> I think it has a lot to do with, just kind of, power hierarchies that have existed for a long time between Europeans and non-Europeans and believing that the West is more educated, that they know more and they know how to do things better. So coming from the West and coming from an institution of higher learning from the West, I think that it's a starting point before they even meet us.

Sam's explanation points to unequal power relations and how they can operate to produce privileged positions, particularly for Westerners in non-Western contexts. However, this perspective requires critical analysis in order to disrupt rather than perpetuate these privileged positions and identities.

Razack (2005) explores how representations of 'race' and whiteness, nationality and identity merge to produce complex relations when Western students go abroad. Similar to Razack's findings, all of the students in this study were immediately aware of some level of a privileged status while overseas. This was manifested in different ways, bringing more concrete understanding to imperialist binaries such as coloniser/colonised, white/black, advanced/backward and beautiful/ugly, and how dominant and subordinate identities are produced. For example, students reflected on the feelings of being treated as 'experts' at the schools; those with light skin and hair were repeatedly told they were beautiful (and furthermore, seeing numerous skin-whitening and bleaching cosmetic products in stores); and, lastly, all of the students discussed feelings of guilt because not only could they for the most part not speak any Thai, but there were instances where local people were also apologising for their 'poor' English language skills. Therefore, even in a non-native-English-speaking country they felt the privilege ascribed to English as a global language, whose power derives from its historical use across the British colonies, the largest of the modern empires, and from its use by the United States (Ashcroft et al., 2000).

It is important to note that, although Thailand was never formally colonised, the students' experiences have relevance within today's postcolonial and neocolonial context, particularly within highly ethno-culturally diverse schools. Razack (2005) argues that, although we are no longer in the colonial era, it is imperative to have an understanding of how 'postcolonial subjects are struggling to decolonize their minds and societies' (p. 91), particularly in settler societies, such as Canada and Australia. If those of us in privileged positions, including pre-service teachers and educators from large Western universities, are not critically aware of colonial legacies, imperial binaries that maintain unequal relations of power will only deepen. Drawing from this overseas experience, we can also make links to our own local contexts. As educators, we must ask ourselves what are the potential assumptions or judgements that are made about children, parents and education systems from different parts of the world. Furthermore, we must also do more than just think critically about our work, but also engage in reflexivity to inform our day-to-day practices.

Implications

> Education never was, is not and never can be neutral or indifferent in regard to the reproduction of the dominant ideology or the interrogation of it. (Freire, 1998, p. 91)

Drawing from the previous discussion and analysis of the students' experiences, I offer two main implications framed around praxis and rethinking educational practices. First, education, and more specifically, preparing to teach global education and social justice curriculum, involves praxis in the Freirean sense, whereby reflection and action occur simultaneously and are mutually important in striving for social change (Freire, 1970). Reflecting on their overseas experiences, some of the students commented on how they had never been to a 'developing country' and how it was eye-opening to learn about poverty. However, while learning about other regions of the world is a valuable component of global education, there is also a need to deconstruct the image of the starving child as Other; poverty, infringements on human rights, and social inequity are not bound by any borders. Therefore, while various experiences and encounters can open our eyes to different realities, we risk ambivalence to injustice if all we take from the learning experience is a sense of 'how lucky we are' or 'how grateful we are for what we have'. Critical reflexivity on the local and the global involves an understanding that inequity exists in all societies, including Western 'developed' societies, and in an increasingly globalised world our actions, practices and ways of living have far-reaching effects. Therefore, praxis may also take us into uncomfortable spaces and challenge us to think in more critical and nuanced ways, so as to consider how we may be implicated in global inequity through our own action or inaction, and to inform how we move forward from there.

Second, reconceptualising childhood involves rethinking childhood educational practices. Within a highly globalised and market-driven world, Kincheloe (2002) contends that a new childhood has emerged that requires a more progressive politics of childhood education. This demands more complex understandings of the cognitive abilities of children that lead to new avenues of adult–child interaction. Similarly, the new sociology of childhood challenges traditional generational assumptions about children's capabilities and positions them as social agents who are simultaneously influenced by, as well as influence, cultures. Therefore, focusing on children's agency also requires consideration of how the existing social structures, such as schools, will support or enable their actions. As a starting point, educators may find it helpful to review studies where adult researchers have positioned children as competent individuals capable of participating in research concerning their lives. Varying methodological approaches engage children at different levels of participation; however, the underlying assumption is that children, including younger children, are capable of identifying issues that are relevant to them, setting research agendas and carrying out research. This approach opens up numerous possibilities for the classroom, as children are provided with more opportunities to have a voice in matters that they consider relevant and meaningful to their lives.

This chapter explores the experiences of pre-service teachers during an overseas placement outside of their own dominant cultural environment. These experiences brought a new level of awareness of the importance of contextualising their understanding of childhood and culture. The analysis of their experiences highlights the importance of deconstructing dominant images of the child as universal, in order to reposition children as social agents and to reconceptualise childhood as socially constructed. This is significant for us as educators because the ways in which we view children and our expectations about childhood affect the ways in which we carry out research, teach and interact with them and their families. Therefore, rather than an end point, this represents an entry point into rethinking educational practices that consider the fluidity of childhood and culture in today's contemporary context.

Considerations

- The new sociology of childhood reveals new possibilities for educational practice. How are your current textbooks and educational resources framed within the dominant discourses of childhood? Do any of these materials challenge these discourses?
- How can particular views of childhood and subsequent educational practices either limit or lead to the empowerment of children to take action for social change?
- In the same way that children's agency is influenced by broader social structures, teachers' agency and ability to act is also affected by existing policies. What are the challenges to adopting alternative approaches for teaching in mainstream educational settings?

- Although it was published over 25 years ago, Peggy McIntosh's seminal paper *White Privilege: Unpacking the Invisible Knapsack* (McIntosh, 1990) is still used in anti-racism education today. What is the relationship between whiteness, power and social privilege? (Refer to the discussion on Critical Race Theory in Chapter 1 for further reading.) Regardless of your background, what privileged space(s) do you occupy?
- How might global education perpetuate, rather than challenge, unequal relationships of power and privilege? What critical pedagogical approaches can we adopt as educators to embrace diversity and challenge inequities?

Of interest

- Teaching and Learning for a Sustainable Future: A Multimedia Teacher Education Program. This is an online professional development program by the United Nations Educational, Scientific and Cultural Organization (UNESCO) that focuses on the interconnectedness of global issues. See http://www.unesco.org/education/tlsf
- Child Friendly Cities UNICEF (see http://childfriendlycities.org/). This website of the United Nations Children's Fund provides information on the Child Friendly Cities initiative and offers examples of projects, as well as good practices and tools, based on principles of child rights and participation.
- Universal Children's Day. The 20th of November is a day dedicated to promoting the ideals and objectives of the Convention on the Rights of the Child. See http://www.un.org/en/events/childrenday

References

Ariès, P. (1962). *Centuries of childhood: A social history of family life* (R. Baldick, Trans.). New York: Knopf. (Original work published 1960).

Ashcroft, B., Griffiths, G. & Tiffin, H. (2000). *Post-colonial studies: The key concepts.* London: Routledge.

Bhabha, H. K. (1994). *The location of culture.* London: Routledge.

Bradley, B. S. (1989). *Visions of infancy: A critical introduction to child psychology.* Cambridge: Polity Press.

Burman, E. (2008). *Deconstructing developmental psychology* (2nd ed.). New York: Routledge.

Cannella, G. S. (1997). *Deconstructing early childhood education: Social justice and revolution.* New York: Peter Lang.

—— (2002). Global perspectives, cultural studies, and the construction of a postmodern childhood studies. In G. S. Cannella & J. L. Kincheloe (Eds.), *Kidworld: Childhood studies, global perspectives, and education* (pp. 3–18). New York: Peter Lang.

Corsaro, W. A. (2015). *The sociology of childhood* (4th ed.). Thousand Oaks, CA: Sage Publications.

Dandy, J. & Pe-Pua, R. (2010). Attitudes to multiculturalism, immigration and cultural diversity: Comparison of dominant and non-dominant groups in three Australian states. *International Journal of Intercultural Relations*, 34(1), 34–46. doi:10.1016/j.ijintrel.2009.10.003

Education Services Australia (ESA) (2008). *Global perspectives: A framework for global education in Australian schools*. Melbourne: Education Services Australia.

Epprecht, M. (2004). Work-study abroad courses in international development studies: Some ethical and pedagogical issues. *Canadian Journal of Development Studies*, 25(4), 687–706. doi:10.1080/02255189.2004.9669009

Foucault, M. (1971). Orders of discourse: Inaugural lecture delivered at the Collège de France. *Social Science Information*, 10(2), 7–30. doi:10.1177/053901847101000201

Freire, P. (1970). *Pedagogy of the oppressed*. Baltimore, MD: Penguin Books.

—— (1998). *Pedagogy of freedom: Ethics, democracy and civic courage*. Lanham, MD: Rowman & Littlefield.

Gaskins, S., Haight, W. & Lancy, D. F. (2007). The cultural construction of play. In A. Göncü & S. Gaskins (Eds.), *Play and development: Evolutionary, sociocultural, and functional perspectives* (pp. 179–202). Mahwah, NJ: Lawrence Erlbaum Associates.

Göncü, A., Jain, J. & Tuermer, U. (2007). Children's play as cultural interpretation. In A. Göncü & S. Gaskins (Eds.), *Play and development: Evolutionary, sociocultural, and functional perspectives* (pp. 155–78). Mahwah, NJ: Lawrence Erlbaum Associates.

Ho, C. (2011). Respecting the presence of others: School micropublics and everyday multiculturalism. *Journal of Intercultural Studies*, 32(6), 603–19. Retrieved from http://dx.doi.org/10.1080/07256868.2011.618106

James, A., Jenks, C. & Prout, A. (1998). *Theorizing childhood*. Cambridge: Polity Press.

James, J. & James, A. (2004). *Key concepts in childhood studies*. London: Sage Publications.

Jorgensen, S. (2010). De-centering and re-visioning global citizenship education abroad programs. *International Journal of Development Education and Global Learning*, 3(1), 23–38. Retrieved from http://ioepress.co.uk/journals/international-journal-of-development-education-and-global-learning

Kincheloe, J. L. (2002). The complex politics of McDonald's and the new childhood: Colonizing Kidworld. In G.S. Cannella & J. L. Kincheloe (Eds.), *Kidworld:*

Childhood studies, global perspectives, and education (pp. 75–121). New York: Peter Lang.

Kirova, A. (2010). Children's representations of cultural scripts in play: Facilitating transition from home to preschool in an intercultural early learning program for refugee children. *Diaspora, Indigenous, and Minority Education, 4*(2), 74–91. doi:10.1080/15595691003635765

LeCompte, M.D. & Schensul, J. J. (1999). *Designing and conducting ethnographic research: Ethnographer's toolkit 1.* Walnut Creek, CA: AltaMira Press.

McIntosh, P. (1990). White privilege: Unpacking the invisible knapsack. *Independent School*, 31–6. Retrieved from http://www.nais.org/Articles/Pages/Independent-School-Magazine.aspx

Ministerial Council on Education, Employment, Training and Youth Affairs (MCEETYA) (2008). *Melbourne declaration on educational goals for young Australians.* Retrieved from http://www.curriculum.edu.au/verve/_resources/National_Declaration_on_the_Educational_Goals_for_Young_Australians.pdf

Organisation for Economic Co-operation and Development (OECD) (2013). *International migration outlook 2013.* Author. doi:10.1787/migr_outlook-2013-en

Razack, N. (2005). 'Bodies on the move': Spatialized locations, identities, and nationality in international work. *Social Justice, 32*(4), 87–104. Retrieved from http://www.socialjusticejournal.org

Said, E. W. (1978). *Orientalism.* New York: Pantheon Books.

—— (1995). *Orientalism* (reprinted with a new afterword). New Delhi: Penguin Books India.

Steinberg, S. R. & Kincheloe, J. L. (2004). Introduction: Kinderculture, information saturation, and the socioeducational positioning of children. In S. R. Steinberg & J. L. Kincheloe (Eds.), *Kinderculture: The corporate construction of childhood* (2nd ed., pp. 1–48). Boulder, CO: Westview Press.

Strauss, A. & Corbin, A. (1998). *Basics of qualitative research: Techniques and procedures for developing grounded theory.* Thousand Oaks, CA: Sage Publications.

Synott, J. P. (2009). *Quality education: Global perspectives for Australian schools.* Terrigal, NSW: David Barlow.

Tudge, J. (2008). *The everyday lives of young children: Culture, class, and child rearing in diverse societies.* New York: Cambridge University Press.

Vedder, P., Horenczyk, G., Liebkind, G. & Nickmans, G. (2006). Ethno-culturally diverse education settings; problems, challenges and solutions. *Educational Research Review*, 1, 157–68. doi:10.1016/j.edurev.2006.08.007

Yazdiha, H. (2010). Conceptualizing hybridity: Deconstructing boundaries through the hybrid. *Formations, 1*(1), 31–8. Retrieved from http://ojs.gc.cuny.edu/index.php/formations/index

Gender and sexuality diversity, policy framings and the construction of the subject

Tania Ferfolja

AUSTRALIAN PROFESSIONAL STANDARDS FOR TEACHERS

Standard 1: Know students and how they learn

This chapter provides understandings about gender and sexuality diversity in order for teachers to be responsive to the needs of their students from diverse backgrounds. It enables them to recognise that the way that texts are formed constructs particular understandings in relation to difference that may or may not be helpful for learning or wellbeing.

> It is not our differences that divide us. It is our inability to recognize, accept, and celebrate those differences. (Audre Lorde)

Introduction

Constructed as a medical, social and psychological pathology, gender and sexuality–diverse individuals and communities have experienced overt and covert discrimination to various degrees for centuries. Depending on time and context, this discrimination was not only interpersonally inflicted but institutionally enacted; that is, inequities were 'built into the system' through federal and state legislation and policy. In the twenty-first century in Australia, discriminatory attitudes towards gender and sexuality diversity have started to lean towards greater equality. Activism by the lesbian, gay, bisexual, transgender and queer (LGBTQ+) communities and their supporters has increased awareness about the discrimination, inequities and marginalisation gender and sexuality–diverse people experience. Many readers may be unaware that the Sydney Gay and Lesbian Mardi Gras, now a public display of celebration and solidarity, began as a protest rally in 1978, one which ended in violence and brutality (Carbery, 1995).

Such events, coupled with political and public education, have resulted in changes to legislation. For example, amendments to federal anti-discrimination legislation were made during the 1980s rendering it illegal to discriminate on the grounds of sexual orientation and gender identity in the delivery of goods and services, employment, education and accommodation, among other things (Australian Human Rights Commission, n.d.). In the first decade of the twenty-first century, further legislative amendments addressing a raft of inequities related to gender and sexuality diversity mean that gender and sexuality–diverse people can now access many (but not all) of the same rights and privileges afforded those who identify as heterosexual. There is also growing political acknowledgement of the historical discrimination endured by gender and sexuality–diverse people; for example, in 2017 several Australian state governments officially apologised to gay men historically convicted of the 'crime' of engaging in consensual, adult, male-to-male sex, previously legislated as a criminal act (ABC News, 2017; Caldwell, 2017). Thus, in the second decade of the twenty-first century, gender and sexuality diversity is increasingly normalised, celebrated and recognised as just another part of human diversity and as a human right (United Nations Educational, Scientific and Cultural Organization [UNESCO], 2012a).

Although such changes have buoyed the access and rights of this community, legislative amendments do not guarantee that 'everything is alright now' for gender and sexuality–diverse people. The situation is complex; despite legislative change and increased social acceptance, discrimination on the grounds of gender and/or sexuality diversity still occurs. Individuals remain vulnerable to homophobic or transphobic harassment in a variety of forms, including verbal and physical abuse as well as subtler, less easily perceptible forms of prejudice, micro-aggressions and inequity (Berman & Robinson, 2010); such abuse is more frequent for trans males and females (Leonard, Pitts, Mitchell, Lyons, Smith, Patel, Couch & Barrett, 2012). Additionally, ongoing public, political and legal argument over issues such as 'gay marriage' (Hall, 2013) demonstrates continued surveillance and structural inequity. However, broadly speaking, in Australia there is growing acceptance, awareness, visibility and, at times, celebration of gender and sexuality diversity. In fact, an ethical turn-around during the last 20 or so years means that discrimination on these grounds is perceived by many as inequitable and morally reprehensible and homo/transphobia is now understood as problematic.

Despite the broader socio-cultural and political context, schools are highly challenging sites for gender and sexuality–diverse individuals, including students and teachers. School-based harassment and bullying of those who are, or are perceived to be, gender and/or sexuality diverse is an internationally recognised yet underaddressed problem (UNESCO, 2012b). As will be shown below, it is vital that schools educate young people to promote a harmonious society that is safe and inclusive for all. To do this, policy, curricula and other resources could convey messages that potentially offer critical guidance to teachers and school administrators; yet, they construct identities in particular ways, some of which may be unhelpful.

This chapter examines how gender and sexuality–diverse subjects are constructed at the time of writing. It does so through website documentation from two Australian public schooling institutions: the New South Wales Department of Education and the Victorian Department of Education and Training. Although space precludes a detailed analysis, the discussion illustrates how education departments constitute particular understandings of gender and sexuality–diverse subjects through their documentation. Before embarking on this discussion, however, it is critical to recognise how discrimination towards gender and sexuality diversity manifests in schools and the potential consequences and limitations this places on all individuals through the surveillance of gender and sexuality. This highlights the urgency for educational institutions to have effective and supportive messaging in this area of equity.

Background

Gender and sexuality diversity in school education

Homophobic harassment discrimination and bullying that is based on a person's *actual* or *perceived* sexual orientation or gender identity.

Transphobic harassment discrimination, bullying, exclusion or other negative behaviour that is directed against people who are trans.

Discrimination the inequitable treatment of and behaviours towards people particularly on the basis of their minority status, such as gender and sexuality diversity.

Homophobic and **transphobic harassment** are common in schools throughout the world and gender and sexuality–diverse students and teachers are frequently the recipients of this **discrimination** (Guasp, 2012; Human Rights Watch, 2011; Kosciw, Palmer, Kull & Greytak, 2013; Takács, 2006; Taylor & Peter, 2011). The situation in Australia is no different, with research pointing to similar histories of ongoing inequities in the nation's schools as far back as the 1990s when studies into this area began to emerge (see, for example, Hillier et al., 1998). More recent research provides evidence that homo/transphobic harassment remains a reality. For instance, Hillier and colleagues, in a national study of 3134 same-sex attracted and gender questioning young people, found that nearly two-thirds had experienced verbal abuse and nearly one-fifth physical abuse based on their perceived or actual sexuality and/or gender non-conformity; most abuse occurred at school (Hillier et al., 2010). Similarly, Robinson and colleagues found that young people are often fearful of 'coming out' at school and many of those who do so experience homophobia. The study found that perpetrators of this abuse included students and teachers, with Personal Development, Health and Physical Education teachers being singled out for comment (Robinson,

Bansel, Denson, Overden & Davies, 2013). This is a disturbing finding considering that it is within this discipline's curriculum that gender and sexuality diversity is generally located. Perhaps the largest Australian study to date of gender and sexuality–diverse youths (in this study, people aged 14–18 years) (Ullman, 2015), points to the ways that gender and sexuality discrimination plays out in schools (see Chapter 4 this volume). Ullman surveyed 704 gender and sexuality–diverse youth nationally. Her research found that participants overwhelmingly claimed that homo/transphobic language was rife in their schools and that such discriminatory language was dealt with inconsistently by staff. Forty-five per cent of participants had witnessed physical harassment of actual, or perceived to be, gender and sexuality–diverse classmates; reportedly, school staff rarely intervened. Ullman found that teachers in schools that explicitly included gender and sexuality diversity in their policies were more likely to intercede and were generally more positive and supportive of gender and sexuality–diverse students.

Experiences of discrimination are not restricted to students. A national study of 159 lesbian and gay–identified teachers found that the vast majority hid their sexuality from students and 80% 'reported that they consciously hid their sexuality at work in some way' (Ferfolja & Stavrou, 2014, p. 35). This highlights how teachers, who relative to students are in positions of power in educational institutions, feel it necessary to 'manage' or hide their diverse sexual identity, reflecting a potentially exclusive workplace culture. Other research supports this finding of marginalisation. As Gray and colleagues eloquently point out, 'LGBTQ[1] teachers exist within a "space of exclusion" that is dominated by discursive mechanisms that (re)produce heteronormativity' (Gray, Harris & Jones, 2016, p. 286) and that this space reflects the broader societal position that is 'not quite accepting, yet not completely intolerant of gender and sexual diversity' (p. 288). Moreover, many gender and sexuality–diverse teachers operate in these institutions without being fully cognisant of the protections available to them (Jones, Gray & Harris, 2014). The potential for discrimination is compounded in religious schools, which remain, according to both state and national legislation, permitted to discriminate on the grounds of sexual orientation (Jones, Gray & Harris, 2014.). The results of silencing and invisibility, or living 'two lives', can have considerable ramifications on daily workplace management, satisfaction and stress of gender and sexuality–diverse teachers.

Homo/transphobic harassment in schools manifest in many ways, including, but not limited to, overt teasing and bullying, physical and/or verbal abuse, ostracism, graffiti, rumour mongering, gossip and/or cyberbullying. Discrimination occurs at all levels of the educational spectrum, from early childhood through to secondary settings (DePalma & Atkinson, 2009; Duke & McCarthy, 2009). Such abuse often results in feelings of non-acceptance, fear and/or anxiety. The repercussions of discrimination can be dire and long-term and may include social isolation, school drop-out, changing schools, truancy, impaired academic performance,

---

1   LGBTQ is an acronym for lesbian, gay, bisexual, transgender and queer. In this chapter, the term 'LGBTQ' has been, in the main, replaced by gender and sexuality–diverse to reflect an inclusion of a broader range of identities who may not identify as LGBTQ.

homelessness, depression and other mental health issues, poor self-esteem, suicide ideation, suicide attempts and suicide completion (DeLay, Hanish, Zhang & Martin, 2016; Hillier, Turner & Mitchell, 2005). In fact, Robinson and colleagues found that 16% of gender and sexuality–diverse young people between the ages of 16 and 27 had attempted suicide (2014, p. ix). Reportedly, many youth suicides are associated with sexuality and gender struggles (Hillier et al., 2010). Suicide attempts by gender and sexuality–diverse youth are four times greater than that of heterosexual youth (Centre for Disease Control and Prevention, 2016) and pre-teens may also respond to homo/transphobic harassment by attempting to, and succeeding in, taking their life (Gander, 2014).

Homo/transphobic harassment is directed at many people in schools, whether or not they currently, in the future, or indeed ever have, identified as gender or sexuality diverse. It also affects all people's life options and ways of being in the world because it is linked to the surveillance of both sexuality and gender and a reductive understanding of what these subjectivities can mean. Thus, homo/transphobia is deeply problematic. Indeed, the reality of homo/transphobia and its ramifications is heavily ensconced in public debate, policy developments and program funding and has in some ways obliged authorities to act (Marshall, 2010); yet, this simultaneously reduces young people to a classification of victim. It is critical to point out that not all gender and sexuality–diverse youth (or teachers) who experience homo/transphobia consider themselves 'victims', nor do these individuals all have negative experiences at school; indeed, some people in some contexts feel supported. Others have been proactive in the fight for justice, using the courts and media, for instance, when they have experienced homophobic discrimination in or by their school (Levy, 2010). The research highlights that it is critical that educators, at all levels, teach students about gender and sexuality diversity. It is only through information, understanding, and changing the negative and limited ways that some people think about diversity that equity and genuine inclusion will become a reality in educational contexts.

Addressing gender and sexuality diversity

Gender and sexuality diversity the full range of gender and sexuality identities that do not fall under cisgendered or cissexual categories. This may include, but is by no means limited to, individuals who identify as lesbian, bisexual, gay, transgender, queer, pan sexual, asexual, and questioning (among others).

Although some teachers pointedly address content related to **gender and sexuality diversity** in their curricula and classrooms, it seems that many actively avoid any reference to the topic. Leonard and colleagues found that over 50% of teachers in Victoria do not include gender and sexuality diversity–related issues in their sex education classes (Leonard, Marshall, Hillier, Mitchell & Ward, 2010). Another Australian study of over 300 secondary sexuality education teachers found that same-sex attraction is not taught at all by 15.5% of the respondents (Smith et al., 2011, p. 18). Additionally, lesbian, gay, bisexual and transgender–related content is poorly included, if at all, in the school curriculum (Hillier et al., 2010). The reasons for teacher avoidance include, but are not limited to: a lack of knowledge, understanding or resources about the topic; its perceived irrelevance to their subject area or their school population; their disapproval of the topic based on personal moral and/or religious beliefs;

a fear that students, parents and/or colleagues may perceive them to be gender or sexuality diverse; a view that it is inappropriate knowledge for children and young people and therefore that delivery is contentious; confusion as to what is permitted and what is not; and, analogous to this, anxiety about potential parental, community and/or employer backlash if they broach content related to gender and sexuality diversity in their classroom (Duffy, Fotinatos, Smith & Burke, 2013; Ollis, 2010; Shannon & Smith, 2015; Smith et al., 2011). Interestingly, no large-scale Australian study has been conducted to date that demonstrates that parents do not want their children to engage with such material; a recent smaller qualitative study indicates that the opposite seems to be the case (see Ferfolja & Ullman, 2017; Ullman & Ferfolja, 2016).

Though some of the above-mentioned concerns are limited, frustrating and reactionary, they are, to a degree, understandable considering the ongoing surveillance of curriculum, teacher professionalism and school autonomy. For instance, the climate towards gender and sexuality–diversity inclusion in school education has undergone considerable interference via political, media and conservative lobby groups, inflaming disagreement and division that benefits no student. For example, as discussed elsewhere (see Ferfolja & Ullman 2017), in 2015, *Gayby Baby*, an award-winning documentary rated PG (parental guidance) was slated to be viewed by high school students across New South Wales on Wear It Purple Day[2]. The intention was to use the film to educate students about gender and sexuality diversity as it pertained to four school-aged children living in lesbian- or gay-headed families. The student viewing was forbidden by the then state Minister for Education in response to a handful of vocal critics and media 'shock jocks' who declared it to be 'promoting' homosexuality (Bagshaw, 2015). The minister claimed that it was 'not part of the curriculum' (McDougall, 2015), despite the fact that there are spaces where teaching about diversity in terms of gender and sexuality is possible.

Similarly, in 2016–2017, education in relation to gender and sexuality diversity regressed nationally. A public backlash organised by vocal religious lobbyists, conservative politicians and media caused the Safe Schools Coalition Australia's education program funded by the federal government to be, by and large, de-funded. The program's intent, in alignment with the National Safe Schools Framework (Ministerial Council on Education, Employment, Training and Youth Affairs [MCEETYA], 2011), was to create inclusive primary and secondary schools for gender and sexuality–diverse individuals. The program was the first of its kind in the country, and considering the harm done by homo/transphobic harassment, as pointed out above, was and is much needed. Its collapse in most states is not surprising; as Shannon and Smith (2015) point out, although the Australian governments at both state and federal levels acknowledge gender and sexuality identities in 'social policy and within anti-discrimination legislation, the notion of queer sexuality and "controversy" within curriculum documents and education department policy perseveres,

---

2   Wear It Purple Day is aimed at raising the awareness of the community in relation to the challenges that gender and sexuality diverse or questioning young people experience. It is a show of solidarity and support that encourages young people to be proud of who they are.

as governments seek to quell any potential panic' (p. 642). It seems that governments generally prefer to separate themselves from, rather than publicly educate or explain, situations that inflame community anxiety, particularly in terms of sexuality and gender diversity. Vocal hostility supported by media controversy is powerful.

Curriculum and classroom silences perpetuate understandings that gender and sexuality–related content is taboo and, by extension, that gender and sexuality–diverse people and relationships are problematic or wrong. Studies have demonstrated that education about gender and sexuality diversity can reduce bullying and increase feelings of safety for these students (Guasp, 2012). Thus, it is critical that teachers include gender and sexuality diversities in their everyday teaching. In many instances, however, the extent to which this is enabled depends on the micro-climate of the school and the institutional support available to teachers, which is reflected in the content of policy, curriculum, guidelines and other institutional documentation. This chapter explores how policy frameworks and guidelines pertaining to gender and sexuality diversity–related content may be facilitating or problematic. The way that issues and identities are framed by educational institutions may create a basis for acceptance and encourage curriculum and pedagogical inclusion; alternatively, the language used and the resulting underlying messages may, at best, promote a risk-averse approach. To examine these framings, it is important to understand some key theoretical concepts, to which this discussion now turns.

Key theoretical concepts

This chapter draws on feminist poststructuralist and Foucauldian theory, including the concepts of language, discourse, subjectivity and power, to briefly review publicly available educational policy and associated guidelines and their inclusion of gender and sexuality–diverse subjects. These theoretical concepts help to illustrate the ways in which official institutional documentation constructs and positions understandings of the individuals on which it focuses.

Feminist poststructuralism a theory of how subjectivity is socially constructed and constituted within discourse. It explores how language, power and discourse intersect, and how they impact, in particular, on gendered subjects. It understands that subjectivities are fluid, contextual and dynamic.

A central tenet of **feminist poststructuralism** is the ability of language to construct our realities. Language is critical to understanding 'social organization, social meanings, power and individual consciousness' (Weedon, 1987, p. 21). It illustrates how individuals are perceived by others and how individuals perceive themselves. For example, a boy who enjoys what are socially constructed as 'soft' or 'feminine' interests, such as ballet or art, may be considered by some people as 'girly', 'effeminate' or 'unmanly'; he may be positioned in deficit to what is constructed as a 'real' male. This language and positioning fails to acknowledge the courage that it takes to challenge the dominant constructions of what it means to be male in broader society. From a different perspective, this child may be described as 'artistic', 'creative', 'capable' and 'brave', as a young man who 'knows what he wants' and is not afraid to claim it. Thus, there are multiple ways of constructing an object or person and the manner in which someone or something is talked about constructs particular knowledges about that person (or thing).

In this way, language is intimately tied to discourse (Foucault, 1978). Burr (1995, p. 48) provides a simple but clear explanation of this concept. She defines discourse as:

> a set of meanings, metaphors, representations, images, stories, statements and so on that in some way together produce a particular version of events. It refers to a particular picture that is painted of an event (or person or class of persons), a particular way of representing it or them in a certain light … a multitude of alternative versions of events is potentially available through language, this means that, surrounding any one object, event, person … there may be a variety of different discourses, each with a different story to tell about the object in question.

Multiple discourses circulate about an object, person or event at any one time and these vie for social power and ascendancy within society. The discourses with most authority are generally supported by social, cultural and political institutions that perpetuate particular knowledges or truths about an object, person or event. However, discourses are not fixed; they are dynamic, contextually and temporally dependent and in constant competition with each other. Thus, the language that is used about a group of people at a particular time and place in history may position them in a specific way that reflects the dominant discourse in that context. However, Foucault (1978) points out that it is not only what is said that constitutes discourse; what is *not* said is equally important. This is of particular relevance when considering how language operates in policy and resource framings, discussed in the next section of this chapter.

Subjectivity – that is, who one is and how one is perceived – is constituted in discourse (and hence by language). Subjectivity is fluid, complex, contradictory, dynamic and contextual. Different discursive positions provide subjects with different amounts of power within a given context. So, for example, in schools the dominant discourse operating in relation to sexuality is heterosexuality and to identify as heterosexual has currency. Both teachers and students police (hetero) sexuality – 'punishing' through various means those who transgress (Foucault, 1978). Thus, if a student positions themselves as heterosexual and is perceived by others to be such, they will be seen as 'normal' and less vulnerable to harassment in terms of this aspect of their subjectivity.

Additionally, the normalcy of heterosexuality is constructed and reinforced through artefacts of the institution, such as, but not limited to, curriculum or policy documents and websites. These have historically overwhelmingly reinforced heterosexuality as the ascendant and dominant discourse. Subjects are constituted in discourses through what is written and spoken or represented about them; thus, for example, policy socially constructs subjects. Although policy may be considered an edict, such documents may be interpreted in various ways, depending on the context and reader, who may cherry-pick, variously interpret, ignore, resist and/or avoid aspects of, or the entirety of, a policy; it does not guarantee particular actions or behaviours (Ball, Maguire & Braun, 2012). Yet this does not mean that policy is worthless. Indeed, it is vital to enable development and change.

In a similar way, resources, guidelines, websites and curriculum documentation construct subjectivities through the language and images they incorporate. It is critical to recognise that none of these documents develop in isolation, but are historically, contextually, culturally, politically and socially infused. As all subjects possess power and agency and are themselves positioned in various discourses, the reading and enactment of these framings is complex and unpredictable.

Methodology

This discussion draws mainly on analysis of Australian, state-based education policy and related guidelines and resources in terms of the inclusion and visibility of gender and sexuality–diverse subjects. As institutional artefacts, these documents have significant potential to contribute to the discourses and enactments in schools in relation to gender and sexuality diversity. The documents were located via key term searches on the New South Wales Department of Education and the Victorian Department of Education and Training websites' policy pages, providing insight into the discursive framings applied in comparable educational contexts. The terms employed to locate the documents related to gender and sexuality diversity, homophobia, transphobia and their synonyms. Researching terms via the departments' websites provided insight into the public face promulgated by each institution in relation to gender and sexuality diversity. Analysis of these texts illustrate the different ways in which gender and sexuality–diverse subjects are constructed and constituted in and by discourses operating in formal, institutionally endorsed documentation.

The texts were retrieved and closely read. They were interrogated using poststructural discourse analysis, where discourses, in the Foucauldian sense, were identified in terms of their socio-cultural and political constructions and their implications in relation to subjectivity, knowledge and agency. Discourse structures the experience of individuals and communities; it offers subject positions by constituting the self and others; and it simultaneously constructs knowledges that circulate, reinforcing power differences between and among subjects in various contexts (Ezzy, 2002). Thus, although no text is all things to all people, they construct and reinforce particular understandings about, and approaches to, gender and sexuality diversity in schools. Some of these appear innocuous, supportive or progressive; others are limited and potentially problematic. What is important to remember is that from a feminist poststructuralist and Foucauldian perspective these discourses construct subjects for whom they speak through both what is written and what remains unsaid (Foucault, 1978). It is to a brief discussion of these texts that this chapter now turns.

Analysis and discussion

The NSW Department of Education framing

The *Homophobia in Schools* policy was the NSW Department of Education's (and its manifestations) only policy specifically related to sexuality-diverse subjects (see Ferfolja, 2013 and 2015 for a detailed analysis). Penned in 1997, and available on the institution's website for nearly two decades, the policy was a memorandum sent to central and secondary school principals in the late 1990s and arose in response to legal action taken by a student subjected to ongoing homophobic abuse that went largely unchecked by the institution (Kendall & Sidebotham, 2004). Importantly, the document explicitly rejected discrimination in schools on the grounds of 'homosexuality' as required by the NSW *Anti-Discrimination Act 1977*. However, it simultaneously constructed 'homosexuals'[3] who may be subjected to discrimination as a difficulty schools may encounter.

Such difficulty was reflected, for example, in: the document's title, which focused on 'homophobia', highlighting the negative about sexuality diversity; the advice for principals who were directed to procedures to deal with 'complaints' and 'concerns about discrimination or harassment'; directives that their staff address 'homophobia' via welfare and curriculum opportunities; and that the police force's gay and lesbian liaison officers could be approached to assist in the implementation of 'anti-violence initiatives'. The policy suggested four (outdated, although when introduced, potentially informative) teaching resources that focused on HIV/AIDS, violence, homophobia and its potential ramifications in youth suicide and concluded with administrative information, including what quickly became obsolete contact details of a 'go to' person.

The discourse prevailing in the policy suggested that homosexuality was a high risk to be managed in schools, as 'homosexual' subjects were targets for harassment and discrimination. 'Homosexuality' was marked, negatively visible and constructed as requiring surveillance and 'protection' (Foucault, 1978). Although perhaps intended to manage risk related to discrimination, the policy's text – through the said and unsaid – constituted a discourse that marginalised its focal subject and, by default, elevated the power and normality of the dominant heterosexual discourse and those constituted within it. Although recently made obsolete, this policy's language constructed 'homosexual' subjects within a discourse of victim, problem, pathology and illness – outmoded and harmful constructions – for nearly two decades.

To inform the writing of this chapter, the NSW Department of Education's new policy library platform was accessed. This platform 'contains all current operational policies in the NSW Department of Education' (see education.nsw.gov.au/policy-library). The library includes several policies, under the umbrella term

---

3   The use of the term 'homosexual' as a generic term referring to same-sex attraction/relations for men and women is outdated; it was historically rejected by many lesbians as a masculinist term and no longer reflects the range of sexuality identities to which many people relate.

Access and Equity, which deal with areas of potential discrimination or marginal-isation. Included within the *Access and Equity* umbrella are policies that relate to 'Aboriginal education, anti-racism, gifted and talented, multi-cultural education and students with disabilities'. Interestingly, no policy under the *Access and Equity* category directly relates to either gender or sexuality broadly or gender or sexu-ality diversity specifically. Such omissions constitute the discourse operating in relation to these areas of identity; institutional silence and invisibility suggests such areas do not warrant consideration or are of little consequence. Omission, either by design or default, conveys a message that these forms of diversity may be too hard, too contentious, too political, or irrelevant or forbidden. Such omission is problematic considering the research detailed earlier in this chapter and else-where that illustrates how both gender and sexuality diversity are areas of ongoing discrimination in schools and can have deleterious effects on students and staff.

A keyword search of the department's policy library's search engine, using terms such as 'homosexual' and 'homophobia', their synonyms and related terms, however, resulted in nine hits linking these terms to *other* departmental policies, guidelines, codes, procedures and implementation documents. These included: the *School Uniform Policy* and its guidelines; *Bullying: Preventing and Responding to Student Bullying in Schools Policy* and its guidelines; *The Code of Conduct; Responding to Allegations Against Employees in the Area of Child Protection; Suspension and Expulsion of School Students – Procedures*; and *Protecting and Supporting Children and Young People Procedures*. A close reading illustrates that reference to gender and sexuality diversity–related terms in these documents occurs in relation to discrimination awareness – that is, as a risk management tool – either reflecting anti-discrimination, legislation to highlight expected compliance or actually defining such legislation. All of these references include the term – generally 'homosexual' or 'transgender' – only fleetingly alongside a string of other potential sites of discrimination, such as 'race', sex, marital status, disability and age. In *Bullying: Preventing and Responding to Student Bullying in Schools Policy* and related guidelines, the terms 'homosexuality' and 'transgender' appear simply to provide a brief definition of what constitutes bullying respectively in each document. There is no articulation of the prevalence of homo/transphobic bullying or the omnipresence of homophobic language in schools and no information that explains that such bullying is often withheld from parents and teachers for fear, by the victim, of being harassed or punished again on these grounds; that is, doubly discriminated against. Sexuality diversity is men-tioned in reactionary and largely negative terms and limiting knowledges through a lens of homophobia.

Mention of the term 'homosexual' in *The Code of Conduct* appears in rela-tion to the illegality of teachers having sexual relationships with students. The Code states: 'It is irrelevant whether the relationship is homosexual or hetero-sexual, consensual or non-consensual or condoned by parents or caregivers' (NSW Department of Education, 2006, p. 3). This same text appears in the doc-ument *Responding to Allegations Against Employees in the Area of Child Protection* (NSW Department of Education and Training, 2010). Although at first glance this may seem innocuous, the positioning of 'homosexual' first in the heterosexual/

homosexual binary, controverts the generally common usage of binary constructs, where the more socially powerful position is articulated first – that is, generally the binary is expressed as heterosexual/homosexual. This positioning in the document implies that this code may be of more relevance to sexuality-diverse individuals, subtly reinforcing the archaic discourse that lesbian and gay people are predatory and have a proclivity to have intimate relationships with minors; in most cases of child sexual abuse the perpetrator is male and the survivor is female (Kaufman & Erooga, 2016).

These patchy allusions to gender and sexuality diversity in the institution's official policy documentation and related resources, available via the website, unfortunately continue to constitute gender and sexuality–diverse subjects and related content in discourses of risk aversion. From a Foucauldian understanding, silences and invisibility perpetuate the discourse that gender and sexuality diversity is of little consequence and/or of lesser importance than other sites of difference. The policy and related documents, although at times mentioning gender and/or sexuality diversity, do not openly foster understanding, dialogue or cultural change. Nor do they produce spaces in which teachers feel secure to undertake equity work related to this topic, which continues to be seen as contentious and risky to broach. Without a strong grounding in policy, and explicit direction that gender and sexuality–diversity inclusion is important and warranted, it is likely that these aspects of diversity will remain hidden or only inconsistently addressed by teachers and schools who have a personal commitment to social justice, rather than a whole-of-system approach. Through its prevailing risk management discourse, these policy allusions do not reflect the contemporary lives of gender and sexuality–diverse individuals who exist in all schools; nor does it facilitate understanding of differences.

The Victorian Department of Education and Training framings

The Victorian Department of Education and Training within its *School Policy and Advisory Guide*, available on its website, has numerous links where gender and/or sexuality diversity is addressed, such as 'Lesbian Students', 'Gender Identity', 'Same Sex Attraction Among Students' and 'Sexuality Education Including Supporting Sexuality Diversity'. The latter, which forms part of the 'whole-school approach to health education', clearly mandates that 'Schools must support and respect sexuality diversity including same sex attraction'[4]. The language used in the wording of these links recognises a range of sexualities, suggesting that not all individuals identify within seemingly fixed, archaic and historically pathologised identity categories such as 'homosexual'. Moreover, these descriptors acknowledge the fluidity of gender and sexuality and its relevance to youth, reflecting contemporary understandings related to these identities. Hyperlinks connect to a site entitled *Health Education Approaches*, which within a section entitled *Sexuality Education*, highlights

4   See http://www.education.vic.gov.au/school/principals/spag/curriculum/Pages/health.aspx

the importance of 'comprehensive' and 'inclusive' sexuality education as being 'compulsory' for all state schools, although options exist for parents or carers to remove their child from sexual health education. Within this section, a hyperlink to a resource entitled *Supporting Sexual Diversity in Schools* is included.

Supporting Sexual Diversity in Schools (Victorian Department of Education and Early Childhood Development, 2008), a policy resource, discursively constructs sexuality-diverse people as valued members of the school community and society. Drawing on the Victorian *Equal Opportunity Act 1995* and the Victorian *Charter of Human Rights and Responsibilities Act 2006*, the document refers to the illegality of discrimination on the grounds of perceived or actual sexual orientation or gender identity, including discrimination based on association. In this way, it draws on broader government legislation to support its discourse of inclusion. It explicitly places the responsibility for education about 'homophobia or discrimination' on schools, stating that, 'Strategies and preventative measures undertaken should be *continuous and proactive*, and should reflect *educative processes within the school*' (p. 6, emphasis added). The document, however, goes beyond discursively positioning sexuality-diverse subjects only as potential victims of homophobia or as people for whom discrimination risks need to be managed, using instead a positive discourse that embraces diversity and inclusion. This is apparent in statements such as:

> Schools have an obligation to ensure they create supportive and relevant educational experiences for their students. The inclusion of all students must be reflected in a school's policies, codes of conduct, curriculum, learning and teaching, student services, organisation and ethos. (p. 6)

There is articulation of the Department's commitment to integrated 'support [of] same-sex attracted young people' and, critically, a directive for a whole-school approach that includes, but goes beyond, bullying and homophobia to a curriculum that demonstrates 'positive inclusion of same-sex attracted young people and same-sex attracted family members' (p. 7). Moreover, examples are provided that move the responsibility for this education beyond the discipline of health or personal development into the realms of other subjects, encouraging teachers of various disciplines to 'include sexually diverse content and themes, for example, studying human rights, investigating events that have resulted in civil improvements for minority groups, and discussing texts that incorporate the theme of same-sex relationships' (p. 7). This approach recognises sexuality to be integral to identity beyond the body by acknowledging the experiences and achievements of gender and sexuality–diverse subjects and constructing them as agentic. They are positioned as active and productive subjects who can, and have, made a valuable contribution to history and society and various human achievements. Although homophobia did and still does exist, so do positive experiences and knowledges about sexuality-diverse subjects, about whom young people should be educated; education decreases homophobia in schools. Hence, this document supports schools to take up discourses that normalise gender and sexuality–diverse subjects, challenging the power and ascendancy historically inherent in heterosexuality by making gender and sexuality diversity part of students' everyday educational and schooling experiences.

Implicit in the document is a direct theoretical connection to Foucault's (1978) concept of the importance of the said and unsaid as constituting discourse. This is illustrated through the document's reference to the impact of any school staff members' 'inaction' around homophobic behaviour and sentiment as 'amount[ing] to an implicit authorisation or encouragement of discrimination or sexual harassment' (p. 6). By not responding to homophobic harassment and by 'turn[ing] a blind eye' (p. 6), one who has power as both adult and, importantly, institutional authority through their role as teacher is perpetuating the acceptability of discriminatory and homophobic discourse. There is meaning in such silence, which the institution highlights in this document.

Critically, the Department paves the way for all government schools to embrace this form of diversity, stating that primary and high schools have opportunities to develop and ensure 'safe and supportive' contexts for 'same-sex attracted young people' (p. 5). Hence, there is recognition of the existence of sexuality-diverse pre-teenage students in schools and acknowledgement of the importance of education to promote understanding; sexuality diversity is constructed as relevant even to young students. Moreover, there is a stated need to provide teachers with professional development opportunities and families with information about the topic, pointing to currently operating external providers and resources. Thus, the strongly inclusive language, the detail of this document and its whole-of-school-community approach illustrates not only the institution's serious intention to tackle homophobia but, moreover, the importance of education and understanding for all. The language used, supportive approach and strong directives reinforce a discourse of inclusion and normalisation for gender and sexuality–diverse people that is being steered by the institution, the Victorian Department of Education and Training.

Implications

Clearly, policy and guiding documents have implications for teachers' work. Teachers in Australia do have legal and, depending on the state in which they teach, institutional support that enables them to address gender and sexuality diversity–related content in their classrooms. The policy approaches mentioned above, despite their differential construction and in some cases limited framing, do provide spaces for teachers to do some work related to gender and sexuality diversity. At the least, they point out that discrimination on the grounds of perceived or actual sexual orientation or transgender identity is prohibited in public institutions by government legislation (although private religious institutions are generally exempt). National declarations like the *Melbourne Declaration on Educational Goals for Young Australians* (MCEETYA, 2008) and international guidelines such as the *International Technical Guidance on Sexuality Education* (UNESCO, 2009) outline the importance of providing all young people with discrimination-free education and/or inclusion of content that addresses all forms of sexual orientation and gender diversities. Most public education institutions stipulate that educators have a duty of care to young people in their charge. Additionally, the new national Health and Physical Education curriculum (Australian Curriculum, Assessment and Reporting Authority, 2014) refers to sexual diversity and the need for inclusion in school curriculum and teacher practice, although inclusion in state-based curriculum is limited (see Ferfolja & Ullman, 2014; Ullman & Ferfolja, 2014).

When directives to undertake this work seem invisible or risky, effective, proactive teachers should note the 'spaces between' in curriculum and policy; these are akin to the metaphor of the 'unseen half' in education discussed in Chapter 1. These spaces (often unseen) hint at the opportunity to broaden the scope and approach of what one teaches. For example, the curriculum may refer to the teaching of 'sexuality' at a particular stage of education. Being aware of the range of sexualities that this term can encompass enables one to be inclusive of diversity; sexuality does not only equate to heterosexuality. One must be cognisant of the discourses in documentation and resources, how they construct subjects and how they potentially contribute to silence and in/equities. It should be noted that teacher positivity towards gender and sexuality diversity enables a greater sense of connection to school and enhances student morale and wellbeing (Ullman, 2016).

The 'reading' and interpretation of any text is influenced by one's discursive positioning; in terms of equity, this means that it is imperative that teachers are aware of diversity, discrimination and its ramifications, how they are positioned in discourse, as well as how educators of future citizens can open doors for young people to a world of opportunity and an appreciation of difference. Integrating gender and sexuality diversity into everyday teaching is critical; educators must go beyond the 'special events' routes so readily taken up by schools to 'address' issues of diversity. For example, celebrating IDAHOT[5] day has its place; however, it should be accompanied and reinforced by classroom inclusions. This should be presented in a developmentally appropriate manner from the early years of schooling. For instance, one may start by including same-sex headed families in discussions about family diversity.

Waiting until young people are adolescents to teach about gender and sexuality diversity, as has historically been the case, is too late, as prejudices are already well formed. These discriminatory attitudes need to be attended to early and across all educational systems. Critical understandings of gender and sexuality diversity would enhance the lives of all young people, as the constraints imposed by dominant discourses of gender and sexuality that demand particular, limiting and narrow ways of being in the world need to be challenged. It is up to teachers, now and in the future, to do this work.

---

5   The International Day Against Homophobia and Transphobia (IDAHOT) is on 17 May and celebrates gender and sexuality diversity worldwide.

Considerations

- How do concepts such as discourse and subjectivity help pre-service teachers better understand teaching and learning materials as well as professional relationships?
- At the time of writing, most Australian states permit private religious institutions to discriminate on the grounds of sexual orientation. What may be the implications of this legislation on students, schools and teachers across all sexual identities?
- Parents are often considered to have rights when it comes to the sexuality education of their child. Do parents have the right to regulate their child's access to what the state deems appropriate knowledge considering the changing nature of society?
- The effectiveness of policy is determined at least partly by the way it is implemented in schools. What kinds of approaches could schools take to implement policy related to gender and sexuality diversity?
- The Victorian Department of Education and Training, at the time of writing, is one of the leaders in Australian public education school systems in terms of gender and sexuality–diversity inclusions. What policies, guidelines or support are available in other states? How do these documents construct gender and sexuality–diverse individuals, families and communities?

Of interest

- International Day Against Homophobia and Transphobia (IDAHOT). This day (17 May) celebrates gender and sexuality diversities worldwide. See http://dayagainsthomophobia.org
- Wear It Purple. This youth-led and youth-focused organisation aims to support gender and sexuality–diverse young people. See http://wearitpurple.org
- *It's Elementary: Talking about Gay Issues in Schools* (D. Chasnoff & H. Cohen, Women's Educational Media, CA). This 'older' video is an entertaining and educational examination of how schools and teachers can talk about sexuality diversity from early childhood through to secondary education settings.
- *Bully.* Documentary 2013. Directed by Lee Hirsch, this documentary follows the lives of a number of students in the United States who are bullied at school – some homophobically – and the impact on them and their families.
- *Born Free and Equal* (Office of the High Commission for Human Rights). This publication concerns sexual and gender identities in international human rights law. See http://www.ohchr.org/EN/NewsEvents/Pages/BornFreeAndEqual.aspx

References

ABC News (2017, April 13). *Tasmanian Government apologises for criminalisation of gay sexual acts*. Retrieved from http://www.abc.net.au/news/2017-04-13/tas-govt-apology-for-laws-criminalising-homosexuality/8443528

Australian Curriculum, Assessment and Reporting Authority (2014). *The Australian Curriculum: Health and Physical Education, Foundation to Year 10*. Retrieved from http://www.australiancurriculum.edu.au/healthandphysicaleducation/Curriculum/F-10

Australian Human Rights Commission (n.d.). *A quick guide to Australian discrimination laws*. Retrieved from http://www.humanrights.gov.au/employers/good-practice-good-business-factsheets/quick-guide-australian-discrimination-laws

Bagshaw, E. (2015, September 2). The truth behind the Gayby Baby ban. *The Sydney Morning Herald*. Retrieved from http://www.smh.com.au

Ball, S. J., Maguire, M. & Braun, A. (2012). *How schools do policy: Policy enactments in secondary schools*. London: Routledge.

Berman, A. & Robinson, S. (2010). *Speaking out: Stopping homophobic and transphobic abuse in Queensland*. Bowen Hills: Australian Academic Press.

Burr, V. (1995). *An introduction to social constructionism*. New York: Routledge.

Caldwell, F. (2017, May 11). *Queensland Premier says sorry to people punished under historical gay sex laws*. Retrieved from http://www.brisbanetimes.com.au/queensland/queensland-premier-says-sorry-to-people-punished-under-historical-gay-sex-laws-20170511-gw289u.html

Carbery, G. (1995). *A history of the Sydney Gay and Lesbian Mardi Gras*. Parkville: Lesbian and Gay Archives Inc.

Centre for Disease Control and Prevention (2016). *Sexual identity, sex of sexual contacts, and health-related behaviors among students in grades 9–12 – United States and selected sites, 2015*. 65(9), 1–202.

DeLay, D., Hanish, L. D., Zhang, L. & Martin, C. L. (2016). Assessing the impact of homophobic name calling on early adolescent mental health: A longitudinal social network analysis of competing peer influence effects. *Journal of Youth Adolescence*, 46, 955–69. doi:10.1007/s10964-016-0598-8

DePalma, R. & Atkinson, E. (2009). 'No outsiders': Moving beyond a discourse of tolerance to challenge heteronormativity in primary schools. *British Educational Research Journal*, 35(6), 837–55. doi:10.1080/01411920802688705

Duffy, B., Fotinatos, N., Smith, A. & Burke, J. (2013). Puberty, health and sexual education in Australian regional primary schools: Year 5 and 6 teacher perceptions. *Sex Education*, 13(2), 186–213. doi:10.1080/14681811.2012.6 78324

Duke, T. S. & McCarthy, K. W. (2009). Homophobia, sexism, and early childhood education: A review of the literature. *Journal of Early Childhood Teacher Education*, 30(4), 385–403. doi:10.1080/10901020903320320

Ezzy, D. (2002). *Qualitative analysis: Practice and innovation.* Sydney: Allen & Unwin.

Ferfolja, T. (2013). Sexual diversity, discrimination and 'homosexuality policy' in New South Wales' government schools. *Sex Education*, 13(2), 159–71. doi:10.1080/ 14681811.2012.697858

—— (2015). LGBT equity and school policy: Perspectives from Canada and Australia. In L. D. Hill, & F. J. Levine (Eds.), *World Education Research Yearbook 2015* (pp. 94–113). New York: Routledge.,

Ferfolja, T. & Stavrou, E. (2014). Workplace experiences of Australian lesbian and gay teachers: Findings from a national survey. *Canadian Journal of Educational Administration and Policy*, 173, 113. Retrieved from http://www.umanitoba.ca/publications/cjeap/pdf_files/qecb7-Ferfolja_Stavrou.pdf

Ferfolja, T. & Ullman, J. (2014). Opportunity lost and (re)written out: LGBTI content in Australia's 'new' National Health and Physical Education curriculum. In S. Gannon & W. Sawyer (Eds.), *Contemporary Issues of Equity in Education*, (pp. 69–87). Newcastle upon Tyne, UK: Cambridge Scholars Publishing.

—— (2017). Gender and sexuality diversity and schooling: Progressive mothers speak out. *Sex Education*, 17(3), 348–62. doi:10.1080/14681811.2017.1285761

Foucault, M. (1978). *The will to knowledge: The history of sexuality: Vol. 1. An introduction* (R. Hurley, Trans.). New York: Vintage Books.

Gander, K. (2014, February 15). US schoolboy who attempted suicide after being bullied for liking 'My little pony' may have permanent brain damage. *The Independent*. Retrieved from http://www.independent.co.uk/news/world/americas/us-schoolboy-who-tried-to-kill-himself-after-being-bullied-for-liking-my-little-pony-may-have-permanent-brain-damage-9110411.html.

Gray, E., Harris, A. & Jones, T. (2016). Australian LGBTQ teachers, exclusionary spaces and points of interruption. *Sexualities*, 19(3), 286–303. doi: 10.1177/1363460715583602.

Guasp, A. (2012). *The experiences of gay young people in Britain's schools in 2012.* London: Stonewall/University of Cambridge.

Hall, B. (2013, December 15). High Court obliged by law to back government on same-sex marriage. *The Age*. Retrieved from http://www.theage.com.au/comment/high-court-obliged-by-law-to-back-government-on-samesex-marriage-20131214-2ze46.html

Hillier, L., Dempsey, D., Harrison, L., Beale, L., Matthews, L. & Rosenthal, D. (1998). *Writing themselves in. A national report on the sexuality, health and well-being of same-sex attracted young people.* Melbourne: Australian Research Centre in Sex, Health and Society, La Trobe University.

Hillier, L., Jones, T. Monagle, M., Overton, N., Gahan, L., Blackman, J. & Mitchell, A. (2010). *Writing themselves in 3: The third national report on the sexuality, health and well-being of same sex attracted young people.* Melbourne: Australian Research Centre in Sex, Health and Society, La Trobe University.

Hillier L., Turner, A. & Mitchell, A. (2005). *Writing themselves in again – 6 years on: The 2nd national report on the sexual health and wellbeing of same-sex attracted young people in Australia.* Melbourne: Australian Research Centre in Sex, Health and Society, La Trobe University.

Human Rights Watch (2011). *'We'll show you you're a woman': Violence and discrimination against black lesbians and transgender men in South Africa.* Retrieved from https:www.hrw.org/report/2011/12/05/well-show-you-youre-a-women/violence-and-discrimination-against-black-lesbians-and

Jones, T., Gray, E. & Harris, A. (2014). GLBTIQ teachers in Australian education policy: Protections, suspicions, and restrictions. *Sex Education,* 14(3), 338–53.

Kaufmann, K. & Erooga, M. (2016). *Risk profiles for institutional child sexual abuse. A literature review.* Sydney, Australia: Royal Commission into Institutional Responses to Child Sexual Abuse.

Kendall, C. & Sidebotham, N. (2004). Homophobic bullying in schools: Is there a duty of care? *Australia & New Zealand Journal of Law & Education,* 9(1), 71–93.

Kosciw, J., Palmer, N., Kull, R. & Greytak, E. (2013). The effect of negative school climate on academic outcomes for LGBT youth and the role of in-school supports. *Journal of School Violence,* 12(1), 45–63. doi:10.1080/15388220.2012.732546

Leonard, W., Marshall, D., Hillier, L., Mitchell, A. & Ward, R. (2010). *Beyond homophobia: Meeting the needs of same-sex attracted and gender questioning (SSAGQ) young people in Victoria. A policy blueprint.* Melbourne: Australian Research Centre in Sex, Health and Society, La Trobe University.

Leonard, W., Pitts, M., Mitchell, A., Lyons, A., Smith, A., Patel, S., Couch, M. & Barrett, A. (2012). *Private lives 2: The second national survey of the health and wellbeing of gay, lesbian, bisexual and transgender (GLBT) Australians. Monograph Series* Number 86. Melbourne: Australian Research Centre in Sex, Health and Society, La Trobe University.

Levy, M. (2010, November 11). Worldwide support for Australia's 'Constance McMillen'. *The Sydney Morning Herald.* Retrieved from http://www.smh.com.au/action/printArticle?id=2037469

Marshall, D. (2010). Popular culture, the 'victim' trope and queer youth analytics. *International Journal of Qualitative Studies in Education,* 23(1), 65–85. doi:10.1080/09518390903447176

McDougall, B. (2015, August 26). Burwood Girls High School: Anger over gay parenting documentary 'Gayby Baby'. *The Daily Telegraph.* Retrieved from http://www.dailytelegraph.com.au

Ministerial Council on Education, Employment, Training and Youth Affairs
(MCEETYA) (2008). *Melbourne declaration on educational goals for young
Australians*. Retrieved from http://www.mceecdya.edu.au/mceecdya/
melbourne_declaration,25979.html

—— (2011). National Safe Schools Framework. Retrieved from https://docs
.education.gov.au/system/files/doc/other/national_safe_schools_
framework.pdf

NSW Department of Education (n.d.). *Policy library*. Retrieved from https://
education.nsw.gov.au/policy-library

—— (2004). *School Uniform Policy*. Retrieved from https://education.nsw.gov.au/
policy-library/policies/school-uniform-policy

—— (2006). The *code of conduct*. Retrieved from https://education.nsw.gov.au/
policy-library/policies/code-of-conduct-policy

—— (2010). *Protecting and supporting children and young people policy*. Retrieved
from https://education.nsw.gov.au/policy-library/policies/protecting-and-
supporting-children-and-young-people-policy

—— (2011). *Bullying: Preventing and responding to student bullying in schools policy*.
Retrieved from https://education.nsw.gov.au/policy-library/policies/
bullying-preventing-and-responding-to-student-bullying-in-schools-policy

NSW Department of Education and Communities (2015). *Suspension and expulsion
of school students – procedures – 2011*. Retrieved from https://education.nsw
.gov.au/policy-library/associated-documents/suspol_07.pdf

NSW Department of Education and Training (1997). *Homophobia in schools*. Retrieved
from https://www.det.nsw.edu.au/policiesinter/atoz/search.do?level

—— (2010). *Responding to allegations against employees in the area of child protection*.
Retrieved from https://education.nsw.gov.au/policy-library/associated-
documents/respondwoutdisc.pdf

Ollis, D. (2010). 'I haven't changed bigots but … ': Reflections on the impact of
teacher professional learning in sexuality education. *Sex Education*, 10(2),
217–30. doi:10.1080/14681811003666523

Robinson, K. H., Bansel, P., Denson, N., Ovenden, G. & Davies, C. (2014). *Growing
up queer: Issues facing young Australians who are gender variant and sexuality
diverse*. Melbourne: Young and Well Cooperative Research Centre.

Shannon, B. & Smith, S. J. (2015). 'A lot more to learn than where babies come
from': controversy, language and agenda setting in the framing of school-
based sexuality education curricula in Australia. *Sex Education*, 15(6),
641–54. doi:10.1080/14681811.2015.1055721

Smith, A., Schlichthorst, M., Mitchell, A., Walsh, J., Lyons, A., Blackman, P. & Pitts,
M. (2011). *Sexuality education in Australian secondary schools 2010, Monograph
Series No. 80*. Melbourne: Australian Research Centre in Sex, Health and
Society, La Trobe University.

Takács, J. (2006). *Social exclusion of young lesbian, gay, bisexual and transgender (LGBT) people in Europe.* Brussels: ILGA-Europe.

Taylor, C. & Peter, T. (2011). *Every class in every school: The first national climate survey on homophobia, biphobia, and transphobia in Canadian schools – Final report.* Toronto, Canada: Egale Canada Human Rights Trust.

Ullman, J. (2015). *Free2Be?: Exploring the schooling experiences of Australia's sexuality and gender diverse secondary school students.* Sydney: Centre for Educational Research, School of Education, Western Sydney University.

—— (2016). Teacher positivity towards gender diversity: Exploring relationships and school outcomes for transgender and gender-diverse students. *Sex Education,* 17(3), 276–89.

Ullman, J. & Ferfolja, T. (2014). Bureaucratic constructions of sexual diversity: 'sensitive', 'controversial' and silencing. *Teaching Education,* 26(2), 145–59.

—— (2016). The elephant in the (class)room: parental perceptions of LGBTQ-inclusivity in K–12 educational contexts. *Australian Journal of Teacher Education,* 41(10), 15–29.

United Nations Educational, Scientific and Cultural Organization (UNESCO) (2009). *International technical guidance on sexuality education: An evidence-informed approach for schools, teachers and health educators.* Retrieved from http://www.unesco.org/new/en/unesco/

—— (2012a). *Born free and equal: Sexual orientation and gender identity in international human rights law.* New York and Geneva: Author.

—— (2012b). *Good policy and practice in HIV and health education. Booklet 8: Education sector responses to homophobic bullying.* Paris: Author.

Victorian Department of Education and Early Childhood Development (2008). *Supporting sexual diversity in schools.* Melbourne: Student Wellbeing and Health Support Division Office for Government School Education, Department of Education and Early Childhood Development. Retrieved from https://www.eduweb.vic.gov.au/edulibrary/public/teachlearn/student/supportsexualdiversity.pdf

Weedon, C. (1987). *Feminist practice and poststructuralist theory.* Oxford: Blackwell.

CHAPTER 4

Regulating 'gender climate'

Exploring the social construction of gender and sexuality in regional and rural Australian schools

Jacqueline Ullman

....

AUSTRALIAN PROFESSIONAL STANDARDS FOR TEACHERS

Standard 4: Create and maintain supportive and safe learning environments

The pedagogical focus of this chapter relates to Standard 4, which acknowledges the importance of inclusive curriculum – where students' and their families' identities are visible within the teaching and learning content – for student participation and engagement. Additionally, this standard recognises the necessity of a safe environment to student wellbeing and academic success.

....

> When I first started dating my girlfriend that I am with now, there were these popular girls in my class who act 'perfect' and have the best boyfriends apparently … There were three teachers standing around either talking to students or each other. These girls actually came over and started throwing pieces of paper at me and they said things like 'pussy licker', 'faggot' and 'go die' … The biggest girl there started kicking me as I was sitting down and all I could feel was thumping in my ribs and legs. (15-year-old girl from regional New South Wales)

> A student drew penises all over my textbook while I was presenting an oral presentation and proceeded to cough the word 'faggot' during the applause … All of the other students (mainly male), besides my group of friends (all female), laughed at his comment and my friends stuck up for me while the teacher rolled her eyes and did nothing towards talking to him, telling him to 'stop it' or punishing him. After returning to my seat I showed my teacher my textbook and she replied, 'Well, just ignore it. We are past that subject anyway'. (16-year-old boy, early school leaver from outer regional Queensland)

Introduction

The school experiences of same-sex attracted (SSA), transgender and gender non-conforming (TGNC) young people have received a great deal of attention in both the mainstream media and academic research in recent years. This increased awareness of the school-based marginalisation faced by some SSA and TGNC students, as well as the importance of supportive teachers, has prompted a number of Australian schools to adopt some degree of anti-homophobia education and to begin to make space for gay/straight alliances (GSAs) or ally groups. In contrast to a school environment historically characterised by the marginalisation and silencing of diverse sexualities and genders, this is a definite move forward. Nevertheless, this style of program can be reductionist in nature, particularly if school-based inclusivity is limited to slogans of 'equal rights' and 'zero tolerance (for homophobia)' or to various symbolic manifestations of support (such as rainbows or wearing purple on a particular day of the year[1]), which lack substance if situated as stand-alone content or single-day events.

Discrimination against young people who identify as SSA may be neatly positioned as 'homophobic', prompting a clear-cut, uncomplicated teacher response (perhaps something along the lines of 'We do not tolerate homophobic language at this school'). In contrast, addressing the everyday, informal and institutionalised marginalisation of students who express their gender outside of school-based norms – expression that may or may not exist alongside same-sex attraction – is less straightforward. Given that, at their core, homophobia and transphobia are constructed around conservative and essentialist notions of gender expression, it is crucial to link anti-homophobia/transphobia education to discussions about gender expression, gender roles, gender stereotypes and the ways in which culture and social context are linked to 'natural' and 'unnatural' expressions of gender.

This chapter examines the reported school experiences of SSA and TGNC Australian teenagers from regional, rural and remote Australia to explore the impact of discourses[2] of gender and sexuality. In particular, this chapter presents an analysis of data from the author's national survey on gender climate in secondary schools, the *Free2Be?* project (Ullman, 2015a), using theories of gender and sexuality to guide interpretation. Although much research in gender and sexuality relies on qualitative methodologies, this chapter suggests that quantitative research can reveal large-scale patterns that have implications for the ways in which schools are organised and for the work of teachers in supporting young people. To begin, this chapter contextualises sexual and gender diversity in schools, the impact of discriminatory practices on student outcomes, and regional/rural Australia as a location of interest for such study.

---

1   I am referring here to the *Wear It Purple* day, wherein staff and students wear purple wristbands or clothing to demonstrate support of lesbian, gay, bisexual, transgender, queer and intersex (LGBTQI) individuals.
2   See Chapter 1 for an in-depth presentation of discourse as a theoretical concept.

Background

School experiences of SSA and TGNC students

Australian SSA and TGNC students report routine social isolation and **marginalisation** in secondary schools, perpetrated
by both peers and school staff, with research indicating that
school-based homophobic and transphobic harassment impacts
between 63% (Robinson, Bansel, Denson, Ovenden & Davies,
2014) and 80% (Hillier et al., 2010) of these young people. Overt
forms of school-based marginalisation include: verbal abuse,
such as homophobic and transphobic slurs; physical intimidation and bullying; psychological intimidation; social isolation;
spreading rumours; and cyberbullying. These experiences are
not only linked to SSA and TGNC students' lowered sense of school belonging
and connection to school (Pearson, Muller & Wilkinson, 2007), but also to diminished educational outcomes, including safety fears (Hillier, Turner & Mitchell,
2005), higher rates of absenteeism (Poteat & Espelage, 2007), difficulty concentrating at school (Blackburn, 2012; Robinson et al., 2014) and lower academic
achievement (Kosciw, Palmer, Kull & Greytak, 2013).

> Marginalisation the process of
> pushing an individual or group
> of individuals to the edges/
> fringes of society. In the case
> of educational marginalisation,
> this refers to systemic,
> institutional maltreatment,
> which includes curricular and
> pedagogical neglect.

Social marginalisation of SSA and TGNC students is compounded by the lack
of curricular mandates and policy requiring the explicit inclusion of diverse sexualities and genders within Australian schools (Duffy, Fotinatos, Smith & Burke,
2013; Ullman & Ferfolja, 2015). This results in many schools remaining silent on
these topics, even within the context of sexual health education (Mitchell, Patrick,
Heywood, Blackman & Pitts, 2014; Smith et al., 2011). Where policy does reference
diverse sexualities and genders, it can be problematic in and of itself, due to the
implicit ways that it reinforces silences. (See Ferfolja, Chapter 3 in this volume,
for a detailed examination of how institutional policy constructs identities in
schools.) In an Australian national survey of 1032 young people identifying as SSA
or TGNC, only 13% said that they had learned about same-sex attraction in sex
education, with 9% reporting having learned that people can experience different genders from their biological sex (Robinson et al., 2014). These numbers echo
findings from a larger national survey, Writing Themselves In (Hillier et al., 2010),
which surveyed 3134 SSA and TGNC young people and found that, while nearly
60% reported learning about heterosexual relationships at school, less than 20%
reported learning about same-sex attraction.

These concerns appear to be compounded for SSA and TGNC young people in
regional and rural locations in Australia (Edwards, 2006; Robinson et al., 2014). In
terms of negative emotional impact, alongside a lowered sense of safety while at
school, the 2010 Writing Themselves In project found higher rates of self-harm, suicidal
ideation and attempts for young people living in regional and rural areas, coupled
with concerns about their future due to experiences of social isolation, discrimination and a lack of local services and support (Hillier et al., 2010). Young people from
these locations described a dearth of visible lesbian, gay, bisexual, transgender, queer

LGBTQI a designation for members of the lesbian, gay, bisexual, transgender, queer and intersex communities, this acronym often also includes the plus sign (+) to acknowledge the growing array of gender and sexuality–diverse identities (e.g. LGBTQI+).

and intersex (**LGBTQI**) community, as well as an air of secrecy surrounding diverse sexualities and genders related to fears of discrimination and violence. More recent findings reiterate this last point, with SSA and TGNC young people from regional and rural locations reporting difficulties meeting other same-sex attracted and gender diverse people and having 'no one to talk to about their sexuality or gender variance' (Robinson et al., 2014, p. viii).

While the social isolation experienced by regional, rural and remote Australian SSA and TGNC young people is partially influenced by the basic statistical likelihood of smaller numbers of LGBTQI individuals in communities with smaller populations[3], it is likely compounded by some of the social features of regional and rural Australia that may be replicated in the school environment. In regional and rural areas, historically linked to agriculture and mining industries, heterosexual marriage and reproduction have represented the continuation and succession of the community (Bryant & Pini, 2011). Accordingly, Bryant and Pini (2011) suggest that rural spaces in Australia have been 'entrenched, defined, and performed as heterosexual spaces' wherein 'moral codes ... community sanction, surveillance, and discipline' have traditionally served to regulate sexual behaviours and maintain the ascendancy of heterosexual relationships (p. 81). Scholars of regional and rural Australia have explored the ways in which these geographic spaces may be distinguished by traditional and conservative views about gender roles (Pini, 2006; Alston, 2005), a patriarchal structure – with males as the primary authority in political, economic, family and social life (Campbell, Mayerfeld Bell & Finney, 2006) – and the affordance of a narrow range of socially acceptable expressions of masculinity to its men and boys (Gottschalk & Newton, 2003). While there is great contextual variety in the social structure of sex/gender norms across regional and rural spaces in Australia, the research gives us cause for concern. As these social spaces shift alongside broader cultural shifts, both nationally and internationally, regional and rural Australia are here viewed as dynamic sites of interest for the exploration of adolescent sexuality and **gender expression**.

Gender expression the external, outward-facing manifestation of one's gender (behaviour, clothing, haircut, body characteristics, voice). This is distinct from one's internal, personal sense of gender identity.

The research project discussed in this chapter investigates the links between students' school climate with regard to diverse sexualities and genders and their sense of wellbeing and connection to the school environment. The following sections outline concepts associated with the theory of social constructionism, which states, broadly, that individuals are active participants in the construction of their perceived social reality and that they co-construct various understandings of the world through repeated social affirmations. Social constructionism offers useful perspectives for understanding the value systems that circulate around gender and sexuality.

---

3   In a national survey of Australian secondary school students aged 16–19 (Mitchell, et al., 2014), 12.8% of males and 19.3% of females indicated that they were attracted to members of the same sex.

Key theoretical concepts

Gender as a social construction

Seen through the lens of **social constructionism**, gender is shaped by and through the society in which we live. Thus, rather than gender being positioned as innate and gender differences as genetically predetermined, 'becoming' male or female is viewed as a social process, learned through culture and culturally specific (Kehily, 2002). Socially acceptable expressions of gender are influenced by multiple contextual factors, including family, religion, geographic location and the media. The dominant way that gender is constructed creates and maintains the notion that men and women are two distinct and fundamentally different groups of people.

Social constructionism a sociological theory which challenges the concept of natural, pre-existing social typologies, such as gender categories, and instead suggests that these are constructed within societies and according to cultural ideals.

A crucial element of socially constructed gender difference is an implied (hetero)sexuality, where individuals are automatically perceived as being attracted to the opposite sex. Adrienne Rich famously coined this assumption 'compulsory heterosexuality', a largely unspoken belief that serves to legitimise heterosexual sex and romantic relationships while simultaneously marginalising same-sex attraction (Rich, 1980, p. 623). This concept was extended by Judith Butler (1990), a feminist poststructural theorist, who coined the term 'heterosexual matrix' to describe the socially constructed coherence between one's biological sex, one's gender and one's assumed (hetero)sexuality. Individuals who do not conform to this set of linear relationships (i.e. sex = gender = sexuality), either because their biological sex does not 'match' their expressed gender or because they are sexually attracted to members of the same sex, challenge this assumption and are, accordingly, viewed as 'unusual'. This framing, referred to as a 'binary opposition', constructs both heterosexual/homosexual and cisgender[4]/transgender subjects as dichotomous in nature, as opposites that are both mutually defining and mutually exclusive, negating the possibility for fluidity of one's expression of gender or sexuality.

Binary oppositions such as these are not value-free. Rather, there is a power dynamic inherent in the social construction of binaries, wherein each pair contains both a dominant and a subordinate position. (See Chapter 1 for a more in-depth discussion of power as a sociological concept.) This power dynamic features in the heterosexual/homosexual binary, where heterosexuality and heterosex are socially positioned as the normative sexuality and sexual behaviour and provide the reference point from which all other sexualities are judged. The cisgender/transgender binary similarly reflects a power differential and is linked to the constructed 'correct' way to express one's biological sex via gender; deviations from this result in social marginalisation proportional to the degree of gender transgression relative to social context.

---

4   Cisgender refers to an individual whose gender identity is aligned with their biological sex (e.g. a biological male with a male gender identity).

Hegemony a sociological concept that describes the way that power is used to maintain social hierarchies. It is the process by which the dominant group maintains its social dominance.

Gender **hegemony** theory offers an explanation for this phenomenon, whereby particular forms of gender expression are viewed as acceptable, normal or better than others. At the heart of the concept of hegemony is the notion that the social order that it implies is largely accepted, even considered 'common sense' (Gramsci, 1971, as cited in McCormack, 2012), thus making inequities and associated power differentials seem normal. Gender hegemony has been taken up by scholars to help understand the social boundaries of acceptable gender expression for men and women and which forms dominate the social order of gender.

In her seminal theoretical critique of the dynamics of gender hierarchy, Connell (1995) coined the term 'hegemonic masculinity' to describe the prevailing 'configuration of gender practice ... which guarantees (or is taken to guarantee) the dominant position of men and the subordination of women' (p. 77). Inherent in this concept is the subordination of particular kinds of masculinities – that is, those perceived as more feminine – and those men who embody these characteristics. Connell writes about subordinated masculinities as including gender non-conforming and same-sex attracted men. By definition, hegemonic masculinity allows for multiple forms of masculinity, but only one of these is dominant.

The (asymmetrical) parallel for women was initially referred to as 'emphasised femininity' by Connell (1987, p. 183). However, more recent work with this concept (Shippers, 2007) has reclaimed the term 'hegemonic femininity', using it to account for the ascendancy of particular forms of femininity over other femininities to 'serve the interests of the gender order and male domination' (p. 94). As Shippers (2007) further explains:

> If hegemonic gender relations depend on the symbolic construction of desire for the feminine object, physical strength and authority as the characteristics that differentiate men from women *and* define and legitimate their superiority and social dominance over women, then these characteristics must remain unavailable to women. To guarantee men's exclusive access to these characteristics, other configurations of feminine characteristics must be defined as deviant and stigmatised. (pp. 94–5, emphasis in original)

Where hegemonic masculinity necessitates a subordinated masculinity, Shippers proposes the concept of 'pariah femininities' as a counter to hegemonic femininity (2007, p. 95). The term 'pariah' is preferred over 'subordinate' because the characteristics associated with this form of femininity are considered not so much *inferior* as they are *contaminating* to the relationship between masculinity and femininity (Shippers, 2007, p. 95). Thus, these characteristics, inclusive of women's gender non-conformity and/or same-sex attraction, are viewed as socially undesirable, threatening and deserving of social sanction.

Schools as gender and sexuality 'construction sites'

Social sanction, occurring via the naming and shaming of difference, is a key facet of the social construction of gender and sexuality in schools. Social construction 'works' via discourse, a particular way of speaking about someone or something that assigns that person or thing certain attributes and situates them or it in a particular social position. Homophobic utterances in the school context provide a useful working example of this phenomenon.

When a student calls a male student a 'poofter' or 'faggot', for example, that student is tapping into a pre-existing discourse of socially acceptable forms of masculinity and employing a set of meanings wherein 'faggot' is constructed in contrast to heteromasculinity (Youdell, 2004) as its better, stronger and more socially successful (Richardson, 2010) opposite. The language invokes a power differential, whereby 'faggot' is positioned as lesser, socially distained and always in opposition to a hegemonic masculine exemplar. School-based homophobia and transphobia 'do' hegemonic masculinity and femininity through the architecture of 'border constructions' (Richardson, 2010, p. 739) – that is, young men and women publicly delineate what they are *not* as a way to highlight what they *are*, or at least what they think they ought to be (e.g. heterosexual and, therefore, 'normal'). This active gendered *performance* (Butler, 1990) scaffolds social arrangements: young men's school-based homophobic practices are enacted and repeated to 'create the illusion of a coherent heterosexual masculinity' (Kehily, 2002, p. 45) and compulsory heterosexuality functions as the 'core ideology for social cohesion in adolescent girl groups' (Durham, 2002, as cited in Payne, 2007, p. 61). Heterosexuality and the deployment of a homogeneous gender script for boys and girls is, therefore, lauded and branded as a 'collective' social achievement.

Classroom peers and teachers are important social actors in this scene since, as Youdell (2004) writes, gender identities and the boundaries of what is socially un/acceptable are re/defined in daily social practices of schooling. Much informal learning regarding gender and sexuality occurs through social rewards and punishments meted out by both teachers and students. Additionally, the typical Australian school implements a formal curriculum in which heterosexuality is reflected as the 'normal', assumed sexuality for all and in which explicit inclusion of diverse sexualities and genders is the exception rather than the rule. Marginalising pedagogical practices, including teachers' failure to publicly and uniformly address homophobic and transphobic language in the classroom (Ullman, 2014), or to affirm gender and sexuality diversity (Ullman, 2017), stand out as additional contributing factors. Hegemonic masculinity and femininity, including the boundaries of 'subordinate masculinities' and 'pariah femininities', is thus an explicit facet of the social learning inherent in K–12 schooling, leading Kehily (2002) to conclude that 'schools can be seen as sites for the *production* of gendered/sexualised identities rather than agencies that passively reflect dominant power relations' (p. 50, emphasis in original).

Failure to perform one's gender 'correctly' often results in negative reinforcement, since gender, particularly in schools, is governed by 'clearly punitive and regulatory social conventions' (Butler, 1988, p. 527). Schools enforce a clear 'gender regime' through organisational and interpersonal means, including formal and informal dress codes, language codes, the attribution of masculine or feminine qualities to key learning areas of the curriculum (Connell, 1996), the 'policing' of masculinities (Martino, 2000) and femininities, and a culture of compulsory hetero-sexuality (Toomey, McGuire & Russell, 2012). Social marginalisation, isolation and even physical bullying are justified in such a setting where the gender/sexuality transgressor can be viewed as 'worthy of punishment for having violated gender norms' and where the enforcer can view themselves as 'rendering gender justice and reaffirming the natural order of gender appropriate behaviour' (Harry, 1992, p. 116, as cited in McCormack, 2012).

Methodology

Sample and measures

Framing gender as socially constructed, it follows on that nuances of this construction are dependent on the dynamics of the social location. Particular boundaries of masculinity and femininity are constructed and deployed differently in different geographic locales, with regional and rural Australia representing an often limiting space in terms of gender expression. Tyler and Fairbrother (2013) have theorised about a particular Australian rural hegemonic masculinity, characterised by physical strength, risk-taking and 'man against nature', and valorised as the 'rural warrior hero' (p. 115). Since gender is relational, it stands to reason that the Australian rural woman cannot or should not possess these same qualities (Tyler & Fairbrother, 2013). On a self-rating measure of gender-stereotypical characteristics, a survey of women from rural and remote towns in Australia rated themselves more highly on measures of 'female characteristics' (e.g. sensitive and emotional) and lower on measures of 'male characteristics' (e.g. superior and bossy) than women from urban centres (Bramston, Rodgers-Clark, Hegney & Bishop, 2000), reflecting essentialist notions of gender difference. Thus, regional and rural Australia present an important location for the exploration of the 'heterosexual matrix' (Butler, 1990) via SSA and TGNC teenagers' school experiences.

The data explored in this chapter are a subset of data from the author's nation-wide *Free2Be?* project (Ullman, 2015a), which explored the school experiences and related outcomes of 704 SSA and TGNC students from across Australia. Data were collected via an online survey with both closed- and open-ended items wherein young people were asked about their teachers' and classmates' treatment of diverse sexualities and gender expression, both as curricular content within class-based lesson plans and in terms of social inclusivity or marginalisation. Measures included original items investigating 'gender climate' (Ullman, 2014) that examined formal (i.e. organisationally enforced) and informal (i.e. socially enforced) 'rules' regarding students' gender expression. Previously validated measures (Mikulsky, 2007) were used to explore other elements of school climate, including the frequency of various forms of homophobia and transphobia at school and teachers' responses to such behaviours. Further, participants were asked about their sense of school wellbeing, connection, safety and motivational outcomes using scale measures from the *Attitudes Towards School Survey* (ATSS) (Department of Education and Early Childhood Development [DEECD], 2012), a measure of general academic self-concept from the *ASDQII* (Marsh, 1990), as well as other stand-alone items.

Participants' postal codes were used alongside the Accessibility/Remoteness Index of Australia (Australian Institute of Health and Welfare, 2004) to identify young people living in regional, rural and remote areas of Australia, based upon proximity to urban centres with a population of more than 5000 people. Outcomes for this participant cohort were examined using bivariate statistical analyses, including mean score comparisons (t-tests), correlations and chi-square tests for the closed-ended survey items and thematic coding for analysis of the open-ended items (Saldana, 2009). Both quantitative and qualitative data were examined in light of the key theoretical concepts as outlined in the earlier sections of this chapter, particularly regarding social and curricular boundaries of acceptable and marginalised masculinities and femininities and links to sexual orientation.

Participants were recruited using targeted advertising on social media (Facebook), where the recruitment post was specifically shown to Australian teens between the ages of 14 and 18 who were either (a) 'interested in' people of the same reported biological sex or (b) had 'liked' LGBTQI-related Facebook pages. According to Facebook tracking, the recruitment statement was posted on 37 568 individual Facebook pages, with 1292 young people clicking through to commence the survey (3.4% response rate[5]). Of these, final numbers were reduced to 704 useable surveys, with 213 of these being from young people from regional and rural Australia (30% of the sample) and all eight states and territories represented.

Mirroring the larger sample, the majority of the sample were female (57%) and older, with 56.7% aged 16 and 17. Most of these young people identified as gay (29%), bisexual (28%) or lesbian (23%), with young women being more likely to identify as bisexual than lesbian. A small number of regional and rural participants (n = 10, 5% of the sample) identified as transgender or gender non-conforming, with five additional participants electing not to nominate a gender preference. Eight regional and rural participants identified as Aboriginal or Torres Strait Islander.

Analysis and discussion

Marking the boundaries: Verbal and physical homophobia and transphobia

Students from regional and rural Australia were significantly more likely to report having heard transphobic language at school within the last month (65% regional/rural students vs. 56% urban students on a yes/no item; $x^2(1)$ = 4.57, $p < .05$), compared to young people in or near urban centres. Likewise,

---

5　While online survey rates typically hover between 20–47% (Nulty, 2008), using Facebook targeted advertising for recruitment results in a much lower response rate. The average click-through rate for Facebook advertisements is 0.90% (Irvine, 2017). By comparison, the 3.4% click-through rate achieved in the current project was deemed as a positive outcome.

these students were significantly more likely to have witnessed physical harassment of their classmates due to perceived non-heterosexuality or gender non-conformity within the last month (55% regional/rural students vs. 43% urban students on a yes/no item; $x^2(1) = 7.59$, $p < .01$). While mean differences in the reported frequency of verbal homophobia, transphobia, physical harassment and teachers' positive interventions in these instances were not statistically significantly different across the two cohorts, the regional and rural students reported higher percentages of extreme negative responses for five of the six items that measured this element of school climate. In other words, larger numbers of regional and rural students reported that their classmates 'always' engaged in homophobic/transphobic behaviours and that their teachers 'never' intervened.

Students' responses to related open-ended items highlighted perceived teacher inaction, with 41% of responses from regional and rural youth describing instances of teachers ignoring homophobic or transphobic language, indicating that teachers did 'nothing', 'didn't care' or 'ignored it'. While nearly 30% of responses detailed teachers intervening to stop the behaviours or language, nearly every account featured teachers attending to the inappropriate timing (e.g. talking out of turn) or use of language, rather than their acknowledgement of the discourses informing the language. In other words, students were told to 'stop' or to 'be quiet' but teachers did not discuss homophobic/transphobic implications of the language or link its use to the active reproduction of normative expectations for gender and sexuality.

Many responses highlighted the everyday nature of the deployment of such language as evidence of daily 'border constructions' (Richardson, 2010, p. 783), where (hetero)masculinities and (hetero)femininities are constructed, in no small part, by the repudiation of non-normative gender expressions. Likewise, the young people alluded to their teachers' tacit acceptance of the daily violence of homophobic/transphobic language due to the very nature of its frequency:

> People at my school call people 'poofters' and 'fags' all the time. When this happens, it's just brushed off easily and no one seems to care. (16-year-old girl from very remote Western Australia)

> The teacher just carried on as though it was normal. It [homophobic language] happens every day. (17-year-old boy from regional New South Wales)

Most troubling were the additional 37 responses (13%) in which teachers were described as actively supporting the homophobia/transphobia by 'laughing along', 'smirking', 'joining in' or otherwise using homophobic or transphobic language themselves, making visible teachers' active participation in the social construction of the dominant gender order:

> Nothing happens. The teachers let it go, as if it is a cultural way of speaking to each other, as if the terms aren't offensive to those who hear them, and to whom it affects. Teachers will often say the phrase 'that's gay' themselves. (16-year-old girl from outer regional South Australia)

Official discourses on diverse sexualities and genders: What's happening in the classroom?

Participants were asked about the inclusion of LGBTQI people, history and current events as a topic of formal classroom learning, with less than one-quarter of students nationwide reporting such education. SSA and TGNC students from regional and rural Australia were significantly less likely to report the inclusion of diverse sexualities and genders within the formal curriculum, $(x^2(2) = 12.72, p < .01)$, with 27% of the urban sample reporting such education compared to 14% of the regional and rural sample. These silences were echoed in policy, with just 13% of regional and rural students confirming the inclusion of sexual orientation within their school's anti-discrimination policy.

Four additional items assessed teachers' and classmates' informal positivity towards or support of SSA and TGNC individuals and associated conversation. On average, participants reported that their classmates and teachers were 'hardly ever'[6] positive about diverse genders and sexualities, with regional and rural students reporting significantly lower incidence of positivity than urban students across three of the four items. Considering the ways in which compulsory heterosexuality (Rich, 1980) and its associated cisgender 'performances' (Butler, 1990) are policed and positioned as a collective social achievement for students (Richardson, 2010), it is not surprising that the most profound differences across the rural and urban cohorts were related to perceived positivity from participants' peers, rather than from their teachers. While teachers may scaffold students' compulsory heterosexuality through their delivery of the formal curriculum, enforcement and communication of formal school policy, and the informal conversations they are willing to have (and the others that they are not), it is the students themselves who are at the front lines of the 'border construction' (Richardson, 2010). Findings suggest tighter border control for young SSA and TGNC students in rural and regional settings, who report significantly less positivity from their peers regarding both same-sex attraction (urban average = 2.23 vs. regional/rural average = 1.99; $t(692) = 2.91, p < .01$) and gender non-conformity (urban average = 1.44 vs. regional/rural average = 1.17; $t(692) = 3.17, p < .01$). Likewise, findings speak to the greater social marginalisation generally reported by TGNC young people who, from the perspective of gender hegemony theory, step further outside the 'border' in their gender transgressions.

Associated school wellbeing, connection and academic outcomes

Given teachers' duty of care to both protect their students as well as provide equitable access to learning, investigating indicators of perceived protection and access provides important insight into the impact of schools' active production of

---

6　All four items measured on a 5-point Likert scale with points: 'Never' (0), 'Hardly ever' (1), 'Some of the time' (2), 'Most of the time' (3) and 'Always' (4).

gendered and sexualised identities (Kehily, 2002) on SSA and TGNC students. In this investigation, students' reported school wellbeing, school connection, motivational outcomes and academic self-concept[7] were viewed as outcome variables, representative of perceived access, safety and connection to the school community. In line with findings related to school climate and gender climate, as detailed above, regional and rural SSA and TGNC students fared worse on every outcome measure than their urban peers, with average (mean) differences large enough to be statistically significant for six of the nine measures (see Table 4.1).

Table 4.1: Mean scores on school wellbeing, connection and motivational outcomes for urban and regional/rural students

Measurement scales	Location		*t-value*	*df*
	Urban (n = 481)	Regional/rural (n = 213)		
School morale[a] (5-item scale)	3.71 (1.40)	3.56 (1.28)	1.33	692
School distress[b] (6-item scale)	4.32 (1.40)	4.53 (1.47)	−1.79	692
Teacher empathy[c] (7-item scale)	3.40 (0.92)	3.17 (0.94)	3.04**	692
Classmate social connection[c] (5-item scale)	3.56 (0.85)	3.34 (0.97)	2.89**	692
School connection (general)[c] (5-item scale)	3.03 (1.11)	2.75 (1.09)	3.00**	692
Confidence in learning[c] (4-item scale)	3.48 (0.92)	3.32 (0.93)	2.13*	692
Motivation to learn[c] (4-item scale)	3.87 (0.94)	3.72 (0.98)	1.92	692
School safety[d] (4-item scale)	2.62 (1.13)	2.97 (1.20)	−3.69***	692
Academic self-concept[e] (8-item scale)	3.36 (1.57)	3.77 (1.61)	−3.00**	628

a 7-point Likert scale measure, where higher numbers indicate **higher morale**
b 7-point Likert scale measure, where higher numbers indicate **higher distress**
c 5-point Likert scale measure, where higher numbers indicate **more positive outcome**
d 5-point Likert scale measure, where higher numbers indicate **less safe school environment**
e 8-point Likert scale measure, where higher numbers indicate **lower academic self-concept**
Note: * = $p \leq .05$; ** = $p \leq .01$; *** = $p \leq .001$. Standard deviations appear in parentheses below means.

7   These variables were measured by the ATSS (DEECD, 2012) and the ASDQII (Marsh, 1990).

Unsurprisingly, these measures of wellbeing, connection, safety and perceived teacher empathy were statistically significantly correlated with measures of school climate (Table 4.2) and gender climate (Table 4.3), with items related to perceived teacher actions (e.g. positive intervention) or expectations shown to have some of the strongest relationships to students' school wellbeing and connection. Taking school morale as an example, measured here as feeling happy, relaxed and positive at school, these two tables highlight the link between regional and rural students' positive school morale and (a) their perception that teachers positively intervene during instances of school-based homophobia and transphobia, (b) their perceptions that teachers and classmates hold less restrictive gender expectations, and (c) their perceptions about their ability to autonomously express their own gender identity without breaking school 'rules'. With regard to gender expectations, as shown in Table 4.3, this relationship was more pronounced for young men in the group, pointing to the stronger impact of these expectations

Table 4.2: Pearson's product moment correlations for school climate with school wellbeing, connection and safety outcomes for regional/rural students

Measurement scales	Verbal homophobia		Verbal transphobia		Physical bullying	
	Freq. (n = 203)	Freq. teacher intervention (n = 175)	Freq. (n = 138)	Freq. teacher intervention (n = 86)	Freq. (n = 110)	Freq. teacher intervention (n = 110)
School morale[a] (5-item scale)	−.15*	.43***	−.08	.21*	−.14	.19*
School distress[b] (6-item scale)	.22**	−.33***	.21*	−.22*	.27**	.27**
Teacher empathy[c] (7-item scale)	−.23**	.42***	−.07	.29**	−.12	.26**
Classmate social connection[c] (5-item scale)	−.20**	.30***	−.16	.13	−.33***	.16
School connection (general)[c] (5-item scale)	−.28***	.44***	−.15	.19	−.16	.23*
School safety[d] (5-item scale)	.40***	−.31***	.26**	−.35**	.41***	−.16

a 7-point Likert scale measure, where higher numbers indicate **higher morale**

b 7-point Likert scale measure, where higher numbers indicate **higher distress**

c 5-point Likert scale, where higher numbers indicate **more positive outcome**

d 5-point Likert scale measure, where higher numbers indicate a **less safe school environment**

Note: * = $p \leq .05$; ** = $p \leq .01$; *** = $p \leq .001$.

Table 4.3: Pearson's product moment correlations for selected gender-climate items with school wellbeing, connection and safety outcomes for regional/rural students

	Teachers' gender expectations[a]		Student's gender expectations[b]		Impact of rules on gender expression[c]
	Males (n = 76)	Females (n = 122)	Males (n = 76)	Females (n = 122)	All regional/rural (n = 213)
School morale (5-item scale)	.48*	.32***	.52***	.29**	.35***
School distress (6-item scale)	−.43**	−.40***	−.55***	−.36***	−.42***
Teacher empathy (7-item scale)	.61**	.44***	.47***	.27**	.41***
Classmate social connection (5-item scale)	.43**	.40***	.38**	.39***	.38***
School connection (general) (5-item scale)	.51***	.42***	.55***	.40***	.38***
School safety (5-item scale)	.50***	.38**	.50***	.45***	.43***

All gender-climate items measured using a nine-point Likert scale, with higher numbers indicating **greater freedom of gender expression**.

a Item read: 'My teachers expect me to act a certain way because I am a girl/guy.'

b Item read: 'Other students expect me to act a certain way because I am a girl/guy.'

c Item read: 'Certain rules at my school make it hard for me to express my gender in the way I would like.'

Note: * = $p \le .05$; ** = $p \le .01$; *** = $p \le .001$.

on their school wellbeing and connection. Given the well-documented causal influence of perceived teacher care on students' academic outcomes (Wentzel, 2009), a finding that has been replicated with cohorts of Australian SSA and TGNC youth (Ullman, 2015b), it is especially disconcerting to see such a strong correlation between young men's perceptions of their teachers' gender expectations and perceived teacher empathy ($r = 0.61$, $p < .01$), measured as teachers' care for the individual's learning.

Open-ended item responses reflected the significant relationships highlighted above between the two climate variables (school climate and gender climate) and reported classroom wellbeing and connection. To an item asking regional and rural students to describe why they had chosen a particular class as their favourite, many described being 'good at' the subject, sharing the class with friends or simply 'liking' the subject. Other responses were more revealing: in just over half (52%) of the 192 closed-ended responses, students reported that their favourite class was one in which they could be free to express themselves (59 responses), where they had a strong connection, either to their teacher (19 responses) or to the students in the class (13 responses), or where they felt 'relaxed' or 'calm' because of a lack of peer or teacher marginalisation (8 responses).

> My teacher treated me just like every other person in the class, and did not hold back on [teaching me] 'feminine' dance moves as she didn't care what gender or orientation I was – I was just a student. I could dance my heart out and not be laughed at or called names for the passion I put into the subject. (16-year-old boy from outer regional Queensland)

It is noteworthy that higher numbers of SSA and TGNC young people from regional/rural Australia reported leaving school prior to graduation (37.5% vs. 29.8%) and were significantly more likely to truant from school ($x^2(4) = 14.43, p < .01$), with 18% of regional and rural students reporting truancy more than 10 times in the month that preceded survey completion as opposed to 10% of young people from urban centres who reported the same. Further, regional and rural young people were significantly less likely than their urban peers to say they would attend university ($x^2(6) = 13.03, p < .05$), with almost half of the urban sample indicating that it was 'very likely' they would attend, compared to just 35% of the regional/rural sample. This finding was echoed in the significant mean difference in reported academic self-concept between the two cohorts ($t(628) = -3.00, p < .01$), with regional/rural SSA and TGNC students' average academic self-concept nearly half a point lower than that of urban students, measured using an eight-point Likert scale. Open-ended items highlighted this relationship; young people frequently spoke of excelling academically and enjoying most the classes in which they experienced teacher support and a lack of social harassment. Likewise, students' descriptions of why they had truanted echoed this relationship; most cited harassment, active bullying related to sexuality and/or gender expression, and marginalisation by teachers as key reasons:

> I was scared to go into class, fearing that, because I have no friends to sit next to, people will find it easier to pick on me. (14-year-old girl from regional New South Wales)

> My classmates make me uncomfortable. I don't fit in. It is more stress attending class than having to catch up on work. (16-year-old girl from outer regional Tasmania)

> I hate that class now because my teacher makes life difficult for me and the other gay person in my class ... I also don't feel that she cares about me or my results enough. (17-year-old girl from regional South Australia)

Implications

While a focus on zero-tolerance strategies for homophobia and transphobia might go part of the way to silencing students' use of such language, these approaches alone cannot account for the powerful social forces that drive the marginalisation of SSA and TGNC individuals. While the inclusion of LGBTQI perspectives in the official K–12 curriculum is an important step in increasing visibility and normalisation, it is not enough. Simply disallowing homophobic and transphobic language and mandating a reductionist anti-homophobia education cannot deconstruct the dominant discourses that surround same-sex attraction and gender non-conformity in schools. (See Ferfolja & Ullman, 2014 for a critique of this framing within the Australian national Health and Physical Education syllabus.)

Educators must be able to discuss with their students, and must themselves understand, the ways in which everyday instances of gender policing construct the social hierarchy and reflect dominant discourses related to gender and sexuality of both the non-normative/subordinate/pariah and the hegemonic ideal. To do this, teachers must be able to recognise gender policing when they see it, from students, colleagues, in the mandated curriculum and within their own pedagogical practices – present not only in the easily identified linguistic forms of homophobia and transphobia, but also in the more mundane organisational elements of formal school life. Educators must be able to identify how curricular inclusions and exclusions, institutional policies and school 'rules' function to both reproduce social inequities related to gender expression and to support the marginalisation of SSA and TGNC students. The sum total of school gender climate has the potential to validate or alienate these and all students, to encourage their sense of belonging and their motivation to succeed at school or to systematically exclude them from the school community and its educational pursuits.

Considerations

- Many SSA and TGNC young people report that their teachers do not identify the homophobic or transphobic discourses present in the language used by their classmates. How does this contribute to the social construction of gender and sexuality at the school level?
- Australian society by and large would not support educators holding racist or sexist viewpoints, yet some would defend teachers' homophobic or transphobic beliefs as a moral or religious right. Should teachers have a right to these beliefs and how might these beliefs manifest in the classroom in ways that impact student wellbeing?
- How do discourses of gender essentialism impact on the school experiences of all students, not just those who identify as SSA or TGNC?

Of interest

- Safe Schools Coalition. This program creates and disseminates tools, resources and support to enable Australian schools to support the safety and inclusivity of students with diverse genders and sexualities. See http://www.safeschoolscoalition.org.au

- *How to support sexual diversity in schools.* This checklist has been designed by the Australian Research Centre in Sex, Health and Society (ARCSHS) to help schools self-evaluate their efforts to support the wellbeing of students with diverse genders and sexualities. See https://www.latrobe.edu.au/arcshs/downloads/arcshs-research-publications/SexualDiversityChecklist.pdf
- The Queering Education Research Institute (QuERI). This independent think tank and research initiative aims to 'bridge the gap between research and practice in the teaching of LGBTQ students and the creation of LGBTQ youth-affirming schools through sociological approaches to understanding education and educational environments'. See http://www.queeringeducation.org

References

Alston, M. (2005). Gender perspectives in Australian rural community life. In C. Cocklin & J. Dibden (Eds.), *Sustainability and change in rural Australia* (pp. 139–56). Sydney: University of New South Wales Press.

Australian Institute of Health and Welfare (2004). *Rural, regional and remote health: A guide to remoteness classifications.* AIHW cat. no. PHE 53. Canberra: Author.

Blackburn, M. (2012). *Interrupting hate: Homophobia in schools and what literacy can do about it.* New York: Teachers College Press.

Bramston, P., Rodgers-Clark, C., Hegney, D. & Bishop, J. (2000). Gender roles and geographic location as predictors of emotional distress in Australian women. *Australian Journal of Rural Health*, 8, 154–60. doi:10.1046/j.1440–1584.2000.00272.x

Bryant, L. & Pini, B. (2011). *Gender and rurality.* London: Routledge.

Butler, J. (1988). Performative acts and gender constitution. *Theatre Journal*, 40(4), 519–31. doi:10.2307/3207893

—— (1990). *Gender trouble: Feminism and the subversion of identity.* New York: Routledge.

Campbell, H., Mayerfeld Bell, M. & Finney, M. (2006). Masculinity and rural life: An introduction. In H. Campbell, M. Mayerfeld Bell & M. Finney (Eds.), *Country boys: Masculinity and rural life* (pp. 1–26). University Park, PA: Pennsylvania State University Press.

Connell, R. W. (1987). *Gender and power: Society, the person and sexuality politics.* Cambridge: Polity.

—— (1995). *Masculinities.* Berkeley, CA: University of California Press.

—— (1996). Teaching the boys: New research on masculinity and gender strategies for schools. *Teachers College Record*, 98(2), 206–35.

Department of Education and Early Childhood Development (DEECD) (2012). *Attitudes towards school survey.* Melbourne: Author.

Duffy, B., Fotinatos, N., Smith, A. & Burke, J. (2013). Puberty, health and sexual education in Australian regional primary schools: Year 5 and 6 teacher perceptions. *Sex Education*, 13(2), 186–213. doi:10.1080/14681811.2012.678324

Edwards, J. (2006). *Coming out alone: An assessment of the needs of same sex attracted youth, their families, and service providers in Western Australia.* Perth: Trinity Outreach Services.

Ferfolja, T. & Ullman, J. (2014). Opportunity lost or (re)written out: LGBTI content in Australia's new national Health and Physical Education curriculum. In M. Somerville & S. Gannon (Eds.), *Contemporary issues of equity in education* (pp. 69–87). London: Cambridge Scholars Publishing.

Gottschalk, L. & Newton, J. (2003). *Not so gay in the bush: 'Coming out' in regional and rural Victoria.* Ballarat: University of Ballarat, Department of Human Services, Grampians Region.

Hillier, L., Jones, T., Monagle, M., Overton, N., Gahan, L., Blackman, J. & Mitchell, A. (2010). *Writing themselves in 3 (WTi3): The third national study on the sexual health and wellbeing of same sex attracted and gender questioning young people.* Melbourne: Australian Research Centre in Sex, Health and Society, La Trobe University.

Hillier, L., Turner, A. & Mitchell, A. (2005). *Writing themselves in again: 6 years on: The second national report on the sexuality, health and well-being of same sex attracted young people in Australia* (Monograph series No. 50). Melbourne: Australian Research Centre in Sex, Health and Society, La Trobe University.

Irvine, M. (2017, September 28). Facebook Ad Benchmarks for Your Industry [Blog post]. Retrieved from: http://www.wordstream.com/blog/ws/2017/02/28/facebook-advertising-benchmarks

Kehily, M. (2002). *Sexuality, gender and schooling: Shifting agendas in social learning.* London: Routledge.

Kosciw, J., Palmer, N., Kull, R. & Greytak, E. (2013). The effect of negative school climate on academic outcomes for LGBT youth and the role of in-school supports. *Journal of School Violence*, 12(1), 45–63. doi:10.1080/15388220.2012.732546

Marsh, H. (1990). The structure of academic self-concept: The Marsh/Shavelson Model. *Journal of Educational Psychology*, 82(4), 623–36. doi:10.1037/0022–0663.82.4.623

Martino, W. (2000). Policing masculinities: Investigating the role of homophobia and heteronormativity in the lives of adolescent school boys. *The Journal of Men's Studies*, 8(2), 213–36. doi:10.3149/jms.0802.213

McCormack, M. (2012). *The declining significance of homophobia: How teenage boys are redefining masculinity and heterosexuality.* Oxford: Oxford University Press.

Mikulsky, J. (2007). *'In or "out?"': An examination of the effects of school climate on same-sex attracted students in Australia.* Doctoral dissertation. University of Sydney Digital Theses (Open Access). Retrieved from http://hdl.handle.net/2123/1969

Mitchell, A., Patrick, K., Heywood, W., Blackman, P. & Pitts, M. (2014). 5th national survey of Australian secondary students and sexual health 2013 (ARCSHS Monograph Series No. 97). Melbourne: Australian Research Centre in Sex, Health and Society, La Trobe University.

Nulty, D. (2008). The adequacy of response rates to online and paper surveys: What can be done? Assessment and Evaluation in Higher Education, 33(3), 301–14. doi: 10.1080/02602930701293231

Payne, E. (2007). Heterosexism, perfection, and popularity: Young lesbians' experiences of the high school social scene. Educational Studies: A Journal of the American Educational Studies Association, 41(1), 60–79. doi:10.1080/00131940701309054

Pearson, J., Muller, C. & Wilkinson, L. (2007). Adolescent same-sex attraction and academic outcomes: The role of school attachment and engagement. Social Problems, 54(4), 523–42. doi:10.1525/sp.2007.54.4.523

Pini, B. (2006). A critique of 'new' rural local governance: The case of gender in a rural Australian setting. Journal of Rural Studies, 22(4), 396–408. doi:10.1016/j.jrurstud.2006.02.002

Poteat, V. P. & Espelage, D. L. (2007). Predicting psychosocial consequences of homophobic victimization in middle school students. Journal of Early Adolescence, 27, 175–91. doi:10.1177/0272431606294839

Rich, A. (1980). Compulsory heterosexuality and lesbian existence. Signs, 5(4), 631–60. doi:10.1086/493756

Richardson, D. (2010). Youth masculinities: Compelling male heterosexuality. The British Journal of Sociology, 61(4), 737–56. doi:10.1111/j.1468–4446.2010.01339.x

Robinson, K. H., Bansel, P., Denson, N., Ovenden, G. & Davies, C. (2014). Growing up queer: Issues facing young Australians who are gender variant and sexuality diverse. Melbourne: Young and Well Cooperative Research Centre.

Saldana, J. (2009). The coding manual for qualitative researchers. Phoenix, AZ: Sage Publications.

Shippers, M. (2007). Recovering the feminine other: Masculinity, femininity and gender hegemony. Theory and Society, 36(1), 85–102. doi:10.1007/s11186-007–9022-4

Smith, A., Schlichthorst, M., Mitchell, A., Walsh, J., Lyons, A., Blackman, P. & Pitts, M. (2011). Sexuality education in Australian secondary schools 2010. Monograph Series No. 80. Melbourne: Australian Research Centre in Sex, Health and Society, La Trobe University.

Toomey, R., McGuire, J. & Russell, S. (2012). Heteronormativity, school climates, and perceived safety for gender non-conforming peers. Journal of Adolescence, 35, 187–96. doi:10.1016/j.adolescence.2011.03.001

Tyler, M. & Fairbrother, P. (2013). Bushfires and 'men's business': The importance of gender and rural hegemonic masculinity. Journal of Rural Studies, 30, 110–19. doi:10.1016/j.jrurstud.2013.01.002

Ullman, J. (2014). Ladylike/butch, sporty/dapper: Exploring 'gender climate' with Australian LGBTQ students using Stage-Environment Fit Theory. *Sex Education*, 14(4), 430–43. doi:10.1080/14681811.2014.919912

—— (2015a). *Free2Be?: Exploring the schooling experiences of Australia's sexuality and gender diverse secondary school students*. Sydney: Centre for Educational Research, School of Education, Western Sydney University.

—— (2015b). 'At-risk' or school-based risk?: Testing a model of school-based stressors, coping responses, and academic self-concept for same-sex attracted youth. *Journal of Youth Studies*, 18(4), 417–33. doi:10.1080/13676261.2014.963539

—— (2017). Teacher positivity towards gender diversity: Exploring relationships and school outcomes for transgender and gender-diverse students. *Sex Education*, 17(3), 276–89. doi:10.1080/14681811.2016.1273104

Ullman, J. & Ferfolja, T. (2015). Bureaucratic constructions of sexual diversity: 'Sensitive', 'controversial' and silencing. *Teaching Education*, 26(2), 145–59. doi:10.1080/10476210.2014.959487

Wentzel, K. (2009). Students' relationships with teachers as motivational contexts. In K. Wentzel & A. Wigfield (Eds.), *Handbook of motivation at school* (pp. 301–22). Mahwah, NJ: LEA.

Youdell, D. (2004). Wounds and reinscriptions: Schools, sexualities and performative subjects. *Discourse: Studies in the Cultural Politics of Education*, 25(4), 477–93. doi:10.1080/0159630042000290973

Part 2

Intersecting Theories for Meaning

Postcolonialism, Critical Race Theory
and Cultural Theory

CHAPTER 5

Destabilising privilege

Disrupting deficit thinking in white pre-service teachers on professional experience in culturally diverse, high-poverty schools

Bruce Burnett and Jo Lampert

AUSTRALIAN PROFESSIONAL STANDARDS FOR TEACHERS

Standard 1: Know students and how they learn

Knowing how students learn in a low socio-economic school is an ongoing process of trial, error and reflection. Furthermore, teaching in low socio-economic schools means that teachers are more likely to come across diversity in linguistic, cultural and religious backgrounds. This chapter provides theoretical grounding to help pre-service and graduate teachers reflect on their own practice when learning how their students learn. In particular, it is critical that teachers understand that white privilege is often a barrier to the learning of all students, particularly in low socio-economic schools.

I found myself standing in my second prac in front of a very different class that included mostly Indigenous and Polynesian kids. They were just so different from me: they walked with a swagger, dressed in baggy jumpers despite sweat dripping down their faces, and spoke to me with edgy attitude. Throughout this four-week placement, I never saw a single parent in any of my classes. 'Most of them just don't care' was the response from my supervising teacher. How was I supposed to make this group of kids excited about colonial-Australian bush poetry with so many of the other teachers' suggestions along the lines of: 'Don't try group work with that class – they don't have the social skills' … 'Just get them to sit and write a lot – it keeps them quiet'?

Introduction

The preceding vignette was Kristie's[1] written response to an early professional placement experience in a school located in a low socio-economic area on the outskirts of Brisbane, Queensland. At that time, Kristie was a high-achieving student in her third year of a four-year Bachelor of Education degree. Because of her high academic achievement, she was invited at the end of her second year of study to participate in the National Exceptional Teaching for Disadvantaged Schools (NETDS) program, an **Initial Teacher Education** program targeting **high-poverty schooling**, a sector that historically has difficulty employing and retaining teachers.

Initial Teacher Education (ITE) Preliminary qualification required for practising/accredited teachers. ITE is also known as pre-service teacher training and occurs at the tertiary level at either an undergraduate Bachelor's or Master's degree level.

High-poverty schooling (also called low socio-economic schooling, urban schooling or disadvantaged schooling) a description of complex school settings characterised by the multiple dimensions of poverty and how these issues impact on education.

This chapter examines the personal reflections and experiences of several pre-service and newly graduated teachers who were involved in the NETDS program. This process of reflexivity documents a series of professional journeys, including descriptions of struggling when their privileged, taken-for-granted ways of being were destabilised, and grappling with tensions related to their own predispositions and values, which are investigated in the context of whiteness and privilege theory (McIntosh, 2012).

The 'comments from the field' that make up the narratives in this chapter all come from participants of the NETDS program. Since 2009, NETDS has created a pathway for the highest-achieving pre-service teachers in selected Australian universities to be better prepared for teaching careers within high-poverty schools. NETDS is designed to deepen pre-service teachers' understandings of the contexts in which they will be teaching. Once invited into the program, the participants complete all of their remaining professional experience placements and a final internship in low socio-economic schools. These schools are selected based on having an Index of Cultural and Social Educational Advantage (ICSEA) level of less than 1000, which is the Australian mean. It is well acknowledged that in Australia teachers are predominantly white and middle-class (Mills, 2012); therefore, time is often taken with NETDS participants to unpack such concepts as Othering, deficit attitudes, Critical Race Theory and whiteness. Teachers, no matter how prepared or well meaning, are not born with the ability to critically self-reflect; nor can it be expected that they automatically recognise their own racialised ideas. By the very nature of their taken-for-grantedness, pre-service teachers' unexamined attitudes towards both poverty and 'race' are often invisible to them and need to be brought to the fore in an ongoing and deliberate way. Social justice education, as explained by scholars such as Arnetha Ball (2009), exposes how crucial it is for good teachers to develop reflexivity as part of their teacher preparation, arguing that it is essential for teachers to interrogate their

---

1   Pseudonyms are used for all reflections. Ethical clearance was approved for this research and all participants provided signed consent.

attitudes prior to entering the classroom and to continue to engage in ongoing dialogue once they are teaching. Hence, it can be argued that white, privileged teachers must engage in continuous reflection of this nature throughout their careers, because trying to understand privilege is an ongoing journey, and at many stages involves one step forward and two steps back.

Background

Many teachers in high-poverty, underserved schools in Australia are white and come from middle-class backgrounds (Mills, 2012); therefore, it is common for teachers to arrive in these classrooms with little knowledge of their students' families and communities. The literature associated with the problems that arise from the cultural mismatch between teachers and students is unequivocal and raises several explicit issues. It is clear that teachers must do more than engage in 'cultural competency' workshops, or learn cultural communication styles. They must deeply reflect on their own cultural identities, and question the taken-for-granted assumptions that come from the belief that dominant ways are 'normal'. As Aveling (2002, p. 121) notes, pre-service teachers 'need to be able to interrogate their own assumptions and racialised subject positions; to understand the codes "they [we] use to construct their own narratives and histories"' (p. 121).

When Aveling (2007, p. 76) and other scholars who write about anti-racism education use the word 'Othering', they refer to the process where students who are constructed as 'different' are often perceived as a problem. In order to understand this though, white teachers are required to unpack how their own cultures come to appear normal in the first place. In particular, the kind of critical reflection suggested to analyse discourses of whiteness requires teachers to think about how identities structure how we hear and what we are 'willing to know' (Dion, 2009). As Mansouri and Jenkins (2010, p. 96) remind us:

> Within the Australian school system, where the majority of teachers, administrators and students are white, whiteness can be seen as the 'norm' and non-white skin colour as the 'Other'. This positioning of white as 'normal' can encourage intercultural relations in which race and racism are 'normalised' and viewed as an inevitable part of the daily existence for students.

How teachers examine their own cultural identities has an especially significant impact if they are teaching in high-poverty schools, where students are less likely to be 'like them' and more likely to be Othered. When Kristie says her first response to students was *They were just so different from me*, she takes up a position of absolute binary, believing that her students' 'different' culture will be altogether 'incommensurable with mainstream education' (Keddie, Gowlett, Mills, Monk & Renshaw, 2012, p. 91). While Kristie knows how to recognise stereotypical responses from fellow teachers when she hears them in the staffroom, she also engages in her own binaried assumptions. However, given the right conditions, Kristie's reflection provides an important 'teachable moment' for her in which she is able to trouble and unsettle her own responses through a critical lens. Indeed, Villegas (2007, p. 374) suggests that:

> To maximise the impact of formal preparation on teacher learning, teacher educators must create ample opportunities early in the program for candidates to examine critically their taken-for-granted beliefs in relation to classroom actions. Without such reflection, many teachers-to-be are unable or unwilling to incorporate new ideas and new habits of thought and action into their teaching, preferring instead to teach based on their taken-for-granted beliefs.

Ideally, pre-service teachers need to re-evaluate their own cultural positions prior to entering the classroom as employed teachers, and it is reasonable to suggest, therefore, that this process must begin during their Initial Teacher Education programs (Lampert and Burnett, 2014). While some evidence suggests that early career teachers waver in their attitudes, sometimes defaulting to previous stereotypical positions once they begin their teaching careers (Lampert, 2012), with mentoring and support, combined with a strong community of practice, teachers can be provided with forums in which to continue their reflective practices (Buchanan et al., 2013). Conversations around issues such as whiteness regularly take place among and between the NETDS pre-service teachers and graduate teachers of the program, who stay connected both in person and through a dedicated social networking site (Burnett and Lampert, 2015).

It is important to note that, although written personal reflections are a critical component, the process itself is much more involved. This chapter focuses on the necessity of connecting such reflections with relevant theoretical concepts, such as whiteness and privilege, which are defined in the following section where we will explain how pre-service and graduate teachers can be guided to think through their own assumptions and, ultimately, work towards a useful understanding of their own position of privilege, using a combination of theory and a highly personalised practice of reflection.

Critical Race Theory (CRT) an interrogation of invisible historical and social constructions of whiteness. It draws on postcolonial theory and cultural studies to focus on the relationships that exist between 'race', racism and power. CRT in education challenges accepted practice and provides a critical theoretical lens through which it is possible to identify normative white privilege and interpret racial inequality.

Whiteness a theoretical position that attempts to unmask and demystify the social construction of 'whiteness' and provide a lens through which to understand the cultural, historical and sociological aspects of privilege and social status

Key theoretical concepts

Drawing on **Critical Race Theory (CRT)** and, in particular, its offshoots, **whiteness** (Frankenberg, 1993) and privilege theory (McIntosh, 2012), this chapter explores specific concepts such as colour blindness and deficit thinking that emerge as important themes in the narratives. In combination, these concepts help explain how schooling practices (and student outcomes) are often contingent on unspoken power relationships having to do with racialised practices and privilege.

Educators have employed CRT as a way to examine how 'race' and ethnicity can be implicit in unequal power relationships between teachers and their students; for instance, by examining the normalised practices of privileged, white teachers who teach students unlike themselves (Ladson-Billings, 1998; see also Chapter 1 in this volume). As an offshoot of CRT, whiteness theory, developed from the work of Ruth Frankenberg (1993), turned the gaze on white teachers to critically reflect on their own privileges, in terms of both 'race' and class. However, privilege can also be afforded by the intersection of gender, age, sexual orientation and social class, which is recognised by the more encompassing privilege theory (McIntosh, 2012). Understanding how privilege operates extends the work required of many teachers, in asking them to look at how their own privileged experiences may produce social inequities with or without intent. In this way, whiteness and privilege theories work together to support a clearer, though more complex, view of how teachers may recognise (and change) their privileged practices where they exist.

These concepts provide useful ways for pre-service teachers to critique their own cultural positioning, how they view their students and, more significantly, how they become responsible for themselves and their actions. As a key element of CRT, whiteness theory promotes an examination of privilege, which through formal and informal dialogue can 'reveal the hegemonic power of a dominant group' and be used as a 'lens through which to analyse the discourse of Whiteness' (Mansouri & Jenkins, 2010, p. 96). In addition, through the recognition of white privilege, pre-service teachers gain a better understanding of how educational policy, curriculum, pedagogy and other institutional school-based practices are developed and enacted in ways that are normalised by the dominant culture. This taken-for-grantedness (Yoon, 2012) is often invisible to many white middle-class teachers, who make assumptions about their students. Privilege theory, therefore, serves as an important way for future teachers to think ahead of time about what they are teaching, how they are teaching it and why this matters. Critically, privilege theory allows pre-service teachers the opportunity to examine the tensions that arise in their own responses and practices.

The process of reflection inherent in understanding privilege is also significant in finding a way to unpack and traverse key deficit presumptions that have widespread impact on the quality of education frequently offered to children and young people in 'disadvantaged' communities. When white privilege is the focus, it is possible to shed light on how, for example, low expectations are frequently (and dangerously) associated with 'race', ethnicity and 'culture', as observed when Kristie recalls comments from the staffroom, such as *most of them just don't care*. (See also Chapter 8 in this volume.) Indeed, as Ladson-Billings (1998, p. 9) states, '[o]ur notions of race (and its use) are so complex that even when it fails to make sense we continue to employ and deploy it'.[2] It is well acknowledged (Luke et al., 2013; Sarra, 2012; Ullucci & Battey, 2011) that teachers' low expectations of culturally diverse students in Australia reproduce existing inequities. What teachers expect of students makes a profound difference. Kristie's opening comment indicates assumptions about students' academic abilities (*don't try group work*), values (*I never saw a single parent in any of my classes*) and social behaviour (*they don't have the social skills*). One of the key elements of CRT is the teacher's ability to

---

2   Hence the use of quotation marks around the word 'race' in this chapter.

'challenge dominant social and cultural assumptions regarding culture and intelligence, language and capability, objectivity and meritocracy' (Yosso, 2002, p. 98). Low expectations, 'dumbing down' and limited subject offerings are just some of the consequences of deficit thinking that construct academic futures for privileged students and limit choices or opportunities for others.

In Australia, the literature around the impact of teachers' high and low expectations has often focused on its impact on Indigenous students. Chris Sarra's 'Stronger Smarter' philosophy has been instrumental in rejecting negative deficit thinking, insisting that high-quality pedagogies that value cultural identity must take centre stage (Sarra, 2011, 2012). Sarra suggests that teachers may not even recognise their low expectations, masked as they sometimes are in a 'dumbed down' curriculum (Perso, 2012) or in low expectations about everything from attendance to abilities and attitudes that sometimes label Indigenous children and families as troublemakers, lazy or worse (Sarra, 2012). Other Indigenous scholars, such as Yunkaporta and McGinty (2009), have also noted the institutional racism that influences individual teachers' low expectations – and an unspoken racism that pressures teachers into negative discourses about Indigenous students (for instance, in Kristie's classroom). Numerous studies identify the expectations of teachers as pivotal, both to the relationships they have with their students and communities, and to the impact that this has on learning (Luke et al., 2013; Phillips, 2011).

The theories associated with CRT also highlight the reasons that deficit ideas or 'discourses of limitations' (Leonardo, 2013, p. 127) are both prevalent and dangerous. Sometimes referred to as 'culture of poverty' arguments, people with limiting beliefs may conclude that 'people of colour are weak and somehow lacking resilience' (Leonardo, 2013, p. 128). The importance of this was alluded to in Kristie's opening reflection, when she touched on how such beliefs are hard to resist, especially for beginning teachers who find themselves thrust into a professional environment heavily weighted by deficit discourses. We suggest that in order to disrupt such inequities, and to encourage the deconstruction of normalised practices, teachers need encouragement to engage in continuous reflection in communities of practice that are challenging, yet safe.

Without making inequality visible, the effects of disadvantage are easily obscured and lost. The myths of meritocracy (Burnett, 2004) can make it seem to teachers that all students, regardless of 'race' or social class, have the same opportunities as each other if they are just smart enough and work hard enough. The injustice of 'colour blindness', where feel-good statements about 'treating all children equally' prevail, is even more damaging if treating all children equally means judging them as though all children's experiences are the same, fair and objective. The issue of colour blindness is one of the most serious issues for teachers, both at the personal level and in terms of policy. As Zamudio, Russell, Rios and Bridgeman (2011, p. 24) ask, 'What then is the role of colorblind policies in maintaining racial inequalities at the institutional level? At the least of these levels these colorblind policies practice social neglect'. Convincing pre-service teachers that it is 'unequal' to treat all students the same is, however, a difficult task, especially since, as noted earlier, dividing the world into 'us' and 'them' is equally dangerous. This becomes a central tension for many teachers – how to both notice and respect difference (i.e. to differentiate) without falling into the trap of assuming differences are always in opposition or making value judgements about these differences as they are imagined through privileged eyes. The problem is not difference in itself, but that in a world of unequal privilege some difference is positioned as 'less' and power relationships become invisible. As the narratives below demonstrate, there is striking evidence of the invisibility of privilege even among these NETDS participants who have been specifically prepared to understand educational disadvantage.

Methodology

The reflections used in this chapter were generated from a number of sources. Some comments were unsolicited, sent to us as emails while our NETDS pre-service teachers were on their professional experience placements. When this was the case, often email conversations continued, and sometimes we linked pre-service teachers to each other to have further in-depth group discussions. Other reflections were solicited. When we had students doing professional experience placements in several remote schools, we were able to ask them specific questions in order to generate dialogue. For instance, we asked them:

- What is it like for white teachers like yourselves when you find yourselves teaching students from cultures other than your own?
- What are your impressions of your students and what are your biggest challenges?
- Does culture matter to your teaching? How?
- Any stories you'd like to tell?

These broad, open-ended questions elicited rich conversations and regularly led to fruitful discussions about whiteness. Another set of data came from the reflections the NETDS pre-service teachers made in their journals, which were kept over the 18 months they were involved with the program. Yet other reflections come from our early career graduate teachers, who are encouraged to (and do) keep in touch both by email and social media.

A key method or aspect associated both with CRT and privilege studies is providing a safe community in which pre-service and early career teachers can express themselves freely about issues related to privilege; we encourage honesty rather than 'perfection'. From the variety of communication, we can see that certain types of discursive communities have particular benefits: participants feel safer telling the very hard stories face to face and in small groups. While email responses elicit more carefully worded reflections, it is important to ensure that participants retain their anonymity.[3] The provision of multiple forums is also critical to creating safe

---

3   Ethical clearance has been granted for this research. Names of those interviewed have been
     changed in this paper, except for Kristie, who has given permission for her real name to be used.

practice, for it is well established that teacher communities have the potential to serve as 'sites of transformative learning' (Yoon, 2012, p. 592). We believe that the process of creating communities of practice allows participants to better reflect on their own positions of privilege in relation to high-poverty schools.

Analysis and discussion

Despite our attempts to present the complex dimensions and impact of poverty on educational opportunity, some of the NETDS pre-service teachers default or 'fall back' on deeply ingrained attitudes and dispositions that can be linked to specific forms of middle-class social capital (Sleeter, 2008). The blending of narrative and theories of social reproduction built into the NETDS model allows the pre-service teachers to reflectively inform their practice within school settings characterised by poverty and disadvantage. Although the narratives of the NETDS pre-service teachers in some cases highlight deeply internalised dispositions that appear 'natural and self-evident' (Shim, 2012, p. 212), the tangible narrative itself allows such ingrained deficit orientations to rise to the surface, to be seen and openly discussed and unpacked. Hence, in this way, the personal serves as a tool through which to interpret daily practice. The following section allows us to discuss in more detail the three main themes that arose from this particular data: colour blindness, defaulting to deficit and disrupting privilege.

Colour blindness

The participants in this study were all part of (or had graduated from) the NETDS program. Interestingly, we found little resistance within the group to the process of examining privilege, yet a strong reluctance to notice 'race'. Levine-Rasky (2013) refers to this reluctance as colour blindness, and suggests that this is one of the ways that whiteness works. Some of the participants' discourse exposed a seemingly 'race-neutral' stance, defaulting to the common belief in the rightness of 'treating all children the same'. For example, Mindy touched on this in the field notes from her second practicum:

> A whole thing started in my classroom one morning when one girl was angry at another one for saying she was Aboriginal when she should have been calling her Indigenous … Which one is actually right? I realised I didn't know what to say, or how to stop the argument. I just had no idea. So I just took the opportunity to tell them it's okay, everybody has the right to their own opinion.

Mindy's comments confirm Yoon's (2012, p. 588) observation that some teachers feel discomfort in responding to racial dynamics in the classroom, and that despite their 'best intentions, may be unsure of what to do'. The children's 'race talk' (Vass, 2013) clearly made Mindy uncomfortable. She quite rightly acknowledged that she had neither the right nor the knowledge to participate in the debate and she attempted to defuse the situation by making 'race' invisible again, encouraging children to discount difference. This response, which possibly comes from fear and a lack of knowledge (Sleeter, 2001), appears to be relatively commonplace among teachers who have neither the background nor the comfort levels to allow conversations about 'race' in the classroom. Critically, this potentially relegates such conversations to the playground. On one level, this may have been appropriate (in fact, the children's argument may not have been the teacher's business), but the dismissal of the interaction highlights Mindy's nervousness and unease related to the topic. Mindy's dilemma – what can she pretend to know and how much should she interfere in what she does not know? – is exacerbated in a school where there are no Indigenous teachers, and nobody from within the culture that the school serves has the requisite power or voice to challenge the situation.

Defaulting to deficit

A second manifestation of unrecognised privilege is the difficulty that even those teachers prepared to work in low socio-economic settings have in letting go of their previous deficit thinking. Much time is taken in the NETDS program to counteract these positions, and participants know, both via theory and through practice, the impact of low expectations and deficit discourses on their students' outcomes. Nonetheless, of all the theoretical positions, it would appear that this one is the hardest to maintain in the field. The deficit discourses are so prevalent that it seems extremely hard for these teachers not to default to deficit language in the classroom and the staffroom, for in these places such deficit responses are so common they come to seem 'normal'. The pre-service teachers themselves recognised through their narratives that they needed to maintain a vigilance to avoid being seduced into focusing on deficit. Yet it is also clear that institutional cultures are often so deeply established within schools that without a strong supportive community of resistance, teachers easily relapse to what appears to be the norm. Kristie's personal narrative describes this during her second practicum:

> I found it a struggle to resist defaulting into what other teachers in the staffroom kept saying: 'the parents don't care'... [W]ere the war stories shared between teachers fact or fiction? There was this one student in my class who always seemed tired, was always late, never wore a uniform, never had pencils or paper and never once for my whole prac completed his homework. I found myself thinking ... '[W]here is this kid's mother? She doesn't care about him at all, let alone his education'.

Here we see Kristie revisiting many of her first impressions, repeating some of the same phrases she previously expressed around parents who *don't seem to care about their children*. She explains this in another reflection as a 'stumbling block' that she needs to keep coming back to in order to put the myth to rest, even in her own mind. Resisting deficit thinking is one of the key areas that indicates the need for honest and ongoing conversations among critical communities of teachers.

Critical reflections presented an opportunity for these pre-service teachers to recognise moments in their own thinking and teaching that represented flashes of misalignment, and set off alarm bells that they might not previously have recognised as troubling. For example, after being allowed to pursue her own uncertainties, Kristie's subsequent reflections illustrate a deeper questioning, one that she continues to pursue now as an early career teacher. Two reflections from Kristie demonstrate the power of this process of reflection. In the first, which she wrote on her second practicum after joining NETDS, we see the common and reinforced assumption that white teachers will be shocked and horrified by what they first encounter in low socio-economic schools:

> Looking back – nothing could have prepared me for this and despite the work we had done in the months leading up to this prac, I still found myself in a state of 'shock' … and the 'calming' words of my supervising teacher didn't help: 'Don't worry, everyone has culture shock when they come here – you'll get used to it'.

For us as teacher educators, asking key questions is more important – and indeed more honest – than pretending to have all the answers. The uncertainties and honesty of the pre-service teachers indicated a vital level of engagement in exploring their own privilege. This was true even when they felt uncertain that they had achieved any progress. However, without ongoing (and supported) dialogue, a shift in perspectives seems very unlikely. With support and through dialogue, Kristie could think with more complexity about her initial experiences. Kristie's next reflection, written several weeks after the first one, is more theorised, more introspective, more layered and complex, even if she as yet has no definitive answers to her questions:

> I know in theory that there is an unconscious nature to our dispositions that results in damaging assumptions and consequent judgement. Perhaps the student's mother actually does care and that's why she is working such long hours. Perhaps she feels uncomfortable with the school? … with me? There are so many possible reasons to explain why this kid's mum is absent from her child's schooling. Yet I'm still having trouble coming to terms with the fact somewhere down inside … I still feel this mother simply doesn't care.

For a new teacher, knowing when you do not 'get it' is often as important as having the answers. We suggest that when the routine of reflection is established, both pre-service teachers and early career teachers are in a position to stop themselves before they jump to their previous default deficit conclusions. As one pre-service teacher, Laurie, recounted, understanding her students sometimes takes an 'unknowing'; a stepping back from automatic certainties based on coming from a culture of privilege:

> There was definitely a moment when I realised I didn't get it. My prac was in a pretty disruptive class with a lot of [bad] behaviour. One day a girl who had gotten in trouble at school came in with her hair – all her long, beautiful hair – cut off. Apparently it had been cut off by her father as punishment for having got in trouble at school. Anyway, I didn't know anything about it – it turns out this isn't uncommon as punishment in her culture – and I think I might have pushed her too far the next week. I didn't realise just how much shame having her hair cut off had caused her – and I just kept on and on at her, making her sit still in her group and making her answer

questions in class when she was just trying to stay a bit invisible and trying really hard to be 'good'. I don't know how I could have known this, but it did make me think about how much I just assumed.

However, not all of the NETDS participants are from middle-class backgrounds. While the majority are privileged in their whiteness, some of the most interesting reflection was done by pre-service teachers who themselves grew up in disadvantaged communities. Interestingly, their journeys into teaching are often quite different from the mainstream. Significantly, despite what they know from their own experience of disadvantage, they too find the deficit stance of schools persuasive. Stephanie discussed these issues in her field notes about her practicum:

> Going onto my third prac, the first person I met was a postgrad student who came to collect me from the office. She said to me 'this school is different' and made several comments about the students she had worked with over the last four days. After arriving in the staffroom and meeting my supervising teacher, the postgrad student mentioned she gets quite uncomfortable at the [nearby] train station and was talking about the fights she had seen while waiting for the train. My supervising teacher said, 'You know, I don't mean to be offensive, but the kids at this school are absolute bogans'. I write this as my first day on prac approaches and I find myself really worried and anxious about the students I will come across. I know this is irrational, to let other people's experiences and opinions guide my thoughts, but it has been extremely difficult to convince myself otherwise (that I won't have any issues with the students). Even though I am perfectly aware of the ways attitudes and side-comments affect teachers' dispositions, I can't help but let it get to me.

Stephanie herself is from the same community near the train station, yet so dominant are the stereotypes about this low socio-economic community that she found herself agreeing with them. Though from her own working-class experience she felt differently, the middle-class values of schooling were powerful enough to both override her experience and make her question what she identified as her own 'common sense'. In Stephanie's case, critical reflection allowed her to go back to what she 'really' believed rather than slide into attitudes that were more powerfully accepted in schools, and to be, as she later put it, 'more true to myself'.

Disrupting privilege

When teachers begin to understand their own privilege, they can revisit what they do and how they do things both inside and outside the classroom. In one instance, an early career teacher, Lois, who was working in a remote community, found herself challenged not only by her own classroom teaching, but also by other school-based and systemic circumstances. Teaching in her classroom, Lois aspired to use culturally appropriate practices and worked hard, for example, to value the culture of her students, but at the same time, she distanced herself from recognising her privilege over her co-workers within the Indigenous community where the school was located. This was not easily resolved because Lois did in fact have privileges as an employed teacher over the local, poorly paid Indigenous Education Workers. Lois emailed the NETDS mentors in her first year as a teacher with this description of her experience:

> There are several younger teachers working here who are really enthusiastic and care about outcomes for the students and a lot of the time this outlook seems to clash with the Indigenous staff ... The Indigenous staff mumble and grumble about issues but don't do anything to try to improve issues; instead they threaten to retire almost every other day. There also seems to be a bit of an issue surrounding what's acceptable for Indigenous staff and non-Indigenous staff – different rules seem to apply and although non-Indigenous staff are compliant with this ... it can wear a bit thin.

Lois remained employed for several years in the same remote community. As time went on, it would have been possible for her to become even more immersed and influenced by the school culture that reinforced a binaried division between the 'real' teachers (i.e. the privileged white teachers) and the 'local' teachers (i.e. the Indigenous Education Workers) who were seen to be working in opposition, with Indigenous culture and knowledge both marginalised and resented in a 'two-race' binary framework (McConaghy, 2000). This 'racism and resentment', which Keddie et al. (2012) recognise as an all too common element of 'race' politics as it plays itself out in schools, can easily go unnoticed in a school culture where it becomes the norm. Lois continued to correspond about these issues for the entire two years of her remote teaching, and transferred eventually to an urban low socio-economic setting. She came in time to revisit many of her first impressions. Interrogating these norms requires constant and regular reflection, as we have found that even the most 'self-aware' of white teachers can easily slide back into normalised positions. Sometimes, after writing them down or talking them through, teachers are taken aback by their own thoughts, which they had forgotten lay shallowly beneath the surface.

Nerida, a graduate teacher, who was working in a remote Indigenous community (in a different location from Mindy), recounted a story about one of her experiences. Her email indicated some degree of cultural awareness, although she appeared less aware of the socially privileged, and somewhat odd, situation in which she found herself within this remote community:

> The students [at this school] were the most amazing kids I've ever met and I miss them every day. The fact that some of them made it to school each day made me so proud. Going to their houses for home visits and seeing some of the living conditions and overcrowding that existed made me understand why attending school was not always considered necessary. There were much bigger issues to address. Myself, along with a couple of other female teachers, were lucky enough to get to organise and manage Women's Business with the grade 7–12 female students. We did the funnest things every week! It was the best experience and it really allowed us to develop such amazing relationships with the girls. We would take them snorkelling, bush walking, reefing, fishing; we would do art, cooking and dancing.

While Nerida found organising Women's Business 'fun', she did not initially reflect on the irony of being a young, white woman teaching Indigenous children Indigenous art and dancing. Like many young teachers who begin their careers in remote communities, Nerida took up the employment persuaded by a complex mix of a desire to 'make a difference', while also to have a 'fun' experience. While Nerida was employed as an early career teacher in a school that finds it very difficult to source teachers at all, and while she was young and entirely new to the remote community (having been raised in a city), she felt entitled very quickly to take a position of authority, and adopts a maternal tone in her reflection. In addition, she adopts a tone of 'knowing', assuming that in a short period of time she can both 'understand' the lives of people in the community and make a difference. Initially, rather than engaging in **reflexivity** around her own whiteness, Nerida's response suggests she is trying to 'know' about Indigenous people instead, something both McConaghy (2000) and Keddie et al. (2012) define as reductionist practice, where 'culture is seen as a knowable, bounded and separate entity' (Keddie et al., 2012, p. 92). In this case, culture is seen as not only knowable, but ownable, with Nerida being positioned (and positioning herself) as the expert. In later correspondence with Nerida, she became less certain of her position in the community, what she indeed 'knew' and even her motives.

> Reflexivity a process of inward contemplation. It refers to the subjective practice of self-examination and how this connects to social behaviour and relationships. It uses understandings of power, situated context and accessibility to interrogate and evaluate one's professional practice.

More than simply journal writing, the pre-service (and early career) teachers who take part in this program engage regularly in reflexivity, thinking regularly and through theory about their own 'automatic and habituated practice(s)' (Schirato & Webb, 2002, p. 255), something they sometimes find challenging and unsettling. Ella, for example, was a graduate teacher working in a remote community when she responded to an email from the NETDS mentors outlining such an experience:

> To address the idea of being a white teacher in a school comprised of over 50% Indigenous students, I think I felt quite insignificant and inferior at times. There is so much 'knowing' happening in your classes and really thick cultural binds that you're on the outer of, and don't have the right to interfere with. I doubt that the students see it that way, as more often than not (in my experience) they had been made to feel less worthy in the education system than their non-Indigenous peers.

Ella's questions are complex. Though she feels *insecure and inferior* she knows, too, that she holds a privileged position of power and *doubts students see it that way*. Ella's comment holds no solutions, but it illustrates a common contradiction or tension held by teachers – that valuing culture and having higher self-expectations are somehow oppositional. The research, however (see for example Sarra, 2012; Perso, 2012), suggests that higher expectations that lead to better outcomes for Indigenous students are strongly correlated when culture is valued and central to teaching.

Implications

As is evident through these examples, guided reflexivity has the potential to deepen teachers' understandings of their own beliefs and practices. Learning is deepest when it involves an intersection between theory and exposure to the field, which helps to unearth the manner in which teachers might need to engage on a lifelong journey of 'unlearning'. While there may be 'no such thing as an unreflective teacher' (Zeichner, 1996, p. 207), we constantly attempt to reinforce the notion that theory remains central to how teachers make meaning of their work.

As Jennifer Obidah (2005, p. 251) points out, for predominantly white, privileged teachers, 'our only recourse is to change ourselves: our preconceived (conscious and unconscious) ... perceptions about our students, and most important, our will to effectively educate our students'. In this chapter, we have drawn on CRT, whiteness and privilege theory to illustrate how pre-service teachers can develop notions of reflexivity allowing them to contemplate their own positions of privilege in relation to the children they teach in low socio-economic schools. The NETDS program has confirmed that no matter how well prepared pre-service teachers are for the realities of high-poverty schools, the inequalities they encounter set up deep and profound personal reactions. Thus, the implications of this chapter extend across mainstream teacher education by showing an example of how positive change can be encouraged using narrative as a catalyst to enrich a community of practice among teachers in low socio-economic schools.

Considerations

- How can teachers engage in difficult and honest discussions about whiteness?
- Why are these conversations important and how can they be sustained over time?
- Can you identify a time when you fell back into deficit thinking? How could you have stopped yourself or changed your perspective?

Of interest

- 'Racism. No way' (NSW Government). See http://www.racismnoway.com.au/
- 'Tackling racism in Australia' (Australian Human Rights Commission). See https://www.humanrights.gov.au/our-work/education/publications/rightsed-tackling-racism-australia
- 'High Expectations' (the work of Chris Sarra). See http://strongersmarter.com.au/wp-content/uploads/2015/01/SSI-HER-Position-Paper-Final-lowres.pdf
- 'Human rights in the school classroom' (Australian Human Rights Commission). See http://www.humanrights.gov.au/education/human-rights-school-classroom

References

Aveling, N. (2002). Student teachers' resistance to exploring racism: Reflections on 'doing' border pedagogy. *Asia-Pacific Journal of Teacher Education*, 30(2), 119–30. doi:10.1080/13598660220135630

—— (2007). Anti-racism in schools: A question of leadership? *Discourse: Studies in the Cultural Politics of Education*, 28(1), 69–85. doi:10.1080/01596300601073630

Ball, A. (2009). Toward a theory of generative change in culturally and linguistically complex classrooms. *American Educational Research Journal*, 46(1), 45–72. doi:10.3102/0002831208323277

Buchanan, J., Prescott, A., Schuck, S., Aubusson, P., Burke, P. & Louviere, J. (2013). Teacher retention and attrition: Views of early career teachers. *Australian Journal of Teacher Education*, 38(3), 112–29. doi:10.14221/ ajte.2013v38n3.9

Burnett, B. (2004). How does othering constitute cultural discrimination? In B. Burnett, D. Meadmore & G. Tait (Eds.), *New questions for contemporary teachers: Taking a socio-cultural approach to education* (pp. 101–12). Sydney: Pearson Education.

Burnett, B. & Lampert, J (2015). Teacher education for high poverty schools in Australia: The National Exceptional Teachers for Disadvantaged Schools Program. In J. Lampert & B. Burnett (Eds.), *Teacher education for high poverty schools.* (pp. 73–94). Springer: New York & London.

Dion, S. (2009). *Braiding histories: Learning from Aboriginal peoples' experiences and perspectives.* Vancouver: UBC Press.

Frankenberg, R. (1993). *White women, race matters: The social construction of whiteness.* Minneapolis, MN: University of Minnesota Press.

Keddie, A., Gowlett, C., Mills, M., Monk, S. & Renshaw, P. (2012). Beyond culturalism: Issues of Indigenous disadvantage through schooling. *Australian Educational Researcher*, 40(1), 91–108. doi:10.1007/s13384-012–0080-x

Ladson-Billings, G. (1998). Just what is critical race theory and what's it doing in a nice field like education? *International Journal of Qualitative Studies in Education*, 11(1), 7–24. doi:10.1080/095183998236863

Lampert, J. (2012). Becoming a socially just teacher: Walking the talk. In J. Phillips & J. Lampert (Eds.), *Introductory Indigenous studies in education: Reflection and the importance of knowing* (pp. 81–96). Sydney: Pearson Education Australia.

Lampert, J. & Burnett, B. (2014). Teacher education for high-poverty schools: Keeping the bar high. In S. Gannon & W. Sawyer (Eds.), *Contemporary issues of equity in education* (pp. 115–28). Newcastle, UK: Cambridge Scholars Publishing.

Leonardo, Z. (2013). Cultural studies, race representation, and education. In Z. Leonardo (Ed.), *Race frameworks: A multidimensional theory of racism and education* (pp. 114–45). New York: Teachers College Press.

Levine-Rasky, C. (2013). *Whiteness fractured.* Burlington, VT: Ashgate.

Luke, A., Cazden, C., Coopes, R., Klenowski, V., Ladwig, J., Lesterm J.,... Wood, A. (2013). *A summative evaluation of the stronger smarter learning communities project.* Brisbane: Queensland University of Technology.

Mansouri, F. & Jenkins, L. (2010). Schools as sites of race relations and intercultural tension. *Australian Journal of Teacher Education*, 35(7), 93–108. doi:10.14221/ ajte.2010v35n7.8

McConaghy, C. (2000). *Rethinking Indigenous education: Culturalism, colonialism, and the politics of knowing.* Flaxton: Post Pressed.

McIntosh, P. (2012). Reflections and future directions for privilege studies. *The Society for the Psychological Study of Social Issues*, 68(1), 194–206. doi:10.1111/ j.1540–4560.2011.01744.x

Mills, C. (2012). When 'picking the right people' is not enough: A Bourdieuian analysis of social justice and dispositional change in pre-service teachers. *International Journal of Educational Research*, 53, 269–77. doi:10.1016/j.ijer .2012.04.001

Obidah, J. (2005). Preparing teachers for 'Monday morning' in the urban school classroom: Reflecting on our pedagogies and practices as effective teachers. *Journal of Teacher Education*, 56(3), 248–55. doi:10.1177/0022487105275920

Perso, T. F. (2012). *Cultural responsiveness and school education with a particular focus on Australia's first peoples: A review and synthesis of the literature.* Darwin: Menzies School of Health Research, Centre for Child Development and Education.

Phillips, J. (2011). *Resisting contradictions: Non-Indigenous pre-service teacher responses to critical Indigenous studies.* PhD thesis, Queensland University of Technology.

Sarra, C. (2011). *Strong and smart: Towards a pedagogy for emancipation.* New York: Routledge.

—— (2012). *Good morning, Mr Sarra: My life working for a stronger, smarter future for our children.* Brisbane: University of Queensland Press.

Schirato, T. & Webb, J. (2002). Bourdieu's notion of reflexive knowledge. *Social Semiotics*, 12(3), 255–68. doi:10.1080/10350330216373

Shim, J. (2012). Pierre Bourdieu and intercultural education: It's not just about lack of knowledge about Others. *Intercultural Education*, 23(3), 209–20. doi:10.1080/ 14675986.2012.701987

Sleeter, C. (2001). Preparing teachers for culturally diverse schools: Research and the overwhelming presence of whiteness. *Journal of Teacher Education*, 52(2), 94–106. doi:10.1177/0022487101052002002

—— (2008). Equity, democracy, and neoliberal assaults on teacher education. *Teaching and Teacher Education*, 24(8), 1947–57. doi:10.1016/j.tate.2008.04.003

Ullucci, K. & Battey, D. (2011). Exposing color blindness/grounding color consciousness. *Urban Education*, 46(6), 1195–1225.doi:10.1177/0042085911413150

Vass, G. (2013). Hear no race, see no race, speak no race: Teacher silence, Indigenous youth and race talk in the classroom. *Social Alternatives*, 32(2), 19–24.

Villegas, A. M. (2007). Dispositions in teacher education: A look at social justice. *Journal of Teacher Education*, 58(5), 370–80. doi:10.1177/0022487107308419

Yoon, I. (2012). The paradoxical nature of whiteness-at-work in the daily life of schools and teacher communities. *Race, Ethnicity and Education*, 15(5), 587–613. doi:10.1080/13613324.2011.624506

Yosso, T. (2002). Toward a critical race curriculum. *Equity and Excellence in Education*, 35(2), 93–107. doi:10.1080/713845283

Yunkaporta, T. & McGinty, S. (2009). Reclaiming Aboriginal knowledge at the cultural interface. *The Australian Educational Researcher*, 36(2), 55–72. doi:10.1007/ BF03216899

Zamudio, M., Russell, C., Rios, F. & Bridgeman, J. (2011). *Critical race theory matters*. New York: Routledge.

Zeichner, K. (1996). *Reflective teaching: An introduction*. Mahway, NJ: L. Erlbaum Associates.

CHAPTER 6

More than cultural celebrations

Indigenous identities in school settings

Marnee Shay

AUSTRALIAN PROFESSIONAL STANDARDS FOR TEACHERS

Standard 1: Know students and how they learn

It is critically important that teachers employ strategies for teaching Aboriginal and Torres Strait Islander students. Equally, it is important to understand and respect Aboriginal and Torres Strait Islander people to promote reconciliation between Indigenous and non-Indigenous Australians (see Standards 1.4 and 2.4). Indigenous education is a national priority. The inclusion of teacher standards that focus on Indigenous education is testament to how important it is for teachers to have access to quality resources to enable best practice in relation to Indigenous education – for both Indigenous and non-Indigenous students. Indigenous identity foregrounds all aspects of Indigenous education.

The 'concept of Aboriginality' and what 'an Aborigine is' has been an ongoing construction of the colonisers, an imposed definition. It is also a political issue for Australia's First Nations peoples, who have been forced to live by legislation created around these constructions answering to variations of it, while at the same time trying to explain to our 'other' (that is, non-Aboriginal Australia) what it actually means to be Aboriginal from our perspectives and based on our lives in the twenty first century. (Heiss, 2012, p. 14)

Introduction

Australian research on Indigenous[1] education has been based on deficit notions of cultural difference as the inhibitor to educational parity between Indigenous and non-Indigenous young people. Research from the 1970s focused on 'why' Indigenous young people were not succeeding in conventional school settings, and 'how' schools could engage and improve outcomes for Indigenous young people. In the following four decades, there has been limited research on the types of learning within which Indigenous young people have subsequently re-engaged after being disengaged.

The research presented in this chapter focuses on the specific Australian schooling site termed '**flexi schools**'. The term describes a model of schooling outside conventional education addressing the needs of disenfranchised young people. There is an array of flexible schooling programs operating in Australia with the distinct aim of re-engagement (te Riele, 2007). Given the high numbers of Indigenous young people disengaging from conventional schooling and the disparity in educational outcomes between Indigenous and non-Indigenous young people (Australian Government, 2013), it is not surprising that there are high numbers of Indigenous young people engaged in flexi schools (Shay, 2013).

> **Flexi schools** a model of schooling outside of mainstream that is aimed at changing the way of delivering schooling to meet the needs of young people.

This chapter presents research from an Aboriginal standpoint, by an Aboriginal researcher. An online survey methodology was used to investigate how leaders of flexi schools were supporting Indigenous young people to remain engaged in education. The focal point of this chapter will be how principals or leaders of flexi schools described their practices that support the needs of Indigenous young people, specifically related to the nurturing of these students' cultural identity. Findings from this online survey of flexi school principals and school leaders are analysed using the theoretical framing of Critical Race Theory (CRT) (Ladson-Billings, 1998; Solorzano & Yosso, 2001) to better understand the ways in which institutionalised discourses of Indigenous 'race' and difference impact the school experiences of Indigenous students via school leaders.

Background

Constructs of cultural identity, a key topic within this chapter, must include the historical context, as this is highly implicated in the current context in Australia. The dominant story that continues to be told in relation to Indigenous Australians is that of hopelessness, cultural deficit and racial inferiority (Sarra, 2011). What is often left out of this story is the brutality, exclusion and genocide that Indigenous

---

[1]   The terms 'Indigenous' and 'Aboriginal and/or Torres Strait Islander' will be used throughout the chapter, as both terms refer to First Nations peoples of Australia.

Australians were subjected to while the nation was being built (Moran, 2005). The first 100 years of colonisation saw Aboriginal people slaughtered in great numbers. By the early 1900s, there was concern that the 'mixed race population' was threatening white racial purity. In the 1930s, assimilation ideology became entrenched in policy and legislation as a response to this 'issue' (Moran, 2005). The policy of assimilation has resulted in devastating consequences for Indigenous people. Assimilationist ideology requires Indigenous people to assume a white cultural identity and to adhere to white cultural values, positioning Indigenous knowledge and cultures as inferior (Townsend-Cross, 2011). It will be argued that this racially motivated discourse continues to remain entrenched in social ideology with a clear impact on teachers' practices in schools.

The process of racialisation of white Australians and Indigenous Australians is intrinsically linked with colonial practices (Harris, Nakata & Carlson, 2013). Phillips (2011) concludes that this construction has occurred in 'specific ways in order to justify colonisation' (p. 147). Moreover, Indigeneity, as in the not too distant past, continues to be viewed as a biological construct. Essentialist notions of culture are very strongly linked with biological constructs of 'race': the racialised categorisation that has long been disproven, yet remains entrenched in Australian discourse in constructions of Indigeneity (Brough et al., 2006). Further, biological constructs of 'race' lead to a black/white binary edifice (Chong-Soon Lee, 1995). The problem with binary thinking is that one of the two binary positions is always viewed or categorised as being superior to the other (Crenshaw, 1995). In reference to the white Australian/Indigenous Australian binary, historical evidence demonstrates with certainty that white Australians are viewed as being superior. This has major implications for school settings, where the majority of the teacher workforce are white middle-class Australians (Santoro & Allard, 2005).

Indigenous cultural identity a complex and emerging construct to describe the ways in which Indigenous peoples identify themselves within colonial contexts.

Critical Race Theory (CRT) an interrogation of invisible historical and social constructions of whiteness. It draws on postcolonial theory and cultural studies to focus on the relationships that exist between 'race', racism and power. CRT in education challenges accepted practice and provides a critical theoretical lens through which to identify normative white privilege and interpret racial inequality.

Indigeniety or **Indigenous cultural identity** must be defined briefly to provide a deeper context to this chapter. The chapter will use **Critical Race Theory (CRT)** to speak back to the racialised discourse that often underpins discussion about Indigeneity. However, it must be understood that Indigenous cultural identity is a complex concept and one that is defined by Indigenous and non-Indigenous Australians in often conflicting, opposing and contradictory ways (Sarra, 2011). It must first be highlighted that Indigenous people have the right to define our identities but the impact of colonisation and 'race' impacts upon the ways in which Indigenous identities are defined and spoken about in public discourse by Indigenous and non-Indigenous peoples (Carlson, 2011; Sarra, 2011).

There is no fixed definition of who an Indigenous person is (Carlson, 2011). However, Indigenous people talk about cultural identities in connection to country, respect for culture, community, family or kin and activism (Harris, Nakata & Carlson, 2013; Kickett Tucker, 2009; Sarra, 2011). The Australian Government offers a three-part definition – an Indigenous person is: a person who identifies as being Aboriginal and/or Torres Strait Islander; a person who is of Aboriginal and/or Torres Strait Islander descent; and, a person who is recognised as Aboriginal and/or Torres Strait Islander in the community in which they live (Carlson, 2011).

An examination of the literature informing this project highlights what engages Indigenous learners in conventional school settings. CRT provides a robust framework for the critical exploration of how 'race' and racism continue to subordinate and oppress students who are other-than-white (Ladson-Billings, 2005). Some CRT scholars would argue that focusing on finding 'what works' for Indigenous students is, in fact, a form of racism. This 'what works' framing implies cultural deficit (e.g. 'much *does not* work') and does not acknowledge deficit present within the educator or education system itself (Ladson-Billings, 1998). Nonetheless, the research presented here is best framed by what is known about supporting educational outcomes for Indigenous students in order to provide a focal point for the questions asked of the flexi school leaders.

A survey of the empirical literature reveals the importance of two key considerations for schools committed to Indigenous student success that are particularly relevant for the purposes of this research: (1) schools working to affirm the cultural identity of their Indigenous students (Armstrong & Buckley, 2011; Kickett-Tucker, 2008; Purdie & Buckley, 2010; Purdie, Tripcony, Boulton-Lewis, Fanshawe & Gunstone, 2000; Rahman, 2010; Russell, 1999; Sarra, 2011) and (2) the impact of school leadership on school outcomes for Indigenous students (Blackley, 2012; Hughes, Khan & Matthews, 2007; Jorgensen, Sullivan & Grootenboer, 2012; Mason, 2009; Sarra, 2007; Winkler, 2010, 2012). Scholars and practitioners argue that it is essential for Indigenous young people to be in an environment that nurtures, affirms and supports their cultural identities as Aboriginal and Torres Strait Islander people. Ensuring that any discussions relating to **Indigenous education** include a consideration of the ways in which cultural identities are constructed is vital in shifting teachers' preconceived conceptions about Indigenous students (Phillips, 2012). Without critical conversations about how educators perceive Indigenous identities, it is inconceivable that educators are able to make considerations in their practices such as embedding Indigenous perspectives or implementing support strategies for Indigenous students. Moreover, the role that school leaders play in leading change in order to improve outcomes for Indigenous students cannot be ignored; if priorities in relation to Indigenous education are not supported by school leaders, it is very difficult, if not impossible, for schools to experience whole-school changes. Accordingly, this chapter hones in on flexi school leaders' feedback on the ways in which they strive to affirm and nurture the cultural identity of Indigenous young people, in line with the two considerations addressed above.

In order to appreciate the complexity of why Indigenous young people are disengaging from conventional schooling at high rates, it is important to understand the broader context and contributing factors of disengagement. There are multiple reasons why young people disengage from education. Some of these reasons

Indigenous education a term commonly used in a colonial context to address educational disadvantage of Indigenous peoples. It can be described differently by Indigenous people.

include: socio-economic background, family situation, poor achievement, language or cultural barriers, and a broad array of school-based factors (McGregor & Mills, 2012). According to recent statistics, 85% of non-Indigenous 20–24-year-olds hold a Year 12 or equivalent qualification (Australian Bureau of Statistics [ABS], 2013). This figure stands in stark contrast to the 61.5% of Indigenous 20–24-year-olds who hold a Year 12 or equivalent qualification, according to the *Close the Gap* progress report (Australian Government, 2017). Neither statistic is particularly encouraging, though the remarkable difference in outcomes for Indigenous young people reaffirms the need for radical new approaches in education. As a whole, these statistics point to the fact that some young Australians attend conventional schools that do not engage them. Young people who disengage from education experience significant short-term and long-term social and economic disadvantage, including social dislocation and overall poorer health outcomes (Wilson, Stemp & McGinty, 2011). This is of particular concern for young people who are already disenfranchised, as is the case for many Indigenous young people. Accordingly, the importance of a place for young people to re-engage in education when they have experienced exclusion and/or disengagement cannot be overstated.

Flexi schools, by and large, are much smaller in size than conventional schools (Mills & McGregor, 2010). Many have multidisciplinary teams that include qualified teachers, social workers, youth workers, counsellors, arts/music workers and outdoor education specialists (Morgan, Pendergast, Brown & Heck, 2014). Though flexi schools vary in relation to community contexts and the demographic of students, there are common themes in relation to how they are described in the literature. Most flexi schools are described as having an 'emphasis on relationships; sense of community and belonging and empowerment of young people' (Shay, 2013, p. 13). Prior to the study reported in this chapter, there were no actual data published on enrolment figures of Indigenous young people in the flexi schooling context.

This chapter presents a glimpse into the ways in which principals and other school leaders from flexi schools in Queensland frame their support in relation to cultural identity and Indigenous learners. This discussion will focus on the first consideration identified in the Indigenous education literature: the need for schools to explicitly nurture and strengthen the cultural identity of Indigenous young people.

Key theoretical concepts

In education, issues of 'race' and racism are largely avoided (Ladson-Billings & Tate, 2006). Despite this avoidance, school failure is often attributed to 'racial' groups (Blackmore, 2010). Paradoxically, school success is rarely attributed to racial groups or is often a taken-for-granted assumption. There is a dire need for education institutions as a whole to critically examine the persistence of racism in advantaging some groups and disadvantaging others. As introduced in Chapter 1, CRT in education has the potential to 'define, expose and address educational problems' (Parker & Lynn, 2002, p. 7). Because issues of 'race' and racism are largely avoided, CRT requires researchers to 'defend positions that are marginal, challenging and some-times plain unpopular' (Hylton, 2012, p. 36). Although CRT scholarship originated from and focuses heavily on issues in the United States, CRT is a relevant theo-retical framework in an Australian context, particularly in Indigenous education research. Due to the racialised discourse that remains entrenched in educational policy, ideology and practice, CRT offers an effective framework of inquiry for analysing educational disparity between Indigenous and non-Indigenous young people.

The core tenets of CRT are grounded in the belief that 'race' and racism mediate every aspect of our lives (Lopez, 2013). While biological and essentialist construc-tions of 'race' have long been disproved (Chong-Soon Lee, 1995; Figueroa, 2012; Ladson-Billings, 1998; Lopez, 2013), Lopez (2013) argues that, 'human fate still rides upon ancestry and appearance' to categorise individuals that we encounter (p. 238). Humans have always constructed how 'race' is categorised (Crenshaw, 1995; Lopez, 2013), disproving the pervasive biological constructs of 'race' that are still consistently referred to. Moreover, Chong-Soon Lee (1995) proposes that 'the term race may be so historically and socially over-determined that it is beyond rehabilitation' (p. 441).

Key CRT scholars such as Lopez (2013) and Ladson-Billings and Tate (2006) agree that 'race' is socially constructed. Notwithstanding, the pervasiveness of racial categorisation based on disproven biological and scientific constructs remains entrenched in all aspects of our societies (Chong-Soon Lee, 1995; Obach, 1999). Crenshaw (1995) argues that these constructions were created by white cultures. The upholding of racialised biological constructions of 'race' by white cultures has resulted in many policies that are premised on the continuation of white superior-ity (Solorzano & Yosso, 2002). This is seen in education systems around the world, where white students continue to experience educational advantage and other-than-white students experience educational disadvantage (Zamudio, Russell, Rios & Bridgeman, 2011).

Memmi (2014) supports the idea that racism's purpose '[I]s both the emblem and the rationalization for a system of social oppression' (p. 92). The common defi-nition of racism is a belief that one ethnic or 'racial' group is superior to another (Solorzano & Yosso, 2001). There are many dominant group advantages that come with this type of racism, including economic, social, political and psychological (Memmi, 2014). Despite this, racism is still perceived as evidenced mainly via sin-ister individual acts perpetrated by ignorant or racist individuals (López, 2003; Parker & Lynn, 2002). The limited scope of individualistic understandings of racism fails to adequately critique how individual, structural and collective acts of rac-ism are constructed (Memmi, 2014). Further, if there is an emphasis only on overt individual acts of racism, subtle and covert systemic racism is often overlooked (Bonilla-Silva, 1997).

The omnipresence of racism in education requires robust discussion and investigation into how racism continues to oppress minority students and those 'of colour' (Hylton, 2012; Ladson-Billings, 1998; Ladson-Billings 2005; López, 2003; Parker & Lynn, 2002; Solorzano & Yosso, 2001; Stefancic & Delgado, 2013). Solorzano and Yosso (2001) argue that a CRT framework in education has five central themes that require particular investigation: 'the centrality and intersectionality of race and racism; the challenge to dominant ideology; the commitment to social justice; the centrality of experiential knowledge; and the interdisciplinary perspective' (pp. 2–3). These themes inform the analysis of the research data presented later in this chapter.

In my position as researcher, I enact two of Solorzano and Yosso's (2001) themes: commitment to social justice and centrality of experiential knowledge. Solorzano and Yosso (2001) conclude that learning from experiential knowledge is not just appropriate but vital in analysing and understanding issues of 'race' and racism. For this reason, stating my own standpoint and experience in relation to my research is appropriate at this point. I proudly identify as an Aboriginal Australian woman who is descended from Wagiman country, Northern Territory (through my mother and grandmother). Through my father I have white Australian heritage with strong Scottish ancestry. I was raised by my mother and have always been told to be proud of being Aboriginal. As an Aboriginal Australian person, I have endured the public schooling system in Australia myself, navigating through very tumultuous times in Australian discourse about what it means to be Aboriginal. Among many examples, I have been questioned about the authenticity of my cultural identity based on my appearance; been told I am smart for being 'one of them'; tolerated sitting in a classroom while a teacher presented archaic images of Aboriginal people in the desert; been accused of only identifying my Aboriginality in order to be the recipient of mythical 'benefits'; and then, returning to the school environment as a teacher, received comments from colleagues wondering whether I had to do the same study as them to gain my qualifications. It is not only my own experiences, but those of my family and community that motivated me to undertake such a study.

Methodology

Survey methodology was used for this small research project. A web-based questionnaire was designed for data collection. The cross-sectional survey design was aimed at finding the trends, attitudes, beliefs and practices of this group at this particular time (Bishop, Berryman, Wearmouth, Peter & Clapham, 2012). Cautions outlined with survey methodologies, such as the inability to reach participants or participants' access to the internet (Creswell, 2008), were not issues in this case because the demographic was principals or lead teachers of schools. The survey included demographic data on the context of the schools and their Indigenous staff and student numbers, some of which are reported here. Further, the survey had a series of open-ended questions linked to the literature on what is known to support Indigenous students in conventional school settings. The findings discussed in this chapter will centre on the responses from one of the survey's open-ended questions, wherein qualitative thematic analysis was used to identify and analyse central themes within the data (Braun & Clarke, 2006).

Instrument

An electronic survey was used to collect data for this research project. Anonymity and security of the data collected was a concern, particularly as it is commonly known that there is still reluctance among educators to engage in critical conversations about issues of 'race'/cultures (Blackmore, 2010). Web-based surveys are known for time and cost efficiency (Fan & Yan, 2010; Mertler, 2002) as well as protection against loss of data (Mertler, 2002). The survey comprised a total of 15 open-ended and closed-ended items (Dawson, 2007), with questions positioned to allow participants the opportunity to critically reflect on power relations or 'race' in relation to their own practices in supporting Indigenous young people. The findings reported in this chapter report on responses to the closed-ended item 'I actively support staff to nurture and strengthen Indigenous young people's cultural identity', which included a follow-up open-ended item asking participants to provide examples of this support.

Participants

Homogeneous sampling was used in this project, involving as it did the selection of participants focusing on two characteristics: being a principal or lead teacher and being in a specific flexi school context in Queensland (Creswell, 2008). For the purpose of identifying participants for this study, the national website developed by Dusseldorp Skills Forum 'Learning Choices' (Dusseldorp Skills Forum, 2013) was used to develop a list of potential participants from those registered on the national database as offering alternative education programs for young people. Invited participants were limited to schools with 'programs [that had been operating] one year or more' and that '[targeted young people] at risk of non-completion' (Dusseldorp Skills Forum, 2013). This selection ensured a variety of established schools or units, with 19 schools identified as potential sites for participants. Of the 19 invited participants, eight responded. The response rate is considered higher than the 30% average for electronic surveys reported in the literature (Cook, Heath & Thompson, 2000; Mertler, 2002).

Analysis and discussion

This section will use CRT to frame the discussion of the ways that flexi school leaders reported nurturing and supporting the cultural identities of Indigenous young people, as this is a crucial element of any school improvement targeting Indigenous education (Sarra, 2011). A CRT analysis conducted by an Aboriginal researcher (myself) provides evidence that the results reported here are not dissimilar to findings discussed in the background section that highlight the ways in which dominant constructions of Indigenous identity continue to impact on Indigenous young people in all school settings.

The demographic data from this study revealed that the statistical average of Indigenous student enrolments across the eight schools surveyed was 31.3%, with schools located in urban, regional and remote community settings (Shay, 2013). In contrast to the Queensland Indigenous population figure of 4.2% (ABS, 2011) and Education Queensland (state schools) Indigenous enrolment figure of 8.69% (Department of Education, Training and Employment, 2014), these findings demonstrate that flexi schools enrol higher than average numbers of Indigenous young people.

All eight principals and school leaders selected 'yes' to the survey item 'I actively encourage staff to nurture and strengthen the cultural identity of Aboriginal and Torres Strait Islander young people'. There were a variety of responses about how educational leaders reported that they are achieving this. Using qualitative thematic analysis, it emerged that the prevalent theme from the data was the practice of cultural celebrations (such as National Aborigines and Islanders Day Observance Committee [NAIDOC] Week), as well as unspecified cultural classes and activities that were positioned as nurturing and strengthening the cultural identity of Indigenous young people. The data also revealed that some leaders of flexi schools encouraged professional development for staff, including inviting Elders to the school, linking to local Aboriginal organisations, and, in one case, the purchase and use of 'Indigenous resources'. This CRT-informed analysis resulted in two key findings, presented below.

Key finding 1: Multiculturalist approaches

A qualitative thematic analysis revealed celebration of culture and cultural activities as the most popular practice of principals in nurturing the cultural identity of Indigenous young people. This is evidence of a superficial and celebratory engagement with the concept of 'multiculturalism', critiqued by Ladson-Billings and Tate (2006) as a distinct form of covert racism. While the concept of multiculturalism is used widely in education reforms and was designed to address issues of racial inequality, its ill-informed application can be problematic in several ways (Blackmore, 2010; Dixson & Rousseau, 2005; Ladson-Billings & Tate, 2006). Ladson-Billings (1998) argues that such approaches to multiculturalism in education began with the explicit purpose of engaging students in critical thinking about constructs of culture (in this example, in the United States). Further, despite having diverse histories and foundations, the term 'multiculturalism' more broadly incorporates concepts such as anti-racism and discrimination as well as the promotion of equal rights (Race, 2011).

In an Australian context, 'official policy of the Commonwealth of Australia is multicultural, and this is given sincere emphasis in goals for education. But [it] is hard to change the monocultural, ethnocentric tradition in schools' (Hickling-Hudson, 2003, p. 3). Within this policy is the inclusion of Indigenous Australians. Conversely, Indigenous peoples have long rejected inclusion in this category since Indigenous histories and the current Indigenous social and political situation are acutely different from the experiences of migrants (Curthoys, 1999). Hickling-Hudson (2003) argues that the demands on teachers are considerable if they are to implement robust multiculturalist practices, such as meeting the needs of children from diverse cultures and designing 'intercultural curriculum' (p. 5).

Sadly, in some cases, educators' understandings of what it means to engage in multicultural education rely upon superficial and stereotypical multiculturalist practices, manifesting primarily through the implementation of activities such as eating 'ethnic or cultural foods, singing songs, or dancing' (Ladson-Billings & Tate, 2006, p. 61). With this in mind, we turn to the first of the flexi school leaders' responses: 'We encourage and support celebrations; cultural activities that are accessible for all young people; acknowledgement and welcome to country and smoking ceremonies' (Flexi school leader, Queensland). This excerpt from the data is one of many examples that evidenced the prevalence of multiculturalist practices in the schools surveyed. The essence of multiculturalism in education is in the promotion of tolerance and oneness; thus, the status of Otherness or difference becomes equal, creating a competitive environment for all minority cultures to be included (Ladson-Billings & Tate, 2006). In an Australian context, despite Indigenous Australians clearly articulating rejection of being in the multicultural category (Hickling-Hudson, 2003), this issue of competing for inclusiveness is articulated through the compulsory categorisation imposed upon us.

Blackmore (2010) discusses the problematic and ineffective nature of using celebratory multiculturalism to address issues of equity in education, as these practices do not effectively disrupt the white culture norm. Instead, these attempts often result in 'soft multiculturalism', wherein white educators are able to celebrate the exotic Other at a personal level without disrupting structural white dominance (Blackmore, 2010, p. 52). An example related to these findings is that white educators can happily 'celebrate' Indigenous cultures through watching traditional dance. Yet, that practice discursively maintains white privilege by controlling when these celebrations occur, how frequently, whether the dancers are paid, how dancers are observed, whether there are any further interactions and whether there is any context in which all students can explore constructs of their own cultures in situ by engaging with such a celebration. These points are not to dismiss activities such as cultural celebrations, which are linked to inclusive education. However, a deeper critique of superficial responses to culture should become an important part of any analyses involving 'race', racism and educational inequality, pushing the boundaries of common practices that need shifting (Ladson-Billings & Tate, 2006).

Without the accompaniment of robust whole-of-school practices in how schools nurture and strengthen the cultural identities of Indigenous young people, celebration of cultures becomes innately intertwined with essentialist notions of 'race' and culture. Essentialist notions of 'race' and culture are also linked with cultural deficit practices based on biological constructs of 'race', which were discussed in the background as being problematic. This is an issue in schools, particularly for Indigenous young people. With many educators wanting to 'get it right', many in fact do not because they (re)present what they think they know about Indigenous people. This is often what is commonly termed 'boomerangs and dots' (cultural artefact and traditional Aboriginal art), whereby stagnant or inaccurate representations of Indigenous peoples and cultures, grounded in the teachers' misinformed perception of Indigenous identities and cultures, surface in classrooms as attempts to 'embed Indigenous perspectives'.

Key finding 2: Colour blindness

Sarra (2011) argues that white perceptions of Indigenous people remain ingrained in racialised deficits grounded in biological constructs of 'race'. Instead, Aboriginal perspectives of being Aboriginal reveal strong connection to land, family, Elders, and a sense of pride about cultural identity. This paradox reveals strong notions of 'race' and racism at play and the overwhelming need for constructions of Aboriginal identity to be critiqued within schools, where the dominant culture holds the power of what is taught, how it is taught and who is teaching it. As one participating principal described, 'Many of our young people choose *not* to differentiate themselves, despite minimal encouragement' (Flexi school leader, Queensland). This quote from the data exposes the importance of Sarra's (2011) research and puts emphasis on constructs of Aboriginal identity. On the one hand, the respondent is placing the responsibility back on Indigenous young people, stating that they don't want to 'differentiate' themselves. Yet, in the same statement there is admission that the school hasn't really encouraged young people to do so. The curious part of this statement is the term 'differentiate'. Differentiate from whom? The presumed answer is the dominant white culture. This statement is loaded with connotations associated with 'colour blindness' in that sameness is valued and Otherness is viewed in a negative light. To elaborate on this term, colour blindness is what CRT scholars identify as the dominant ideal (Dixson & Rousseau, 2005). However, colour blindness supports 'racial'/cultural inequality through its imposition of sameness ideals when, in fact, structural subordination ensures that we are not all the same (Dixson & Rousseau, 2005). Moreover, overlooking the cultural identity of a person who is other-than-white implies there is something wrong with this (Dixson & Rousseau, 2005).

Implications

The above section presented a CRT-informed analysis of findings from a small study on how leaders of flexi schools are nurturing and strengthening the cultural identity of Indigenous young people. Historical and contemporary cultural constructions of Indigenous and non-Indigenous identity position Indigenous Australians within a deficit discourse while non-Indigenous identities remain undisrupted and silently dominant. The analysis revealed three main concerns about how Indigenous students are perceived by flexi schools. First, definitions of culturally appropriate activities put an emphasis on cultural celebrations, which, according to the literature, often results in superficial 'multiculturalist' approaches that are problematic, and covert forms of racism. Second, while the literature is emphatic that Indigenous young people need to have their cultural identity nurtured and affirmed in schools, there was little evidence of this in this study. Third, some principals and lead teachers prefer to believe there should be no differentiation between students. Clearly the concept of colour blindness is an issue for schools. The implications of this discussion will follow.

There are multiple implications of this study for flexi schools, which enrol high numbers of Indigenous young people. Key findings one and two suggest an urgent need for all staff in flexi schools to be supported to develop their skills and knowledge in working with Indigenous young people and to embrace the complexity of cultural constructs of Indigenous and non-Indigenous Australian identity. However, there are further implications that impact on all educators. Currently, there are two major policy changes that mandate that all Australian educators (1) embed Indigenous perspectives as a cross-curriculum priority in all discipline areas (Australian Curriculum, Assessment and Reporting Authority, 2014) and (2) understand and respect Indigenous cultures and histories and know how to effectively teach Indigenous students as per the mandated national teacher standards (Australian Institute for Teaching and Leadership [AITSL], 2013). With limited training provided at a teacher-education level and patchy opportunities for current teaching staff to engage in professional development, how then are teachers able to ensure they have the skills to embed Indigenous knowledge and know how to teach Indigenous students?

Though Indigenous identities are complex, we also know that non-Indigenous Australians' view of Indigenous identities differs greatly from an Aboriginal perspective (Sarra, 2011). The implication here is that teachers must avoid making assumptions about Indigenous students based on their misinformed biological constructionist understanding of Indigenous identity. This includes defaulting to racialised assumptions that a student is not Indigenous because they have fair skin, or that because a student is Indigenous and/or has dark skin they will be from the bush or know how to perform corroboree. As would be best practice with all students, educators should get to know their Indigenous students, and their families, as individuals with individual strengths and goals. Making assumptions about students based on disproven biological constructs is a form of racism that has no place in Australian schools.

No Australian is immune to exposure to the deficit discourses that have constructed Indigenous identities and the normative, racialised discourses that have constructed white Australians. These discourses have been (re)produced through school curricula, media, politics and social interactions. Phillips (2012) argues that teachers must know their own cultural framework because how they are positioned impacts on whether 'interpretation, knowledge and commitments will compel or constrain ... [their] actions or choices' (p. 140). Teachers need to engage in critical thinking when it comes to their own practices and capacity to reflect critically on their own cultural standpoint. Teachers who are non-Indigenous must understand they do have a cultural standpoint that requires interrogation and critical reflection (Phillips & Lampert, 2012). With the mandates being implemented by AITSL and the National Curriculum, teachers will need to find their own learning opportunities to develop their understanding of self and recognition of biases, with an eye for reflection on how these might impact their interactions with Indigenous young people. Further, teachers need to be critical of the sources they are using to educate both themselves and their students, to ensure they do not present essentialist representations of Indigenous cultures, such as 'boomerangs and dots'. Finally, in flexi schools where there are high numbers of Indigenous young people, these mandates provide an ideal opportunity for educators to engage with robust and innovative practices that provide all young people the opportunity to explore their own cultural identities.

On a personal level, as an Aboriginal woman who is a teacher, I conclude by wanting to instil a sense of empowerment to effect change within any reader who was confronted by the ideas presented in this chapter. Though many teachers may unknowingly absorb and internalise misperceptions about Indigenous peoples and cultures, many of our people are diverse, strong and proud. The research as presented in this chapter highlights the following implications for teachers:

- Learn from examples in practice where non-Indigenous educators work *with* and not *over* Indigenous people.
- Reach out to Indigenous communities represented in their schools – including Indigenous communities located in urban areas – to begin to form (and in many cases continue to nurture) meaningful relationships.
- Be privileged by the local knowledge available and offer your hand in partnership with the local community, who are the experts on their own lives.
- Challenge yourself to question what you think you know and be open to realising that you may need to unlearn what you think you know about Indigenous peoples.
- Most importantly, understand that knowing the prolific history of this country, which dates back over 40 000 years, will enrich the experiences of and give meaning to all Australian students.

Considerations

- What is your understanding of Indigenous cultural identity? How have you come to know what you know?
- Have you ever made assumptions about a student based on their appearance?
- Do you know what your cultural standpoint is and how it impacts on your teaching practices?

Of interest

- An overview of the Australian Professional Standards for Teachers is included on the Australian Institute of Teaching and School Leadership website. See https://www.aitsl.edu.au/teach/standards
- Inclusion of Indigenous histories and cultures is a national cross-curriculum priority. More information on this can be found in *Australian Curriculum Priority: Aboriginal and Torres Strait Islander Histories and Cultures*. See http://www.australiancurriculum.edu.au/crosscurriculumpriorities/Aboriginal-and-Torres-Strait-Islander-histories-and-cultures

- Australian Government (2017). *Closing the Gap Prime Minister's Report 2017*. See https://www.pmc.gov.au/sites/default/files/publications/ctg-report-2017.pdf
- Uluru Statement from the Heart, Indigenous peoples, 2017. See https://www.referendumcouncil.org.au/sites/default/files/2017-05/Uluru_Statement_From_The_Heart_0.PDF
- For any educators wanting to learn about Australian history, including significant events that have impacted on Indigenous peoples, the *First Australians* series (2006), from Australia's television channel SBS, is a good place to start.
- Dr Anita Heiss is an accomplished Aboriginal author. In her memoir, *Am I Black Enough for You?* (Bantam Random House, 2012), Dr Heiss discusses her experiences in relation to her Aboriginal identity. This Aboriginal-authored teaching resource is useful for teachers interested in exposing their students to a forthright, personal account of the discourses that surround indigeneity in Australia.

References

Armstrong, S. & Buckley, S. (2011). An investigation into the attendance and retention of Aboriginal and Torres Strait Islander students: Research and theory about what works. Paper presented at the Research Conference 2011. Indigenous education: Pathways to success Conference proceedings. Retrieved October 2013 from http://research.acer.edu.au/cgi/viewcontent.cgi?article=1120&context=research_conference

Australian Bureau of Statistics (ABS) (2011). *Population, Aboriginal and Torres Strait Islander Queenslanders*. Queensland Treasury and Trade, 30 June 2011. Retrieved from http://www.oesr.qld.gov.au/products/briefs/pop-atsi-qld-2011/pop-atsi-qld-2011.pdf

—— (2013). *Reflecting a nation: Stories from the 2011 census, 2012–2013*. Retrieved November 2014 from http://www.abs.gov.au/ausstats/abs@.nsf/Latestproducts/2071.0Main%20Features552012%E2%80%932013?opendocument&tabname=Summary&prodno=2071.0&issue=2012%962013&num=&view=

Australian Curriculum, Assessment and Reporting Authority (2014). *Australian Curriculum, Assessment and Reporting Authority*. Retrieved November 2014 from http://www.acara.edu.au/default.asp

Australian Government (2013). *Closing the gap: Prime Minister's report 2013*. Retrieved November 2014 from http://www.fahcsia.gov.au/sites/default/files/documents/02_2013/00313-ctg-report_fa1.pdf

—— (2014). *Closing the gap: Prime Minister's report*. Retrieved November 2014 from http://www.dpmc.gov.au/publications/docs/closing_the_gap_2014.pdf

—— (2017). *Closing the Gap Prime Minister's Report 2017*. Retrieved from closingthegap.pmc.gov.au/sites/default/files/ctg-report-2017.pdf

Australian Institute for Teaching and School Leadership (AITSL) (2013). *Australian professional standards for teachers*. Retrieved November 2014 from http://www.aitsl.edu.au/australian-professional-standards-for-teachers/standards/list

Bishop, R., Berryman, M., Wearmouth, J., Peter, M. & Clapham, S. (2012). Professional development, changes in teacher practice and improvements in Indigenous students' educational performance: A case study from New Zealand. *Teaching and Teacher Education*, 28(5), 694–705. doi:10.1016/j.tate.2012.02.002

Blackley, G. (2012). The necessity for individual responsibility to improve Indigenous education. *Professional Learning Sabbaticals*. Retrieved from http://www.sabbaticals.aitsl.edu.au/sites/www.sabbaticals.aitsl.edu.au/files/field/final/graham_blackley_professional_learning_sabbatical_report.pdf

Blackmore, J. (2010). 'The Other within': Race/gender disruptions to the professional learning of white educational leaders. *International Journal of Leadership in Education*, 13(1), 45–61. doi:10.1080/13603120903242931

Bonilla-Silva, E. (1997). Rethinking racism: Toward a structural interpretation. *American Sociological Review*, 62(3), 465–80. doi:10.2307/2657316

Braun, V. & Clarke, V. (2006). Using thematic analysis in psychology. *Qualitative Research in Psychology*, 3(2), 77–101. doi:10.1191/1478088706qp063oa

Brough, M., Bond, C., Hunt, J., Jenkins, D., Shannon, C. & Schubert, L. (2006). Social capital meets identity: Aboriginality in an urban setting. *Journal of Sociology*, 42(4), 396–411. doi:10.1177/1440783306069996

Carlson, B. (2011). *The politics of identity: Who counts as Aboriginal today?* PhD thesis, University of New South Wales.

Chong-Soon Lee, J. (1995). Navigating the typology of race. In K. Crenshaw, N. Gotanda, G. Peller & K. Thomas (Eds.), *Critical race theory: The key writings that formed the movement* (pp. 441–8). New York: The New Press.

Cook, C., Heath, F. & Thompson, R. (2000). A meta-analysis of response rates in web- or internet-based surveys. *Educational and Psychological Measurement*, 60(6), 821–36. doi:10.1177/00131640021970934

Crenshaw, K. (1995). Race, reform and retrenchment: Transformation and legitimation in anti-discrimination law. In K. Crenshaw, N. Gotanda, G. Peller & K. Thomas (Eds.), *Critical race theory: The key writings that formed the movement* (pp. 103–26). New York: The New Press.

Creswell, J. (2008). *Educational research: Planning, conducting, and evaluating quantitative and qualitative research* (3rd ed.). Upper Saddle River, NJ: Pearson.

Curthoys, A. (1999). An uneasy conversation: Multicultural and Indigenous discourses. In G. Hage & R. Couch (Eds.), *The future of Australian multiculturalism* (pp. 277–93). Sydney: University of Sydney Press.

Dawson, C. (2007). *A practical guide to research methods.* Oxford: How To Books.

Department of Education Training and Employment. (2014). *Educational statistics and information.* Retrieved November 2014 from http://education.qld.gov.au/schools/statistics/enrolments.html

Dixson, A. D. & Rousseau, C. K. (2005). And we are still not saved: Critical race theory in education ten years later. *Race, Ethnicity and Education, 8*(1), 7–27. doi:10.1080/1361332052000340971

Dusseldorp Skills Forum. (2013). *Learning choices.* Retrieved from http://www.learningchoices.org.au/about.html

Fan, W. & Yan, Z. (2010). Factors affecting response rates of the web survey: A systematic review. *Computers in Human Behavior, 26*(2), 132–9. doi: http://dx.doi.org/10.1016/j.chb.2009.10.015

Figueroa, P. (2012). *Education and the social construction of 'race'.* Retrieved from http://QUT.eblib.com.au/patron/FullRecord.aspx?p=982037

Harris, M., Nakata, M. & Carlson, B. (Eds.). (2013). *The politics of identity: Emerging indigeneity.* UTSePress. Retrieved September 2014 from http://epress.lib.uts.edu.au/research/bitstream/handle/10453/21913/Politics%20of%20Identity.pdf?download=1#page=28&zoom=auto,-265,411

Heiss, A. (2012). *Am I black enough for you?* NSW: Bantam Random House.

Hickling-Hudson, A. (2003). Multicultural education and the postcolonial turn. *Policy Futures in Education, 1*(2), 381–401. Retrieved November 2014 from http://eprints.qut.edu.au/1796/1/1796.pdf

Hughes, P., Khan, G. & Matthews, S. (2007). Leaders: Acting to improve outcomes for Indigenous students. Paper presented at The Leadership Challenge: Improving Learning in Schools, conference proceedings. Retrieved from http://www.acer.edu.au/documents/RC2007_ConfProceedings.pdf

Hylton, K. (2012). Talk the talk, walk the walk: Defining critical race theory in research. *Race, Ethnicity and Education, 15*(1), 23–41. doi:10.1080/13613324.2012.638862

Jorgensen, R., Sullivan, P. & Grootenboer, P. (2012). *Pedagogies to enhance learning for Indigenous students: Evidence-based practice.* Retrieved from http://QUT.eblib.com.au/patron/FullRecord.aspx?p=1083719

Kickett-Tucker, C. S. (2008). How Aboriginal peer interactions in upper primary school sport support Aboriginal identity. *Australian Journal of Indigenous Education, 37,* 138–51.

—— (2009). Moorn (Black)? Djardak (White)? How come I don't fit in Mum? Exploring the racial identity of Australian Aboriginal children and youth. *Health Sociology Review, 18*(1), 119–136.

Ladson-Billings, G. (1998). Just what is critical race theory and what's it doing in a nice field like education? *International Journal of Qualitative Studies in Education,* 11(1), 7–24. doi:10.1080/095183998236863

—— (2005). The evolving role of critical race theory in educational scholarship. *Race, Ethnicity and Education,* 8(1), 115–19. doi:10.1080/1361332052000341024

Ladson-Billings, G. & Tate, W. (2006). Toward a critical race theory in education. In A. Dixson & C. Rousseau (Eds.), *Critical race theory in education: All God's children got a song* (pp. 11–31). New York: Routledge.

López, G. R. (2003). The (racially neutral) politics of education: A critical race theory perspective. *Educational Administration Quarterly,* 39(1), 68–94. doi:10.1177/0013161x02239761

Lopez, I. (2013). The social construction of race. In R. Delgado & J. Stefancic (Eds.), *Critical race theory: The cutting edge* (Vol. 3, pp. 238–48). Philadelphia, PA: Temple University Press.

Mason, J. (2009). MindMatters, leadership and community partnerships. *Independent Education,* 39(1), 24–5.

McGregor, G. & Mills, M. (2012). Alternative education sites and marginalised young people: 'I wish there were more schools like this one'. *International Journal of Inclusive Education,* 16(8), 843–62. doi:10.1080/13603116.2010.529 467

Memmi, A. (2014). *Racism.* Minneapolis, MN: University of Minnesota Press.

Mertler, C. (2002). Demonstrating the potential for web-based survey methodology with a case study. *American Secondary Education,* 30(2), 49.

Mills, M. & McGregor, G. (2010). *Re-engaging students in education: Success factors in alternative schools.* Brisbane: Youth Affairs Network Queensland.

Moran, A. (2005). White Australia, settler nationalism and Aboriginal assimilation. *Australian Journal of Politics and History,* 51(2), 168–93. doi:10.1111/j.1467-8497.2005.00369.x

Morgan, A., Pendergast, D., Brown, R. & Heck, D. (2014). The art of holding complexity: A contextual influence on educator identity and development in practice in a system of alternative 'flexi' schools. *Reflective Practice: International and Multidisciplinary Perspectives.* doi:10.1080/14623943.2014 .900020

Obach, B. K. (1999). Demonstrating the social construction of race. *Teaching Sociology,* 27(3), 252.

Parker, L. & Lynn, M. (2002). What's race got to do with it? Critical race theory's conflicts with and connections to qualitative research methodology and epistemology. *Qualitative Inquiry,* 8(1), 7–22. doi:10.1177/107780040200800102

Phillips, J. (2011). *Resisting contradictions: Non-Indigenous pre-service teacher responses to critical Indigenous studies.* Brisbane: Queensland University of Technology. Retrieved from http://eprints.qut.edu.au/46071/

—— (2012). Indigenous education in Australia. In S. Carrington & J. Macarthur (Eds.), *Teaching in inclusive school communities* (pp. 139–60). Milton: John Wiley & Sons Australia.

Phillips, J. & Lampert, J. (2012). *Introductory Indigenous studies in education* (2nd ed.). Sydney: Pearson.

Purdie, N. & Buckley, S. (2010). *School attendance and retention of Indigenous Australian students.* Canberra: Australian Institute of Family Studies.

Purdie, N., Tripcony, P., Boulton-Lewis, G., Fanshawe, J. & Gunstone, A. (2000). *Positive self-identity for Indigenous students and its relationship with school outcomes.* Retrieved from http://www.aboriginalstudies.com.au/content/uploads/2012/07/2000-Purdie-etalDETYA-Self-Identity-and-Outcomes.pdf

Race, R. (2011). *Multiculturalism and education.* New York and London: Continuum.

Rahman, K. (2010). Addressing the foundations for improved Indigenous secondary student outcomes: A South Australian qualitative study. *Australian Journal of Indigenous Education*, 39(1), 65–76.

Russell, D. (1999). The importance of identity in the retention and attainment of Aboriginal students at secondary school: Some research findings. *Australian Journal of Indigenous Education*, 27(1), 10–19.

Santoro, N. & Allard, A. (2005). (Re)Examining identities: Working with diversity in the pre-service teaching experience. *Teaching and Teacher Education*, 21(7), 863–73. doi:http://dx.doi.org/10.1016/j.tate.2005.05.015

Sarra, C. (2007). Stronger, Smarter, Sarra. *Teacher: The National Education Magazine*, 32–4, 36–8, 40–1.

—— (2011). *Strong and smart – Towards a pedagogy for emancipation: Education for First Peoples.* Oxon: Routledge.

Shay, M. (2013). *Practices of alternative schools in Queensland in supporting Aboriginal and Torres Strait Islander young people to remain engaged in education.* Unpublished Master of Education thesis, University of the Sunshine Coast.

Solorzano, D.G. & Yosso, T. J. (2001). From racial stereotyping and deficit discourse toward a critical race theory in teacher education. *Multicultural Education*, 9(1), 2–8.

—— (2002). Critical race methodology: Counter-storytelling as an analytical framework for education research. *Qualitative Inquiry*, 8(1), 23–44. doi:10.1177/107780040200800103

Stefancic, J. & Delgado, R. (2013). *Critical race theory: The cutting edge.* Retrieved from http://QUT.eblib.com.au/patron/FullRecord.aspx?p=1210896

te Riele, K. (2007). Educational alternatives for marginalised youth. *The Australian Educational Researcher*, 34(3), 53–68. doi:10.1007/BF03216865

Townsend-Cross, M. (2011). Indigenous education and Indigenous studies in the Australian academy: Assimilationism, critical pedagogy, dominant culture learners and Indigenous knowledges. In G. Dei (Ed.), *Indigenous philosophies and critical education* (pp. 68–79). New York: Peter Lang.

Wilson, K., Stemp, K. & McGinty, S. (2011). Re-engaging young people with education and training: What are the alternatives? *Youth Studies Australia*, 30(4), 32–9.

Winkler, M. (2010). Taking action on Indigenous education. *Education Horizons*, 11(2), 18–20.

—— (2012). Hidden treasures: Recognising the value of Indigenous educators. *Education Horizons*, 12(2), 20–1.

Zamudio, M., Russell, C., Rios, F. & Bridgeman, J. L. (2011). *Critical race theory matters: Education and ideology*. Retrieved from http://QUT.eblib.com.au/patron/FullRecord.aspx?p=592906

CHAPTER 7

Silences in growing up bi/multilingual in multicultural globalised societies

Educators', families' and children's views of negotiating languages, identity and difference in childhood

Criss Jones Díaz

....

AUSTRALIAN PROFESSIONAL STANDARDS FOR TEACHERS

Standard 1: Know students and how they learn

This chapter develops understandings of bi/multilingual children's and families' experiences of growing up bi/multilingual, identity negotiation and hybrid cultural practices. It highlights the ways in which children's bi/multilingual identities are closely linked to their use of languages in everyday life, within contexts of diversity, difference and marginalisation.

Standard 7: Engage professionally with colleagues, parents/carers and the community

This chapter supports educators to engage with colleagues and families about the importance of bi/multilingualism and the new potentialities of multiple identity negotiation of cultural and linguistic practices across family, community and educational settings.

....

> At the beginning of the year they would talk a lot more in Spanish/Vietnamese/ Cantonese and now they express themselves in English, they avoid their home language. (Early childhood educator, questionnaire response)

Introduction

In Australian educational contexts, there exist silences around bi/multilingual children's experiences of learning and using a minority language and identity negotiation. These silences mask our understandings of children's decreasing capacity to retain adequate levels of bilingual/multilingual proficiency due to the early exposure to dominant English-only early childhood and primary education. This is also shaped by global, political, social and economic factors in which English as a global language has a major impact on children's emerging identities, which are a 'work in progress', constantly negotiated, renegotiated and constructed within social and linguistic contexts.

The data examined in this chapter are based on a study that attempts to disrupt some of these silences by documenting Latin American Australian children's and families' views about their bi/multilingual experiences, identity negotiation and hybrid cultural practices, often ignored or dismissed by educators. The findings demonstrate ways in which the children's bi/multilingual identity is closely linked to the use of languages in everyday life, within contexts of difference and marginalisation in growing up bi/multilingual. By drawing on conceptual frameworks of cultural studies, I examine concepts of cultural hybridity, diaspora and Bhabha's (1994) 'third space' to show how interracial/interethnic families negotiated their use of languages and constructions of identity in a globalised world in which English dominates social institutions, cultural discourses and linguistic practices. Drawing on concepts of discourse and subjectivity, these views are contrasted against early childhood and primary educators' awareness levels of the children's understandings and experiences of the minority status of Spanish spoken as their home language. The discussion highlights how understandings of identity are unacknowledged in shaping children's and families' views of negotiating two or more languages in education. This chapter concludes with implications for practice for future mainstream and languages teachers. It offers new ways of thinking about bi/multilingualism, children's languages learning and identity negotiation to critically highlight the ideological issues of language linked to constructions of identity.

Background

The significance of linguistic and cultural diversity in Australia

Bi/multilingual possessing the ability to speak more than one language for communicative purposes across a range of social and cultural contexts.

In the world today, there are by far more **bi/multilinguals** than monolinguals (Romaine, 2013). In Australia, over 19% of the population over five years of age speaks a language other than English at home (Australian Bureau of Statistics, 2012). The diversity of languages and cultures represented in early childhood and school settings throughout Australia is characteristic of Australia's multicultural and multilingual society. Much of Australia's linguistic diversity is found in the rich mosaic of cultural, social and economic capital produced in languages. Australia's cultural and linguistic diversity is of national significance and this forms the basis of what is currently Australia's social policy of multiculturalism. Therefore, as Australia becomes a more globalised and diverse nation, the role languages play forms a significant part of Australia's multilingual and multicultural identity. However, this diversity must not come at the cost of globalising agendas that impact on identity, language retention and learning in Australia.

English as global linguistic currency

Within the last 50 years, English has become a powerful global language. It is now the second most extensively spoken language in the world, with more speakers of English as a second language than there are 'native' English speakers (Blommaert, 2010). Consequently, it is recognised by the United Nations as either an official or dominant language in more than 60 countries and enjoys prominence in an additional 20 (Crystal, 2010, p. 370). In this global contemporary context, everyday economic, social, cultural and linguistic practices do not escape the influences of globalisation. The impact of fast-paced for-profit agendas, competitive modes of production, consumerism, communication and digital technologies, media and popular culture results in the rise of increased prominence of English as a global linguistic currency.

Hence, English as a global language has a major impact on children's emerging identities, which are constantly being constructed and reconstructed, negotiated and transformed across diverse social, cultural and linguistic contexts. This is of major significance for bi/multilingual families and communities, as normative English-only agendas from negative community attitudes, media, and educators and other professionals result in families abandoning their home language in preference for speaking English to their children. The idea that the home language is an impediment to their children's educational success and economic advancement may be a major contributing factor to families opting to speak only English to their children in order for them to more readily take up opportunities to participate in an ever-increasing competitive globalised world (Jones Díaz, 2014; Schwartz, 2010).

Bi/multilingual families who place value on the retention of their home language/s as a vehicle to affirm cultural identity may grapple with uncertainties of language choice and code switching with their children on a daily basis. They may also deal with the complexities of identity formation, language use and their children's perceptions, attitudes and dispositions towards use of the home language/s (Jones Díaz & Harvey, 2007). These issues, combined with children's possible rejection of their home language, are of concern for bi/multilingual families and educators who are aware of the social, cultural, intellectual, linguistic and economic gains in being bi/multilingual, including the benefits to family cohesion (Pacini-Ketchabaw, Bernhard & Freire, 2001). Nevertheless, these benefits are not readily known to many families and educators. (See also Chapter 12 in this volume.) Therefore, bi/multilingual families in educational settings are silenced in their capacity 'to raise concerns and issues regarding their children's bilingual trajectory' (Jones Díaz, 2016, p. 39).

Silences in growing up bi/multilingual and negotiating identity

In educational settings in Australia, bi/multilingual children's and youth's experiences of growing up with more than one language and negotiating more than one identity are often silenced. These silences can be attributed to the lack of research investigating how broader sociological factors associated with language retention and identity construction may play a significant role in facilitating or inhibiting children's/youth's potential in being bi/multilingual. Such silences can eclipse understandings of the challenges families and communities face in assisting children/youth to retain adequate proficiency levels of their home language/s. This is particularly pertinent as early childhood and school settings, where identity construction is continuously changing, renegotiated and transformed, could contribute significantly to children's capacity to develop proficiency in their home language/s. Furthermore, the scarcity of research into early childhood language shift in Australia within fields of education has resulted in ongoing silences around children's decreasing abilities to retain their home languages while attending early childhood settings (Jones Díaz & Harvey, 2007). This chapter attempts to disrupt some of these silences by documenting children's and families' views and perspectives about their bi/multilingual experiences, **identity negotiation** and hybrid cultural practices. It draws attention to such silences by reporting on educators' observations and awareness levels of children's understandings and experiences of the minority status of their home language/s.

Identity negotiation the shifting and transformative experiences of belonging or not belonging across different and often contested cultural, linguistic and social practices within multiple cultural fields.

Socio-critical perspectives in bi/multilingualism, languages education and identity work

As discussed in Chapter 1, Bourdieu's theory of social practice, which emphasises capital, habitus and field, can be applied to the production of inequality at macro and micro levels in education. Adopting Bourdieusian perspectives, studies from Canada and the United Kingdom on language and inequality in education have examined how multilingual practices and discourses are shaped by, and constituted in, the legitimisation of power relations among cultural groups (Heller, 2012). These studies demonstrate how pedagogical discourses shape language practices through processes of legitimisation embedded in curriculum, pedagogy and policy. They also show 'how children and adults unwittingly contribute to the reproduction of hegemonic relations through bi/multilingual or monolingual discursive practices' (Jones Díaz, 2016, p. 40).

In Australia, research adopting a critical stance towards languages education and bilingual children's experiences of negotiating identity in a minority language remains limited (Jones Díaz, 2013). Nevertheless, there are some emerging studies that critically examine the views and experiences of children from Latin American backgrounds of growing up bi/multilingual and biliterate (see Cole, 2012; Jones Díaz, 2011). Still, in educational and community settings, ways in which equity, identity negotiation and power relations impact on children's attitudes towards their home language/s remain underacknowledged and under-researched. For many bi/multilingual children, experiences of their languages and literacies encountered in family and community settings represent the multiplicity of linguistic and cultural practices embedded in everyday social practices (Beecher & Jones Díaz, 2014; Jones Díaz, 2011). These experiences have major influences on their location in normative discourses associated with language, gender, 'race', class, ethnicity and religion. This chapter, therefore, offers significant contributions to understanding bi/multilingual children's experiences of inequality and marginalisation in relation to the negotiation of identity that cuts across different cultural, linguistic practices within multiple cultural fields.

Key theoretical concepts

In examining the relationship between identity and language retention, the discussion that follows draws on Hall's (1993, 1996) concepts of identity negotiation and Bhabha's (1994, 1998) 'third space' to inform understandings of how bi/multilingual children and their families negotiate transformative and often contested identities in their everyday lived experiences. Furthermore, the theoretical concepts (such as discourse, power and subjectivity) informed by poststructural theory help illustrate how language and social practices produce interactions that provide meanings about the world. Through these meanings, children's understandings about themselves are closely tied to how they negotiate the use of their languages in different situations.

> **Third space** the place where cultural and linguistic straddling affirms new and hybrid identities marked by 'race', gender and class.

Growing up bi/multilingual and negotiating multiple and transformative identities

As outlined in Chapter 1, Hall (1994, 1996) conceptualises identity from four related viewpoints in terms of the relationship between culture and identity. The first position, he argues, is related to shared culture and allegiance in which mutual histories and cultural practices bind together forms of solidarity and imagined homogeneity within individuals and groups. For Hall, this shared collective builds on imagined homogeneity to form fixed boundaries that yield power relations between the 'insiders' and 'outsiders'. This focus illustrates the social and political specificity of identity in constructing marginalised groups.

The second position argues that identities are constructed outside of difference and their struggle for validity is legitimised through their capacity to exclude. As a consequence, every identity has its 'margin'. Therefore, the unity that identity treats as a necessary foundation for homogeneity is not natural. Unity in this sense is a socially constructed form of closure (Hall, 1996). Social identity is constituted in power and the 'unities' through which identities are constructed occur within the processes of power and exclusion.

Hall's third position on identity is concerned with the positional and unstable aspect of identity in which processes of identification are never complete but are transformative. For bi/multilingual children, processes of becoming may be multi-layered and complex as they encounter multiple social, cultural and linguistic experiences embedded in family life, educational and community settings. Hall (1996) argues that identity is an act of articulation and subject to the play of difference, and that the marking of symbolic boundaries is important. He argues that for diasporic communities, questions of difference always exist in the background where thinking and acting with difference rather than against it are profoundly crucial (Hall, 2012, in Jones Díaz, 2016). He suggests that identities are about using the resources of history, language and culture in the processes of becoming, rather than being. This focus on identity is a useful tool to apply to this study, as it permits an investigation into the important relationships between languages, cultures and history in the construction of bi/ multilingual identity in children and adults.

Finally, Hall's fourth position (1996) claims that identities are constantly changing as a result of globalised labour markets, population mobility, immigration, diversity, and socio-economic and political instability. Within this unsteadiness, identities are 'increasingly fragmented and fractured; multiply constructed across different, often intersecting and antagonistic discourses, practices and positions' (p. 4). From this perspective, he argues that because identities are constituted within representation and discourse, we need to understand how they are produced in specific historical, economic, social and institutional sites. In addition, Hall articulates how power constructs identities that emerge as a result of difference, rather than unity. It is this focus on identity that goes beyond traditional meanings of identity as fixed and stable to incorporate contemporary ideas of identity as shifting and relational, constituted in power, exclusion and fragmentation (Bhabha, 1994; Hall, 1993).

Theoretical tools that articulate transformative aspects of identity in relation to cultural practice can provide deeper understandings about the ways in which bi/multilingual children use languages to locate and negotiate multiple identities within different cultural and social practices across family, educational and community contexts.

Cultural hybridity the lending and borrowing between different cultural practices, experienced through multiple contradictions, connections and possibilities. Cultural adaptation, intermarriage, intergenerational change and globalisation give rise to these forms of cultural mixing. 'Cultural hybridity' counters understandings of ethnicity as discrete and bounded and acknowledges the fluidity of cultural forms.

Diaspora the voluntary or forced scattering of a cultural group over different historical and political eras and geographic locations. Within a contemporary context, 'diaspora' refers to transnational migration movements linked to globalisation, embedded in a social condition, entailing a particular form of consciousness and sense of identity.

Negotiating hybrid identities and the third space in the Latin American Australian diaspora

In cultural studies, concepts of cultural hybridity and diaspora critically inform understandings about how the negotiation of identity is connected to language retention, particularly in terms of growing up bi/multilingual, mediated by language, 'race', ethnicity, gender and class. They describe the contemporary cultural reality and mixed cultural and 'racial' identities shared by many of the participants in this study from Latin American Australian backgrounds.

Cultural hybridity is the two-way borrowing and lending between cultures (Rosaldo, 1995). As cultural, linguistic and social practices overlap, meaning is constructed from within past and present cultural histories, linguistic repertoires and life trajectories. As Jones Diaz (2016, p. 42) points out, 'For many Latin Americans living outside Latin America in super-diverse societies, identity transformation and difference are negotiated within contexts of cultural heterogeneity'. This is experienced through the multiple contradictions, connections and possibilities derived from traversing across multiple cultures and language practices. Still, within the spaces of cultural heterogeneity, identity and difference are negotiated as daily life is made up of constant forms of adaptation and contradictions in living in two or more cultures (Acosta-Belén & Santiago, 1998).

Bhabha's (1994) concept of the 'third space' is influenced by ideas of adaptation and transformation created as a result of difference, which is then negotiated in social practices and discourses (Jones Diaz, 2016). He argues that 'minorities or marginalised subjects have to construct their histories from disjunct and fragmented archives and to constitute their subjectivities and collectivities through attenuated, dislocated and exclusionary practices' (Bhabha, 1998, p. 39).

Discourse, power and subjectivity

The concepts of discourse, power and subjectivity offer useful tools for examining how bi/multilingual identities are not only constructed within social categories of identity, but are also subjected to broader contextual realities formed through relationships and taken-for-granted assumptions about the world. These realities are also in accordance with the social processes, norms and values that operate in contexts of diversity and difference. As discussed in Chapter 1, discourses are meaning systems that make use of language to represent and constitute our reality of the world and social experiences. Discourses embody relationships that constitute individuals' lived experiences and power relations. Groups of ideas, statements and ways of thinking that express social values are also constructed in discourse. The possibility of thought is not only constrained by, but also produced through, discourse (Ball, 2013). Discourses operating in society sustain power and authority and compete against each other, vying for more recognition and acceptance. Discourses that uphold the status quo afford individuals who comfortably take up positions in these discourses relative power.

Poststructural and cultural theories highlight subjectivity as critical in the social construction of the 'self' (McNay, 2013). The 'self' is viewed as an active and conscious thinking subject whose understandings, interpretations and meanings about the world and the social relations between people, institutions and social practices influence everyday lived experiences. Hence, children and adults are capable of shifting and changing their thinking and behaviours according to the social field in which they are participating. They are also able to position themselves in the normalising discourses that govern that particular field. For example, in English-only educational settings, bi/multilingual children's home language/s are often ignored or dismissed due to a singular preoccupation with English (Gogolin, 2011).

Methodology

The participants in this study comprised of 25 children and 39 family members from Spanish-speaking Latin American Australian backgrounds, living in Sydney. The children attended educational and community settings. The families represented diverse family structures, including extended, blended and interethnic/ interracial families. This also included various income levels, with most parents working in a range of skilled and non-skilled occupations. In addition, 34 educators working in prior-to-school and school settings from the inner-west, south-west and eastern suburbs of Sydney participated (Jones Díaz, 2016).

The data presented in this chapter are taken from a smaller sample of these children and parents.[1] The parents included Raul, Carol, Camilla, Alicia, Clarissa, José, Jenny and Miryam, and there were two children – Jack and Emilio.[2] Of the 34 caregivers and teachers from the broader study, this chapter reports on data from two selected childcare workers, one teacher's assistant, two primary classroom teachers, one early childhood teacher, one English as an additional language (EAL) teacher and two directors of early childhood settings.

The data collection methods included questionnaires, semi-structured interviews, participant observations, researcher field notes, reflective journals, children's work samples and the collection of documentation.[3] The study included the documentation and analysis of young children's Spanish and English bilingual experiences in varied social contexts, such as day-to-day family life, education and community settings. The families and their children were the centre of this study, and their perspectives about negotiating languages and identity construction in various cultural practices were the primary concern of the investigation.[4] In addition, the data analysis involved an examination of how power relations and discursive practices that operate in educational and community settings impact on children's negotiation of identity and the retention of Spanish (Jones Díaz, 2016).

---

1   In order to protect the identity of the participants, the names used in this chapter are pseudonyms.

2   The children and the adults in this study are not related. Clarissa's, Jenny's and Alicia's children and Jack's parents were not interviewed in the broader study. The children of the remaining parents were not included, as they did not raise specific issues relevant to the focus of this chapter.

3   The data analysed in this chapter draw on the questionnaires and semi-structured interviews only.

4   Data relating to caregiver and teacher attitudes towards bilingualism and language retention were also analysed in the larger study. For the purposes of this chapter, the discussion pertains only to some of the voices of the caregivers/teachers, children and families in this research.

Thematic discourse analysis techniques were used to analyse the data from the questionnaires and interviews, informed by feminist, critical and cultural theories framed within poststructural concepts. However, the data presented in this chapter are analysed from a cultural studies and poststructuralist lens through which concepts of cultural hybridity, diaspora, the 'third space', discourse and subjectivity are applied to investigate how the children and adults negotiated their identities and languages as bi/multilingual Latin American Australians. Therefore, the study draws on 'the accounts of the participants and the analysis was evidence-driven and theoretically informed' (Jones Díaz, 2016, p. 44. See also Davis, 1995; Patton, 2002).

In the context of this study, I am interested in how children and adults negotiate their multiple and often contradictory identities marked by language, 'race', ethnicity, class and gender. The public and personal spaces that I traverse and the discursive ideologies and multiple identities that shape my subjectivity as a researcher, academic and mother of bilingual and interracial children play a pivotal role in this study's examination of silences and inequalities that exist in multilingual educational, family and community settings. Moreover, as a bilingual Anglo-Australian, the daily lived experiences of identity transformation and change involve the careful navigation of the intersections of 'race', language, gender and class. The experiences and reflections shared in the conversations between the participants highlighted for me 'the significance of reflexivity in the research process, as the interplay of my membership in the field in which I am researching is bounded by personal, professional and scholarly pursuits and complexities' (Jones Díaz, 2016, p. 44).

Analysis and discussion

In the discussion that follows, three themes are highlighted: children's and families' views about their bi/multilingual experiences, identity negotiation and hybrid cultural practices; the silences in Afro-Indigenous Latino/a identity in the Latin American Australian diaspora; and, educators' knowledge of children's experiences of growing up bi/multilingual and their awareness levels of children's perceptions of the minority status of their home language/s.

Children's and families' views about their bi/multilingual experiences: Shared allegiance through cultural and language practice

The parents and children in this study expressed feelings of belonging to a cultural minority in which shared cultural and language practices were pertinent. In Jenny's family, the languages and dialects spoken include Mandarin, Cantonese, Shanghaiese, Portuguese and Spanish. Within this multilingual context her children were exposed to six languages (including English) in varying degrees. In the extract below, it is apparent that Jenny worked hard to promote her children's

Uruguayan identity as she described her husband's reaction to the eldest daughter's insistence on being 'Chinese':

> Because she speak[s] more Chinese. 'Always I'm Chinese'. When she says that, my husband says 'No, you are [from] Uruguay' ... I said look, you are Uruguay China [Uruguayan Chinese] or Australian ... I don't want that she [only] knows the China ... You are from China country ... You are from Uruguay ... [But] she says, 'I'm Chinese' ... She always speaks Chinese, Chinese. All the family [speak] Chinese. But her mother [does] not [speak] much ... Spanish. So I said, no you're Spanish but you can't speak [it].

Jenny's desire for her children to identify with both her partner's Uruguayan side and her family's Chinese heritage was minimised by her daughter's identity claim, 'I'm Chinese'. Much of Jenny's struggle with identity politics between her partner and her daughter was located in her daughter's construction of her Chinese identity being contingent upon her proficiency in Mandarin. Despite Jenny's daughter learning Spanish at a Spanish Community Language School, Jenny's efforts to challenge her, 'no you're Spanish but you can't speak [it]', was an attempt to destabilise language as the singular site for identity construction to promote some allegiance to her Latin American heritage. These concepts of identity as shared cultural practice can be applied to draw attention to the role of language in the negotiation of identity and cultural practice. In this case, Jenny's focus on her daughter's limited Spanish was recognition that identity is not necessarily contingent upon language.

While language was problematic for Jenny in terms of getting her daughter to recognise her Latin American heritage, for other parents it was the vehicle through which identity and Latin American cultural practices were affirmed. Below, Alicia reflected on why speaking Spanish to her children was important:

Es solamente parte del día de[l] vivir. Es como una prolongación de nosotros mismos ... porque es la identidad que estamos proyectando a los hijos ...	It's all part of my daily life. It's like an extension of ourselves... because it's our identity that we project onto our children ...

Alicia's reasons for speaking Spanish to her children were mainly due to her desire for them to know about their heritage. For Alicia, identity is the means through which her children come to know and respect their family: 'Y ... entonces ellos van ... a saber quiénes son, um, sus padres, ellos mismos. Creo que en parte que ellos honren su entorno, su familia y nosotros' [And so they know who they are, their parents, themselves. I think it's how they give respect towards their family]. Alicia's views of identity were congruent with Hall's (1993, 1996) framework of identity as a site for belonging and shared solidarity. For Alicia, Spanish was a means by which her children were able to know and respect her culture, which she believed was constructed through language.

Jenny's and Alicia's views on the relationship between identity and speaking Spanish to their children illustrate Hall's (1996) primary position of identity, which emphasises solidarity and shared allegiance through which cultural codes and practices become affirmed and legitimised. These perspectives illustrated the significance of language and cultural practices in the construction of shared identity.

Identities are multiple, hybridised and transformative

Various forms of linguistic, cultural and racial hybridity were evident in the ways that the children and the parents in this study negotiated the 'third space', positioning them in multiple, hybridised, transformative and often competing discourses of identity. Below José, Miryam and Camilla reflected on their children's identity:

Primero lo que tienen que saber es, esa esencia, primero para poder … identificados como australianos … Primero que todo … no titubean en, qué son, quiénes son o de dónde son, o qué cultura vienen. (José)	First, they need to know their heritage, primarily so that they can … identify as Australians … From this … they won't get confused about who they are or where they are from, or what culture they come from. (José)

In the extract below, Miryam acknowledged her daughter's Australian identity and also added that her daughter was aware of her Latin American background. She expressed her desire for her daughter to simultaneously identify as a bilingual with her Latin American background:

Aunque nosotros siempre decimos que ella es Australiana y su lengua es español e inglés, y todo pero, nos gusta que también sienta que ella es, sus raíces son, son … vienen de nosotros.	Even though we always say that she is Australian, and her language is Spanish and English, we like her to feel that her roots are, are … they come from us.

Camilla was open about alternatives that her child might construct. However, she also emphasised her daughter's negotiation of two cultural worlds: 'No sé, ella está creciendo así, se forma sus ideas. Pero a mí me parece que ella está en las dos cul-turas' [I don't know, she is growing up like this, she can form her ideas. But for me it appears that she is in both cultures].

As discussed previously, the fluidity of identity location is often located in the 'third space' (Bhabha, 1994, 1998). This defines an 'in-between' location that negotiates two competing discursive worlds. Grossberg (1997) suggests that images of the 'third space' are marked by the notion of 'border crossing', which highlights an in-betweenness through which subjects transcend and transform their identities. For the children in this study, what it meant to be Latin American carried multiple meanings and discursive practices. The multiple and hybrid identity claims made by the parents, as in the case of José, Miryam and Camilla about their children's identity, highlight the similarities and differences from their perspectives.

Identity builds on power and exclusion

As discussed, an important function of identity is its capacity to build homogeneous boundaries upon which imagined unity and sameness operate to construct closure and exclusion. Within this process, power relations are constructed through hegemonic identities that are able to sustain themselves (Hall, 1996). Below, Clarissa reflected on her experiences of persistent questioning from others about her Australian identity:

> I never cease to answer the question of where are you from, and when I say Australia, they say, yes but where are your parents from? I go Australia, oh yes but where are your grandparents from, and they want to go through my whole history of family history before they will actually accept that I'm Australian.

Hall (1996) suggests that identity negotiation is also linked to how we might be represented and accepted by others through meanings that position individuals and collective identities as subjects through which we make sense of ourselves and our experiences. The ways in which 'racial' identity is read by others, based on assumptions about a particular ethnic or racial group, is an example of signifying practices. Clarissa's experience of being marked in this way influenced the process of identity negotiation. For Clarissa, this constant interrogation of her family history meant that her identity as Australian was scrutinised because she appeared to be non-Anglo-Australian. This form of scrutiny operated to exclude Clarissa from being represented as Australian.

Identity politics also emerged in the data of some of the children and adults. Below, struggles over identity claims were apparent for Jack in his contestation of his friend Emilio's identity claim as an Australian. I asked Emilio and Jack about where their parents were from:

> **CRISS:** So where is your mum from? (to Emilio)
>
> **EMILIO:** Argentiiiiina (emphasises the 'i' in Argentina).
>
> **CRISS:** Where's your dad from?
>
> **EMILIO:** Chile.
>
> **CRISS:** So do you know ... (to Jack)
>
> **JACK:** I know where my mother and my dad are from.
>
> **CRISS:** Where are they from?
>
> **JACK:** Darwin.
>
> **EMILIO:** But that's from Australia!

Jack was of a Malaysian, Chinese and Anglo-Australian background and his parents were born in Darwin. Emilio's astonished reaction to Jack's parents being born in Darwin, 'that's from Australia!', suggests that he was drawing on racialised assumptions through which Jack's identity claim as Australian is not legitimated. Since Emilio named his parents' nationalities, perhaps he expected Jack to do the same. For Emilio, it appeared that Jack's Asian appearance required him to name his parents' Asian heritage rather than their Australian birthplace.

While identity claims can be a useful strategy in the struggle for voice and identity, Emilio's contestation of Jack's identity claim is a form of identity politics that is divisive and exclusive. Papastergiadis (2013) argues that identity politics is considered to be a cause rather than a symptom of the narrowing of political horizons. An example of this can be found in an extreme form of identity politics, 'essentialism', which gives an appearance of fixed difference based on some form of biological or cultural 'uniqueness', as in the case of Emilio's reaction to Jack's response.

Diaspora, identity and silences in Afro-Indigenous Latino/a identity

In this study, the participants' cultural histories revealed silences in Indigenous and Afro hybrid identities, often intersected with linguistic and racial hybridity, racism, poverty and hardship. The cultural histories of Alicia and Carol were forged in the memories of their Indigenous grandparents. Carol's memories of her grandmother's prohibition of speaking Quechua, 'nunca lo ha practicado porque su madre no le dejaba ... porque eran "cholos"' [she never spoke it because her mother would not let her ... because they were 'cholos'], illustrates the intersection of colonisation, racism and language. 'Cholo' is a racialised term that exists in Peru to describe people of hybridised Indigenous descent. It is used throughout the Andes to denote a person of mestizo or Indigenous descent who speaks Spanish and identifies culturally and economically with urban Spanish-speakers (Lipski, 1994). Carol's grandmother prohibited her mother from speaking Quechua, as a way of denying their Indigenous background and assimilating to dominant Peruvian Spanish-speaking culture.

Alicia, on the other hand, used her grandmother's indigeneity as a talking point to stimulate interest in her son about Peru:

Y hay palabras [que] son en Quechua ... así que ... este hay cuentos ... que yo yo le [a mi hijo] explico yo lo que es que la abuelita ha vivido en las montañas ...	And there are words in ... Quechua ... like there are stories ... that I explain to him [my son] that's where his grandmother ... had lived in the mountains ...

Alicia drew on a cultural narrative about place and its connection to language as a way of promoting her mother's Indigenous identity to her son. Alicia's grandmother spoke Quechua but not Spanish. Her mother understood Quechua but she did not speak it.

The Afro-Latino/a Caribbean diaspora

The Latin American experience comprises many diasporas derived from a post-colonial context of Spanish colonisation and subordination of Africans and Indigenous Americans. Hence, migration experiences in this study exemplify the diverse cultural history of the Latin American diaspora, representing the contemporary cultural reality of blended or mixed cultural and racial identities evident in multicultural urban societies such as Australia.

Raul, who was born in the Dominican Republic, has a cultural history embedded in an Afro-Latino/a diaspora. Below, he told of how a political policy of 'Blanquismo' [whitening process] manipulated the race relations in his country through the classification of people according to skin colour.[5]

> Yes people were socially classified according to their skin colour. They were mulattos, mestizos, negroes that descended from the slaves of Africa. There in the Dominican Republic, there are different names for people according to [skin] colour, *so you remember what colour you are* [Raul's emphasis].

Raul's remark, 'so you remember what colour you are', exemplifies how such forms of racism produce power relations constituted in identity politics that denied the heterogeneous reality of Dominican life. This encompasses everyday experiences of African, Latino/a and Indigenous Taina heritage where spaces of multiple cultural, social and racial differences co-exist (Nyberg Sørensen, 2001). Yet, despite this reality, discourses of Dominican national identity adopted nineteenth-century racialising categories of essentialised difference. According to Alvar, (1987, cited in Young, 1995, p. 177), there are 128 words in Spanish for different combinations of mixed 'race'.

In the stories of Carol and Alicia, Indigenous languages and identity feature as important threads to everyday life that are passed down to their children. Similarly for Raul, in the cultural histories of the Afro-Latino/a diaspora the African presence is strong. Despite the apparent large-scale miscegenation that has resulted in a hybridised state of Indigenous, African and European influences, these histories and narratives emerge as powerful testaments of struggle, perseverance, adaptation and survival.

Educators' awareness levels of children's experiences of growing up bi/multilingual: Children's location in discourses of monolingualism

In this study, discourses of monolingualism were apparent in the educators' observations of children's reluctance to speak their home language. They reported that the bi/multilingual children with whom they worked felt ashamed and embarrassed to speak their home language, as the data below illustrate:

> They are not fully fluent in their home language. They are embarrassed. It's not cool! (Primary teacher)

---

5   Identity in the Dominican Republic has, until recently, been the site for political manipulation. There is a history of politically driven identity politics through the dictatorship of General Rafael Leónidas Trujillo Molina (1930–61). In combination with the ruling elite, Trujillo's dictatorship silenced and denied the Afro-Latino/a identity by telling the people that, despite the colour of their skin, they were white, Catholic and 'Hispanic' (Nyberg Sørensen, 2001).

It's about having confidence being able to speak in your home language. (Teacher's assistant: La Escuelita)

Children feeling uneasy/shy to speak their home language. (Childcare worker: ECE)

Children are reluctant. Parents are very reserved about admitting it. (EAL primary teacher)

Some children are beginning to reply to parents in English even though they are spoken to in the home language. (Teacher director: ECE)

Children arrived with little or no English, now speak English at the school and at home. We no longer hear them speak their home language. (Director: ECE)

At the beginning of the year they would talk a lot more in Spanish/Vietnamese/ Cantonese and now they express themselves in English, they avoid their home language. (ECE teacher: questionnaire response)

Parents [are] informing carers that their children are speaking more English than their home language and/or refusing to speak their language. (CCCs[6]: ECE)

To be able to communicate successfully at school, children often drop their home language. (Primary teacher)

Children's reluctance and shame in speaking their home language is an illustration of their location in discourses of monolingualism as they felt 'shy', 'reluctant', 'uneasy', 'threatened', 'exposed to teasing or ridicule', 'withdrawn', 'embarrassed' and 'lacking in confidence' when they spoke their home languages. The awareness that 'their home language may be a minority language' illustrates their capacity for thinking about and locating themselves in normalising discourses of monolingualism. These discourses sustain inequitable power relations between languages, reifying the dominance of English as natural and normal. Such normative monolingual language and communication practices are constructed around the use of one language: usually English. In the above extracts, the children's perceptions of their home language/s suggest that for bi/ multilingual children, their subjectivity is highly influenced by constructions of normative monolingualism. Hence, such monolingual discourses evident in the children's subjectivities, also apparent in many educational settings (Jones Díaz, 2013), propose challenges to educators as they look for ways of assisting children in using their home languages.

Implications

The findings in this chapter have critically disrupted the silences surrounding bi/ multilingual children's and families' experiences of growing up bi/multilingual.

---

6   CCCs refers to the qualification of a diploma-trained childcare worker.

Documented are the perspectives of families and children in view of how they experienced their identities as shifting and transformative in the context of monolingualism, shared cultural practices, power relations, marginalisation and difference. The analysis drew on Hall's (1994, 1996) framework of identity to highlight concepts such as belonging, solidarity, collectivity and transformation to illustrate the significance of language and cultural practices in the construction of identity and bi/multilingualism. The data also revealed the applicability of Bhabha's (1994, 1998) 'third space' in understanding how identity is transformative and changeable, often intersected with linguistic and racial hybridity, racism and marginalisation. Building on these understandings of identity, this chapter also examined children's awareness of the minority status of their home language/s, informed by normative monolingual discourses in which issues of power and language impacted on the children's views of their linguistic differences, positioning them in discourses of monolingualism through which they experience their identities and subjectivities of being bi/multilingual.

For teachers working with bi/multilingual children and families, it is important to recognise the varied and shifting contexts through which identities are expressed. Through this process, understandings of the impact of contemporary global expressions of language and cultural practice will create transformative and responsive pedagogy, curriculum and policy. In order for this to occur, it is important that parental anxieties regarding children's bi/multilingual experience are acknowledged. This involves sensitive and critical engagement with families about issues of rising global English within discursive frames of English-only monolingualism. It includes encouraging families to continue to speak their home language/s, so that in growing up bi/multilingual in Australia, apart from economic, intellectual and familial benefits, there are new potentialities of multiple-identity negotiation of cultural and linguistic practices; affirmation; and belonging to communities, cultural groups and educational settings.

Considerations

- If you are from a bi/multilingual background, how did you experience the negotiation of your languages as you were growing up? How was this linked to your social and cultural identity in shaping how you positioned yourself in monolingual discursive practices?
- You are working or on practicum in an early childhood or school setting and the bi/multilingual families are reluctant to share their experiences and/or concerns about their children's learning and use of languages. How do you approach these families so that you can engage in a positive, supportive and responsive conversation about bi/multilingualism and identity negotiation?

Of interest

- The DVD *Growing Up Bilingual in Australia: An Investment* provides an over-view of the benefits of bi/multilingualism and ways in which educators can facilitate children's growth as confident bi/multilingual citizens. See http://ecsc.org.au/resources
- The video clip *More than 250 Indigenous Languages at Risk of Disappearing* reports on language revival programs where linguistics and educators are working to save the many Indigenous languages that are at risk of disappearing. See https://www.sbs.com.au/ondemand/video/450701379810/more-than-250-indigenous-languages-at-risk-of-disappearing

References

Acosta-Belén, E. & Santiago, C. E. (1998). Merging borders: The remapping of America. In A. Darder & R. D. Torres (Eds.), *The Latino studies reader: Culture, economy and society* (pp. 29–42). Malden, MA: Blackwell.

Australian Bureau of Statistics (2012). *Cultural diversity in Australia: Reflecting a nation: Stories from the 2011 census, 2012–2013.* Retrieved from http://www.abs.gov.au/AUSSTATS/abs

Ball, S. J. (2013). *Foucault, power, and education.* London: Routledge.

Beecher, B. & Jones Díaz, C. (2014). Extending literacies through partnerships with families and communities. In L. Arthur, J. Ashton & B. Beecher (Eds.), *Diverse literacies in the early years: Implications for practice* (pp. 41–64). Sydney: ACER.

Bhabha, H. (1994). *The location of culture.* London: Routledge.

—— (1998). Culture's in between. In D. Bennett (Ed.), *Multicultural states: Rethinking difference and identity* (pp. 29–47). London: Routledge.

Blommaert, M. (2010). *The sociolinguistics of globalisation.* Cambridge: Cambridge University Press.

Cole, D. R. (2012). Latino families becoming-literate in Australia: Deleuze, literacy and the politics of immigration. *Discourse: Studies in the Cultural Politics of Education,* 33(1), 33–46. doi:org/10.1080/01596306.2012.632160

Crystal, D. (2010). *The Cambridge encyclopedia of language.* Cambridge: Cambridge University Press.

Davis, K. (1995). Qualitative theory and methods in applied linguistics research. *TESOL Quarterly,* 29(3), 427–53. doi.org/10.2307/3588070

Gogolin, I. (2011). The challenge for superdiversity for education in Europe. *Education Enquiry,* 2(2), 239–49.

Grossberg, L. (1997). *Bringing it all back home: Essays on cultural studies*. Durham, NC: Duke University Press.

Hall, S. (1993). Cultural identity in question. In S. Hall, D. Held & T. McGrew (Eds.), *Modernity and its futures* (pp. 273–316). Cambridge: Polity Press.

—— (1994). Cultural identity and diasporas. In P. Williams & L. Chrisman (Eds.), *Colonial discourse and post-colonial theory* (pp. 392–403). New York: Columbia University Press.

—— (1996). Who needs 'identity'? In S. Hall & P. du Gay (Eds.), *Questions of cultural identity* (pp. 1–17). London: Sage Publications.

—— (2012). Avtar Brah's Cartographies: Moment, method, meaning. *Feminist Review*, 100(1), 27–38. doi:10.1057/fr.2011.65

Heller, M. (2012). Sociolinguistic perspectives on language and multilingualism in institutions. In S. Gardner and M. Martin-Jones (Eds.), *Multilingualism, discourse and ethnography*. New York: Routledge.

Jones Díaz, C. (2011). Children's voices: Spanish in urban multilingual and multicultural Australia. In K. Potowski & J. Rothman (Eds.), *Bilingual youth: Spanish in English-speaking societies* (pp. 251–81). Amsterdam: John Benjamins. doi.org/10.1075/sibil.42.16jon

—— (2013). Institutional, material and economic constraints in languages education: Unequal provision of linguistic resources in early childhood and primary settings in Australia. *International Journal of Bilingual Education and Bilingualism*. 17(3), 272–86. doi:10.1080/13670050.2012.754400

—— (2014). Languages and literacies in childhood bilingualism: Building on cultural and linguistic capital in early childhood education. In L. Arthur, J. Ashton & B. Beecher (Eds.), *Diverse literacies in the early years: Implications for practice* (pp. 106–25). Sydney: ACER.

—— (2016). Growing up bilingual and negotiating identity in globalised and multicultural Australia: Exploring transformations and contestations of identity and bilingualism in contexts of cultural hybridity and diaspora. In D. Cole & C. Woodrow (Eds.), *Superdimensions in globalisation and education*. Springer: New York.

Jones Díaz, C. & Harvey, N. (2007). Other words, other worlds: Bilingual identities and literacy. In L. Makin, C. Jones Díaz & C. McLaughlan (Eds.), *Literacies in childhood: Challenging views, challenging practice* (2nd ed., pp. 71–86). Sydney: Elsevier.

Lipski, J. M. (1994). *Latin American Spanish*. London: Longman.

McNay, L. (2013). *Foucault: A critical introduction*. Maldan, MA: Polity Press.

Nyberg Sørensen, N. (2001). There are no Indians in the Dominican Republic: The cultural construction of Dominican identities. In K. Fog Olwig & K. Hastrup (Eds.), *Sitting culture: The shifting anthropological object* (pp. 292–310). London and New York: Routledge.

Pacini-Ketchabaw, V., Bernhard, J. K. & Freire, M. (2001). Struggling to preserve home language: The experiences of Latino students and families in the Canadian school system. *Bilingual Research Journal*, 25(1/2), 115–45.

Papastergiadis, N. (2013). The homeless citizen, In C. McCarthy, W. Crichlow, G. Dimitriadis, N. Dolby (Eds.), *Race, identity and representation in education* (2nd ed., pp. 117–36). London: Routledge.

Patton, M. Q. (2002). *Qualitative research and evaluation methods* (3rd ed.). Thousand Oaks, CA: Sage Publications.

Romaine, S. (2013). The bilingual and multilingual community. In T. K. Batia & W. C. Ritchie (Eds.), *The handbook of multilingualism and bilingualism* (2nd ed., pp. 443–65). Oxford: Blackwell.

Rosaldo, R. (1995). *Foreword, Hybrid cultures: Strategies for entering and leaving modernity*. Minneapolis, MN: University of Minnesota Press.

Schwartz, M. (2010). Family language policy: Core issues of an emerging field. In L. Wei (Ed.), *Applied linguistics review*. New York: Walter de Gruyter. doi:org/10.1515/9783110222654.171

Young, R. J. C. (1995). *Colonial desire: Hybridity in theory, culture and race*. London: Routledge.

CHAPTER 8

'Disaffected' youth

Intersections of class and ethnicity

Mohamed Moustakim

AUSTRALIAN PROFESSIONAL STANDARDS FOR TEACHERS

Standard 1: Know students and how they learn

This chapter helps the reader to understand how students with diverse linguistic, cultural, religious and socio-economic backgrounds experience the issues of disaffection and its impact on their education. It also highlights the importance of having broad knowledge and understanding of how culture, cultural identity and linguistic background affect the education of students from diverse backgrounds.

> I used to think I was poor, then they told me I wasn't poor, I was needy. Then they told me it was self-defeating to think of myself as needy, I was deprived. Then they told me deprived was a bad image, I was underprivileged. Then they told me under-privileged was over-used, I was disadvantaged. I still don't have a dime, but I have a great vocabulary. (Feiffer, cited in Pilger, 1989, p. 237)

Introduction

Dominant ways of understanding disproportionately low academic outcomes for students from Indigenous and other minority groups fail to locate the debate about learner engagement and academic achievement in the wider context of social inequality. Instead, they continue to attribute students' disconnection from schooling to their cognitive, emotional and behavioural deficits or in terms of a moral underclass culture in their communities. However, considerable international evidence suggests that socio-economic status (SES), or class, and ethnicity can have significant effects on social and educational outcomes (Blanden, Hansen & Machin, 2008; Blanden & Macmillan, 2016).

According to Blanden et al. (2008, p. 7), there is a 'very clear pathway from childhood poverty to reduced employment opportunities, with earnings estimated to be reduced by between 15 and 28% and the probability of being in employment at age 34 reduced by between 4 and 7%'. Their British study found clear links between children and young people receiving free school meals (FSM) and low academic achievement, with students from Black and minority groups more likely to receive FSM.[1] Such inequities are not limited to the United Kingdom. Ford (2013) uses the concept of 'locked-in inequality' to draw parallels between the enduring educational disadvantage of Black students in Britain and the persistent and systemic achievement gap between Indigenous and non-Indigenous students in Australia. This is particularly apparent in the Northern Territory, as evidenced by the National Assessment Program in Literacy and Numeracy (NAPLAN) (Ministerial Council for Education, Early Childhood Development and Youth Affairs, 2009), which shows a persistent achievement gap in reading, numeracy and writing for Years 3, 5 and 9, between 2001 and 2009.

Ethnicity and indigeneity add to the layering of disadvantage resulting from low SES, and students from Indigenous and other disadvantaged minority groups are more likely to be described as disaffected (Osler & Starkey, 2005; Gillborn, 2015) and to face inequalities in education (Ford, 2013; Gray & Beresford, 2008; Harrison & Greenfield, 2011; Keddie, Gowlett, Mills, Monk & Renshaw, 2013). Definitions of disaffection distinguish between active and passive disaffection, with passive disaffection characterised by underachievement and withdrawal and active disaffection characterised by complete disconnection from schooling through truancy, exclusion or early school leaving (Parsons, 2005; Allan, 2015). However, as will be discussed in this chapter, the term 'disaffection' has acquired different definitions in a variety of formal and informal educational contexts, rendering its meaning ambiguous.

This chapter draws on research conducted in a secondary school in the United Kingdom to analyse dominant understandings of youth 'disaffection' captured in the stories of a teacher, a learning mentor and a group of six young people considered to be 'at risk' of dropping out of school. It argues that the intersecting inequalities resulting from the categories of class, ethnicity and indigeneity have marginalising effects on students from minority groups; these effects are explored through the schooling experiences of Black young people in Britain, with some parallels drawn to Indigenous students in Australia. The theoretical concepts of habitus, capital and field (Bourdieu, 1986) are used in the chapter to make sense of how class is played out in schools. Ethnicity, as a category, is discussed in the light of dominant deficit discourses on the underachievement of

---

1   In the United Kingdom, entitlement to FSM is means-tested and is offered to students whose parent(s) are in receipt of certain benefits, such as Income Support or Job Seekers Allowance.

Black young men in the United Kingdom and references are made to research on addressing issues of Indigenous disadvantage in Australian schools (Harrison & Greenfield, 2011; Keddie et al., 2013) with strikingly similar concerns (Ford, 2013; Gillborn, 2008).

This chapter explores how the quality of students' experiences of schooling was identified as contingent upon two factors: 1) being treated with respect by school staff and 2) teachers' critical awareness of the marginalising effects of 'racialised' deficit representations of students from Black and minority groups. Disconnection from learning emerged as a rational response to difficult pedagogic relations with teachers and the school uniform was a visible site of collective resistance to school norms and the expression of solidarity with peers.

Background

At the time this research was conducted at a secondary school in south London, a moral panic about 'troublesome' youth, sparked by sensationalist media report- ing about a spate in youth gangs, gun and knife crime, had gripped the nation. Moreover, high levels of truancy and a perceived lack of interest in education by a large number of young people were seen by policy makers as linked to crim- inality (Blanden et al., 2008). While asserting that the rise in youth crime had nothing to do with poverty, the then British Prime Minister Tony Blair blamed it on the growing influence of a 'distinctive Black culture' among British young people (Wintour & Vikram, 2007, para. 1). Blair's incendiary remark epitomised the demonising representations of Black young people as a moral underclass whose abject exclusion from mainstream society was not only self-inflicted, but had a corruptive influence on British society (Levitas, 2010). There are paral- lels here with the experiences of youth from racialised minority backgrounds in Australia, where despite evidence of victimisation, media reporting cast the 'problem' with the victims. For example, Windle (2008) analysed newspaper reports during intense media focus on three events involving African youth between September and December 2007, triggered by two racist attacks on two young Sudanese refugees and violent arrests made by police at a housing estate in Melbourne. Although African young people were at the receiving end of the violent attacks, frequent references in the articles to 'ethnic, youth, gang and conflict' (p. 563) turned the victims into perpetrators through the use of racial- ised labels.

As the epigraph to this chapter suggests, labels applied to socially con- structed categories of people have a tendency to change over time. So-called 'at-risk' youth, for example, have been positioned in a particular discourse. As discussed in Chapter 1, discourses operate to construct categories of classifi- cation that position subjects in ways that marginalise or privilege identities. In this instance, youth 'at risk' are described variously as 'disaffected', 'disengaged', 'disconnected' and 'NEET' (not in education, employment or training), among

other labels. These understandings have become embedded in many teachers'
and other welfare professionals' pedagogic discourse. Watson (2011) suggests
that teachers use terms such as 'at risk', 'disadvantaged' and 'urban' to talk
about Indigenous and minority students without making explicit
references to 'race'. Although the term '**disaffection**' has been
used to refer to students' absenteeism, disruptive behaviour
and disengagement from learning in schools for some time, it
increasingly appeared more prominent in the British education policy discourse following concerns raised by the House
of Commons Select Committee on Education and Employment,
which estimated the number of disaffected students at 8% of all
14–16-year-olds, and as being predominantly male from Black
backgrounds. The report also made a link between this group of young people
and criminality (House of Commons, 1998).

> Disaffection a state that is
> associated with academic
> underachievement and
> withdrawal. Active disaffection
> refers to disconnection from
> school through truancy,
> exclusion or early school
> leaving.

From around this period, the term 'disaffection' began to conflate a variety
of meanings and became synonymous with any behaviour that was perceived to
deviate from the norm. However, as Osler and Starkey point out, 'Young people
from minority ethnic communities, refugees and other newly-arrived students are
more likely to be characterised as disaffected and are often poorly served by their
schools' (2005, p. 196). Indeed, some teachers locate explanations of socially disadvantaged students' disproportionately low academic achievement as evidence
of personal deficit as a result of their dysfunctional families. To illustrate, Hatton,
Munns and Dent (2006) contrasted three Australian schools' pedagogical responses
to children in poverty in terms of their capacity to contribute to socially just outcomes and found that:

> While the deficiencies teachers perceive in these families are often no more than a
> failure to be middle-class, they are used to explain low levels of academic achieve-
> ment. These perceptions condition the classroom life of students from 'bad' fami-
> lies; they bear the brunt of the teachers' hostility towards their 'deficiencies'. (2006,
> p. 43)

Not only do these representations have the effect of constructing deviant identities with marginalising consequences for young people, they also fail to consider
the impact of the structure of schooling and socio-economic factors on academic
attainment, despite well-documented evidence to support this (Blanden et al.,
2008; Ford, 2013; Gray & Beresford, 2008).

Several policies and initiatives introduced to redress academic inequality and
reduce the high level of exclusions from schools of children and young people
from Indigenous and minority groups have had little effect (Keddie et al., 2013;
Warren, 2005). As will be discussed in the next sections of this chapter, despite the
good intentions of most teachers to make a difference to the social outcomes for
students from marginalised groups, the uncritical development and subsequent
enactment of culturalist policies and initiatives at the school level runs the risk of
further entrenching social divisions.

Key theoretical concepts

Class the ranking of social groups on the basis of socio-economic status measures, such as education, occupation and income. Traditional class distinctions have included upper class, middle class and working class.

Ethnicity a group of people who are identified as sharing historical experiences often associated with a geographic place of origin, with distinctive cultural, linguistic or religious characteristics.

Inequalities resulting from the intersecting categories of social **class**, **ethnicity** and 'race' contribute to disproportionately low educational outcomes for students from working-class and minority groups. The section begins with a discussion on how the allied theoretical concepts of forms of capital, habitus and field (Bourdieu, 1986) can provide useful tools for explaining low academic achievement for students from low SES groups. This is followed by an examination of the negative effects of racialisation and deficit representations of students from minority groups on their experiences of schooling (Keddie et al., 2013; Mills & Keddie, 2012).

Capital, habitus, field and educational outcomes

As discussed in Chapter 1, Bourdieu's theory of social practice incorporates three key tenets: capital, habitus and field. Capital is broken down into cultural, social and economic forms, which can be transferred or converted into different forms depending on the context. Economic capital is purchasing power that allows individuals to acquire material goods and enables them to access resources and services that permit them to secure comfortable living and relatively superior life chances to those who have limited economic capital. However, the effect of SES, an aspect of economic capital, is not always a strong indicator of academic achievement and future life chances.

Still less obvious are the manifestations of cultural and social forms of capital. To begin, cultural capital refers to skills, dispositions, attitudes and other cultural assets that are passed down from parents to their children. For instance, parents from middle-class English-speaking backgrounds tend to instil English literacy practices legitimised in formal schooling. Research evidence has shown that cultural capital confers advantages on some children while disadvantaging others in schools. Research by Tramonte and Willms (2010) found that cultural capital had a positive effect on reading literacy, sense of belonging at school and occupational aspirations.

Moreover, Bourdieu (1986) divides cultural capital into three forms: embodied, objectified and institutionalised. The 'embodied' form of cultural capital relates to acquired knowledge and understanding culminating in dispositions of the body as well as of the mind (Bourdieu, 1986). This type of cultural capital is typically measured by researchers in terms of the number of visits to a museum or a play, time spent reading and hours spent engaged in cultural activities outside school (Gaddis, 2014). The 'objectified' form of capital relates to the possession of cultural resources such as books, paintings and so on. The use of the internet was not prevalent in Bourdieu's time and one could argue that it has made access to more objectified forms of capital than Bourdieu could have imagined. The 'institutionalised' form of capital relates to qualifications gained from formal institutions, such as schools, colleges and universities. These confer a certain status on the bearer and are easily convertible to economic capital through the possibility of gaining salaried employment. Combined, these forms of cultural capital confer prestige and honour on the bearer when others recognise them as having legitimate symbolic value.

Often, the level of cultural capital is aligned with the extent of social capital. Social capital consists of the network of connections or memberships that an individual has access to. If one has access to a network of people in powerful positions, one has the advantage of possibly accessing privileged information or opportunity. Another example of social capital is that it can provide information about how to navigate the education system when dealing with schools, and even provide useful contacts for securing apprenticeships or employment opportunities.

The relationship between cultural and social capitals and educational achievement is mediated by habitus (Gaddis, 2014). Habitus is the set of dispositions, beliefs and values that inform students' participation in education. It is the 'durable set of dispositions that people carry within them that shapes their attitudes, behaviours and responses to given situations' (Webb, Shirato & Danaher, 2003, p. 27). The possession of privileged culture is said to shape an individual's habitus by giving him/her a sense of confidence and entitlement. Habitus also refers to the general sense of self-esteem and belief in one's abilities based on feedback on successes and failures, but it is also future-oriented, and as such shapes aspirations (Gaddis, 2014).

The field represents a set of social relations between social actors who are positioned within a social context according to the levels of capital that they possess. Their actions within the field are also influenced by the rules that regulate that particular social context. Bourdieu also highlights the importance of symbolic capital as 'the form that the various species of capital assume when they are perceived and recognized as legitimate' (Bourdieu, 1989, p. 17). He used the metaphor of life as a game and the social world as a field where individuals use cultural, social and economic resources, or forms of capital, to participate in the game.

Teachers play an important role in helping students make sense of their life experiences, gain confidence and develop a positive sense of self-worth. However, as will be highlighted in the following sections, despite the good intentions behind some teachers' and school-based initiatives, they at times produce unintended consequences of further marginalising students from disenfranchised groups (Keddie et al., 2013; Mills & Keddie, 2012).

Racialisation and deficit representations of students from marginalised groups

Critical to this discussion is the **racialisation** and deficit representations of students from marginalised groups in policy responses to low academic achievement. Watkins (2011) argues that differential academic achievements between groups of students cannot always be reduced to ethnicity. What has received less attention

Racialisation the process of representing individuals or groups through the prism of racial or ethnic stereotypes.

from policy makers, she argues, are 'the networks of interrelations between bodies, minds and material objects' (Watkins, 2011, p. 853) at the micro level of teaching and learning. In other words, the complexities of teaching and learning in schools with increasing diversity call for a more sophisticated understanding of the in-school and out-of-school factors that influence students' experiences of schooling.

Indeed, as the data presented in this chapter demonstrate, the enactment of policy responses to achievement gaps can potentially have unintended and undesirable effects on the pedagogic relations at the school level. This is because they run the risk of promoting culturalism or cultural reductionism that adopts an essentialist view of ethnicity and culture and contributes to perpetuating rather than ameliorating disadvantage (Keddie et al., 2013).

As mentioned earlier in this chapter, a number of initiatives have been introduced in the United Kingdom to raise and maximise academic engagement among Black boys. Similarly, in Australia, several initiatives focused on equity and cultural awareness have been developed to redress inequality in education and in society at large between Indigenous and non-Indigenous students. In both countries, many of these policies have striking similarities. For example, in the United Kingdom, 'Black Boys Can' was introduced in some schools, aimed specifically at Black students, in an attempt to raise their aspirations and to motivate them to want to learn. While many of these initiatives were well received by students and their parents, they were nevertheless couched in culturalist assumptions that focused more on differences between categories of students than on the many experiences and struggles that young people growing up in a metropolis shared. Commenting on attempts to redress inequality between Indigenous and non-Indigenous students through similar policies and initiatives deployed in Australian schools, Keddie et al. (2013) argue that very few teachers critically examine the homogenising effects implicit in culturalist approaches to engaging Indigenous students. Culturalism promotes a view of culture as a 'knowable, bounded and separate entity ... that makes appeals to notions of tradition as remote, past and exotic' (McConaghy, as cited in Keddie et al., 2013, p. 92; see also Chapter 9 in this volume). This produces the unintended outcome of reinforcing stereotypical deficit representations of Black and Indigenous young people. Hence it is important that teachers engage critically with the meanings, assumptions and implications of equity-focused initiatives for minority groups at the policy enactment level in schools.

Methodology

Although the school where the research reported upon in this chapter took place was located in a highly affluent area, the majority of students who attended came from an enclave of working-class communities occupying adjacent social housing or from poorer inner-city neighbouring boroughs located elsewhere in south London. The income gap between the dwellers of the grand Victorian houses surrounding the school and the working-class communities in the estates built in the 1960s widened between the 1980s and the early part of the twenty-first century, culminating in a stark juxtaposition of affluence and deprivation. During this period, the population profile of the council tenants also changed, from almost exclusively white to predominantly Black and minority communities. The proportion of students from this group accounted for 58% of the total school population. Four out of every 10 students were eligible for free school meals and more than 42% spoke a first language other than English. The school faced a wide range of difficulties associated with staff changes, the quality of teaching and learning and, consequently, low student achievement. This was also compounded by concerns over the behaviour of many students. A range of interventions were introduced to engage students in learning and to improve their behaviour. One of these initiatives was the Alternative Education Programme, which was developed by the learning mentor and other teaching and support staff in an attempt to re-engage Years 10 and 11 students in learning.

Students who participated in the research had poor attendance and demonstrated challenging behaviour and low academic achievement. The 'typicality' (Cohen, Manion & Morrison, 2000, p. 103) of this group of students, in terms of the difficult relations they had with schooling, made it an ideal sample to investigate the processes through which some young people become disengaged from learning. The primary data set consisted of transcripts from a focus group and semi-structured interviews with six young people, a teacher and a learning mentor. Out of the six male participants who took part in the focus group and one-to-one interviews, one was white and five were of Black descent. Four were 15 and one had just turned 16 years of age.

Gutteridge (2002) defined a list of behaviours and dispositions, identified by teachers involved in a large study aimed at defining disaffection, and provided interesting insights into how some teachers define disconnection from learning. The set of behaviours could be summarised as: failure to heed teachers' instructions; task avoidance; lack of engagement in classroom activities; infringement of school uniform requirements; and lack of motivation. These behaviours were a useful starting point for discussions with the research participants at the beginning of the one-to-one and focus group interviews.

Additional data were generated through the notes made after each interview, which proved helpful during subsequent data analysis. The analysis involved a recursive process consisting of post-interview discussions with the participants, to identify how patterns in data related to aspects of in-school and out-of-school factors that contributed to students' disaffection, as they perceived them.

Analysis and discussion

Intersections of class, ethnicity and schooling

Naming 'race' or ethnicity as a factor to be considered in the academic achievement of students is problematic, as Omi and Winant (2002) point out:

> There is a continuous temptation to think of race as something fixed, concrete, and objective. And there is also an opposite temptation to imagine race as a mere illusion, a purely ideological construct which some ideal non-racist social order would eliminate. (p. 7)

Gillborn (2000, 2015) argues that naming 'race' explicitly is not the real issue, but it is how it is used, the context in which it is used and with what effects on others that should be closely examined. He suggests that a useful question to ask is whether the naming of 'race' has clear implications for 'race' and ethnic equality. Commenting on 'racial' categories deployed in education discourse, Gillborn argues that racialisation is 'spurious' when it is deliberately used to make links with crime statistics or other deficit representations of racialised groups, but there are times when de-racialising the discourse can have equally adverse effects on 'racial' and ethnic equality. For example, when education policy discourses are de-racialised in a liberal attempt to raise achievement among 'all' students, exclusion and oppression in schools and in the wider society are reproduced (Gillborn, 2015). There are, however, times when racialisation in discourse is 'legitimate'; for example, when using ethnic monitoring as a basis for deploying interventions to address equality issues in education (Gillborn, 2015). In a similar vein, commenting on the appallingly high numbers of African-Caribbean young men who are subjected to school exclusions, far more than any other group, Warren (2005) asserts that 'Given this knowledge, it is difficult for the education community to claim ignorance, and therefore an unwitting responsibility for the racialised and racialising effects of educational practices' (p. 244). He argues that such ignorance amounts to institutionalised forms of racism in schools and that de-racialising the discourse, despite the evidence of enduring inequalities in education outcomes, constitutes a blatant omission.

It is, however, important to be mindful that the categories of ethnicity and 'race' in particular, are complex, fluid and far from being homogeneous (Mills & Keddie, 2012; Watkins, 2011). Perhaps due to this complexity, the descriptions and explanations given by the teachers about the factors influencing marginalised students' experiences in the school where this research took place were often fraught with ambiguity and contradictions.

Class, ethnicity and implications for schooling: Promoting anti-discriminatory practice in schools

When asked to comment on definitions of a disaffected student, the teacher and the learning mentor in this study suggested that these definitions were reductive in their narrow focus on the individual characteristics of students as they did not take into account other factors that influenced the difficult relations that some young people had with education. Moreover, they both suggested that they could not see any connection between ethnicity and academic engagement. However, their descriptions were fraught with stereotypical generalisations about the negative influences that Black young men were exposed to. For example, the teacher blamed rap music for its negative influence on students due to its glorification of antisocial behaviour. Reference was also made by the learning mentor to a prevalent conception among Black young people of education being irrelevant due to a supposed belief that social divisions were such that gaining qualifications did not guarantee better career prospects. He attributed this to the influence of disillusioned older members of the Black 'community' whose experiences of institutional racism alienated them from mainstream society. He also made a link between disconnection from school and criminality by suggesting that some young people were seduced by the immediate gratification that drug dealing provided to those who were willing to truant and act as go-betweens for drug dealers and their clients. Such sweeping remarks embody discourses that ascribe social identities to young people based on a deficit model and echo policy makers' discourses on the vulnerabilities of disaffected Black young men to criminality, discussed earlier in this chapter.

The teacher and learning mentor argued that the link between ethnicity and academic outcomes was not clear-cut due to the demographic profile of the school where Black students were in the majority. However, 73% of the students who were excluded from the school in the preceding two years were from Black backgrounds. The teacher pointed out that white parents were more likely than Black parents to 'play the system' by getting their children statemented[2] to safeguard against permanent exclusion. He stated:

> Many males are disaffected. Many females, Black and white, are disaffected. The difference comes when an awful lot of white English – I'll start with the white English. When their children become disaffected, they know how to play the game. They get their children statemented. Whereas an awful lot of Black parents don't and so they fall through, because they don't have the backup. (Excerpt from the interview transcript, Teacher)

The teacher is referring here to an assumed familiarity with the lengthy and at times cumbersome application procedures for statementing students. He also suggested that some parents influenced their children in ways that encouraged their engagement with learning, through involvement in completing homework, reading and regular attendance at Parents' and Teachers' Night. Active parental involvement in children's education, which the teacher attributed to white parents, gave students the possibility to understand and operate more successfully within the cultural norms and expectations of the school. Bourdieu (1986) argued that children's tastes and appreciation for privileged cultural forms acquired through socialisation, and specifically through parental influence, gave them advantages in an educational system that valorises highbrow culture. However, as will be discussed in the next section, the values and norms expressed by young people through, for example, the continual infringement of the school uniform code could

2   In the United Kingdom, statementing is a formal process of identifying students as having special educational needs, which can relate to emotional, social or behavioural difficulties as well as physical and sensory disabilities. This requires a statutory assessment under the *Education Act 1996*, which, once granted, makes it more difficult for schools to exclude students.

be interpreted as acts of solidarity among students in the collective resistance to mainstream school culture.

School uniform as a visible site of collective resistance

The main reasons given by young people for their lack of enthusiasm for schooling were focused on pedagogic relations with teachers, their perceptions of the curriculum being irrelevant and the influences that they, as a group, exerted on each other, although only the first point is discussed here. (For further reading, see Moustakim, 2011.) The students' stories pointed to the importance of the mutuality of respect in pedagogic relations with teachers. Respect was cited as an important element in their characterisation of a good teacher and not only led to reciprocation on their part, it also determined their level of engagement with a subject. Young people used words such as 'friendliness', 'respect', 'humour' and an 'easy-going attitude' to describe the qualities of a 'nice' teacher. On the other hand, 'disrespect', 'sarcasm' and 'rudeness' were used to describe a teacher who was not considered to be 'nice'. Their descriptions suggest that, while subject preference was a motivating factor in their level of enthusiasm for learning, their perception of a 'nice' teacher determined the extent of their engagement with learning. This echoes Warren's (2005) accounts of how the young men in his study negotiated what he called 'asymmetrical economies of respect' (p. 249) in their relations with teachers whose inconsistent and disproportionate enforcement of discipline led to differential treatments of individual young men by different teachers. Respect was tied to power relations between young people and their teachers, mediated through school discourse conventions and expressed in a set of rules that permeated all aspects of teaching and learning. The teachers were involved in regulating and monitoring young people's adherence to conventions relating to a wide range of school activities, from assessment to the management of space and young people's presentation and behaviour in school. Furthermore, Black young men were often subjected to 'greater surveillance and control' (Youdell, 2003, p. 97). This engendered a sense of unfairness and created an atmosphere of disrespect and withdrawal. The young people explained that their resistance to teachers' demands for conformity in school was due to their reluctance to be labelled as 'neek' by peers. One of the definitions of a 'neek' given by the students was: 'Yeah they would like have their trousers high, shirt tucked in, long tie. They always sit in the front and always do their homework. They raise their hands to speak and always want to please the teacher' (James, Year 10).

The ascription of the label 'neek' was a counter-discourse to the teachers' discourse of disaffection, and represented students who complied with school expectations as undesirable. Neeks were subjected to taunts and bullying. Solidarity was evident in the students' adherence to group norms, which deviated from the expectations of the school. The conformity demands placed on students were a major source of conflict, usually around the expectation to wear the uniform correctly. The struggle between the teachers and students over the correct way to wear the uniform was relentless. In addition to the strategies used by the students to challenge teachers' authority through overt and covert means in class, the uniform offered a visible site of collective resistance. Many young people wore the trousers far below the hips or wore shoes with the laces undone and ties almost undone so that only two stripes were revealed rather than four, as required by the school uniform code.

The enforcement of the school uniform code began at the school gate each morning. It was a ritual that involved teachers making students take off their trainers, put on their school shoes, which were normally kept in the school bag, pull up their trousers and do their ties up to a specification. In his seminal work on **youth resistance**, Clarke (1976) argues that youth oppositional performances embody 'interventions' against cultural domination. The students were simultaneously challenging the authority of teachers, while exerting pressure on peers to not conform to the school's normative expectations. O'Donnell and Sharpe state that 'Schools engage in what is sometimes a losing battle to counterbalance the collective influence of the peer group, particularly the male peer group' (O'Donnell & Sharpe, 2000, p. 89). Moreover, Hebdidge (2005) argues that the spectacular oppositional performances displayed by young people are attempts to gain independence from the dominant adult culture and 'represent creative attempts to try to win autonomy or space from dominant cultures' (p. 55). However, although the students referred to as 'neek' faced derision and ridicule from peers, they understood the rules of the 'game' well and the dispositions, values and attitudes, or habitus, they had gained from their cultural milieu enabled them to respond appropriately to the choices and requirements they had to negotiate in school (Webb, Sherato & Danaher, 2003).

> **Youth resistance** young people's refusal to conform to school norms and expectations expressed through oppositional behaviour, such as not complying with the rules and specifications for wearing the school uniform.

Implications

The discussion in this chapter has mainly focused on the significance of class and ethnicity on students' academic outcomes and experiences of schooling. In order to disrupt the reproduction of class privilege in schools, it is important for teachers to develop a critical understanding of how cultural capital, field and habitus are played out in schools. They should provide supportive classroom environments that value difference and promote mutual respect. Teachers must also be prepared to challenge discourses and practices that normalise and sustain social inequality.

Drawing on Thompson's (2012) Personal, Cultural and Structural (PCS) model of anti-discriminatory practice, the discussion that follows points to three areas in which educators can challenge this discrimination. The model suggests that discrimination potentially comes from different sources, including ourselves, termed as 'personal'; our interactions with others, defined as 'cultural'; and how institutions, such as schools, are organised, referred to as 'structural'.

The personal part of the PCS model requires teachers to engage critically in personal reflexivity in relation to their understandings of equity and diversity issues; that is, to reflect on their own attitudes, values and beliefs in relation to difference and diversity and raise questions about the implications of these for their professional practice. This is because our background knowledge and experience of the social world influence how we see and relate to others. The linguistic, cultural and social diversity in contemporary schools, in countries such as Australia and the United Kingdom, requires teachers to develop critical awareness of the implications of this diversity for their daily interactions with students and their communities. This is particularly important given that research on Australian pre-service teachers' understandings of diversity points to a mismatch between their life experiences and those of their students (Mills & Keddie, 2012). As discussed by Lampert and Burnett in Chapter 5, a lack of critical awareness of equity and diversity issues may result in pre-service teachers making inaccurate assumptions about their students and their communities.

In a study that examined pedagogical relationships between teachers and children from low SES and Indigenous backgrounds in three Australian primary schools, Hatton et al. (2006) found that where teachers viewed children's 'poverty as deficiency', and not 'poverty as poverty' (Connell, 1993, cited in Hatton et al., 2006, p. 48), the education outcomes for students were very poor. However, in schools where teachers had overt political commitments to making a difference in the lives of their students and their communities, the students' achievements and experiences of schooling were much better. Hatton et al. (2006) argued that in schools where students achieved low academic outcomes, staffroom culture supported the view of poverty as deficiency and promoted the lowering of expectations from their students.

The latter point relates to Thompson's (2012) cultural dimension of anti-discriminatory practice. He argues that in order to address discrimination at the cultural level, teachers must be prepared to challenge others' sexist, racist, homophobic or similar stereotypical representations and practices in professional contexts and beyond. Banter is often used in the staffroom cultures, which Hatton and colleagues (2006) describe as the insidious effects of stereotypical representations of the minority Other, which can only be discouraged through critique and constructive challenge.

The structural dimension of the PCS model of anti-discriminatory practice relates to identifying and redressing implicit and explicit institutional barriers to equity and fairness in professional practice. Barriers to achieving equitable outcomes may result from the enactment of policies that disadvantage members of certain minority groups. For example, in the Australian context, one of the main reasons for the enduring achievement gaps between Indigenous and non-Indigenous students was the axing of bilingual education in the 1990s, which substantially reduced the number of Aboriginal teachers (Ford, 2013), estimated to be at less than 1% of the total number of Australian teachers (Keddie et al., 2013). The Australian Government introduced the 'More Aboriginal and Torres Strait Islander Teachers Initiative' (MATSITI, 2012) with the aim of increasing Aboriginal people's participation and retention in the teaching profession. However, it is important to examine critically the culturalist assumptions that underpin some equity initiatives (Keddie et al., 2013). As noted by Keddie and colleagues, teachers should engage critically with equity-focused policies or strategies introduced by governments. They argue that this is a necessary requirement that permits movement beyond the notions of culturalism and racial incommensurability that homogenise indigeneity within and against dominant white norms.

Conclusion

Evidence from research conducted in Britain and in Australia shows that the intersections of class, ethnicity and 'race' exacerbate the disproportionality of low educational outcomes for students from Black, Indigenous and minority groups. However, dominant discourses about students' underachievements continue to locate explanations of educational inequality in the affective, behavioural and cognitive deficits of young people and fail to take into account other highly significant in-school and out-of-school factors that can determine success or failure in education. One of the key in-school factors cited by young people who took part in the research reported on in this chapter pointed to the significance of the influence of peers on their disconnection from learning. Of more importance, however, was that the extent of their engagement with curriculum subjects was contingent on the quality of the relationships they had with their teachers.

Some of the out-of-school factors considered in this chapter are ethnicity and social class. It is clear that Pierre Bourdieu's theoretical concepts of habitus, field and capital still provide useful lenses for examining how social class is played out in schools, particularly with reference to how school exclusions are mitigated by parents who know how to 'play' the system.

It is imperative for teachers to engage critically with equity-focused policy responses to differential educational outcomes between students. This is because, despite their well-meaning intentions, some initiatives embody culturalist assumptions that emphasise racial difference and incommensurability rather than a common human right to a good education, irrespective of ethnic or 'racial' background.

To engage in anti-discriminatory practice, teachers, particularly those with limited understanding of the impact of inequity, should start with examining their own values and beliefs about equity and diversity issues. This is important because they will teach students from diverse backgrounds and different identities. Teachers should also be prepared to challenge structural barriers that can limit students' potential for development and growth. Only then can they be assured that they are providing an inclusive education for all children.

Considerations

- Cultural capital has strong effects on education outcomes. How might schools provide opportunities for students to exchange forms of capital through pedagogy, curriculum and policy?
- What does culturalism mean? What are its effects on students from minority groups?

- Why is it important for teachers to examine critically the assumptions upon which some of the equity-focused initiatives are based?

Of interest

- Longitudinal Surveys of Australian Youth (LSAY). See http://www.lsay.edu.au/aboutlsay
- 'Race discrimination' (Australian Human Rights Commission). See https://www.humanrights.gov.au/race-discrimination
- 'Children and schooling' (Department of the Prime Minister and Cabinet – Indigenous Affairs). See http://www.indigenous.gov.au/children-and-schooling

References

Allan, D. (2015). Mediated disaffection and reconfigured subjectivities: The impact of a vocational learning environment on the re-engagement of 14–16-year-olds. *International Journal on School Disaffection*, 11(2), 45–65. doi.org/10.18546/IJSD.11.2.03

Blanden, J., Hanson, K. & Machin, S. (2008). *The GDP cost of the lost earning potential of adults who grew up in poverty*. York, UK: Joseph Roundtree Foundation. Retrieved from: https://www.org.uk/report/gdp-cost-lost-earning-potential-adults-who-grew-poverty

Blanden, J. & Macmillan, L. (2016). Educational inequality, educational expansion and intergenerational mobility. *Cambridge University Press Journal of Social Policy*, 45(4), 589–614. doi:10.1017/S004727941600026X

Bourdieu, P. (1986). The forms of capital. In J. Richardson (Ed.), *Handbook of theory and research for the sociology of education*. London: Routledge.

—— (1989). Social space and symbolic power. *Sociological Theory*, 7, 14–25. doi:10.2307/202060

Clarke, J. (1976). Style. In S. Hall & T. Jefferson (Eds.), *Resistance through rituals: Youth subcultures in post-war Britain*. London: Hutchinson.

Cohen, L., Manion, L. & Morrison, K. (2000). *Research methods in education* (5th ed.). London: Routledge.

Ford, M. (2013). Achievement gaps in Australia: What NAPLAN reveals about education inequality in Australia. *Race Ethnicity and Education*, 16(1), 80–102. doi:10.1080/13613324.2011.645570

Gaddis, M. (2014). The influence of habitus in the relationship between cultural capital and academic achievement. *Social Science Research*, 42(1), 1–13. doi:10.1016/j.ssresearch.2012.08.002

Gillborn, D. (2000). Anti-racism: From policy to praxis. In B. Moon, S. Brown & M. Ben-Peretz (Eds.), *Routledge international companion to education.* London: Routledge.

—— (2008). *Racism and education: Coincidence or conspiracy?* Abingdon, UK: Routledge.

—— (2015). Intersectionality, critical race theory, and the primacy of racism. *Qualitative Inquiry,* 21(3), 277–87. doi:10.1177/1077800414557827

Gray, J. & Beresford, Q. (2008). A 'formidable challenge': Australia's quest for equity in Indigenous education. *Australian Journal of Education,* 52(2), 35–49. doi:10.1177/000494410805200207

Gutteridge, D. (2002). Identifying disaffection. *Journal of Pedagogy, Culture and Society,* 10(2), 161–8. doi:10.1080/14681360200200137

Harrison, N. & Greenfield, M. (2011). Relationship to place: Positioning Aboriginal knowledge and perspectives in classroom pedagogies. *Critical Studies in Education,* 52(1), 65–76. doi:10.1080/17508487.2011.536513

Hatton, E., Munns, G. & Dent, J. N. (2006). Teaching children in poverty: Three Australian primary school responses. *British Journal of Sociology of Education,* 17(1), 39–52. doi:10.1080/0142569960170103

Hebdidge, D. (2005). The function of subculture. In S. During (Ed.), *The cultural studies reader* (2nd ed.). London: Routledge.

House of Commons (1998). *Select Committee on Education and Employment fifth report: Tackling disaffection.* London: Author. Retrieved from http://www.publications.parliament.uk/pa/cm199798/cmselect/cmeduemp/498v/ee0503.htm

Keddie, A., Gowlett, C., Mills, M., Monk, S. & Renshaw, P. (2013). Beyond culturalism: Addressing issues of Indigenous disadvantage through schooling. *Australian Educational Researcher,* 40(1), 91–108. doi:10.1007/s13384-012-0080-x

Levitas, R. (2010). Introduction: Inequality and social exclusion. In A. Walker, D. Gordon, R. Levitas, P. Phillimore, C. Phillipson, M. E. Salomon & N. Yeates (Eds.), *The Peter Townsend reader* (pp. 270–4). London: Policy Press.

Mills, C. & Keddie, A. (2012). 'Fixing' student deficit in contexts of diversity: Another cautionary tale for pre-service teacher education. *International Journal of Pedagogies and Learning,* 7(1), 9–19. doi:10.5172/ijpl.2012.7.1.9

Ministerial Council for Education, Early Childhood Development and Youth Affairs (2009). *NAPLAN reading Indigenous and non-Indigenous 2009.* Retrieved from http://www.mceecdya.edu.au/verve/_resources/NAPLAN2009-Indig-Reading.pdf

More Aboriginal and Torres Strait Islander Teachers Initiative (2012). *More Aboriginal and Torres Strait Islander Teachers Initiative (MATSITI).* Retrieved November 2014 from http://matsiti.edu.au/

Moustakim, M. (2011). Reproducing disaffection. *International Journal on School Disaffection*, 8(2), 14–23. Retrieved from http://web.b.ebscohost.com/ehost/pdfviewer/pdfviewer?sid=b672d4dd-5e53–4a7c-8088-e5a765612e78%40sessionmgr111&vid=2&hid=102

O'Donnell, M. & Sharpe, S. (2000). *Uncertain masculinities: Youth, ethnicity and class in contemporary Britain*. London: Routledge.

Omi, M. & Winant, H. (2002). Racial formation. In P. Essed & D. Goldberg (Eds.), *Race critical theories*. Oxford: Blackwell.

Osler, A. & Starkey, H. (2005). Violence in schools and representations of young people: A critique of government policies in France and England. *Oxford Review of Education*, 31(2), 195–215. doi:10.1080/03054980500117728

Parsons, C. (2005). School disaffection: Perspectives from across Europe. *The International Journal on School Disaffection*, 3(2), 39–43. Retrieved from http://web.b.ebscohost.com/ehost/pdfviewer/pdfviewer?sid=bfae1502–4eb6–4b47–9313-d52dfa93f79f%40sessionmgr114&vid=1&hid=102

Pilger, J. (1989). *A secret country*. London: Jonathan Cape.

Thompson, N. (2012). *Anti-discriminatory practice: Equality, diversity and social justice*. Basingstoke, UK: Palgrave Macmillan.

Tramonte, L. & Willms, J. D. (2010). Cultural capital and its effects on education outcomes. *Economics of Education Review*, 29(2), 200–13. doi:10.1016/j. econedurev .2009.06.003

Warren, S. (2005). Resilience and refusal: African-Caribbean young men's agency, school exclusions and school-based mentoring programmes. *Race, Ethnicity and Education*, 8(3), 243–59. doi:10.1080/13613320500174283

Watkins, M. (2011). Complexity, reduction, regularities and rules: Grappling with cultural diversity in schooling. *Continuum*, 25(6), 841–56. doi:10.1080/1030431 2.2011.617876

Watson, D. (2011). Urban but not too urban: Unpacking teachers' desires to teach urban students. *Journal of Teacher Education*, 62(1), 23–34. doi:10.1177/0022487110379216

Webb, J., Shirato, T. & Danaher, G. (2003). Bourdieu and secondary schools. In *Understanding Bourdieu* (pp. 105–26). Sydney: Allen & Unwin.

Windle, J. (2008). The racialization of African youth in Australia. *Social Identities: Journal for the Study of Race, Nation and Culture*, 14(5), 533–66. doi:10.1080/13504630802343382

Wintour, P. & Vikram D. (2007, April 12). Blair blames spate of murders on black culture. *The Guardian*. Retrieved from http://www.theguardian.com/politics/2007/apr/12/ukcrime.race

Youdell, D. (2003). Identity traps or how black students fail: The interaction between biographical, sub-cultural and learner identities. *British Journal of Sociology of Education*, 24(1), 3–20. doi:10.1080/01425690301912

Part 3

Using Critical Theory

CHAPTER 9

Culture, hybridity and globalisation

Rethinking multicultural education in schools

Megan Watkins

AUSTRALIAN PROFESSIONAL STANDARDS FOR TEACHERS

Standard 1: Know students and how they learn

1.3 Students with diverse linguistic, cultural, religious and socio-economic backgrounds

This chapter will develop teachers' knowledge of theory relevant to understanding the cultural complexity of the student populations of the schools in which they teach and of the broader community beyond. It will encourage them to rethink established practices around multicultural education and to avoid forms of cultural essentialising that can have repercussions for student learning.

I don't have a culture, miss. I'm not different. (Alice[1], aged 9 years)

Introduction

In writing this chapter I am reminded of the 2014 downing of flight MH17 in the Ukraine. This was a tragic event, but one that resonates with many of the themes to be examined here around culture, hybridity and globalisation, their impact on schooling and the preparedness of teachers and students to meet the challenges

---

1   Pseudonyms are used to refer to the school and all research participants in this chapter.

they pose, some of which I see encapsulated in the young student's comment that opens this chapter. MH17 was a Malaysian Airlines flight en route to Kuala Lumpur from Amsterdam. It was carrying 298 passengers and crew of varying nationalities, though predominantly Dutch, Malaysian and Australian. Some on board had dual citizenship. Many others were resident in various countries on a permanent or temporary basis. Passengers were travelling for various reasons: holiday, work, study, family reunion. The plane was also carrying the passengers' luggage and various possessions, manufactured and purchased in numerous sites across the globe. Together with this, the plane 'carried' less tangible items: the expertise, for example, of those travelling to Melbourne for an international AIDS conference; the transnational contacts those and other passengers had forged in the pursuit of their work and travel. This global connectedness is, of course, repeated thousands of times over on a daily basis in journeys across the globe. Malaysian Airlines itself, while a national carrier, operates as a transnational business, having links with numerous airlines worldwide. This illustrates not only how globalisation operates through transnational flows of people, goods, services, capital and labour, but of culture itself: the complex entanglements of ideas, understandings and practices resulting in a hybrid mix that is characteristic of the everyday reality for many. Other aspects of globalisation that the downing of flight MH17 serves to highlight include the speed with which information, images and commentary flashed around the globe through the resources of digitised news and social media; and the almost immediate reaction of governments worldwide and supranational agencies, such as the United Nations, drawing on their own international networks, forms of communication and surveillance, to condemn, assess and assist. Yet, together with this tragic event demonstrating the globalised nature of the world in which we live, it also serves to highlight quite the opposite – the tenacity of the nation as a conceptual frame. In fact the plane's very downing was a result of conflict over national allegiance, ethnic divisions and territorial disputes. This firming of boundaries is also enacted in other ways: the counting of the dead and the priority national governments give to those they claim as theirs.

The event is insightful, therefore, in what it reveals about the push and pull of the global and the national and how we are all enmeshed in processes of cultural flux and fixity, which brings me back to the comment that opened this chapter. Alice, the little girl who made this remark, was in a Year 3 class in an ethnically diverse school in the outer-western suburbs of Sydney participating in a project around multicultural education. Alice's teacher had set students the task of compiling digital photo stories about their cultural backgrounds, highlighting their country of birth and aspects of 'their culture's' customs and food. Alice, of Anglo-Australian background, however, was a little confused. She did not feel she could complete the task because, as she explained, 'I don't have a culture, miss. I'm not different'. How is it that Alice can make a statement like this? What does it reveal about her place in the world – or at least how she sees it? There is little of the global connectedness that has just been described or affinity with the cultural diversity characteristic of Australia as a multicultural nation. To Alice, culture represents difference, something of which she is not a part. Multicultural education, it seems, has not been as inclusive as intended, not only setting Alice apart from her class-mates, whom she sees as 'different', but, in the process, casting them as Other, quite distinct from the Anglo mainstream.

This chapter puts multicultural education under the spotlight. It examines how it has been influenced by understandings of culture and ethnicity that framed early policies of multiculturalism and how increasing cultural complexity resulting from globalisation and mass migration requires us to reconsider how we engage with issues around cultural diversity in schooling. This is especially pertinent within an Australian context, with the National Curriculum requiring teachers to promote intercultural understanding in relevant subjects across the curriculum (Australian Curriculum, Assessment and Reporting Authority [ACARA], 2013). But to what extent does intercultural understanding differ from current programs of multicultural education? Following a discussion of these issues and the theoretical concepts that assist us to make sense of their ramifications for education, we will examine how these ideas play out in schools by considering recent research in this area into how teachers and students are grappling with these ideas.

Background

Multiculturalism: policy and practice

'Multiculturalism' is a term that has various meanings. To many it is simply used to refer to Australia's **cultural diversity** – that we are a society comprised of many 'different cultures'. To others, multiculturalism has a quite specific meaning, denoting particu-lar policies and practices involved in managing that diversity. In a sense it functions as a term of both description and prescrip-tion (Kalantzis, 2013, p. 92), and it is important to make a distinc-tion between the two, given these very different meanings. Not all nations with culturally diverse populations, for instance, have pol-

> **Cultural diversity** the varying nature of socio-cultural experience that includes: class, ethnicity, gender, sexuality, religion etc. Although the focus in this chapter is on cultural diversity as it pertains to ethnicity, it is important to recognise culture as a broader term with various meanings.

icies of multiculturalism that encourage both cultural maintenance among migrant groups and the recognition and respect of the practices in which they engage. Also, those countries that do, may apply the term 'multiculturalism' quite differently. In Sweden, for example, where since 1974 multiculturalism has been enshrined in the constitution, it is a term applied quite broadly, encompassing diversity in terms of gender, nationality, ethnicity, colour, age, sexuality and dis/ability. In Australia, multiculturalism has a much narrower focus. Both in its description of society and in relation to particular policies and programs, 'culture' in 'multiculturalism' generally equates to ethnicity, conceived in terms of distinct and cohesive eth-nic communities, and quite separate from our understandings of Indigenous cul-tures. This distinction is maintained especially in terms of policy to ensure that the different issues pertaining to migrant and Aboriginal Australians are addressed accordingly and that full recognition is given to the latter as Australia's original inhabitants. Multiculturalism, therefore, relates to the cultural or ethnic diversity stemming from immigration to which policies of multiculturalism, dating back to the 1970s, give recognition. This is in contrast to earlier policies of assimilation and integration that sought to either erase or suppress cultural difference, following Australia's increasing levels of immigration after World War II. In addition to cultural recognition, policies of multiculturalism are also designed to counter discrimination and ensure equal access and opportunity within society (Department of Social Services [DSS], 2011).

Despite what many would view as the success of multiculturalism in Australia, and studies demonstrating broad acceptance of cultural diversity (Ang, Brand, Noble & Sternberg, 2006; Dunn, Forrest, Burnley & McDonald, 2004), multiculturalism has always been 'a contested policy and concept' (Koleth, 2010, p. 2). This seemed particularly the case during John Howard's prime ministership, with a weakening in government commitment evident in his abolition of the Office of Multicultural Affairs and the renaming of the Department of Immigration and Multiculturalism to that of Immigration and Citizenship. Criticism of multiculturalism also increased following 9/11 and the threat of global terrorism associated with the rise of Islamic fundamentalism. Critics of multiculturalism argue its emphasis on cultural maintenance has resulted in social fragmentation, heightening risks to national security. Although such criticism has led to many conservative commentators questioning the viability of multiculturalism (Akerman, 2001; Albrechtsen, 2002), in 2011 the federal Labor government issued a multicultural policy, restating its commitment to key principles of cultural recognition and anti-discrimination (DSS, 2011). This has been followed by the Turnbull Liberal government's 2017 statement, *Multicultural Australia: United, Strong, Successful* (DSS, 2017).

The key difference between this 2017 document and the 2011 policy is the omission of any reference to multiculturalism. Instead, this more recent statement gives emphasis to multicultural Australia in a descriptive sense, seemingly distancing itself from multiculturalism's perceived association with social fragmentation. The document highlights the importance of social cohesion and worryingly frames support for Australia's cultural diversity with concerns over global terrorism and the need for stronger border protection. In doing so, ethnic difference is cast as a potential threat to Australia's security, providing only qualified support for a multicultural Australia. Malcolm Turnbull's ascendency to prime minister, therefore, saw little change in the conservatism that characterised the government of Tony Abbott (2013–15), who in 2013 similarly qualified his support for Australia's cultural diversity. With specific reference to skilled migrants – a preferred category of immigration over family reunion and humanitarian programs – Abbott remarked that they 'come here to join us, not to change us' (Liberal Party of Australia, 2013). Whether it is possible for a nation, and a perceived dominant culture, to remain 'intact' alongside a program of immigration, however regulated, is a matter we'll return to below, but it seems particularly unrealistic, given our earlier discussion of globalisation, that any nation, anywhere, could be resistant to change, or indeed would want to be! A further name change to the Department of Immigration and Citizenship, replacing the latter with *Border Protection*, alongside the Australian Attorney-General George Brandis's attempt in March 2014 to dilute protections within the Commonwealth *Racial Discrimination Act* 1975 by claiming that 'people have a right to be bigots' (Harrison & Swan, 2014, p. 1), indicates a lack of government commitment to multiculturalism.

Yet, critique of multiculturalism is not simply the preserve of the political right. Left-leaning commentators and academics also have reservations about multiculturalism, at least in terms of how it has operated as public policy. Such critiques are not levelled at the cultural diversity of Australia's population but rather at how it is conceived and managed. Cultural theorist Ien Ang (2001; 2014), for example, is critical of the ways in which policies and practices of multiculturalism tend to essentialise ethnicity as if it is the single determinant of an individual's identity rather than one of a range of contributing factors along with class, gender, sexuality, religion, age, education – not to mention individual experience. Such a process is often attributed to the identity politics formulated in response to assimilatory policies that thwarted any expression of cultural identification beyond the Anglo mainstream (Watkins & Noble, 2014). In asserting a particular ethnic identity, important especially in lobbying government for services and resources for marginalised communities, Ang (2001, p. 11) feels 'that very identity is also the name of a potential prison house'. In saying this, she is not trying to devalue the powerful sense of belonging individuals and groups attach to such forms of identification, but to question the ways in which ethnicity is then cast as the defining feature of identity, reified as stable and unchanging, which becomes a marker of difference, creating artificial boundaries between people (Watkins & Noble, 2014). It is this view of ethnicity that she feels is characteristic of multiculturalism, evident in its seemingly inclusive logic of recognition but which results in the kind of understanding that Alice (above) exhibits wherein she equates culture with difference. Multiculturalism is also critiqued for operating as a moralising discourse in that ethnic difference is to be respected and celebrated with a focus on the food and customs of the exotic Other through events such as the now ubiquitous multicultural day (Youdell, 2012). Such activities many dismiss as banal forms of cosmo-multiculturalism (Hage, 1998; Noble & Poynting, 2000) that serve to obscure a more meaningful focus on racism and forms of structural inequality that remain unchecked amid the celebration.

The inclusion of intercultural understanding in Australia's National Curriculum as a capability to be promoted across various subjects could be interpreted as an attempt to address what some view as the shortcomings of **multicultural education**, at least in terms of a more critical interrogation of questions of cultural identification. In contrast, the intent of intercultural understanding is to encourage critical reflection upon one's own cultural identity, its contextual variability and the numerous factors, beyond ethnicity, that are constitutive of its ongoing production. These insights are then to be utilised in interaction with others whom we may perceive as different (ACARA, 2013, p. 86). Also, whereas multiculturalism is associated with the cultural diversity of Australia's migrant populations, intercultural understanding seeks a broader engagement, inclusive of Indigenous cultures.

Multicultural education
an umbrella term that in Australia refers to a range of programs in schools, designed to meet the needs of migrant and refugee students and their families and to promote intercultural understanding across the curriculum.

Interestingly, given the long history of multiculturalism in Australia, and the traction of the term in public discourse, it seems unusual it is not given prominence in the documentation on intercultural understanding. In fact there is only one reference in passing to multicultural education as one of a number of fields from which intercultural understanding originates (ACARA, 2013, p. 85).

In Europe, where interculturalism has a much higher profile, it is now favoured by many as a more inclusive concept than multiculturalism. Some, however, critique interculturalism as simply a backlash against multiculturalism, and that its emergence, given government concerns over social cohesion since 9/11, may represent a return to assimilation in another guise. The degree to which intercultural understanding, as it is understood in an Australian context, actually differs from multiculturalism is not clear. 'Inter', for example, seems to suggest boundaries to be crossed, and so the immutability of culture, and 'understanding' could signify both an intellectual engagement – understanding how identities are shaped – and an ethical stance – involving empathy and an unreflexive valuing of cultural difference – not dissimilar to multiculturalism (Watkins, Lean, Noble & Dunn, 2013). If intercultural understanding within the National Curriculum intends to foreground the former, and steer clear of the slippage from an ethical stance into the type of moralising of which multiculturalism is often accused, greater clarification of its intent is needed. Also, teachers require the necessary intellectual and critical capacities to engage in the forms of cultural analysis with their students that can shed light on the hyperdiversity with which schools and the broader Australian community are now faced. It is here that theory has an important role to play.

Key theoretical concepts

Theorising cultural complexity

Globalisation a term used to refer to the transnational flows of people, capital, goods, information and technology exacerbated by advances in transport and computer technology.

Cultural hybridity the lending and borrowing between different cultural practices, experienced through multiple contradictions, connections and possibilities. Cultural adaptation, intermarriage, intergenerational change and globalisation give rise to these forms of cultural mixing. Cultural hybridity counters understandings of ethnicity as discrete and bounded and acknowledges the fluidity of cultural forms.

There are a range of different, yet related, theoretical perspectives that are useful in exploring issues of cultural complexity, in particular critical and cultural theory around cultural identity, postcolonialism, **globalisation**, transnationalism and cosmopolitanism. Each of these, in one way or another, has influenced sociological thought in this area, together with other disciplines across the humanities and social sciences, such as cultural studies and anthropology. All of these are given some consideration here as we develop the necessary theoretical tools to think through some of the implications of cultural diversity for schooling and to provide a foundation for interpreting the research to be presented later in this chapter. To some extent we have already touched on some of these theoretical perspectives in our discussion of multiculturalism and intercultural understanding. Ang, for example, draws on the work of postcolonial theorist Homi K. Bhabha in her critique of multiculturalism and theorisation of **cultural hybridity**.

Postcolonialism is a theoretical perspective that focuses on the cultural legacy of colonialism, questions this raises about self and national identity, and the persistence of colonial thinking and white domination in postmodern contexts. Cultural theorist Stuart Hall has also informed Ang's work. He similarly makes use of postcolonial theory in grappling with questions of cultural identity and his insights about the role of theory are particularly pertinent here. He points out that, in trying to make sense of key issues around culture and society, it is important to make a 'detour through theory'[2] (cited in Ang, 2001, p. 168). Both theorists, however, caution against theory for theory's sake, explaining how theory needs to be 'put to work' to help us move beyond approaching issues from a purely personal perspective and to think more broadly in understanding the complex nature of the world in which we live. How, for example, would we respond to Alice? There's not much point in trying to explain postcolonial theory to a nine-year-old, however relevant, but it would be extremely useful to draw on the insights it and cultural theory more broadly provide in helping her to rethink how she understands culture. It would be helpful, for example, to ask: What is culture? – a question we'll now attempt to answer, but one that is not as straightforward as it might seem.

Cultural theorist Raymond Williams described culture as 'one of the two or three most complicated words in the English language' (Williams, 1983, p. 87) and, in 1952, anthropologists Kroeber and Kluckhohn identified 164 different definitions of the word (Kroeber & Kluckhohn, 1952). Clearly, 'culture' can be understood in many different ways. It is a term we attach to 'something' of various sizes and scales, from the global to the local and operating at the level of society, the individual and everything in between. Processes of globalisation, for example, have led many to refer to the existence of a global culture (Featherstone, 1990) and it is a term we typically use in relation to different nations, such as Australian or American culture. It is also a term we assign to certain social groupings, such as 'working-class culture' or 'youth cultures', and to smaller subsets or subcultures, such as 'punk culture' or 'emo culture'. It is a term used to describe certain lifestyles, such as 'consumer culture'. We similarly see it applied in discussion of institutions, such as 'workplace culture' and 'academic culture', or religions, such as Islamic, Christian or Jewish culture. It may even denote an emotional climate, such as a culture of fear, and it is common within New Age literature to refer to one's 'personal culture'. Culture is also a term used to explain what would otherwise be conceived of as political or economic (Yúdice, 2003). Politicians and the media use it on a regular basis as an explanation for various social problems: the culture of entitlement, for example, used by conservative politicians to explain a reliance on welfare, the root cause of which may be structural unemployment.

Clearly 'culture' is a term that is understood in a variety of ways and is used to serve a number of different purposes. What is similar to each is that 'culture' denotes a certain coherence in terms of meanings, values and practices; it signifies commonality. But, in grouping 'like' together we are also engaged in processes of

2   Others, such as Lawrence Grossberg, make a similar point. See Ang (2001, p. 168) for a discussion of these ideas.

differentiation, what sociologist Eviatar Zerubavel refers to as 'contrasting yet complementary cognitive acts of lumping and splitting' (Zerubavel, 1996, p. 421). Such processes help us to make sense of the world, but at the same time can be reductive if we view the categories that order our thinking as truths rather than simply a matter of perception. In general terms, this represents the difference between the theoretical paradigms of structuralism and poststructuralism; the former focusing on systematising experience and its categorisation, and the latter the contestation of these categories and the rejection of such wholesale systematicity (see Chapter 1 in this volume). Structuralist thought, however, has been influential across a range of different disciplines. Given its prominence during the first half of the twentieth century, it had a major impact on fledgling disciplines, such as anthropology and sociology. Anthropological inquiry sought the identification of different cultures and the systematic relations that characterised them. This is a view of culture that persists to this day and is evident in policies of multiculturalism, which tend to give recognition to what are viewed as distinct cultural traits. Reference is made, for example, to the Chinese community or the Lebanese community as if all those who possess either a Chinese or Lebanese heritage can be thought of as homogeneous groups engaged in similar practices and with similar world views. Such understandings have long since been critiqued within anthropology and sociology (Watkins & Noble, 2014). In the late 1960s, anthropologist Fredrik Barth critiqued the idea of ethnicity as a primordial category. He highlighted its social constructedness and the ways in which ethnic boundaries are maintained through processes of inclusion and exclusion by both those within and those outside a group (Watkins & Noble, 2014). These ideas around the social constructedness of ethnicity have been developed by many others, most notably sociologist Rogers Brubaker, who, in his account of 'ethnicity without groups', reminds us that, 'ethnicity, race and nationhood exist only in and through our perceptions, interpretations, categorisations and identifications. They are not things *in* the world but perspectives *on* the world' (Brubaker, 2002, p. 174, emphasis in original).

Postcolonial thought is clearly influential here. It emphasises a blurring of ethnic categories, with Homi K. Bhabha (2004) referring to the 'third space', the intermingling of cultures and the formation of hybrid identities; understandings attuned to the impact of globalisation and its resultant transnational flows that challenge conceptions of culture as fixed and unchanging (see Chapters 1 and 7 in this volume). But what is the impact of these ideas on educational practice and, in particular, how multicultural education operates in schools? Norma Gonzalez writes that, 'While many anthropologists may bemoan the essentialism and reification of bounded and shared cultural traits … the reality is that academic critical discourses have been slow to penetrate curricular practices in schools' (Gonzalez, 1999, p. 431). This comment was written almost 20 years ago and yet very little seems to have changed. We see these same ideas recycled in classrooms on a daily basis. Educational rhetoric may be littered with references to the promotion of 'global citizenship' and 'intercultural understanding', but if students are to develop more cosmopolitan dispositions of openness to others and the critical capacities to make sense of the hyperdiversity around them – both within the national frame and beyond – teachers need to be able to broker the requisite knowledge to enable them to do so. They need to be able to respond to the kind of comment that Alice made. Culture is not simply about difference, it is as much about what we have in common. The boundary markers that we put in place to separate us are, by and large, artificial. In light of this, it would be useful to bear in mind the comments of social anthropologist Marilyn Strathern (1995, p. 153), who points out that 'The nice thing about culture is that everyone has it'.

Methodology

In recent research conducted in schools as part of the Rethinking Multiculturalism/ Reassessing Multicultural Education (RMRME) Project (Watkins & Noble, 2014), understandings about culture and ethnicity similar to those expressed by Alice were found to be quite prevalent. Before we take a closer look at some of these and then focus on how teachers in one school approached multicultural education, I want to give a brief account of the methodologies we employed in collecting these data. RMRME involved a range of methodologies – quantitative and qualitative – and so, as a whole, it used a mixed-method approach. Initially, a survey of NSW public school teachers was conducted to collect data on the cultural and linguistic diversity of the teaching population and practices around multicultural education (see Watkins et al., 2013). These data were then used with teachers in the 14 project schools involved in the study, which were a mix of primary/secondary, of high and low socio-economic status (SES), high and low LBOTE[3] and from a spread of urban and rural areas. We matched these data with those collected from the surveys of all staff in each of these schools to allow them to see how their own school fared in comparison to the state overall.

These comparative surveys operated as useful baseline data to help schools formulate site-specific projects around issues related to multicultural education. Five-member research teams comprised of teachers and executives in each school devised research plans, collecting data in the process of implementing projects to evaluate their effectiveness. The data collection techniques they employed involved surveys and/or focus groups of staff, parents and/or students, observations of events and classroom practice, analyses of documents and/or student work samples and attendance records, depending on the nature of the project they undertook. Together with the other RMRME researchers, my job was to conduct a meta-analysis of these projects. To do this, we conducted interviews with the principals, and focus groups with the research teams, before and after the implementation of the projects, questioning all involved about the process, together with collecting observational data related to their specific projects. Prior to the

---

3   LBOTE is an acronym for language background other than English. Schools classified as high LBOTE in this study were those with populations of LBOTE students over 60%; mid-range were those with populations of LBOTE students of 30–59%; and low were those with populations of LBOTE students of below 30%.

research teams devising their research plans and conducting their projects, all were involved in training around action – practitioner-based – research, working through processes of planning, acting, observing and reflecting (NSW Department of Education and Training, 2010). Other aspects of the training included discussing readings around some of the theory considered in this chapter, particularly around conceptions of culture, ethnicity and multiculturalism and the relation between globalisation and cultural hybridity. In the next section, I consider the project that was undertaken in one of these schools, examining the degree to which the research team was able to engage with the ideas they encountered in the training. In conducting the meta-analysis, our role was not to intervene in the action research but to investigate how the research teams were able to put theory into practice. Before examining this, I will draw on some of the focus group data collected from students as, together with the surveys and the various data-collection techniques used in the meta-analysis of the action research projects, separate focus groups were held in each of the project schools with students, parents and teachers to find out the forms of cultural identification they employed and to gauge their understanding of and attitudes towards cultural diversity.

Analysis and discussion

Approaches to multicultural education

Alice's comment, which frames discussion in this chapter, was drawn from data in a pilot project undertaken prior to RMRME and we were keen to see if other students held similar understandings in the schools involved in this project. As indicated, the students who volunteered to participate were from both primary and secondary schools and were mainly aged between 10 and 12 years in the former and between 14 and 16 years in the latter. Students offered a range of responses when asked about what they understood by the term 'culture'. Very often, however, the same focus on culture as difference that Alice displayed was evident. Some responses include:

> It means like different types of nationalities and all that. (Miranda, low SES, low LBOTE secondary school)

> It means different countries and what they believe in, like their country. (Madison, high SES, mid LBOTE primary school)

> What they believe in, kind of. (Lucas, mid SES, low LBOTE secondary school)

> How they do stuff in their country, what food they would eat. (Jillian, low SES, low LBOTE primary school)

> Well, culture means from a different country, like their background is a different culture than our background. (Elise low SES, low LBOTE primary school)

When I asked Elise if I had a culture given I was born in Australia, she was a little confused and her friend Vera helped her out:

Well, depends, as you said, you were born in Australia and if you have a culture, like say your parents were born in a different country and then they had a culture and then their parents had a culture, so then you would have a culture because their parents have culture and so do your grandparents. So you would have a culture because they are from a different country or they were born in a different country.[4]

Clearly, 'culture' is understood here as something quite separate from the Anglo mainstream. It is associated with ethnic difference, however far removed, rather than simply the varying social processes constitutive of individual subjectivity. But how is it that such views are so prevalent? Our previous discussion around culture and ethnicity is useful here. We can see, for example, both Zerubavel's (1996, p. 421) notion of 'lumping and splitting' and Brubaker's complementary notion of 'groupism' (Brubaker, 2002) evident in these remarks; how these students engage in processes of differentiation around culture, which multicultural discourse has itself encouraged.

The action research conducted in schools was designed to challenge this tendency towards groupism and the type of essentialising of ethnicity it engenders. Multicultural education encompasses a range of programs: inclusive curriculum, community liaison, ESL (English as a second language) or EAL/D (English as an additional language or dialect) support, anti-racism and community language. Its goal, therefore, is not only to meet the needs of LBOTE students but to ensure all students develop capacities in successfully navigating cultural complexity. The project to be examined here was undertaken in a primary school that was focusing on community liaison with the intent of improving the participation of LBOTE parents in their school community. While the school's research team participated in the RMRME training, their level of engagement with the theory they encountered and their ability to apply it in the context of the project they devised and implemented was disappointing. This was not the case with all schools. In many there were far more successful programs than that presented here. (See Watkins & Noble 2014; 2016 for accounts of schools where this is the case.) The rationale for examining this particular school's attempt to rethink their approach to multicultural education is to allow you to analyse what was a typical whole-school activity in relation to multicultural education – something you may have encountered yourself as either a school student or trainee teacher – and for you to use the theoretical tools we have discussed to think through what conceptions of culture it promotes.

The school in question is located in the affluent eastern suburbs of Sydney. It has a small, high SES, low LBOTE (just 22%) student population. Of the LBOTE population, the vast majority are French-speaking, with increasing numbers speaking Japanese, Mandarin and Cantonese. Many of the parents of these students are on temporary visas; highly paid professionals who are resident in Australia for two or three years before moving elsewhere, given the transitory and transnational nature of their employment. The research team led by the principal, Samira, was keen to increase the involvement of these and other LBOTE parents in the school, particularly at Parents' and Citizens' meetings, which were generally only attended by

4   See Watkins and Noble (2016) for further discussion of these data.

Anglo parents. There was also some concern about racism at the school, particularly towards the increasing number of children from various Asian backgrounds who, in comparison to those of European backgrounds, were treated by some as a less acceptable 'difference' within the school community. While, ostensibly, the aim of the school's project was to increase the participation of LBOTE parents, it was felt that lifting their profile in the school would have pay-offs in terms of countering this racism. The degree to which the project was successful in meeting these aims, however, seemed negligible. The research team decided that the course of action they would take would be to hold what they referred to as 'multicultural cafes' at the school, which proved to be a more sophisticated take on the multicultural day. In effect, it involved all classes from Years 3 to 6 choosing a country and investigating its 'culture', including aspects of language, traditional dress, music, history, various customs and especially food. This was incorporated into the curriculum over two terms. As Samira explained, 'I want to generate an understanding, an appreciation of the different cultures ... I want them to appreciate the multiple sort of diversity that would be in every child's heritage'. This seemed an attempt to engage with ideas around cultural hybridity, but understood as a patchwork of different cultures.

On the day itself, each of the Years 3–6 classes set up a cafe in their room serving food and conducting activities related to aspects of the culture of the country they had investigated. These countries included China, France, Spain, Italy, Australia, England and the United States. The audience for these activities, and the customers in the cafes, were K–2 students, who moved from class (country) to class (country), complete with a passport that had to be stamped on entry to each. Parents had been notified well in advance of the day and some attended, assisting students and teachers in preparing and serving food. This constituted their involvement. In the 'China' classroom, for example, one mother of Chinese background was busy steaming dumplings and passing them to the 'Chinese' students to serve. In discussion with the research team following the event, it was considered 'a positive start' and a 'success', as Andrea, a teacher, explained, because 'the kids were immersed in that culture'. The team, however, was disappointed by the limited involvement of parents, but Andrea pointed out that 'the multicultural cafes will continue onto next year and that will evolve into a greater forum to involve *multicultural parents*' (emphasis added).

To what extent, however, had this event – and the data the team collected from student surveys and parent focus groups (which few attended) in evaluating it – shifted teachers' understandings of culture and, even more importantly, those of their students and the parents they had hoped to involve? Culture, it seemed, was still very much perceived as bounded and static, with activities on the day simply reinforcing this point. Multicultural education, yet again, provided the rationale for the celebration and – in the process – the instantiation of difference. It seems highly likely that activities such as these, as well-meaning as they are, led to the equation of culture with difference that the students in the focus groups discussed above exhibited. The school's multicultural cafes are representative of the cosmo-multiculturalism that Hage (1998) critiques but, at the same time, is quite distinct from the actual cosmopolitan lifestyles of some of the so-called 'multicultural parents', whose transnational lifestyles were more commensurate with a cosmopolitanism suggesting truly hybrid forms of cultural identification rather than belonging to 'this' or 'that' culture. The day itself, in fact, presented plenty of opportunities for a more nuanced examination of culture with students as did, no doubt, the lessons conducted in advance. In the 'China' room, for example, one of the activities for the K–2 students – while eating their dumplings – was to watch excerpts from the Walt Disney animated movie *Mulan*, replete with the Chinese characters speaking in American accents. Rather than presenting this as a realistic depiction of 'Chinese culture' – which clearly it was not – it could have acted as a useful stimulus for young children to discuss globalisation, hybrid identities and more fluid conceptions of culture, with questions being posed such as: Where was this movie made? What type of accents do the characters have? Who are the actors who are voicing the characters? (Eddie Murphy, an African-American actor, and Pat Morita, a Japanese-American actor, both voice characters.) Is this a Chinese or an American movie? Is it both or neither? Do you think people of other nationalities were involved in its making? What's the difference between nationality and culture? What is similar/different in culture between China, as depicted in the film, and China today? What connections do we have with China today and in the past? What aspects of culture do we share? What do travel, technology, migration do to culture? Yet such questioning did not eventuate. Instead, given students were in the 'China' room, this was presented as an example of 'Chinese culture'.

The readings the research team had undertaken, both during the training and as part of a literature review they were encouraged to undertake, also seemed to have had limited effect on broadening their perspectives on culture and any reflexive capacity in relation to their practices around multicultural education. While most indicated that they relished the opportunity, with Richard (a participant) pointing out that, 'I think the last time we had done something like this [academic reading] was when we were at uni', when interviewed separately Samira indicated she actually encountered 'massive resistance' from the team given the time and level of commitment required to undertake the readings and conduct research. The point here is not to critique these teachers but to think through how they could have reflected on the action they undertook – an important aspect of professional practice and key to successful action research. Clearly, what was needed was far more than just commitment. Though important – especially given the busy nature of teachers' day-to-day responsibilities in classrooms – rethinking multicultural education requires a far stronger intellectual and critical engagement with the theoretical tools that can bring new insights to our conceptions of culture and to making effective interventions in improving the practice of multicultural education in a time of increasing cultural complexity in schools.

Implications

So what are the implications for teaching of the theory and research findings presented here? This chapter has offered a critique of multiculturalism and certain practices around multicultural education that both the theory and research conducted in schools would suggest is justified. So, does this now mean multiculturalism has reached its use-by date and that multicultural education should be disbanded in schools? Despite problematic aspects of policy and practice, multiculturalism in Australia has, by and large, been very successful. Since World War II, over seven million people have migrated to Australia and one in four of Australia's population is now born overseas (Australian Government Department of Immigration and Border Protection, 2014). This presents a considerable demographic shift, and one accomplished with relatively little social disharmony. Australia, however, is very different from what it was in the 1970s when policies of multiculturalism were first introduced. Given intergenerational change, intermarriage and increasing globalisation leading to greater cultural and linguistic diversity, polices of multiculturalism may need to be rethought, as does multicultural education. What is required is a far more robust multicultural education that moves beyond a simplistic recognition and valorisation of difference to one that assists all students to acquire the capacities to effectively navigate the complexity in their midst. This is dependent on practitioners having not only the knowledge and skills to think critically about the challenges that globalisation and cultural hybridity pose for schools and their communities but also the ability to devise effective curricula and programs in light of this. These are complex issues that all teachers, from pre-K to Year 12 and beyond, need to engage with so that when they are confronted with comments such as Alice's the theoretical tool kit they have acquired in the course of their professional learning stands them in good stead to respond accordingly.

Considerations

- Multicultural days in schools may act as positive community events, but in what ways can they be supplemented with activities in classrooms to move beyond tokenism and to prevent the kinds of problems discussed in the research findings presented here?
- Teachers across Australia are now required to promote intercultural understanding. What do you think intercultural understanding involves? Refer to the documentation on the ACARA website at https://www.australiancurriculum .edu.au/f-10-curriculum/general-capabilities/intercultural-understanding. Using the theoretical understandings presented here, conduct your own analysis of these materials.
- The Melbourne Declaration calls for students to become 'responsible global and local citizens' (Ministerial Council on Education, Employment, Training and Youth Affairs, 2008, p. 9). What do you understand by global citizenship? Is there any conflict between notions of national and global citizenship?
- Do laws prohibiting racial vilification impinge upon free speech? Does everyone have a right to be a bigot? How might multicultural education respond to the issues these questions raise?

Of interest

- Acquaint yourself with the relevant policies around multicultural education and anti-racism in New South Wales schools. See https://education.nsw.gov.au/policy-library/policies/multicultural-education-policy and https://education.nsw.gov.au/policy-library/policies/anti-racism-policy
- Do not leave behind your engagement with theoretically informed scholarship when you complete your training. Compile a bibliography of readings on issues related to multicultural education, add it to your professional portfolio and build on it as a useful source of information throughout your career as a teacher.
- To find out more about the RMRME project, read its research reports and access other relevant research around multicultural education. See http://www.multiculturaleducation.edu.au
- A wealth of teaching resources to combat racism in schools can be found at http://www.racismnoway.com.au

References

Akerman, P. (2001, September 18). Opening our doors to a wave of hatred. *The Daily Telegraph*, p. 22.

Albrechtsen, J. (2002, September 4). Defend to the death our Western ways. *The Australian*, p. 13.

Ang, I. (2001). *On not speaking Chinese: Living between Asia and the West*. London: Routledge.

—— (2014). Beyond Chinese groupism: Chinese Australians between assimilation, multiculturalism and diaspora. *Ethnic and Racial Studies*, 37(7), 1184–96. doi:1 0.1080/01419870.2014.859287

Ang, I., Brand, J., Noble, G. & Sternberg, J. (2006). *Connecting diversity*. Sydney: Special Broadcasting Service.

Australian Curriculum, Assessment and Reporting Authority (ACARA) (2013). *General capabilities in the Australian Curriculum*. Retrieved February 2013 from http://www.australiancurriculum.edu.au/GeneralCapabilities/Pdf/Overview

Australian Government Department of Immigration and Border Protection (2014). *Fact Sheet 4 – More than 65 years of post-war migration*. Retrieved from https://www.immi.gov.au/media/fact-sheets/04fifty.htm

Bhabha, H. K. (2004). *Location of culture*. London: Routledge.

Brubaker, R. (2002). Ethnicity without groups. *European Journal of Sociology*, 43(2), 163–89. doi:10.1080/17449057.2011.574389.

Department of Social Services (DSS) (2011). *The people of Australia: Australia's multicultural policy.* Canberra: Author.

—— (2017). *Multicultural Australia: United, strong, successful. Australia's multicultural statement.* Canberra: Author.

Dunn, K. M., Forrest, J., Burnley, I. & McDonald, A. (2004). Constructing racism in Australia. *Australian Journal of Social Issues,* 39(4), 409–30. Retrieved from http://search.informit.com.au/documentSummary;dn=937672105564037; res=IELHSS

Featherstone, M. (1990). Global culture: An introduction. In M. Featherstone (Ed.), *Global culture: Nationalism, globalisation and modernity* (pp. 1–14). London: Sage.

Gonzalez, N. (1999). What will we do when culture does not exist anymore? *Anthropology and Education Quarterly,* 30(4), 431–5. doi:10.1525/aeq.1999 .30.4.431

Hage, G. (1998). *White nation.* Sydney: Pluto Press.

Harrison, D. & Swan J. (2014, March 24). Attorney-General Brandis: People do have a right to be bigots. *The Sydney Morning Herald,* p. 1.

Kalantzis, M. (2013). The cultural deconstruction of racism: Education and multiculturalism. *Sydney Studies in Society and Culture,* 4, 90–9.

Koleth, E. (2010). *Multiculturalism: A review of Australian policy statements and recent debates in Australia and overseas.* Research Paper No. 6, Parliamentary Library, Parliament of Australia.

Kroeber, A. & Kluckhohn, C. L. (1952). *Culture: A critical review of concepts and definitions.* Cambridge, MA: Papers of the Peabody Museum of Archaeology and Ethnology. Retrieved from https://www.zotero.org/bohemicus/items/ itemKey/MWMDK4M2

Liberal Party of Australia (2013). Tony Abbott – Address to the 2013 federal Coalition campaign launch. Retrieved from www.liberal.org.au/latest-news/2013/08/25/tony-abbott-address-2013-federal-coalition-campaign-launch

Ministerial Council on Education, Employment, Training and Youth Affairs (2008). *Melbourne Declaration on Educational Goals for Young Australians.* Melbourne: Author.

Noble, G. & Poynting, S. (2000). Multicultural education and intercultural understanding: Ethnicity, culture and schooling. In S. Dinham & C. Scott (Eds.), *Teaching in context* (pp. 56–81). Melbourne: ACER Press.

NSW Department of Education and Training (2010). *Action research in education guidelines.* Sydney: Author.

Strathern, M. (1995). The nice thing about culture is that everyone has it. In M. Strathern (Ed.), *Shifting contexts: Transformations in anthropological knowledge* (pp. 151–76). London: Routledge.

Watkins, M., Lean, G., Noble, G. & Dunn, K. (2013). *Rethinking multiculturalism: Reassessing multicultural education. Project report number 1: Surveying NSW public school teachers.* Sydney: University of Western Sydney.

Watkins, M. & Noble, G. (2014). *Rethinking Multiculturalism/Reassessing Multicultural Education Project Report Number 3: Knowledge Translation and Action Research.* Institute for Culture and Society: University of Western Sydney.

—— (2016). Thinking beyond recognition: Multiculturalism, cultural intelligence and the professional capacities of teachers. *Review of Education, Pedagogy and Cultural Studies,* 38(1), 42–57. doi:10.1080/10714413.2016.1119642

Williams, R. (1983). *Keywords: A vocabulary of culture and society.* New York: Oxford University Press.

Youdell, D. (2012). Fabricating 'Pacific Islander': Pedagogies of expropriation, return and resistance and other lessons from a 'Multicultural Day'. *Race Ethnicity and Education,* 2, 141–55. doi:10.1080/13613324.2011.569243

Yúdice, G. (2003). *The expediency of culture: Uses of culture in the global era.* Durham, NC: Duke University Press.

Zerubavel, E. (1996). Lumping and splitting: Notes on social classification. *Sociological Forum,* 11(3), 421–33. doi:10.1007/BF02408386

Acknowledgements

This article draws on research that was funded by the Australian Research Council, the NSW Department of Education (DoE) and the former NSW Institute of Teachers (NSWIT). I would like to acknowledge the generous support of each body and also the assistance of the other chief investigators involved in the project: Professors Greg Noble and Kevin Dunn, Western Sydney University and our partner investigators (Nell Lynes, Eveline Mouglalis and Amanda Bourke, NSW DoE and Robyn Mamouney, NSWIT).

CHAPTER 10

Social class and the classroom

A reflection on the role of schooling and mothering in the production and reproduction of disadvantage and privilege

Kate Huppatz

> We were upper middle class. Because of Dad's income we were reasonably comfortable and probably a bit higher than the average. We got to go to private Catholic schools as kids and then I was sent to a private girls' school in the city, because we lived in the country, and then university. So we were probably upper middle class. (Peta, a middle-class mother)

Introduction

The preceding interview excerpt shows how closely schooling is tied to social class. Here, the interviewee links her middle-class status to the privilege of private schooling and tertiary education, along with her father's income. Interestingly, while Peta was asked to discuss her class history, she was not specifically questioned about her schooling history at this point – this is an inference that the interviewee, as well as many others who participated in a study of mothering practices, made independently. This chapter reiterates and unpacks this connection in a description and appropriation of **Pierre Bourdieu**'s sociology of education. While many of us may recognise, as Peta did, a connection between social class and schooling, Bourdieu's abstractions allow both researchers and teachers to better understand, articulate and respond to the complexities of this association. Beginning with an outline of some of the ways in which Bourdieu has been taken up within contemporary education research, this chapter highlights the strengths of Bourdieu's theory of social practice. Making use of his concepts, as well as the approaches of Annette Lareau, Diane Reay, Gill Crozier and David James, this chapter explores the classed dimensions of school choice in an analysis of mothers' orientations to 'private' and 'public' schooling. In doing so, it argues against 'the end of class' thesis, the now popular notion that class is irrelevant for understanding contemporary experience. The chapter proposes that the frame of social class helps to capture processes of inequality and identity formation in relation to education, and that this has implications for understandings of mothering, family involvement in schooling, socially responsible teaching practice and social policy targeted at disadvantage in education.

> **Pierre Bourdieu** a French sociologist, anthropologist, philosopher and public intellectual whose substantial body of work concerned the dynamics of power in society. He developed a methodology for understanding people's actions and decisions as social practices, creating a theory of practice and a cultural analysis of social class.

Background

Contemporaneously, social theorists and commentators tend to see education as an avenue for either producing and reproducing disadvantage and privilege or reducing inequalities (Marks & McMillan, 2003). The relationship between inequalities and education is therefore widely recognised, but it is also a complicated and vexing issue on which there is no agreement; disadvantage grows without any wide-ranging established solutions. There are, however, frequently used terms and concepts that give reference to educational inequality across academic, popular and political arenas; and, for the most part, the relationship between education and inequality has been understood via the concept 'socio-economic status'. This is a concept that recognises stratification in the education system but tends to sidestep the role of identity and culture. The popularity of this concept is due to a widely held contention that **social class**

> **Social class** an identity category or position formed within relationships of social inequality marked by access to social, cultural and economic resources.

is a 'living dead' or 'zombie' category, a category that still circulates but is no longer relevant (Beck, 2001). This 'end of class' thesis is the notion, prominent in individualisation theories, that class culture is irrelevant in a neoliberal society where students are increasingly framed as 'individuals', 'customers' and 'competitors', and where students' learning outcomes are seen as the responsibility of parents. This 'classless society' thesis is frequently taken up in political discourse and this means that other markers of social inequality, such as race, ethnicity and rurality, or the more generic concept 'social exclusion', tend to be the focus of education policy (Reay, 2010, p. 397).

This emphasis on other markers of difference, in combination with an antipathy for the class concept, has resulted in social class experiencing a 'fluctuating presence' (Reay, 2010, p. 397) in policy. Divisions tend to be framed in terms of 'a deprived minority on the one hand and a large mainstream on the other' (Reay, 2010, p. 397), which dramatically oversimplifies the dynamics of the relationship between inequality and education. However, alongside individualising discourses and oscillating policy approaches, there has been a revival of interest in sociological theories of class, in part provoked by an increased academic engagement with the cultural theory of French sociologist Pierre Bourdieu. Bourdieu's sociology of education was very popular in the 1970s and 1980s (Jenkins, 2002, p. 115), became less so in the 1990s, but has experienced a kind of renaissance since the early 2000s. At a time when there has been an overemphasis on educational outcomes, Bourdieu's theorising has redirected interest to 'the processes through which these educational patterns are created and reproduced' (Lareau, 1987, p. 73). A series of Bourdieu's articles and books – the most famous of these is perhaps *Distinction* (Bourdieu, 1984) – highlight the significance of culture, including the culture of education institutions and the culture of families, for producing and reproducing privilege and disadvantage.

Lareau is one of the best known scholars in education sociology who adapts Bourdieu's concepts to understand how parenting and schooling practices reproduce privilege. For example, in the 1980s Lareau carried out qualitative research on family–school relationships in white working-class and middle-class schools in the United States. In her analysis of data acquired through participant observation and in-depth interviews with the parents, teachers and principals of children in the first and second grades, Lareau argues that class position and culture have much to do with the level of parental involvement in schools. She therefore proposes that Bourdieu's concept of 'cultural capital' is useful for explaining social class differences in children's experiences of schooling. As was explained in Chapter 1 of this volume, and will be explored further later in this chapter, capital, habitus and field are the key concepts that form the foundation of Bourdieu's theory. Lareau (1987) suggests that 'the social and cultural elements of family life that facilitate compliance with teachers' requests can be viewed as a form of cultural capital', and that it is middle-class families who are more likely to hold this capital (p. 73). Appropriate information is circulated and parental social networks are established via middle-class culture, and this shapes middle-class parents' behaviours so that they are in line with schools' expectations (Lareau, 1987, p. 82).

More recently, for her book *Unequal Childhoods*, Lareau (2011) carried out observational and interview research with 12 families (from a larger study of 88 children,
who were in the third grade at the initiation of the study) and the staff at their children's schools to examine parents' labour practices as well as the reciprocal relationships between parents and children. In this study, Lareau applies Bourdieu's
theoretical model and finds that parents differ in their parenting strategies and
the extent and manner in which they survey and involve themselves in their children's education. What is more, Lareau finds there to be both working-class and
middle-class styles of parenting. Using Bourdieu's terminology, Lareau (2011, p. 12)
finds that orientations to parenting are aspects of family habitus, which means
that class 'shapes the logic of child rearing in the home'. Working-class parents
tend to practise a cultural logic that she terms 'the accomplishment of natural
growth' (Lareau, 2011, p. 12); parents expect their children's development to progress in a natural way, if provided with the basic necessities. For example, an aspect
of this 'natural growth' approach is that working-class parents facilitate children's
informal play in their homes and nearby areas. Working-class parents also tend to
rely on educators to provide children with the learning support they need. Middle-
class parents, in contrast, engage in 'concerted cultivation', which is the 'deliberate
and sustained effort to stimulate children's development and to cultivate their
cognitive and social skills … parents actively fostered and assessed their children's
talents, options and skills' via the scheduling of activities, 'hovering' over children,
reasoning with children and 'intervening on their behalf' (Lareau, 2011, p. 238).

Unfortunately, Lareau finds that working-class and middle-class parenting
practices are not only oriented differently, but are also valued differently. Perhaps
due to the dominance of individualism in American society, concerted cultivation
is attributed greater value than the more constrained working-class approach. This
is problematic for working-class children's experiences in formal schooling environments as school staff expect parents to take up 'concerted cultivation' despite
the fact that the labour that is involved in concerted cultivation is exhausting
for parents and children, sometimes creates tension between parents and children, fosters entitlement among the wealthy, and encourages individualism at the
expense of family (Lareau, 2011).

Reay, Crozier and James' (2011) study of white middle-class urban schooling
experiences is informed by the Bourdieusian assumption that education informs
the habitus and that in studying individuals it is possible to understand 'social
practices, spaces, positions and relations' (p. 22). However, Reay and her co-authors
take a different approach to Lareau, in that they deliberately target middle-class
families who eschew the status quo by expressing an ideological commitment to
public education and sending their children to government schools. Reay and her
co-authors carried out in-depth interviews with 125 white middle-class families
who have children in attendance at inner-city public schools in three cities within
the United Kingdom. Demographic data were also collected in interviews with 68
middle-class young people (most of whom were over 18), who lived in the same
areas, to explore their school experiences but also the ways in which their identities
and perspectives were constructed as similar to, or different from, their parents'

identities and perspectives. Reay and her co-authors found that even though these progressive parents are supportive of multicultural school environments, they also 'face the perils of middle-class acquisitiveness' in that the 'multi-ethnic other' has become a source of 'multicultural capital'; affluent families extract 'value from, as they find value in, their multi-ethnic "other"' (p. 8). Reay and her co-authors conclude, somewhat pessimistically, that this is because these middle-class parents are facing very difficult structural inequalities, which they have little chance of overcoming; 'the wider social context of structural injustices throws up impossible moral dilemmas and leads to all sorts of morally inconsistent behaviour' (p. 9). The weight of economic uncertainty bears down on middle-class parents and this leads to a dilemma if they want to do what is best for both their child and for the wider, multicultural community. If they choose to facilitate their child's success in a global economy by exposing their child to ethnic Others, then they are reproducing distance between themselves and those they extract value from (Others become objects more than 'subjects' through this practice), which works against multiculturalism. On the other hand, if they choose not to extract value for their children, and embrace diversity in a more genuine, non-profit-seeking manner, they risk producing children who have fewer life chances.

Key theoretical concepts

Pierre Bourdieu's theoretical approach

The appeal of Bourdieu's approach is that it connects individual practices to wider social patterns; his concepts have enabled researchers to unpack the family orientations to parenting and schooling that are implicated in reoccurring education divisions. So far, an examination of Lareau and Reay and her co-authors' articulations of Bourdieu's theory has highlighted the usefulness of two of his concepts: habitus and capital. While all three of Bourdieu's concepts, namely habitus, capital and field, are pertinent and interlinked, this discussion will focus on the first two concepts. For the purpose of this chapter, all that needs to be understood about the field concept is that field refers to a space of social action, and that these spaces are characterised by their own unique rules and norms, sets of positions and struggles for capital. For example, for Bourdieu (1996), the family is a social field, along with the 'field of education' and the 'intellectual field' (Bourdieu, 1977), and these fields all overlap with each other and are interrelated in terms of their relationships to the classed habitus and various capitals.

Habitus

The habitus concept is perhaps most central to Bourdieu's theory of practice. The habitus is 'understood as a system of lasting, transposable dispositions which, integrating past experiences, functions at every moment as a *matrix of perceptions, appreciations, and actions*' (Bourdieu, 1977, p. 83, emphasis in original). The past (and present) experiences that shape this matrix include family and school experiences.

The family structures the habitus and this shaping mediates school experience, but school experiences also impact the habitus:

> the habitus acquired in the family underlies the structuring of school experiences (in particular the reception and assimilation of the specifically pedagogical message), and the habitus transformed by schooling, itself diversified, in turn underlies the structuring of all subsequent experiences. (Bourdieu, 1977, p. 87)

The family and schooling are therefore connected in their substantive roles in the production of a child's identity and future trajectory.

For Bourdieu, social distance is a key aspect of stratification. Dispositions of the habitus, informed by present and past positions in the social structure, including the family and school, connect to objective positions within different fields of action, which are marked by social distance. Dispositions assure this distance because they are also marked by:

> so many reminders of this distance and of the conduct required in order to 'keep one's distance' or to manipulate it strategically, whether symbolically or actually, to reduce it (easier for the dominant than for the dominated), increase it, or simply maintain. (Bourdieu, 1977, p. 82)

Our attitudes to mobility – whether we take chances, strive for change or accept things as they are – are informed by our classed experiences. The habitus, structured by the family and schooling, is implicated in the positioning of individuals; practice is linked to structure.

Capital

Bourdieu uniquely conceptualises wealth as cultural and symbolic as well as economic. As the introduction to this book highlights, Bourdieu generally refers to wealth as 'capital' and capital exists in several species as well as subspecies, including: economic capital (money and property rights); social capital (profitable social connections that may be transferred into economic capital or institutionalised as a title of social honour); and cultural capital. Of all the capitals, cultural capital is perhaps Bourdieu's most unique conceptual contribution and it is an important focus for his sociology of education because it refers to cultural knowledge and competencies and can exist in an embodied state (as the dispositions of the habitus), in the objectified state (as cultural goods, such as books) or in the institutionalised state (in educational qualifications).

For Bourdieu, cultural capital in the institutionalised state also implies cultural capital in the embodied state, as schooling is the primary means by which cultural capital is cultivated and reproduced (Bourdieu, 1986, p. 47). Here is where Bourdieu's sociology of education most clearly relates class culture and education to power. He argues that children from wealthy backgrounds achieve greater schooling success because the learned skills and competencies that are valued in the education system are the cultural capitals that belong to the elite, established through familial cultural cultivation (Bourdieu & Passeron, 1977). This privileging of elite skills within education institutions does not occur because the cultures of the middle and upper classes are inherently more valuable, rather, this process occurs because the middle and upper classes occupy superior statuses within social fields. Those who hold power have capital that is misrecognised as legitimate and so it becomes 'symbolic capital'. This arbitrary imposition of privileged class culture occurs via the symbolic violence of 'pedagogic action' (carried out by those with pedagogic authority), 'diffuse education' (e.g. via peer groups), 'family education' and 'institutional education' (e.g. via schools) (Jenkins, 2002, p. 105).

In order to study the processes whereby inequalities in education are produced and reproduced, it is therefore necessary not only to consider variations in economic investments and outcomes for students, it is also necessary to consider the role of the family for cultural inculcation. Researchers must take into account 'that the scholastic yield from educational action depends on the cultural capital previously invested by the family', as this is 'the best hidden and socially most determinate educational investment' (Bourdieu, 1986, p. 48). Studying the family helps to resist the 'natural' depiction of privileged academic success. The research on mothering practices discussed in the next section of this chapter, considers not only the role of the family in schooling inequalities but also the role of elite schools in Australia's education system, as these institute cultural capital as well as social capital (the establishment of social proximity socially instated by the name of the school) via a kind of 'collective magic' (Bourdieu, 1986, p. 51).

> **Mothering** the performance of nurturing or protective activities. Mothering is usually, but not always, associated with the mother–child relationship. 'Good motherhood' is an ideological disposition that mothers are encouraged to take up through representations and commonly held understandings of motherhood and mothering.

Methodology

In the following analysis, Bourdieu's concepts will be applied to make sense of discussions of school choice with 39 mothers. These data were collected via semi-structured, in-depth interviews for a broader research project which explored how mothers actively participate in 'class making' through parenting and consumption practices, as well as how notions of 'good mothering' and 'bad mothering' are implicated in the making of classed subjects. The interviews ranged from 30 minutes to two hours and elicited information about maternal experience, including: maternal '*orientations* to culture' (Silva, Warde & Wright, 2009, p. 301, emphasis in original); consumption and social media; the regulation of maternal identities and practices; maternal isolation; and gender relationships. The interview questions therefore focused on issues such as parent-to-child disciplinary practices, school choice, breastfeeding, social networking and economic resources, work/life balance, child care and unpaid household labour. Participants for this study were recruited via advertisements in local papers and at community centres, creches and early childhood centres. Snowball sampling was also utilised after initial contact was made with a number of the participants. The interviewees were from working-class, middle-class and upper-class backgrounds and from

> **School choice** the school selection process that is enabled by the marketisation and privatisation of education as well as specific family resources.

a range of locations in New South Wales; however, the majority of the participants (approximately 60%) were middle-class and lived in Western Sydney. The
class positions of participants, as identified for this project, were informed by
their own understandings of their locations, as well as family income, occupation, education and, when interviews were face to face, participants' embodied
attributes (dress, accent and so forth). Although the following analysis is mostly
based on the comments of 14 of the mothers who have school-age children,
aspects of the narratives from some of the mothers with younger children are
also included since they communicated established ideas regarding their children's futures.

Analysis and discussion

Private education has become central to the reproduction of privilege in many parts
of the world. In Australia, there has been a pattern that has mirrored international
trends in that by the mid-1990s, education had become a commodity rather than
a social good, and parents were being encouraged to exercise choice and seek out
advantage by 'purchasing schooling'. In Australia, federal funding by successive
governments has been organised so that non-government schools have prospered
while government schools remain insufficiently resourced. As a result, the private
sector has expanded greatly, as more and more (mostly middle-class) parents have
chosen to send their children to non-government schools, while the public sector has stalled in its development (Aitchison, 2010, p. 93). This means that there
exists a divide in terms of the resources and funding allocated to government and
non-government schools and also in terms of the social class backgrounds of those
who attend them.

    This divide makes private schooling a contentious topic, and among the moth-
ers interviewed for this project there are avid supporters of the system as well as
those who find it deeply problematic. Whatever their stance, all of the mothers
expressed an opinion on the benefits and costs of both public and private schooling, and that includes the mothers of children who had not yet reached school age.
What is more, the middle and upper classes in particular seem to share a certain
orientation to their children's education experiences and outcomes. There is therefore a clear 'homology' (Bourdieu, 1977, p. 86), or systematic similarity, in their
perspectives on, and actions in relation to, schooling. This was most obvious in
discussions around school choice and family–school relations. This section of the
chapter focuses on these mothers' narratives and is therefore organised according
to these themes.

Choosing private education

School choice appears to be a fraught issue for many mothers, particularly when
weighing up the costs and benefits of a private education. Interestingly, the two
interviews that express this best were with mothers who have achieved mobility

and perhaps feel the precariousness of social class more keenly. For example, when asked if she will send her children to a public or private school, Helen, a middle-class mother (from a working-class background), replied:

> If they instil discipline, it may help them study. And there is also some social pressure around it too, from friends. They say, 'What school are you sending your kids to?' Like my friend told me that she put her child on the wait list for an exclusive school and I thought, 'Oh my God, I'm a terrible mother' – I hadn't thought about it and had been more relaxed about it and hadn't put them first ... [I thought,] 'What might happen to them?'

Here Helen describes how she failed to recognise the importance of private schooling for class distinction and so she was reminded via social pressure to 'keep one's distance' (Bourdieu, 1977), rather than returning to her working-class background. As Bourdieu asserts, classed individuals are frequently reminded by their peers that it is important to keep social distance between themselves and differently grouped Others. The right choice for affluent mothers therefore often involves both symbolic and spatial segregation or 'exclusivity'. As Reay (2010) points out, private schooling segregates affluent children from poorer children, protecting their educational achievements (p. 401).

In this narrative, it is also possible to see some of the concerns that arise for middle-class mothers in making school choices. Reay and her co-authors (2011) argue that these concerns develop because high stakes are involved; the capacity to make choices in relation to multiple aspects of social life, including schooling, 'lies at the heart of white middle-class identity' (p. 1). These concerns intensify as social reproduction for the middle classes in vulnerable global economies becomes less certain. The anxiety that Helen expressed is a hidden psychic element to social class that is most likely to occur when faced with the proposition of slipping into working-classness ('What might happen to them?').

School choice therefore takes a great deal of largely invisible labour – physical labour (visiting schools, researching curriculum, and so on), but also 'emotion work' (managing the guilt and anxiety for both children and adults around choice and entry requirements) (Aitchison, 2010, p. 91). In managing this risky process, Sasha (an upper-middle-class mother who is also from a working-class background) took the extreme action of christening her child, to provide greater choice, and to free up the family's economic resources to invest in other modes of class reproduction, such as the ownership of property:

> **SASHA:** We don't feel that, even though my husband earns pretty good money, that we should sacrifice the majority of a big wage to send her to a private school when really a public or a Catholic education would have been just as fine. She [Sasha's daughter] probably needs some help in the future, so with buying a house or something else as opposed as to all this money you're spending. But other people are very different.

> **FACILITATOR:** Okay, so if you can't get her into a Catholic school, she might go to a public school?

SASHA: Yeah, I mean there's good public schools in this area in regards to primary, but I think we would like to send her to a Catholic, so that's the first preference. I got her christened Catholic for that reason.

Again, evident in this narrative is a concern that class privilege might slip away if the schooling choice process is not managed properly. Although this mother has christened her child as insurance, she also states that she lives in a 'good area' and so her spatial positioning operates as a safety net in this process.

As the interviews progressed it became clear that the labour of school choice is mostly the responsibility of mothers (Aitchison, 2010). This is a result of the specific ways in which mothering is constructed in Australia. We live in a culture where women still take up less paid employment than men, but do the lion's share of unpaid labour in the home, including concerted cultivation activities like school shopping. As Bourdieu (1986) recognises, effective transmission of capital is a time-consuming activity. It is as much about the investment of time as it is about the quantity of capital that a family has to pass on, and so it is unsurprising that this hidden labour falls on mothers (p. 54). Another explanation of the gendering of this labour is that to appropriately manage school choice is to do 'good mother-hood' (Aitchison, 2010), an essential aspect of middle-class femininity (Goodwin & Huppatz, 2010). As the first interview narrative makes clear, the appropriate school choice displays discernment and self-sacrifice (which Helen felt she hadn't achieved, she 'hadn't put them first'), qualities that have long been conceptualised as elements of good motherhood as opposed to bad motherhood (Helen exclaimed, 'Oh my God, I'm a terrible mother!'). Therefore, despite being framed by many authors as classed objects, women consciously or unconsciously govern processes that reproduce family class positions; they are active subjects in the production of family class distinction.

Discipline and morality

Those who chose private schooling frequently expressed a desire to ensure their children became disciplined subjects. You will recall that Helen stated that the advantage of a private high school is, 'if they [the private schools] instil discipline, it may help them [students] study'. Similarly, Linda, a middle-class mother (from a working-class background), stressed that a private school would ensure success because peers would be disciplined: 'A private school would provide them more focus on what their strengths are; more resources, more support to success, peers that are focused'. The purpose of this institutional discipline is therefore to pro-mote *self*-discipline. Gillian, a middle-class mother, commented on the ways in which self-discipline has paid off among her peer group:

Both my husband and I went to private schools. At the time, when I was at school I was not too fussed about being there. But I look back now and the people that were of the same age that went off to the public high school, I can see differences. Just differences in outlook and I guess also the discipline in a private school and the adherence to a code and rules and that sort of thing. It's just the sort of thing … we

> err more to that. Once you get out in the workplace, you can't just do what you like.
> So you've got to have grounding somewhere along the line.

Self-discipline, fostered by private schooling, is therefore valued by the elite because it orients children towards the future. As Bourdieu (1986, p. 48) argues, self-discipline, in the form of 'self-improvement' and at the cost of time and involving renunciation and sacrifice, is central to the cultivation of cultural capital. In addition, by emphasising the significance of self-discipline, these parents are using the language of individualisation. The individual student is seen as responsible for their own success, as seen in the statement 'you can't just do what you like'. These parents are therefore writing class out of school success while they are, at the same time, engaging in a classed practice; individualism and social class are simultaneously produced and class privilege is 'misrecognised' as individual success. This is one of the contradictions of the current schooling environment.

Self-discipline is not only a disposition that cultivates cultural capital, it is also a moral attribute. This is clear in a number of the interview excerpts, including Isabelle's (an upper-class mother), which emphasises the disadvantages of public schooling and the link between discipline and 'manners':

> They [public schools] actively do not promote courtesy. Children are permitted to be rude to one another. And unless it's able to be inferred as bullying, it receives no mention, no reprimand.

Discussion of self-discipline can easily slip into discussion of manners because one is seen to produce the other and both are seen as part of the moral economy and implicated in class distinction. As Reay and her co-authors (2011) state, morality has become particularly important for the middle classes:

> Middle-classness is seen to be embedded within a range of virtues and positive attributes such as ambition, sense of entitlement, educational excellence, confidence, competitiveness, hard work and deferred gratification ... the middle-classes have now replaced the working classes as 'the moral identifier'. (p. 12)

Again, by ensuring that their children obtain the aptitude for self-discipline, a moral, middle-class disposition of the habitus, these mothers are ensuring the reproduction of social class.

Choosing public education

The mothers who chose public education for their children were not necessarily less invested in social class than those who chose private schooling. A number of these mothers talked about their satisfaction with their local public schools; however, this was largely in reference to primary rather than high school education and perhaps discipline, morality and individualism are less important for the fashioning of middle-class children than they are for middle-class adolescents. Indeed, a number of these parents mentioned the possibility of sending their children to private high schools. In addition, for many, particularly middle-class, mothers, the satisfaction with the public system stems from the influence of location on school environment. Many mothers actually moved into areas that they perceived as respectable so that they could have access to reputable schools. For example, the importance of a 'good area' for school choice was highlighted in Sasha's interview, and in Peta's (a middle-class mother) interview:

> We looked at the education system here at this suburb. And this is one of [the] reasons why we moved here. Good principal, walking distance to school. It also came to finances as well – we didn't think we could afford it [private school] and we didn't want a religious school.

This type of response indicates that, not only is there a division between public and private schools, there also exists a divide between public schools that are located in respectable middle-class locations and those that are not. Reay (2010) argues that, in this way, the emphasis on school choice has left 'the working classes stranded in an increasingly segregated system mediated in many cases by housing costs and the ability to move house' (p. 401). In the Sydney context, for example, where geography starkly articulates social distance, spatial location is pertinent to the creation of schooling inequalities.

Choice as resistance

Another pattern in the school choices of mothers was a deliberate renunciation of the private system. For example, Marion (a working-class mother) stated:

> **MARION:** I think if you have good public schools then that's where they should be going.

> **FACILITATOR:** Yes. Okay. So money didn't come into it?

> **MARION:** Well either way I think it's a waste of money. Each to their own but I think if a good public school … the curriculum's the same for Christ's sake. It's just the uniform's a bit nicer and, if you're paying a lot of money, they're going to get to have instruments. That's what the public schools lack, they don't get bands and things like that … I think a bit about the private school as well, it's a bit of that aspirational middle class, 'We're all a bit better than everybody else' thing, I do.

Here, Marion is questioning the status quo and perhaps even attempting to elevate her position by questioning the assumption that affluent schooling is superior. Perhaps more surprisingly, similar sentiments were expressed by some of the middle-class mothers, demonstrating that not all of the middle classes fit the same mould. Some explicitly rejected private schooling, despite having the resources to access this type of education, thereby engaging in an unusual and 'risky' practice for middle-class parents. For example, Lucinda (an upper-class mother from a working-class background) stated:

> I would rather send her to a public school. Because I was at a private school myself in high school. I went there on a scholarship, so not as a fee paying student. Boy I hated it… Because I was a non-fee paying student and everyone knew it. Because all the girls there had perfectly sized uniforms; I wore the same one from Year 7 to

Year 11. You know, they were all athletic and could swim and had people pick them up after school and I did not match any of that.

This mother therefore has 'insider' knowledge in that she attended a private school, but her habitus did not fit with that of the dominant culture. This experience makes her question the class system and so she is reluctant to reproduce a culture of privilege.

Alice's (a middle-class mother) rejection of private education is also a result of her schooling experiences, but hers was a positive experience in the public system. She reported a broader ideological commitment to public education, despite other family members encouraging her to pursue private education for her daughter:

Both of us believe in the public education system ... my mum was saying, 'Oh you've got to get her to [name of private school] and she can get a scholarship if she learns to play the bassoon'. The bassoon! I mean like talk about challenges of motherhood! I do not want a reed instrument in my house. Please, no, anything but that! ... I mean, I think at this point in time her going to the local school that we can walk to, that we can get involved in and frankly, that there'll be a lot of other kids like her ... I mean, there is an element there of, I suppose what I think exists in the private education system; it's not all about this, but there is a strong driver around class aspiration.

In their own research on school choice in urban public schools, Reay and her co-authors (2011) found a similarly oriented group of parents whom they characterise as representing 'a bolder, more risk-taking white middle-class cohort, and simultaneously, perhaps a more hopeful open one' (p. 7). In Reay and her co-authors' study, parents expressed what the authors perceive to be 'communitarian' sentiments; they see value in their children mixing with children from a wide range of cultural backgrounds. However, the relationship that these parents have with public schooling is not straightforward. Their engagement with cultural Others is beneficial for their children, who are global citizens, and so this practice also improves their children's positions. This means that Reay and her co-authors' participants were primarily engaged with the ethnic Other rather than the classed Other; working-class children and families were still kept at a distance despite sharing the same schooling community and so social divisions did not disappear. In contrast, within the present Australian study, there was less evidence of seeking out benefit from the ethnic Other, and perhaps more positively, a direct resistance to class stratification (although the findings might have indicated otherwise if this group was explicitly targeted within the research, as was the case in Reay and her co-authors' study).

Family–school relationships

The middle-class mothers with children in attendance at public schools often reported a high level of involvement in the school community, even though they were not questioned about this. For example, Sia, a middle-class mother from a working-class background, stated:

I'm on the P&C, so I have a lot of personal and professional benefits with being on that. So I can sort of push my own agenda politically if I want to with regards to the state education fund being cut. So, that empowers me to be able to make change. So, that wider community from that aspect is great.

This practice seems to be about managing the risky business of engaging with public education. For example, Peta, a middle-class mother, stated:

We have discussed sending them to a private high school if we have more money and then we will look for a grammar school. We would try and find a good private school. We might even move house to be near a good school. If I thought there were any problems with the local school, then I'd go. Plus I go into the school and do reading groups and that allows my son to see me being involved and I get an idea of what happens in the classroom. And he is proud and all the kids know I'm his mum.

Reay and her co-authors (2011) found a similar pattern in their study of middle-class parents who send their children to public schools in the United Kingdom. The parents they interviewed were heavily involved in school governance and day-to-day life and this was a way of contributing to community (as Sia also articulated), but at the same time it worked to manage the risky business of investing in the public rather than the private system (as Peta discussed). In an environment where schooling is not immune to 'commodification and economising', schools are similar to the stock market: 'they require vigilance and careful monitoring in order to maintain their value and ensure a profit' (Reay et al., 2011, p. 151). Parents must be prepared to redirect their educational investment if stocks suddenly drop, and so volunteering time to school activities is also about school surveillance.

Implications

This research, with the aid of Bourdieu's concepts, and in combination with other Bourdieusian studies on school choice, demonstrates that families, particularly mothers, have a complicated relationship with their children's schooling experiences, and that this relationship is important for the making of social class identities and practices. Class culture interacts with private schooling in order to produce self-disciplined, morally superior subjects who have high stocks of cultural capital. As a result, parents, especially middle-class mothers, spend much time agonising over school choice, calculating risks and benefits and enacting strategies (such as moving house, volunteering at school or christening their child) to safeguard their children from working-classness. In these ways, mothers attempt to look after their children's best interests, but at the same time, they are implicated in the reproduction of an unequal class system (as well as good mothering ideology).

Social class, therefore, matters. While schools and teachers should not be blamed for the prioritisation of middle-class culture, it is important for teachers to be aware of the role of class power and privilege in the production of curriculums, orientations to parenting, and school cultures, and to be reflexive about the ways in which parents and teachers may contribute to the reproduction of inequalities. It is important, especially within the public system, to be aware that families are divided in the resources that they bring to their child's schooling experience and that this can have serious ramifications for the ways in which a child engages with their peers, their teachers, the institution and the school work itself. At the pre-service level, teachers need sociological understandings so that they can critically identify the divisions that might exist in their future schools. Moreover, strategies need to be developed at the classroom and school level to deal with these divisions. Reflexive policy action that acknowledges class culture, rather than only giving reference to 'socio-economic status' or other divisions, is also of utmost importance.

Considerations

- What was the school choice process like for you and your family? Can you apply Bourdieu's concepts to your own experience?
- How is parental involvement in schooling implicated in the production of class divisions?
- What are some of the factors that cause tension between public and private schooling?
- Why is it important for teachers to be aware of class divisions?

Of interest

- The Organisation for Economic Co-operation and Development (OECD) offers statistics and commentary on the public/private divide in Australia. See http://www.oecd.org/edu/education-at-a-glance-19991487.htm

References

Aitchison, C. (2010). Good mothers go school shopping. In S. Goodwin & K. Huppatz (Eds.), *The good mother: Contemporary motherhoods in Australia* (pp. 89–110). Sydney: University of Sydney Press.

Beck, U. (2001). Interview with Ulrich Beck (with Don Slater and George Ritzer). *Journal of Consumer Culture*, 1(2), 261–77. doi:10.1177/146954050100100209

Bourdieu, P. (1977). *Outline of a theory of practice* (R. Nice, Trans.). Cambridge: Cambridge University Press.

—— (1984). *Distinction: A social critique of the judgement of taste*. London: Routledge.

—— (1986). The forms of capital. In J. E. Richardson (Ed.), *Handbook of theory of research for the sociology of education* (pp. 241–58). New York: Greenwood Press.

—— (1996). The family as a realized category. *Theory, Culture and Society*, 13(3), 19–26. doi:10.1177/026327696013003002

Bourdieu, P. & Passeron, J. C. (1977). *Reproduction in education, society and culture*. London: Sage.

Goodwin, S. & Huppatz, K. (2010). *The good mother: Contemporary motherhoods in Australia*. Sydney: Sydney University Press.

Jenkins, R. (2002). *Pierre Bourdieu* (Rev. ed.). London and New York: Routledge.

Lareau, A. (1987). Social class differences in family–school relationships: The importance of cultural capital. *Sociology of Education*, 60(2), 73–85.

—— (2011). *Unequal childhoods: Race, class and family life* (2nd ed.). Berkeley and Los Angeles, CA: University of California Press.

Marks, G. & McMillan, J. (2003). Declining inequality? The changing impact of socio-economic background and ability on education in Australia. *British Journal of Sociology*, 54(4), 453–71. doi:10.1111/j.1468–4446.2003.00453.x

Reay, D. (2010). Sociology, social class and education. In M. W. Apple, S. J. Ball & L. A. Gandin (Eds.), *Routledge international handbook of the sociology of education* (pp. 396–404). New York: Routledge.

Reay, D., Crozier, G. & James, D. (2011). *White middle-class identities and urban schooling*. Basingstoke: Palgrave Macmillan.

Silva, E., Warde, A. & Wright, D. (2009). Using mixed methods for analysing culture: The cultural capital and social exclusion project. *Cultural Sociology*, 3(2), 299–316. doi:10.1177/1749975509105536

CHAPTER 11

Digital literacies

Understanding the literate practices of refugee kids in an after-school media club

Karen Dooley

AUSTRALIAN PROFESSIONAL STANDARDS FOR TEACHERS

Standard 1: Know students and how they learn

The understandings developed in the chapter examine the ways that students learn in high-diversity, high-poverty settings. In addition, this chapter relates to content and teaching strategies for Arts and English learning areas of the curriculum.

Schools can enable kids in high-poverty areas to access digital technologies and media production. Consider the opportunities Dana[1] took up at MediaClub:

> It is about 3:20 p.m. on the sixth Thursday of Term 2. Fourteen kids, each with a laptop, are in the school library. Most are sitting at a cluster of tables in one corner of the room. They are watching a teacher demonstrate how to burn a CD. After the demonstration, the kids begin working on their media production projects. For the last six weeks they have been using GarageBand to compose a song that will be burned to a group CD at the end of term.
>
> Meanwhile, 12-year-old Dana is sitting on the other side of the library. She does not seem to have been participating in the demonstration but has been typing on her laptop, copying handwritten words from a notebook onto a PowerPoint slide.
>
> I ask several questions of Dana: What are the words? Where did the idea come from? When do you work on these slides? Do you have any other slides like these?

---

1   All names are pseudonyms selected by the researcher from a list of the most common girls' names in the Democratic Republic of the Congo.

192

Dana says that the 'words are [my] own'. She shows me a slide with a list of bands. She says that the presentation is self-initiated; it is 'my own idea'. She says '[I] only do it at MediaClub', but then adds that she has also been using the library computers to work on her PowerPoint presentation at lunch time. Further, this is not her only slideshow; she has 'another one started'.

Dana then goes back to her typing. When she has finished copying from her notebook, she experiments with layout and fonts. Then she adds a title slide, typing 'By Dana'. After that, she inserts images of hearts, girls and flowers. She puts her headphones on and sings quietly while looking at her slides. I ask Dana whether she will present the slideshow to anyone. She says she will put it on a USB and show her family. When I mention Dana's self-initiated PowerPoint project to the media teacher, she says that Dana tried to do something similar during last year's GarageBand module.

Introduction

MediaClub was an after-school **media arts** program. It was open to young people at a high-diversity, high-poverty outer-suburban primary school. The club ran for 14 terms as part of the URLearning (URL) research project (Woods, Levido, Dezuanni & Dooley, 2014) and the 'media club kids' were accustomed to participant observer researchers like me working alongside them. Each term, approximately 16–20 young people signed up, with about 50% returning repeatedly. Dana was one of the 'regulars'.

Media arts the component of an arts curriculum concerned with the ways that communications media, such as mobile technologies and the internet, are used creatively to produce and receive ideas and stories.

In this chapter, I look at some of the literacy benefits of MediaClub for students such as Dana and her friend, Brinella. Both girls had arrived in Australia as refugees from the Democratic Republic of the Congo (DRC).

Before proceeding, it is worth clarifying some of the language choices in this chapter, specifically the term 'kids/young people of refugee background'. My intent in using this term is to mark that a young person's life is more than their experience of forced displacement, asylum-seeking, and re-settlement. In using the term 'kids', as opposed to 'students', I highlight the difference between MediaClub as a relatively informal educational site, albeit on school grounds, and the formal classroom. By the term 'young person', I refer to both 'kids/students' (under 13) and 'teens/students' (older than 13). While my study was conducted in a primary school with young people less than 13 years old, much of what I have to say is of relevance also to teens.

After-school programs have been organised in Australia, as in other Western countries of refugee resettlement, to address the disadvantage faced by young people of refugee background. Most of these programs seem to have been homework clubs, such as the Refugee Action Support (RAS) program of the University of Western Sydney (Ferfolja, Vickers, McCarthy, Naidoo & Brace, 2011). Homework programs directly target the formal academic needs of young people of refugee background.

In contrast, MediaClub was not designed specifically for refugee kids, nor linked to the classroom, even though it occurred on school grounds. Rather, MediaClub was an after-school space designed for kids in Years 4–7 (age 9½–12½) who had an interest in media production. The club was envisaged as a space for skilling kids up as digital media experts, not only for school, but also for their families and communities. However, there was much more to MediaClub than skilling up; as it was put by one of the regulars, the club was also a 'place to hang out with friends' (Woods et al., 2014).

'Hanging out' is integral to the life of kids and teens, but is not necessarily viewed positively by adults. Parents and teachers may see it as a waste of time (Ito et al., 2010). Indeed, as a tutor in a drop-in homework club myself some years earlier, I had been uneasy about the 'hanging out', worried about lost homework opportunities. I recall thinking, 'I wish they'd stop looking at the photos on their phones and start working on their assignments!' At the time, I thought the young people's interest in digital photography was a resource that teachers could capitalise on in classroom literacy instruction. But I was uncomfortable about kids simply 'hanging out' during homework club time.

It is a small step from adult preoccupation with academic activity to actively discouraging hanging out in after-school programs (Ito et al., 2010). This was not a step we took in MediaClub; we did not view hanging out and skilling up as incompatible. Rather, we were interested in MediaClub as a space for skilling up *and* hanging out. In this chapter, then, I address the question: What are the literacy benefits of participation in an after-school media club where hanging out is at least as important as skilling up?

Media club a common supplementary education activity that provides young people with opportunities to use and learn digital literacies.

More specifically, I look at some of the literacy benefits that Dana and Brinella seemed to gain from their participation in MediaClub. In doing so, I use a sociological model of literacy education. This model has been created from concepts developed by French sociologist Pierre Bourdieu, namely: field, capital and habitus. The model makes it possible to look at the benefits of MediaClub in a deep and systematic fashion. As a result, I offer new understandings to the literature on after-school programs for young people of refugee background. First, however, I look at what is already known in the literature about these programs.

Background

After-school clubs and kids of refugee background

In recent years, sizeable cohorts of young people of refugee background have entered Australian schools, many with substantial educational needs that may be unfamiliar to their teachers. These students generally speak Standard Australian English as an additional language or dialect (EAL/D) and are among the most disadvantaged of students (Vickers & McCarthy, 2011; Creagh, 2014a, 2014b).

Official data on National Assessment Program in Literacy and Numeracy (NAPLAN) subsume refugee students into the category Language Background Other Than English (LBOTE). This category includes affluent students who have arrived in Australia after uninterrupted experiences in high-quality schools as well as students of refugee background who have little, no, or severely interrupted education. In short, students of refugee background are invisible in national testing data (Creagh, 2016). However, interrogation of Year 9 NAPLAN data from Queensland (Creagh, 2014a, 2014b) is cause for consideration. It shows that the mean score of students on refugee visas was within the national minimum standard band but well below the mean for the total cohort. Furthermore, the scores of students of refugee background were the lowest of all students in the population. In contrast, children of skilled migrants were achieving above the total cohort mean. In other words, while skilled migrants were outperforming all other students, refugee students were underperforming them. These results are consistent with international findings which show that, while the top 25% of migrants outperforms the top 25% of Australian-born students in reading, the bottom 25% performs below the bottom 25% of locally born students. Refugees are likely to be over-represented in the lowest performing group (Vickers & McCarthy, 2011).

There have been several approaches to meeting the educational needs of refugee students. One is focused on describing learning challenges and developing pedagogic responses to these (e.g. Miller, 2007; Oliver, Haig & Grote, 2009; Miller & McCallum, 2014; McBrien, Birman & Dooley, 2017). It advises teachers about how to better serve refugees within the mainstream classroom. Another approach has focused on academic support. The RAS program of after-school **literacy** tutoring (Ferfolja et al., 2011) is an example of such an approach. Evaluations of RAS demonstrated that this program not only improved the academic skills of refugee students, but also developed the pedagogic skills and professional capabilities of the pre-service teacher tutors (e.g. Naidoo, 2011). Applying **Bourdieusian** concepts, the researchers involved in that program have argued that RAS interrupts the reproduction of disadvantage through schooling. The program effects change in students' dispositions to school and equips them with both the cultural resources valued in the school and the social resources for getting ahead; that is, with cultural capital and social capital. Moreover, it equips tutors with knowledge, skills and behaviours valued in disadvantaged schools; that is, with 'teacher capital' (Ferfolja, 2009; Naidoo, 2009).

Homework clubs are only one type of **after-school program** that seems to be beneficial for young people. In Australia (Woods et al., 2014), as in the United States (Ito et al., 2010) and the United Kingdom (MacBeth et al., 2001), after-school programs are proliferating. While some of these programs are located in libraries, museums and other civic spaces, others, such as MediaClub, are attached to schools. Large-scale research from the United Kingdom, involving more than 8000 students from 52 schools

Literacy communication practices, in print or on digital platforms, that involve linguistic, visual, audio and other modes for making meaning. It is important to note that some literate practices are more valued than others in school.

Pierre Bourdieu a French sociologist, anthropologist, philosopher and public intellectual whose substantial body of work concerned the dynamics of power in society. He developed a methodology for understanding people's actions and decisions as social practices, creating a theory of practice and a cultural analysis of social class.

After-school programs supplementary education provided outside of school hours.

(MacBeth et al., 2001), points to the benefits of these programs. While some of the after-school programs focused on school subjects (e.g. Maths Club) and others did not (e.g. African Drumming Group), results demonstrated that after-school programs of any kind were associated with improved academic performance. Perhaps most noteworthy, ethnic minority students participated more and benefited most from participation.

In the United States, relevant research has looked at outcomes of out-of-school new media activity (Ito et al., 2010). It highlights friendship-building among teens as they hang out with new media and consume popular culture products – even covertly – in school spaces. It also indicates that media or computer clubs are conducive to intense interest-driven engagement with digital media.

From this brief review of the extant literature, it can be concluded that within an after-school media club, where 'hanging out' is validated as a potentially rich learning activity, academic outcomes are only some of the possible benefits. This was a consideration in the design of MediaClub. The intent was to give kids opportunities for media production that might be taken into their everyday lives as well as the classroom—an aim that remains important given evidence of a deepening divide between the digital 'haves' and 'have nots' (Rowsell, Morrell & Alvermann, 2017). From the review it is apparent, too, that Bourdieusian concepts have been useful for understanding schooling after refugee resettlement. Therefore, I use these same theoretical perspectives in this chapter as I seek to add to the empirical literature from my analysis of the literacy benefits of MediaClub for kids of refugee background.

Key theoretical concepts

A sociological model of literacy education

Bourdieu developed a field theory through more than 40 years of research on mechanisms of social suffering and inequality in 1950s Algeria and mid–late twentieth century France. A 'field' denotes a relatively autonomous social space; for example, the field of education with its particular logic of academic merit and practices. Within a field, social agents (such as students in the field of education), occupy positions of more or less power according to the value endowed on their resources in that field (for instance, their mastery of particular forms of language in the classroom). The greater the value, the more 'capital' the agent has to yield in struggles for dominance in the field. Through experience of the social relations in the field, agents build up a 'habitus' or set of dispositions to act in certain ways; for example, a student who has positive experiences around learning in education may approach assessment tasks keenly and with greater confidence.

Research with young Sudanese men of refugee background in the United States illustrates how literacy education reproduces social disadvantage (Perry, 2007). It shows that the young men made extensive use of English literacy for: religious purposes, such as reading the Bible; interpersonal communication through letters, email and notes; community newsletters, letters to the editor, websites and books; and for minutes, invitations, ledgers and other community organisation tasks. Moreover, these young men had been educated in English in the Kakuma Refugee Camp in Kenya for more than a decade and had earned the Kenya Certificate of Secondary Education. Yet, in the United States, where they were required to take basic English classes, they struggled; for example, they could not complete skill-and-drill worksheets. Unable to pass English certification tests, they were unable to graduate from college. These difficulties seem to reflect differences in school-ing practices. In Kakuma, students typically repeated after the teacher and copied from the chalkboard; these were not the practices of their US schools. Mismatches like these have been reported in studies with young people of refugee background in Australia, although for some young people the challenge arises from histories of little or severely interrupted schooling rather than mismatches between schooling practices (e.g. Naidoo, 2009; Dooley, 2012).

A Bourdieusian understanding of literacy education explains the position in which the young Sudanese found themselves. It begins with the observation that certain forms of communicative practice are privileged over others: 'literacy' is widely thought of as 'forms of communicative practice that are ... understood to be somehow different from other forms of communicative practice' (Heller, 2008, p. 54). In other words, while literacy can be understood as communicative practice, only some forms of communicative practice count as 'literacy' for the purposes of schooling.

Historical accounts show that with the rise of the capitalist nation-state, the forms of communicative practice that were privileged as 'literate' were those that involved ways of thinking thought to be suited to the pursuit of social order and progress. In this way, 'literacy' was distinguished from everyday language practices. This represents what Brian Street (1984) referred to as an 'autonomous' model of literacy. It assumes that literacy is a unified and universal cognitive skill implicated in development of logic, rationality, empathy and other supposed benefits. With the rise of the back-to-basics movement in literacy education and NAPLAN, the auton-omous model of literacy has not only persisted but gained new vigour. One aim of the research project reported here was to develop alternatives to the autonomous model in place in local schools (Luke, Woods & Dooley, 2011).

Schooling and literacy are closely connected because the privileged and privileg-ing practices of communication considered to be 'literate' generally require formal instruction and active learning in a way that everyday literacies do not. Much of this instruction occurs within the institution of formal education. In Bourdieusian terms, literacy education is understood as a discursive field constructed within a given socio-historical context (Heller, 2008).

The notion of field refers to a social space within which agents with different portfolios of resources, and therefore power, compete for resources (Bourdieu & Wacquant, 1992). The field of literacy education is institutionalised through

> the production of specialized materials, the development of dedicated technologies and the identification of particular practices, and the regulation of the distribution of all of the above in specific sites, involving selected actors. (Heller, 2008, p. 55)

The skill-and-drill worksheets with which the Sudanese young people in the US study struggled are an example of the specialised materials through which the field of literacy education is institutionalised. The decontextualised drill and skill activities involving those texts that were so difficult for the young men are an example of the practices selected as literate. Regulation of the distribution of these practices occurs through the certifying exams that were holding the young men back.

In any field, certain resources are valued – that is, they work as 'capital'. Mastery of the registers of English valued in Australian schools, for example, bestows 'linguistic capital' (a subspecies of cultural capital) on students. This capital is at stake in the field of literacy education – that is, it is the profit on offer in the field. But linguistic capital also enables students to act powerfully in the classroom (e.g. to speak with authority); in this sense, it is a 'weapon' in the struggle for legitimation through schooling (Bourdieu & Wacquant, 1992). Economic, social and cultural subspecies of capital are all relevant for understanding education. Research with Puerto Rican families in the US has identified resources of all these different types that work as capital in the field of literacy education (Compton-Lilly, 2007). Specifically, economic capital refers to possessions with monetary value, such as computers, electronic devices and educational toys. The maldistribution of these resources for literacy learning is a source of inequity for young people of refugee background who may not have the same kinds of access to these resources as their peers (McBrien et al., 2017). Social capital refers to connections with family members, teachers, peers, community members and others. It refers not only to young people's social skills, networks and interactions as such, but also to access to resources that young people gain through their social relationships (e.g. advice about going to the library that an educated mother might provide to her daughter's friend). Cultural capital takes three forms. Embodied capital (1) refers to dispositions to such things as reading the 'right' books, acting appropriately in reading lessons and saying the 'right' things about reading. Objectified reading capital (2) includes the production of artefacts that are taken as evidence of reading proficiency; for example, a completed sheet of comprehension questions. Institutionalised reading capital (3) refers to credentials that are taken as proof of reading proficiency (e.g. a NAPLAN result). Finally, any of these capitals may be converted to 'symbolic capital'. This is the capital of fame, reputation and recognition that comes with possession of considerable quantities of some other form of capital (Bourdieu, 2000). In schools, with their competitive and meritocratic logic and practices, 'intelligence' and a reputation as a 'high achiever' are examples of the symbolic capital enjoyed by some.

In this time of globalisation, the state can be understood as 'a switchboard' that is playing a critical role in 'structuring access to and the distribution of economic, social, cultural and symbolic capital, including language' (Billings, 2014, p. 17). In Australia, NAPLAN is one means by which the state is structuring and distributing capital within the field of literacy education. The autonomous model of literacy education is the ideological force of this structuring work. Literacy has been tied closely to economic activity and understood in autonomous terms. Hence, dominant discourse construes literacy as measurable communicative skills for economic participation, and literacy education as an ideologically neutral field for the transmission of those skills (Heller, 2008). However, inequitable outcomes persist. With respect to reading, for instance, re-invigorated autonomous models have seen the roll-out of comprehension skills programs in low-achieving schools. But these programs do not deliver the substantive intellectual content and connections to students' everyday worlds that are a key to sustainable achievement (Luke et al., 2011).

One's knowledge of one's place in school contexts of a field such as literacy education can be understood as habitus (Naidoo, 2009). **Habitus** is a set of dispositions to act in certain ways (Bourdieu, 2000). The habitus consists not only of cognition but also of bodily memory of one's experience within the social relations of a field and shapes one's expectations and orientations into the future. It is implicated in social reproduction because those who know themselves to be positioned tenuously in the field tend to select out of the educational competition. In the case of refugees, habitus dynamics are complex. While refugee young people may not have the habitus rewarded in the literate field, their families are often highly school-oriented. They are disposed to invest their (often meagre) economic, social and cultural capital heavily in the education of their children (Naidoo, 2009). The RAS research has shown that after-school homework clubs disrupt the reproductive work of the school by creating after-school spaces that appeal to the pro-school dispositions of the family while changing (or transforming) the individual habitus of the children to privileged and privileging forms of literate practice. Within these spaces, young people of refugee background can deploy their capitals (e.g. social connections) to acquire the cultural capitals valued in classroom contexts of the literate field. These theoretical understandings are useful for the data presented and examined here.

Habitus a set of dispositions to act in certain ways.

Methodology

The URL project was conducted in a high-diversity, high-poverty school, with 23 different cultural backgrounds represented in an enrolment of about 600. Aboriginal and Torres Strait Islander students constituted 15% of the population and EAL/D students, 10%. Approximately 6% of the population was eligible for the EAL/D program, including refugees from Burma, the DRC and Afghanistan. Many of the students of all ethnic backgrounds were affected by poverty; the number of children in the lowest quartile of socio-educational advantage was more than double the national average, while the number in the highest quartile was only a fraction of that average.

MediaClub was not tied directly to the assessable curriculum content of the school program. It was, therefore, what has been described in research from the United Kingdom as a 'non-subject' after-school program (MacBeth et al., 2001), akin to the Art Club, Dance Club, Music Club, African Drumming Group and other 'aesthetic' programs documented by that research. During the four years MediaClub ran as part of the URL project, content included: film-making; Lego robotics; GarageBand; stop motion animation; media remix (photography, film-making and web page building); comics; digital publishing (ebooks, posters, photography and film-making); podcasting and radio production; video games; macro photography; and iPad-based storytelling (Woods et al., 2014). The three main activities were:

Each MediaClub workshop ran for two hours. The three main activities were:

- group time (25 minutes) – expectations introduced, concepts taught and skills demonstrated
- independent work time (one hour) – individual, pair or small-group work on projects with the support of peer and adult experts
- group sharing time (15 minutes) – project work shared for peer and teacher feedback.

Each term culminated in a Showcase activity, such as an exhibition of student work, or in the case of the GarageBand module, the burning of the kids' songs to a group CD. Work on the Showcase piece commenced at the outset of the module; kids returned to the piece repeatedly as they learned new things.

The data I use in this chapter were produced by several URL researchers during MediaClub workshops. The URL project was informed by the principles of design-based research. In this approach, researchers typically work with practitioners to create and test an educational innovation in a real setting. Among other things, this enables analyses of authentic learning and teaching interactions (Design-based Research Collective, 2003). At MediaClub, participant-observer methods were used, along with interviews and artefact collection. Dana and Brinella were two of the students I came to know during my two years at the club.

As DRC-born Australians, Dana and Brinella were part of a small but rapidly growing community. A summary of data collected by the Australian Bureau of Statistics (Australian Government, n.d.) indicates that there were only 270 DRC-born people in Australia at the time of the 2001 census and 2576 at the time of the 2011 census, a figure that had risen to 4097 by the time of the 2016 Census. Nearly all were humanitarian entrants. Around about the time of data collection, unemployment was high and income low in the DRC-born community: the unemployment rate was nearly 25% and median individual income was $274 per week, in contrast to less than 6% and $577 per week for the total Australian population.

Like other DRC-born Australians, Dana and Brinella were multilingual. They were part of an Australian community that uses languages that include: French, the official language of the DRC; the languages of DRC ethnic groups; the cross-border language, Kiswahili; English; and other languages learned in countries of first asylum and after resettlement (Ndhlovu, 2013). Brinella had been in Australia for eight years in comparison to Dana's four years of residence in Australia. Educationally, this is salient, for it takes five to seven years for EAL/D learners to attain an average level of achievement. This period is extended to about 10 years for those with interrupted schooling and trauma (Thomas & Collier, 1997) – the experience of many DRC-born young people.

The analyses I present here draw on: (1) observations of MediaClub work-shops; (2) interviews with Dana and Brinella and with the school's EAL/D teacher; and (3) artefacts (teachers' work plans, children's project planning materials and completed media products). During analysis, I first scanned the entire data set and extracted all the data from the modules in which Dana and Brinella partici-pated. I then put all the data for each term together. Next, I read the file for each term. To ensure literal comprehension, I checked points of ambiguity with another URL researcher. While reading, I highlighted data pertaining to Dana and Brinella. These data were then interrogated with analytic questions: What is the learning here? What are the literacy benefits? The findings are presented in the next section of this chapter. Bourdieusian theory is used to interpret the findings.

Analysis and discussion

Here, I look at three key findings: (1) the structured program developed media pro-duction knowledge and skills transferable to home and classroom; (2) the struc-tured media production activity was a context for new and existing friendship; and (3) the program provided an opportunity for students to initiate their own literacy projects.

Development of transferable media production knowledge and skills

MediaClub was a structured program of media production. The GarageBand mod-ule, for instance, included instruction in: musical concepts (e.g. tempo, lyrics, song structure); software skills (i.e. how to operate GarageBand); and use of GarageBand for music production (e.g. midi instruments, recording voice and instrumentation, and mixing). Like the other kids at MediaClub, Dana and Brinella learned skills that were on offer.

By way of example, consider Brinella. For her, learning was an essential compo-nent of MediaClub: 'I think it just gives me more experience because I really love singing so I think that it just gives me more experience. It can just teach you what you don't know'. Brinella spoke of what she had learned: 'I learned about … tempo. I didn't know … if your music was too loud it make it like, destruction [distortion], I think it was'. Moreover, Brinella was able to imagine taking what she learned home to teach her sister. She could also imagine transferring her MediaClub learning to the classroom: 'in our classroom we're recording ballads, so I can like show them all the distortions and stuff'. This was consistent with our goal of skilling kids up as media experts.

The kids' media products enjoyed local distribution through Showcase events. The work of all the kids was on display during these events; all enjoyed the acclaim of parents, school administration and peers. This was especially so for Brinella at the end of the remix term. The video Brinella produced with a friend that term was featured during the formal segment of the Showcase event, with Brinella being asked to introduce the video to the audience. Recognition was also on offer within the supportive environment of MediaClub. For example, during week one of the GarageBand modules, I heard the lead teacher commend Dana on her achievements during the previous year's GarageBand module: 'You did a good one last time, I remember'.

What are the literacy benefits here? MediaClub can be understood as a local context within the field of literacy education. Within this context, communicative practice in multiple modes counted as literacy – the oral, written, visual and audio among these. Moreover, the written mode was not privileged as it is in classroom contexts where the structuring effects of the national literacy testing regimen are felt most strongly. Within this context, Dana and Brinella acquired the embodied cultural capital of media production skills. This capital was converted into the symbolic capital of status and recognition during workshops and at Showcase events. To the extent that they were transferred into the formal classroom program, the media production skills learned at MediaClub could be valued as embodied cultural capital in the classroom context, too. Moreover, they could be converted into symbolic capital, especially if the MediaClub kids worked as media experts.

Media production as a context of new and existing friendship

MediaClub offered opportunities for socialising while learning. Some projects were amenable to pair-work or small-group work, as occurred with Brinella and Dana's remix video. In other cases, kids worked on individual projects, but learned collaboratively, as occurred during the GarageBand module. During the first week of that module, for instance, the lead teacher demonstrated how to select and copy samples and then directed the kids to spend the first part of independent work time doing the same. She went on to say, 'You can help others if you were here before [last year]'. At this point, I saw Dana assist Brinella. A little while later, I heard Brinella say, 'Now I get it'. For some kids, this was a new context for existing friendship; for others, it was a context for new friendships.

Consider Dana. When I asked her why she went to MediaClub, she responded, 'to have fun, to meet new people'. In other words, Dana saw MediaClub as a place where she could enjoy herself and also make friends. When I spoke with the EAL/D teacher about this, she said that many of the refugee parents in the school were examples of what she called 'the thinking parent'. By this she meant parents who 'really see education as of critical importance to the future ... understanding that this is the key'. These parents, she observed, were 'very supportive' of 'extra-curricular or outside-of-school hours activities' because of the opportunities to learn English and hence 'to maximise the students' potential to grasp everything they can from education'. The teacher nominated MediaClub as 'a case in point', noting that it provided opportunities for becoming 'more fluent much faster' because the kids are 'exposed to English for longer'. The kids' friendship was pivotal:

> There's also sometimes the thought [on the part of parents of refugee background]
> that they're better with their friends than coming home to mum and little brother,
> or baby sister, or whoever, because they're going to make friends, get out into the
> community, and use their English in a manner that will assist the family long term.
> So the parents are quite keen and supportive of such activities.

What might be the literacy benefits here? In Bourdieusian terms, the EAL/D teacher is suggesting that parents of refugee background expect friendship to enable their kids to acquire linguistic capital in English for contexts within the fields of formal education. There is hope of converting this capital into the institutional capital of credentials and hence into capital that will secure the family's future. In conditions of economic disadvantage, there is hope of education working transformatively rather than reproductively. This is the hope of habitus attuned to the hierarchical and competitive structures of educational fields. In this situation, family support works as social capital; it is a resource invested in the hope of academic benefit. To clarify, Bourdieu drew attention to the access to resources young people enjoyed as a result of their parents' social connections As a result, educators have observed that young people build their own social capital by developing and maintaining relationships with people who can help them succeed and get ahead. In other words, family relationships may work as social capital.

Self-initiated practice within the media production space

From the opening vignette it is evident that Dana took the opportunity of two GarageBand modules to work on self-initiated PowerPoint slideshows, paying homage to her favourite bands. This everyday literate practice occurred when the kids were supposed to be consolidating their GarageBand compositions. Moreover, it was a practice Dana worked on during free time in the library outside of MediaClub.

Although covert media use has been observed in school (Ito et al., 2010), there was little of it at MediaClub. Dana's self-initiated projects were notable for their rarity. From the data it is not possible to ascertain why Dana engaged in these projects. But what is clear is that she used MediaClub as an opportunity to pursue projects that mattered to her, as indeed she used the school library. During the remix module, for example, Dana produced a set of photographs of herself. She told me that these were for her modelling portfolio; she wanted to be a model like some other Congolese girls.

Dana's PowerPoint projects seemed to apply capabilities she had developed in class – skills and knowledge valued as capital in classroom contexts of the literate field. This is a dynamic that has been observed in the literature on the cultural practices of schooling (Zhang, 2007). The point is that embodied cultural capital from school is taken into everyday contexts by young people. Moreover, the projects made use of economic literacy capital available at school. For at least some kids in this high-poverty area, school was a critical site of access to such capital – an institution that redressed inequities in the distribution of digital technologies

(Rowsell et al., 2017). What is evident, though, is that Dana took cultural capital from school contexts of literacy to other contexts. In the case of the remix module, this seemed to be an imaginary dynamic: the embodied and objectified cultural capital of Dana's photography skills and her remix project were integral to imagined participation in the literate practices of the modelling world.

Discussion

This chapter has examined the literacy benefits of participation in an after-school media club where 'hanging out' is at least as important as skilling up. It adds to the literature in three ways. First, MediaClub was like after-school homework clubs in that it developed knowledge and skills able to be 'converted' into capital in classroom contexts within the field of literacy education (Naidoo, 2009; Ferfolja et al., 2011). However, there is a point of difference. In the case of homework clubs, the capital value of the knowledge and skills developed in the after-school setting is more or less assured because the club supports young people with tasks set by the school. In contrast, MediaClub tasks were not directly linked to the classroom literacy program. The value of the knowledge and skills acquired in MediaClub – the capital the kids were able to bring into play in that context within the field of literacy education – could not be taken for granted. It was dependent on such things as school and teacher response to the structuring work of the national regimen of literacy testing; this was a school under pressure to improve test performance on print basics.

Second, as described in the literature on young people and new media (Ito et al., 2010), the media production activities of MediaClub were a space for 'hanging out' with friends old and new. But where 'hanging out' is often viewed somewhat suspiciously by some adults, my analyses suggest that for some – the EAL/D teacher, and possibly parents of refugee background – this activity is viewed differently. For them, 'hanging out' was a means of acquiring capital in the service of a transformative experience of schooling. As was noted earlier, school experiences can be designed to interrupt the reproductive work of schooling – in this case, to open up opportunities for disadvantaged students.

Third, there is the question of the directionality of flows of literate practice. The literature on the literate practices of young people of refugee background has been focused on flows from community contexts into school; in particular, the disadvantage that arises from blockages to such. Hence, there are calls for educational institutions in the West to find ways of incorporating the everyday literate practices of young people of refugee background (e.g. Perry, 2007). My analyses here have highlighted flows in the other direction. Some of the knowledge and skills valued as capital in the field of literacy education might flow from the school into other contexts. The big issue here is that of digital inclusion. New media literacies are integral to growing up in the second decade of the twenty-first century (Ito et al., 2010). During 2009–14, the URL project worked on the premise that the school has a role in enabling kids in a high-poverty area to participate in media cultures of home, community and beyond – a premise that remains important (Rowsell et al., 2017). Irrespective of whether this was what was actually happening in

Dana's case, her self-initiated projects and the use she made of the remix project give glimpses of what such a dynamic might look like.

Implications

Young people of refugee background and their teachers of literacy education face significant challenges. Schooling in general and literacy education in particular are implicated in the reproduction of the social inequality experienced by these young people. This is evident in the over-representation of young people of refugee background among the lowest scoring groups on national literacy testing. It has long been known that the most disadvantaged of EAL/D learners require the richest of literacy programs (Thomas & Collier, 1997); for EAL/D learners of refugee backgrounds, this includes programs of digital and multimodal literacy (Christie & Sidhu, 2002). For these learners, print basics are essential but insufficient. As the digital communications revolution deepens, literacy education should do even more: it needs to provide students whose lives are affected by poverty with access to the technologies and practices of everyday life in digital worlds of literacy. Approaches are likely to vary from level to level of the school system.

In the early years there is currently considerable interest in the potential of tablet technology. Teachers are exploring ways of incorporating this technology into their classroom practices, both as a means of teaching the print basics (e.g. phonics apps) and for teaching multimodal interactive literacies (e.g. story apps, bookmaking apps, storytelling apps and drawing tools). There has long been a flow of literacy materials from the early years classroom to the home: storybooks, readers, felt stories, puppets and so forth are sent home with kids to promote literate practices privileged in school. More recently, there have been efforts to enable literacies to flow the other way: from home and community to the early years classroom (e.g. Kenner, 2000; Beecher & Jones Díaz, 2014). Digital technologies are now part of this mix.

A recent study in several kindergartens in low and mixed socio-economic areas added iPad tablets to the literacy materials children could take home (Dezuanni, Dooley, Gattenhof & Knight, 2015). In the classroom, the children learned operational and software skills and literate practices (e.g. how to capture ideas through photographs). At the same time, however, teachers sought to learn from the ways families and children used the technology at home. The aim was a two-way flow of literate practices to skill the children up for digital worlds while enabling mastery of the print basics, which are privileged in early years contexts in the field of literacy education. These pedagogic conditions would seem to be rich in potential for young children of refugee background.

In the primary and secondary years, after-school programs are increasingly common (Woods et al, 2014). Homework clubs are well established as programs of supplementary academic support that enable young people of refugee background to complete their schoolwork. When they are designed for young people of refugee background, these programs create a space within which the experience and educational beliefs of the young people and their families have value as capital. This helps disrupt the reproductive work of schooling (Naidoo, 2009). After-school programs that are not linked directly to schoolwork and are not designed specifically for young people of refugee background may serve a complementary function. But these effects are complex. To understand them, thinking tools such as the Bourdieusian concepts I have used here are helpful. Like all the perspectives introduced in this volume, Bourdieusian concepts are of practical value to teachers: they enable us to think systematically and deeply about educational phenomena and, in doing so, to go beyond what seems obvious.

Considerations

- How might teachers make the knowledge and skills developed at MediaClub valuable in the classroom? Given national literacy testing, how feasible is this?
- What knowledge and skills do teachers require in order to build on young people's everyday literate practices?
- Should teachers bring everyday practices into the curriculum? Does the teacher run the risk of dismissing or appropriating young people's lived experiences?

Of interest

Would you like to find out more about young people of refugee background in Australian schools?

- *Global trends. Forced displacement in 2015.* This publication presents many thought-provoking statistics. It puts current refugee crises in Australia in historical and global perspective. See http://www.unhcr.org/576408cd7.pdf
- *New and Emerging Communities in Western Australia* (Government of Western Australia, 2012). This publication describes communities like that of DRC Australians as 'new and emerging communities'. These are all communities that have formed in Australia since 2001. The publication defines the term 'new and emerging community' and provides information about key characteristics, including educational attainment and English language proficiency. See https://www.omi.wa.gov.au/StatsInfoGuides/Documents/lga_guides/New_and_Emerging_Communities.pdf
- *The Democratic Republic of Congo-born Community* (Australian Government Department of Social Services, 2014). This publication provides a snapshot of the Congolese community in Australia. See https://www.dss.gov.au/our-responsibilities/settlement-and-multicultural-affairs/programs-policy/a-multicultural-australia/programs-and-publications/community-information-summaries/the-democratic-republic-of-congo-born-community

References

Australian Government (n.d.). *Community information summary: Democratic Republic of the Congo-born community*. Retrieved September 2014 from http://www .dss.gov.au/sites/default/files/documents/02_2014/democratic_republic_ congo.pdf

Beecher, B. & Jones Díaz, C. (2014). Extending literacies through partnerships with families and communities. In L. Arthur, J. Ashton & B. Beecher (Eds.), *Diverse literacies in the early years: Implications for practice*. Sydney: ACER.

Billings, S. (2014). *Language, globalization and the making of a Tanzanian beauty queen*. Bristol: Multilingual Matters.

Bourdieu, P. (2000). *Pascalian meditations*. Cambridge: Polity Press.

Bourdieu, P. & Wacquant, L. J. D. (1992). *An invitation to reflexive sociology*. Cambridge: Polity Press.

Christie, P. & Sidhu, R. (2002, May 21). Responding to globalisation: Refugees and the challenges facing Australian schools. *Mots Pluriels*. Retrieved from http://www.arts.uwa.edu.au/MotsPluriels/MP2102pcrs.html

Compton-Lilly, C. (2007). The complexities of reading capital in two Puerto Rican families. *Reading Research Quarterly*, 42(1), 72–98. doi:10.1598/RRQ.42.1.3

Creagh, S. (2014a). A critical analysis of problems with the LBOTE category on the NAPLAN test. *Australian Educational Researcher*, 41, 1–23. doi:10.1007/ s13384-013-0095-y

—— (2014b). National standardised testing and the diluting of English as a second language (ESL) in Australia. *English Teaching: Practice and Critique*, 13(1), 24–38. Retrieved from http://edlinked.soe.waikato.ac.nz/research/journal/ view.php?article=true&id=913&p=1

—— (2016). A critical analysis of the Language Background Other Than English (LBOTE) Category in the Australian national testing system: A Foucauldian perspective. *Journal of Education Policy*, 31(3), 275–89. doi:1080/02680939.2015.1066870.

Design-based Research Collective (2003). Design-based Research: An emerging paradigm. *Educational Researcher*, 32(1), 5–8. doi:10.3102/001318 9X032001005

Dezuanni, M., Dooley, K., Gattenhof, S. & Knight, L. (2015). *iPads in the early years: Developing literacy and creativity*. New York: Routledge.

Dooley, K. (2012). Positioning refugee students as intellectual class members. In F. McCarthy & M. H. Vickers (Eds.), *Refugee and immigrant students: Achieving equity in education* (pp. 3–20). Charlotte, NC: Information Age.

Ferfolja, T. (2009). The Refugee Action Support program: Developing understandings of diversity. *Teaching Education*, 20, 395–407. doi:10.1080/10476210902741239

Ferfolja, T., Vickers, M. H., McCarthy, F., Naidoo, L. & Brace, E. (2011). *Crossing borders: African refugees, teachers and schools*. Canberra: Australian Curriculum Studies Association.

Heller, M. (2008). Pierre Bourdieu and 'literacy education'. In J. Albright & A. Luke (Eds.), *Pierre Bourdieu and literacy education* (pp. 50–67). New York: Routledge.

Ito, M., Baumer, S., Bittanti, M., Boyd, D., Cody, R., Herr-Stephenson, B., Horst, H. A., Lange, P. G. … Pascoe, C. J. (2010). *Hanging out, messing around and geeking out*. Cambridge, MA: MIT Press.

Kenner, C. (2000). *Home pages: Literacy links for bilingual children*. Stoke-on-Trent, UK: Trentham Books.

Luke, A., Woods, A. & Dooley, K. (2011). Comprehension as social and intellectual practice: Rebuilding curriculum in low socioeconomic and cultural minority schools. *Theory Into Practice*, 50(2), 157–64. doi:10.1080/00405841.2011.558445

MacBeth, J., Kirwan, T., Myers, K., McCall, J., Smith, I., McKay, E. … & Pocklington, K. (2001). *The impact of study support: A report of a longitudinal study into the impact of participation in out-of-school hours learning on the academic attainment, attitudes and school attendance of secondary school students*. Research Report RR273. Colegate, Norwich: Department for Education and Skills. Retrieved from http://dera.ioe.ac.uk/4624/1/RR273.pdf

McBrien, J., Birman, D. & Dooley, K. (2017). Cultural and academic adjustment of refugee youth. Introduction to the special issue. *International Journal of Intercultural Relations*, 60, 104–8.

Miller, J. (2007). Teaching refugee learners with interrupted education in science: Vocabulary, literacy and pedagogy. *International Journal of Science Education*, 31(4), 571–92. doi:10.1080/09500690701744611

Miller, J. & McCallum, M. (2014). *Intensive language scaffolding across the curriculum: An EAL literacy model*. Melbourne: Monash University.

Naidoo, L. (2009). Developing social inclusion through after-school homework tutoring: A study of African refugee students in Greater Western Sydney. *British Journal of Sociology of Education*, 30(3), 261–73. doi:10.1080/01425690902812547

—— (2011). School-university-community partnerships. In T. Ferfolja, M. H. Vickers, F. McCarthy, L. Naidoo & E. Brace, *Crossing Borders: African refugees, teachers and schools* (pp. 73–90). Melbourne: Common Ground.

Ndhlovu, F. (2013). Language nesting, superdiversity and African diasporas in regional Australia. *Australian Journal of Linguistics*, 33(4), 426–48. doi:10.1080/07268602.2013.857573

Oliver, R., Haig, Y. & Grote, E. (2009). Addressing the educational challenges faced by African refugee background students: Perceptions of West Australian stakeholders. *TESOL in Context*, 19(1), 23–38. Retrieved from http://www.tesol.org.au/Publications

Perry, K. (2007). Sharing stories, linking lives: Literacy practices amongst Sudanese refugees. In V. Purcell-Gates (Ed.), *Cultural practices of literacy: Case studies of language, literacy, social practice, and power* (pp. 57–84). Mahwah, NJ: Lawrence Erlbaum Associates.

Rowsell, J., Morrell, E. & Alvermann, D. E. (2017). Confronting the digital divide: Debunking brave new world discourses. *The Reading Teacher*, 71(2), 157–65.

Street, B. (1984). *Literacy in theory and practice*. Cambridge: Cambridge University Press.

Thomas, W. P. & Collier, V. (1997). *School effectiveness for language minority students*. Washington DC: National Clearinghouse for Bilingual Education.

Vickers, M. H. & McCarthy, F. (2011). Crossing borders: Into the future. In T. Ferfolja, M. H. Vickers, F. McCarthy, L. Naidoo & E. Brace, *Crossing borders: African refugees, teachers and schools* (pp. 105–13). Melbourne: Common Ground.

Woods, A., Levido, A., Dezuanni, M. & Dooley, K (2014). Running a MediaClub – What's involved? And why would you bother? *Literacy Learning: The Middle Years*, 22(3), 18–23.

Zhang, G. M. (2007). Multiple border crossings: Literacy practices of Chinese American bilingual families. In V. Purcell-Gates (Ed.), *Cultural practices of literacy: Case studies of language, literacy, social practice, and power* (pp. 85–98). Mahwah, NJ: Lawrence Erlbaum Associates.

Acknowledgements

This chapter reports data collected as part of an Australian Research Council-funded project (2009–2014). I owe a debt of gratitude to the MediaClub kids and families, volunteers, assistants, artists and teachers. I thank the teachers, students and administrators at the school and the parents and Indigenous Elders. I also acknowledge my research colleagues Vinesh Chandra, John Davis, Beryl Exley, Katherine Doyle, Michael Dezuanni, Amanda Levido, Allan Luke, Kathy Mills, Wendy Mott and Annette Woods of Queensland University of Technology and John McCollow and Lesley MacFarlane of the Queensland Teachers' Union.

CHAPTER 12

Reflections on language and literacy

Recognising what young people know and can do

Jacqueline D'warte

....

AUSTRALIAN PROFESSIONAL STANDARDS FOR TEACHERS

Standard 1: Know students and how they learn

This chapter illustrates the importance of being responsive to the learning strengths and needs of students from diverse linguistic, cultural, religious and socio-economic backgrounds.

Standard 4: Create and maintain supportive and safe learning environments

The chapter also highlights strategies to support inclusive student participation and engagement in classroom activities.

   The tensions and complexities that play out in teaching and learning for culturally and linguistically diverse (CALD) student communities around the world are highlighted in this chapter. The standards above are considered in the offering of explicit research-informed ways to acknowledge and build on the broad language resources students already possess. Practical applications for *knowing* CALD students and *how they learn* and evidence of how classrooms can *maintain a creative and supportive environment* that facilitates *student participation and engagement* are detailed. Being open to the idea that students do bring myriad knowledges, skills and understandings to school, and that these associated knowledges are easily revealed and can be explicitly connected to school curriculum, is a crucial starting point for teaching and learning. This thinking and related practice is fundamental to becoming a reflective practitioner, one who prepares young people to lead successful and productive lives by acknowledging and building on their linguistic potential.

....

Well, my teacher got a different insight into us, and where we are at, and it's fun to know what other people are learning and how their life is and what they speak. (Year 6 student)

Introduction

Diversity is an increasingly prominent feature of schools and society. Western education systems in particular are made up of communities of young people who come from diverse cultural, religious, linguistic and educational backgrounds. Scholarship (Blommaert, 2010) purports that these young people's linguistic capabilities and cultural experiences are increasingly diverse and dynamic. Yet, as the student comment above helps illustrate, societal and institutional mandates have been slow to recognise the complexity of language/s and literacies across all domains of students' lives. Instead, common educational policies and practices continue to focus on promoting the universal individual development of English literacy, compared and measured by high-stakes, traditional tests. Rarely are the resources and repertoires of students called on in supporting this endeavour.

However, common educational theory compels teachers to recognise what students bring to school and asks that teachers build on that knowledge in service of classroom learning. Therefore, teachers must be open to the idea that students bring myriad knowledges, skills and understandings to school, that these knowledges, skills and understandings are easily revealed, and that there are transparent connections between them and the mandated school curriculum.

This chapter employs elements of Bourdieu's theory of practice as a lens through which to view **classroom research** undertaken with young people, aged 10–14, in five Australian classrooms. Teachers and students in these classrooms became ethnographers of their own language practices; they critically examined the ways they used language and literacies in their everyday worlds and reflected on how and in what ways these languages and literacies may support in-school learning. The interlocking 'thinking tools' (Bourdieu & Wacquant, 1989, p. 50) of habitus, field and capital are applied in considering how the 'unseen half' (see Chapter 1 in this volume) may begin to become visible when changes are made to educational curricula, teacher pedagogies and classroom practices.

Classroom research
empirical research conducted
in educational settings.

Background

Socially, culturally and linguistically diverse classrooms and measures of 'success'

Recent scholarship challenges us to reconsider old notions of diversity and the established categories and patterns that came with migration and the movement of people. The recent notion of super-diversity (Vertovec, 2007) characterises tremendous increases across categories in patterns of immigration. Essentially, the global flows of people are changing profoundly, and numbers of migrants are steadily growing, bringing together ever greater numbers of people from different socio-economic, cultural, religious, linguistic and educational backgrounds. These patterns are reflected in many contemporary classrooms, which are complex, multicultural and multilingual and include diverse students from migrant, refugee and Indigenous backgrounds. Contemporary global conditions offer evidence of ongoing and purposeful movement among language varieties (Blommaert, 2010). We now consider languages as being in contact and mutually influencing each other; what we call 'translingual' communication (Canagarajah, 2011) is everywhere and involves ever-wider groups of people.

However, many argue that educational policy and practice around the learning of English in educational settings is sustained and influenced by a view of language as a bound structure, with set mental linguistic structures and features. This is in the face of evidence that twenty-first-century classrooms across the English-speaking world and beyond are increasingly places that consist of speakers of many different languages and versions of English. In Australia, for example, a significant history and ongoing presence of Indigenous languages has been added to by the inclusion of people from over 100 countries from around the world, speaking over 200 different languages. Commonly, English, like many other languages, is influenced by ideological, historical and political constructions tied to nationhood. English is viewed as a circumscribed system that links particular communities and wields considerable power (Woolard, Schieffelin & Kroskrity, 1998). In this framing, one version of English is considered 'standard'; this version is positioned as superior to other forms and comes to signal belonging.

Prompted by the complexity and diversity within twenty-first-century classrooms, and also by increasing local and global accountability measures, many English-speaking countries, such as the United States, Australia and England, have developed new language arts curricula[1] and assessment measures. The Australian Curriculum: English (Australian Curriculum, Assessment and Reporting Authority, 2012), for example, acknowledges Australian students' linguistic diversity and identifies three key strands underpinning the study of English in Australia: Language, Literacy and Literature. However, new policies, new curricula, and the focus on local, national and international benchmarks are presenting complex challenges for language and literacy educators. Increasing pressure is being placed on students and teachers to demonstrate evidence of English language and literacy proficiency in very short time frames. Many scholars argue that these conditions are hindering rather than supporting teachers' capacities to respond to difference. It is in this context that many researchers and educational practitioners continue to explore ways to meet the educational needs of diverse student populations. Ongoing evidence has demonstrated that multilingualism, plurality and transnationality do

---

1   In the United States, this includes the Common Core Standards; in Australia, the Australian
      Curriculum; and in the United Kingdom, the National Curriculum for England.

not translate into equality and equity for many diverse and marginalised young people. Inequality in schooling is undeniable (Luke, 2008), particularly for those who speak languages other than English, or use varieties or forms of English that are not considered 'standard', as in the case of Aboriginal English.

A focus on assets

Many scholars have turned their attention to the ways children are socialised into particular understandings and usages of language and literacies from their homes and communities, and the impact of these on their schooling (Heath 2012; Moll, Amanti, Neff & González, 2005; Somerville, 2013). This work has identified what have been commonly termed cultural 'mismatches' in ways of using language at home and school. This work has helped to elucidate (mis)understandings that have led some teachers to underestimate the abilities of children, particularly children from cultural backgrounds outside of the dominant cultural group/s. Likewise, this work has prompted scholars and educators to consider issues of power, equity and justice in relation to particular forms of language and literacies, and what happens when language and literacies do not align with the mainstream language and literacy practices valued and tested in school (Gee, 2004; Martinez, Morales & Aldana, 2017). Practices not aligned with mainstream practices valued in school receive unequal access or opportunity (Gutiérrez, Morales & Martínez, 2009), particularly when they lie outside of what is considered to be mainstream 'standard' English. Diversity is often undervalued, positioned as deficit or difficult, and sometimes made invisible. Culturally and linguistically diverse student populations frequently encounter negative assumptions about their abilities to perform linguistically and academically (Comber, 2016). As a consequence, students' language and literacy experiences and learning are often not reflected in what they do in school, and their communicative competence is erased or narrowed, especially under the influence of high-stakes testing (Rymes, 2010). Multilingual and CALD students are often subjected to reductive remedial literacy programs that fail to recognise their repertoires of practice (Gutiérrez & Rogoff, 2003) and, therefore, learning can be inhibited.

Evidence suggests that measures of 'success' both in school and in everyday life depend on which forms of language and literacies one commands. On the other hand, recent work has also suggested important possibilities for connecting home and school language and learning experiences (Hull & Schultz, 2002; Orellana, 2016). Research on the experiences of young people and the dynamic literacy practices that accompany them, both in and out of school settings, offer us new understandings about literacies. Children from CALD backgrounds have been shown to possess language repertoires that can be a resource for literacies in English and for enhanced educational practice that takes into account: multiple modes of expression (Rennie, 2009); code switching and switching between languages (Martínez, 2010); and linguistic invention (Pennycook, 2010). The research and thinking presented in this chapter builds on this body of work.

Diverse classrooms bring new learning opportunities. As access to local and global Others improves, new practices, texts and genres are being continually created in increasingly new environments, encouraging the development of new ways of thinking about teaching and language. A sociological lens has long offered many educational scholars the opportunity to develop ongoing knowledge and understandings about meeting the needs of diverse school populations. This chapter outlines how agency and voice for groups and individuals who have traditionally been marginalised in educational practice and social life are crucial for learning. It considers how the framing of **linguistic and cultural diversity** by educational institutions can acknowledge students' strengths and support actions that disrupt deficit discourses, empowering students and teachers to make assets visible and enhance learning. To analyse these frameworks, it is important to understand some key theoretical concepts. It is to a further explanation of these concepts that this chapter now turns.

> **Linguistic and cultural diversity** a broad and inclusive descriptor that denotes diverse language, ethnic background, nationality and religion of a community.

Key theoretical concepts

> **Pierre Bourdieu** a French sociologist, anthropologist, philosopher and public intellectual whose substantial body of work concerned the dynamics of power in society. He developed a methodology for understanding people's actions and decisions as social practices, creating a theory of practice and a cultural analysis of social class.

As discussed in Chapter 1, **Pierre Bourdieu** was interested in relations of power; his work increasingly focused on how these relations are reproduced in education and, in turn, how they manifest inequality within educational discourses, policies and pedagogies. Many scholars have written about and interpreted Bourdieu's significant body of work. **Bourdieu's theory of practice** (1977, 1990), in particular, offers a lens through which to view the micro and macro dimensions of educational practice and policy (see also Chapters 8, 10 and 11 in this volume for ways that other authors have applied Bourdieu). For example, educators use Bourdieu's (1990) concepts of capital, habitus and social fields to examine how history, socialisation, language, knowledge, culture and traditions acquired over time (i.e. capital) influence character, disposition, ways of thinking and doing (i.e. habitus) and, in turn, reveal agency, position and action in educational arenas (i.e. social fields), such as classrooms, schools and the larger educational landscape.

> **Bourdieu's theory of practice** a theory that synthesises societal structures and individual dispositions as a way to account for how the world is made and transformed.

Although these concepts are briefly presented as separate notions in the following discussion, it is crucial to stress that within Bourdieusian scholarship the concepts of habitus, capital and field are necessarily interrelated, both conceptually and empirically (Bourdieu & Wacquant, 1992).

Educational scholarship continues to reveal how language is inextricably linked to students' identities, experiences and, most importantly, opportunities to learn. Bourdieu experienced a duality of language from an early age. As a young child growing up in a small village in the Pyrenees, he used the Béarn dialect of home, but French was the language of school and the language of the prestigious universities he attended. In the following discussion, language is positioned as a form of capital that does not always have a universal value; language is also a form of habitus that is brought into the social field of education. Bourdieu offers a way to see how language is taken up in the social field of education. Macro structures that constitute the field (such as federal and state agendas, societal mandates), and the related micro structures (such as classroom assessments and classroom pedagogies) position the language practices and experiences people bring to the educational field, and assign them a value. In turn, these structures and this positioning affect the practices and pedagogies (interactions, groupings, methods of instruction and choice of language instruction) enacted in the field. In essence, these features can work to enhance or undermine capital and, by extension, evolve the habitus of both students and teachers. These concepts inform and are themselves informing; they are relational, and they offer a way to think about our social worlds. These sociological theories can illuminate the ways in which educators' perspectives function to shape the social phenomena around them, and the way educators not only view but practise language and literacy education.

Capital and language

The term 'capital' is usually associated with economic and monetary exchange. Bourdieu extends this association to include myriad assets that are transformed and exchanged within and across different fields. Bourdieu's notion of capital presents itself in three ways: economic, cultural and social. Economic capital refers to the traditional commercial exchange. Cultural capital is acquired over time, accumulated through knowledge, language, skills, family background and taste, and is transferred into privilege that some people acquire as part of their life experiences. It may or may not yield social, political and economic power across different social institutions and social practices. Social capital refers to social networks, relations, religion and culture; it is also a source of knowledge, power and exchange in the field and is acquired over time (Bourdieu, 1977). Social capital involves access to social networks, institutions, relationships, recognition and resources that are accrued to individuals or groups as a result of group membership and mutual acquaintance. These forms of capital vary as required by the field in which they operate. According to Bourdieu, capital is power and a source of exchange; through processes of transfer and conversion, one kind of capital is transferred into another. Language is viewed as one form of capital that sits within a larger fusion of modes of capital that make up one's habitus.

Linguistic capital takes various forms, a variety of language resources that make up the different human dispositions that influence the way we act, think and carry out our daily lives. Bourdieu (1990) explained language as being a form of embodied cultural capital that is internalised; a part of one's being representing a means of communication and self-presentation acquired from one's surrounding culture. As language cannot stand alone and is part of the habitus of a person, it is important to consider how the particular languages or language forms and practices people employ may rest within fields, such as the wider educational institution or the classroom. In educational settings, some languages and some practices are perceived as linguistically or socially equal to those that hold most power in the field and others are not.

Generally, one dominant language and/or standard form of language is legitimised and privileged. Speakers of dominant languages may inherit and have access to this legitimate language through the capital they inherit from families and through educational inclusion and opportunity. The language practices and experiences of the poor, working-class, marginalised, and linguistically and culturally diverse may have less value. These ways of speaking and doing may not be legitimated in the social fields of education and in classrooms most specifically, and, in turn, may not become capital that offers access to power. Linguistic capital, then, is: embodied; acquired over time; acquired through instruction; facilitated by agency; valued, if given legitimacy, in a particular field; and expressed through the habitus.

Habitus and language

Bourdieu (1990, p. 53) defines habitus as 'complex and multidimensional'. He suggests that habitus encompasses an individual's internal and external life, the conscious and unconscious mind, and proposes that structures and agency occur in concert to inform one's habitus. Habitus helps to shape an individual's present and future practices. In essence, it connects the individual with the social world. As mentioned in the previous paragraph, language is an interpretive element of habitus that people bring to the field of education. Therefore, one's practices are both a result of one's habitus and a consequence of how one may be positioned in the field and how well one knows and can participate in its associated social arena.

In thinking about language, the concept of habitus can be used to consider the multiple identities of young people in schools. Young people bring complex combinations of history, affiliation, identity and linguistic competence to the social fields. Although many young people possess comprehensive linguistic tool kits (Orellana, 2009), everyday language and literacy practices are often seen by teachers and youth themselves as inferior to school language practices (Gutiérrez, Morales & Martínez, 2009) and, as such, this linguistic capital holds little power in the educational field. It is imperative for educators to engage in critical reflection that examines how speakers of non-dominant languages, or non-standard dialects or accents, are viewed. It can be suggested that a teacher's habitus is the main driver of their pedagogical actions and decisions, with associated impact on students' academic growth and potential. An examination of one's habitus can offer new ways to view alternative possibilities, relationships and practices that may impact on students' participation and, indeed, their habitus, making practices that are invisible, visible. Teachers may ask: How do I view my students' language and literacy practices? Are they recognised in my interactions, pedagogical choices and assessment decisions? How do students view themselves? These critical examinations may also help to begin to address equality and equity for many diverse and marginalised young people.

The conditions that generate and organise social practices form dispositions and, in turn, these dispositions adapt to suit the outcome, event or social situation in which they operate (Bourdieu, 1990). In relation to language teaching, there is the potential for diverse ways of knowing, interacting, speaking, thinking and composing to be recognised or, indeed, ignored. Looking through this frame, we can work to examine the complex histories, interplays, activities and connections that link many young people with communities across social fields. Their activities and connections provide them with opportunities to engage in diverse multimodal, socio-cultural and socio-linguistic practices in their everyday worlds. These practices and experiences are realised both spontaneously and generatively in daily social practices, within a variety of social contexts.

We might ask: How do these practices and experiences position young people in the social and cultural fields of education? One's habitus influences one's actions; how particular groups of young people are viewed or perceived may consciously and unconsciously influence what teachers do, what they say and how they teach. Equally, this informs and develops students' habitus, how they perceive themselves, their abilities, identities and notions of belonging in this social field. A critical reflection on the role of habitus may help educators to see how the education field functions to reproduce and legitimate inequalities while maintaining the status quo, perhaps leading us to question: How are those in power consciously or unconsciously working to exclude?

Social field and language

Bourdieu used the term 'field' to describe the structured environment and operational space where interactions occur. The field is a source of valued cultural capital and, within any social field, others evaluate forms of capital. Those who construct the field have the greatest power within that field and they often possess the power to negotiate, value and transform capital. The structured educational field is extensive, formed by a macro array of institutions, all operating within an agreed system of structured social positions and regulations (Bourdieu & Wacquant, 1992). The educational field is an interconnected network, a landscape that includes many stakeholders, government agencies and departments, school districts, schools and classrooms. These are interconnected fields that administer policy, practices and the setting of agendas, working in concert to set the rules and operations in this social field.

In the educational field, teachers are placed in positions that require them to recognise and evaluate students' capital. In considering language in this framing, Bourdieu's notion that capital does not exist and function except in relation to the field is foregrounded. A change of position in the field has to follow the rules that regulate the distribution of capital and how that capital is accumulated. According to Bourdieu, the 'game' that occurs in social spaces or the field is competitive. The field is not a level 'playing field', so to speak; some individuals come with particular forms of valued capital and are therefore advantaged. They bring particular assets to the 'game', assets that, in turn, can be used to advance their capital. The larger structures, rules, histories and values within the field serve to decide what capital is valued and therefore position some as more successful than others. In relation to linguistic capital, educators must consider what language is recognised:

specifically, what scripts, genres, ways of talking, thinking and doing are not only employed but, more importantly, valued in their field, and how these are then reproduced by students and measured by their teachers, producing positional hierarchy in the classroom. Positions of advantage are driven by the acquisition and accumulation of linguistic resources that are deemed valuable (e.g. English speaker or speaker of 'standard English') and that are necessary in assigning positions of privilege (e.g. confident school student and language learner) and success within the educational field, through, for example, targeted literacy benchmarks.

What is further considered in this discussion is that the physical and social space of the field structures the habitus. Bourdieu argued that practices and discourses of education are embodied in those that dominate and possess power in the field; in other words, the field orientates its inhabitants. It can be argued that, although the field is dominated by larger structures, rules, histories and values, agency and change can still occur within the field. How then do we create equitable classrooms and curriculum that value and take up students' habitus and, further, enable teachers to critically reflect on their own habitus? What practices and exchanges within the social field of schools and classrooms help us to do this? This chapter now turns to research that offers one way to begin to address these questions.

Methodology

This research (D'warte, 2014) involved two urban primary schools and two urban high schools in Australia. Participants included five classroom teachers and four English as a second language (ESL) teachers, as well as 105 students from two Year 5/6 composite classes, one Year 6 class, one Year 7 class and one Year 8 class. English-only speakers, those from language backgrounds other than English (LBOTE) and students who spoke one or more languages other than English were represented in these five classrooms. In total, these young people spoke 31 different languages and dialects. Research data were comprised of audio-recorded student and teacher interviews, transcriptions, curriculum artefacts, student work samples, and audio recordings and field notes from classroom lesson observations. Contrastive thematic analysis across the data set provided evidence for the research findings presented here.

The research encompassed multiple phases. Initially, individual interviews were conducted with participating teachers, wherein they discussed their careers and shared their experiences of teaching CALD, multilingual students. Teachers expressed their views about the kinds of linguistic practices and experiences they assumed their students engaged with in their homes and wider community. They also identified possible links between students' home and school practices. Interviews were then conducted with students in groups of four to six. Students identified the languages they spoke and those they were studying either formally or informally. They shared the multimodal language and literacy practices they engaged in; that is, how, when and with whom, and in what language/s they were reading, writing, talking, listening and viewing. Students reflected on whether their shared practices and experiences were called upon in school.

The second phase of this research involved in-classroom work. First, student data were collated and teachers in each classroom shared both quantitative and qualitative data sets with their students. Data comprised quantitative tables that sought information about the languages spoken, languages studied, students' every-day multimodal experiences and/or practices, engagement in translation/ language brokering practices, what students translated or brokered, and where, when and with whom. Qualitative data comprised representative student comments about bilingualism, translation/language brokering (in multiple languages and across modes in English), connections, if any, between everyday language use and English study in school, and general comments about language learning and language use.

Students and teachers applied a critical analysis to their data, which became the object of study, and they further explored the ways they used language in their everyday lives. Students continued to observe their language practices and ex-periences and added to the initial data set with their teachers. Designing graphic representations, role-playing, comparing and contrasting with others in their classes, and talking with parents and the larger community enabled them to ana-lyse their everyday encounters at the social, cultural, textual and word level. In the final phase of this work, teachers capitalised upon students' newly revealed understandings and skills to design English units, lessons and activities aligned to English outcomes. These included, for example, researching and creating an audio-visual representation of family histories, designing a multilingual cyberbullying campaign, and researching and presenting multilingual folktales and fairy-tales.

In the following analysis, Bourdieu's theoretical frame facilitates critical under-standings of how the linguistic and cultural skills and abilities of a diverse group of students were viewed in the broader educational context and then applied in class-rooms. It offers an opportunity to consider the particular ways these classrooms inhibited or promoted equitable learning outcomes for students. The findings pre-sented here situate language as a strong form of capital and examine teachers' and students' recognition and valuing of students' pre-existing linguistic habitus. The analysis considers how recognition of students' linguistic capital was realised, and began to transform the field, influencing what teachers did, what they said and how they taught. A critical reflection on the role of habitus elucidates how the education field of these classrooms functioned to legitimise linguistic equality and worked to include students' myriad knowledges, skills and understandings.

Analysis and discussion

These young people and their teachers transformed their everyday practice and exchanges by actively examining the diverse multimodal, socio-cultural and socio-linguistic practices in their everyday worlds. This transformation required teachers' active development of new curriculum and pedagogies that enabled stu-dents' 'repertoires of linguistic practice' to be revealed. Teachers not only asked students to share their practices and experiences in informal interviews, they continued to work with, and elaborate on, the information they collected. Classroom work began with students being presented with their interview data in the form of graphs and tables. Data revealed almost all students were surprised by what they could do, as represented by the comment below:

> Yeah! Me, us, we all do lots of stuff, lots of languages, lots of ways of using language and 'skill' yeah [addressed to researcher]? I didn't know that. (Year 5/6 student)

Almost all students were unaware of their linguistic dexterity and the value of being able to switch codes and registers with regularity. In each classroom, the initial data set became active and dynamic; students offered new and additional information not shared in initial interviews; interactive whiteboards enabled new information to be added. These classroom examinations and analyses engaged students in being **ethnographers** of their own language practices and experiences. They were asked what these data revealed about their class, what was surprising or interesting about these data, and what may have been missing. They considered what influenced the type of language they used or the ways in which they communicated with others; what connections, if any, could be made between their everyday language and literacy experiences; and what they were learning and doing in their English lessons. Teachers' and students' collaborative examination of what they knew and could do facilitated the exploration and development of new curriculum and pedagogies for language and literacy learning.

Linguistic ethnography a theoretical and methodological development centred on the study of language, communication and the social world. It considers language and the social world to be mutually shaping and analyses situated language, offering insights into the mechanisms and dynamics of social and cultural production in everyday activity.

Exchange and agency in the field

Common in educational discourse is a desire to extend students' potential; to move young individuals along a continuum that builds on what they know by developing and extending their knowledge, understandings and skills. The aim is to deepen students' existing social and cultural capital and apply these to both pre-existing and new cultural practices that become transferable across social fields. In the classrooms discussed here, teachers in the social field of their immediate classrooms employed transformative and reflexive practices and curriculum that were centred on first recognising, then building on, students' foundational language knowledge and experiences. Knowledge was being co-constructed *with students* and *about students*. For many of the students in the study, their home language was not English or was outside the Standard Australian English (SAE). However, these students and their teachers acknowledged their linguistic capital in this field, exploring how it could be leveraged in the service of learning in real and meaningful ways.

As articulated, Bourdieu argues that those who construct the field have the greatest power within the field. In this study, students served as ethnographers of their own language practices, wherein their languages, voices, histories and world views were included, validated and given power and prestige. As bearers of the knowledge about the ways of thinking and doing, students had power and agency in the social field of their classroom, and this continued to influence their views throughout this study. Most importantly, it began to influence how they viewed themselves.

> Wow, I'm talking about language – like we said before – it's visual, it's viewing, it's listening; I'm clever. (Year 7 student)

For teachers, fields rest within fields. For example, these fields include: the classroom, the school, policies and practices that define teaching, centralisation of much of the English curriculum, and the field of assessment that relates associations of success with measurable outcomes and larger social and economic language policies (local and national tests and assessment tasks). As teachers learned what their students knew and could do, they revised lessons and included curriculum that changed the interaction in the immediate field. They positioned students as active participants; these young people's practices and experiences were valued in and of themselves as well as recognised as valuable resources for learning. Evidence from the final teacher and student interviews revealed the ways in which participants saw this work as transformative, as having increased both teachers' and students' expectations of students' abilities, leading to the development of more cognitively challenging curriculum that engaged students.

> Well, I just learned so much about my kids and what they could do and I think they learned so much about themselves and together we made our classroom more interesting and engaging. (Year 5/6 teacher)

Reflections on habitus

Bourdieu argues that our perceptions, thoughts and, by extension, actions come to be and continue to develop as a result of our histories and the surrounding social and political discourses that most often become internalised ways of knowing and doing. The languages and practices that are valued and considered standard are formed by complex understandings of the social world, informed by the dominant culture and context that sustains them. Many scholars have argued that the existing social structure is perpetuated and reproduced in school. Teachers' habitus is informing and informs what happens in classrooms; as Bourdieu suggests, habitus is both conscious and unconscious, concerns the internal and external life, and helps shape an individual's present and also future practices. Examination of teachers' and students' habitus and the role they play in shaping learning in the educational field requires careful and critical consideration.

Student habitus

> I speak Vietnamese – I'm embarrassed. I feel like I'm not learning. It makes me feel like I'm not good at speaking English. (Year 5 student)

The comment above, shared during the review of the initial data, suggests that, for this student, the language of home and school were in conflict. Identity, agency and power are crucial constructs that need to be considered in literacy learning.

If learning is the acquisition and appropriation of ideas, hearing students' voices can lead us to consider how identities are shaped by, and in turn shape, the social and cultural contexts of school literacy learning. Comparative analysis of student data revealed a considerable change in many students' views about their language skills, practices and experiences at the conclusion of this project. Entry data revealed little acknowledgement or recognition that using two languages was a valuable ability and something that required considerable skill, or something that should be acknowledged in school. The ability to use two languages had little value for these young people when this research began.

> I don't feel the need to read and write it [Chinese] now. I guess I kind of adapted to the Australian culture. It is not part of school. No one knows or cares. (Year 8 student)

Unfortunately, for some other students, ongoing discussions with the researcher and their teacher about the skill and linguistic dexterity inherent in a variety of practices such as translating, for example, did little to disrupt the hierarchical power relations ingrained in their habitus. The representative student comments included in this discussion suggest that students' embodied disposition encompassed a view that their cultural capital or linguistic assets had little or no value in this field and therefore offered them little opportunity for success.

> If being bilingual is so clever, how come I am always failing in English? Sometimes I can't speak really well and sometimes I speak fast and I can't really see the word really clear. But sometimes my mum's like, 'You have to be brave and do it yourself'. (Year 7 student)

However, analysis revealed some students' increasing surprise and, for others, reluctant delight at their own abilities – as the student comment below suggests. Data also revealed an emerging critical awareness of how their language/s were not only used, but also valued, within their classrooms and the wider society. While some parents were worried that this work would inhibit students' English language ability, most parents were surprised and pleased that their children were talking about, and studying, their everyday language practices. Multilingual, multidialectal and 'non-standard' varieties of English were acknowledged and framed as assets rather than deficits.

> Well, I talked about it with Mum; I told her how I am really clever and I should be proud of myself. (Year 7 student)

As students continued to make their everyday language use visible, their capacity to be experts and authentic chroniclers of their own lives and experiences was showcased. Students were given the opportunity to analyse and document their everyday communication at the text and word level and this supported them in seeing how these understandings could be transferred to their study of English.

> I didn't know my knowledge could benefit me in classroom learning. (Year 6 student)

At the conclusion of this study, evidence suggests that, common across schools, was the view that this work had a positive influence on classroom culture, student identity and confidence. A noticeable shift in teachers' expectations of their students' abilities was also evident.

Teacher habitus

Paulo Freire (2005) argues that educators must employ active critical consciousness in order to become learners of students' habitus. Teachers may hold unconscious views about certain minority groups and their language practices, views that are influenced by external pressures, such as mandated curriculum requirements and assessment measures. A considerable body of research details how teachers' habitus may impact on students' language learning (Delpit, 1995; Luke, 2007). Analysis of the initial interviews with teachers involved in the research revealed some understandings of students' everyday language worlds; however, most teachers were not fully aware of the range of students' dynamic multimodal, multilingual linguistic practices and experiences. The extent and complexity of these practices were greatly underestimated, as reflected in the following teacher comments:

> I know that many students speak a language other than English at home, but I am not sure they use it in complex or sophisticated ways. (Year 7 teacher)

For the most part, the field has a significant impact on teachers' habitus. Teachers' lives and their work are closely aligned to the expectations of the field. As English is the most valuable commodity in the field of education, students who are native speakers of English are considered to possess valuable capital within that field. The analysis presented here revealed that teachers' views of students' capacities continued to change. This was evident via significant increases in teachers' expectations of students' abilities.

> I learned so much about my students. I didn't realise all the things they were doing, their understandings and the skills they had. (Year 6 teacher)

Bourdieu argues that the habitus is generative of practices and, in this study, teachers' practices changed. As students and teachers continued to study students' everyday practices, teachers came to see the range and complexity of students' translating/language-brokering experiences; of particular note was the realisation that translating written and spoken texts for grandparents was a common practice. Teachers began to see how students traversed multiple registers, and how they used a variety of media to communicate, how they employed critical literacy skills in discussing the dominance of English in Australia and how particular languages and speakers of other languages were viewed in the Australian context. This shared knowledge, practice and experience led teachers to design increasingly complex lessons and activities that engaged them in creating a variety of multilingual and multimodal texts. Students developed intercultural competencies and metalinguistic awareness as they applied their knowledge and expanded their repertoires of language use. Students focused on register, the ways in which language changes for different audiences and purposes, a key outcome that students work towards in their study of English.

Implications

This work not only revealed students' linguistic complexities but was also agentive in addressing the powerful ways of knowing that students must master to perform linguistically and academically. These authentic contexts offered opportunities for students to build further knowledge about how language and literacies work and are adapted for classroom learning and further afield: across and around practices, communities and countries. This pedagogy began to incorporate the repertoires, knowledge and practices that diverse students bring to school while engaging them in learning 'dominant capitals' necessary for success. It worked to address and counter the evident notions of deficit expressed by some teachers and students.

Studying the everyday worlds of students in school offers a valuable opportunity for teachers and students to listen, learn, think and make meaning together. Classroom work was transformed, collective awareness deepened and learning was enhanced. This chapter cannot claim, however, that because teachers grew to know their students better, identities were transformed and inequities were addressed. It does not claim that there was, or will be, a lasting effect on students' and teachers' habitus or that the field was significantly changed. As Bourdieu makes us aware, complex interplays and relationships sustain dominant educational policy and practice. While things may have briefly changed in this social field, multilingualism, plurality and transnationality do not translate into equality and equity for many diverse and marginalised young people.

This work was a first step in enabling teachers to develop a more detailed understanding of and engagement with their students' habitus and provided an opportunity for teachers to reflect on their own habitus. It facilitated a process that supported teachers to begin to work towards what Luke describes as a 'principled, culturally and linguistically sensitive, sociologically grounded *evidence-based teaching*' (2008, p. 302, emphasis in original).

> My experience has continued to confirm my view that most students do not see complexity in their everyday practices and in my classrooms. I believe this has been compounded by my inability to support them in revealing this to themselves, or even revealing it to myself. (Year 6 teacher)

Tensions and complexities play out in teaching and learning as diverse student communities around the world continue to work to meet linear and hierarchical models of English language and literacy. The broad language resources students already possess must be a starting point in studying English. Social and cultural experiences are invaluable to the processes of language and literacy teaching, and learning and schools offer some potential to redress equity and promote change. Educators must reflect on their own subject-position, biases, privileges and limitations in order to give voice to marginalised Others. Teachers' habitus is one of the main drivers of their pedagogical actions and decisions and can therefore facilitate academic growth. It is essential to uncover the value, complexity and power of everyday language practices in order to address broader issues of equity and discrimination as they play out in diverse classrooms.

Considerations

- Consider your own experience of language and literacy learning. How were languages other than English viewed or treated in your school setting? How did the classroom teaching work to include or exclude the participants?
- How will you reveal what students know and can do in your classroom? What kinds of prevalence will students' language and literacy practices have in your social fields and how could you build on students' linguistic capital?
- How will you reflect on your own habitus, particularly as you address the powerful ways of knowing that students must master to perform linguistically and academically in your setting? How will you support others in reflecting on their habitus?

Of interest

- D'warte, J. (2014). Exploring linguistic repertoires: Multiple language use and multimodal acting in five classrooms. *Australian Journal of Language and Literacy*, 37(1), 21–30.
- Orellana, M., Martínez, D., Lee, C. & Montano, E. (2012). Language as a tool in diverse forms of learning. *Linguistics and Education*, 23(4), 373–8.

References

Australian Curriculum, Assessment and Reporting Authority (2012). *The Australian Curriculum, English Version 4.0*. Sydney: Author.

Blommaert, J. (2010). *The sociolinguistics of globalization*. Cambridge: Cambridge University Press.

Bourdieu, P. (1977). *Outline of a theory of practice* (R. Nice, Trans.). Cambridge: Cambridge University Press.

—— (1990). *The logic of practice* (R. Nice, Trans.). Oxford: Polity Press.

Bourdieu, P. & Wacquant, L. (1989). Towards a reflexive sociology: A workshop with Pierre Bourdieu. *Sociological Theory*, 71(1), 26–63. Retrieved from http://web.b.ebscohost.com/ehost/

—— (1992). *Invitation to reflexive sociology*. Chicago: University of Chicago Press.

Canagarajah, A. S. (2011). Translanguaging in the classroom: Emerging issues for research and pedagogy. *Applied Linguistics Review*, 2, 1–28. doi:org/10.1515/9783110239331.1

Comber, B. (2016). *Literacy, place, and pedagogies of possibility*. Routledge: New York.

Delpit, L. (1995). *Other people's children: Cultural conflict in the classroom*. New York: New Press.

D'warte, J. (2014). Exploring linguistic repertoires: Multiple language use and multimodal activity in five classrooms. *Australian Journal of Language and Literacy*, 37(1), 21–30. Retrieved from http://www.alea.edu.au/resources/AJLL

Freire, P. (2005). *Education for critical consciousness*. London: Continuum.

Gee, J. P. (2004). *Situated language and learning: A critique of traditional schooling*. New York: Routledge.

Gutiérrez, K. D., Morales, P. Z. & Martínez, D. C. (2009). Remediating literacy: Culture, difference, and learning for students from nondominant communities. *Review of Research in Education*, 33(1), 212–45. doi:org/10.3102/0091732X08328267

Gutiérrez, K. & Rogoff, B. (2003). Cultural ways of learning: Individual traits or repertoires of practice. *Educational Researcher*, 32(5), 19–25.

Heath, S. B. (2012). *Words at work and play: three decades in family and community life.* Cambridge: Cambridge University Press.

Hull, G. & Schultz, K. (Eds.). (2002). *School's out! Bridging out-of-school literacies with classroom practice*. New York: Teachers College Press.

Luke, A. (2007). Pedagogy as gift. In J. Albright & A. Luke (Eds.), *Pierre Bourdieu and literacy education* (pp. 67–91). New York: Routledge.

—— (2008). Race and language as capital in school: A sociological template for language education reform. In R. Kubota & A. Lin (Eds.), *Race, culture and identities in second language education* (pp. 286–308). London: Routledge.

Martinez, D. C., Zitlali Morales, P. & Aldana, U. S. (2017). Leveraging students' communicative repertoires as a tool for equitable learning. *Review of Research in Education*, 41(1), 477–99.

Martínez, R. A. (2010). Spanglish as literacy tool: Toward an understanding of the potential role of Spanish-English code-switching in the development of academic literacy. *Research in the Teaching of English*, 45(2), 124–49. Retrieved from http://www.ncte.org/journals/rte

Moll, L., Amanti, C., Neff, D. & González, N. (2005). Funds of knowledge for teaching: Using a qualitative approach to connect homes and classrooms. In *Funds of knowledge: Theorizing practices in households, communities, and classrooms* (pp. 71–88). Lawrence Erlbaum Associates. doi:10.4324/9781410613462

Orellana, M. F. (2016). *Immigrant children in transcultural spaces: Language, learning, and love*. New York: Routledge.

—— (2009). *Translating childhoods: Immigrant youth, language, and culture*. New York: Rutgers University Press.

Pennycook, A. (2010). *Language as a local practice*. London: Routledge.

Rennie, J. (2009). Diversity in different times. *Literacy Learning: The Middle Years*, 17(3), 11–17. Retrieved from http://www.alea.edu.au/resources/literacy-learning-the-middle-years-ll

Rymes, B. (2010). Classroom discourse analysis: A focus on communicative repertoires. In N. H. Hornberger & S. L. McKay (Eds.), *Sociolinguistics and language Education* (pp. 528–46). Bristol: Multilingual Matters.

Somerville, M. (2013). Place, storylines and the social practices of literacy. *Literacy*, 47(1), 10–16. doi:org/10.1111/j.1741–4369.2012.00677.x

Vertovec, S. (2007). Super-diversity and its implications. *Ethnic and Racial Studies*, 30(6), 1024–54. doi:org/10.1080/01419870701599465

Woolard, K., Schieffelin, B. & Kroskrity, P. (1998). *Language ideologies: Practice and theory*. London: Oxford University Press.

CHAPTER 13

Final ruminations on the 'unseen half'

Jacqueline Ullman, Criss Jones Díaz and Tania Ferfolja

AUSTRALIAN PROFESSIONAL STANDARDS FOR TEACHERS

Standard 3: Plan for and implement effective teaching and learning

Standard 5: Assess, provide feedback and report on student learning

While the APST Standards do not explicitly refer either to processes of reflection or to teachers as reflexive practitioners, we take the position that strong, critical teaching practices, particularly in the areas of planning and implementation (Standard 3) and assessing student learning (Standard 5), require teachers to employ theoretical perspectives in their decision-making processes.

> When people lack a critical understanding of their reality, apprehending it in fragments which they do not perceive as interacting constituent elements of the whole, they cannot truly know that reality ... It is thus possible to explain conceptually why individuals begin to behave differently with regard to objective reality, once that reality has ceased to look like a blind alley and has taken on its true aspect: a challenge which human beings must meet. (Freire, 1972, pp. 104–6)

> Rather than defining teacher work through the narrow language of professionalism, a critical pedagogy needs to ascertain more carefully what the role of teachers might be as cultural workers engaged in the production of ideologies and social practices ... [who] embrace a practice that is capable of revealing the historical, ideological, and ethical parameters that frame its discourse and implications for the self, society, culture and the other. (Giroux, 2005, p. 71)

Making the 'unseen' seen

In Chapter 1, the 'unseen half' was introduced as a metaphor for both the diversity of children and families who are, in many ways, insufficiently catered for in early childhood, primary and secondary education, as well as for the unseen, taken-for-granted inclusion and privilege inherent in an education system that is designed for a socially constructed, normative student. In the chapters that followed, the authors problematised elements of normativity in education and worked to make the unseen 'seen' through their analysis of the diverse schooling experiences of preschoolers, children, adolescents and their families. While each of these chapters could have been positioned as a summative description of an issue, the incorporation of sociological theory as an analytical and reflexive tool provided a more nuanced understanding of the issues under investigation. Each chapter highlighted the ways in which theory functions to 'value-add', providing depth, a richer perspective and a move away from the superficiality of description and taken-for-granted knowledge to a critical approach.

Sociological theories enabled authors to reposition understandings of diversity in relation to 'race', ethnicity, Indigenous understandings, culture, language, socio-economic status, dis/ability, sexuality and gender, as well as notions of childhood – and explored the ways in which Othering constructs discourses of deficit, which silence marginalised subjectivities and knowledges. In Part 1 of the book, poststructuralist theoretical concepts assisted in destabilising taken-for-granted understandings and revealed the often unequal, but always contextual and shifting, power dynamics inherent in the discourses that are constituted both inside education and more broadly. These concepts facilitated a questioning about whose voices and knowledges are privileged in educational settings and exposed how educational institutions often reproduce inequities. In Part 2, cultural studies, Critical Race Theory and postcolonialism provided the means to examine the racialised dimensions of educational institutions and underscored the criticality of questioning racial privilege and associated marginalisation across all levels of social, cultural and educational life. These chapters applied theory to problematise assessments of knowledge and/or ability and shifted the focus from deficit to the contributions, strengths and resilience of 'racially', culturally and linguistically diverse children and youth. Lastly, critical theory, here characterised primarily by the work of Pierre Bourdieu in Part 3 of the book, enabled authors to critique the social landscape of society through the exposure of historical and economic influences on social and cultural oppression. Critical theory enabled an exploration of the cultural complexities of schools and their communities, and was used to reveal a reflexive and socially responsible teaching practice characterised by an exposure of cultural and class-based privilege.

In this final chapter, we would like to extend the metaphor of the 'unseen half' a step further by exploring how sociological theory itself is 'unseen' in early childhood, primary and secondary educational contexts, at least outside of pre-service teacher education and academia itself. When stories about education settings, educational-related issues or educational research findings enter the public milieu via the media, there is rarely any explicit acknowledgement of the theoretical perspectives that might have informed the analysis of the story, issue or 'problem'. We propose that ignoring these theoretical influences is due less to a lack of theoretical presence and more to theory's unfortunate relegation to the background as bland, unintelligible, irrelevant or even elitist. Thus, everyday conversations about the state of play in schools and early childhood settings, conversations to which most people feel empowered to contribute given their own schooling histories, tend to focus more on the *what* – the summative – than the *why* or *how*.

Further, the impact of sociological theory on the everyday work of educators also remains firmly situated in the unseen. Through the course of a typical lesson or learning experience, unless explicitly stated, it is unclear to students or other observing professionals how educators use sociological theories to inform, direct or reflect on their work. As Darling-Hammond (2006, p. 300) argues, 'Much of what teachers need to know to be successful is invisible to lay observers'; thus, the body of knowledge that includes theoretical understandings and their integration into practice is unseen. This is of particular salience considering the personal impact of inspirational teachers on pre-service educators' preconceptions and understandings of the profession (Korthagen, 2010b). When pre-service teachers remember these educators, they reflect on their passion, their flexibility, their content knowledge and their relationships with students rather than their use of sociological theory to inform their pedagogical practices. As pre-service teacher educators, we have never heard our own students fondly reflect on their inspirational teachers' consideration of sociological perspectives in their pedagogy, community interactions or professional relationships!

This is not due to teachers' lack of theoretical application but rather to the invisibility of sociological theory in the practice of teaching, where teaching quality is determined by a set of tangible, visible practices and interactions, and where the theory informing these remains, most often, imperceptible and unmentioned. In short, sociological perspectives rarely visibly sit at the 'coalface' of the classroom; rather they remain 'unseen' and, in doing so, find additional purchase as unimportant or impractical. This view of theory is often reinforced for new educators by teaching colleagues whose practice remains uninformed by sociological theory (Korthagen, 2010b). This legacy is continued when beginning teachers, likewise, marginalise sociological theory as irrelevant to practice rather than useful and *necessary* in the dynamic world of twenty-first-century education.

To move the discussion and practice forward, we stress the affordances of exposing crucial, potentially 'unseen' links between theoretically-informed analyses of pedagogical practices and pre-service teachers' perceptions about a particular social or educational phenomenon that impacts learners (Kessels & Korthagen, 1996). In line with Korthagen (2010a), we believe working from a place of personal idea-building or theorising is a natural, easy inroad to fluency with sociological theory. Ongoing reflective and reflexive practices that are explicitly informed by sociological theories not only develop understanding and a deeper sensitivity to the diverse lived experiences of young people, but bridge the unproductive gap between theory as a stand-alone body of knowledge and **praxis** itself. It is to this link between teachers' reflective and reflexive practice and sociological theory that this discussion now turns.

> **Praxis** the unity between theory and practice or theoretically-informed action.

Theoretical perspectives for reflective and reflexive practice

Reflection involves making connections between theory and practice. Through this process, teachers challenge the various unproductive discourses co-constructed through pedagogical practices by unravelling normative assumptions constituted in social practices, institutions and social structures. In contrast, **reflexivity** transcends reflection through its inclusion of a critical awareness of the 'self' and recognition of the multiplicity of inter-relations between power and knowledge (Giroux, 2005). D'Cruz, Gillingham and Melendez (2007) argue that reflexive practitioners (including teachers) are constantly engaged in self-critique and questioning of both their own knowledge claims and those of others as they engage in social interaction and micro practices of knowledge and power. Therefore, an understanding of the relationship between reflective practice and reflexivity enables teachers to effectively adopt reflective and critical dispositions in their work, particularly with marginal communities, to bring about social justice and equity in their pedagogical practice.

> **Reflexivity** a process of inward contemplation. It refers to the subjective practice of self-examination and how this connects to social behaviour and relationships. It uses understandings of power, situated context and accessibility to interrogate and evaluate one's professional practice.

Reflective practice leads to reflexivity

In his paper on reflective teaching and the importance of integrating both theory and empirical research into reflective practice, Rodriguez-Valls (2014) describes how educators may fall into a rut of either duplicating or eliminating 'what we experienced as students, what we saw other teachers doing, and what administrators tried to implement in schools', stressing that, on the contrary, quality teaching is informed by an active process of 'refining and questioning previous practices' (p. 300). This process of refining and questioning is at the heart of reflective practice, which has long been positioned as an important part of the teaching process (Darling-Hammond, 2000).

Reflection is characterised by the deliberate consideration of various classroom challenges, struggles and successes, incorporating both evaluation and contemplation. In order for teachers' reflective practice to be transformative, processes of *reflexivity* are fundamental to the acquisition of greater awareness of both the self-as-teacher and the classroom community. These processes include a turning outward: to be able to see beyond the actions of a single student or class and recognise how students' actions are situated within a much broader socio-political network of relationships, causes and effects. Of paramount importance in this process, as argued by Freire (1972), is the understanding that reflexivity brings together these processes to simultaneously focus on reflection and liberatory praxis. In order for this to occur, teachers engage in self-critique to go beyond locating their biases and normative assumptions to locating their own position of privilege and power in their involvement with students, families and colleagues. Hence, the recognition that there are multiple interrelationships between dimensions of power, knowledge and subjectivity leads to praxis, the foundation of critical pedagogical practices. Succinctly put, in the words of Freire, praxis is: 'reflection and action upon the world in order to transform it' (Freire, 1972, p. 28).

Subsequently, for pre-service teachers, not only learning about sociological theory but also being explicitly taught about how to use this learning in the processes of critical reflection and reflexivity are fundamental to developing praxis. As Darling-Hammond (2000) writes:

> Individuals who have had no powerful teacher education intervention often maintain a single cognitive and cultural perspective that makes it difficult for them to understand the experiences, perceptions, and knowledge bases that deeply influence the approaches to learning of students who are different from themselves. The capacity to understand another is not innate; it is developed through study, reflection, guided experience, and inquiry. (p. 171)

Thus, Darling-Hammond advocates for applying theoretical principles to classroom problems as a means of contextualising the issues, concerns or problems at hand while also disrupting habits of drawing generalisations about practice. This positioning of the reflective teacher as a scholar of theory has been echoed in more recent writing on the topic, where Rodriguez-Valls (2014) notes that a reflective teacher, one who creates 'theory-based practices', 'must argue before she/ he teaches' (p. 300). Scholarship in theory is an essential ingredient of reflective practice and reflexivity since it is in this argument, this provision of a rationale, defence of practice, and situation of personal experiences within the macrocosm where teacher growth and understanding occur.

It is in this shift that teacher practices move from mere teaching method to the complexities of *pedagogy* – a move from a static, prescribed set of actions to a dynamic interplay between 'teachers, learners and instructional materials during the process of teaching and learning' (Richard & Renandya, 2002, p. 6). Incorporating theoretical perspectives into reflective and reflexive practice is necessary for true critical pedagogical practice, framed by Giroux (2005) as 'forms of cultural production that are inextricably historical and political' (p. 74). Seen this way, such practice is bigger than any one teacher or student, any single classroom or any one school in any given town. It is political work requiring a critical consciousness (or as Freire [1972] would put it – *concientizacao*): an acknowledgement that each classroom or educational setting, and the teachers and learners within it, are actively situated within much larger educational, historical, political, economic and social realities. Thus, the addition of sociological perspectives can expand educators' conceptualisations of their own work – from agents of the state, whose role involves translating externally designed curriculum documentation into lesson plans and benchmarking student outcomes – to highly influential, creative and resourceful political agents for social justice and equity.

Protective qualities of theory

Incorporating sociological theory into practice and reflection affords a number of beneficial outcomes, including serving as a protective factor for educators by working as a shield against the daily occupational stresses of teaching. Teacher burnout, characterised by lowered self-belief regarding one's teaching abilities, lowered personal investment in students, and feelings of futility in one's work, as well as emotional exhaustion, impacts one in four beginning teachers in Australia (Richardson, Watt & Devos, 2013). Korthagen (2010b) writes about the ways in which new teachers' feelings of 'frustration, anger and bewilderment' can lead to a sense of having been unprepared by teacher education programs and a subsequent turn towards teaching colleagues as reasonable role models who understand the daily pressures of their profession (p. 670). Despite this support, up to one-third of all new teachers will leave the teaching profession within their first five years of employment (Ewing & Manuel, 2005).

In Stephen Brookfield's (1995) seminal book *Becoming a Critically Reflective Teacher*, he speaks to the protective quality of engaging with theoretical literature, framing it as a 'psychological and political *survival necessity*, through which teachers come to understand the link between their private [teaching] struggles and broader political processes' (Brookfield, 1995, pp. 37–8, emphasis added). He notes that a theoretical understanding of how student behaviours and teacher expectations are situated within a larger set of societal norms about what is acceptable or unacceptable in the classroom can help to shift the shaming and blaming of teachers and students that is rife both inside and outside of educational settings. Theoretical understandings may reveal different ways of seeing, reading and interpreting the context or phenomenon; thus, a sociologically informed analysis may alleviate educators' feelings of guilt and blame and ease the emotional burden of personalising classroom challenges. For example, rather than position a student's challenging behaviour as an interpersonal problem, applying sociological perspectives to look beyond what is immediately presenting itself can provide relief and insight. Marginalising talk, such as 'Johnny is a lost cause', and negative self-talk, such as 'I am an awful teacher', are typical and debilitating psychological responses to difficult situations for many new teachers. Rather than responsibility for a failed lesson plan resting squarely on the new teachers' shoulders (or the shoulders of a particularly challenging student or group of students), bringing a critical consciousness to bear on the incident, one informed by sociological theory, allows for greater emotional detachment, frees the affective space from blame and affords new perspective on the context, within both the microcosm (e.g. the realities of students' lives) and macrocosm (e.g. societal and cultural influences). As Darling-Hammond (2000) articulates, applying theoretical principles to problems in specific contexts 'helps teachers understand more deeply the many variables that influence their work' (p. 171), many of which are externally situated and beyond the educator's immediate control.

Freedom from blame or negative self-beliefs allows educators to reframe classroom challenges or 'failures' as opportunities for learning, wherein teachers can draw on sociological theoretical understandings to offer alternative or innovative approaches. In turn, this outlook aids in teacher flexibility, enhancing avenues for creative practice. To incorporate such theoretical approaches inevitably results in a wider range of possibilities for pedagogy. Where teachers employ a greater range of movement in their teaching repertoire, making independent, creative decisions drawn from theoretical knowledge, and moving beyond teacher guides and 'tool-boxes of tricks', they gain confidence in their own abilities. In contrast, teaching that follows a prescribed format fails to allow room for classroom challenges or cohort 'mis-fit'.

It would appear that teaching from a place of theoretical awareness is empowering outside the classroom 'trenches' as well. Knowledge of sociological theory can further enhance understanding and critical assessment of externally produced curricular mandates, policy, and all manner of reporting and institutional bureaucracy, as well as buffer the negative impact of public scrutiny and commentary. Teaching is one of the more surveilled professions in the Western world, a position that, over time, has chipped away at teachers' freedoms, professional sensibilities and autonomy, depriving teachers of the 'trust characteristic of professionals' (Bushnell, 2003, p. 252). Understanding the historical, political and gendered elements of educators' current social position can further safeguard these professionals from the pressures of their daily bureaucratic demands by offering perspective, a certain depersonalisation and distance from their potentially negative psychological impact.

Our final point here is perhaps our most important. Incorporating sociological theories into reflective and reflexive teaching practices can preserve the core social justice perspective that we hope most pre-service teachers hold dear as they enter the profession. It can be challenging for new educators to remain aware of the theoretical influences they were exposed to during their teacher education, particularly when such material seems to go against prevailing conditions in the classroom (Waghorn & Stevens, 1996). There exists a strong pull for beginning teachers, particularly those in practicum teaching situations involving intensive observation, to set aside their own ideas about teaching approaches informed by theory, suspend their own judgement and adopt 'less desirable ways of teaching', evidencing what has been described by Tabachnick and Zeichner as a 'washout effect' (Tabachnick and Zeichner, 1984, as cited in Waghorn & Stevens, 1996, p. 171). We propose that this steady erosion of educators' beliefs, most probably inclusive of things like a love of students, a respect for diversity and an altruistic desire to change the world, can be protected through a steady inoculation of sociological theory. Continually dipping into the literature and bringing such writings to bear on teaching practice reminds teachers of the 'unseen' and inspires their continuous efforts to shine their light, making the 'unseen' seen.

Considerations

- Thinking about your experiences either as an educator or as a student, what stands out for you as evidence of social inequity in schooling? How might some of the sociological theories or theoretical concepts aid in your interpretation and understanding of that phenomenon?
- What does the concept of the 'unseen half' mean to you? What or who do you think remains 'unseen' to your fellow practitioners?
- While sociological theories aid educators in their understanding of social phenomena and of schooling as a social institution, these theories can also be used to generate proactive responses to inequitable practices. In what ways might you use some of the concepts covered in this book within your own professional practice to generate practical solutions to 'real-world' issues?

Of interest

- *RISE: International Journal of Sociology of Education.* This open-access online academic journal publishes theoretical and empirical educational research that incorporates relevant sociological theories and has a drive to contribute to social transformation and overcome social inequities through education. See http://www.hipatiapress.info/hpjournals/index.php/rise
- *Sociology of Education.* This academic journal publishes quarterly on studies in the sociology of education and human social development. In particular, published work examines how social institutions, and individuals' experiences within them, impact educational processes and social development. See http://soe.sagepub.com
- Study.com's online course on *Praxis Sociology.* This online short course contains a series of animated instructional videos on key sociological theories and associated areas of human diversity, such as: sex and gender, 'race' and ethnicity, socio-economic status, and age. See http://study.com/academy/course/praxis-ii-sociology-test.html

References

Brookfield, S. (1995). *Becoming a critically reflective teacher*. San Francisco, CA: Jossey-Bass.

Bushnell, M. (2003). Teachers in the schoolhouse panopticon: Complicity and resistance. *Education and Urban Society*, 35(3), 251–72. doi:10.1177/0013124503035003001

Darling-Hammond, L. (2000). How teacher education matters. *Journal of Teacher Education*, 51(3), 166–73. doi:10.1177/0022487100051003002

—— (2006). Constructing 21st century teacher education. *Journal of Teacher Education*, 57(3), 300–14. doi:10.1177/0022487105285962

D'Cruz, H., Gillingham, P. & Melendez, S. (2007). Reflexivity, its meanings and relevance for social work: A critical review of the literature. *British Journal of Social Work*, 37, 73–90. doi:10.1093/bjsw/bcl001

Ewing, R. & Manuel, J. (2005). Retaining early career teachers in the profession: New teacher narratives. *Change: Transformations in Education*, 8(1), 1–16.

Freire, P. (1972). *Pedagogy of the oppressed*. Middlesex, UK: Penguin Books.

Giroux, H. (2005). *Border crossings: Cultural workers and the politics of education* (2nd ed.). New York: Routledge.

Kessels, J. & Korthagen, F. A. J. (1996). The relationship between theory and practice: Back to the classics. *Educational Researcher*, 25(3), 17–22. doi:10.3102/0013189X025003017

Korthagen, F. A. J. (2010a). Situated learning theory and the pedagogy of teacher education: Towards an integrative view of teacher behaviour and teacher learning. *Teacher Education*, 26, 98–106. doi:10.1016/j.tate.2009.05.001

—— (2010b). The relationship between theory and practice in teacher education. *International encyclopedia of education* (pp. 669–75).

Richard, J. C. & Renandya, W. A. (2002). Approaches to teaching. In J. C. Richard & W. A. Renandya (Eds.), *Methodology in language teaching: An anthology of current practice* (pp. 1–5). Cambridge: The Press Syndicate of the University of Cambridge.

Richardson, P., Watt, H. & Devos, C. (2013). Types of professional and emotional coping among beginning teachers. In M. Newberry, A. Gallant & P. Riley (Eds.), *Emotion and school: Understanding how the hidden curriculum influences relationships, leadership, teaching, and learning (advances in research on teaching)* (Vol. 18, pp. 229–53). Bingley, UK: Emerald Group.

Rodriguez-Valls, F. (2014). Reflective teaching: Theory within classroom practices. *Teaching Education*, 25(3), 294–308. doi:10.1080/10476210.2014.889669

Waghorn, A. & Stevens, K. (1996). Communication between theory and practice: How student teachers develop theories of teaching. *Australian Journal of Teacher Education*, 21(2), 70–81. doi:10.14221/ajte.1996v21n2.7

Index